# HIGH-PERFORMANCE INTERACTIVE GRAPHICS:

# Modeling, Rendering and Animating

# For IBM PCs® and Compatibles

Lee Adams

**TAB BOOKS Inc.**

Blue Ridge Summit, PA

## Notes on the Cover

The color photographs on the cover are examples of graphics produced by the demonstration programs inside the book. Exposure was 1/4 second at f2.8 using Agfachrome 100 RS color slide film. The camera was a 35mm Pentax K1000 fitted with a 2x teleconverter on a standard 1:2 50mm lens. A tripod and remote shutter cable release were employed to minimize camera vibration. The graphics were generated on an IBM Enhanced Color Display.

The photographs in the main body of the book are halftones taken from black and white prints produced with Kodak Plus-X Pan film. Exposure was 1/4 second at f2.8 for wire-frame models and solid object models. For fully-shaded models, exposure was 1/4 second at f3.4.

FIRST EDITION
THIRD PRINTING

Printed in the United States of America

Library of Congress Cataloging in Publication Data

Adams, Lee
High performance interactive graphics : modeling, rendering, and animating for IBM PCs and compatibles / by Lee Adams.
p.  cm.
Includes index.
ISBN 0-8306-2879-7 (pbk.)
1. Computer graphics.  I. Title.
T385.A33   1987

TAB BOOKS Inc. offers software for sale. For information and a catalog, please contact TAB Software Department, Blue Ridge Summit, PA 17294-0850.

Questions regarding the content of this book should be addressed to:

Reader Inquiry Branch
TAB BOOKS Inc.
Blue Ridge Summit, PA 17294-0214

# Contents

# Acknowledgments

The author is grateful to Quadram Corporation for generously providing a QuadEGA+ enhanced graphics adapter for the author's use during preparation of the book.

Special appreciation is extended to the fine people who prepared IBM's BASIC Version 3.21 Reference manual. Their diligent attention to detail and accuracy in documenting the various instructions in BASIC is an achievement which should not go unrecognized. Their hard work made the author's task more manageable.

# *Notices*

MS, GW, GW-BASIC, Microsoft BASIC, MS-DOS, Microsoft are trademarks of Microsoft Corporation.

Tandy is a registered trademark of Tandy Corp./Radio Shack

QuickBASIC is a trademark of Microsoft Corporation.

TurboBASIC is a trademark of Borland International, Inc.

IBM, IBM PC, PCjr, IBM Personal Computer XT, IBM Personal Computer AT, RT, Personal System/2, IBM BASIC, and PC-DOS are trademarks of International Business Machines Corporation.

Quadram and QuadEGA+ are trademarks of Quadram Corp.

COMPAQ is a trademark of COMPAQ Computer Corp.

Kodak and Plus-X Pan are trademarks of Kodak.

Agfachrome is a trademark of Agfa-Gevaert.

Panasonic Business Partner is a trademark of Panasonic Industrial Co.

Commodore is a trademark of Commodore Electronics, Ltd.

Leading Edge is a trademark of Leading Edge Hardware Products Inc.

Tech PC is a trademark of Tech Personal Computers.

PC's Limited is a trademark of PC's Limited

Sanyo is a trademark of Sanyo Business Systems Corp.

AT&T is a trademark of AT&T.

Epson is a trademark of Epson America, Inc.

Heath is a trademark of Heath Co.

Kaypro is a trademark of Kaypro Corp.

NEC is a trademark of NEC Information Systems.

Mitac is a trademark of Mitac International.

Blue Chip is a trademark of Blue Chip Electronics, Inc.

Wyse is a trademark of Wyse Technology.

Zenith is a trademark of Zenith Data Systems.

Xerox is a trademark of Xerox Corp.

AMT is a trademark of American Micro Technology.

Texas Instruments is a trademark of Texas Instruments.

Tandon is a trademark of Tandon Corp.

Hewlett-Packard is a trademark of Hewlett-Packard Co.

NCR is a trademark of NCR Corp.

Cordata is a trademark of Cordata.

ITT is a trademark of ITT Information Systems.

PC Designs is a trademark of PC Designs.

Atronics is a trademark of Atronics International, Inc.

BTurbo is a trademark of Basic Time, Inc.

Computerland BC88 is a trademark of Computerland.

Franklin is a trademark of Franklin Computer Corp.

USA Micro is a trademark of USA Micro.

Victor is a trademark of Victor Technologies, Inc.

Microstar is a trademark of Microstar.

QIC is a trademark of QIC Research.

Olivetti is a trademark of Olivetti USA.

Packard Bell is a trademark of Packard Bell.

QSP is a trademark of QSP, Inc.

Rose Hill is a trademark of Rose Hill Systems.

Televideo is a trademark of Televideo Systems, Inc.

Unisys is a trademark of Unisys Corp.

# Introduction: How to Use This Book

This book provides you with the knowledge you need to master the exciting fields of modeling, rendering, and animating on your personal computer.

You will learn how to create accurate 3D images of real objects, and you will have the choice of displaying the images on the screen as transparent wire-frame models or as solid models. By changing a few lines of program code, you will be able to rotate the model and move your viewpoint closer to or farther away from the model. You will learn how to create fully-shaded models by instructing your computer to calculate the position of the light source, and with a few keystrokes you can change the location of the light. You will learn three different high-speed methods for animating the models which you have created.

## WHO SHOULD USE THIS BOOK?

If you use a microcomputer and you are interested in computer graphics, then you will want to read this book. If you are new to computing, the exciting world of computer-generated images is waiting for you to explore. If you are an experienced computer user, this book will show you some high-performance graphics tricks that you may have thought impossible with an off-the-shelf personal computer. If you are a professional programmer or software author, you will learn some useful techniques for upgrading your graphics. If you use a professional CAD system, this book will give you valuable insight into the concepts and al-

gorithms found in many expensive CAD (computer-aided-design) software packages.

## ABOUT THE BOOK

This book has been designed as a learning tool. If you want to turn back corners of pages which interest you so you can quickly find them again, go right ahead. You might find it helpful to highlight portions of the text with a marker pen. Writing your own insights and observations into the margins can be helpful, too.

### What the Book Strives to Do

The book attempts to teach you modeling, rendering, and animating on IBM-compatible microcomputers in the context of a modular programming environment and properly structured BASIC code. Using the learn-by-example style of teaching, 44 professional-caliber demonstration programs are provided for you to run on your personal computer.

Emphasis is placed on helping you understand the concepts behind the programs. Once you learn what makes a program tick, you are well on your way to creating your own original software for modeling, rendering, and animating. Using the information presented in this book, you will be able to generate accurate displays of architectural design, industrial parts, packaging design, drafting projects, vehicle design . . . the list of topics is limited only by your imagination! Because a modular structured programming approach is used throughout the book, you will find it easy to convert the concepts to other programming languages such as C, Pascal, and Assembly Language.

## SPECIAL FEATURES OF THE BOOK

The book is organized in a linear format. Important fundamentals covered near the beginning of the text become the cornerstones for more advanced applications. Using a modular programming philosophy, independent routines which perform specific assigned tasks are grouped together to create advanced programs which produce spectacular graphics on your personal computer.

Every program listing is presented in a standalone form. Simply type it in and it is ready to run, no matter what type of IBM-compatible computer or what version of BASIC you are using. A special configuration module in each program enables the software to adapt itself to produce the best graphics possible using your particular graphics adapter, display monitor, and version of BASIC.

Every program is accompanied by a photograph of an actual monitor display, so you can compare the results produced by your own microcomputer. A rich selection of drawings provides the background information you need in order to understand how each program works. A thoughtful, in-depth, written analysis of each program gives you a line-by-line description of the logic involved.

If you wish to select only topics of specific interest to your programming requirements, a comprehensive table of contents and a detailed index will direct you to the pages which contain the information you are seeking.

## HOW THE BOOK IS ORGANIZED

The material in the book is organized into five broad sections for your ready reference.

PART ONE introduces you to graphics fundamentals. You will learn about the exciting graphics potential of different microcomputers, graphics adapters, display monitors, and versions of BASIC. You are taught the graphics instructions and modular programming techniques which form the foundation for high-performance modeling, rendering, and animating on your personal computer. You will learn how to manage your keyboard effectively, and you will see innovative methods for managing the screen.

PART TWO opens up the exciting world of modeling on your microcomputer. You will learn the underlying concepts of 3D models, including automatic hidden surface removal. You will see how to rotate, scale, and move a computer-generated image. Demonstration programs show you how to produce fundamental shapes like cubes, pyramids, prisms, spheres, cylinders, and the helix. You will be shown an efficient algorithm for generating smooth curves in 3D. You will learn how to use surface mapping to plot graphics onto the surface of containers such as cylinders, spheres, and cubes.

PART THREE discusses rendering: techniques of illumination and shading for microcomputers. You are introduced to important fundamental concepts as implemented on professional systems. The exciting techniques of halftoning and line dithering are used to create a range of shades, and a matrix algorithm for computer-controlled shading is explained. Demonstration programs show you how to use your personal computer to create computer-shaded models of cubes, spheres, cylinders, and polyhedrons. You will explore advanced topics such as mirror reflections and shadows. Smooth shading capabilities of personal computers are clarified.

PART FOUR gives you the programming tools to create high-speed animation on your microcomputer. First, you get a general overview of the animation capabilities of various microprocessors, graphics adapters, monitors, and versions of BASIC. Then you will learn how to create software sprite animation at up to six FPS (frames per second). You can experiment with full-screen frame animation at 10 FPS to 18 FPS. Routines for producing real-time animation on your EGA or Color/Graphics Adapter provide you with the expertise you need to create live-action programs.

PART FIVE explores some practical uses for modeling, rendering, and animating on your personal computer. A trio of demonstration programs shows you how to display a complex industrial part in transparent wire-frame form, solid model form, and computer-shaded model form. Two sample programs introduce you to the exciting field of package design: techniques for creating a soft drink container and a photographic film carton are presented. A fully interactive CAD program lets you create drafting designs, experiment with computer-generated curves, and save your drawings to diskette for later editing. You will learn how to simulate flight through 3D airspace in an aerospace engineering simulation using real-time animation.

## WHAT YOU NEED TO USE THE BOOK

The demonstration programs will automatically adapt themselves to produce the best graphics possible on your particular computer. A special configuration module in each program is used to identify the type of graphics adapter and monitor you are using. The program then chooses the best screen mode, depending on the version of BASIC being used.

### Software Requirements

If you have BASIC, you have everything you need. The programs are written in IBM BASICA, and every program is 100% compatible with GW-BASIC, COMPAQ BASIC, and Microsoft BASICA. The programs will also run under the QuickBASIC and TurboBASIC compilers.

### Equipment Requirements

If you have an IBM-compatible personal computer, you have everything you need. The programs are written for the IBM PC, IBM PC XT, IBM Personal Computer AT, IBM RT, IBM PCjr, and IBM Personal System/2. Any microcomputer which is compatible with these models will run the demonstration programs. The list of compatibles includes Tandy, COMPAQ, Panasonic, Leading Edge, Tech PC, Commodore, PC's Limited, AT&T, Epson, Heath, Kaypro, NEC, Mitac, Blue Chip, Sanyo, Wyse, Zenith, Xerox, AMT, Texas Instruments, Tandon, Hewlett-Packard, NCR, Cordata, ITT, PC Designs, Atronics, BTurbo, Computerland BC88, Franklin, USA Micro, Victor, Microstar, QIC, Olivetti, Packard Bell, QSP, Rose Hill, Televideo, Unisys, and others.

If you have a Color/Graphics Adapter in your microcomputer, the programs will run in the $320 \times 200$ 4-color mode. If you have an EGA (enhanced graphics adapter), the programs will run in the $640 \times 350$ 16-color mode with the enhanced display monitor and they will run in the $640 \times 200$ 16-color mode with the standard color display monitor. If you have a PCjr, the programs run in the $640 \times 200$ 4-color mode. A Tandy will run the programs just as if it were a PCjr. If you are using an IBM Personal System/2 computer, you may wish to use the $640 \times 350$ 16-color mode. Most other IBM-compatible microcomputers will run the programs in the $320 \times 200$ 4-color mode.

Refer to Chapter One for a discussion of the relationship between graphics adapter, display monitor, and version of BASIC.

## THE COMPANION DISKETTE

The companion diskette to HIGH-PERFORMANCE INTERACTIVE GRAPHICS is jam-packed with demonstration programs from the main body of the book. Using the diskette, you can begin immediately to tap directly into the high-energy graphics discussed in the book. There is no need to spend your time keying in the program listings when the author has already done all the work for you!

The programs on the companion diskette are ready to load and run on your IBM-compatible personal computer using IBM BASICA, IBM Cartridge BASIC, GW-BASIC, COMPAQ BASIC, and Microsoft BASICA. You can display the program source codes on your monitor and you can print out the program listings on your printer. The companion diskette is an excellent learning aid.

The programs are stored on the companion diskette using BASIC's compressed tokenized format. You get 44 programs in all. . . over 6000 lines of valuable source code! Only 8192 bytes remain unused on the diskette; it is 98% full, giving you real value for your money.

If you use Microsoft QuickBASIC or Borland TurboBASIC, all you need do is make the simple changes discussed in Appendix C and Appendix D, and the programs on the companion diskette will run at blazing speeds on your microcomputer.

Refer to the order coupon at the back of the book for more details.

## THE COMPUTERS USED TO CREATE THE DEMONSTRATION PROGRAMS

The demonstration programs in the book were created on an IBM PC using IBM DOS 3.20, IBM BASICA 3.21, an IBM Enhanced Color Display monitor, and a Quadram QuadEGA+ enhanced graphics adapter. The programs were developed for the $640 \times 350$ 16-color mode and the $640 \times 200$ 16-color mode using this hardware/software configuration.

In order to develop the programs for the $320 \times 200$ 4-color mode of the Color Graphics Adapter, IBM DOS 2.10 and IBM BASICA 2.10 were used to force the graphics adapter into the CGA mode.

To develop the programs for the $640 \times 200$ 4-color mode, IBM Cartridge BASIC J1.00 was used on an IBM PCjr using an IBM PCjr Color Display and IBM DOS 2.10.

The operating system should be IBM DOS or Microsoft MS-DOS or equivalent. IBM DOS is readily available through your local IBM dealer. IBM BAS-ICA is included on the IBM DOS diskette, but IBM BASICA will work only on genuine IBM microcomputers. MS-DOS is available at most retail computer outlets and is usually included as part of the package when you purchase an IBM-compatible microcomputer. Either GW-BASIC or Microsoft BASICA is usually included with the MS-DOS diskette, both of which will run on IBM-compatible microcomputers and on genuine IBM microcomputers.

## VERIFICATION OF PROGRAM RESULTS

In order to check the graphics produced by the demonstration programs under a diverse range of conditions, the author has run the programs under the following BASIC interpreters: IBM BASICA 3.21, IBM BASICA 2.10, GW-BASIC 2.0, GW-BASIC 3.2, and COMPAQ BASIC 2.0. The programs have been tested with the following BASIC compilers: Microsoft Quick-BASIC 2.0 and Borland TurboBASIC 1.0.

A variety of different microcomputers were tested, including an IBM PC, an IBM PCjr, an IBM Personal Computer AT, an IBM 3270, a Tandy 1000 SX, a COMPAQ Deskpro, a Panasonic FX-600 Business Partner, a Commodore PC-10, and others. To ensure graphics adapter compatibility, the programs were tested with a Quadram QuadEGA+ Enhanced Graphics Adapter, an IBM Color/Graphics Monitor Adapter, an IBM Extended Color/Graphics Adapter, and a variety of IBM-compatible color/graphics cards, including COMPAQ, Tandy, Panasonic, AT&T, and others. Monitors which were tested included an IBM Enhanced Color Display monitor, an IBM Color Display monitor, a Tandy CM-10 RGB Monitor, a Tandy CM-5 RGB Monitor, an Amdek Video-300A monochrome display, a Sysdyne Enhanced Color Display monitor, an IBM 5270 Color Display monitor, an IBM PCjr Color Display, a Panasonic monochrome display, and others.

## IF YOU INTEND TO ADAPT MATERIAL FROM THIS BOOK

If you intend to adapt any material from this book for your own professional purposes, or if you intend to use the information in this book to write marketable software, you should read the following three paragraphs:

The author's best efforts have been used to prepare the material and the program listings contained in this book. These efforts include the development, research, and thorough testing of the demonstration programs to determine their effectiveness and accuracy.

However, many different brands of personal computers are available. Many different languages (and many different versions of BASIC) are being used on those computers. In addition, the program listings in this book can be applied to a wide range of CAD uses. Some of these potential applications are just plain fun, but other applications are very serious ones indeed.

In recognition of this diversity of applications, the author is unable to make any absolute guarantees to you that the information and program listings in this book will solve your specific design, engineering, or simulation problems. You will find many powerful programming techniques in this book, but if you intend to adapt the material for your own purposes, you should thoroughly test the programs before you rely upon their accuracy.

# List of Demonstration Programs

*Bonus program included on companion diskette only.

**Appendix programs not included on companion diskette.

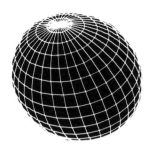

# 1

# *System Resources*

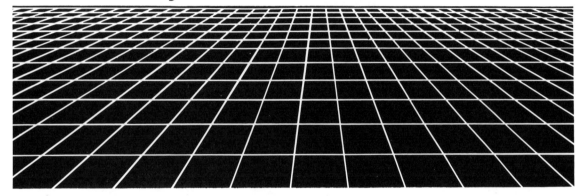

If you are interested in producing high-performance interactive graphics on your IBM personal computer or compatible, you will be pleased to learn that most of the spectacular techniques used by expensive CAD systems are easily implemented on your off-the-shelf microcomputer. The 3D perspective formulas are consistent, no matter whether used on a $60,000 CAD graphics workstation or on your home computer. Similarly, algorithms for hidden surface removal, computer-controlled shading, and high-speed animation all adhere to universal principles of graphics. These principles are not as difficult to use as many programmers think. In fact, as you will soon see, many of these exciting graphics techniques are very simple in concept. The key to producing sophisticated images on your personal computer is knowing how to mix and match different graphics techniques.

## UNIVERSAL PRINCIPLES

The mathematics for modeling and rendering on microcomputers are generally universal in their application. After all, the functions of sine, cosine, multiplication, division, addition, and subtraction will yield the same result on an IBM PC and a Tandy 1000SX

and a Compaq DeskPro and a . . . well, you get the picture.

Simply stated, the laws of geometry, trigonometry, vector multiplication, cumulative association, and other mysterious-sounding disciplines are unchanging. Math is math, wherever it is found. (Or, stated in computerese, arithmetic operators are arithmetic operators, wherever found.) Whether you choose to write your programs in BASIC, C, Pascal, or Assembly Language, the graphics math in this book will give you consistently good results.

The formulas that you will find in this programming manual are written in IBM BASICA, which is virtually identical to GW-BASIC, Compaq BASIC, Microsoft BASICA, Borland TurboBASIC, and Microsoft QuickBASIC. However, if you prefer to program in C, Pascal, or Assembly Language you will find it a straightforward task to adapt the math formulas to your favorite programming language. BASIC is used in order to make the techniques of modeling, rendering, and animating on microcomputers available to as many programmers as possible. Although C, Pascal, and Assembly Language each offer unique advantages to the programmer, almost everyone has some familiarity with BASIC. The converse is not necessarily true.

The logic, logical operators, relational operators, and fundamental structures used in interactive graphics are also universal. An IF. . .THEN decision is consistent in all programming languages and on all IBM-compatible personal computers. A loop is a loop no matter what language you use. And a subroutine is a subroutine, whether you call it a subprogram as QuickBASIC does or a procedure as Assembly Language does.

Similarly, the fundamental concepts of computer graphics are universal, especially within the world of bit-mapped graphics displays. This is the type of graphics display used on IBM personal computers and compatibles. You can use a key matte color to build a solid model on your screen just as effectively on an IBM PCjr as on an IBM Personal Computer AT. You can create a standalone subroutine which checks if a surface is visible or hidden just as easily in IBM BASICA as you can in Microsoft QuickBASIC or, for that matter, C, Pascal, or Assembly Language. Again, the simple vector math used in such a hidden surface routine is universal because the concept of a surface perpendicular is universal.

So, mathematics, logic, and graphics concepts are generic. That's the good news. The other side of the coin is that the actual implementation of these principles on specific graphics adapters and on specific monitors is often not universal.

## HARDWARE-SPECIFIC GRAPHICS

The computer hardware places a top limit on the quality of the graphics which you can generate on your particular system. Three hardware components are critical to graphics programming. They are, in order of importance, the graphics adapter, the display monitor, and the size of RAM memory.

### The Graphics Adapter

The graphics adapter determines the number of colors and the degree of resolution in the display image. There are four main types of graphics adapters present on IBM personal computers and IBM-compatibles: the standard Color/Graphics Adapter, the Enhanced Graphics Adapter, the PCjr/Tandy video subsystem, and the IBM Personal System/2 graphics adapters.

On a standard Color/Graphics Adapter or compatible, the $320 \times 200$ 4-color mode is most often used for interactive graphics. Although the $640 \times 200$ mode provides better resolution and more detail, the limitation of only two available colors imposes severe problems for the shading routines and the hidden surface removal routines, both of which are essential for producing fully-shaded solid models on microcomputers.

On an Enhanced Graphics adapter (EGA) a $640 \times 200$ 16-color mode can be generated with a standard color display monitor (SCD). If you have an enhanced color display monitor (ECD), you can produce a $640 \times 350$ 16-color display. These two graphics modes permit highly detailed images in both 2D and 3D. Although both the EGA and the Color/Graphics Adapter provide a mechanism for producing fully-shaded solid models, in some instances the coarser resolution of the Color/Graphics Adapter will mean that an area fill algorithm will fail when used inside a very small surface. This situation can be circumvented by simply drawing the image at a larger scale, although this solution is not always a viable option, especially if you want to display four simultaneous views of the model.

The PCjr video subsystem contains some elements of both the Color/Graphics Adapter and the EGA. The most useful screen is the $640 \times 200$ 4-color mode. The Tandy 1000 contains a graphics card virtually identical to the PCjr video subsystem.

Although the VGA on the IBM Personal System/2 series is capable of better performance, it fully supports the EQA modes.

### The Display Monitor

The display monitor places a cap on the capabilities of the graphics adapter. There are three main types of display monitors available in the world of IBM-compatible microcomputers: a composite monochrome display, a standard RGB color display, and an enhanced color display.

Needless to say, a composite monochrome display monitor is the most restrictive. It will never display colors, only shades of a monochrome hue, usually amber or green. Although you can achieve spectacular results on a mono monitor with the shading routines discussed in this book, there are some programmers who feel something is missing if color is not present.

A standard RGB monitor is called a standard color display (SCD) by IBM. An RGB monitor can produce 16 distinctly different hues. It achieves this by mixing the red, green, and blue pixels, each of which can be set at normal or high intensity, giving you 16 different permutations. Light is additive in essence. If you mix red, green, and blue, your eye is deceived into perceiving the result as pure white. It is interesting to note that paint and dyes are subtractive in essence, not additive. If you mix red, green, and blue paint, for example, you get a muddy gray.

When connected to a standard color display monitor, an Enhanced Graphics Adapter can generate 16 colors in the $640 \times 200$ mode. A Color/Graphics Adapter attached to a standard color display monitor can generate four colors in the $320 \times 200$ mode. By using the halftoning matrix discussed in Part Three of this book, your Color/Graphics Adapter can produce eight or more shades between any two colors, giving it the potential to produce fully-shaded solid images on a standard color display. An EGA can also invoke halftoning, although a different technique is used.

An enhanced color display monitor can display all the modes and colors that can be displayed on a standard RGB monitor, plus an enhanced mode. Because the enhanced color display (ECD) can generate 350 horizontal lines, an EGA can produce a $640 \times 350$ 16-color mode in this configuration. You can connect an ECD to your Color/Graphics Adapter, but you can only generate the $320 \times 200$ 4-color mode and the $640 \times 200$ 2-color mode with the CGA, so the extra potential of the enhanced color display monitor will not be used by the Color/Graphics Adapter.

It has been noted that exceptions test a rule; they neither prove nor disprove it. The exceptions in the world of display monitors are the IBM PCjr and the Tandy 1000. The IBM PCjr Color Display was especially designed to be used with the PCjr. Although the PCjr can produce a $640 \times 200$ 4-color mode, the PCjr Color Display monitor is physically limited to a $400 \times 200$ resolution by its large .63 mm dot size (pitch). In other words, the cathode ray tube (screen) of the PCjr Color Display contains only 400 pixel positions across each of its 200 horizontal lines. That is the reason why you will often see a rainbow-like effect in a vertical line on a PCjr Color Display. The pixel positions don't quite match the positions in the $640 \times 200$ screen buffer in memory, so the manner in which the pixels are being mixed on the screen varies from row to row. On the other hand, IBM's standard color display monitor (SCD) contains an actual physical resolution of $640 \times 200$ pixels with a .43 dot pitch, matching exactly the $640 \times 200$ output of the Color/Graphics Adapter. IBM's enhanced color display

(ECD) contains a physical CRT resolution of $640 \times 350$ pixels with a .31 dot pitch, matching the $640 \times 350$ optimum output of the EGA.

The Tandy CM-10 RGB Monitor and the Tandy CM-5 RGB Monitor were designed to be used with the Tandy 1000SX microcomputer. The CM-10 monitor is capable of generating four colors in the $640 \times 200$ mode, but the CM-5 can produce only two colors in this mode. If you are using a CM-5 monitor with your Tandy 1000, you should use the $320 \times 200$ 4-color mode for running the programs in this book, because the halftoning routines and the hidden surface removal routines require three drawing colors and one erasing color.

The monitors used by the IBM Personal System/2 support all EGA and CQA modes.

## SOFTWARE

As you have learned, the hardware places a physical limit on the quality of graphics possible on your particular computer. By using Assembly Language you can always achieve this maximum graphics potential, but programming in Assembly Language requires considerable expertise. There are other, easier languages available. The easiest is probably BASIC, although C and Pascal can become almost second nature to many programmers.

The full range of screen modes which can be produced by a Color/Graphics Adapter or an EGA is readily available through BASIC. The version of BASIC which you are using determines the screen modes available to you. Refer to Fig. 1-1. Whereas the hardware places a physical limit on the graphics capabilities of your computer system (refer to Fig. 1-2), the software places a logical limit on the graphics capabilities of your personal computer.

### A Graphics Standard

The common denominator for graphics is the Color/Graphics Adapter standard. Simply stated, every version of BASIC can generate SCREEN 1 and SCREEN 2.

### SCREEN 1, 2

SCREEN 1 is the $320 \times 200$ 4-color graphics mode. SCREEN 2 is the $640 \times 200$ 2-color graphics mode. Every IBM personal computer and every IBM-compatible microcomputer can generate these two modes. SCREEN 1 and SCREEN 2 are supported by

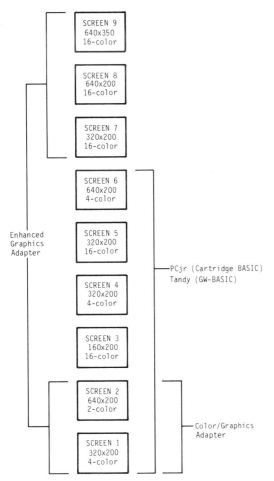

Fig. 1-1. Graphics modes available through BASIC on a Color/Graphics Adapter, an Enhanced Graphics Adapter (EGA), and a PCjr video subsystem. The Tandy 1000 series is fully compatible with the PCjr's video capabilities.

IBM BASICA versions 2.0, 2.10, 3.0, 3.1, 3.21, and 3.3 (and newer). SCREEN 1 and SCREEN 2 are also supported by Compaq BASIC, GW-BASIC, Microsoft BASICA, Borland TurboBASIC, and Microsoft Quick-BASIC. Whether you have a genuine IBM PC, an IBM XT, an IBM Personal Computer AT, an IBM PCjr, a Compaq Deskpro, a Tandy 1000SX, or any other compatible, you can invoke SCREEN 1 and SCREEN 2. It is handy to know about this SCREEN 1 compatibility, as you will soon discover.

### SCREEN 3, 4, 5, 6

The next four graphics modes, SCREEN 3,

SCREEN 4, SCREEN 5, and SCREEN 6, are available on the IBM PCjr using Cartridge BASIC and on Tandy computers using GW-BASIC. Refer to Fig. 1-3. SCREEN 3 is the $160 \times 200$ 16-color mode. Because of its poor resolution, it is not recommended for serious graphics programming. SCREEN 4 is identical to SCREEN 1, except that the SCREEN 4 $320 \times 200$ 4-color mode does not use the same color attribute strategy as SCREEN 1. SCREEN 5 is the $320 \times 200$ 16-color mode. This mode is useful for animation, where color is often more important than resolution. SCREEN 6 is the $640 \times 200$ 4-color mode, which is useful for modeling and rendering because of its high resolution. Although the IBM BASIC Compiler 2.0 supports SCREEN 4, SCREEN 5, and SCREEN 6, neither the QuickBASIC nor TurboBASIC compilers support these modes. Both the PCjr and Tandy can generate SCREEN 1 and SCREEN 2, of course.

### SCREEN 7, 8, 9

Graphics modes SCREEN 7, SCREEN 8, and SCREEN 9 are unique to the EGA. They are fully supported by IBM BASICA 3.21, Microsoft QuickBASIC 2.0, and TurboBASIC 1.0. Refer to Fig. 1-4. SCREEN 7 is the $320 \times 200$ 16-color mode. SCREEN 8 is the $640 \times 200$ 16-color mode. SCREEN 9 is the $640 \times 350$ 16-color mode. With your EGA, you can reallocate color values in these modes through the PALETTE instruction. Multiple graphics pages are available, making it easy for you to produce different types of animation or to write graphics to a hidden page. And if your EGA carries 256K of display memory, you can choose from 64 available colors for the 16 colors which you wish to display in the $640 \times 350$ mode. Versions of IBM BASICA prior to 3.21 do not support the enhanced graphics modes of the EGA, although you could use BASICA 2.10, for example, to drive your EGA in either SCREEN 1 or SCREEN 2. Refer to Fig. 1-5. Appendix E provides a display memory map for the EGA.

### SCREEN 11, 12

Graphics modes 11 and 12 are supported by the IBM Personal System/2 series of microcomputers. SCREEN 11 is the $640 \times 480$ 2-color mode. SCREEN 12 is the $640 \times 480$ 16-color mode. Borland Turbo-BASIC 1.0 was the first version of BASIC to support these modes.

IBM HARDWARE VIDEO MODES

| MODE | DESCRIPTION | WIDTH | PAGE SIZE | COLORS | ADAPTER | MONITOR | DOS MODE | BASIC MODE |
|---|---|---|---|---|---|---|---|---|
| 0 | A | 40 | 2K | 2/16 gray | CGA,PCjr | COMP | BW40 | 0 |
| 1 | A | 40 | 2K | 2/16 | CGA,EGA,PCjr | SCD,ECD,PCjr | C040 | |
| 2 | A | 80 | 4K | 2/16 gray | CGA,PCjr | COMP | BW80 | |
| 3 | A | 80 | 4K | 2/16 | CGA,EGA,PCjr | SCD,ECD,PCjr | C080 | |
| 4 | 320x200 | 40 | 16K | 4 | CGA,EGA,PCjr | SCD,ECD,PCjr | | 1 or 4 |
| 5 | 320x200 | 40 | 16K | 4 gray | CGA,PCjr | COMP | | |
| 6 | 640x200 | 80 | 16K | 2 | CGA,EGA,PCjr | SCD,ECD,PCjr | | 2 |
| 7 | A | 80 | 4K | B/W | EGA/MA | MONO | MONO | |
| 8 | 160x200 | 20 | 16K | 16 | PCjr | PCjr | | 3 |
| 9 | 320x200 | 40 | 32K | 16 | PCjr | PCjr | | 5 |
| 10 | 640x200 | 80 | 32K | 4 | PCjr | PCjr | | 6 |
| 11 12 | | | | | | | | |
| 13 | 320x200 | 40 | 32K | 16 | EGA | SCD,ECD | | 7 |
| 14 | 640x200 | 80 | 64K | 16 | EGA | SCD,ECD | | 8 |
| 16 | 640x350 | 80 | 64K/112K | 16/64 | EGA | ECD | | 9 |
| 15 | 640x350 | 80 | 64K | B/W 4 | EGA | MA | | 10 |

(Bracket labels on BASIC MODE column: modes 0, 1 or 4, 2 → "BASICA 2.00, 2.10, 3.00, 3.10"; modes 3, 5, 6 → "Cartridge BASIC"; modes 7, 8, 9, 10 → "BASICA 3.21")

* EGA statements SCREEN, PALETTE, PCOPY apply to BASICA modes 7, 8, 9, 10.

Professional Graphics Controller

| | DESCRIPTION | WIDTH | PAGE SIZE | COLORS | ADAPTER | MONITOR |
|---|---|---|---|---|---|---|
| -- | 640x480 | 80 | 300K | 256/4096 | IBM PGC | IBM PM |
| -- | 640x480 | 80 | 150K | 16/64 | IBM PGC | IBM PM |

Personal System/2 series

| | DESCRIPTION | WIDTH | PAGE SIZE | COLORS | ADAPTER | MONITOR | | BASIC MODE |
|---|---|---|---|---|---|---|---|---|
| -- | 640x480 | 80 | 38K | 2 | MCGA or VGA | PS/2 | | 11 |
| -- | 640x480 | 80 | 150K | 16 | MCGA or VGA | PS/2 | | 12 |

Fig. 1-2. Hardware video modes in IBM-compatible microcomputers. Hardware modes are listed in left column. BASIC modes are listed in right column. Not all Personal System/2 modes are shown.

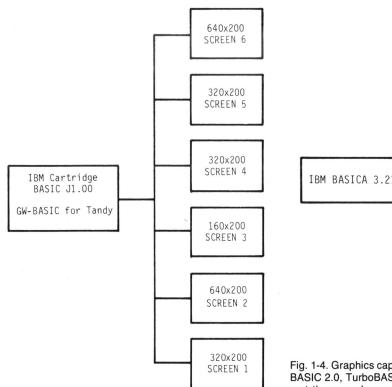

Fig. 1-3. Graphics capabilities of IBM Cartridge BASIC J1.00 for the PCjr and GW-BASIC 2.0 through 3.2 for the Tandy.

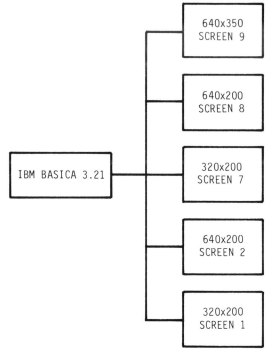

Fig. 1-4. Graphics capabilities of IBM BASICA 3.21. Quick-BASIC 2.0, TurboBASIC 1.0 and newer versions also support these modes.

## GRAPHICS MEMORY MAPPING

All IBM personal computers and compatibles adhere to a generic memory layout scheme when it comes to memory allocation. This layout is physically modified by the amount of RAM present and by the type of graphics adapter installed. The memory layout is logically modified by the memory requirements of the software being used.

A knowledge of memory conditions is useful for writing animation programs and for using machine code subroutines with your BASIC programs. If you are using interpreted BASIC with an IBM PC, XT, AT or compatible, the allocation of run-time memory in your computer is graphically depicted in Fig. 1-6. Examples of interpreted BASIC are IBM BASICA, GW-BASIC, Compaq BASIC, and Microsoft BASICA. If you are using a compiled BASIC such as Microsoft QuickBASIC 2.0, then Fig. 1-7 portrays your memory map. (Another example of a BASIC compiler is Borland TurboBASIC 1.0.)

Note that RAM is normally limited to 640K bytes, ending at address A0000 hex. A full 256K bytes of memory beginning at A0000 hex is reserved for an EGA. If a standard Color/Graphics Adapter is installed, it normally occupies 16K of memory beginning at B8000 hex. Both an EGA and a CGA cannot be used simultaneously, although an EGA which is emulating

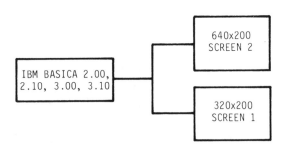

Fig. 1-5. Graphics capabilities of IBM BASICA versions 2.00, 2.10, 3.00, and 3.10. Many versions of Compaq BASIC, GW-BASIC, and Microsoft BASICA offer identical graphics modes.

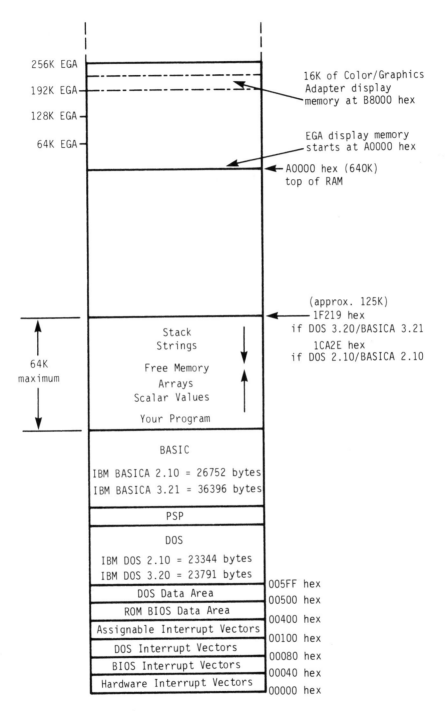

Fig. 1-6. Interpreted BASIC memory map for an IBM PC, XT, AT or compatible showing locations of DOS, BASIC, and graphics adapter display memory.

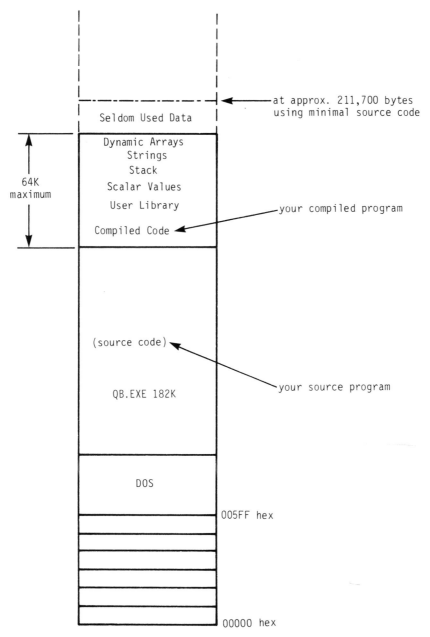

Fig. 1-7. Compiled BASIC memory map for an IBM PC, XT, AT or compatible using QuickBASIC 2.0. When using either QuickBASIC or TurboBASIC, both your original source code and the resultant compiled code are stored simultaneously in RAM.

the CGA mode of SCREEN 1 will use the B8000 hex address for that purpose.

By referring to Fig. 1-6, you can see that the memory used by interpreted BASIC usually ends somewhere around 115K or 125K, depending upon the version of DOS and BASIC being used. If you have 384K or 512K or 640K of RAM in your computer, you can often put the remaining memory to good use. You

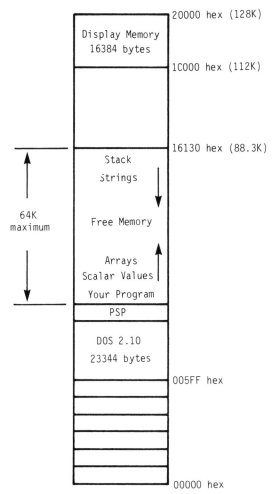

```
                    ┌─────────────┐ 20000 hex (128K)
                    │Display Memory│
                    │ 16384 bytes │
                    ├─────────────┤ 1C000 hex (112K)
                    │             │
                    │             │
                    │             │
      ┌             ├─────────────┤ 16130 hex (88.3K)
      ↑             │    Stack    │
      │             │   Strings   ↓│
      │             │             │
  64K │             │ Free Memory │
maximum│            │             │
      │             │   Arrays    ↑│
      │             │Scalar Values│
      │             │ Your Program│
      ↓             ├─────────────┤
                    │     PSP     │
                    ├─────────────┤
                    │  DOS 2.10   │
                    │ 23344 bytes │
                    ├─────────────┤ 005FF hex
                    │             │
                    │             │
                    │             │
                    │             │
                    │             │
                    └─────────────┘ 00000 hex
```

Fig. 1-8. Memory map of an IBM PCjr using Cartridge BA-SIC J1.00. The BASIC is stored on the cartridge, which is actually an extension of ROM memory.

can store graphics pages here for utilization in high-speed animation programs and for slideshow presentation graphics. You can store a simulated screen buffer in this memory and reconfigure BASIC to write on this hidden page, which is especially useful if you are using a standard Color/Graphics Adapter. You can store assembly language subroutines here. Some of these options are discussed in Part Four.

If you are using QuickBASIC or TurboBASIC, on the other hand, your free RAM does not begin until approximately the 200K point. For more information about QuickBASIC, you may wish to read Appendix C. For more information about TurboBASIC, read Appendix D.

On an IBM PCjr the size of free unused memory is smaller. Refer to Fig. 1-8. IBM PCjr Cartridge BA-SIC J1.00 is essentially an extension of ROM memory, so no RAM is needed as is required when using BASICA on a PC, XT, AT, or compatible. However, the number of extra graphics pages is much more limited on a PCjr than on other microcomputers. A Tandy 1000 uses the same graphics mapping strategy as the PCjr, except that RAM is used to hold GW-BASIC. In addition, much more RAM is available for extra graphics pages.

It is interesting to note that only one graphics page is available on a standard Color/Graphics Adapter. The reason for this is simple. The $320 \times 200$ 4-color mode requires 16384 bytes to store the color attributes for all 64000 pixels. ($320 \times 200 = 64000$ pixels; 64000 pixels $\times$ 2 bits-per-pixel = 128000 bits; 128000/8 = 16000 bytes. 384 bytes in the buffer are unused, except to round out the memory address to a convenient paragraph boundary.) The $640 \times 200$ 2-color mode also requires 16384 bytes. The Color/Graphics Adapter contains only 16384 bytes of display memory, so only one graphics page is available. However, there are easy ways around this limitation. (For a detailed discussion of extra pages and hidden pages using the Color/Graphics Adapter, refer to the author's first book, *High-Speed Animation and Simulation for Microcomputers*, available at your book store or direct from TAB BOOKS, Inc.)

The extra graphics pages available on the IBM PCjr and the Tandy 1000 are added progressively lower and lower in memory by BASIC, with the lowest page always being defined as page 0. The extra graphics pages available on an EGA are added progressively higher and higher in graphics memory, with the lowest page being page 0. If you use your own drivers to place graphics pages in dynamic RAM, then you can situate them anywhere you want, of course. The discussion about animation in Part Four will introduce some interesting routines concerning graphics pages and dynamic memory.

## A TEAM APPROACH TO GRAPHICS

As you have seen, the caliber of graphics which can be produced on your particular personal computer is limited by the weakest link in the chain, so to speak. It is a team approach. Every member of your hardware/software team has a role to play. If you have an enhanced color display monitor connected to a standard Color/Graphics Adapter, then it is the Color/

Graphics Adapter which will limit the graphics to either $320 \times 200$ 4-color or $640 \times 200$ 2-color, even though the monitor can produce a $640 \times 350$ 16-color image. If you have a standard RGB monitor attached to an EGA, then it is the monitor that will limit the EGA.

The reality of hardware limitations is the bad news. The good news is that you can achieve outstanding modeling, rendering, and animation with any graphics adapter, with any display monitor, and with any version of BASIC. This book shows you how. By using the high-performance routines in this book, your choices are between good, better, and best, depending upon your hardware/software configuration. And that's not such a bad choice.

## SUMMARY

In this chapter you learned that math, logic, and fundamental graphics concepts are generic and universal for all microcomputers. You also learned that the implementation of those graphics features is dependent upon hardware capabilities. The graphics adapter and monitor display determine the limit of graphics quality on your computer system. You saw that although the hardware imposes physical limits upon graphics generation, the programming language imposes logical limits. Although you can reach the full graphics potential of your computer by using Assembly Language, it is more productive to use the appropriate version of BASIC to achieve the same results. You discovered that the EGA and the PCjr video subsystem each contain a variety of special graphics modes, although both can also produce the standard SCREEN 1 graphics mode of the Color/Graphics Adapter.

The next chapter will identify the fundamental graphics instructions in BASIC which you can use to build the sophisticated programs described later in the book.

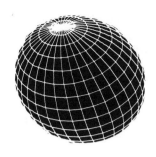

# 2

# *Graphics Instructions*

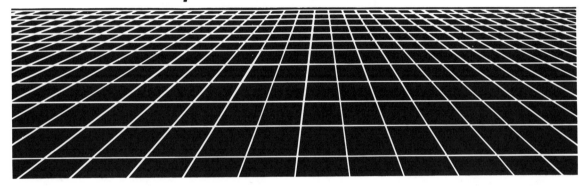

Although BASIC is endowed with an outstanding selection of graphics instructions, only a modest number of instructions is required to create high-performance interactive graphics programs. The sophistication of the graphics program is derived from how you interpose the various instructions, not from the complexity or simplicity of the individual instructions themselves.

The graphics instructions that you will use throughout this book fall into four categories: environmental instructions, graphics primitives, alphanumeric primitives, and bit pumps.

Environmental instructions are BASIC commands such as SCREEN, COLOR, PALETTE, WINDOW SCREEN, and VIEW. These types of instructions serve to establish a general graphics environment on your computer system. They determine the screen resolution and the number of colors available. They determine the scale of your images, and so forth.

Graphics primitives are fundamental drawing instructions. They include commands such as PSET, LINE, and PAINT. You may be surprised to learn that these three instructions are all the graphics primitives required for producing sophisticated programs of modeling, rendering, and animating on your personal computer. Of course, the ability to use the halftoning capabilities of the PAINT instruction and the dithering capabilities of the LINE instruction serves to greatly increase the usefulness of these two instructions. Simply stated, LINE and PAINT are the two workhorses of modeling and rendering programs.

**Alphanumeric Primitives.** Alphanumeric primitives are fundamental text and labeling instructions. They include commands such as LOCATE and PRINT.

**Bit Pumps.** Bit pump instructions are megacommands which move large blocks of graphics data. They include commands such as GET, PUT, and PCOPY. They are useful for saving and retrieving images to/from diskette, for high-speed animation, and for manipulating entire pages of graphics.

## YOUR GRAPHICS TOOLKIT

The handful of instructions described in this chapter gives you a very powerful graphics toolkit. The definitions which follow are by no means a comprehensive discussion of all the graphics commands available in BASIC (or in any other programming language, for that matter). As the saying goes, it is not what you have got that counts, but how you use it. Far better to use a few instructions well. Far better to reach the full power of a few instructions than to stumble along with an unwieldy, large selection of graphics instructions and barely scratch the surface of their potential.

Your graphics toolkit falls into the four categories of instructions described earlier: environmental instructions, graphics primitives, alphanumeric primitives, and bit pumps. It seems appropriate to take a

few moments to become familiar with these powerful graphics instructions and learn how they can help you to generate sophisticated programs.

## ENVIRONMENTAL INSTRUCTIONS

INSTRUCTION: **SCREEN**

PURPOSE: The SCREEN instruction sets the screen mode. Refer to Fig. 2-1. Depending upon your hardware and the version of BASIC which you are using, you can select from up to five graphics screen modes

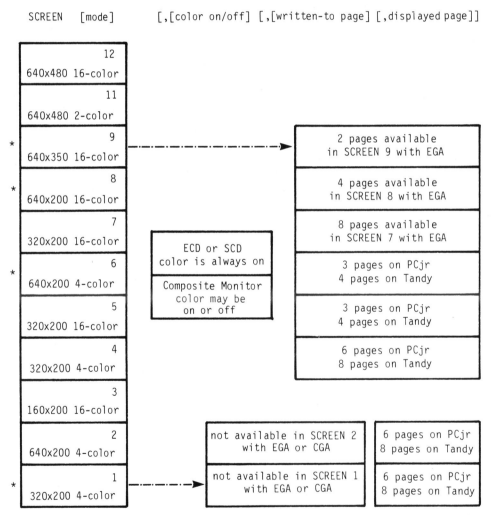

Fig. 2-1. Options available with the SCREEN instruction, depending upon the version of BASIC, the type of display monitor, and the kind of graphics adapter. Asterisks indicate the main graphics modes used in this book for modeling and rendering.

on an EGA, up to two graphics modes on a CGA, and up to six graphics modes with a PCjr video subsystem or Tandy graphics card. The SCREEN instruction can also be used to enable or disable the color on a composite monitor; with an RGB color display or enhanced color display the color is always on, however. When using IBM BASICA 3.21, IBM PCjr Cartridge BASIC, GW-BASIC, QuickBASIC, and TurboBASIC, the final two arguments in the SCREEN instruction can be used to determine the location of the written-to graphics page and the displayed page. The written-to page does not have to be the same as the displayed page. This means you can be drawing graphics on a hidden page while displaying a different page on your monitor. This capability is useful for high-speed real-time animation and for preparation of instant banners. Versions of IBM BASICA prior to 3.21 do not support the page arguments. The Color/Graphics Adapter supports only one graphics page, although in Part Four you will learn an innovative way around this limitation.

SYNTAX: **SCREEN mode, color on/off, written-to page, displayed page**

EXAMPLE: SCREEN 1 establishes the $320 \times 200$ 4-color mode. SCREEN 8,,0,0 sets up the $640 \times 200$ 16-color mode on an EGA with page 0 as the written-to page and page 0 as the displayed page. SCREEN 6,,1,0 invokes the $640 \times 200$ 4-color mode on a PCjr or Tandy with page 0 as the displayed page and all graphics being drawn on hidden page 1. You can omit any of the arguments, but you must include the commas before any argument which you do include. For example, SCREEN,,0,1 would serve to change the written-to and displayed pages without altering the screen mode or the color signal parameters.

WARNINGS: Attempting to invoke any mode other than SCREEN 1 or SCREEN 2 on a Color/Graphics Adapter will cause an error and halt program execution. Attempting to invoke SCREEN 9 on an EGA which is attached to a standard color display will cause an error and halt the program. An enhanced color display monitor is required to generate the $640 \times 350$ SCREEN 9 mode. The CGA is limited to modes 1 and 2. The EGA is limited to modes 1, 2, 7, 8, 9, and 10. (SCREEN 10, which is a monochrome graphics mode, is not used in this book.) The PCjr and Tandy are limited to modes 1, 2, 3, 4, 5, and 6. The error produced when an illegal screen mode is requested is very useful for writing graphics programs which will run on virtually any hardware/software configuration,

as you will learn in Chapter 5.

COMMENTS: Microsoft, Borland, and IBM refer to the written-to graphics page as the a-page (for active page). They call the displayed page the v-page (for visual page). The color on/off nature of the video signal is called color burst by the television industry. On your personal computer, a 1 value disables the color burst on a composite monitor, a 0 value turns on the color signal.

INSTRUCTION: **COLOR**

PURPOSE: The COLOR instruction establishes the colors that will be available for graphics primitives and for alphanumerics. It also establishes the generic background color of the display screen (in all modes) and the border color (in text mode). Refer to Fig. 2-2 for an overview of the standard colors which are available on IBM-compatible personal computers. Regrettably, the COLOR instruction expects to see its arguments in a different format for each of three different screen modes.

SYNTAX FOR SCREEN 0 TEXT MODE: **COLOR background, foreground, border**

SYNTAX FOR SCREEN MODES 1 AND 2: **COLOR background, palette**

SYNTAX FOR SCREEN MODES 3,4,5,6,7,8,9: **COLOR foreground, background**

EXAMPLE: **SCREEN 1,0:COLOR 0,1** sets up the $320 \times 200$ 4-color mode. The 0 argument establishes color 0 (black) as the background color. The 1 argument in-

| 0 BLACK | 8 GRAY |
|---------|--------|
| 1 BLUE | 9 LIGHT BLUE |
| 2 GREEN | 10 LIGHT GREEN |
| 3 CYAN | 11 LIGHT CYAN |
| 4 RED | 12 LIGHT RED |
| 5 MAGENTA | 13 LIGHT MAGENTA |
| 6 BROWN | 14 YELLOW |
| 7 WHITE | 15 INTENSE WHITE |

Fig. 2-2. The standard palette of hardware and display colors on IBM and IBM-compatible microcomputers.

vokes palette 1, which defines 0 as black, 1 as cyan, 2 as magenta, 3 as white. There are only two palettes available in SCREEN 1.

EXAMPLE: **SCREEN 8,,0,0:COLOR 7,0** establishes the 640 × 200 16-color mode on an EGA. The 7 argument invokes color 7 (normal white) as the foreground color for alphanumerics. The 0 argument defines black as the background color.

EXAMPLE: **SCREEN 6,,0,0:COLOR 7,0** invokes the 640 × 200 4-color mode on a PCjr or a Tandy. Normal white (7) is the foreground color for alphanumerics. Black is the background color.

EXAMPLE: **SCREEN 0:COLOR 14,9,1** sets up the text mode. The alphanumerics will display in yellow (color 14); the background will be light blue (color 9); the border color of the screen will be dark blue (color 1). **COLOR 7** would flip the alphanumerics to white while preserving the background and foreground colors.

WARNINGS: In a graphics screen mode, the border color is always the same as the background color. In a text mode, the border color can be the same or different from the background color.

COMMENTS: Refer to Fig. 2-3 for a summary of the range of argument values which are legal for the COLOR instruction. You should note that even on a Color/Graphics Adapter, you can display all 16 colors in the text mode.

INSTRUCTION: **PALETTE**

PURPOSE: The PALETTE instruction is used to choose which hardware colors will be assigned to the available color attribute selections. Refer to Fig. 2-4 for a graphic explanation of this concept. In the 320 × 200 4-color mode, four standard colors are available, numbered as attributes 0, 1, 2, 3. The hardware color black is assigned to attribute 0; hardware color cyan is assigned to attribute 1; hardware color magenta is assigned to attribute 2; hardware color bright white is assigned to attribute 3. On an EGA, PCjr, or Tandy the PALETTE instruction will change these assignments to other hardware colors of your choosing.

SYNTAX: **PALETTE attribute number, hardware color**

EXAMPLE: You could use **PALETTE 1,14** to assign yellow to attribute 1. Whenever you ask for color attribute 1 you would get yellow (hardware color 14).

WARNINGS: Versions of IBM BASICA prior to 3.21 do not support the PALETTE instruction and will produce an error message. IBM BASICA 3.21, GW-BASIC (on a Tandy), IBM Cartridge BASIC, Microsoft QuickBASIC, and Borland TurboBASIC do support the PALETTE instruction. A Color/Graphics

```
SCREEN 1   320x200 4-color
┌─────────────────────────────────────┐
│ COLOR [background] [,[palette]]      │
│        0-15            0-1           │
└─────────────────────────────────────┘

SCREEN 6 640x200 4-color
┌─────────────────────────────────────┐
│ COLOR [foreground] [,[background]]   │
│        1-3             0-15          │
└─────────────────────────────────────┘

SCREEN 8  640x200 16-color
┌─────────────────────────────────────┐
│ COLOR [foreground] [,[background]]   │
│        1-15            0-15          │
└─────────────────────────────────────┘

SCREEN 9 640x350 16-color
┌─────────────────────────────────────┐
│ COLOR [foreground] [,[background]]   │
│        1-15            0-63          │
└─────────────────────────────────────┘
```

Fig. 2-3. Options available with the COLOR instruction.

Adapter will not support a PALETTE instruction. An EGA and the PCjr video subsystem (and the Tandy graphics adapter) support the PALETTE instruction.

COMMENTS: It is important to understand the difference between a color attribute and a hardware color. The hardware colors never change. On most graphics adapters, you have a total of 16 hardware colors available. Period. The color attributes are arguments that you use with the COLOR or LINE instruction, for example, and they can change (on an EGA or PCjr). A color attribute simply refers to one of the hardware colors. Which one it refers to is up to you.

INSTRUCTION: **WINDOW SCREEN**

PURPOSE: The WINDOW SCREEN instruction allows you to redefine the logical coordinates of the display screen. These new logical coordinates are called world coordinates. The actual screen coordinates are called physical coordinates. Specialized routines in BASICA are used to map the world coordinates onto the physical screen.

SYNTAX: **WINDOW SCREEN (upper left)-(lower right)**

EXAMPLE: **WINDOW SCREEN (−399,−299)-(400, 300)** establishes a world coordinate system consisting of 800 horizontal units and 600 vertical units. Coordinate 0,0 would be located at the center of the screen. Note that 0 counts as a point on the screen, which is why the upper left coordinate is −399 and not −400, for example. If you wanted to plot a point at 0,0 the WINDOW SCREEN routine would actually place it

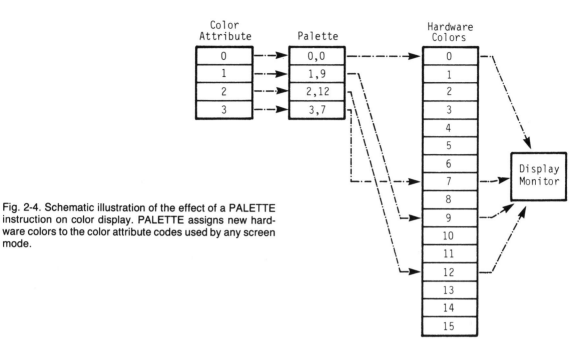

Fig. 2-4. Schematic illustration of the effect of a PALETTE instruction on color display. PALETTE assigns new hardware colors to the color attribute codes used by any screen mode.

at 160,100 on the 320 × 200 4-color screen, at 320,100 on the 640 × 200 16-color screen, and at 320,175 on the 640 × 350 16-color screen. This attribute is handy for writing graphics programs that will execute correctly in any screen mode, as you will learn in Chapter 5.

WARNINGS: Although WINDOW SCREEN preserves the orientation of the screen, the rudimentary WINDOW instruction swaps the Y values, making Y smallest at the bottom of the screen. Use WINDOW SCREEN for 3D graphics. Because of the math routines used by BASIC, an error message (math overflow) will be generated if your world coordinates are less than − 32768 or greater than + 32767. Refer to Appendix B for code fragments which demonstrate a manual method for WINDOWING which overcomes this limitation (and which is useful for C, Pascal, and Assembly Language programming).

COMMENTS: Refer to Fig. 2-5 for a graphic description of the output of the WINDOW SCREEN instruction. Most microcomputer display screens (and all television screens) have a physical aspect ratio of 4:3. In particular, for every four inches of horizontal display, you have three inches of vertical display. This ratio must be preserved for accuracy in 3D modeling, which is why the **WINDOW SCREEN (− 399, − 299)- (400, 300)** instruction is used throughout this book. As a matter of interest, any set of world coordinates

which preserve the 4:3 aspect ratio would be acceptable, but would change the scale of the model. Any other non 4:3 world coordinates would distort the model, making it either too tall and narrow or too short and squat. (For a detailed discussion on how to use the WINDOW SCREEN instruction for panning, zooming, and roaming through a graphics database, refer to the author's first book, *High-Speed Animation and Simulation for Microcomputers,* available at your favorite bookstore or direct from TAB BOOKS, Inc.)

INSTRUCTION: **VIEW**

PURPOSE: The VIEW instruction is useful for installing multitasking graphics windows on the display screen. You can use it too simultaneously display different views of the same 3D model, for example, as you will learn in Part Two. The VIEW routine merely maps world coordinates onto a specified rectangle on the display screen, the size of which you predefine.

SYNTAX: **VIEW (upper left, lower right), color fill, border line**

EXAMPLE: **VIEW (0,0)-(160,100)** would map normal physical screen coordinates into a logical rectangle which is the upper left quarter of the display screen. If you wanted a point at 319,199 (on the 320 × 200 4-color screen), the VIEW routine would place it at 160,100 on the display screen. If you wanted to place

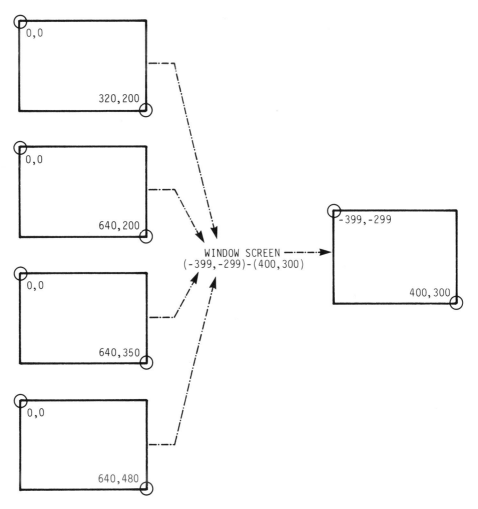

Fig. 2-5. The WINDOW SCREEN instruction redefines the logical coordinates of the screen. Refer to the sample source code in Appendix B for an explanation of how oversized x and y ranges are scaled down to fit the actual physical coordinates of the screen.

a point at the logical center of the viewport, you would ask for 160,100. The VIEW routine would map it to the logical center of your viewport, at 80,50. Refer to Fig. 2-6.

WARNINGS: Note that BASIC maps the entire display screen into the rectangle defined by the VIEW instruction. You are getting a mini-screen, so to speak. The arguments for VIEW cannot be outside the boundaries of the actual physical screen. In the 320 × 200 4-color mode, for example, the arguments for VIEW cannot be less than 0,0 nor greater than 319,199. In addition, when you invoke a CLS instruction to clear the screen, only the area within an active VIEW viewport will be

blanked. Use VIEW without any arguments to disable a viewport.

COMMENTS: If you assign a color attribute to the color fill argument, the rectangle which you have defined with a VIEW instruction will be filled with that color. If you assign a color attribute value to the border line argument, BASIC will draw a border in that color around the viewport (if there is room). Any time you change SCREEN modes the viewports are eliminated. Refer to Appendix B for an example of code which invokes a viewport using a manual method (which is also useful for C, Pascal, and Assembly Language programming).

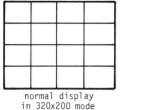 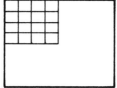

normal display
in 320x200 mode

VIEW (0,0)-(160,100)

Fig. 2-6. The VIEW instruction causes graphics to be mapped onto a logical miniaturization of the screen whose size is defined by the arguments in the VIEW instruction. This technique is useful for generating simultaneous different views of the same model.

## GRAPHICS PRIMITIVES

INSTRUCTION: **PSET**

PURPOSE: The PSET instruction is used to place a single point on the display screen.

SYNTAX: **PSET (x-coordinate, y-coordinate), color**

EXAMPLE: **PSET (95,160),3** will place a dot in color 3 at location 95,160.

WARNINGS: If you do not include the color argument, then BASIC will use the foreground color as the default value.

COMMENTS: PSET is often used to identify the starting point for a long series of lines which draw a polygon.

INSTRUCTION: **LINE**

PURPOSE: The LINE instruction draws a straight line between any two points on the display screen. By using the styling option, dotted lines and dashed lines in a variety of colors can be drawn, thereby giving you the capability for line dithering. Line dithering is the technique of eliminating the harsh surface outlines between two halftone-shaded surfaces.

SYNTAX: **LINE (start)-(end), color, box, style**

EXAMPLE: **LINE (0,0)-(160,100),2** draws a line in magenta from the upper left corner to the center of the 320 × 200 4-color screen.

EXAMPLE: **LINE (0,0)-(160,100),2,B** produces a rectangle whose upper left corner is at 0,0 and whose lower right corner is at 160,100.

EXAMPLE: **LINE (0,0)-(160,100),2,,&HAAAA** draws a dotted line. Refer to Fig. 2-8. This styling option is useful for line dithering when you are rendering solid, fully-shaded 3D models. It is discussed in detail in Part Three. The value &HAAAA is actually AAAA hex, which is 10101010 10101010 binary. A point is plotted for every 1 value; no point is plotted for each 0 value. Whereas 10101010 10101010 creates a dotted line, the value 11001100 11001100 creates a dashed line.

EXAMPLE: **LINE-(200,175),3** draws a line from the last referenced point to 200,175 in color 3. This version of the LINE instruction is useful for creating lengthy polygonal lines.

WARNINGS: BASIC will automatically clip lines whose endpoints fall outside the display screen, but this clipping routine is limited to values greater than − 32767 and less than 32768, otherwise an error message is generated. Refer to Fig. 2-7. Appendix B contains source code for a 2D line clipping routine which does not suffer from this limitation (and which is also useful for programming in C, Pascal, and Assembly Language).

COMMENTS: The LINE instruction is one of the two workhorses of modeling and rendering on microcomputers. IBM and Microsoft refer to the hex styling argument as a 16-bit integer mask.

INSTRUCTION: **PAINT**

PURPOSE: The PAINT instruction provides area fill, sometimes called region fill and flood fill. You can use PAINT to fill any square, rectangle, polygon, circle, or oval. It is one of the two workhorses of modeling and rendering on microcomputers.

SYNTAX: **PAINT (x-coordinate, y-coordinate), fill color, boundary color**

EXAMPLE: **PAINT (160,100),2,3** will use 160,100 as

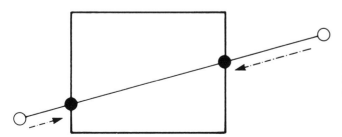

Fig. 2-7. BASIC will automatically clip line segments which fall outside the legal range of screen coordinates. Refer to the source code in Appendix B for an explanation of the mathematics involved.

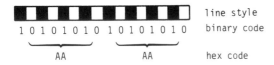

line style

10101010 10101010   binary code

AA        AA          hex code

Fig. 2-8. Line styling. A four-digit hex code is used to represent a two-byte binary code. If the binary bit is 1, the pixel is set to the color called by the LINE instruction. If the binary bit is 0, no action is taken. By varying the binary bit patterns, various dotted and dashed line styles can be plotted.

a starting point and will fill with color 2 until it encounters a border consisting of color 3. Refer to Fig. 2-9. The fill color can be defined as a special code which describes a pixel pattern. This technique is the basis for halftoning, which allows you to create eight or more shades between any two single colors. See Part Three for more on this technique (which is called tiling by IBM and Microsoft).

WARNINGS: If the starting point is located on the boundary, then no area fill will occur. If the starting point is located outside of the boundary, then the background screen will be filled, but not the polygon's interior. If the boundary does not completely encircle the polygon, then the area fill will spill outside the polygon and corrupt other areas of the display screen.

COMMENTS: The area fill routine in BASIC is one of the marvels of the language. It can fill odd-shaped polygons just as easily as simple shapes like rectangles and circles. It can even handle peninsulas and islands in a polygon. Only one quirk in BASIC's fill algorithm is of importance to graphics programmers: if BASIC checks a horizontal line and determines that the entire line is already in the color to be painted, then the area fill routine will stop, even though other sections of the polygon require filling. Although this contingency rarely occurs, it can be easily overcome by

specifying two or more starting points. You are probably already aware that it is not an easy task to write a good fill routine. The algorithm used by BASIC incorporates a number of proven algorithms, including left/right checking, up/down checking, and alternate horizontal zoning analysis (to handle peninsulas and islands). Although no algorithm can be expected to handle every conceivable scenario, the advanced algorithm developed by Microsoft (used in IBM BASICA, IBM Cartridge BASIC, GW-BASIC, Compaq BASIC, Microsoft BASICA, and Microsoft QuickBASIC) is probably one of the best. The algorithm used by Borland TurboBASIC is also very efficient.

## ALPHANUMERIC PRIMITIVES

INSTRUCTION: **LOCATE**

PURPOSE: The LOCATE instruction is used to reposition the alphanumeric cursor to any legal location on the display screen.

SYNTAX: **LOCATE row, column, visible/hidden**

EXAMPLE: **LOCATE 10,1** would reposition the cursor at the tenth row down and the first horizontal column. On the 320 × 200 4-color screen, there are 25 horizontal rows, starting with row 1 at the top of the screen and finishing with row 25 at the bottom of the screen. The 320 × 200 screen supports 40 vertical columns, starting with column 1 at the left of the screen and ending with column 40 at the right of the screen. This means you can print 40 alphanumeric characters across the screen. The 640 × 200 screen supports 25 horizontal rows and 80 vertical columns. This means you can print 80 alphanumeric characters across the screen. If you were to invoke LOCATE 20,10,0 in the text mode the cursor would be located at row 20 (near the bottom of the screen), column 10 (one quarter of the distance across the screen), and the cursor would

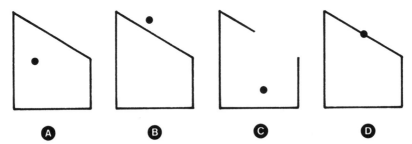

Fig. 2-9. PAINT instruction. In example (a) the polygon will be filled. The background, not the polygon, will be painted in example (b). The area fill will spill over and corrupt the rest of the screen in example (c). If the polygon's border is the same color as the PAINT boundary choice, no area fill will occur in example (d).

be invisible (caused by the 0 argument). Using the 1 argument would make the cursor visible again. The cursor is always visible in the graphics mode.

WARNINGS: Although you can print alphanumerics on line 24, many BASICs will scroll the text up to line 23 as soon as <Enter> is pressed. Some EGAs will leave the text on line 24.

COMMENTS: If you are using multiple graphics pages, you should keep in mind that you have only one cursor at your disposal. If you flip pages, the cursor always stays with the written-to page. If you change written-to pages, the cursor switches to the new written-to page, but retains its present row/column position. You can alter the shape of the cursor in the text mode with two arguments appended to the end of the LOCATE instruction; refer to your BASIC manual for details.

INSTRUCTION: **PRINT**

PURPOSE: The PRINT instruction is used to place alphanumerics on the display screen. You use LOCATE first to identify the starting position.

SYNTAX: **PRINT data**

EXAMPLE: **PRINT "This word"** would display the alphanumerics which are enclosed inside the double quotes.

EXAMPLE: **PRINT C** would display the arithmetic value of C, whatever that value is. However, note that **PRINT "C"** would merely print a letter C on the screen.

EXAMPLE: **PRINT A$** would display an alphanumeric string defined by A$, which could be an entire sentence.

WARNINGS: When you use LOCATE to define the starting location for a subsequent PRINT instruction, you should note that BASIC actually prints an arithmetic variable at the next location. If the variable is positive, a blank space is left before the value of the variable is printed. If the variable is negative, a minus sign is placed in this otherwise blank space. Unless you use a LOCATE instruction, each subsequent PRINT instruction will begin printing at the next row down, flush left.

COMMENTS: The PRINT instruction normally displays alphanumerics in the foreground color, which is usually white. If you are using a Color/Graphics Adapter, you can change the color of the alphanumerics. **DEF SEG:POKE &H4E,2** would cause alphanumerics to be displayed in magenta (color 2) when using IBM BASICA. Your options are limited to colors 1, 2, or 3 when using this POKE technique, however. If you are using an EGA with IBM BASICA 3.21 or QuickBASIC or TurboBASIC, you can change the foreground color with the COLOR instruction. The same applies to IBM Cartridge BASIC on the PCjr and GW-BASIC on the Tandy. The PALETTE instruction can also be used to revise the color of the alphanumerics, of course.

## BIT PUMP INSTRUCTIONS

INSTRUCTION: **GET**

PURPOSE: The GET instruction captures graphics data from a rectangle in the displayed page (the screen buffer) and stores the data in a one-dimensional array inside the BASIC workspace.

SYNTAX: **GET (upper left corner)-(lower right corner), name of array**

EXAMPLE: **GET (10,20)-(160,100),ARRAY1** would save the image inside the rectangle whose upper left corner is at 10,20 and whose lower right corner is at 160,100. The array's name is ARRAY1. Refer to Fig. 2-10.

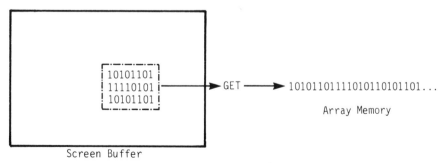

Fig. 2-10. The GET instruction reads the data contents of a screen buffer within a rectangle defined by the GET argument. The data is stored in a graphic array inside BASIC's workspace. A PUT instruction takes the data from the array and places it at any location in the screen buffer.

WARNINGS: An array must be dimensioned with the DIM instruction before the GET instruction is used. The discussion of software sprite animation techniques in Part Four will clarify this methodology. If you are using GW-BASIC, you should remember that GW-BASIC accepts only physical screen coordinates.

COMMENTS: The GET instruction is useful for high-speed animation using graphic arrays, sometimes called software sprite animation. It is also used to capture the portion of the screen to be saved on diskette by the CAD graphics editor demo program in Chapter 25.

INSTRUCTION: **PUT**

PURPOSE: The PUT instruction retrieves a graphic image which has been previously saved in an array by a GET instruction. The PUT instruction will place the image back on the display screen at any legal location.

SYNTAX: **PUT (location), name of array, logical operator**

EXAMPLE: **PUT (160,100),ARRAY1,PSET** would place the array called ARRAY1 at position 160,100 on the display screen. Refer to Fig. 2-10. In other words, the upper left corner of the rectangular array would be positioned at 160,100. The PSET argument means the array will cover any graphics already at the location. Other arguments are possible which provide the ability to produce odd-shaped array graphics. These advanced techniques are discussed in Part Four.

WARNINGS: If you are using GW-BASIC, you should use only physical screen coordinates.

COMMENTS: The PUT instruction is useful for high-speed software sprite animation. It is used in conjunction with GET and DIM, as discussed in detail in Part Four. (For sophisticated examples of high-speed animation using the GET/PUT instructions, refer to the author's first book, *High-Speed Animation and Simu-*

*lation for Microcomputers*, available at your favorite bookstore or direct from TAB BOOKS, Inc.)

INSTRUCTION: **PCOPY**

PURPOSE: The PCOPY instruction copies the contents of one graphics page to another graphics page. This bit pump instruction is available on IBM BASICA 3.21 with an EGA, GW-BASIC on a Tandy, and IBM Cartridge BASIC on a PCjr. It is also available with Quick-BASIC with an EGA. TurboBASIC 1.0 has no PCOPY statement.

SYNTAX: **PCOPY source page, target page**

EXAMPLE: **PCOPY 1,0** would transfer the graphics contents of page 1 to page 0. The contents of the source page are undamaged during the procedure.

WARNINGS: This function is unavailable on a Color/Graphics Adapter, although in Part Four you will learn about an innovative way to overcome this limitation.

COMMENTS: When using an EGA, PCOPY will work only with screen modes 0, 7, 8, 9, 10. When using a PCjr or a Tandy, PCOPY will work with screen modes 0, 1, 2, 3, 4, 5, 6.

**EXPERIMENTATION**

This chapter provides an introduction to the graphics instructions that you will be using later in the book. You will be learning more about the instructions, particularly the PAINT instruction, when rendering techniques are discussed in Part Three.

Your best reference is and will always be your BASIC manual. Many programmers experience difficulty understanding the sometimes mysterious explanations found in many manuals, but hands-on experimentation will always clear up any misunderstanding.

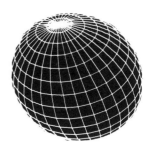

# 3

# Modular Programming

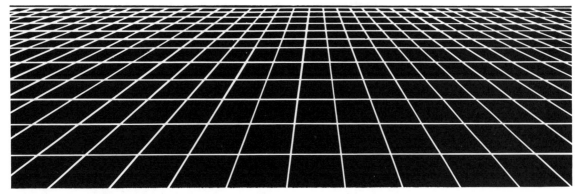

If you want to supercharge your programs, use modular programming.

Any program can be written, tested, and debugged quicker if you use modular programming techniques. This is especially true for graphics programs. In addition, the resulting program will normally be more compact, easier to read and revise, and will produce higher quality graphics. It would have been impossible to create the high-performance demonstration programs in this book without using a modular programming approach. Modular programming can take a very complicated idea and make it easy to understand.

## WHAT IS MODULAR PROGRAMMING?

What is modular programming? It is two things. First, it is an attitude towards writing programs. Second, it is a set of skills and techniques that you employ while you are writing programs.

Simply stated, modular programming involves using separate subroutines to accomplish separate tasks within the overall environment of the whole program. A modular program consists of a main routine which calls upon a number of separate subroutines to help

it get the job done.

The opposite of modular program code is inline code. Refer to Fig. 3-1. Instead of jumping to a separate subroutine to accomplish a specific task, the code which produces the desired result is written right into the main routine. This approach will eventually lead to the infamous "spaghetti code" that you have probably already seen or read about.

## PROGRAMMING ALTERNATIVES

Although you can achieve good results with either inline code or modular code, you will expend much more effort and time if you use the inline code approach. It is difficult to keep the logical structure of your program straight in your mind when the program is a convoluted mixture of unrelated routines. As your program grows in size, as any serious interactive graphics program must, you will find it increasingly difficult to make changes in your code. And the changes you do make will often produce unexpected results.

When you use a modular approach to programming, however, you are forced to be organized in your thinking and in your code writing. If you use a stand-

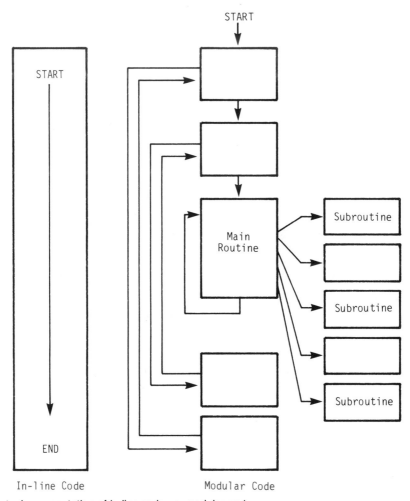

START

START

Main
Routine

Subroutine

Subroutine

Subroutine

END

In-line Code

Modular Code

Fig. 3-1. Conceptual representation of in-line code vs. modular code.

alone subroutine to calculate 3D coordinates, for example, you know that the subroutine expects to receive certain input when it is called and it will always give you consistent output. A 3D formula subroutine, for example, expects to receive the world coordinates of the model you wish to draw. When you return to your main routine, the 3D formula subroutine will give you the x,y coordinates for the display screen. Needless to say, this regimen forces you to adopt an organized approach to creating the 3D image on the screen.

### The 90/10 Rule

There is an old saying among successful programmers. They say that 10% of the program code usually

performs 90% of the computing while the program is running. This is especially true in graphics programs. Using a modular approach to programming means that you will have a separate subroutine for each separate graphics function. If you find that you are making very heavy use of your 3D formulas subroutine, for example, you can work on optimizing that particular routine. And because it is a separate standalone subroutine, you can revise and edit it without worrying about corrupting other parts of your program. If unexpected things start happening, you know exactly where the problem originates.

Using a modular approach also provides an opportunity for improved formatting of your programs. Formatting refers to the way in which the program code

22

is arranged on the display screen or when it is printed out. You will read more about formatting later in this chapter.

Best of all, a modular approach to programming keeps things simple. This means you can concentrate on the really important things such as logical structure and decision-making techniques. In other words, modular programming makes it easy for you to take full advantage of the tools which BASIC (or Pascal, C, or Assembly Language) places at your disposal.

## THE BASIC PROGRAMMING LANGUAGE

BASIC provides three types of high-powered programming tools which you can use to create graphics programs: statements, numeric expressions, and numeric operators.

If you are like most programmers, you have probably been using these tools in your programming without the bother of having to understand their generic names. It is like many things in the real world, these tools work whether or not you take the time to delve into the theory which explains why they work.

## HIGH-POWERED TOOL NO. 1:
## NUMERIC EXPRESSIONS

A numeric expression is simply another name for a number (or a value). It can be a numeric constant such as 4, −512, or 32767. Or it can be a numeric variable such as A, SR1, or C%. A numeric expression can be either an integer value or a floating point value. Unless you tell it otherwise, BASIC will use floating point values for all calculations. This is what programmers mean when they say default. BASIC defaults to floating point, although integer calculations are much faster.

What is an integer? It is a whole number. That is, it never contains any decimal point. Because BASIC uses two bytes of memory to store an integer, the number cannot be greater than +32767 nor less than −32768.

What is a floating point number? Simply stated, it is a number with a decimal point in it. BASIC uses scientific notation to store floating point numbers in memory. This means a floating point number can be very large or very small, much larger or much smaller than an integer. BASIC uses floating point numbers which are accurate to six digits, which means a floating point number can be as negative as 10E−38 or as positive as 10E+38 (these mysterious notations are

simply a scientist's way of writing 10 with 38 zeros). BASIC requires 4 bytes of memory to store a single precision number.

All of the demonstration programs in this book use floating point numbers. Although math calculations are much quicker with integer numbers, 3D formulas need the extra accuracy provided by floating point numbers, as you will see in Part Two. To be specific, the programs use BASIC's default condition of single-precision floating point numbers, which are accurate to six digits and which contain up to seven digits. You can also instruct BASIC to use double-precision floating point numbers, which are accurate to 16 digits and which contain up to 17 digits, but this degree of accuracy is very time-consuming. (TurboBASIC can handle numbers in a different way. Refer to Appendix D.)

Numeric expressions (numbers) are manipulated by numeric operators. So, what is a numeric operator?

## HIGH-POWERED TOOL NO. 2:
## NUMERIC OPERATORS

The numeric operators which BASIC provides fall into four main categories: relation operators, arithmetic operators, logical operators, and function operators.

### Relation Operators

Relation operators are decision-making operators. They are often used in conjunction with IF...THEN statements. The symbol < and the symbol > and the symbol = are relation operators. For example, the statement IF A>B THEN GOSUB 500 means that the program will branch to line 500 if A is greater than B. The statement IF A<B THEN GOSUB 500 will branch if A is less than B. Relation operators can be combined as in IF A> =B THEN... which is understood to mean if-A-is-greater-than-or-equal-to-B. The program will branch if either condition or if both conditions are true.

### Arithmetic Operators

Arithmetic operators are mathematical. The addition symbol + is an arithmetic operator. The subtraction symbol − and the multiplication symbol * and the division symbol / are also arithmetic operators. Other, seldom used arithmetic operators include the exponential symbol ^ and the integer division symbol \. For example, A^2 means A squared. A^3 is A cubed.

### Function Operators

Function operators are closely related to arithmetic operators. Function operators are trigonometric, or geometric, or mathematical functions such as sine, cosine, square root, and so forth. As you can see, a function is simply a group of arithmetic operators which produces a specific result. Although you can use BASIC to predefine your own customized function operators, BASIC has a number of useful function operators already built-in. These include SIN for sine and COS for cosine, among others.

### Logical Operators

Logical operators are used to check for true and false conditions. Logical operators are useful for making decisions about program flow. As you will see in Part Four, logical operators are also very handy for creating some spectacular effects with graphic arrays and software sprite animation. Logical operators include NOT, AND, OR, XOR, IMP, and EQV.

### HIGH-POWERED TOOL NO. 3: STATEMENTS

A statement is an instruction such as GOSUB, IF ...THEN, CLS, and so on. IBM BASICA, IBM Cartridge BASIC, GW-BASIC, Compaq BASIC, Microsoft BASICA, Microsoft QuickBASIC, and Borland TurboBASIC all have a rich vocabulary of powerful, yet easy-to-use, statements. IBM BASICA 3.21, for example, provides over 160 different statements, 19 of which are graphics oriented. Microsoft QuickBASIC 2.0 provides over 150 different statements. TurboBASIC 1.0 offers over 170 statements.

Some BASIC statements are used in conjunction with logical operators. The PUT statement uses a logical operator as one of its arguments when it places a graphic array on the display screen, as you will see in Part Four and Part Five. The IF...THEN statement often uses a relation operator to render a decision about program flow (i.e., IF A>B THEN...).

The GOSUB statement is important to modular programs, obviously. It is used to jump to a subroutine from the main routine. RETURN is used to branch back to the main routine from the subroutine.

The FOR...NEXT statement is useful for counting loops in graphics programs, especially animation programs. For example, a set of instructions regulated by FOR T = 1 TO 20 would be executed 20 times. The FOR...NEXT statement can be nested, which means

that one counting loop can be placed inside another counting loop. Refer to Fig. 3-2. This is a handy way to keep your graphics programs compact, as you will later learn in Part Two.

The READ...DATA pair of statements is useful for retrieving values from a graphics database. This technique is referred to by professional CAD systems as a linked list approach to the database. As you begin to learn about 3D modeling in Part Two, you will see the world coordinates for the model which you want to draw are stored in a database. The READ statement permits the program to fetch these items from the database.

### FORMATTING YOUR PROGRAMS

Modular programming makes it easy to format your programs. Formatting is the process of organizing the layout of your programs at the source code level. Formatting refers to the way your program listing looks when you view it on the display screen or when you print it out on your printer.

Proper program formatting achieves two results. First, a properly formatted graphics program runs faster. Second, a properly formatted program is easier for you to read and revise.

Refer to Fig. 3-3 as you read this section. Notice

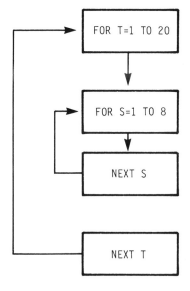

Fig. 3-2. Nested loops. The T loop will execute 20 occasions. The S loop will execute 160 occasions (8 occasions for each of 20 T loops = 160).

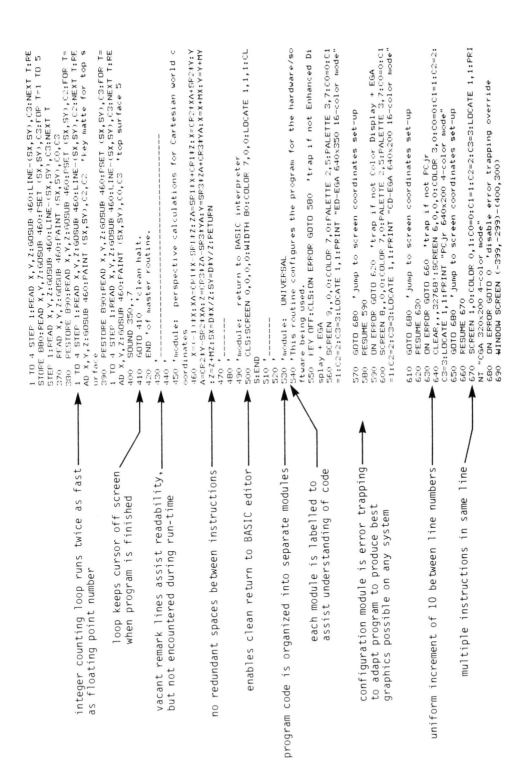

Fig. 3-3. Line formatting principles for readable, structured source code.

how vacant remark lines have been used to separate the various subroutines of the program. These vacant lines aid in program readability, but they are never encountered by the program during run-time, so no speed is lost. Notice, on the other hand, that no extra spaces have been left inside the statements, where it would slow down run-time speed. Where a number of statements are included on one line, they are butted up against each other, separated by only a colon. Where a comma is used as a delimiter, no redundant space is included after the comma.

Many of the program lines in Fig. 3-3 contain more than one statement. There is no reason to put each statement on a separate line. In fact, BASIC executes faster if groups of statements are placed on the same line. In addition, it makes sense to group related statements together on the same line. It is easier to follow the logic flow when you group them together.

Each line number increments by ten. Line 200 is followed by line 210, for example. While you are building and testing the program, this approach makes it easy for you to add new lines between existing lines. It also makes it easy to read the program in spite of BASIC's tendency to wrap long statements onto the next display line. You can tell where the next program line starts because it always starts with a line number which is ten units greater than the previous line number.

The program listing illustrated in Fig. 3-3 has been printed out to a line length of 60 characters. This was achieved by the keyboard command WIDTH "LPT1:",60:LLIST. Otherwise, BASIC would print out your program to a line length of 80 characters, which doesn't leave you much space in the left and right margins. Space in the margins is handy for making changes in pen or pencil while you are working on a complicated graphics program.

You can see from Fig. 3-3 how proper line formatting lends itself to modular programming and how modular programming lends itself to proper line formatting. They go hand in hand.

## OPTIMIZED CODE

Optimized code is program code which has been crafted to run as efficiently as possible. For graphics programs, this usually means the program has been crafted to run as fast as possible. The demonstration programs in this book use a number of optimizing techniques which you can use in your own programming.

## Optimizing the Math

Some arithmetic operations in BASIC are much quicker than others. When you wish to square a number, it is much quicker to multiply the number by itself than to square it in BASIC. In other words, $X*X$ executes faster than $X^2$. Division executes very slowly in BASIC (as it also does in Pascal, C, and Assembly Language). If you want to divide a number by two, it makes more sense to write $X*.5$ than to write $X/2$.

Integer math will sometimes execute 100 times faster than floating point math. Although it is possible to rewrite all of the 3D formulas, all of the hidden surface removal formulas, and all of the computer-controlled shading formulas in this book in integer math, it would make the code more difficult to understand.

## Optimizing Decision-Making

The most often-used statement for making a decision is the IF. . .THEN statement. If a number of conditions are being tested, you should always test the most likely condition first. Why waste time checking rare conditions before you check a likely condition? Simply check the likely one first, then carry on with program execution if the test is positive. If the test is negative, then you can take the time (i.e., you must take the time) to check among the less likely conditions. The 2D interactive graphics editor demo program in Part Five provides a fast-running demonstration of this technique. (For an example of optimized keyboard controls in a flight simulation environment, refer to the author's first book, *High-Speed Animation and Simulation for Microcomputers*, available at your favorite bookstore or direct from TAB BOOKS, Inc.)

## Optimizing Trapping

All of the demonstration programs in this book use key trapping. When a program is running, you simply touch F2 to exit back to BASIC. Although this is handy during program development because it lets you quickly start up and stop a program, it is very wasteful of time. When you write your own programs, you should remove the ON KEY statement which enables key trapping once you have thoroughly debugged your program. It takes time for BASIC to check the keyboard buffer between each statement it executes. Instead, simply use an INKEY$ variable in your keyboard subroutine, as demonstrated in Chapter 25. (If you are using QuickBASIC, refer to Appendix C for more discussion about this. If you are using TurboBASIC, read Appendix D.)

### Optimizing Subroutines

Contrary to what you may have heard, it does not make any difference to the BASIC interpreter where your subroutines are located in your program. No matter where they are situated, on the first occasion they are called with a GOSUB statement BASIC must search through the program until it finds the subroutine. BASIC then memorizes where that subroutine is located. On subsequent GOSUB statements, BASIC jumps directly to the subroutine. So it won't make your programs run any faster if you put your subroutines right next to the main routine that calls them.

### HOW TO DEBUG GRAPHICS PROGRAMS

A strong advantage of using BASIC while you are learning about writing graphics programs is BASIC's ability to point out your programming bugs. In interpreted BASIC, the program will halt at an error and will display the offending line. A short description of the error is usually displayed too. In compiled BASIC this same process occurs during compilation.

A word of caution is in order here. Always save your program on diskette before you run it for the first time. Otherwise, if your computer locks up when you attempt to run a new program, you'll lose your only copy of the program (in RAM memory) when you reboot your microcomputer.

### Common Garden-Variety Bugs

A number of familiar errors seem to keep popping up again and again during the development of high-performance graphics programs. After a while, you will become accustomed to these common error messages and to the corrective measures required to remedy the situation.

Figure 3-4 outlines the most common error messages and suggested remedial action. If you don't have the companion diskette and you are typing in the program listings from the book, the error which you will encounter most often is "Syntax error". This usually means a simple typing error. When you are writing your own programs, it can either mean a simple typing error or it can mean you have used improper language. The solution is to carefully read the statements in the offending line until you spot your oversight. Referring to your BASIC manual is often helpful. Even the best professional programmers get caught by syntax errors more often than they would care to admit, including this author.

Some of the descriptions in Fig. 3-4 may seem mysterious now. Their meaning will become clearer as you progress through the book. You might want to fold back the corner of the page so you can easily refer back to Fig. 3-4 when you encounter error messages during the demonstration programs.

### Easy Bugs vs. Tough Bugs

It is easy enough to clean up a bug-ridden program when BASIC guides you through it, of course. The really tough part of the job comes when the program listing adheres to all of BASIC's syntax requirements, but the program results are not what you want (or what you expect!). Graphics programs either work right or they don't . . . there is no middle ground. Because their results are right there on the display screen for everyone to see, it is pretty obvious when they are not working correctly.

### PERFORMANCE ERRORS

Performance errors can be tricky to correct in a graphics program. There are a limited number of programmer's oversights which seem to be the prime culprits, however. Regrettably, BASIC's error-trapping editor cannot help you identify these errors, you've got to find these bugs and stomp on them yourself.

First, make certain your concepts are correct. Obviously, it doesn't matter if you have used correct syntax for COS (the cosine function) if what was required was a sine function. Some programmers, this author included, maintain that getting the conceptual component of a program right is the most challenging part of programming.

Next, ensure that every subroutine is concluded with a RETURN statement. Otherwise, the program falls through to an undesired location in the code.

If your computer hangs when you try to run the program, use Ctrl-Break to return to the BASIC editor (use Fn-Break on the PCjr). BASIC will tell you

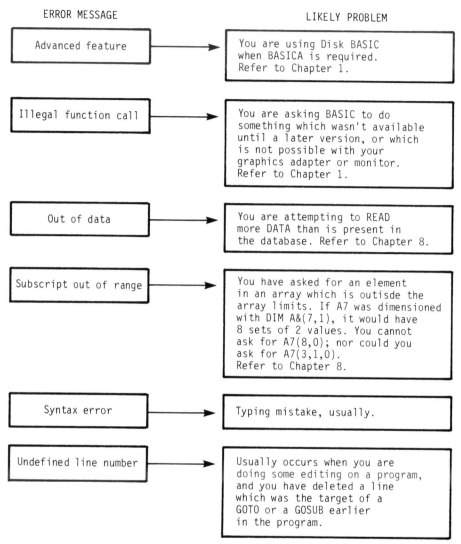

| ERROR MESSAGE | LIKELY PROBLEM |
|---|---|
| Advanced feature | You are using Disk BASIC when BASICA is required. Refer to Chapter 1. |
| Illegal function call | You are asking BASIC to do something which wasn't available until a later version, or which is not possible with your graphics adapter or monitor. Refer to Chapter 1. |
| Out of data | You are attempting to READ more DATA than is present in the database. Refer to Chapter 8. |
| Subscript out of range | You have asked for an element in an array which is outisde the array limits. If A7 was dimensioned with DIM A&(7,1), it would have 8 sets of 2 values. You cannot ask for A7(8,0); nor could you ask for A7(3,1,0). Refer to Chapter 8. |
| Syntax error | Typing mistake, usually. |
| Undefined line number | Usually occurs when you are doing some editing on a program, and you have deleted a line which was the target of a GOTO or a GOSUB earlier in the program. |

Fig. 3-4. Common error messages experienced with graphics-oriented programs.

what line number was being executed when you pressed Break. Start your bug search in this area. If your computer locks up, on the other hand, you will have to use Ctrl-Alt-Del to reboot. In severe cases you will have to turn off the power supply to regain control of your computer. In these two situations, use the foolproof debugging technique discussed at the end of this section.

Check that you aren't using the same variable name to refer to two different variables. In complicated graphics programs, this situation can easily occur. You

may want to read Appendix A for more information on this.

If you have just made a change and the program suddenly begins to run incorrectly, go back and check the line you just edited. Many BASICs will leave off the invisible character for the line-feed-carriage-return function when your statement finishes at the exact end of the line. If so, use <Enter> to put the character back in. (IBM BASICA 3.21 is notorious for this.)

If you want to be certain a particular section of code is executing, place a BEEP statement in it. You can always remove the BEEP later. You can also use PRINT statements at critical locations to display alphanumerics which tell you what's happening as the program is executing. This technique is effective for debugging math-oriented subroutines which generate interim math values.

If you have used the DEFINT statement anywhere in the program, delete it in order to be certain that you haven't accidentally declared another variable as an integer when it needs to be floating point. (If you use DEFINT T, then T will be an integer, but T4A will also be an integer.) If the program output is still unchanged, re-insert the DEFINT instruction.

### A Fool-proof Debugging Technique

If you are really stuck, there is only one thing you can do. Put breakpoints in the code. Fortunately, this final resort never fails. Starting near the beginning of the program, add an endless loop such as:

```
590   BEEP:LOCATE 10,1:PRINT "OK to here."
600   GOTO 600
```

which cleanly halts the program. If your program runs correctly up to the breakpoint, move the breakpoint to a point further along. Keep up this strategy until you isolate the area where the bug is located.

### SUMMARY

You learned in this chapter that modular programming is efficient and effective in any programming language. You saw that BASIC offers a rich selection of powerful, yet easy-to-use, instructions. You learned specific ways to optimize, format, and debug your programs.

The next chapter discusses innovative ways to manage your keyboard in an interactive context.

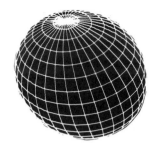

# 4

# *Managing The Keyboard*

An interactive graphics program responds to your input by changing the image being displayed. In turn, you respond to the image by either accepting the model or by requesting further changes. Interactivity is a two-way street. It is a dynamic process.

## TOOLS FOR INTERACTING

The reciprocal nature of an interactive graphics program means that you must have some way of communicating with the computer. Four tools are usually used for interacting with a graphics program: a mouse, a light pen, a digital pad, and a keyboard. Because not everyone has a mouse, a light pen, or a digital pad, the demonstration programs in this book employ the keyboard for all interactive input. After all, every microcomputer is sold with a keyboard as standard equipment.

Likewise, the reciprocal nature of an interactive graphics program means that the computer must have some way of communicating with you. Six tools are usually used by programs to interact with the user. These tools are: graphics on the display screen, alphanumerics on the display screen, sound, graphics produced on paper by a plotter, alphanumerics produced on paper by a standard printer, and graphics saved as an image file on diskette.

The demonstration programs in the book rely primarily upon the display screen to interact with you. Both graphics and alphanumerics are used by the programs to communicate with you. Occasionally, sound is used to alert you to some occurrence or activity. You will also learn how to save graphics images on diskette and how to retrieve them later. (If you have access to a plotter, or even a standard dot matrix or ink jet printer, you can generate a permanent paper copy of the display image. Refer to the GRAPHICS screen print instruction in your DOS manual for more on this.)

## LEVELS FOR INTERACTING

A graphics program can be interactive at two different levels. First, the interactivity can occur at the programmer's level. During program development, you simply halt the program, display the source code on the display screen, and edit the variables which will change the image on which you are working.

Second, interactivity can occur at the user's level. In this instance the end-user does not have access to the source code (and probably would not understand it even if access were available). The program is essentially complete and polished. The user interacts with the graphics program while it is running. As the programmer, you are responsible for constructing a variety of subroutines which the end-user can invoke by keyboard commands.

Because this book is a guide for programmers, most of the demonstration programs are interactive at the programmer's level (i.e., at the source code level). As you gain more expertise in modeling, rendering, and animating with your personal computer, you will find that you can halt a program and quickly edit a few variables to create the results you seek. No book on high-performance interactive graphics would be complete, however, without a solid example of interactivity at the user level. The CAD graphics editor in Chapter 25 is a stand-alone demonstration program which illustrates a dynamic user interface in a complex graphics environment. Chapter 26 provides code which creates a fully-interactive real-time animation of an aerospace vehicle in 3D airspace.

## MANAGING THE KEYBOARD

Whether you interact with the graphics program at the source code level or at the user's level, you must find effective and efficient ways of managing the keyboard. Each level of interaction implies a specific set of keyboard techniques. You are probably already familiar with the source code level techniques if you have done any kind of programming at all.

## KEYBOARD MANAGEMENT
## AT SOURCE CODE LEVEL

As you will soon discover, the demonstration programs in this book have been designed for easy modification. If you are using a BASIC interpreter such as IBM BASICA, IBM Cartridge BASIC, GW-BASIC, Compaq BASIC, or Microsoft QuickBASIC, simply touch F2 to start a program. (Tandy users touch Alt-R.) If you wish to stop a program that is running, simply touch F2 again. By using F2 as a toggle switch, you can quickly start and stop any program. This makes experimentation a breeze with interpreted BASIC. Plus, as an added bonus, you are always returned to the proper editing mode (the 80-column text mode); whereas if you use the Break key to exit a program, you are left stranded in whatever graphics mode the program was using.

## Interpreters

Interacting with the program is straightforward with interpreted BASIC. You use the LIST command to display a section of source code on the screen. Then you use the EDIT command to display the particular line you wish to change. By using the cursor arrow keys and the DEL key you can easily modify the line. Touch the F2 key and your program is immediately up and running, giving you immediately feedback on your changes.

Simply stated, interpreted BASIC is probably the most efficient programming language for initial development of graphics programs.

## Compilers

If you are using a BASIC compiler such as Quick-BASIC or TurboBASIC, you reap the advantage of much quicker run-time speeds. Interacting with the program at the source code level is almost, but not quite, as easy as with interpreted BASIC. With Quick-BASIC, for example, you use the cursor arrow keys to scroll past portions of source code to the line you wish to edit. After editing the line, you simply touch the F5 key to compile the code into memory. Once compilation is complete (a 200-line program can be compiled in 15 seconds), you press Ctrl-R to run the program. Again, while the program is running, all you need do is touch F2 to return to the QuickBASIC editor. TurboBASIC operates in a similar manner, with slight differences.

## KEYBOARD MANAGEMENT
## AT THE END-USER LEVEL

Managing the keyboard while a program is running is a substantive programming challenge, even for professional programmers. The user must be protected from the onerous chore of having to understand the workings of the source code. The source code must be protected from fatal errors introduced by inappropriate keyboard requests from the user. With a little planning, however, the manner in which the user interacts with the program via the keyboard can be a pleasant and productive experience. This interaction is often called the user interface.

## The Keyboard Buffer

The hardware and the ROM/BIOS of your computer take care of capturing keystrokes while a program is running. It stores these keystrokes in a keyboard buffer. As the programmer, it is your job to retrieve these keystrokes from the keyboard buffer and use them to control the activities of your program.

The keyboard buffer used by BASIC can hold a maximum of 15 keystrokes. Refer to Fig. 4-1. The first keystroke into the buffer is also the first one taken out by your program. For example, if you type A B C D on the keyboard, when your program retrieves a keystroke from the keyboard buffer the first character it will encounter will be an A, then a B, and so on.

If the user attempts to enter more than 15 keystrokes before your program has removed any characters from the keyboard buffer, the computer will beep. The extra keystroke is lost; it is not saved anywhere.

As you can see in Fig. 4-1, special keystrokes such as < Enter>, ALT, CTRL, INS, and so forth can be stored in the keyboard buffer. It is easy for the user to enter these special keys; simply use the keyboard. It is a bit trickier for the programmer to retrieve these special characters from the keyboard buffer. Fortunately, BASIC provides some powerful tools to help manage the keyboard.

### The INKEY$ Statement

The INKEY$ statement in both interpreted and compiled BASIC will retrieve one (and only one) keystroke from the keyboard buffer. When you use the instruction K$ = INKEY$, for example, the top character in the keyboard buffer is assigned to the variable K$. It is at this point that a keystroke is retrieved from the keyboard buffer. From this point on there are a variety of algorithms you can use to check the identity of this variable. The most useful is the IF...THEN statement.

The algorithm IF K$ = "A" THEN... will check if the character A is present. This simple statement can be used to check for any standard uppercase alphabetic character from A to Z, any standard lowercase alphabetic character from a to z, or any standard numerical character, among others. You can also check if the spacebar was pressed by using the statement, IF K$ = " " THEN... provided that you place a space between the two sets of quotation marks.

If your program pauses for input from the user, there are a number of clever algorithms you can use to control this scenario. The following example will

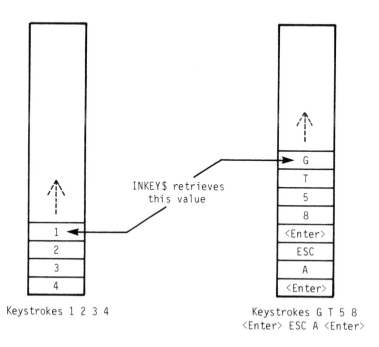

Keystrokes 1 2 3 4

Keystrokes G T 5 8
<Enter> ESC A <Enter>

INKEY$ retrieves this value

Fig. 4-1. Keyboard buffer. The INKEY$ instruction checks the contents of the keyboard buffer on a first-in first-out basis. Only one keystroke is retrieved by INKEY$ on each occasion the INKEY$ instruction is used by a program.

pause until the user presses any key.

```
590  K$ = INKEY$
600  IF K$ = " " THEN 590
```

Line 590 checks the keyboard buffer. Line 600 determines the identity of the character, if it is nul (i.e., no key has been pressed) the program loops back to line 590. Note that there is no space between the two sets of quotation marks. You could accomplish the same thing with the following example.

```
600  K$ = INKEY$:WHILE
       K$ = " ":K$ = INKEY$:WEND
```

If you want a specific key to be pressed before your program will continue, you might use an algorithm such as the following example. Simply put, line 600 will loop back to 590 if the keystroke is any character other than G, including the nul character.

```
590  K$ = INKEY$
600  IF K$ < > "G" THEN 590
```

Alternatively, if you wish the G key to be pressed before your program will continue, you could use the following example. Line 600 loops back to 590 until the G keystroke is received.

```
590  K$ = INKEY$
600  IF K$ = "G" THEN 700 ELSE 590
```

The INKEY$ instruction is also useful for emptying the keyboard buffer. Unless you specifically retrieve keystrokes from the buffer, they will remain there, even after the program has ended. An unexpected character in the keyboard buffer could throw your program offstep if the user has been striking the keyboard when you didn't expect it.

To empty the keyboard buffer before you ask the user for input, you could use the following algorithm. Line 600 keeps looping back to line 590 if it finds any character besides nul in the keyboard buffer.

```
590  K$ = INKEY$
600  IF K$ < > " " THEN 590
```

Although other statements such as INPUT and INPUT$ can be used to read the keyboard, the INKEY$ instruction is very efficient and very effective for most graphics applications. Refer to your BA-SIC manual for more information about INPUT and INPUT$.

The examples in this chapter assign the INKEY$ value to the variable K$. You can use any other variable of your choosing, such as A$ = INKEY$, T6B$ = INKEY$, LETTER$ = INKEY$, and so on. K$ = INKEY$ is used throughout this book for consistency.

## KEYBOARD CONVENTIONS

Over the years a number of familiar keyboard conventions have become established. Refer to Fig. 4-2. For example, ESC or F1 is often used as a key to request help, which is usually provided either as a full-page help screen or as a few lines of alphanumerics on the existing screen. The <Enter> key is often used as a method for the user to accept a default condition or to simply continue program execution. The spacebar has become more commonplace ever since the introduction of QuickBASIC, which uses it instead of the <Enter> key to execute commands. The cursor arrow keys are often used to move the alphanumeric cursor and to control the movement of a crosshair (as demonstrated by the CAD graphics editor in Chapter 25).

Although these conventions lend a professional polish to your program, you require a more sophisticated tool than INKEY$ to incorporate these keyboard conventions into your interactive graphics programs.

## ASCII CHARACTER CODES

Keystrokes are stored in the keyboard buffer as ASCII character codes. In the earlier example the character A would be stored inside the buffer as ASCII character 075. In BASIC, you can code this as either "A" or CHR$(075) or CHR$(75). The ability to address characters by their ASCII codes is helpful in dealing with special keys. The following example will check for the <Enter> key:

```
600  K$ = INKEY$:IF K$ = CHR$(013) THEN . . .
```

The following algorithm searches for the ESC key.

```
600  K$ = INKEY$:IF K$ = CHR$(027) THEN . . .
```

The next example detects the backspace key.

```
600  K$ = INKEY$:IF K$ = CHR$(008) THEN . . .
```

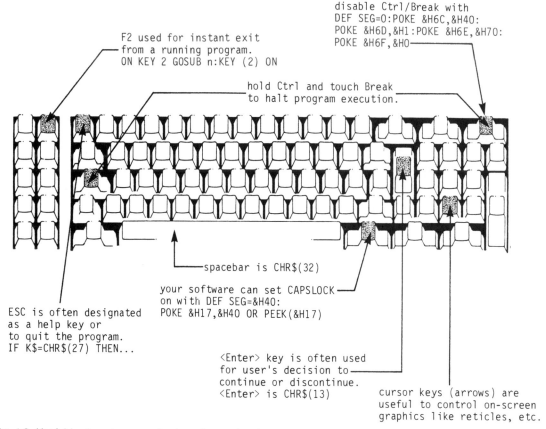

F2 used for instant exit
from a running program.
ON KEY 2 GOSUB n:KEY (2) ON

disable Ctrl/Break with
DEF SEG=0:POKE &H6C,&H40:
POKE &H6D,&H1:POKE &H6E,&H70:
POKE &H6F,&H0

hold Ctrl and touch Break
to halt program execution.

spacebar is CHR$(32)

your software can set CAPSLOCK
on with DEF SEG=&H40:
POKE &H17,&H40 OR PEEK(&H17)

ESC is often designated
as a help key or
to quit the program.
IF K$=CHR$(27) THEN...

<Enter> key is often used
for user's decision to
continue or discontinue.
<Enter> is CHR$(13)

cursor keys (arrows) are
useful to control on-screen
graphics like reticles, etc.

Fig. 4-2. Useful keyboard ergonomics for software developers.

To check for the spacebar, you could use the following algorithm.

**600 K$ = INKEY$:IF K$ = CHR$(032) THEN . . .**

The following algorithm looks for the TAB key.

**600 K$ = INKEY$:IF K$ = CHR$(9) THEN . . .**

## EXTENDED ASCII CODES

The really professional keystrokes are composed of not one, but two ASCII codes. Refer to Fig. 4-3. Retrieving these keystrokes from the keyboard buffer is a two-step procedure. First, you must check to see if the character string retrieved by INKEY$ is composed of two ASCII codes. Second, if it is, then you must determine the identity of the second code. The first ASCII code in a two-code string is normally CHR$(0).

By referring to the appendices in your BASIC manual you can identify the extended ASCII codes for exotic keystrokes such as CTRL-F1, ALT-F6, INS, DEL, ALT-Q, and the four cursor arrow keys, among many others. Figure 4-3 summarizes these useful keys for you.

Suppose you wished to designate the keystroke combination of ALT-Q for a particular purpose, perhaps to Quit a part of the program. If this combination of keys was pressed by the user, it would show up in the keyboard buffer as a two-character string composed of CHR$(0) and CHR$(16).

If you wished to designate the cursor-arrow keys for a particular function, you could poll the keyboard buffer for the cursor-right arrow key by checking for CHR$(0) and CHR$(77). The following algorithm will identify an extended ASCII code.

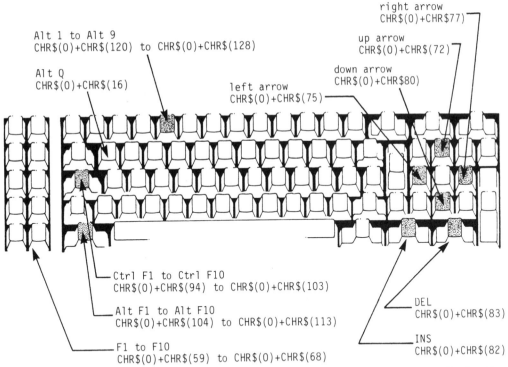

Alt 1 to Alt 9
CHR$(0)+CHR$(120) to CHR$(0)+CHR$(128)

Alt Q
CHR$(0)+CHR$(16)

right arrow
CHR$(0)+CHR$77)

up arrow
CHR$(0)+CHR$(72)

down arrow
CHR$(0)+CHR$80)

left arrow
CHR$(0)+CHR$(75)

Ctrl F1 to Ctrl F10
CHR$(0)+CHR$(94) to CHR$(0)+CHR$(103)

Alt F1 to Alt F10
CHR$(0)+CHR$(104) to CHR$(0)+CHR$(113)

F1 to F10
CHR$(0)+CHR$(59) to CHR$(0)+CHR$(68)

DEL
CHR$(0)+CHR$(83)

INS
CHR$(0)+CHR$(82)

Fig. 4-3. An understanding of how to use extended keyboard codes gives you the capability to use professional keystroke combinations in your programs.

```
580 K$ = INKEY$
590 IF LEN(K$) = 2 THEN K$ = RIGHT$(K$,1)
600 IF K$ = CHR$(16) THEN . . .
```

In the preceding example, line 590 checks to see if the length of the string retrieved from the buffer is 2. If so, the RIGHT$ statement in BASIC is used to determine the identity of the second code in an array composed of the two-character string. Line 600 checks if ALT-Q is the keystroke. Line 600 checks for CHR$(16) because ALT-Q is composed of CHR$(0) and CHR$(16).

Similarly, to check for the cursor-right arrow key, you would use the following algorithm.

```
580 K$ = INKEY$
590 IF LEN(K$) = 2 THEN K$ = RIGHT$(K$,1)
600 IF K$ = CHR$(77) THEN . . .
```

Again, simply refer to Fig. 4-3 as you develop your program. By using extended ASCII codes you gain access to a wider variety of keystrokes. As an added bonus, your user interface takes on a more professional polish.

Some of the demonstration programs throughout the book use <Enter> to solicit your input while the program is running. Others use ESC to ask if you wish to return to BASIC when it has been determined the program requires either a different graphics adapter or a different version of BASIC than found on your computer system. The CAD graphics editor in Part Five uses a full-function user interface with cursor-arrow keys, <Enter>, ESC, and so forth.

### KEY TRAPPING

The ON KEY and KEY ON statements in BASIC are used to trap keystrokes. While a program is running, BASIC checks after each statement to see if a specific keystroke has occurred. The F2 key is used throughout this book to enable you to exit from a running program. This is invoked with the following code.

**600 ON KEY (2) GOSUB 1000:KEY (2) ON**

Thereafter, whenever F2 is pressed, BASIC immediately acts upon it. The keystroke never appears in the keyboard buffer, so you do not have to use INKEY$ to check for it. Although this technique is handy for breaking out of ill-behaved programs during development and testing, it is time-consuming because of BASIC's need to check for the key after each and every instruction it executes. Other keys besides F2 can be invoked. Refer to your BASIC manual for further details.

## SUMMARY

In this chapter you learned that interactive graphics programs require two-way communication between the computer and the user. You discovered that the keyboard is the primary tool used by the user to communicate with the program. You saw that the display screen is the primary tool used by the computer to communicate with the user. You learned that interaction can occur at two levels: the programmer's level and the end-user's level. You saw innovative ways to manage the keyboard with the INKEY$ statement and with extended ASCII codes.

The next chapter discusses methods of managing the display screen.

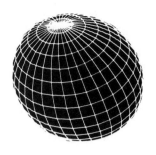

# 5

# *Managing The Screen*

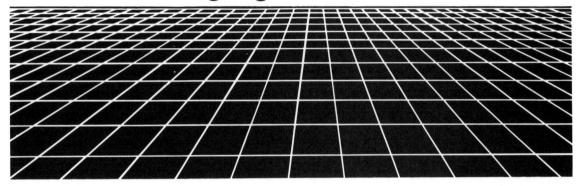

Graphics programs can make or break their reputation by the images they produce on the display screen. It is vital that the screen is managed effectively, in terms of both hardware and software. As a graphics programmer, managing the screen is your responsibility.

## GRAPHICS COMPATIBILITY

Across the family of IBM personal computers and compatibles there exists a wide range of display monitors, graphics adapters, and screen modes. As you learned in Chapter 1, there is some variation in compatibility between hardware capabilities on different computer models. In order to create high-performance interactive graphics programs which will execute correctly on more than just one type of microcomputer, a method must be found to make a program universal. In particular, graphics programs must be written in a manner that will guarantee similar graphics on the display screen, no matter whether the graphics adapter is a Color/Graphics Adapter, an EGA, a PCjr video subsystem, a Tandy graphics adapter, or the MCGA or VGA of the IBM Personal System/2 models.

It goes without saying that it would be impracti-

cal for you to create separate versions of the program in order to run it on different brands or models of microcomputers. In addition, as a graphics programmer, you do not always have the luxury of knowing in advance which particular hardware/software combination will be used with your program.

### Graphics Drivers

Fortunately, BASIC contains graphics drivers for a variety of different screen modes. For example, as long as you specify the coordinates for the endpoints of a line, BASIC will automatically draw that line in the correct position on either the $320 \times 200$ screen, the $640 \times 200$ screen, the $640 \times 350$ screen, or any other screen mode supported by your version of BASIC. What is a graphics driver? A graphics driver is a section of machine code which manages graphics in a particular screen mode on a particular graphics adapter.

### A Graphics Standard

Provided that either IBM BASICA, IBM Cartridge BASIC, GW-BASIC, Compaq BASIC, Microsoft BASICA, Microsoft QuickBASIC, or

Borland TurboBASIC is being used on an IBM-compatible microcomputer with a graphics adapter, you can rely upon the fact that the 320 × 200 4-color screen and the 640 × 200 2-color screen are available. SCREEN 1 and SCREEN 2 are the ad hoc graphics standard. Simply stated, if a computer doesn't support SCREEN 1 and SCREEN 2, then it's not IBM-compatible. Period.

Although you could ensure the compatibility of your graphics programs by always writing them in the 320 × 200 4-color mode, this tactic would not take advantage of the EGA's enhanced modes: the 640 × 200 16-color mode and the 640 × 350 16-color mode. Neither would this approach take advantage of the capabilities of the PCjr and the Tandy line of computers: the 640 × 200 4-color mode.

## GRAPHICS UNIVERSALITY

In order to create a universal graphics program, two problems must be overcome. First, the hardware must be configured to operate at its fullest graphics potential. There is no purpose in having an EGA if you only use the 320 × 200 mode. Second, the software must be capable of generating graphics in whatever screen mode has been established on the hardware. In both cases, you can use BASIC to solve the problem.

## Software Universality

The WINDOW SCREEN statement in BASIC can be used with any screen mode which is supported by your version of BASIC. Refer to Fig. 5-1. When you establish a particular set of world coordinates, such as WINDOW SCREEN ( – 399, – 299)-(400,300), for example, these coordinates will be mapped onto the display screen no matter whether the screen mode being used is 320 × 200, or 640 × 200, or 640 × 350. These world coordinates are called device-independent coordinates, because they operate independently of the hardware (i.e., the graphics adapter).

As you will learn in the next chapter, WINDOW

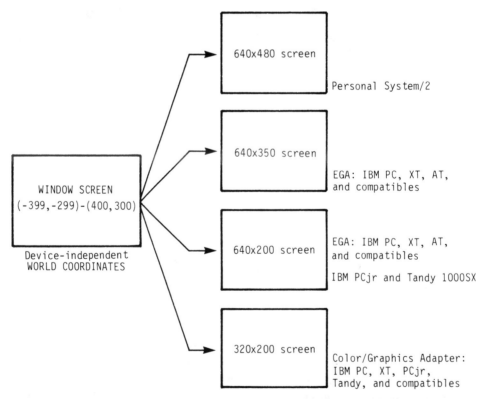

Fig. 5-1. If device-independent world coordinates are employed in graphics programs, the programmer can rely upon BASIC's WINDOW SCREEN instruction to map the graphics onto either the 640 × 480, 640 × 350, 640 × 200, or 320 × 200 screen.

SCREEN (−399, −299)-(400,300) is a very efficient method for dealing with 3D models on a personal computer. It is used in the demonstration programs throughout this book. The ratio of x-coordinates to y-coordinates in this logical configuration is 800:600, or 4:3. This 4:3 ratio is identical to the width-to-height ratio of a display monitor. Refer to Fig. 5-2. By maintaining this 4:3 ratio as you transfer your 3D model to the 2D display screen, you avoid any visual distortion, as you will discover in Part Two.

If you are using a Color/Graphics Adapter and you have invoked the 320 × 200 4-color mode, any request to draw a line from (−399, −299) to (0,0) will actually draw a line on the display screen at physical coordinates (0,0) to (160,100).

If you are using a PCjr or Tandy and you have invoked the 640 × 200 4-color mode, any request to draw a line from (−399, −299) to (0,0) will actually draw a line on the display screen at physical coordinates (0,0) to (320,100).

If you are using an EGA and you have invoked the 640 × 350 16-color mode, a request to draw a line from (−399, −299) to (0,0) will actually draw a line on the display screen at physical coordinates (0,0) to (320,175).

If you are using an IBM Personal System/2 computer and you have invoked the 640 × 480 16-color mode, any request to draw a line from (−399, −299) to (0,0) will actually draw a line on the display screen at physical coordinates (0,0) to (320,240).

In other words, if you specify device-independent world coordinates which ask BASIC to construct a line from the logical upper left corner to the logical center of the world coordinates screen, BASIC will make the necessary calculations and draw the line from the ac-tual upper left corner to the actual center of the physical screen. Although this transposition appears somewhat magical, it is nothing more than simple mathematics. For a code fragment (written in BASIC) which mimics the WINDOW SCREEN instruction by mapping world coordinates onto a physical display screen, refer to Appendix B. The algorithm in Appendix B is also useful if you are using C, Pascal, or Assembly Language, where automatic mapping is not provided as it is in IBM BASICA, IBM Cartridge BASIC, GW-BASIC, Compaq BASIC, Microsoft BASICA, Microsoft QuickBASIC, and Borland TurboBASIC.

Provided you establish a logical set of device-independent screen coordinates by using the WINDOW SCREEN instruction, you can write your graphics program knowing that it will execute correctly in any screen mode. If you are using 3D graphics, you can use WINDOW SCREEN (−399, −299)-(400,300), as the programs do in this book. If you are creating 2D graphics, you could use WINDOW SCREEN (0,0)-(640,200) to write programs that will execute properly and uniformly in all available screen modes: the 320 × 200 mode, the 640 × 200 mode, the 640 × 350 mode, the 640 × 480 mode, and other screen modes supported by BASIC.

### Hardware Universality

BASIC also provides a method to ensure that the fullest graphics potential of the hardware will be used by your program. Not only must your program determine which graphics adapter is present, but your program must determine which version of BASIC is being used. BASICA 2.1, for example, supports only

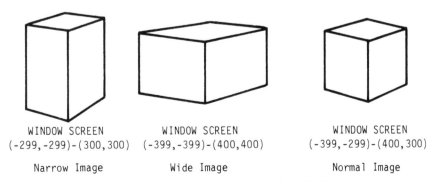

|  |  |  |
|---|---|---|
| WINDOW SCREEN (-299,-299)-(300,300) | WINDOW SCREEN (-399,-399)-(400,400) | WINDOW SCREEN (-399,-299)-(400,300) |
| Narrow Image | Wide Image | Normal Image |

Fig. 5-2. The world coordinate system must match the 4:3 aspect ratio of the display monitor, otherwise the 3D image will be distorted when BASIC maps the graphics onto the screen buffer.

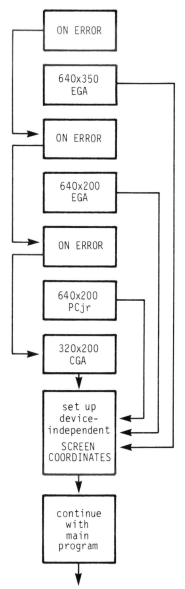

Fig. 5-3. Schematic representation of a universal compatibility module designed to adapt itself to run on any graphics adapter with any monitor using various versions of BASIC.

ports but which the CGA does not support. You are limited by the lowest common denominator, as you learned in Chapter 1.

The schematic representation in Fig. 5-3 illustrates an algorithm which will set up the best screen mode on any IBM-compatible microcomputer using any designated version of BASIC. The key to the algorithm is BASIC's ON ERROR statement.

### Trapping the Error

If you ask BASIC to set up a screen mode which is not supported by the graphics adapter or which is not supported by the version of BASIC being used, then BASIC will generate an error message and the program will halt. By trapping this error with the ON ERROR statement, you can control what happens next. And what happens next is to simply keep trying different screen modes until you find one which is supported by both the graphics adapter and the version of BASIC you are using. Once the screen mode is established, WINDOW SCREEN is used to set up the world coordinates and program execution begins. (If you are anxious to see how the actual source code is written for this algorithm, skip ahead to the first demonstration program in Chapter 8.)

In addition, once your program has determined a viable screen mode, it can use that information to assign color attributes. If the actual drawing code uses variables for color attributes, these variables can mean different things to different graphics adapters. The same drawing code, therefore, can be used successfully with a Color/Graphics Adapter, an EGA, a PCjr video subsystem, a Tandy graphics adapter, and so forth.

### Hardware/Software Universality

By using the ON ERROR algorithm to first establish the best graphics mode supported by the hardware and software which is present, and by then using the WINDOW SCREEN instruction to invoke a logical set of device-independent world coordinates, you can write high-performance interactive graphics programs which will run on any member of the IBM family of personal computers and compatibles. With such a regime in place, you can now turn your attention to other aspects of screen management.

### MULTITASKING GRAPHICS WINDOWS

Any graphics program can display multiple views

SCREEN 1 and SCREEN 2 even if an EGA is attached, so you cannot expect the EGA to exhibit SCREEN 8 if BASICA 2.1 is being used as the graphics driver. Similarly, if BASICA 3.21 is being used with a Color/Graphics Adapter, there is no point in asking for SCREEN 8, which BASICA 3.21 sup-

of the same object by using BASIC's VIEW instruction. Although this is not multitasking in the literal sense of the word, it provides a powerful tool for modeling, rendering, and animation on your personal computer.

As you learned in Chapter 2, the VIEW statement maps the coordinates from the entire display screen into a mini-screen located anywhere inside the physical display screen. These mini-screens are called viewports. By drawing one view of the model inside one viewport and then drawing a different view of the same model inside a different viewport located elsewhere on the screen, you can display different views simultaneously. The coding for this technique is first introduced in the demonstration program in Chapter 8. It is this technique which permits multiple views of the soft drink container design in Chapter 24, as well as the film carton package design demonstration program in the same chapter. In addition, this algorithm allows you to independently animate each model, as the advanced demonstration program in Chapter 28 illustrates.

## TECHNIQUES FOR TITLING

In many instances, you will want to place alphanumeric labels and titles on the graphics images produced by your program. You may also need to use witness lines, arrows, and leader lines. (These are the various dimensioning markers and arrow pointers that are found on many drafting drawings. Refer to Chapter 25.)

Although you can simply use the LOCATE and PRINT statements to place labels and titles on the display screen, in many cases this will produce undesirable results. If you are attempting to place the label over existing graphics, the black background portion of the alphanumeric character will obliterate the background graphics. This looks amateurish and is simply an overwrite of the label or title.

A better method is to superimpose the label over the existing graphics. Even when you are using the built-in ROM/BIOS alphanumerics which BASIC provides, this superimposition is easy to accomplish. Here's how. Before you begin creating any graphics, set up the appropriate graphics screen mode, then display the alphanumeric titles and labels which you will be using later and save them as graphic arrays. To su-

perimpose the label over your graphics image, simply use PUT (x,y),arrayname,OR. The OR logical operator will superimpose the white alphanumeric characters over the background graphics without the unpleasant black bar which occurs when you merely use PRINT. (To see coding for saving and retrieving graphics arrays, refer to Part Four.)

The PUT,OR approach will work equally well for any oversized titles which you create. (For a detailed discussion of oversized titles refer to the author's first book, *High-Speed Animation and Simulation for Microcomputers*, available at your favorite bookstore or order direct from TAB BOOKS, Inc.)

## TEXT INCOMPATIBILITIES

Although the various graphics screen modes in the IBM family of personal computers and compatibles will support alphanumerics, the PRINT instruction can easily run into problems of incompatibility. The $320 \times 200$ mode provides for 40 characters in each of 25 lines. The $640 \times 200$ mode provides for 80 characters in each of 25 lines. The line count is identical, but the width discrepancy in characters per line can cause problems.

If you PRINT an alphanumeric phrase which runs past position 40, for example, the remaining characters will wrap around onto the next line in the $320 \times 200$ mode, although the phrase will be displayed on a single line in the $640 \times 200$ or $640 \times 350$ mode.

Two methods of getting around this situation can be used. First, the programmer can ensure that all titles and labels fall within the first 40 positions in any line. This approach is used by most of the demonstration programs in the book. Second, the programmer can use variables which fluctuate to meet the needs of the particular screen mode being used. This approach is demonstrated in the graphics editor demonstration program in Part Five.

Also of interest is the fact that some EGAs will permit you to display alphanumerics on line 24, while many Color/Graphics Adapters will scroll the material up to line 23 as soon as the statement is completed (or as soon as <Enter> is pressed). It seems wise to avoid PRINTing any alphanumerics on line 24. Both CGAs and EGAs will support non-scrollable alphanumerics on line 25, however, if the soft key display has been disabled by the KEY OFF instruction.

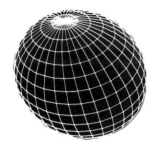

# 6

# *Concepts of 3D Graphics*

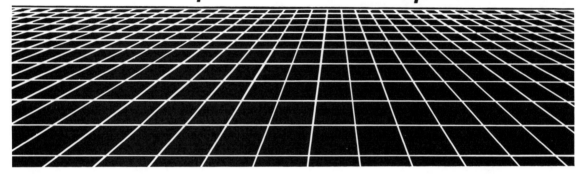

Real objects have three dimensions: height, width, and depth. An image on a computer display screen which simulates the height, width, and depth of an object is said to be three-dimensional or 3D. In computer graphics, such an image on a display screen is called a 3D model. The creation of the image is called modeling. The addition of shading, highlights, textures, and shadows is called rendering.

Although modeling and rendering go hand in hand, you must be able to generate a 3D model before you can render the shading. The chapters in Part Two will provide you with the tools you need to produce 3D models of virtually any shape. The chapters in Part Three will show you how to add shading to your models. In particular, Part Three illustrates source code which allows your microcomputer to calculate the light levels and automatically shade your models for you. Part Four teaches you how to add movement to your fully-shaded models by animating them.

## WORLD COORDINATES

The fundamental shape of the model which you wish to display is expressed as X,Y,Z coordinates. Refer to Fig. 6-1. By using a coordinate axis system, the three dimensions of height, width, and depth can be defined. By convention, the X axis is used to represent the left-right dimensions; the Y axis is used to denote up-down; and the Z axis depicts near-far depth. As Fig. 6-1 shows, the viewpoint is initially located at position 0,0,0 (where X = 0 Y = 0 Z = 0). The viewpoint is the position of you, the viewer.

No matter what shape of model is desired, each important position on the 3D model can be expressed as an X,Y,Z set of coordinates. Each X,Y,Z triplet will refer to only one unique location within the 3D space of the axis system.

The first step in modeling an object is to define the world coordinates of the object. These world coordinates are the fundamental shape or design of the model. World coordinates are also called absolute coordinates, cartesian coordinates, and model space coordinates. In essence, world coordinates form the database of the model's design.

The X,Y,Z axis system is called world coordinate space. It represents the real world, independent of your program and independent of your microcomputer. The X,Y,Z coordinates in the 3D axis system of world coordinate space are sometimes referred to as device-independent coordinates.

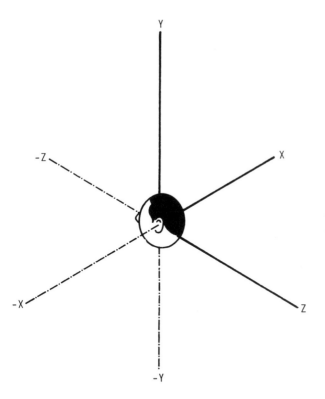

Fig. 6-1. The x,y,z axes used to identify 3D device-independent world coordinates. X is to the viewer's right; – X is left. Y is up; – Y is downward. – Z is ahead; Z is behind the viewer.

## GENERATING 3D MODELS

There are three conceptual stages in the generation of 3D models on personal computers. Refer to Fig. 6-2. First, the fundamental shape of the model (as it exists in the generic X,Y,Z axis system) is defined as WORLD COORDINATES. Second, the fundamental model is spinned and then moved to a new location in the 3D axis system to provide the point of view that is desired. The spin is called rotation. The move is called translation. Rotation and translation produce VIEW COORDINATES. Third, projection formulas are used to generate the image on the display screen, thereby creating DISPLAY COORDINATES.

The WORLD COORDINATES and VIEW COORDINATES are device-independent coordinates. These coordinates will be identical no matter what graphics adapter or display monitor you are using. The DISPLAY COORDINATES, however, are device-dependent. You must take into consideration the screen mode (i.e., 320 × 200 or 640 × 200 or 640 × 350) before you begin plotting the display coordinates onto the screen.

The WORLD COORDINATES consist of a triplet of X,Y,Z coordinates. The VIEW COORDINATES consist of a rotated and translated triplet of X,Y,Z coordinates. The final 2D DISPLAY COORDINATES are composed of a doublet of X,Y coordinates because the display screen uses only an x-coordinate and a y-coordinate to plot points.

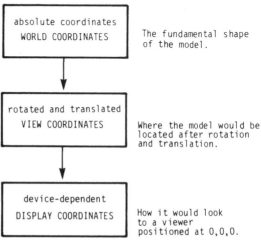

Fig. 6-2. The sequence of conceptual steps required to generate 3D models on a personal computer.

## Model Components

Every 3D model contains certain components, as shown in Fig. 6-3. A vertex is a corner: an intersection of two or more lines. Vertices are groups of intersections. An area on the model is called a surface. Surfaces may be flat or curved, rectangular or polygonal, visible or hidden. A surface which is invisible is called a hidden surface. The computer code or algorithm which calculates whether a particular surface can be seen or not is called a hidden surface routine. Naturally, a line which is not visible is called a hidden line. Any line on a 3D model can be called an edge.

The most important parts of a 3D model are vertices and surfaces. If you know the vertex coordinates, you can draw the model. You can then determine the orientation of the various surfaces on the model and shade them according to the position of the light source.

## Instancing

Figure 6-4 illustrates in a visual context the three steps for generating 3D models. You are not limited to a single object, of course. You could create numerous instances of the same object from the same original world coordinates. This is called instancing and it is demonstrated by the interior design program in Chapter 27 which draws five different chairs from a single set of world coordinates. When used in this format, it is called static instancing (because it is stationary). An enemy aircraft in a flight simulation environment would be an example of dynamic instancing (because it moves). (For an example of flight simulation source code, refer to the author's first book,

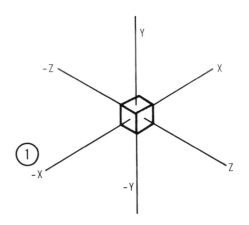

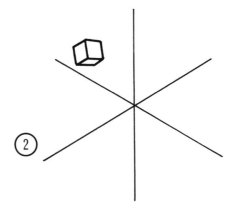

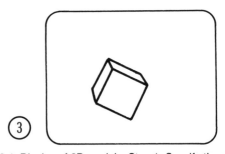

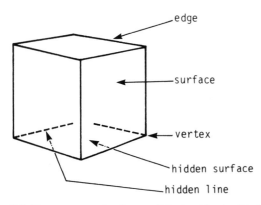

Fig. 6-3. The components of a parallelepiped (a six-sided 3D model).

Fig. 6-4. Display of 3D models. Step 1: Specify the shape of the model as WORLD COORDINATES (also known as model space, absolute coordinates, cartesian coordinates, and device-independent coordinates). Step 2: Rotate and move the model to an appropriate position to obtain VIEW COORDINATES. Step 3: Use geometric formulas to transpose the model to the two-dimensional screen DISPLAY COORDINATES (also known as projection coordinates).

*High-Speed Animation and Simulation for Microcomputers,* available from your favorite bookstore or order direct from TAB BOOKS, Inc.)

### Sub-objects

It is also common practice to create complex 3D models from groups of smaller, simpler components called sub-objects. Sub-objects are common geometric models such as cubes, cones, cylinders, spheres, parallelepipeds, and so forth. Some professional CAD systems rely heavily upon the sub-object approach and supply built-in sub-objects for the user's use, while other systems expect the user to build the model from scratch, so to speak. Both approaches have benefits and drawbacks.

### DISPLAY OPTIONS

A number of different images can be created from the world coordinates. Refer to Fig. 6-5. The simplest image is the transparent wire-frame model. This is comparable to the connect-the-dot puzzles you used to doodle with as a child. The vertexes are simply connected by lines. The shape of the model is accurate, but no effort is directed towards hidden surface removal. In many cases transparency is desirable. Because you can see right through the model, you can ascertain if you have drawn it correctly and if internal parts are correctly located.

Transparent wire-frame models often suffer from problems of ambiguity, however. Simply stated, they are sometimes confusing to the viewer. Refer to Fig. 6-6. We humans are not accustomed to having X-ray vision, after all.

The ambiguity of a transparent wire-frame model can be overcome by deleting the surfaces which should be hidden. This act is called hidden surface removal. The resultant solid model pictured in Fig. 6-5 is also called a line drawing, a solid surface model, or a polygon mesh model. The final step, of course, is to add shading and highlights, creating a fully-shaded model. This final step is called rendering.

### 3D MATHEMATICS

In conceptual terms, the mathematics required for creating and manipulating 3D models on microcomputers is straightforward. Obviously, no mathematical formulas are required for inputting the world coordinates. You can think of these world coordinates as raw coordinates or as a simple database.

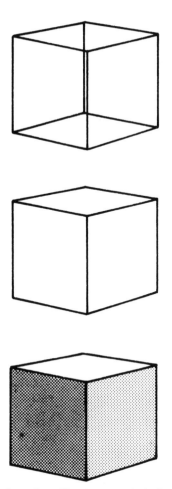

Fig. 6-5. Display options. Top: transparent wire-frame model. Center: solid model (also called line drawing, solid surface, polygon mesh). Bottom: fully-shaded model.

The trigonometric functions of sine and cosine are used to rotate the model. Simple addition and subtraction are used to translate the rotated model. Once rotation and translation have been used to create the VIEW COORDINATES, geometry is used to transform the 3D image to the 2D display screen. The next chapter gives you a blow-by-blow description of the 3D formulas.

### CONCEPT VERSUS CODE

If you grasp the concept of 3D models on microcomputers, you have the problem licked. Given a choice between understanding either the concept or the source code, the concept must win. If you under-

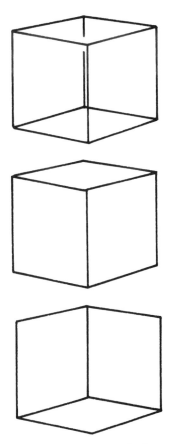

Fig. 6-6. Ambiguity of transparent wire-frame models can create confusion at the display coordinate level. The wire-frame model (top) can be interpreted as either being tilted upward or tilted downward.

stand the concept, you can always eventually figure out how the source code works. Unfortunately, the reverse is not always true.

Figure 6-4 sums up the concepts of 3D graphics on personal computers.

First, you define the shape of the object in world coordinate space, which you can think of as a database space, if you like. This shape is expressed as WORLD COORDINATES.

Second, you spin the model and then move it in order to create the point of view you want. Remember, the viewpoint is always located at X,Y,Z coordinates 0,0,0 within the 3D axis system, so you must move the model to get the particular viewing angle you seek. How the model looks at this location is called VIEW COORDINATES.

And third, you use simple geometry to place the 3D image onto your 2D display screen. The coordinates on the display screen are called DISPLAY COORDINATES.

## SUMMARY

In this chapter, you studied the concepts of 3D models. You learned that three steps are required to create a 3D image on the display screen. You read about WORLD COORDINATES, VIEW COORDINATES, and DISPLAY COORDINATES. You learned that 3D models can be displayed as either transparent wire-frame models, solid models, or fully-shaded models.

The next chapter introduces the 3D formulas that you will be using to draw and manipulate models.

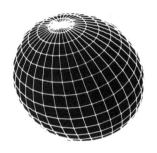

# 7

# *Manipulation of Models*

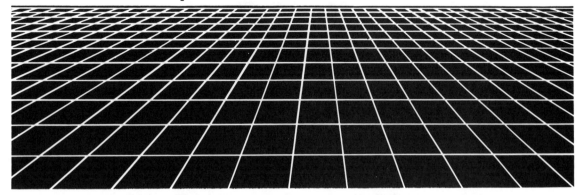

The WORLD COORDINATES of any model describe the fundamental design or the shape of the object. The model must be manipulated in order to provide a desirable view.

## 3D ALGORITHMS

The fragment of program source code in Fig. 7-1 provides complete flexibility for the manipulation of models. As you learned in the previous chapter, three stages occur during the preparation of a 3D image on your computer's display screen. First, a database of WORLD COORDINATES for the model must be provided. Second, the model is rotated and translated to an appropriate location, resulting in a set of VIEW COORDINATES (which give you the view you want). The rotations are based on the spherical coordinate system. (See Fig. 7-1.) Third, the rotated and translated 3D model is transposed to the 2D display screen by projection formulas which create DISPLAY COORDINATES.

If you provide the X,Y,Z WORLD COORDINATES as input to the algorithm in Fig. 7-1, you will receive SX,SY DISPLAY COORDINATES as output.

### Rotation Formulas

The first manipulation performed by the algorithm in Fig. 7-1 is rotation. The model is subjected to yaw rotation, which is a spin to the left or to the right. The SR1 variable in the formula denotes the sine of the yaw angle R1 which has been declared in another area of the 3D program. The CR1 variable refers to the cosine of the yaw angle R1. The X,Y,Z variables are the WORLD COORDINATES. The XA,YA,ZA variables are simply temporary interim variables to hold the changing values of the WORLD COORDINATES as they pass through the formulas on their way to becoming VIEW COORDINATES.

The next rotation performed by the algorithm in Fig. 7-1 is roll, which is a spin in a clockwise or counterclockwise direction. The SR2 variable denotes the sine of the roll angle R2. The CR2 variable denotes the cosine of the roll angle R2.

The final rotation undertaken by the 3D algorithm is pitch, which is a spin in a forward or backward direction. The SR3 variable is the sine of pitch angle R3. The CR3 variable is the cosine of pitch angle R3.

The effect of rotation on the display image is illustrated in Fig. 7-2. By adjusting the values of the

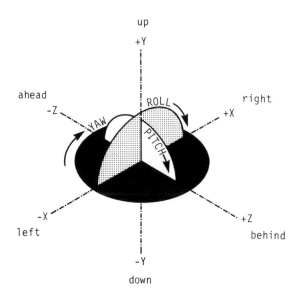

CARTESIAN COORDINATE SYSTEM:
world coordinates for 3D modeling
on microcomputers

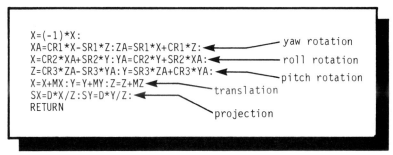

Fig. 7-1. The three components of the 3D algorithm: rotation, translation, and projection.

angles for yaw, roll, and pitch you can rotate the model to any angle in 3D space. For a discussion of the matrix math which underlies the rotation formulas, you may wish to turn to Appendix B.

**Translation Formulas**

The second manipulation performed by the algorithm in Fig. 7-1 is translation. The model can be translated, or moved, along each of the three axes in the 3D coordinate system. Because the viewer is always located at the 0,0,0 origin of the axis system, the model must be moved to a position which will give an

appropriate point of view.

The variable MX defines the distance to be moved along the x-coordinate, which is left-right movement. This variable has been declared in an earlier portion of the 3D program. The variable MY refers to the distance to be moved along the y-coordinate, which is up-down movement. The variable MZ designates the distance to be moved along the z-coordinate, which is near-far movement. Refer to Fig. 7-3.

**Projection Formulas**

The third major manipulation performed by the

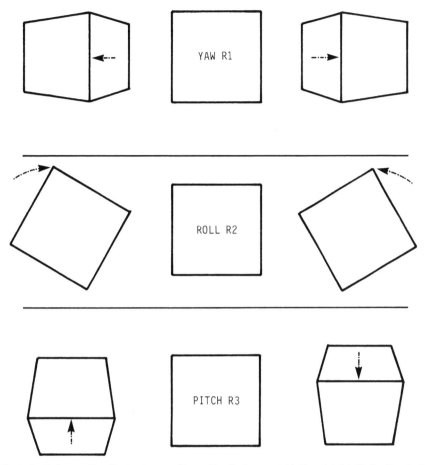

Fig. 7-2. The effect of rotation on the display image. Yaw will spin the model left and right. Roll will spin the model clockwise or counterclockwise. Pitch will spin the model forward or backward.

algorithm in Fig. 7-1 is projection. The VIEW COORDINATES which have been created by the rotation and translation formulas must be modified for the 2D display screen. Although the rotation and translation formulas are the result of a complicated series of matrix functions and sine/cosine trigonometric calculations, the projection formulas are simply high-school math.

The geometry involved in taking the 3D VIEW COORDINATES and plotting their location as DISPLAY COORDINATES on a 2D screen is shown in Fig. 7-6 and Fig. 7-7. As you can see, Fig. 7-6 concerns the y-coordinate on the display screen, which is always called SY in this book. Figure 7-7 refers to the x-coordinate on the display screen, which is always labelled SX in this book.

The geometrical algorithm for the projection for-

mulas assumes that a flat 2D transparent screen has been placed between the viewer and the 3D model being observed. This transparent screen is called a picture plane by artists and illustrators. The distance between the viewer and the model is expressed as Z, which is the near-far coordinate. The distance between the viewer and the display screen is expressed as D.

Because the viewing scenario can be interpreted as two right angle triangles, the ratios of various sides and angles is consistent. In Fig. 7-6, for example, the values of Y, Z, and D are known. It becomes relatively straightforward to use geometry to solve the unknown value of SY (the DISPLAY COORDINATE).

$SY/D = Y/Z$ expresses the equality of the ratio of the sides of the two right angle triangles in Fig. 7-6. Simple transposition produces $SY = D*Y/Z$. You can apply the same geometry to the triangles in Fig. 7-7

49

in order to prove the validity of the SX projection formula.

## ANGULAR DISTORTION

The variable D in the projection formulas refers to the distance between the viewer and the display screen. This factor is important in determining the angular distortion of the resultant display image. Refer to Fig. 7-4.

If the distance D is too large, the model will appear flat. It will not look lifelike. Lines which recede into the distance will not get smaller or converge on each other like they do in real life.

If the distance D is too small, the model will appear distorted and overly angular, as Fig. 7-4 illustrates. Again, the image will mock rather than mimic real life. The reason for this angular distortion resides in the physical design of the human eye. Refer to Fig. 7-5. People normally possess a 60 degree field of vision. If you are standing too close to a large building, for example, you cannot see it all in just one glance; you must pan your eyes along it. The angular distortion in a 3D display image is caused by trying to display too much of the object in relation to the distance between the viewpoint and the model. To solve the problem, simply move the viewer back from the picture plane.

## RADIANS VS. DEGREES

Angles for yaw, roll, and pitch are always measured as radians in 3D formulas. Just as there are 360 degrees in a full circle, there are $2\pi$, or roughly 6.28 radians in a circle. Although degrees are more familiar to most people, the assignment of 360 degrees to

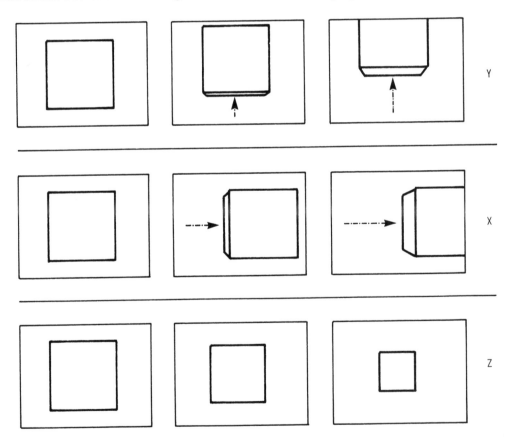

Fig. 7-3. The effect of translation on the display image. Y translation will move the model higher or lower. X translation will move the model left or right. Z translation will move the model closer to the viewer or farther from the viewer.

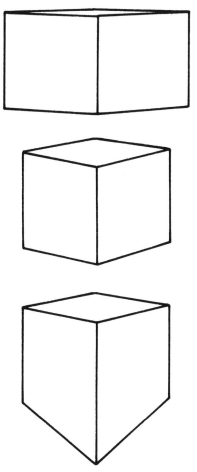

Fig. 7-4. The effect of angular perspective (D) on the display image. Top: D is too large; the model is flattened. Center: D is in the correct range; the shape of the model is similar to real-world conditions. Bottom: D is too small; the model is distorted.

ter way around the circle); 180 degrees equals about 3.14 radians (halfway around the circle); 270 degrees equals about 4.17 radians (three-quarters of the way around the circle); and 360 degrees equals about 6.28 radians (completely around the circle).

## THE ROTATION-TRANSLATION SEQUENCE

There is no reason preventing you from switching the order of the various rotation and translation subsets in the 3D formula set shown in Fig. 7-1. Different sequences will produce different images on the display screen, however.

The formulas presented in Fig. 7-1 are best suited for typical 3D models. The resulting image on the display screen can be imagined thus: pretend you are holding a cube at arms' length. If you twist and turn the cube by bending your wrist, you are able to view the model in different positions. Your viewpoint is not changing; the position of the model is changing. Refer to Fig. 7-8. Similarly, the formulas will twist and turn the model on the display screen and leave the viewpoint unchanged.

However, if the model is translated before it is rotated, the viewpoint does appear to change. You are now walking around the room, turning your hips as you twist the model with your hand and wrist. It's an entirely different ball game. Refer to Fig. 7-9. By reordering the formulas so that the MX, MY, and MZ factors are added before the model is rotated, a global 3D environment is introduced. Simply stated, the viewpoint moves when the model moves. This environment is useful for programs which simulate an architectural walk-through or which simulate vehicle movement or flight.

## SCALING CONSIDERATIONS

By using the WINDOW SCREEN statement in BASIC, you can safely ignore many of the difficulties caused by scaling. As you learned, the MZ factor in the 3D formulas controls how near you are to the model along the z-coordinate. If you are very close, the model will be very large, perhaps larger than the display screen. The automatic line clipping performed by the WINDOW SCREEN instruction will resolve any parts of the model which fall outside the range of the display screen coordinates.

As you discovered in Chapter 2, however, the math used by BASIC's WINDOW SCREEN statement

represent a full sweep around a circle is an arbitrary one. There is no logical or mathematical reason for using 360 degrees in preference to, say, 226 degrees. This lack of mathematic support for the 360 degree regime causes some problems for computers (and mathematicians!).

Radians are based upon the relationships between the various elements found in a unit circle. A unit circle is simply a circle with a radius of one unit. If you wish a detailed description of the derivation of radians, you may wish to read Appendix B. For now, however, all you need to understand is that 0 degrees equals 0 radians; 90 degrees equals about 1.57 radians (quar-

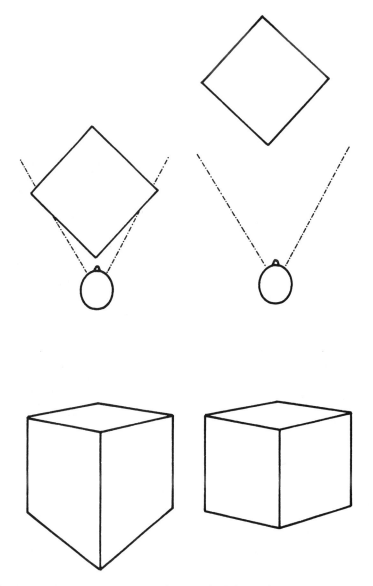

Fig. 7-5. Angular distortion in 3D computer images. Left: viewpoint is located too near the model. Right: model is fully located within the 60 degree field of vision.

will limit the legal range of coordinates to minimum −32768 and maximum +32767. This limitation is suitable for most modeling and rendering programs.

Appendix B provides a code fragment which performs a windowing function with floating point numbers. It is, for all intent and purposes, impossible to overload this code. In addition, the algorithm used by the code in Appendix B is universal and can be adapted for use in C, Pascal, and Assembly Language.

## SUMMARY

In this chapter you learned that a comprehensive set of 3D formulas will provide you with the capability to rotate, translate, and display a 3D model. You discovered how to control angular distortion.

The next chapter shows you demonstration programs which introduce three different methods for hidden surface removal and which demonstrate four ways to display a 3D model.

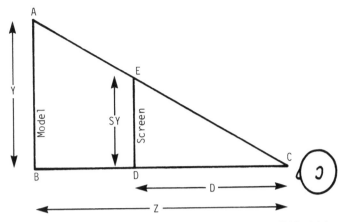

Fig. 7-6. Calculation of Y projection coordinates. Geometry is used to compute the SY (height) coordinates on the display screen.

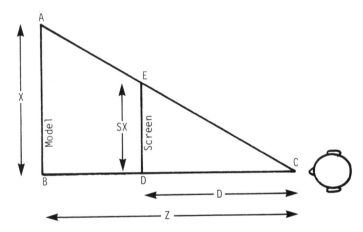

Fig. 7-7. Calculation of X projection coordinates. Geometry is used to compute the SX (width) coordinates on the display screen.

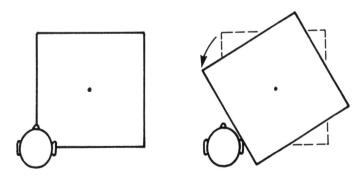

Fig. 7-8. Effect of rotation when model is rotated before translation. Sorting the formulas in this order is useful for viewing models, objects, and sub-objects.

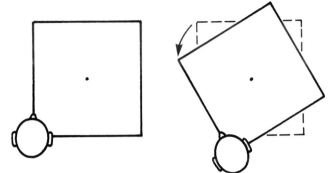

Fig. 7-9. Effect of rotation when model is translated before rotation. Sorting the formulas in this order is useful for flight simulation.

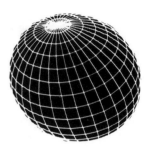

# 8

# *The Cube*

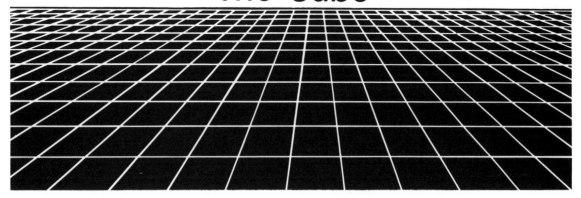

A parallelepiped is a solid with six surfaces, each of which is a parallelogram. A cube is the simplest parallelepiped. Each of its six sides is a square. All six sides are the same size. The cube provides a suitable starting point for exploring the mechanics of modeling on your personal computer.

## TRANSPARENT WIRE-FRAME CUBE

Figure 8-1 illustrates the screen output of the demonstration program in Fig. 8-2. To run this program from the companion diskette, type **LOAD "A-01.BAS",R**. Although only a simplistic cube is drawn, the program contains a number of important principles which will persist throughout the book.

As you learned in Chapter 3, modular programming is an important part of interactive graphics programs. Note the layout of the demonstration program. The master routine, which begins at line 180, is near the start of the program for easy readability. Even before the master routine begins executing, however, line 140 sends the program to the configuration module located later in the program listing.

## The Configuration Module

The configuration module begins at line 380. As you learned in Chapter 5, the ON ERROR instruction in BASIC can be used to configure the hardware and software to produce the best graphics possible on your particular computer system. Line 400 sets up the error trapping. Then, when line 410 attempts to invoke the 640 × 350 mode, the program will skip to line 430 if your computer determines that line 410 is illegal for your particular combination of hardware and software. The 640 × 350 mode requires an EGA and an enhanced color display monitor.

Line 440 sets up another error trap. Line 450 attempts to set up the 640 × 200 16-color mode. This screen mode requires an EGA and a standard color display monitor. If an error occurs, the program simply jumps to line 470.

Line 480 sets up the third error trap. Line 490 attempts to set up the 640 × 200 4-color mode for the PCjr and Tandy microcomputers. If this is illegal, program control jumps to line 510.

After these screen modes have failed, the final re-

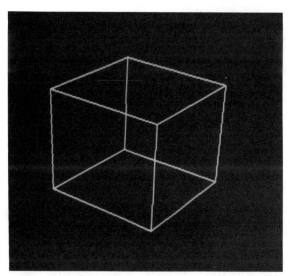

Fig. 8-1. The display image produced by the demonstration program in Fig. 8-2.

DINATES. The master routine uses a RESTORE instruction to ensure that the correct line in the database is being addressed as each surface is being drawn.

Refer to line 190, for example, which draws the bottom surface of the cube. First, the database pointer is assigned with the RESTORE 650 instruction. Line 650 in the database is being used now. Next, the first X,Y,Z values in the database are retrieved. The program jumps to a subroutine at line 310, which is the 3D formulas you learned about in the previous chapter. Then, a point is plotted using the PSET statement. A FOR. . .NEXT loop is used to draw the four lines which make up the bottom surface of the cube. On each pass through the loop, a set of X,Y,Z WORLD COORDINATES are retrieved from the database, they are sent to the 3D formulas, and they are drawn as a LINE on the display screen.

This process is repeated until all six surfaces of the cube have been drawn.

sort is the graphics standard of the 320 × 200 4-color mode. This screen mode is invoked by line 520.

A short alphanumeric comment in the upper left corner of your display screen informs you which screen mode has been invoked on your particular microcomputer system.

No matter which screen mode is established by the configuration module, program control eventually shifts to line 540, which invokes the appropriate WINDOW SCREEN environment, as discussed in Chapter 2. Next, line 550 establishes the F2 key as a bail-out key. If you touch F2 while the program is running, the program immediately executes line 350, which cleans up the programming environment and returns you to the 80-column text mode.

Line 560 sends the program back to the beginning of the program.

## The Master Routine

When you run this program, note the order in which the various surfaces of the cube are drawn on the display screen. The bottom of the cube is drawn first. Then the two back sides are drawn, then the two front panels. The final surface to be drawn is the top of the transparent wire-frame cube. The program beeps to let you know it has completed the cube.

Each surface is represented by a separate line in the database, which begins at line 640. The database is composed of triplets of X,Y,Z WORLD COOR-

## Assigning Variables

A separate module is used to assign the variables used by the demonstration program in Fig. 8-2. It is located at line 590. Line 600 assigns values to the D factor (angular perspective) and the yaw/roll/pitch angles. Remember, all angles are expressed as radians. As you can see in line 600, the cube is pushed back 350 units away from the viewing position (MZ = −350). It is pushed straight back; both MX and MY are set to a value of 0.

Line 610 is used to generate the sine and cosine values of the various viewing angles defined in line 600.

## Experimentation

After you've finished typing in the demonstration program and got it running correctly, you may wish to play around with it to gain a better understanding of how it works. Try changing the value of MZ in line 600. Move the model closer to the viewpoint by setting MZ to −250, for example. In addition, by modifying the value of D in line 600, you can see firsthand how the angular distortion is affected by this variable.

The database and the drawing code in this program are very inefficient, but they are easy to understand in this format. Before this chapter is concluded, you will learn a much more effective way to structure the database and the code which actually does the drawing.

Fig. 8-2. Transparent wire-frame model.

```
100 'Program A-01.BAS   Transparent cube.
110 'Does not remove any hidden surfaces.
120 '_____
130 '
140   GOTO 400    'configure system
150   GOSUB 600   'assign scalar data
160 '_____
170 '
180 'master routine:   draw cube
190   RESTORE 650:READ X,Y,Z:GOSUB 310:PSET (SX,SY),C3:FOR T=
1 TO 4 STEP 1:READ X,Y,Z:GOSUB 310:LINE-(SX,SY),C3:NEXT T   '
bottom surface 0
200   RESTORE 660:READ X,Y,Z:GOSUB 310:PSET (SX,SY),C3:FOR T=
1 TO 4 STEP 1:READ X,Y,Z:GOSUB 310:LINE-(SX,SY),C3:NEXT T   '
surface 1
210   RESTORE 670:READ X,Y,Z:GOSUB 310:PSET (SX,SY),C3:FOR T=
1 TO 4 STEP 1:READ X,Y,Z:GOSUB 310:LINE-(SX,SY),C3:NEXT T   '
surface 2
220   RESTORE 680:READ X,Y,Z:GOSUB 310:PSET (SX,SY),C3:FOR T=
1 TO 4 STEP 1:READ X,Y,Z:GOSUB 310:LINE-(SX,SY),C3:NEXT T   '
surface 3
230   RESTORE 690:READ X,Y,Z:GOSUB 310:PSET (SX,SY),C3:FOR T=
1 TO 4 STEP 1:READ X,Y,Z:GOSUB 310:LINE-(SX,SY),C3:NEXT T   '
surface 4
240   RESTORE 700:READ X,Y,Z:GOSUB 310:PSET (SX,SY),C3:FOR T=
1 TO 4 STEP 1:READ X,Y,Z:GOSUB 310:LINE-(SX,SY),C3:NEXT T   '
top surface 5
250   BEEP   'cube complete
260   GOTO 260   'clean halt.
270   END 'of master routine.
280 '_____
290 '
300 'module:   perspective calculations for Cartesian world c
oordinates
310   X=(-1)*X:XA=CR1*X-SR1*Z:ZA=SR1*X+CR1*Z:X=CR2*XA+SR2*Y:Y
A=CR2*Y-SR2*XA:Z=CR3*ZA-SR3*YA:Y=SR3*ZA+CR3*YA:X=X+MX:Y=Y+MY
:Z=Z+MZ:SX=D*X/Z:SY=D*Y/Z:RETURN
320 '_____
330 '
340 'module:   return to BASIC interpreter
350   CLS:WINDOW:SCREEN 0,0,0,0:WIDTH 80:COLOR 7,0,0:CLS:LOCA
TE 1,1,1:END
360 '_____
370 '
380 'module:   UNIVERSAL
390 'This routine configures the program for the hardware/so
ftware being used.
```

```
400   KEY OFF:CLS:ON ERROR GOTO 430   'trap if not Enhanced Di
splay + EGA
410   SCREEN 9,,0,0:COLOR 7,0:PALETTE 2,5:PALETTE 3,7:C0=0:C1
=1:C2=2:C3=3:LOCATE 1,1:PRINT "ED-EGA 640x350 16-color mode"

420   GOTO 530   'jump to screen coordinates set-up
430   RESUME 440
440   ON ERROR GOTO 470   'trap if not Color Display + EGA
450   SCREEN 8,,0,0:COLOR 7,0:PALETTE 2,5:PALETTE 3,7:C0=0:C1
=1:C2=2:C3=3:LOCATE 1,1:PRINT "CD-EGA 640x200 16-color mode"

460   GOTO 530   'jump to screen coordinates set-up
470   RESUME 480
480   ON ERROR GOTO 510   'trap if not PCjr
490   CLEAR,,,32768!:SCREEN 6,0,0,0:COLOR 3,0:C0=0:C1=1:C2=2:
C3=3:LOCATE 1,1:PRINT "PCjr 640x200 4-color mode"
500   GOTO 530   'jump to screen coordinates set-up
510   RESUME 520
520   SCREEN 1,0:COLOR 0,1:C0=0:C1=1:C2=2:C3=3:LOCATE 1,1:PRI
NT "CGA 320x200 4-color mode"
530   ON ERROR GOTO 0   'disable error trapping override
540   WINDOW SCREEN (-399,-299)-(400,300)
550   ON KEY (2) GOSUB 350:KEY (2) ON   'F2 key to exit progra
m
560   GOTO 150   'return to main program
570   '————————
580   '
590   'module:  assign variables
600   D=1200:R1=5.68319:R2=6.28319:R3=5.79778:MX=0:MY=0:MZ=-3
50   '3D parameters
610   SR1=SIN(R1):CR1=COS(R1):SR2=SIN(R2):CR2=COS(R2):SR3=SIN
(R3):CR3=COS(R3):RETURN
620   '————————
630   '
640   'module:  database of Cartesian XYZ world coordinates fo
r 3D cube (sorted as bottom surface 0, surface 1, surface 2,
 surface 3, surface 4, top surface 5)
650   DATA  30,-30,30,  30,-30,-30,  -30,-30,-30,  -30,-30,30
,  30,-30,30,  0,-30,0
660   DATA  30,30,-30,  -30,30,-30,  -30,-30,-30,  30,-30,-30
,  30,30,-30,  0,0,-30
670   DATA  -30,30,-30,  -30,30,30,  -30,-30,30,  -30,-30,-30
,  -30,30,-30,  -30,0,0
680   DATA  -30,30,30,  30,30,30,  30,-30,30,  -30,-30,30,  -
30,30,30,  0,0,30
690   DATA  30,30,30,  30,30,-30,  30,-30,-30,  30,-30,30,  3
0,30,30,  30,0,0
700   DATA  -30,30,-30,  30,30,-30,  30,30,30,  -30,30,30,  -
```

58

```
30,30,-30,  0,30,0
710 '_____
720 '
730  END 'of program code
```

## HIDDEN SURFACE REMOVAL

The previous demonstration program was notable for its complete inability to remove surfaces which should have been hidden. Obviously, you should not be able to see the surfaces located at the back of the cube.

There are three main methods for hidden surface removal on microcomputers: the *radial presort method*, the *radial sort method*, and the *plane equation method*. All three methods are based upon the surfaces of a cube. Refer to Fig. 8-3. Each method employs the principle of back-surface elimination, sometimes called culling.

### The Radial Presort Method

If a programmer decides in advance the direction from which the model will be viewed, then the program needs only to draw the visible surfaces. The database can contain only the WORLD COORDINATES for the visible surfaces. This approach to hidden surface removal produces an apparently solid model, which is in fact only a shell. This technique is called the *radial presort method*, because the direction (radial angle) has been predefined, permitting the WORLD COORDINATES to be presorted.

### The Radial Sort Method

Where the programmer must do all the work in the radial presort method, the computer does all the work in the *radial sort method*. The database contains the WORLD COORDINATES for all surfaces of the model. The program determines which surfaces are visible or hidden, depending upon the viewing angle. This approach is more versatile, permitting you to generate numerous different views of the model from a single database.

### The Plane Equation Method

If the programmer is careful when retrieving WORLD COORDINATES from the database, the failure-proof plane equation method can be used to remove hidden surfaces. By using vector multiplication it is possible to determine if a point is on one side or the other side of any particular plane. And because a surface on the cube is a plane, this approach can be used to determine if the viewpoint is on one side or the other side of the surface. This relationship determines whether the surface can be seen or not. Appendix B provides a detailed discussion of vector math and planes.

### Other Methods

The three methods just described are object-space methods. Each method of hidden surface removal makes a decision based upon the model itself. Other methods which make their decisions based upon characteristics of the 2D display image are called image-space methods. Although these methods can be very effective, they require extremely large amounts of memory, because huge arrays must be established in memory in order to keep track of the depth orientation for each and every pixel on the display screen. This pixel technique is known as the depth-sort algorithm (or, in its more comprehensive form, the depth-buffer algorithm). If you are interested in these image-space techniques, refer to the many university texts currently available.

### SOLID CUBE: RADIAL PRESORT METHOD

Figure 8-4 illustrates the screen output of the demonstration program in Fig. 8-5. To run this program from the companion diskette, type **LOAD "A-02.BAS",R**. The cube is represented as a solid model, even though all the surfaces are drawn as in the previous demonstration program.

As you watch the program executing, you will see that a key matte is first prepared for each surface. A key matte can be thought of as an area that is cleared of all other graphics in preparation to receive the desired image. The term key matte is derived from the special effects branch of the film industry.

### How Key Matte Works

The cube is drawn in white against a black background. The surfaces of the cube are, in effect, black

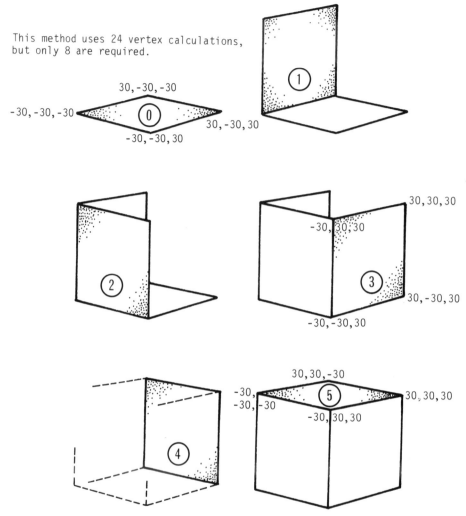

This method uses 24 vertex calculations, but only 8 are required.

30,-30,-30

-30,-30,-30

(0)

30,-30,30

-30,-30,30

(1)

(2)

(3)

30,30,30

-30,30,30

30,-30,30

-30,-30,30

(4)

30,30,-30

-30, -30,-30

(5)

30,30,30

-30,30,30

Fig. 8-3. Plane surfaces and vertex coordinates for a 3D cube.

surfaces which are outlined in white. By using a unique color different from colors used to draw the model, you can safely erase an area so that you can draw a clean surface in that area. First, the erasing color (color 2) draws the outline of the surface. Then the outlined area is filled with the erasing color. Because the erasing color (color 2) is not used for any other purpose in the image, it will cleanly erase all existing graphics inside the outline. Next, the outline is redrawn in the correct drawing color, which is white (color 3). Finally, the surface is filled with black (color 0). By using this key matte technique, you ensure that nearer surfaces will always cover surfaces which are farther away, provided that the nearest surfaces are drawn last.

Note the master routine, which begins at line 180. The surfaces of the cube are always drawn in the same order: first, the bottom is drawn; then the back two panels are drawn; then the front two panels; finally, the top panel is constructed. Because the surfaces are always drawn in this sequence by the master routine, the cube can only be viewed from a limited number of angles. If you spin the model 180 degrees, for example, the back surfaces will be drawn last and will not be covered by the front surfaces.

Although the demonstration program in Fig. 8-5 has its limitations, it introduces the vital concept of the key matte technique. The key matte approach will be used for the rest of the book. As a surface model-

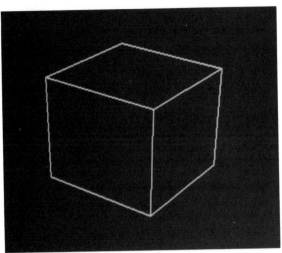

Fig. 8-4. The display image produced by the demonstration program in Fig. 8-5.

ing routine, it can be used to draw a surface of any shape on any model. Refer to Fig. 8-6 for a schematic representation of the logic involved.

## SOLID CUBE: RADIAL SORT METHOD

Figure 8-7 illustrates the screen output of the demonstration program in Fig. 8-8. To run this program from the companion diskette, type **LOAD "A-03.BAS",R**. Unlike the previous demonstration program, this cube can be rotated a full 360 degrees and the invisible surfaces will remain correctly hidden. After you have keyed in the program and it is running correctly, simply press < Enter > when you are prompted and the cube will be redrawn at a new angle. By continuing to press < Enter > you can eventually rotate the solid cube all the way around to its original angle. The four sides of the solid cube have been marked with Roman numerals to help you keep

Fig. 8-5. Solid model using the radial pre-sort method of hidden surface removal.

```
100 'Program A-02.BAS    Solid cube.
110 'Uses radial pre-sort method of hidden surface removal.
120 '_____
130 '
140   GOTO 460   'configure system
150   GOSUB 660   'assign scalar data
160 '_____
170 '
180 'master routine:  draw cube using radial pre-sort method
 of hidden surface removal
190   RESTORE 710:READ X,Y,Z:GOSUB 370:PSET (SX,SY),C2:FOR T=
1 TO 4 STEP 1:READ X,Y,Z:GOSUB 370:LINE-(SX,SY),C2:NEXT T:RE
AD X,Y,Z:GOSUB 370:PAINT (SX,SY),C2,C2  'key matte for botto
m surface
200   RESTORE 710:READ X,Y,Z:GOSUB 370:PSET (SX,SY),C3:FOR T=
1 TO 4 STEP 1:READ X,Y,Z:GOSUB 370:LINE-(SX,SY),C3:NEXT T:RE
AD X,Y,Z:GOSUB 370:PAINT (SX,SY),CO,C3  'bottom surface 0
210   RESTORE 720:READ X,Y,Z:GOSUB 370:PSET (SX,SY),C2:FOR T=
1 TO 4 STEP 1:READ X,Y,Z:GOSUB 370:LINE-(SX,SY),C2:NEXT T:RE
AD X,Y,Z:GOSUB 370:PAINT (SX,SY),C2,C2  'key matte for surfa
ce 1
220   RESTORE 720:READ X,Y,Z:GOSUB 370:PSET (SX,SY),C3:FOR T=
1 TO 4 STEP 1:READ X,Y,Z:GOSUB 370:LINE-(SX,SY),C3:NEXT T:RE
AD X,Y,Z:GOSUB 370:PAINT (SX,SY),CO,C3  'surface 1
230   RESTORE 730:READ X,Y,Z:GOSUB 370:PSET (SX,SY),C2:FOR T=
1 TO 4 STEP 1:READ X,Y,Z:GOSUB 370:LINE-(SX,SY),C2:NEXT T:RE
AD X,Y,Z:GOSUB 370:PAINT (SX,SY),C2,C2  'key matte for surfa
ce 2
```

```
240   RESTORE 730:READ X,Y,Z:GOSUB 370:PSET (SX,SY),C3:FOR T=
1 TO 4 STEP 1:READ X,Y,Z:GOSUB 370:LINE-(SX,SY),C3:NEXT T:RE
AD X,Y,Z:GOSUB 370:PAINT (SX,SY),C0,C3   'surface 2
250   RESTORE 740:READ X,Y,Z:GOSUB 370:PSET (SX,SY),C2:FOR T=
1 TO 4 STEP 1:READ X,Y,Z:GOSUB 370:LINE-(SX,SY),C2:NEXT T:RE
AD X,Y,Z:GOSUB 370:PAINT (SX,SY),C2,C2   'key matte for surfa
ce 3
260   RESTORE 740:READ X,Y,Z:GOSUB 370:PSET (SX,SY),C3:FOR T=
1 TO 4 STEP 1:READ X,Y,Z:GOSUB 370:LINE-(SX,SY),C3:NEXT T:RE
AD X,Y,Z:GOSUB 370:PAINT (SX,SY),C0,C3   'surface 3
270   RESTORE 750:READ X,Y,Z:GOSUB 370:PSET (SX,SY),C2:FOR T=
1 TO 4 STEP 1:READ X,Y,Z:GOSUB 370:LINE-(SX,SY),C2:NEXT T:RE
AD X,Y,Z:GOSUB 370:PAINT (SX,SY),C2,C2   'key matte for surfa
ce 4
280   RESTORE 750:READ X,Y,Z:GOSUB 370:PSET (SX,SY),C3:FOR T=
1 TO 4 STEP 1:READ X,Y,Z:GOSUB 370:LINE-(SX,SY),C3:NEXT T:RE
AD X,Y,Z:GOSUB 370:PAINT (SX,SY),C0,C3   'surface 4
290   RESTORE 760:READ X,Y,Z:GOSUB 370:PSET (SX,SY),C2:FOR T=
1 TO 4 STEP 1:READ X,Y,Z:GOSUB 370:LINE-(SX,SY),C2:NEXT T:RE
AD X,Y,Z:GOSUB 370:PAINT (SX,SY),C2,C2   'key matte for top s
urface
300   RESTORE 760:READ X,Y,Z:GOSUB 370:PSET (SX,SY),C3:FOR T=
1 TO 4 STEP 1:READ X,Y,Z:GOSUB 370:LINE-(SX,SY),C3:NEXT T:RE
AD X,Y,Z:GOSUB 370:PAINT (SX,SY),C0,C3   'top surface 5
310   BEEP   'cube complete
320   GOTO 320   'clean halt.
330   END 'of master routine.
340 '_____
350 '
360 'module:   perspective calculations for Cartesian world c
oordinates
370   X=(-1)*X:XA=CR1*X-SR1*Z:ZA=SR1*X+CR1*Z:X=CR2*XA+SR2*Y:Y
A=CR2*Y-SR2*XA:Z=CR3*ZA-SR3*YA:Y=SR3*ZA+CR3*YA:X=X+MX:Y=Y+MY
:Z=Z+MZ:SX=D*X/Z:SY=D*Y/Z:RETURN
380 '_____
390 '
400 'module:   return to BASIC command level
410   CLS:WINDOW:SCREEN 0,0,0,0:CLS:WIDTH 80:END
420 '_____
430 '
440 'module:   UNIVERSAL
450 'This routine configures the program for the hardware/so
ftware being used.
460   KEY OFF:CLS:ON ERROR GOTO 490   'trap if not Enhanced Di
splay + EGA
470   SCREEN 9,,0,0:COLOR 7,0:PALETTE 2,5:PALETTE 3,7:C0=0:C1
=1:C2=2:C3=3:LOCATE 1,1:PRINT "ED-EGA 640x350 16-color mode"

480   GOTO 590   'jump to screen coordinates set-up
```

```
490    RESUME 500
500    ON ERROR GOTO 530   'trap if not Color Display + EGA
510    SCREEN 8,,0,0:COLOR 7,0:PALETTE 2,5:PALETTE 3,7:C0=0:C1
=1:C2=2:C3=3:LOCATE 1,1:PRINT "CD-EGA 640x200 16-color mode"

520    GOTO 590   'jump to screen coordinates set-up
530    RESUME 540
540    ON ERROR GOTO 570   'trap if not PCjr
550    CLEAR,,,32768!:SCREEN 6,0,0,0:COLOR 3,0:C0=0:C1=1:C2=2:
C3=3:LOCATE 1,1:PRINT "PCjr 640x200 4-color mode"
560    GOTO 590   'jump to screen coordinates set-up
570    RESUME 580
580    SCREEN 1,0:COLOR 0,1:C0=0:C1=1:C2=2:C3=3:LOCATE 1,1:PRI
NT "CGA 320x200 4-color mode"
590    ON ERROR GOTO 0   'disable error trapping override
600    WINDOW SCREEN (-399,-299)-(400,300)
610    ON KEY (2) GOSUB 410:KEY (2) ON   'F2 key to exit progra
m
620    GOTO 150   'return to main program
630    '_____
640    '
650    'module:   assign variables
660    G=0:D=1200:R1=5.68319:R2=6.28319:R3=5.79778:MX=0:MY=0:M
Z=-350   '3D parameters
670    SR1=SIN(R1):CR1=COS(R1):SR2=SIN(R2):CR2=COS(R2):SR3=SIN
(R3):CR3=COS(R3):RETURN
680    '_____
690    '
700    'module:   database of Cartesian XYZ world coordinates fo
r 3D cube (sorted as bottom surface 0, surface 1, surface 2,
 surface 3, surface 4, top surface 5)
710    DATA  30,-30,30,  30,-30,-30,  -30,-30,-30,  -30,-30,30
,  30,-30,30,  0,-30,0
720    DATA  30,30,-30,  -30,30,-30,  -30,-30,-30,  30,-30,-30
,  30,30,-30,  0,0,-30
730    DATA  -30,30,-30,  -30,30,30,  -30,-30,30,  -30,-30,-30
,  -30,30,-30,  -30,0,0
740    DATA  -30,30,30,  30,30,30,  30,-30,30,  -30,-30,30,  -
30,30,30,  0,0,30
750    DATA  30,30,30,  30,30,-30,  30,-30,-30,  30,-30,30,  3
0,30,30,  30,0,0
760    DATA  -30,30,-30,  30,30,-30,  30,30,30,  -30,30,30,  -
30,30,-30,  0,30,0
770    '_____
780    '
790    END 'of program code
```

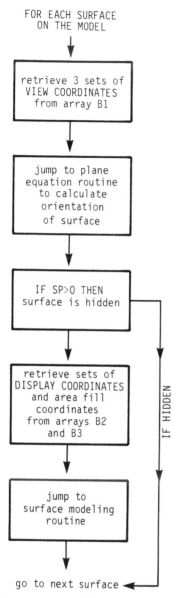

FOR EACH SURFACE
ON THE MODEL

↓

retrieve 3 sets of
VIEW COORDINATES
from array B1

↓

jump to plane
equation routine
to calculate
orientation
of surface

↓

IF SP>O THEN
surface is hidden

↓                    IF HIDDEN

retrieve sets of
DISPLAY COORDINATES
and area fill
coordinates
from arrays B2
and B3

↓

jump to
surface modeling
routine

↓

go to next surface ←

Fig. 8-6. The mechanics of hidden surface removal on 3D models using the plane equation method.

tine. Note line 440, which redefines the sine and cosine values after the view angle has been altered.

The master routine always draws the bottom surface of the cube first. Then, line 210 sends the program to a special subroutine at line 1000. This subroutine uses IF...THEN statements to determine which of the four sides of the cube should be drawn next. By analyzing the view angle, the subroutine knows which side of the cube is at the back of the cube; it instructs the main routine to draw the back sides first, of course. The subroutine also sets the surface counter variable, L, to zero. Control is then returned to the master routine at the appropriate point in the drawing sequence by a RETURN linenum statement. You can think of L as a flag which keeps track of how many surfaces have been completed. The flag concept will be used as a handy method of program control in later demonstration programs.

Line 290 illustrates how the radial sort method of hidden surface removal works. After drawing a surface, the L counter is incremented. If L is 4, then all four sides have been drawn and the program can finish by drawing the top surface. If L is less than 4, additional sides must then be drawn.

Although the radial sort method of hidden surface removal is effective, it is very dependent upon the shape of the model. A cube has surfaces which are at 90 degrees to each other. A triangle or prism would

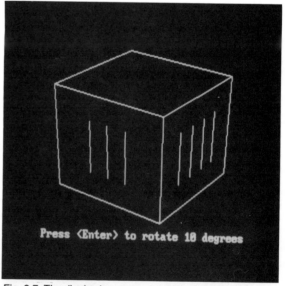

Fig. 8-7. The display image produced by the demonstration program in Fig. 8-8.

track of which side you are viewing during rotation.

The code which controls the rotation of the cube is located at lines 410 through 450. When you touch <Enter> the value of R1, which is the yaw viewing angle, is changed. The screen is cleared and the program jumps back to the beginning of the drawing rou-

Fig. 8-8. Solid model using the radial sort method of hidden surface removal.

```
100 'Program A-03.BAS      Solid cube.
110 'Uses radial sort method of hidden surface removal.
120 '_____
130 '
140   GOTO 590    'configure system
150   GOSUB 790   'assign scalar data
160 '_____
170 '
180 'master routine:  draw 3D cube using radial sort method
of hidden surface removal
190   RESTORE 860:READ X,Y,Z:GOSUB 500:PSET (SX,SY),C2:FOR T=
1 TO 4 STEP 1:READ X,Y,Z:GOSUB 500:LINE-(SX,SY),C2:NEXT T:RE
AD X,Y,Z:GOSUB 500:PAINT (SX,SY),C2,C2  'key matte for botto
m surface
200   RESTORE 860:READ X,Y,Z:GOSUB 500:PSET (SX,SY),C3:FOR T=
1 TO 4 STEP 1:READ X,Y,Z:GOSUB 500:LINE-(SX,SY),C3:NEXT T:RE
AD X,Y,Z:GOSUB 500:PAINT (SX,SY),C0,C3  'bottom surface 0
210   GOSUB 1000  'jump to radial sort routine
220   RESTORE 870:READ X,Y,Z:GOSUB 500:PSET (SX,SY),C2:FOR T=
1 TO 4 STEP 1:READ X,Y,Z:GOSUB 500:LINE-(SX,SY),C2:NEXT T:RE
AD X,Y,Z:GOSUB 500:PAINT (SX,SY),C2,C2  'key matte for surfa
ce 1
230   RESTORE 870:READ X,Y,Z:GOSUB 500:PSET (SX,SY),C3:FOR T=
1 TO 4 STEP 1:READ X,Y,Z:GOSUB 500:LINE-(SX,SY),C3:NEXT T:RE
AD X,Y,Z:GOSUB 500:PAINT (SX,SY),C0,C3  'surface 1
240   READ X,Y,Z:GOSUB 500:PSET (SX,SY),C3:READ X,Y,Z:GOSUB 5
00:LINE-(SX,SY),C3  'detail on surface 1
250   L=L+1:IF L=4 THEN 380  'if four surfaces done, jump to
top surface
260   RESTORE 890:READ X,Y,Z:GOSUB 500:PSET (SX,SY),C2:FOR T=
1 TO 4 STEP 1:READ X,Y,Z:GOSUB 500:LINE-(SX,SY),C2:NEXT T:RE
AD X,Y,Z:GOSUB 500:PAINT (SX,SY),C2,C2  'key matte for surfa
ce 2
270   RESTORE 890:READ X,Y,Z:GOSUB 500:PSET (SX,SY),C3:FOR T=
1 TO 4 STEP 1:READ X,Y,Z:GOSUB 500:LINE-(SX,SY),C3:NEXT T:RE
AD X,Y,Z:GOSUB 500:PAINT (SX,SY),C0,C3  'surface 2
280   FOR T=1 TO 2 STEP 1:READ X,Y,Z:GOSUB 500:PSET (SX,SY),C
3:READ X,Y,Z:GOSUB 500:LINE-(SX,SY),C3:NEXT T  'detail on su
rface 2
290   L=L+1:IF L=4 THEN 380  'if four surfaces done, jump to
top surface
300   RESTORE 910:READ X,Y,Z:GOSUB 500:PSET (SX,SY),C2:FOR T=
1 TO 4 STEP 1:READ X,Y,Z:GOSUB 500:LINE-(SX,SY),C2:NEXT T:RE
AD X,Y,Z:GOSUB 500:PAINT (SX,SY),C2,C2  'key matte for surfa
ce 3
310   RESTORE 910:READ X,Y,Z:GOSUB 500:PSET (SX,SY),C3:FOR T=
```

```
1 TO 4 STEP 1:READ X,Y,Z:GOSUB 500:LINE-(SX,SY),C3:NEXT T:RE
AD X,Y,Z:GOSUB 500:PAINT (SX,SY),CO,C3   'surface 3
320   FOR T=1 TO 3 STEP 1:READ X,Y,Z:GOSUB 500:PSET (SX,SY),C
3:READ X,Y,Z:GOSUB 500:LINE-(SX,SY),C3:NEXT T 'detail on su
rface 3
330   L=L+1:IF L=4 THEN 380   'if four surfaces done, jump to
top surface
340   RESTORE 930:READ X,Y,Z:GOSUB 500:PSET (SX,SY),C2:FOR T=
1 TO 4 STEP 1:READ X,Y,Z:GOSUB 500:LINE-(SX,SY),C2:NEXT T:RE
AD X,Y,Z:GOSUB 500:PAINT (SX,SY),C2,C2  'key matte for surfa
ce 4
350   RESTORE 930:READ X,Y,Z:GOSUB 500:PSET (SX,SY),C3:FOR T=
1 TO 4 STEP 1:READ X,Y,Z:GOSUB 500:LINE-(SX,SY),C3:NEXT T:RE
AD X,Y,Z:GOSUB 500:PAINT (SX,SY),CO,C3   'surface 4
360   FOR T=1 TO 4 STEP 1:READ X,Y,Z:GOSUB 500:PSET (SX,SY),C
3:READ X,Y,Z:GOSUB 500:LINE-(SX,SY),C3:NEXT T  'detail on su
rface 4
370   L=L+1:IF L=4 THEN 380 ELSE 220  'if four surfaces done,
 jump to top surface else jump to next surface
380   RESTORE 950:READ X,Y,Z:GOSUB 500:PSET (SX,SY),C2:FOR T=
1 TO 4 STEP 1:READ X,Y,Z:GOSUB 500:LINE-(SX,SY),C2:NEXT T:RE
AD X,Y,Z:GOSUB 500:PAINT (SX,SY),C2,C2  'key matte for top s
urface
390   RESTORE 950:READ X,Y,Z:GOSUB 500:PSET (SX,SY),C3:FOR T=
1 TO 4 STEP 1:READ X,Y,Z:GOSUB 500:LINE-(SX,SY),C3:NEXT T:RE
AD X,Y,Z:GOSUB 500:PAINT (SX,SY),CO,C3   'top surface 5
400   BEEP:LOCATE 2,1:PRINT "Press <Enter> to rotate 10 degre
es."
410   K$=INKEY$
420   IF K$<>CHR$(13) THEN 410
430   R1=R1-.17454:IF R1<0 THEN R1=R1+6.28319
440   SR1=SIN(R1):CR1=COS(R1):SR2=SIN(R2):CR2=COS(R2):SR3=SIN
(R3):CR3=COS(R3)
450   CLS:LOCATE 3,1:PRINT "View angle:"R1"radians":GOTO 190
460   END 'of master routine.
470   '_____
480   '
490   'module:   perspective calculations for Cartesian world c
oordinates
500   X=(-1)*X:XA=CR1*X-SR1*Z:ZA=SR1*X+CR1*Z:X=CR2*XA+SR2*Y:Y
A=CR2*Y-SR2*XA:Z=CR3*ZA-SR3*YA:Y=SR3*ZA+CR3*YA:X=X+MX:Y=Y+MY
:Z=Z+MZ:SX=D*X/Z:SY=D*Y/Z:RETURN
510   '_____
520   '
530   'module:   return to BASIC interpreter
540   CLS:WINDOW:SCREEN 0,0,0,0:WIDTH 80:COLOR 7,0,0:CLS:LOCA
TE 1,1,1:END
550   '_____
560   '
```

```
570 'module:  UNIVERSAL
580 'This routine configures the program for the hardware/so
ftware being used.
590  KEY OFF:CLS:ON ERROR GOTO 620  'trap if not Enhanced Di
splay + EGA
600   SCREEN 9,,0,0:COLOR 7,0:PALETTE 2,5:PALETTE 3,7:C0=0:C1
=1:C2=2:C3=3:LOCATE 1,1:PRINT "ED-EGA 640x350 16-color mode"

610   GOTO 720  'jump to screen coordinates set-up
620   RESUME 630
630   ON ERROR GOTO 660  'trap if not Color Display + EGA
640   SCREEN 8,,0,0:COLOR 7,0:PALETTE 2,5:PALETTE 3,7:C0=0:C1
=1:C2=2:C3=3:LOCATE 1,1:PRINT "CD-EGA 640x200 16-color mode"

650   GOTO 720  'jump to screen coordinates set-up
660   RESUME 670
670   ON ERROR GOTO 700  'trap if not PCjr
680   CLEAR,,,32768!:SCREEN 6,0,0,0:COLOR 3,0:C0=0:C1=1:C2=2:
C3=3:LOCATE 1,1:PRINT "PCjr 640x200 4-color mode"
690   GOTO 720  'jump to screen coordinates set-up
700   RESUME 710
710   SCREEN 1,0:COLOR 0,1:C0=0:C1=1:C2=2:C3=3:LOCATE 1,1:PRI
NT "CGA 320x200 4-color mode"
720   ON ERROR GOTO 0  'disable error trapping override
730   WINDOW SCREEN (-399,-299)-(400,300)
740   ON KEY (2) GOSUB 540:KEY (2) ON  'F2 key to exit progra
m
750   GOTO 150  'return to main program
760 '_____
770 '
780 'module:  assign variables
790   D=1200:R1=5.68319:R2=6.28319:R3=5.79778:MX=0:MY=0:MZ=-3
50  '3D parameters
800   DEFINT T,L
810   L=0 'number of surfaces drawn
820   SR1=SIN(R1):CR1=COS(R1):SR2=SIN(R2):CR2=COS(R2):SR3=SIN
(R3):CR3=COS(R3):RETURN
830 '_____
840 '
850 'module:  database of Cartesian XYZ world coordinates fo
r 3D cube (sorted as bottom surface 0, surface 1, surface 2,
 surface 3, surface 4, top surface 5)
860   DATA  30,-30,30,  30,-30,-30,  -30,-30,-30,  -30,-30,30
,  30,-30,30,  0,-30,0
870   DATA  30,30,-30,  -30,30,-30,  -30,-30,-30,  30,-30,-30
,  30,30,-30,  0,0,-30
880   DATA  0,15,-30,  0,-15,-30
890   DATA  -30,30,-30,  -30,30,30,  -30,-30,30,  -30,-30,-30
```

```
,   -30,30,-30,  -30,0,0
900   DATA  -30,15,-10,  -30,-15,-10,  -30,15,10,  -30,-15,10

910   DATA  -30,30,30,  30,30,30,  30,-30,30,  -30,-30,30,  -
30,30,30,  0,0,30
920   DATA  -10,15,30,  -10,-15,30,  0,15,30,  0,-15,30,  10,
15,30,  10,-15,30
930   DATA  30,30,30,  30,30,-30,  30,-30,-30,  30,-30,30,  3
0,30,30,  30,0,0
940   DATA  30,15,15,  30,-15,15,  30,15,5,  30,-15,5,  30,15
,-5,  30,-15,-5,  30,15,-15,  30,-15,-15
950   DATA  -30,30,-30,  30,30,-30,  30,30,30,  -30,30,30,  -
30,30,-30,  0,30,0
960   '_____
970   '
980   'module:  radial sort subroutine
990   'this routine determines the farthest surfaces based upo
n view angle and draws those surfaces first, eventually cove
ring them with nearer surfaces.
1000   IF (R1>=4.61239) AND (R1<6.18319) THEN L=0:RETURN 220
1010   IF (R1>=3.04159) AND (R1<4.61239) THEN L=0:RETURN 260
1020   IF (R1>=1.47049) AND (R1<3.04159) THEN L=0:RETURN 300
1030   IF (R1>=6.18319) OR (R1>=0) AND (R1<1.47049) THEN L=0:
RETURN 340
1040   BEEP:LOCATE 1,1:PRINT "Radial sort routine failure."
1050   GOTO 1050
1060   '_____
1070   '
1080   END 'of program code
```

present difficulties for the programmer who insists upon using the radial sort method. You would be reduced to using trial and error in order to determine which surfaces should be hidden in what range of view angles. Is there a better way? Yes. It is the plane equation method, which works effectively for all models, no matter what their shape.

## SOLID CUBE: PLANE EQUATION METHOD

Figure 8-9 illustrates the screen output of the demonstration program in Fig. 8-10. To run this program from the companion diskette, type **LOAD "A-04.BAS",R**. The program introduces four important new concepts. First, it uses the extremely efficient plane equation method of hidden surface removal. Second, it introduces an optimized database. Third, it produces six different simultaneous views of the same model. Fourth, it utilizes a separate subrou-

tine to model a solid surface. It is this optimized modeling prototype that will form the foundation for most of the demonstration programs in the book.

### The Plane Equation Formulas

The subroutine which determines whether a particular surface is visible or hidden is located at line 1150. Like all elegant solutions, it is short. Simply stated, it determines the orientation of the plane (which is the surface). By comparing this orientation to the viewpoint located at 0,0,0, you know if you are looking at the front side or the back side of the plane. Because the plane is located on a convex model (a cube), if you are looking at the back side of the surface, obviously the surface should be invisible. You should only be able to see the front side, which is the outer side, of each surface on the cube.

It is important that the proper coordinates be

68

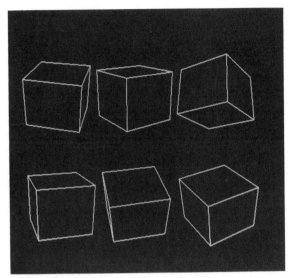

Fig. 8-9. The display image produced by the demonstration program in Fig. 8-10.

provided as input for the hidden surface routine. The model must be rotated and translated before the routine can make a correct decision concerning visibility of surfaces. In addition, the VIEW COORDINATES which describe the surface must be provided to the routine in a consistent manner. The hidden surface routine expects these coordinates to be located in a counterclockwise sequence around the outline of the surface (the plane). When this condition is met, the SP variable generated by the routine can be used to test for visibility. If SP is greater than 0, the surface is hidden.

The formulas used by the hidden surface routine at line 1150 are based upon matrix multiplication. If you are mathematically inclined, you may wish to read Appendix B for a detailed explanation. Otherwise, you can rest assured that the plane equation method of hidden surface removal provides a fail-safe method for determining the visibility of any plane in the 3D coordinate system.

Fig. 8-10. Multiple simultaneous views of a solid 3D model using the plane equation method of hidden surface removal.

```
100 'Program A-04.BAS    Six simultaneous views of cube.
110 'Demonstrates use of viewports to display simultaneous v
iews of cube with hidden surfaces removed by plane equation
method.
120 '_____
130 '
140   GOTO 780     'configure system
150   GOSUB 980    'assign variables
160 '_____
170 '
180 'master routine:   simultaneous views of cube
190   R1=4.46141:VIEW (W1,W7)-(W2,W8):GOSUB 1200:GOSUB 300
200   R1=3.76325:R3=6.00009:VIEW (W3,W7)-(W4,W8):GOSUB 1200:G
OSUB 300
210   R1=4.16325:R3=.48319:VIEW (W5,W7)-(W6,W8):GOSUB 1200:GO
SUB 300
220   R1=3.40009:R3=5.89778:VIEW (W1,W9)-(W2,W10):GOSUB 1200:
GOSUB 300
230   R1=3.34159:R3=5.49778:VIEW (W3,W9)-(W4,W10):GOSUB 1200:
GOSUB 300
240   R1=5.29239:R3=5.59778:VIEW (W5,W9)-(W6,W10):GOSUB 1200:
GOSUB 300
250   GOTO 250  'clean halt
260   END 'of main routine
270 '_____
280 '
```

```
290 'module:  calculate and store vertex coordinates
300   RESTORE 1080  'beginning of database
310   FOR T=0 TO 7 STEP 1:READ X,Y,Z:GOSUB 690:B1(T,0)=X:B1(T
,1)=Y:B1(T,2)=Z:B2(T,0)=SX:B2(T,1)=SY:NEXT T  'load vertex v
iew coordinates into array B1, load vertex display coordinat
es into array B2
320   FOR T=0 TO 5 STEP 1:READ X,Y,Z:GOSUB 690:B3(T,0)=SX:B3(
T,1)=SY:NEXT T  'load area fill origin display coordinates i
nto array B3
330 '_____
340 '
350 'module:  draw 6 surfaces of cube
360 'surface 0 routine
370   X1=B1(7,0):Y1=B1(7,1):Z1=B1(7,2):X2=B1(0,0):Y2=B1(0,1):
Z2=B1(0,2):X3=B1(3,0):Y3=B1(3,1):Z3=B1(3,2):GOSUB 1160:IF SP
>0 THEN 420  'retrieve view coordinates, jump to plane equat
ion routine, test if surface hidden
380   X1=B2(7,0):Y1=B2(7,1):X2=B2(0,0):Y2=B2(0,1):X3=B2(3,0):
Y3=B2(3,1):X4=B2(6,0):Y4=B2(6,1):X5=B3(0,0):Y5=B3(0,1):GOSUB
 1300  'assign display coordinates and jump to solid surface
 modeling routine
390 '_____
400 '
410 'surface 1 routine
420   X1=B1(6,0):Y1=B1(6,1):Z1=B1(6,2):X2=B1(5,0):Y2=B1(5,1):
Z2=B1(5,2):X3=B1(4,0):Y3=B1(4,1):Z3=B1(4,2):GOSUB 1160:IF SP
>0 THEN 470
430 X1=B2(6,0):Y1=B2(6,1):X2=B2(5,0):Y2=B2(5,1):X3=B2(4,0):Y
3=B2(4,1):X4=B2(7,0):Y4=B2(7,1):X5=B3(1,0):Y5=B3(1,1):GOSUB
1300
440 '_____
450 '
460 'surface 2 routine
470   X1=B1(3,0):Y1=B1(3,1):Z1=B1(3,2):X2=B1(2,0):Y2=B1(2,1):
Z2=B1(2,2):X3=B1(5,0):Y3=B1(5,1):Z3=B1(5,2):GOSUB 1160:IF SP
>0 THEN 520
480 X1=B2(3,0):Y1=B2(3,1):X2=B2(2,0):Y2=B2(2,1):X3=B2(5,0):Y
3=B2(5,1):X4=B2(6,0):Y4=B2(6,1):X5=B3(2,0):Y5=B3(2,1):GOSUB
1300
490 '_____
500 '
510 'surface 3 routine
520   X1=B1(0,0):Y1=B1(0,1):Z1=B1(0,2):X2=B1(1,0):Y2=B1(1,1):
Z2=B1(1,2):X3=B1(2,0):Y3=B1(2,1):Z3=B1(2,2):GOSUB 1160:IF SP
>0 THEN 570
530 X1=B2(0,0):Y1=B2(0,1):X2=B2(1,0):Y2=B2(1,1):X3=B2(2,0):Y
3=B2(2,1):X4=B2(3,0):Y4=B2(3,1):X5=B3(3,0):Y5=B3(3,1):GOSUB
1300
540 '_____
```

```
550  '
560  'surface 4 routine
570    X1=B1(7,0):Y1=B1(7,1):Z1=B1(7,2):X2=B1(4,0):Y2=B1(4,1):
Z2=B1(4,2):X3=B1(1,0):Y3=B1(1,1):Z3=B1(1,2):GOSUB 1160:IF SP
>0 THEN 620
580  X1=B2(7,0):Y1=B2(7,1):X2=B2(4,0):Y2=B2(4,1):X3=B2(1,0):Y
3=B2(1,1):X4=B2(0,0):Y4=B2(0,1):X5=B3(4,0):Y5=B3(4,1):GOSUB
1300
590  '_____
600  '
610  'surface 5 routine
620    X1=B1(1,0):Y1=B1(1,1):Z1=B1(1,2):X2=B1(4,0):Y2=B1(4,1):
Z2=B1(4,2):X3=B1(5,0):Y3=B1(5,1):Z3=B1(5,2):GOSUB 1160:IF SP
>0 THEN 640
630  X1=B2(1,0):Y1=B2(1,1):X2=B2(4,0):Y2=B2(4,1):X3=B2(5,0):Y
3=B2(5,1):X4=B2(2,0):Y4=B2(2,1):X5=B3(5,0):Y5=B3(5,1):GOSUB
1300
640    SOUND 550,.7   'model is complete
650    RETURN
660  '_____
670  '
680  'module:   perspective calculations
690    X=(-1)*X:XA=CR1*X-SR1*Z:ZA=SR1*X+CR1*Z:X=CR2*XA+SR2*Y:Y
A=CR2*Y-SR2*XA:Z=CR3*ZA-SR3*YA:Y=SR3*ZA+CR3*YA:X=X+MX:Y=Y+MY
:Z=Z+MZ:SX=D*X/Z:SY=D*Y/Z:RETURN
700  '_____
710  '
720  'module:   return to BASIC interpreter
730    CLS:WINDOW:SCREEN 0,0,0,0:WIDTH 80:COLOR 7,0,0:CLS:LOCA
TE 1,1,1:END
740  '_____
750  '
760  'module:   UNIVERSAL
770  'This routine configures the program for the hardware/so
ftware being used.
780    KEY OFF:CLS:ON ERROR GOTO 810   'trap if not Enhanced Di
splay + EGA
790    SCREEN 9,,0,0:COLOR 7,0:PALETTE 2,5:PALETTE 3,7:C0=0:C1
=1:C2=2:C3=3:LOCATE 1,1:PRINT "ED-EGA 640x350 16-color mode"

800    GOSUB 1240:GOTO 910   'jump to screen coordinates set-up

810    RESUME 820
820    ON ERROR GOTO 850   'trap if not Color Display + EGA
830    SCREEN 8,,0,0:COLOR 7,0:PALETTE 2,5:PALETTE 3,7:C0=0:C1
=1:C2=2:C3=3:LOCATE 1,1:PRINT "CD-EGA 640x200 16-color mode"

840    GOSUB 1250:GOTO 910   'jump to screen coordinates set-up
```

```
850    RESUME 860
860    ON ERROR GOTO 890   'trap if not PCjr
870    CLEAR,,,32768!:SCREEN 6,0,0,0:COLOR 3,0:CO=0:C1=1:C2=2:
C3=3:LOCATE 1,1:PRINT "PCjr 640x200 4-color mode"
880    GOSUB 1250:GOTO 910   'jump to screen coordinates set-up

890    RESUME 900
900    SCREEN 1,0:COLOR 0,1:CO=0:C1=1:C2=2:C3=3:GOSUB 1260:LOC
ATE 1,1:PRINT "CGA 320x200 4-color mode"
910    ON ERROR GOTO 0  'disable error trapping override
920    WINDOW SCREEN (-399,-299)-(400,300)  'establish device-
independent screen coordinates
930    ON KEY (2) GOSUB 730:KEY (2) ON  'F2 key to exit progra
m
940    GOTO 150  'return to main program
950 '_____
960 '
970 'module:   assign variables
980    D=1200:R1=5.68319:R2=6.28319:R3=5.79778:MX=0:MY=0:MZ=-2
70  '3D parameters
990    DIM B1 (7,2)  '8 sets of XYZ view coordinates
1000   DIM B2 (7,1)  '8 sets of SX,SY display coordinates
1010   DIM B3 (5,1)  '6 sets of SX,SY fill coordinates
1020   XL=.57735:YL=.57735:ZL=.57735  'xyz components of unit
 vector for angle of incidence used in illumination algorith
m
1030   SR1=SIN(R1):CR1=COS(R1):SR2=SIN(R2):CR2=COS(R2):SR3=SI
N(R3):CR3=COS(R3)
1040   RETURN
1050 '_____
1060 '
1070 'module:   database of 8 sets of XYZ world coordinates f
or cube vertices
1080   DATA  30,-30,30,   30,30,30,   -30,30,30,   -30,-30,30,
30,30,-30,   -30,30,-30,   -30,-30,-30,   30,-30,-30
1090 '_____
1100 '
1110 'module:   database of 6 sets of XYZ world coordinates f
or area fill origins for 6 surfaces of cube
1120   DATA  0,-30,0,   0,0,-30,   -30,0,0,   0,0,30,   30,0,0,
0,30,0
1130 '_____
1140 '
1150 'module:   plane equation method of hidden surface remov
al
1160   SP1=X1*(Y2*Z3-Y3*Z2):SP1=(-1)*SP1:SP2=X2*(Y3*Z1-Y1*Z3)
:SP3=X3*(Y1*Z2-Y2*Z1):SP=SP1-SP2-SP3:RETURN
1170 '_____
```

```
1180 '
1190 'module:  re-assign sine and cosine rotation matrices
1200   SR1=SIN(R1):CR1=COS(R1):SR2=SIN(R2):CR2=COS(R2):SR3=SI
N(R3):CR3=COS(R3):RETURN
1210 '_____
1220 '
1230 'module:  viewport parameters for 640x350, 640x200, 320
x200
1240   W1=1:W2=319:W3=152:W4=470:W5=320:W6=639:W7=1:W8=174:W9
=175:W10=349:RETURN
1250   W1=1:W2=319:W3=152:W4=470:W5=320:W6=639:W7=1:W8=99:W9=
100:W10=199:RETURN
1260   W1=1:W2=159:W3=76:W4=235:W5=160:W6=319:W7=1:W8=99:W9=1
00:W10=199:RETURN
1270 '_____
1280 '
1290 'module:  solid surface modeling
1300   LINE (X1,Y1)-(X2,Y2),C2:LINE-(X3,Y3),C2:LINE-(X4,Y4),C
2:LINE-(X1,Y1),C2:PAINT (X5,Y5),C2,C2:LINE (X1,Y1)-(X2,Y2),C
3:LINE-(X3,Y3),C3:LINE-(X4,Y4),C3:LINE-(X1,Y1),C3:PAINT (X5,
Y5),C0,C3:RETURN
1310 '_____
1320 '
1330   END 'of program code
```

## The Optimized Database

If you check the database at line 1080, you will see that it is much smaller than the databases in the previous three demonstration programs. This database includes the eight corners (vertices) which make up a cube. Refer to Fig. 8-11. The previous databases were very redundant. They were structured as groups of lines, so that many vertices were repeated because one vertex can be the endpoint for three different lines.

Note lines 990, 1000, and 1010. Memory is set aside inside BASIC's workspace for three arrays. These arrays are used to hold the output of the 3D perspective formulas. Array B1 will eventually contain eight sets of X,Y,Z VIEW COORDINATES, which are the eight corners of the cube. Array B2 will eventually contain eight sets of SX,SY DISPLAY COORDINATES, which are the eight corners of the cube. Array B3 will eventually hold six sets of X,Y,Z area fill coordinates. (There are six surfaces, so six sets of area fill start points are required.)

This approach to organizing the WORLD COORDINATES database results in code which executes more efficiently. Lines 290 through 320 precalculate all the coordinates which will be used later in the program. These assorted WORLD COORDINATES, DISPLAY COORDINATES, and area fill coordinates are temporarily saved in arrays. Note the use of the variable T in the counting loop to assign the appropriate location within each array. The coordinates are retrieved from the arrays at the time they are needed and in the order they are needed to describe the various surfaces which will be presented to the hidden surface removal routine.

You can see how this optimized approach works by referring to lines 360 through 380, which draws surface number 0. Surface number 0 is the first surface to be drawn: the bottom of the cube. Remember, computer numbering begins at 0, not 1. Line 370 retrieves three sets of VIEW COORDINATES from array B1. These coordinates are ordered in a counterclockwise direction around the outline of surface 0. The instruction GOSUB 1160 jumps to the hidden surface routine. The IF SP...THEN statement determines if the surface is visible or hidden.

Line 380 retrieves the appropriate DISPLAY COORDINATES from array B2. Then the area fill

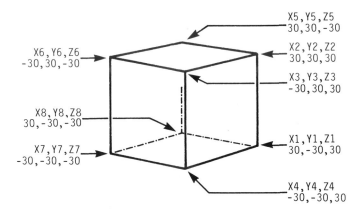

Fig. 8-11. Assignment of counter-clockwise vertex coordinates.

Note: To use plane equation visibility test, coordinates must be inspected in a counterclockwise order as viewed form the outside of the model.

X5,Y5,Z5
30,30,-30

X2,Y2,Z2
30,30,30

X6,Y6,Z6
-30,30,-30

X3,Y3,Z3
-30,30,30

X8,Y8,Z8
30,-30,-30

X1,Y1,Z1
30,-30,30

X7,Y7,Z7
-30,-30,-30

X4,Y4,Z4
-30,-30,30

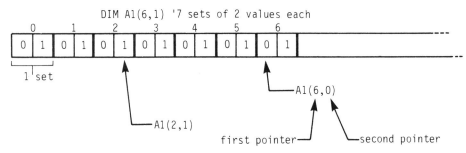

Fig. 8-12. An array is a table composed of sets of values. The first pointer identifies the set being referenced. The second pointer identifies the value being referenced within the set.

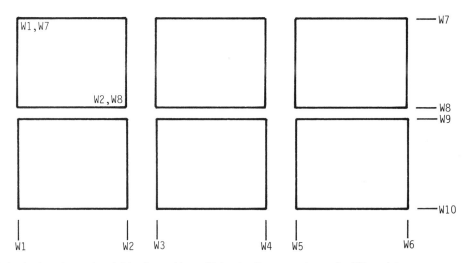

Fig. 8-13. Assigning viewport variables to enable multiple simultaneous views of a 3D model.

coordinates are retrieved from array B3. These coordinates are sent to the modeling subroutine at line 1300. This modeling subroutine uses the coordinates to draw a key matte and then to draw the finished solid surface. Because every surface on the cube is a four-sided polygon, it makes sense to use the same code via a subroutine, thereby eliminating the need to write the same instructions into each surface's drawing code.

| W1 | W2 | W3 | W4 | W5 | W6 | W7 | W8 | W9 | W10 | |
|---|---|---|---|---|---|---|---|---|---|---|
| 1 | 319 | 152 | 470 | 320 | 639 | 1 | 174 | 175 | 349 | EGA 640x350 |
| 1 | 319 | 152 | 470 | 320 | 639 | 1 | 99 | 100 | 199 | EGA + PCjr 640x200 |
| 1 | 159 | 76 | 235 | 160 | 319 | 1 | 99 | 100 | 199 | CGA 320x200 |

Fig. 8-14. Viewport boundaries for the 640 × 350 screen, the 640 × 200 screen, and the 320 × 200 screen.

### How Arrays Work

An array is simply a group of sets. If an array named A1 is dimensioned as DIM A1(7,1) it will contain 8 sets of 2 values each. (Remember, computers begin counting at 0, not 1.) An array dimensioned as DIM A1(7,2) will contain 8 sets of 3 values each.

Refer to Fig. 8-12. To point at one of the sets, you manipulate the first number in the array descriptor. To point at the third set, you would specify A1(2,0). The value 2 identifies the third set. The value 0 identifies the first value in the third set. A1(2,1) would identify the second value in the third set. A1(2,3) would identify the fourth value in the third set.

### MULTIPLE SIMULTANEOUS VIEWS

The demonstration program in Fig. 8-10 generates six views of the solid cube. Because the program supports the 320 × 200 screen, the 640 × 200 screen, and the 640 × 350 screen, some careful preparation is needed to ensure that the viewports are located at the correct position on each screen mode.

The module at line 1230 assigns appropriate values to the variables W1, W2, W3, W4, W5, W6, W7, W8, W9, and W10. Refer to Fig. 8-13. These ten variables are sufficient to describe all the upper left and lower right corners needed by six different VIEW statements. These variables are assigned as needed by each screen mode when the particular screen mode is set up by the configuration module. Refer to Fig. 8-14.

### A UNIVERSAL ALGORITHM

The overall methodology used by the demonstration program in Fig. 8-10 is versatile and effective. Refer to Fig. 8-15. This approach can be applied to models of all shapes and sizes. This technique will provide a fundamentally sound approach for producing

models which can be rendered as fully-shaded objects and which can be animated, if desired.

If you are typing in the demonstration programs, you will find that many of the programs in this part of the book use the same algorithms. By simply changing the database and a few lines in the actual drawing code, you can save yourself a lot of time at the keyboard.

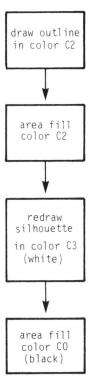

Fig. 8-15. The graphics functions of the surface modeling routine. First, a key matte is used to obliterate all distant images. Then, the surface is redrawn in color C3 and filled with color C0.

# 9

# *Geometric Modeling*

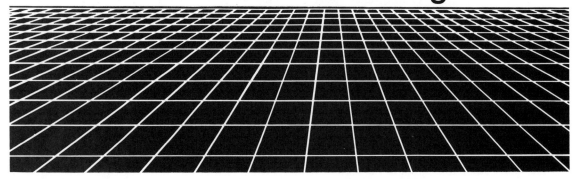

The generic modeling program introduced in the previous chapter can be easily modified to create other geometric shapes. These shapes can be used as sub-objects to build more complicated models. The shapes are also useful to illustrate more advanced techniques of modeling on your personal computer. Because the plane equation method of hidden surface removal is used, these new shapes can be constructed as solid models which can be viewed from any direction. Each demonstration program shows you six different views of the same model using the viewport routines discussed in the previous chapter.

If you are typing the programs from the listings in the book, you can modify the program (see Fig. 8-10) from the previous chapter, rather than retyping the listings in this chapter in their entirety. Often, the only code which changes is the module which precalculates the vertex coordinates, the actual drawing code, and the databases.

## THE SOLID PYRAMID

A tetrahedron is a three-sided pyramid resting upon a base, yielding a total of four sides. Refer to Fig. 9-1. By using a quick sketch of the 3D axis system,

or by using a top elevation view, you can easily determine the WORLD COORDINATES for the pyramid. (A top elevation view is a sketch which depicts how the model would appear if you were directly above it looking down.)

Figure 9-2 illustrates the screen output of the demonstration program in Fig. 9-3. To run this program from the companion diskette, type **LOAD "A-05.BAS",R.**

Note the code from line 290 to line 320. The size of the arrays and the number of coordinates have been modified from the algorithm used for the cube which was drawn in the previous chapter. The actual drawing code, which runs from line 350 to line 530, draws only four surfaces. Because each of these surfaces is a triangle, and not a four-sided polygon, the surface modeling routine at line 1190 has been modified to draw three lines instead of four lines. As you can see, it would be a straightforward task to modify the surface modeling routine to draw polygon surfaces of almost any shape.

The database for the area fill starting points is at line 1020. These WORLD COORDINATES have been estimated by trial and error, which is not a very professional approach. The fully-shaded solid pyramid in

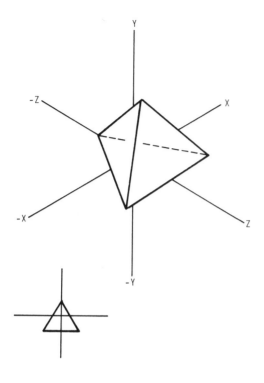

Fig. 9-1. World coordinates of the tetrahedron (four-sided pyramid).

Part Three uses a mathematical method of calculating the location of the area fill coordinates which is more precise than the guesstimate approach used here.

Of particular interest are the two solid pyramids in the lower left corner. One pyramid is located in front of the other and obscures part of the more distant model. This spatial arrangement functions correctly in this demonstration program only because the nearer pyramid is drawn after the pyramid it obscures. Chapter 13 will introduce a number of algorithms to deal with multiple models and obscured surfaces.

## THE SOLID PRISM

Prisms come in all shapes and sizes. The most familiar shape is a five-sided, or pentagonal, prism. Figure 9-4 shows the conceptual location of a pentagonal prism within the 3D coordinate axis system. Ten vertices are required to create a 3D model, because each end of the object is constructed around five corners.

Figure 9-5 shows the screen output of the demonstration program in Fig. 9-6. To run this program from the companion diskette, type **LOAD "A-06.BAS",R.**

Note line 310, which loads ten sets of vertex VIEW COORDINATES into array B1 and ten sets of vertex DISPLAY COORDINATES into array B2. Again, remember that the computer counts from 0 to

Fig. 9-2. The display image produced by the demonstration program in Fig. 9-3.

Fig. 9-3. Tetrahedron (3D pyramid).

```
100 'Program A-05.BAS    Six simultaneous views of pyramid.
110 'Uses plane equation method to remove hidden surfaces.
120 '_____
130 '
140   GOTO 680    'configure system
150   GOSUB 880   'assign variables
160 '_____
170 '
180 'master routine:   simultaneous views of pyramid
190   R1=3.66141:VIEW (W1,W7)-(W2,W8):GOSUB 1100:GOSUB 300
200   R1=3.46325:R3=4.88319:VIEW (W3,W7)-(W4,W8):GOSUB 1100:G
OSUB 300
210   R1=3.26141:R3=.30319:VIEW (W5,W7)-(W6,W8):GOSUB 1100:GO
SUB 300
220   R1=2.80009:R3=5.89778:VIEW (W1,W9)-(W2,W10):GOSUB 1100:
GOSUB 300
230   R1=3.64159:R3=6.22239:VIEW (W3,W9)-(W4,W10):GOSUB 1100:
GOSUB 300
240   R1=5.29239:R3=2.84159:VIEW (W5,W9)-(W6,W10):GOSUB 1100:
GOSUB 300
250   GOTO 250 'clean halt
260   END 'of main routine
270 '_____
280 '
290 'module:   calculate and store vertex coordinates
300   RESTORE 980  'beginning of database
310   FOR T=0 TO 3 STEP 1:READ X,Y,Z:GOSUB 590:B1(T,0)=X:B1(T
,1)=Y:B1(T,2)=Z:B2(T,0)=SX:B2(T,1)=SY:NEXT T  'load vertex v
iew coordinates into array B1, load vertex display coordinat
es into array B2
320   FOR T=0 TO 3 STEP 1:READ X,Y,Z:GOSUB 590:B3(T,0)=SX:B3(
T,1)=SY:NEXT T  'load area fill origin display coordinates i
nto array B3
330 '_____
340 '
350 'module:   draw 4 surfaces of pyramid
360 'surface 0 routine
370   X1=B1(0,0):Y1=B1(0,1):Z1=B1(0,2):X2=B1(2,0):Y2=B1(2,1):
Z2=B1(2,2):X3=B1(1,0):Y3=B1(1,1):Z3=B1(1,2):GOSUB 1060:IF SP
>0 THEN 420  'retrieve view coordinates, jump to plane equat
ion routine, test if surface hidden
380   X1=B2(0,0):Y1=B2(0,1):X2=B2(2,0):Y2=B2(2,1):X3=B2(1,0):
Y3=B2(1,1):X4=B3(0,0):Y4=B3(0,1):GOSUB 1200  'assign display
 coordinates and jump to solid surface modeling routine
390 '_____
400 '
```

```
410 'surface 1 routine
420   X1=B1(0,0):Y1=B1(0,1):Z1=B1(0,2):X2=B1(1,0):Y2=B1(1,1):
Z2=B1(1,2):X3=B1(3,0):Y3=B1(3,1):Z3=B1(3,2):GOSUB 1060:IF SP
>0 THEN 470
430 X1=B2(0,0):Y1=B2(0,1):X2=B2(1,0):Y2=B2(1,1):X3=B2(3,0):Y
3=B2(3,1):X4=B3(1,0):Y4=B3(1,1):GOSUB 1200
440 '_____
450 '
460 'surface 2 routine
470   X1=B1(1,0):Y1=B1(1,1):Z1=B1(1,2):X2=B1(2,0):Y2=B1(2,1):
Z2=B1(2,2):X3=B1(3,0):Y3=B1(3,1):Z3=B1(3,2):GOSUB 1060:IF SP
>0 THEN 520
480 X1=B2(1,0):Y1=B2(1,1):X2=B2(2,0):Y2=B2(2,1):X3=B2(3,0):Y
3=B2(3,1):X4=B3(2,0):Y4=B3(2,1):GOSUB 1200
490 '_____
500 '
510 'surface 3 routine
520   X1=B1(2,0):Y1=B1(2,1):Z1=B1(2,2):X2=B1(0,0):Y2=B1(0,1):
Z2=B1(0,2):X3=B1(3,0):Y3=B1(3,1):Z3=B1(3,2):GOSUB 1060:IF SP
>0 THEN 540
530 X1=B2(2,0):Y1=B2(2,1):X2=B2(0,0):Y2=B2(0,1):X3=B2(3,0):Y
3=B2(3,1):X4=B3(3,0):Y4=B3(3,1):GOSUB 1200
540   SOUND 550,.7  'model is complete
550   RETURN
560 '_____
570 '
580 'module:   perspective calculations
590   X=(-1)*X:XA=CR1*X-SR1*Z:ZA=SR1*X+CR1*Z:X=CR2*XA+SR2*Y:Y
A=CR2*Y-SR2*XA:Z=CR3*ZA-SR3*YA:Y=SR3*ZA+CR3*YA:X=X+MX:Y=Y+MY
:Z=Z+MZ:SX=D*X/Z:SY=D*Y/Z:RETURN
600 '_____
610 '
620 'module:   return to BASIC interpreter
630   CLS:WINDOW:SCREEN 0,0,0,0:WIDTH 80:COLOR 7,0,0:CLS:LOCA
TE 1,1,1:END
640 '_____
650 '
660 'module:   UNIVERSAL
670 'This routine configures the program for the hardware/so
ftware being used.
680   KEY OFF:CLS:ON ERROR GOTO 710  'trap if not Enhanced Di
splay + EGA
690   SCREEN 9,,0,0:COLOR 7,0:PALETTE 2,5:PALETTE 3,7:C0=0:C1
=1:C2=2:C3=3:LOCATE 1,1:PRINT "ED-EGA 640x350 16-color mode"

700   GOSUB 1140:GOTO 810  'jump to screen coordinates set-up

710   RESUME 720
```

```
720    ON ERROR GOTO 750    'trap if not Color Display + EGA
730    SCREEN 8,,0,0:COLOR 7,0:PALETTE 2,5:PALETTE 3,7:C0=0:C1
=1:C2=2:C3=3:LOCATE 1,1:PRINT "CD-EGA 640x200 16-color mode"
740    GOSUB 1150:GOTO 810    'jump to screen coordinates set-up

750    RESUME 760
760    ON ERROR GOTO 790    'trap if not PCjr
770    CLEAR,,,32768!:SCREEN 6,0,0,0:COLOR 3,0:C0=0:C1=1:C2=2:
C3=3:LOCATE 1,1:PRINT "PCjr 640x200 4-color mode"
780    GOSUB 1150:GOTO 810    'jump to screen coordinates set-up

790    RESUME 800
800    SCREEN 1,0:COLOR 0,1:C0=0:C1=1:C2=2:C3=3:GOSUB 1160:LOC
ATE 1,1:PRINT "CGA 320x200 4-color mode"
810    ON ERROR GOTO 0    'disable error trapping override
820    WINDOW SCREEN (-399,-299)-(400,300)    'establish device-
independent screen coordinates
830    ON KEY (2) GOSUB 630:KEY (2) ON    'F2 key to exit progra
m
840    GOTO 150    'return to main program
850    '_____
860    '
870    'module:    assign variables
880    D=1200:R1=5.68319:R2=6.28319:R3=5.79778:MX=0:MY=0:MZ=-1
80    '3D parameters
890    DIM B1 (3,2)    '4 sets of XYZ view coordinates
900    DIM B2 (3,1)    '4 sets of SX,SY display coordinates
910    DIM B3 (3,1)    '4 sets of SX,SY fill coordinates
920    XL=.57735:YL=.57735:ZL=.57735    'xyz components of unit
vector for angle of incidence used in illumination algorithm

930    SR1=SIN(R1):CR1=COS(R1):SR2=SIN(R2):CR2=COS(R2):SR3=SIN
(R3):CR3=COS(R3)
940    RETURN
950    '_____
960    '
970    'module:    4 sets of XYZ world coordinates for pyramid
980    DATA  -30,-25,25,  30,-25,25,  0,-25,-25,  0,25,8
990    '_____
1000   '
1010   'module:    4 sets of XYZ world coordinates for area fill
 origins for 4 surfaces of pyramid
1020   DATA  0,-25,8,  0,0,17,  6,0,3,  -7,0,3
1030   '_____
1040   '
1050   'module:    plane equation method of hidden surface remov
al
1060   SP1=X1*(Y2*Z3-Y3*Z2):SP1=(-1)*SP1:SP2=X2*(Y3*Z1-Y1*Z3)
```

```
:SP3=X3*(Y1*Z2-Y2*Z1):SP=SP1-SP2-SP3:RETURN
1070 '_____
1080 '
1090 'module:   re-assign sine and cosine rotation matrices
1100   SR1=SIN(R1):CR1=COS(R1):SR2=SIN(R2):CR2=COS(R2):SR3=SI
N(R3):CR3=COS(R3):RETURN
1110 '_____
1120 '
1130 'module:   viewport parameters for 640x350, 640x200, 320
x200
1140   W1=1:W2=319:W3=152:W4=470:W5=320:W6=639:W7=1:W8=174:W9
=175:W10=349:RETURN
1150   W1=1:W2=319:W3=152:W4=470:W5=320:W6=639:W7=1:W8=99:W9=
100:W10=199:RETURN
1160   W1=1:W2=159:W3=76:W4=235:W5=160:W6=319:W7=1:W8=99:W9=1
00:W10=199:RETURN
1170 '_____
1180 '
1190 'module:   solid surface modeling for 3-sided polygon
1200   LINE (X1,Y1)-(X2,Y2),C2:LINE-(X3,Y3),C2:LINE-(X1,Y1),C
2:PAINT (X4,Y4),C2,C2:LINE (X1,Y1)-(X2,Y2),C3:LINE-(X3,Y3),C
3:LINE-(X1,Y1),C3:PAINT (X4,Y4),C0,C3:RETURN
1210 '_____
1220 '
1230   END 'of program code
```

9 to arrive at ten sets of coordinates. Line 320 loads seven sets of area fill coordinates into array B3. By referring to Fig. 9-4 you can see that a 3D pentagonal prism contains only seven surfaces: five sides and two ends.

The actual drawing code is located from line 350 to line 680. When required, it calls upon two different surface modeling routines. The routine at line 1350 constructs a four-sided polygon surface. The routine at line 1390 constructs a five-sided polygon surface. The ends of the prism are five-sided; the side panels are four-sided.

The database of area fill WORLD COORDINATES is located at line 1170. These coordinates were obtained from an elevation view drawing of the model.

## THE POLYHEDRON MIDDLECRYSTAL

A polyhedron is a multi-sided solid model. A middlecrystal is constructed from various midsections of a cube. Refer to Fig. 9-7. This is one of the most complicated geometric models which could be considered as a sub-object. Figure 9-8 shows the screen output of the demonstration program in Fig. 9-9. To run this program from the companion diskette, type **LOAD "A-07.BAS",R.**

A polyhedron middlecrystal is composed of 14 surfaces, which can be defined by 12 vertices (or corners). The database for the 12 vertices was derived from a sketch similar to Fig. 9-7. A 3D paper model was constructed to assist the author in conceptualizing the problem. The database for the 14 area fill coordinates, located at line 1510, was derived from elevation views of the middlecrystal which were drawn freehand.

Note that there are two types of surfaces on the middlecrystal: four-sided surfaces and three-sided surfaces. The surface modeling routine at line 1690 is called by the drawing code to create four-sided polygons. The surface modeling at line 1730 is called to draw the three-sided polygons.

If you experiment with different values for R1 and R3 in line 240 (which sets the view angle for the polyhedron in the lower right corner of the screen), you can spin the model to a position where the area fill

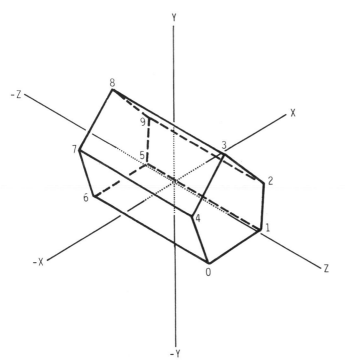

Fig. 9-4. World coordinates for the 3D prism.

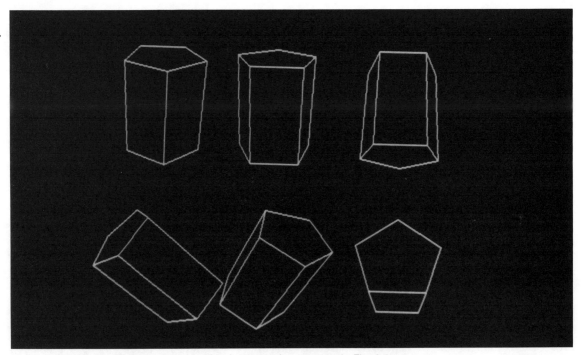

Fig. 9-5. The display image produced by the demonstration program in Fig. 9-6.

Fig. 9-6. Prism.

```
100 'Program A-06.BAS    Six simultaneous views of pentagona
l prism.
110 'Uses plane equation method of hidden surface removal.
120 '_____
130 '
140   GOTO 830    'configure system
150   GOSUB 1030   'assign variables
160 '_____
170 '
180 'master routine:   simultaneous views of prism
190   R1=4.46141:VIEW (W1,W7)-(W2,W8):GOSUB 1250:GOSUB 300
200   R1=3.76325:R3=5.88319:VIEW (W3,W7)-(W4,W8):GOSUB 1250:G
OSUB 300
210   R1=3.76325:R3=.48319:VIEW (W5,W7)-(W6,W8):GOSUB 1250:GO
SUB 300
220   R1=4.46141:R2=.78319:R3=5.68319:VIEW (W1,W9)-(W2,W10):G
OSUB 1250:GOSUB 300
230   R1=3.34159:R2=5.88319:R3=5.49778:VIEW (W3,W9)-(W4,W10):
GOSUB 1250:GOSUB 300
240   R1=0:R2=0:R3=4.99778:VIEW (W5,W9)-(W6,W10):GOSUB 1250:G
OSUB 300
250   GOTO 250  'clean halt
260   END 'of main routine
270 '_____
280 '
290 'module:   calculate and store vertex coordinates
300   RESTORE 1130  'beginning of database
310   FOR T=0 TO 9 STEP 1:READ X,Y,Z:GOSUB 740:B1(T,0)=X:B1(T
,1)=Y:B1(T,2)=Z:B2(T,0)=SX:B2(T,1)=SY:NEXT T  'load vertex v
iew coordinates into array B1, load vertex display coordinat
es into array B2
320   FOR T=0 TO 6 STEP 1:READ X,Y,Z:GOSUB 740:B3(T,0)=SX:B3(
T,1)=SY:NEXT T  'load area fill origin display coordinates i
nto array B3
330 '_____
340 '
350 'module:   draw 7 surfaces of prism
360 'surface 0 routine
370   X1=B1(5,0):Y1=B1(5,1):Z1=B1(5,2):X2=B1(6,0):Y2=B1(6,1):
Z2=B1(6,2):X3=B1(7,0):Y3=B1(7,1):Z3=B1(7,2):GOSUB 1210:IF SP
>0 THEN 420  'retrieve view coordinates, jump to plane equat
ion routine, test if surface hidden
380   X1=B2(5,0):Y1=B2(5,1):X2=B2(6,0):Y2=B2(6,1):X3=B2(7,0):
Y3=B2(7,1):X4=B2(8,0):Y4=B2(8,1):X5=B2(9,0):Y5=B2(9,1):X6=B3
(0,0):Y6=B3(0,1):GOSUB 1390  'jump to 5-sided polygon solid
surface routine
```

```
390 '_____
400 '
410 'surface 1 routine
420   X1=B1(0,0):Y1=B1(0,1):Z1=B1(0,2):X2=B1(6,0):Y2=B1(6,1):
Z2=B1(6,2):X3=B1(5,0):Y3=B1(5,1):Z3=B1(5,2):GOSUB 1210:IF SP
>0 THEN 470 'retrieve view coordinates, jump to plane equat
ion routine, test if surface hidden
430   X1=B2(0,0):Y1=B2(0,1):X2=B2(6,0):Y2=B2(6,1):X3=B2(5,0):
Y3=B2(5,1):X4=B2(1,0):Y4=B2(1,1):X5=B3(1,0):Y5=B3(1,1):GOSUB
 1350  'assign display coordinates and jump to 4-sided polyg
on solid surface modeling routine
440 '_____
450 '
460 'surface 2 routine
470   X1=B1(1,0):Y1=B1(1,1):Z1=B1(1,2):X2=B1(5,0):Y2=B1(5,1):
Z2=B1(5,2):X3=B1(9,0):Y3=B1(9,1):Z3=B1(9,2):GOSUB 1210:IF SP
>0 THEN 520
480 X1=B2(1,0):Y1=B2(1,1):X2=B2(5,0):Y2=B2(5,1):X3=B2(9,0):Y
3=B2(9,1):X4=B2(2,0):Y4=B2(2,1):X5=B3(2,0):Y5=B3(2,1):GOSUB
1350
490 '_____
500 '
510 'surface 3 routine
520   X1=B1(2,0):Y1=B1(2,1):Z1=B1(2,2):X2=B1(9,0):Y2=B1(9,1):
Z2=B1(9,2):X3=B1(8,0):Y3=B1(8,1):Z3=B1(8,2):GOSUB 1210:IF SP
>0 THEN 570
530 X1=B2(2,0):Y1=B2(2,1):X2=B2(9,0):Y2=B2(9,1):X3=B2(8,0):Y
3=B2(8,1):X4=B2(3,0):Y4=B2(3,1):X5=B3(3,0):Y5=B3(3,1):GOSUB
1350
540 '_____
550 '
560 'surface 4 routine
570   X1=B1(3,0):Y1=B1(3,1):Z1=B1(3,2):X2=B1(8,0):Y2=B1(8,1):
Z2=B1(8,2):X3=B1(7,0):Y3=B1(7,1):Z3=B1(7,2):GOSUB 1210:IF SP
>0 THEN 620
580 X1=B2(3,0):Y1=B2(3,1):X2=B2(8,0):Y2=B2(8,1):X3=B2(7,0):Y
3=B2(7,1):X4=B2(4,0):Y4=B2(4,1):X5=B3(4,0):Y5=B3(4,1):GOSUB
1350
590 '_____
600 '
610 'surface 5 routine
620   X1=B1(4,0):Y1=B1(4,1):Z1=B1(4,2):X2=B1(7,0):Y2=B1(7,1):
Z2=B1(7,2):X3=B1(6,0):Y3=B1(6,1):Z3=B1(6,2):GOSUB 1210:IF SP
>0 THEN 670
630 X1=B2(4,0):Y1=B2(4,1):X2=B2(7,0):Y2=B2(7,1):X3=B2(6,0):Y
3=B2(6,1):X4=B2(0,0):Y4=B2(0,1):X5=B3(5,0):Y5=B3(5,1):GOSUB
1350
640 '_____
```

```
650 '
660 'surface 6 routine
670   X1=B1(0,0):Y1=B1(0,1):Z1=B1(0,2):X2=B1(1,0):Y2=B1(1,1):
Z2=B1(1,2):X3=B1(2,0):Y3=B1(2,1):Z3=B1(2,2):GOSUB 1210:IF SP
>0 THEN 690  'retrieve view coordinates, jump to plane equat
ion routine, test if surface hidden
680   X1=B2(0,0):Y1=B2(0,1):X2=B2(1,0):Y2=B2(1,1):X3=B2(2,0):
Y3=B2(2,1):X4=B2(3,0):Y4=B2(3,1):X5=B2(4,0):Y5=B2(4,1):X6=B3
(6,0):Y6=B3(6,1):GOSUB 1390  'jump to 5-sided polygon solid
surface routine
690   SOUND 550,.7  'model is complete
700   RETURN
710 '_____
720 '
730 'module:   perspective calculations
740   X=(-1)*X:XA=CR1*X-SR1*Z:ZA=SR1*X+CR1*Z:X=CR2*XA+SR2*Y:Y
A=CR2*Y-SR2*XA:Z=CR3*ZA-SR3*YA:Y=SR3*ZA+CR3*YA:X=X+MX:Y=Y+MY
:Z=Z+MZ:SX=D*X/Z:SY=D*Y/Z:RETURN
750 '_____
760 '
770 'module:   return to BASIC interpreter
780   CLS:WINDOW:SCREEN 0,0,0,0:WIDTH 80:COLOR 7,0,0:CLS:LOCA
TE 1,1,1:END
790 '_____
800 '
810 'module:   UNIVERSAL
820 'This routine configures the program for the hardware/so
ftware being used.
830   KEY OFF:CLS:ON ERROR GOTO 860  'trap if not Enhanced Di
splay + EGA
840   SCREEN 9,,0,0:COLOR 7,0:PALETTE 2,5:PALETTE 3,7:C0=0:C1
=1:C2=2:C3=3:LOCATE 1,1:PRINT "ED-EGA 640x350 16-color mode"

850   GOSUB 1290:GOTO 960  'jump to screen coordinates set-up

860   RESUME 870
870   ON ERROR GOTO 900  'trap if not Color Display + EGA
880   SCREEN 8,,0,0:COLOR 7,0:PALETTE 2,5:PALETTE 3,7:C0=0:C1
=1:C2=2:C3=3:LOCATE 1,1:PRINT "CD-EGA 640x200 16-color mode"

890   GOSUB 1300:GOTO 960  'jump to screen coordinates set-up

900   RESUME 910
910   ON ERROR GOTO 940  'trap if not PCjr
920   CLEAR,,,32768!:SCREEN 6,0,0,0:COLOR 3,0:C0=0:C1=1:C2=2:
C3=3:LOCATE 1,1:PRINT "PCjr 640x200 4-color mode"
930   GOSUB 1300:GOTO 960  'jump to screen coordinates set-up
```

```
940    RESUME 950
950    SCREEN 1,0:COLOR 0,1:C0=0:C1=1:C2=2:C3=3:GOSUB 1310:LOC
ATE 1,1:PRINT "CGA 320x200 4-color mode"
960    ON ERROR GOTO 0   'disable error trapping override
970    WINDOW SCREEN (-399,-299)-(400,300)   'establish device-
independent screen coordinates
980    ON KEY (2) GOSUB 780:KEY (2) ON  'F2 key to exit progra
m
990    GOTO 150   'return to main program
1000 '_____
1010 '
1020 'module:   assign variables
1030    D=1200:R1=5.68319:R2=6.28319:R3=5.79778:MX=0:MY=0:MZ=-
270   '3D parameters
1040    DIM B1 (9,2)  '10 sets of XYZ view coordinates
1050    DIM B2 (9,1)  '10 sets of SX,SY display coordinates
1060    DIM B3 (6,1)  '7 sets of SX,SY fill coordinates
1070    XL=.57735:YL=.57735:ZL=.57735  'xyz components of unit
 vector for angle of incidence used in illumination algorith
m
1080    SR1=SIN(R1):CR1=COS(R1):SR2=SIN(R2):CR2=COS(R2):SR3=SI
N(R3):CR3=COS(R3)
1090    RETURN
1100 '_____
1110 '
1120 'module:   database of 10 sets of XYZ world coordinates
1130    DATA  -18,40,24,  18,40,24,  28,40,-9,  0,40,-30,  -28
,40,-9,  18,-40,24,  -18,-40,24,  -28,-40,-9,  0,-40,-30,  2
8,-40,-9
1140 '_____
1150 '
1160 'module:   database of 7 sets of XYZ world coordinates f
or area fill origins
1170    DATA  0,-40,0,  0,0,24,  23,0,7,  15,0,-19,  -15,0,-19
,  -23,0,7,  0,40,0
1180 '_____
1190 '
1200 'module:   plane equation method of hidden surface remov
al
1210    SP1=X1*(Y2*Z3-Y3*Z2):SP1=(-1)*SP1:SP2=X2*(Y3*Z1-Y1*Z3)
:SP3=X3*(Y1*Z2-Y2*Z1):SP=SP1-SP2-SP3:RETURN
1220 '_____
1230 '
1240 'module:   re-assign sine and cosine rotation matrices
1250    SR1=SIN(R1):CR1=COS(R1):SR2=SIN(R2):CR2=COS(R2):SR3=SI
N(R3):CR3=COS(R3):RETURN
1260 '_____
1270 '
```

```
1280 'module:   viewport parameters for 640x350, 640x200, 320
x200
1290   W1=1:W2=319:W3=152:W4=470:W5=320:W6=639:W7=1:W8=174:W9
=175:W10=349:RETURN
1300   W1=1:W2=319:W3=152:W4=470:W5=320:W6=639:W7=1:W8=99:W9=
100:W10=199:RETURN
1310   W1=1:W2=159:W3=76:W4=235:W5=160:W6=319:W7=1:W8=99:W9=1
00:W10=199:RETURN
1320 '_____
1330 '
1340 'module:   solid surface modeling for 4-sided polygon
1350   LINE (X1,Y1)-(X2,Y2),C2:LINE-(X3,Y3),C2:LINE-(X4,Y4),C
2:LINE-(X1,Y1),C2:PAINT (X5,Y5),C2,C2:LINE (X1,Y1)-(X2,Y2),C
3:LINE-(X3,Y3),C3:LINE-(X4,Y4),C3:LINE-(X1,Y1),C3:PAINT (X5,
Y5),C0,C3:RETURN
1360 '_____
1370 '
1380 'module:   solid surface modeling for 5-sided polygon
1390   LINE (X1,Y1)-(X2,Y2),C2:LINE-(X3,Y3),C2:LINE-(X4,Y4),C
2:LINE-(X5,Y5),C2:LINE-(X1,Y1),C2:PAINT (X6,Y6),C2,C2:LINE (
X1,Y1)-(X2,Y2),C3:LINE-(X3,Y3),C3:LINE-(X4,Y4),C3:LINE-(X5,Y
5),C3:LINE-(X1,Y1),C3:PAINT (X6,Y6),C0,C3:RETURN
1400 '_____
1410 '
1420   END 'of program code
```

routine fails. This is because the coordinates for the area fill start point were derived from an elevation drawing and therefore are not absolutely accurate. This model is the last one in this book which uses this freewheeling approach. Subsequent modeling projects, including the fully-shaded version of the middlecrystal in Chapter 16, use a failure-proof mathematical method for locating the area fill coordinates on surfaces of any shape and size.

Although the database approach to building a middlecrystal is efficient and effective, a middlecrystal can also be constructed by using the same techniques used to create a sphere in the next chapter.

## PLANES OF COINCIDENCE AND SYMMETRY

Figure 9-10 shows the screen output of the demonstration program in Fig. 9-11. To run this program from the companion diskette, type **LOAD** **"A-08.BAS",R.**

This demonstration program illustrates an easy and effective method for handling intersecting planes. By breaking each plane into two components, you can model the intersection.

Note that this program does not use any hidden surface routine other than the radial presort method described in Chapter 8. The planes which are farthest

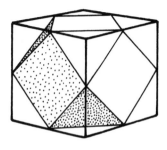

Fig. 9-7. World coordinates for a middlecrystal polyhedron, derived from midsections of a cube.

87

Fig. 9-8. The display image produced by the demonstration program in Fig. 9-9.

Fig. 9-9. Middlecrystal polyhedron.

```
100 'Program A-07.BAS    Six simultaneous views of polyhedro
n.
110 'Uses plane equation method of hidden surface removal.
120 '_____
130 '
140   GOTO 1170    'configure system
150   GOSUB 1370    'assign variables
160 '_____
170 '
180 'master routine:   simultaneous views of polyhedron
190   R1=4.46141:VIEW (W1,W7)-(W2,W8):GOSUB 1590:GOSUB 300
200   R1=3.76325:R3=6.00009:VIEW (W3,W7)-(W4,W8):GOSUB 1590:G
OSUB 300
210   R1=3.96325:R3=.48319:VIEW (W5,W7)-(W6,W8):GOSUB 1590:GO
SUB 300
220   R1=3.30009:R3=5.89778:VIEW (W1,W9)-(W2,W10):GOSUB 1590:
GOSUB 300
230   R1=3.34159:R3=5.49778:VIEW (W3,W9)-(W4,W10):GOSUB 1590:
GOSUB 300
240   R1=5.29239:R3=5.59778:VIEW (W5,W9)-(W6,W10):GOSUB 1590:
```

```
       GOSUB 300
250    GOTO 250   'clean halt
260    END 'of main routine
270    '_____
280    '
290    'module:  calculate and store vertex coordinates
300    RESTORE 1470   'beginning of database
310    FOR T=0 TO 11 STEP 1:READ X,Y,Z:GOSUB 1080:B1(T,0)=X:B1
(T,1)=Y:B1(T,2)=Z:B2(T,0)=SX:B2(T,1)=SY:NEXT T   'load vertex
 view coordinates into array B1, load vertex display coordin
ates into array B2
320    FOR T=0 TO 13 STEP 1:READ X,Y,Z:GOSUB 1080:B3(T,0)=SX:B
3(T,1)=SY:NEXT T   'load area fill origin display coordinates
 into array B3
330    '_____
340    '
350    'module:  draw 14 surfaces of middle crystal polyhedron
360    'surface 0 routine
370    X1=B1(1,0):Y1=B1(1,1):Z1=B1(1,2):X2=B1(10,0):Y2=B1(10,1
):Z2=B1(10,2):X3=B1(7,0):Y3=B1(7,1):Z3=B1(7,2):GOSUB 1550:IF
 SP>0 THEN 420   'retrieve view coordinates, jump to plane eq
uation routine, test if surface hidden
380    X1=B2(1,0):Y1=B2(1,1):X2=B2(10,0):Y2=B2(10,1):X3=B2(7,0
):Y3=B2(7,1):X4=B2(4,0):Y4=B2(4,1):X5=B3(0,0):Y5=B3(0,1):GOS
UB 1690   'assign display coordinates and jump to solid surfa
ce modeling routine
390    '_____
400    '
410    'surface 1 routine
420    X1=B1(0,0):Y1=B1(0,1):Z1=B1(0,2):X2=B1(1,0):Y2=B1(1,1):
Z2=B1(1,2):X3=B1(2,0):Y3=B1(2,1):Z3=B1(2,2):GOSUB 1550:IF SP
>0 THEN 470
430    X1=B2(0,0):Y1=B2(0,1):X2=B2(1,0):Y2=B2(1,1):X3=B2(2,0):Y
3=B2(2,1):X4=B2(3,0):Y4=B2(3,1):X5=B3(1,0):Y5=B3(1,1):GOSUB
1690
440    '_____
450    '
460    'surface 2 routine
470    X1=B1(2,0):Y1=B1(2,1):Z1=B1(2,2):X2=B1(4,0):Y2=B1(4,1):
Z2=B1(4,2):X3=B1(5,0):Y3=B1(5,1):Z3=B1(5,2):GOSUB 1550:IF SP
>0 THEN 520
480    X1=B2(2,0):Y1=B2(2,1):X2=B2(4,0):Y2=B2(4,1):X3=B2(5,0):Y
3=B2(5,1):X4=B2(6,0):Y4=B2(6,1):X5=B3(2,0):Y5=B3(2,1):GOSUB
1690
490    '_____
500    '
510    'surface 3 routine
520    X1=B1(5,0):Y1=B1(5,1):Z1=B1(5,2):X2=B1(7,0):Y2=B1(7,1):
```

```
     Z2=B1(7,2):X3=B1(8,0):Y3=B1(8,1):Z3=B1(8,2):GOSUB 1550:IF SP
     >0 THEN 570
     530 X1=B2(5,0):Y1=B2(5,1):X2=B2(7,0):Y2=B2(7,1):X3=B2(8,0):Y
     3=B2(8,1):X4=B2(9,0):Y4=B2(9,1):X5=B3(3,0):Y5=B3(3,1):GOSUB
     1690
     540 '_____
     550 '
     560 'surface 4 routine
     570   X1=B1(8,0):Y1=B1(8,1):Z1=B1(8,2):X2=B1(10,0):Y2=B1(10,1
     ):Z2=B1(10,2):X3=B1(0,0):Y3=B1(0,1):Z3=B1(0,2):GOSUB 1550:IF
      SP>0 THEN 620
     580 X1=B2(8,0):Y1=B2(8,1):X2=B2(10,0):Y2=B2(10,1):X3=B2(0,0)
     :Y3=B2(0,1):X4=B2(11,0):Y4=B2(11,1):X5=B3(4,0):Y5=B3(4,1):GO
     SUB 1690
     590 '_____
     600 '
     610 'surface 5 routine
     620   X1=B1(9,0):Y1=B1(9,1):Z1=B1(9,2):X2=B1(11,0):Y2=B1(11,1
     ):Z2=B1(11,2):X3=B1(3,0):Y3=B1(3,1):Z3=B1(3,2):GOSUB 1550:IF
      SP>0 THEN 670
     630 X1=B2(9,0):Y1=B2(9,1):X2=B2(11,0):Y2=B2(11,1):X3=B2(3,0)
     :Y3=B2(3,1):X4=B2(6,0):Y4=B2(6,1):X5=B3(5,0):Y5=B3(5,1):GOSU
     B 1690
     640 '_____
     650 '
     660 'surface 6 routine
     670   X1=B1(4,0):Y1=B1(4,1):Z1=B1(4,2):X2=B1(2,0):Y2=B1(2,1):
     Z2=B1(2,2):X3=B1(1,0):Y3=B1(1,1):Z3=B1(1,2):GOSUB 1550:IF SP
     >0 THEN 720
     680 X1=B2(4,0):Y1=B2(4,1):X2=B2(2,0):Y2=B2(2,1):X3=B2(1,0):Y
     3=B2(1,1):X4=B3(6,0):Y4=B3(6,1):GOSUB 1730
     690 '_____
     700 '
     710 'surface 7 routine
     720   X1=B1(0,0):Y1=B1(0,1):Z1=B1(0,2):X2=B1(10,0):Y2=B1(10,1
     ):Z2=B1(10,2):X3=B1(1,0):Y3=B1(1,1):Z3=B1(1,2):GOSUB 1550:IF
      SP>0 THEN 770
     730 X1=B2(0,0):Y1=B2(0,1):X2=B2(10,0):Y2=B2(10,1):X3=B2(1,0)
     :Y3=B2(1,1):X4=B3(7,0):Y4=B3(7,1):GOSUB 1730
     740 '_____
     750 '
     760 'surface 8 routine
     770   X1=B1(8,0):Y1=B1(8,1):Z1=B1(8,2):X2=B1(7,0):Y2=B1(7,1):
     Z2=B1(7,2):X3=B1(10,0):Y3=B1(10,1):Z3=B1(10,2):GOSUB 1550:IF
      SP>0 THEN 820
     780 X1=B2(8,0):Y1=B2(8,1):X2=B2(7,0):Y2=B2(7,1):X3=B2(10,0):
     Y3=B2(10,1):X4=B3(8,0):Y4=B3(8,1):GOSUB 1730
     790 '_____
```

```
800 '
810 'surface 9 routine
820    X1=B1(5,0):Y1=B1(5,1):Z1=B1(5,2):X2=B1(4,0):Y2=B1(4,1):
Z2=B1(4,2):X3=B1(7,0):Y3=B1(7,1):Z3=B1(7,2):GOSUB 1550:IF SP
>0 THEN 870
830 X1=B2(5,0):Y1=B2(5,1):X2=B2(4,0):Y2=B2(4,1):X3=B2(7,0):Y
3=B2(7,1):X4=B3(9,0):Y4=B3(9,1):GOSUB 1730
840 '_____
850 '
860 'surface 10 routine
870    X1=B1(3,0):Y1=B1(3,1):Z1=B1(3,2):X2=B1(11,0):Y2=B1(11,1
):Z2=B1(11,2):X3=B1(0,0):Y3=B1(0,1):Z3=B1(0,2):GOSUB 1550:IF
 SP>0 THEN 920
880 X1=B2(3,0):Y1=B2(3,1):X2=B2(11,0):Y2=B2(11,1):X3=B2(0,0)
:Y3=B2(0,1):X4=B3(10,0):Y4=B3(10,1):GOSUB 1730
890 '_____
900 '
910 'surface 11 routine
920    X1=B1(6,0):Y1=B1(6,1):Z1=B1(6,2):X2=B1(3,0):Y2=B1(3,1):
Z2=B1(3,2):X3=B1(2,0):Y3=B1(2,1):Z3=B1(2,2):GOSUB 1550:IF SP
>0 THEN 970
930 X1=B2(6,0):Y1=B2(6,1):X2=B2(3,0):Y2=B2(3,1):X3=B2(2,0):Y
3=B2(2,1):X4=B3(11,0):Y4=B3(11,1):GOSUB 1730
940 '_____
950 '
960 'surface 12 routine
970    X1=B1(9,0):Y1=B1(9,1):Z1=B1(9,2):X2=B1(6,0):Y2=B1(6,1):
Z2=B1(6,2):X3=B1(5,0):Y3=B1(5,1):Z3=B1(5,2):GOSUB 1550:IF SP
>0 THEN 1020
980 X1=B2(9,0):Y1=B2(9,1):X2=B2(6,0):Y2=B2(6,1):X3=B2(5,0):Y
3=B2(5,1):X4=B3(12,0):Y4=B3(12,1):GOSUB 1730
990 '_____
1000 '
1010 'surface 13 routine
1020    X1=B1(11,0):Y1=B1(11,1):Z1=B1(11,2):X2=B1(9,0):Y2=B1(9
,1):Z2=B1(9,2):X3=B1(8,0):Y3=B1(8,1):Z3=B1(8,2):GOSUB 1550:I
F SP>0 THEN 1040
1030 X1=B2(11,0):Y1=B2(11,1):X2=B2(9,0):Y2=B2(9,1):X3=B2(8,0
):Y3=B2(8,1):X4=B3(13,0):Y4=B3(13,1):GOSUB 1730
1040    SOUND 550,.7:RETURN
1050 '_____
1060 '
1070 'module:   perspective calculations
1080    X=(-1)*X:XA=CR1*X-SR1*Z:ZA=SR1*X+CR1*Z:X=CR2*XA+SR2*Y:
YA=CR2*Y-SR2*XA:Z=CR3*ZA-SR3*YA:Y=SR3*ZA+CR3*YA:X=X+MX:Y=Y+M
Y:Z=Z+MZ:SX=D*X/Z:SY=D*Y/Z:RETURN
1090 '_____
1100 '
```

```
1110 'module:  return to BASIC interpreter
1120  CLS:WINDOW:SCREEN 0,0,0,0:WIDTH 80:COLOR 7,0,0:CLS:LOC
ATE 1,1,1:END
1130 '_____
1140 '
1150 'module:  UNIVERSAL
1160 'This routine configures the program for the hardware/s
oftware being used.
1170  KEY OFF:CLS:ON ERROR GOTO 1200  'trap if not Enhanced
Display + EGA
1180  SCREEN 9,,0,0:COLOR 7,0:PALETTE 2,5:PALETTE 3,7:C0=0:C
1=1:C2=2:C3=3:LOCATE 1,1:PRINT "ED-EGA 640x350 16-color mode
"
1190  GOSUB 1630:GOTO 1300  'jump to screen coordinates set-
up
1200  RESUME 1210
1210  ON ERROR GOTO 1240  'trap if not Color Display + EGA
1220  SCREEN 8,,0,0:COLOR 7,0:PALETTE 2,5:PALETTE 3,7:C0=0:C
1=1:C2=2:C3=3:LOCATE 1,1:PRINT "CD-EGA 640x200 16-color mode
"
1230  GOSUB 1640:GOTO 1300  'jump to screen coordinates set-
up
1240  RESUME 1250
1250  ON ERROR GOTO 1280  'trap if not PCjr
1260  CLEAR,,,32768!:SCREEN 6,0,0,0:COLOR 3,0:C0=0:C1=1:C2=2
:C3=3:LOCATE 1,1:PRINT "PCjr 640x200 4-color mode"
1270  GOSUB 1640:GOTO 1300  'jump to screen coordinates set-
up
1280  RESUME 1290
1290  SCREEN 1,0:COLOR 0,1:C0=0:C1=1:C2=2:C3=3:GOSUB 1650:LO
CATE 1,1:PRINT "CGA 320x200 4-color mode"
1300  ON ERROR GOTO 0  'disable error trapping override
1310  WINDOW SCREEN (-399,-299)-(400,300)  'establish device
-independent screen coordinates
1320  ON KEY (2) GOSUB 1120:KEY (2) ON  'F2 key to exit prog
ram
1330  GOTO 150  'return to main program
1340 '_____
1350 '
1360 'module:  assign variables
1370  D=1200:R1=5.68319:R2=6.28319:R3=5.79778:MX=0:MY=0:MZ=-
270  '3D parameters
1380  DIM B1 (11,2)  '12 sets of XYZ view coordinates
1390  DIM B2 (11,1)  '12 sets of SX,SY display coordinates
1400  DIM B3 (13,1)  '14 sets of SX,SY fill coordinates
1410  XL=.57735:YL=.57735:ZL=.57735  'xyz components of unit
 vector for angle of incidence used in illumination algorith
m
```

```
1420    SR1=SIN(R1):CR1=COS(R1):SR2=SIN(R2):CR2=COS(R2):SR3=SI
N(R3):CR3=COS(R3)
1430    RETURN
1440  '_____
1450  '
1460  'module:   12 sets of XYZ world coordinates
1470    DATA  -30,0,30,  0,-30,30,  30,0,30,  0,30,30,  30,-30
,0,  30,0,-30,  30,30,0,  0,-30,-30,  -30,0,-30,  0,30,-30,
 -30,-30,0,  -30,30,0
1480  '_____
1490  '
1500  'module:   14 sets of XYZ world coordinates for area fil
l origins
1510    DATA  0,-30,0,  0,0,30,  30,0,0,  0,0,-30,  -30,0,0,
0,30,0,  20,-20,20,  -20,-20,20,  -20,-20,-20,  20,-20,-20,
 -20,20,20,  20,20,20,  20,20,-20,  -20,20,-20
1520  '_____
1530  '
1540  'module:   plane equation method of hidden surface remov
al
1550    SP1=X1*(Y2*Z3-Y3*Z2):SP1=(-1)*SP1:SP2=X2*(Y3*Z1-Y1*Z3)
:SP3=X3*(Y1*Z2-Y2*Z1):SP=SP1-SP2-SP3:RETURN
1560  '_____
1570  '
1580  'module:   re-assign sine and cosine rotation matrices
1590    SR1=SIN(R1):CR1=COS(R1):SR2=SIN(R2):CR2=COS(R2):SR3=SI
N(R3):CR3=COS(R3):RETURN
1600  '_____
1610  '
1620  'module:   viewport parameters for 640x350, 640x200, 320
x200
1630    W1=1:W2=319:W3=152:W4=470:W5=320:W6=639:W7=1:W8=174:W9
=175:W10=349:RETURN
1640    W1=1:W2=319:W3=152:W4=470:W5=320:W6=639:W7=1:W8=99:W9=
100:W10=199:RETURN
1650    W1=1:W2=159:W3=76:W4=235:W5=160:W6=319:W7=1:W8=99:W9=1
00:W10=199:RETURN
1660  '_____
1670  '
1680  'module:   solid surface modeling for 4-sided polygon
1690    LINE (X1,Y1)-(X2,Y2),C2:LINE-(X3,Y3),C2:LINE-(X4,Y4),C
2:LINE-(X1,Y1),C2:PAINT (X5,Y5),C2,C2:LINE (X1,Y1)-(X2,Y2),C
3:LINE-(X3,Y3),C3:LINE-(X4,Y4),C3:LINE-(X1,Y1),C3:PAINT (X5,
Y5),C0,C3:RETURN
1700  '_____
1710  '
1720  'module:   solid surface modeling for 3-sided polygon
1730    LINE (X1,Y1)-(X2,Y2),C2:LINE-(X3,Y3),C2:LINE-(X1,Y1),C
```

```
  2:PAINT (X4,Y4),C2,C2:LINE (X1,Y1)-(X2,Y2),C3:LINE-(X3,Y3),C
  3:LINE-(X1,Y1),C3:PAINT (X4,Y4),C0,C3:RETURN
  1740 '_____
  1750 '
  1760   END 'of program code
```

Fig. 9-10. The display image produced by the demonstration program in Fig. 9-11.

from the viewpoint are drawn first. The nearest planes are constructed last, thereby obscuring the more distant surfaces.

## CATEGORIES OF GEOMETRIC MODELS

A surprisingly diverse variety of geometric shapes exists. Refer to Fig. 9-12. Many are solid shapes in their own right, such as the four-sided and the five-sided pyramid. Others are derived from more commonplace shapes. Both the six-sided octahedron and the 14-sided middlecrystal are derived from the everyday cube.

Even the lowly cube has been given the ostentatious label of hexahedron by mathematicians. The base of a solid pyramid is called a frustrum.

If you have a conceptual grasp of geometric solids (and a healthy imagination!), it becomes easy to construct all sorts of shapes. A helix, for example, can be created by simply moving around the surface of a cylinder, as the next chapter will demonstrate. By slicing through a cube, you can generate assorted oblique planes. Quite often, the programming solution to an apparently difficult shape resides in conceptualizing the shape as being derived from one of the standard polyhedra shown in Fig. 9-12. It then is a straightforward task to derive the database from points found on or within the commonplace shape, much as the octahedron is found within the cube.

### SUMMARY

In this chapter you learned how to create solid 3D models of a pyramid, a prism, a middlecrystal, and planes of symmetry. You saw that modifications to the pre-calculation code, the drawing code, and the database were the only major changes required in order to draw different geometric models.

The next chapter describes methods for creating solid spheres and cylinders with automatic removal of hidden surfaces.

Fig. 9-11. Planes of coincidence and symmetry.

```
  100 'Program A-08.BAS     Planes of coincidence & symmetry.
  110 'Uses radial pre-sort method of hidden surface removal.
  120 '_____
  130 '
  140   GOTO 550    'configure system
```

```
150   GOSUB 750   'assign variables
160   '_____
170   '
180   'module:   calculate and save vertexes
190   RESTORE 830   'beginning of database
200   FOR T=0 TO 17 STEP 1:READ X,Y,Z:GOSUB 460:B2(T,0)=SX:B2
(T,1)=SY:NEXT T  'load vertex display coordinates into array
 B2
210   FOR T=0 TO 7 STEP 1:READ X,Y,Z:GOSUB 460:B3(T,0)=SX:B3(
T,1)=SY:NEXT T  'load area fill origin display coordinates i
nto array B3
220   '_____
230   '
240   'main routine:   draw 4 intersecting planes
250   'surface 0 routine
260   X1=B2(0,0):Y1=B2(0,1):X2=B2(8,0):Y2=B2(8,1):X3=B2(17,0)
:Y3=B2(17,1):X4=B2(16,0):Y4=B2(16,1):X5=B3(0,0):Y5=B3(0,1):G
OSUB 910   'assign display coordinates and jump to solid surf
ace modeling routine
270   'surface 1 routine
280   X1=B2(1,0):Y1=B2(1,1):X2=B2(9,0):Y2=B2(9,1):X3=B2(17,0):
Y3=B2(17,1):X4=B2(16,0):Y4=B2(16,1):X5=B3(1,0):Y5=B3(1,1):GO
SUB 910
290   'surface 2 routine
300   X1=B2(2,0):Y1=B2(2,1):X2=B2(10,0):Y2=B2(10,1):X3=B2(17,0
):Y3=B2(17,1):X4=B2(16,0):Y4=B2(16,1):X5=B3(2,0):Y5=B3(2,1):
GOSUB 910
310   'surface 3 routine
320   X1=B2(3,0):Y1=B2(3,1):X2=B2(11,0):Y2=B2(11,1):X3=B2(17,0
):Y3=B2(17,1):X4=B2(16,0):Y4=B2(16,1):X5=B3(3,0):Y5=B3(3,1):
GOSUB 910
330   'surface 7 routine
340   X1=B2(7,0):Y1=B2(7,1):X2=B2(15,0):Y2=B2(15,1):X3=B2(17,0
):Y3=B2(17,1):X4=B2(16,0):Y4=B2(16,1):X5=B3(7,0):Y5=B3(7,1):
GOSUB 910
350   'surface 6 routine
360   X1=B2(6,0):Y1=B2(6,1):X2=B2(14,0):Y2=B2(14,1):X3=B2(17,0
):Y3=B2(17,1):X4=B2(16,0):Y4=B2(16,1):X5=B3(6,0):Y5=B3(6,1):
GOSUB 910
370   'surface 5 routine
380   X1=B2(5,0):Y1=B2(5,1):X2=B2(13,0):Y2=B2(13,1):X3=B2(17,0
):Y3=B2(17,1):X4=B2(16,0):Y4=B2(16,1):X5=B3(5,0):Y5=B3(5,1):
GOSUB 910
390   'surface 4 routine
400   X1=B2(4,0):Y1=B2(4,1):X2=B2(12,0):Y2=B2(12,1):X3=B2(17,0
):Y3=B2(17,1):X4=B2(16,0):Y4=B2(16,1):X5=B3(4,0):Y5=B3(4,1):
GOSUB 910
410   SOUND 550,.7
```

```
420   GOTO 420
430 '_____
440 '
450 'module:   perspective calculations
460   X=(-1)*X:XA=CR1*X-SR1*Z:ZA=SR1*X+CR1*Z:X=CR2*XA+SR2*Y:Y
A=CR2*Y-SR2*XA:Z=CR3*ZA-SR3*YA:Y=SR3*ZA+CR3*YA:X=X+MX:Y=Y+MY
:Z=Z+MZ:SX=D*X/Z:SY=D*Y/Z:RETURN
470 '_____
480 '
490 'module:   return to BASIC interpreter
500   CLS:WINDOW:SCREEN 0,0,0,0:WIDTH 80:COLOR 7,0,0:CLS:LOCA
TE 1,1,1:END
510 '_____
520 '
530 'module:   UNIVERSAL
540 'This routine configures the program for the hardware/so
ftware being used.
550   KEY OFF:CLS:ON ERROR GOTO 580   'trap if not Enhanced Di
splay + EGA
560   SCREEN 9,,0,0:COLOR 7,0:PALETTE 2,5:PALETTE 3,7:C0=0:C1
=1:C2=2:C3=3:LOCATE 1,1:PRINT "ED-EGA 640x350 16-color mode"

570   GOTO 680   'jump to screen coordinates set-up
580   RESUME 590
590   ON ERROR GOTO 620   'trap if not Color Display + EGA
600   SCREEN 8,,0,0:COLOR 7,0:PALETTE 2,5:PALETTE 3,7:C0=0:C1
=1:C2=2:C3=3:LOCATE 1,1:PRINT "CD-EGA 640x200 16-color mode"

610   GOTO 680   'jump to screen coordinates set-up
620   RESUME 630
630   ON ERROR GOTO 660   'trap if not PCjr
640   CLEAR,,,32768!:SCREEN 6,0,0,0:COLOR 3,0:C0=0:C1=1:C2=2:
C3=3:LOCATE 1,1:PRINT "PCjr 640x200 4-color mode"
650   GOTO 680   'jump to screen coordinates set-up
660   RESUME 670
670   SCREEN 1,0:COLOR 0,1:C0=0:C1=1:C2=2:C3=3:LOCATE 1,1:PRI
NT "CGA 320x200 4-color mode"
680   ON ERROR GOTO 0   'disable error trapping override
690   WINDOW SCREEN (-399,-299)-(400,300)   'establish device-
independent screen coordinates
700   ON KEY (2) GOSUB 500:KEY (2) ON   'F2 key to exit progra
m
710   GOTO 150   'return to main program
720 '_____
730 '
740 'module:   assign variables
750   D=1200:R1=3.34159:R2=0:R3=5.59778:MX=0:MY=0:MZ=-300   '3
D parameters
```

```
760    DIM B2 (17,1)    '18 sets of SX,SY display coordinates
770    DIM B3 (7,1)     '8 sets of SX,SY fill coordinates
780    SR1=SIN(R1):CR1=COS(R1):SR2=SIN(R2):CR2=COS(R2):SR3=SIN
(R3):CR3=COS(R3)
790    RETURN
800    '_____
810    '
820    'module:   18 sets of XYZ world coordinates
830    DATA  0,50,30,  21,50,21,  30,50,0,  21,50,-21,  0,50,-
30,  -21,50,-21,  -30,50,0,  -21,50,21,  0,-50,30,  21,-50,2
1,  30,-50,0,  21,-50,-21,  0,-50,-30,  -21,-50,-21,  -30,-5
0,0,  -21,-50,21,  0,50,0,  0,-50,0
840    '_____
850    '
860    'module:   8 sets of XYZ world coordinates for area fill
origins
870    DATA  0,0,10,  10,0,10,  10,0,0,  10,0,-10,  0,0,-10,
-10,0,-10,  -10,0,0,  -10,0,10
880    '_____
890    '
900    'module:   solid surface modeling
910    LINE (X1,Y1)-(X2,Y2),C2:LINE-(X3,Y3),C2:LINE-(X4,Y4),C2
:LINE-(X1,Y1),C2:PAINT (X5,Y5),C2,C2:LINE (X1,Y1)-(X2,Y2),C3
:LINE-(X3,Y3),C3:LINE-(X4,Y4),C3:LINE-(X1,Y1),C3:PAINT (X5,Y
5),C0,C3:RETURN
920    '_____
930    '
940    END 'of program code
```

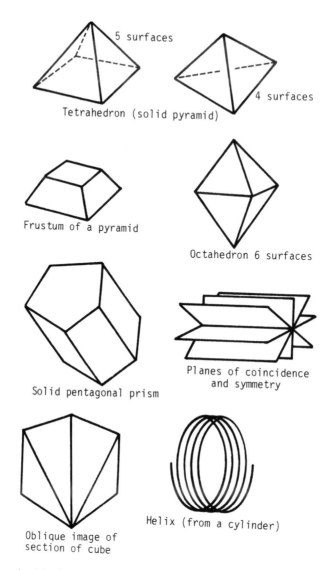

Fig. 9-12. Classification of polyhedra.

98

# 10

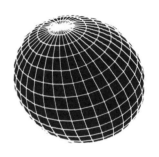

# Sphere, Cylinder, and Helix

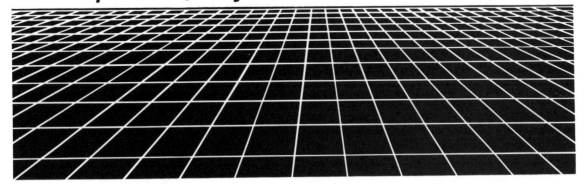

Surprisingly, a graphics program which creates a sphere or cylinder does not need much of a database. As a matter of interest, a database of only one value would be sufficient. This is because assorted points on the surface of the sphere and cylinder can be identified by sine and cosine calculations if the radius is known.

## THE SOLID SPHERE

Although it is possible to draw 3D spheres in a variety of formats, including transparent wire-frame and depth-clipped wire-frame, if the sphere is to be shaded by the computer the model must be comprised of distinct separate surfaces (planes). When each small plane on the surface of the sphere is shaded to the appropriate light level, the overall image of a fully-shaded sphere is obtained. The better the resolution of display produced by your graphics adapter and display monitor, the smaller the individual planes on the surface of the sphere can be.

The previous programs used R1 to represent yaw, R2 to represent roll, and R3 to represent pitch. Two more angle variables, R4 and R5, are introduced in the sphere program. Refer to Fig. 10-1. R4 is the an-

gle being swept around the equator of the sphere, beginning at the right (or eastern) axis. R5 is the angle being swept around the longitudinal arcs of the sphere, beginning at the top polar region (northern axis). Refer to Fig. 10-2.

If the radius is known, the coordinates of any point produced by R4 or R5 can be calculated. If R5 is 0, for example, the sine of R5 will be 1 and the cosine will be 0. In other words, one coordinate will be at maximum potential and the other coordinate will be 0. If R5 shifts to 1.57079 (which is 90 degrees), sine R5 becomes 0 and cosine R5 becomes 1. The interplay of sine and cosine will draw a perfect arc as each value shifts from minimum to maximum.

In addition, you can map the surface of the sphere by using a simple radian diagram such as Fig. 10-3. The starting point for the sweep is always 0 radians (or 6.28319 radians), no matter whether you are manipulating R4 or R5.

The methodology for producing a solid sphere made up of small surfaces is based upon the concept of belts. Refer to Fig. 10-3. First, R5 is swept down to a specified point which is the top of the belt. Then, while R5 is held constant, R4 is swept around the sphere. Second, R5 is swept down to a specified point

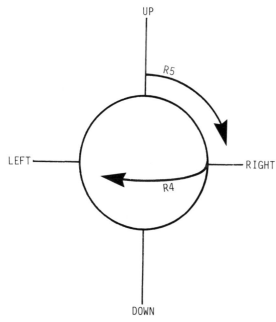

Fig. 10-1. Generation of longitudinal and latitudinal lines on a 3D sphere by trigonometric functions.

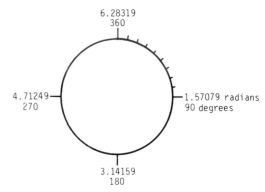

Fig. 10-3. Location of latitudinal lines on a 3D sphere, expressed as radians.

**"A-09.BAS",R.** The image produced by the program is called a polygon mesh sphere, because it is composed of a mesh of polygons. On a genuine IBM PC with an 8088 microprocessor running at 4.77 MHz, the demonstration program takes 8 minutes 12 seconds to complete the sphere. An IBM AT or compatible will punch it out in under 4 minutes.

The program uses an alphanumeric display in the upper left corner to keep you informed of the sweep calculation procedure. As the program draws the polygon surfaces around each belt, the value of SP is displayed for each surface. Remember, if SP is greater than zero, the surface is hidden.

The module beginning at line 210 draws the three-sided polygons which make up the north polar region of the sphere. This module calls the surface mapping routine at line 890 which uses R4 and R5 to compute the appropriate coordinates. The module also calls the standard 3D perspective formulas at line 940. The sur-

which is the bottom of the belt. Then, while R5 is again held steady, R4 is swept around the sphere. By saving the incremental coordinates of both sweeps around the sphere, the top sweep and the bottom sweep can be joined, yielding the fragmented belt illustrated in Fig. 10-4. Each fragment is a four-sided surface which can be subjected to the standard plane equation test for visibility. Refer to Fig. 10-5.

Figure 10-6 shows the screen output of the demonstration program in Fig. 10-7. To run the program from the companion diskette, type **LOAD**

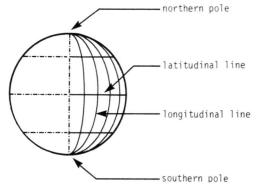

Fig. 10-2. Components of a sphere.

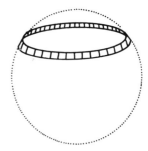

Fig. 10-4. A latitudinal sweep around the sphere produces 36 polygons which create a belt around the sphere. Each polygon can be subjected to the plane equation formulas to test for visibility.

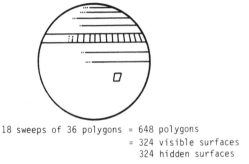

18 sweeps of 36 polygons = 648 polygons
                        = 324 visible surfaces
                          324 hidden surfaces

Fig. 10-5. The 3D polygon mesh sphere is comprised on 648 individual planes, each of which must be tested by the hidden surface routine.

face mapping routine at line 890 generates raw WORLD COORDINATES which must be converted to VIEW COORDINATES and DISPLAY COORDINATES by the perspective formulas at line 940. The module also calls upon the subroutine at line 850 to draw a single sweep of polygons around the north polar vertex.

The module beginning at line 280 draws the belts around the waist of the sphere. This module calls the surface mapping routine at line 890, as well as the standard 3D perspective formulas at line 940. The module then calls the full belt-drawing routines at line 840 and 850 which draw the top and bottom sweeps of the belt. The loop uses the variable Q1 to count 36 polygons around the belt. The variable Q2 is used to provide an alphanumeric display which keeps you informed concerning which surface is currently being drawn by the program.

Note line 290, which sets R5 to .17453, which is 10 degrees down from the north polar point. Line 300 then uses the routine at line 840 to calculate coordinates at 10 degree increments around the R4 arc for the top of the sweep and the routine at line 850 finds the points along the bottom of the sweep.

The module at line 370 draws the south polar three-sided polygons in a manner similar to that used to create the north polar region.

As the program executes, a short beep is emitted after each belt is completed. It is interesting to watch the value of SP getting larger and larger. When it exceeds 0, the surfaces are invisible. As the sweep continues around the back of the sphere, SP gets smaller and smaller until it once again becomes negative and

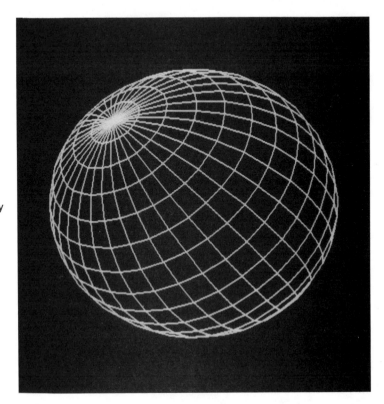

Fig. 10-6. The display image produced by the demonstration program in Fig. 10-7.

Fig. 10-7. Polygon mesh sphere.

```
100 'Program A-09.BAS     Polygon mesh sphere.
110 'Uses plane equation method of hidden surface removal.
120 '_____
130 '
140   GOTO 1030     'configure system
150   GOSUB 1240    'assign variables
160 '_____
170 '
180 'main routine:   calculate/store coordinates for belts ar
ound sphere
190 '_____
200 '
210 'step one:   north polar area
220   R5=0:R4=0:X=30:GOSUB 890:GOSUB 940:B11(0,0)=X:B11(0,1)=
Y:B11(0,2)=Z:B21(0,0)=SX:B21(0,1)=SY   'north pole
230   X=30:R5=.17453:R4=0:GOSUB 850
240   SOUND 350,.7:LOCATE 2,1:PRINT "Modeling solid surfaces"
:FOR Q1=0 TO 35 STEP 1:Q2=Q1+1:IF Q2>35 THEN Q2=0
250   LOCATE 3,1:PRINT Q1" ":GOSUB 470:NEXT Q1:LOCATE 4,1:PR
INT "                "
260 '_____
270 '
280 'step two:   polygon surfaces on belts around sphere
290   R5=.17453:FOR T2=1 TO 16 STEP 1
300   X=30:R4=0:GOSUB 840:X=30:R5=R5+.17453:R4=0:GOSUB 850
310   SOUND 350,.7:LOCATE 2,1:PRINT "Modeling solid surfaces"
:FOR Q1=0 TO 35 STEP 1:Q2=Q1+1:IF Q2>35 THEN Q2=0   'draw bel
t
320   LOCATE 3,1:PRINT Q1" ":GOSUB 700:NEXT Q1   'draw belt
330   LOCATE 4,1:PRINT "                "
340   NEXT T2
350 '_____
360 '
370 'step three:   south polar area
380   R5=3.14159:R4=0:X=30:GOSUB 890:GOSUB 940:B11(0,0)=X:B11
(0,1)=Y:B11(0,2)=Z:B21(0,0)=SX:B21(0,1)=SY   'south pole
390   X=30:R5=2.96706:R4=0:GOSUB 850
400   SOUND 350,.7:LOCATE 2,1:PRINT "Modeling solid surfaces"
:FOR Q1=0 TO 35 STEP 1:Q2=Q1+1:IF Q2>35 THEN Q2=0
410   LOCATE 3,1:PRINT Q1" ":GOSUB 570:NEXT Q1:LOCATE 4,1:PR
INT "                "
420   SOUND 550,10:LOCATE 2,1:PRINT "Program completed.      "
:LOCATE 3,1:PRINT "     "
430   GOTO 430
440 '_____
450 '
```

```
460  'module:  draw 3-sided polygon for polar area
470   X1=B12(Q2,0):Y1=B12(Q2,1):Z1=B12(Q2,2)
480   X2=B12(Q1,0):Y2=B12(Q1,1):Z2=B12(Q1,2)
490   X3=B11(0,0):Y3=B11(0,1):Z3=B11(0,2)
500   GOSUB 1350:LOCATE 4,1:PRINT SP:IF SP>0 THEN RETURN
510   SX1=B22(Q2,0):SY1=B22(Q2,1)
520   SX2=B22(Q1,0):SY2=B22(Q1,1)
530   SX3=B21(0,0):SY3=B21(0,1):SX4=SX1:SY4=SY1
540   X4=X1+.5*(X2-X1):Y4=Y1+.5*(Y2-Y1):Z4=Z1+.5*(Z2-Z1):X=X3
+.6*(X4-X3):Y=Y3+.6*(Y4-Y3):Z=Z3+.6*(Z4-Z3)
550   SX5=D*X/Z:SY5=D*Y/Z
560   GOSUB 1390:RETURN   'north polar area completed
570   X1=B12(Q1,0):Y1=B12(Q1,1):Z1=B12(Q1,2)
580   X2=B12(Q2,0):Y2=B12(Q2,1):Z2=B12(Q2,2)
590   X3=B11(0,0):Y3=B11(0,1):Z3=B11(0,2)
600   GOSUB 1350:LOCATE 4,1:PRINT SP:IF SP>0 THEN RETURN
610   SX1=B22(Q2,0):SY1=B22(Q2,1)
620   SX2=B22(Q1,0):SY2=B22(Q1,1)
630   SX3=B21(0,0):SY3=B21(0,1):SX4=SX1:SY4=SY1
640   X4=X1+.5*(X2-X1):Y4=Y1+.5*(Y2-Y1):Z4=Z1+.5*(Z2-Z1):X=X3
+.6*(X4-X3):Y=Y3+.6*(Y4-Y3):Z=Z3+.6*(Z4-Z3)
650   SX5=D*X/Z:SY5=D*Y/Z
660   GOSUB 1390:RETURN   'south polar area completed
670  '_____
680  '
690  'module:  draw one 4-sided polygon surface on sphere
700   X1=B11(Q1,0):Y1=B11(Q1,1):Z1=B11(Q1,2)
710   X2=B11(Q2,0):Y2=B11(Q2,1):Z2=B11(Q2,2)
720   X3=B12(Q2,0):Y3=B12(Q2,1):Z3=B12(Q2,2)
730   GOSUB 1350:LOCATE 4,1:PRINT SP:IF SP>0 THEN RETURN   'te
st if hidden
740   SX1=B21(Q1,0):SY1=B21(Q1,1)
750   SX2=B21(Q2,0):SY2=B21(Q2,1)
760   SX3=B22(Q2,0):SY3=B22(Q2,1)
770   SX4=B22(Q1,0):SY4=B22(Q1,1)
780   X=X1+.5*(X3-X1):Y=Y1+.5*(Y3-Y1):Z=Z1+.5*(Z3-Z1)   'diago
nal midpoint of polygon's view coordinates
790   SX5=D*X/Z:SY5=D*Y/Z   'area fill coordinates
800   GOSUB 1390:RETURN   'jump to solid surface modeling rout
ine
810  '_____
820  '
830  'module:  calculate/store vertices for sweep 1, sweep 2
840   SOUND 350,.7:LOCATE 2,1:PRINT "Calculating sweep 1
  ":FOR T=0 TO 35 STEP 1:LOCATE 3,1:PRINT T" ":X=30:GOSUB 890
:GOSUB 940:B11(T,0)=X:B11(T,1)=Y:B11(T,2)=Z:B21(T,0)=SX:B21(
T,1)=SY:R4=R4+.17453:NEXT T:RETURN   'sweep 1 coordinates
850   SOUND 350,.7:LOCATE 2,1:PRINT "Calculating sweep 2
```

```
     ":FOR T=0 TO 35 STEP 1:LOCATE 3,1:PRINT T" ":X=30:GOSUB 890
     :GOSUB 940:B12(T,0)=X:B12(T,1)=Y:B12(T,2)=Z:B22(T,0)=SX:B22(
     T,1)=SY:R4=R4+.17453:NEXT T:RETURN   'sweep 2 coordinates
860  '_____
870  '
880  'module:   calculation of world coordinates for 3D sphere

890  SR4=SIN(R4):CR4=COS(R4):SR5=SIN(R5):CR5=COS(R5)
900  X1=SR5*X:Y=CR5*X:X=CR4*X1:Z=SR4*X1:RETURN
910  '_____
920  '
930  'module:   perspective calculations
940  X=(-1)*X:XA=CR1*X-SR1*Z:ZA=SR1*X+CR1*Z:X=CR2*XA+SR2*Y:Y
     A=CR2*Y-SR2*XA:Z=CR3*ZA-SR3*YA:Y=SR3*ZA+CR3*YA:X=X+MX:Y=Y+MY
     :Z=Z+MZ:SX=D*X/Z:SY=D*Y/Z:RETURN
950  '_____
960  '
970  'module:   return to BASIC interpreter
980  CLS:SCREEN 0,0,0,0:WIDTH 80:COLOR 7,0,0:CLS:LOCATE 1,1,
     1:END
990  '_____
1000 '
1010 'module:   UNIVERSAL
1020 'This routine configures the program for the hardware/s
oftware being used.
1030  KEY OFF:CLS:ON ERROR GOTO 1070   'trap if not Enhanced
Display + EGA
1040  SCREEN 9,,0,0:COLOR 7,0:PALETTE 1,8:PALETTE 2,1:PALETT
E 3,9:PALETTE 4,11:PALETTE 5,7:PALETTE 6,37:PALETTE 7,7:PALE
TTE 8,56:PALETTE 9,34:PALETTE 10,20:PALETTE 11,5:PALETTE 12,
44:PALETTE 13,46:PALETTE 14,55:PALETTE 15,63
1050  C0=0:C1=12:C2=9:C3=7:LOCATE 1,1:PRINT "ED-EGA 640x350
16-color mode"
1060  GOTO 1170  'jump to screen coordinates set-up
1070  RESUME 1080
1080  ON ERROR GOTO 1110  'trap if not Color Display + EGA
1090  SCREEN 8,,0,0:COLOR 7,0:PALETTE 1,0:PALETTE 2,1:PALETT
E 3,9:PALETTE 4,7:PALETTE 8,4:PALETTE 9,2:C0=0:C1=8:C2=9:C3=
7:LOCATE 1,1:PRINT "CD-EGA 640x200 16-color mode"
1100  GOTO 1170  'jump to screen coordinates set-up
1110  RESUME 1120
1120  ON ERROR GOTO 1150  'trap if not PCjr
1130  CLEAR,,,32768!:SCREEN 6,0,0,0:COLOR 3,0:PALETTE 1,8:PA
LETTE 3,7:C0=0:C1=1:C2=2:C3=3:LOCATE 1,1:PRINT "PCjr 640x200
 4-color mode"
1140  GOTO 1170  'jump to screen coordinates set-up
1150  RESUME 1160
1160  SCREEN 1,0:COLOR 0,1:C0=0:C1=1:C2=2:C3=3:LOCATE 1,1:PR
```

```
INT "CGA 320x200 4-color mode"
1170  ON ERROR GOTO 0  'disable error trapping override
1180  WINDOW SCREEN (-399,-299)-(400,300)
1190  ON KEY (2) GOSUB 980:KEY (2) ON  'F2 key to exit progr
am
1200  GOTO 150  'return to main program
1210  '_____
1220  '
1230  'module:  assign variables
1240  D=1200:R1=6.19592:R2=.5235901:R3=5.39778:MX=0:MY=0:MZ=
-150  '3D parameter
1250  DEFINT Q:Q1=0:Q2=0
1260  X=0:Y=0:Z=0:R4=6.28319:R5=6.28319
1270  DIM B11(35,2):DIM B12(35,2)  'two sweeps 36 sets xyz v
iew coords
1280  DIM B21(35,1):DIM B22(35,1)  'two sweeps 36 sets sx,sy
 display coords
1290  SR1=SIN(R1):CR1=COS(R1):SR2=SIN(R2):CR2=COS(R2):SR3=SI
N(R3):CR3=COS(R3)
1300  SR4=SIN(R4):CR4=COS(R4):SR5=SIN(R5):CR5=COS(R5)
1310  RETURN
1320  '_____
1330  '
1340  'module:  plane equation method of hidden surface remov
al
1350  SP1=X1*(Y2*Z3-Y3*Z2):SP1=(-1)*SP1:SP2=X2*(Y3*Z1-Y1*Z3)
:SP3=X3*(Y1*Z2-Y2*Z1):SP=SP1-SP2-SP3:RETURN
1360  '_____
1370  '
1380  'module:  solid surface modeling of 4-sided polygon
1390  LINE (SX1,SY1)-(SX2,SY2),C2:LINE-(SX3,SY3),C2:LINE-(SX
4,SY4),C2:LINE-(SX1,SY1),C2:PAINT (SX5,SY5),C2,C2
1400  LINE (SX1,SY1)-(SX2,SY2),C3:LINE-(SX3,SY3),C3:LINE-(SX
4,SY4),C3:LINE-(SX1,SY1),C3:PAINT (SX5,SY5),C0,C3:RETURN
1410  '_____
1420  '
1430  END 'of program code
```

the polygon surfaces become visible. A longer tone announces the final completion of the sphere.

Of particular interest is the method used by this program to identify the location of area fill start points. Note line 780, which uses simple math to determine the center of the 3D polygon described by three sets of VIEW COORDINATES. If you draw a four sided polygon on a scrap of paper with VIEW COORDINATES X1,Y1,Z1 through X4,Y4,Z4, you can easily figure out how this little algorithm works. Line 790 uses the standard projection formulas to convert this point to SX,SY DISPLAY COORDINATES. This technique is much more accurate than the manual method used in previous chapters. Because this approach is mathematically sound, the area fill will never spill over into other areas of the screen because the start point will always be located within the limits of the polygon and will always be located on the surface

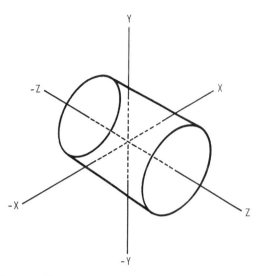

Fig. 10-8. Orientation of the cylinder in world coordinate space.

of the plane defined by the polygon.

This program provides a good opportunity to test the accuracy of your display monitor. If the 3D sphere is not a perfect circle on your monitor, you may wish to adjust the V-Size control (the vertical size control). This adjustment is usually performed by turning the knob found at the back of the monitor. On some monitors you will require a small tool (called a tweaker by technicians) in order to turn a knob recessed in the chassis. Use a hand mirror to watch the display screen as you turn the knob.

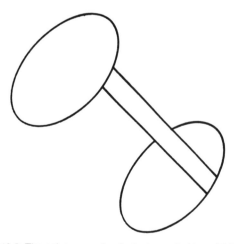

Fig. 10-9. The polygon mesh cylinder is created from 36 four-sided polygons.

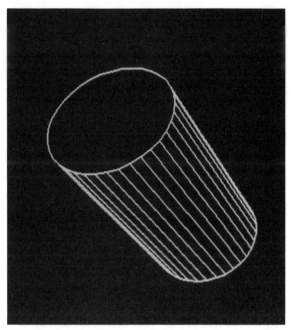

Fig. 10-10. The display image produced by the demonstration program in Fig. 10-11.

## THE SOLID CYLINDER

The conceptualization of a cylinder in the 3D axis system is illustrated in Fig. 10-8. The arcs which form the ends of the cylinder can be manufactured by sweeping the R5 factor around the z-axis. You can think of the cylinder as a single belt of four-sided polygons, as shown in Fig. 10-9.

Figure 10-10 shows the screen output of the demonstration program in Fig. 10-11. To run this program from the companion diskette, type **LOAD "A-10.BAS",R.**

As the program executes, an alphanumeric display in the upper left corner keeps you informed as the coordinates are generated for the top sweep and the bottom sweep. Each sweep corresponds to an end of the cylinder. By connecting the corresponding coordinates on each end, the four-sided surfaces which comprise the solid cylinder can be created.

As the program draws the solid surfaces, the alphanumerics tell you which surface is being drawn and what its SP factor value is. The program emits a tone when complete.

Because the model was initially aligned along the z-axis, the values of yaw and pitch in line 900 are adjusted to provide a more pleasing view of the cylinder.

Fig. 10-11. Polygon mesh cylinder. (For QuickBASIC version see Appendix C. For TurboBASIC version see Appendix D.)

```
100 'Program A-10.BAS     Polygon mesh cylinder.
110 'Uses plane equation method of hidden surface removal.
120 '_____
130 '
140   GOTO 690     'configure system
150   GOSUB 900    'assign variables
160 '_____
170 '
180 'main routine
190   SOUND 350,.7:R5=0:R4=0:FOR T=0 TO 35 STEP 1:LOCATE 2,1:
PRINT "Sweep 1 coordinate"T"   ":X=30:GOSUB 550:Z=Z+60:GOSUB
600:B11(T,0)=X:B11(T,1)=Y:B11(T,2)=Z:B21(T,0)=SX:B21(T,1)=SY
:R5=R5+.17453:NEXT T  'near end of cylinder
200   SOUND 350,.7:R5=0:R4=0:FOR T=0 TO 35 STEP 1:LOCATE 2,1:
PRINT "Sweep 2 coordinate"T"   ":X=30:GOSUB 550:Z=Z-60:GOSUB
600:B12(T,0)=X:B12(T,1)=Y:B12(T,2)=Z:B22(T,0)=SX:B22(T,1)=SY
:R5=R5+.17453:NEXT T  'far end of cylinder
210   SOUND 350,.7:FOR Q1=0 TO 35 STEP 1:Q2=Q1+1:IF Q2>35 THE
N Q2=0
220   LOCATE 2,1:PRINT "Solid surface"Q1"         "
230   GOSUB 400:NEXT Q1
240   SOUND 350,.7:LOCATE 2,1:PRINT "Solid end of cylinder.
    "
250   X1=B11(0,0):Y1=B11(0,1):Z1=B11(0,2):X2=B11(25,0):Y2=B11
(25,1):Z2=B11(25,2):X3=B11(11,0):Y3=B11(11,1):Z3=B11(11,2)
260   GOSUB 1010:IF SP>0 THEN 350
270   FOR Q1=0 TO 35 STEP 1:Q2=Q1+1:IF Q2>35 THEN Q2=0
280   SX1=B21(Q1,0):SY1=B21(Q1,1):SX2=B21(Q2,0):SY2=B21(Q2,1)

290   LINE (SX1,SY1)-(SX2,SY2),C2:NEXT Q1
300   X=0:Y=0:Z=60:GOSUB 600:PAINT (SX,SY),C2,C2
310   FOR Q1=0 TO 35 STEP 1:Q2=Q1+1:IF Q2>35 THEN Q2=0
320   SX1=B21(Q1,0):SY1=B21(Q1,1):SX2=B21(Q2,0):SY2=B21(Q2,1)

330   LINE (SX1,SY1)-(SX2,SY2),C3:NEXT Q1
340   X=0:Y=0:Z=60:GOSUB 600:PAINT (SX,SY),C0,C3
350   SOUND 650,10:LOCATE 2,1:PRINT "Program completed.
    ":LOCATE 4,1:PRINT "                    "
360   GOTO 360
370 '_____
380 '
390 'module:   draw one 4-sided polygon on surface of cylinde
r
400   X1=B11(Q1,0):Y1=B11(Q1,1):Z1=B11(Q1,2)
410   X2=B11(Q2,0):Y2=B11(Q2,1):Z2=B11(Q2,2)
420   X3=B12(Q2,0):Y3=B12(Q2,1):Z3=B12(Q2,2)
```

```
430    GOSUB 1010:LOCATE 4,1:PRINT SP:IF SP>0 THEN RETURN    'te
st if hidden
440    SX1=B21(Q1,0):SY1=B21(Q1,1)
450    SX2=B21(Q2,0):SY2=B21(Q2,1)
460    SX3=B22(Q2,0):SY3=B22(Q2,1)
470    SX4=B22(Q1,0):SY4=B22(Q1,1)
480    X=X1+.5*(X3-X1):Y=Y1+.5*(Y3-Y1):Z=Z1+.5*(Z3-Z1)    'diago
nal midpoint of polygon's view coordinates
490    SX5=D*X/Z:SY5=D*Y/Z   'area fill coordinates
500    GOSUB 1050  'jump to solid surface modeling routine
510    RETURN
520    '_____
530    '
540    'module:   calculation of world coordinates for 3D cylind
er
550    SR4=SIN(R4):CR4=COS(R4):SR5=SIN(R5):CR5=COS(R5)
560    X1=SR5*X:Y=CR5*X:X=CR4*X1:Z=SR4*X1:RETURN
570    '_____
580    '
590    'module:   perspective calculations
600    X=(-1)*X:XA=CR1*X-SR1*Z:ZA=SR1*X+CR1*Z:X=CR2*XA+SR2*Y:Y
A=CR2*Y-SR2*XA:Z=CR3*ZA-SR3*YA:Y=SR3*ZA+CR3*YA:X=X+MX:Y=Y+MY
:Z=Z+MZ:SX=D*X/Z:SY=D*Y/Z:RETURN
610    '_____
620    '
630    'module:   return to BASIC interpreter
640    CLS:SCREEN 0,0,0,0:WIDTH 80:COLOR 7,0,0:CLS:LOCATE 1,1,
1:END
650    '_____
660    '
670    'module:   UNIVERSAL
680    'This routine configures the program for the hardware/so
ftware being used.
690    KEY OFF:CLS:ON ERROR GOTO 730  'trap if not Enhanced Di
splay + EGA
700    SCREEN 9,,0,0:COLOR 7,0:PALETTE 1,8:PALETTE 2,1:PALETTE
 3,9:PALETTE 4,11:PALETTE 5,7:PALETTE 6,37:PALETTE 7,7:PALET
TE 8,56:PALETTE 9,34:PALETTE 10,20:PALETTE 11,5:PALETTE 12,4
4:PALETTE 13,46:PALETTE 14,55:PALETTE 15,63
710    C0=0:C1=12:C2=9:C3=7:LOCATE 1,1:PRINT "ED-EGA 640x350 1
6-color mode"
720    GOTO 830  'jump to screen coordinates set-up
730    RESUME 740
740    ON ERROR GOTO 770 'trap if not Color Display + EGA
750    SCREEN 8,,0,0:COLOR 7,0:PALETTE 1,0:PALETTE 2,1:PALETTE
 3,9:PALETTE 4,7:PALETTE 8,4:PALETTE 9,2:C0=0:C1=8:C2=9:C3=7
:LOCATE 1,1:PRINT "CD-EGA 640x200 16-color mode"
760    GOTO 830  'jump to screen coordinates set-up
```

```
770    RESUME 780
780    ON ERROR GOTO 810   'trap if not PCjr
790    CLEAR,,,32768!:SCREEN 6,0,0,0:COLOR 3,0:PALETTE 1,8:PAL
ETTE 3,7:C0=0:C1=1:C2=2:C3=3:LOCATE 1,1:PRINT "PCjr 640x200
4-color mode"
800    GOTO 830   'jump to screen coordinates set-up
810    RESUME 820
820    SCREEN 1,0:COLOR 0,1:C0=0:C1=1:C2=2:C3=3:LOCATE 1,1:PRI
NT "CGA 320x200 4-color mode"
830    ON ERROR GOTO 0   'disable error trapping override
840    WINDOW SCREEN (-399,-299)-(400,300)
850    ON KEY (2) GOSUB 640:KEY (2) ON   'F2 key to exit progra
m
860    GOTO 150   'return to main program
870    '_____
880    '
890    'module:   assign variables
900    D=1200:R1=5.89778:R2=0:R3=.58539:MX=0:MY=0:MZ=-350   '3D
 parameter
910    DEFINT Q:Q1=0:Q2=0
920    X=0:Y=0:Z=0:R4=6.28319:R5=6.28319
930    DIM B11(35,2):DIM B12(35,2)   'two sweeps 36 sets xyz vi
ew coords
940    DIM B21(35,1):DIM B22(35,1)   'two sweeps 36 sets sx,sy
display coords
950    SR1=SIN(R1):CR1=COS(R1):SR2=SIN(R2):CR2=COS(R2):SR3=SIN
(R3):CR3=COS(R3)
960    SR4=SIN(R4):CR4=COS(R4):SR5=SIN(R5):CR5=COS(R5)
970    RETURN
980    '_____
990    '
1000   'module:   plane equation method of hidden surface remov
al
1010   SP1=X1*(Y2*Z3-Y3*Z2):SP1=(-1)*SP1:SP2=X2*(Y3*Z1-Y1*Z3)
:SP3=X3*(Y1*Z2-Y2*Z1):SP=SP1-SP2-SP3:RETURN
1020   '_____
1030   '
1040   'module:   solid surface modeling of 4-sided polygon
1050   LINE (SX1,SY1)-(SX2,SY2),C2:LINE-(SX3,SY3),C2:LINE-(SX
4,SY4),C2:LINE-(SX1,SY1),C2:PAINT (SX5,SY5),C2,C2
1060   LINE (SX1,SY1)-(SX2,SY2),C3:LINE-(SX3,SY3),C3:LINE-(SX
4,SY4),C3:LINE-(SX1,SY1),C3:PAINT (SX5,SY5),C0,C3:RETURN
1070   '_____
1080   '
1090   END 'of program code.
```

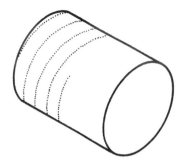

Fig. 10-12. Geometric origin of a helix.

The main routine is located from line 180 to line 360. Line 190 calculates the VIEW COORDINATES and DISPLAY COORDINATES for the sweep which forms the top of the cylinder. Array B11 holds the X,Y,Z VIEW COORDINATES. Array B21 holds the SX,SY DISPLAY COORDINATES.

Line 200 calculates and saves the VIEW COORDINATES and DISPLAY COORDINATES for the sweep which forms the bottom of the cylinder. Array B12 holds the X,Y,Z VIEW COORDINATES. Array B22 holds the SX,SY DISPLAY COORDINATES.

The Q1 loop from line 210 to line 230 retrieves the appropriate VIEW COORDINATES and submits them to the hidden surface routine. If the surface is visible, the appropriate DISPLAY COORDINATES are retrieved and the surface modeling routine at line 400 is called. Of special interest is line 480, which calculates the midpoint of the 3D polygon described by the VIEW COORDINATES. Line 490 converts this point to 2D DISPLAY COORDINATES for the screen. This point is used as the area fill start point. Because it is mathematically derived, it is always 100% accurate and eliminates any possibility of area fill failure.

The key concept in the main routine is the use of the variable Q1 to denote the location of the various points around each end of the sphere. Using Q1 instead of writing out a section of code for each point from 1 to 36 keeps the source code compact. The module at line 390 simply uses Q1 as a reference point to retrieve the appropriate coordinates along each sweep as may be required to construct a particular four-sided polygon on the surface of the sphere.

The Q1 loop from line 270 to line 300 draws the end of the cylinder as a key matte in color C2. The Q1 loop from line 310 to line 340 draws the end in the correct finished color C3 and invokes area fill in color

C0. The code which determines if the end is visible or hidden is located in lines 250 and 260. Line 250 retrieves three sets of VIEW COORDINATES in counterclockwise order for submission to the hidden surface routine at line 1010. The program draws only one end of the cylinder. You can easily modify it to draw the other end also.

## HELIX

A helix is a corkscrew shape that is derived from a cylinder. Refer to Fig. 10-12. This geometric shape can be easily constructed by sweeping the R5 factor while incrementing the z-coordinate.

Figure 10-13 shows the screen output of the demonstration program in Fig. 10-14. To run this program from the companion diskette, type **LOAD "A-11.BAS",R.**

The ZZ variable in line 200 is the decrementer. As each point is plotted around the surface of the cylinder, ZZ is added to the z-coordinate, pushing the point farther away from you in 3D space. The program employs the standard R4 and R5 module at line 250, as well as the standard 3D perspective formulas at line 300.

You may wish to experiment with this program by decrementing the radius of the cylinder during each pass through the loop in line 200. Instead of holding X constant at 30 units, you can create a true corkscrew by reducing X. In addition, you can see that the T loop in line 200 is 124 counts in length. By changing 124 to 324, for example, you can draw an elongated helix. It is left as an interesting exercise for you to try this out on your own computer.

Fig. 10-13. The display image produced by the demonstration program in Fig. 10-14.

Fig. 10-14. Helix in 3D.

```
100 'Program A-11.BAS    Helix.
110 'Demonstrates 3D helix derived from cylinder formulas.
120 '_____
130 '
140   GOTO 400    'configure system
150   GOSUB 610   'assign variables
160 '_____
170 '
180 'main routine
190   LOCATE 2,1:PRINT "Computer-generated helix."
200   R5=0:R4=0:ZZ=60:X=30:GOSUB 260:Z=Z+ZZ:GOSUB 310:PSET (S
X,SY),C3:FOR T=0 TO 124 STEP 1:X=30:ZZ=ZZ-.4:GOSUB 260:Z=Z+Z
Z:GOSUB 310:LINE-(SX,SY),C3:R5=R5+.17453:LOCATE 3,1:PRINT T:
NEXT T
210   SOUND 650,10:LOCATE 3,1:PRINT "     "
220   GOTO 220
230 '_____
240 '
250 'module:   calculation of world coordinates for 3D cylind
er
260   SR4=SIN(R4):CR4=COS(R4):SR5=SIN(R5):CR5=COS(R5)
270   X1=SR5*X:Y=CR5*X:X=CR4*X1:Z=SR4*X1:RETURN
280 '_____
290 '
300 'module:   perspective calculations
310   X=(-1)*X:XA=CR1*X-SR1*Z:ZA=SR1*X+CR1*Z:X=CR2*XA+SR2*Y:Y
A=CR2*Y-SR2*XA:Z=CR3*ZA-SR3*YA:Y=SR3*ZA+CR3*YA:X=X+MX:Y=Y+MY
:Z=Z+MZ:SX=D*X/Z:SY=D*Y/Z:RETURN
320 '_____
330 '
340 'module:   return to BASIC interpreter
350   CLS:SCREEN 0,0,0,0:WIDTH 80:COLOR 7,0,0:CLS:LOCATE 1,1,
1:END
360 '_____
370 '
380 'module:   UNIVERSAL
390 'This routine configures the program for the hardware/so
ftware being used.
400   KEY OFF:CLS:ON ERROR GOTO 440   'trap if not Enhanced Di
splay + EGA
410   SCREEN 9,,0,0:COLOR 7,0:PALETTE 1,8:PALETTE 2,1:PALETTE
 3,9:PALETTE 4,11:PALETTE 5,7:PALETTE 6,37:PALETTE 7,7:PALET
TE 8,56:PALETTE 9,34:PALETTE 10,20:PALETTE 11,5:PALETTE 12,4
4:PALETTE 13,46:PALETTE 14,55:PALETTE 15,63
420   C0=0:C1=12:C2=9:C3=7:LOCATE 1,1:PRINT "ED-EGA 640x350 1
6-color mode"
```

```
430    GOTO 540  'jump to screen coordinates set-up
440    RESUME 450
450    ON ERROR GOTO 480  'trap if not Color Display + EGA
460    SCREEN 8,,0,0:COLOR 7,0:PALETTE 1,0:PALETTE 2,1:PALETTE
 3,9:PALETTE 4,7:PALETTE 8,4:PALETTE 9,2:C0=0:C1=8:C2=9:C3=7
:LOCATE 1,1:PRINT "CD-EGA 640x200 16-color mode"
470    GOTO 540  'jump to screen coordinates set-up
480    RESUME 490
490    ON ERROR GOTO 520  'trap if not PCjr
500    CLEAR,,,32768!:SCREEN 6,0,0,0:COLOR 3,0:PALETTE 1,8:PAL
ETTE 3,7:C0=0:C1=1:C2=2:C3=3:LOCATE 1,1:PRINT "PCjr 640x200
4-color mode"
510    GOTO 540  'jump to screen coordinates set-up
520    RESUME 530
530    SCREEN 1,0:COLOR 0,1:C0=0:C1=1:C2=2:C3=3:LOCATE 1,1:PRI
NT "CGA 320x200 4-color mode"
540    ON ERROR GOTO 0  'disable error trapping override
550    WINDOW SCREEN (-399,-299)-(400,300)
560    ON KEY (2) GOSUB 350:KEY (2) ON  'F2 key to exit progra
m
570    GOTO 150  'return to main program
580    '_____
590    '
600    'module:  assign variables
610    D=1200:R1=5.89778:R2=0:R3=.58539:MX=0:MY=0:MZ=-350   '3D
 parameters
620    ZZ=60  'depth control factor
630    DEFINT Q:Q1=0:Q2=0
640    X=0:Y=0:Z=0:R4=6.28319:R5=6.28319
650    SR1=SIN(R1):CR1=COS(R1):SR2=SIN(R2):CR2=COS(R2):SR3=SIN
(R3):CR3=COS(R3)
660    SR4=SIN(R4):CR4=COS(R4):SR5=SIN(R5):CR5=COS(R5)
670    RETURN
680    '_____
690    '
700    END 'of program code.
```

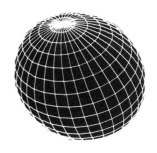

# 11

# *Meshes and Free-Form Curves*

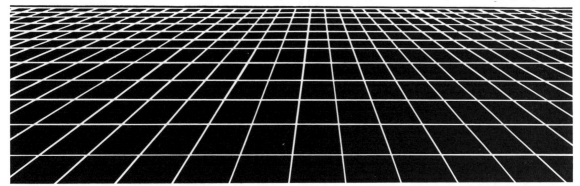

Most objects in the real world contain curves which are neither as symmetrical nor as predictable as the sphere and the cylinder discussed in the previous chapter. Your personal computer is capable of producing smooth free-form curves in either 2D or 3D at varying degrees of curvature.

## CUBIC PARAMETRIC CURVES

The most useful form of free-form curve is the cubic parametric curve. Refer to Fig. 11-1. The curve starts at a designated location and ends at another designated location. The shape of the curve is regulated by control points.

Each control point acts like a magnet, pulling the line away from its intended destination, the endpoint. By manipulating the location of the two control points, you can adjust the shape of the curve.

When a free-form curve is generated in 3D, it is usually in the form of a mesh. This technique is valuable when objects such as automobile designs are being prepared on a microcomputer. Refer to Fig. 11-2. If long, continuous curves are required, the programmer merely utilizes the finishing endpoint for one free-form curve as the starting endpoint for the next free-

form curve. Although free-form curves can be generated with more than two control points, the mathematical formulas involved become very complex and time consuming.

The formulas required to produce a free-form curve are derived from matrix multiplication of a cubic parameter. In its theoretical form, the formula is:

$$C(T) = T\ T\ T\ B \begin{bmatrix} P1 \\ P2 \\ P3 \\ P4 \end{bmatrix}$$

$$\text{where } B = \begin{bmatrix} -1 & 3 & -3 & 1 \\ 3 & -6 & 3 & 0 \\ -3 & 3 & 0 & 0 \\ 1 & 0 & 0 & 0 \end{bmatrix}$$

The variable T is allowed to vary from 0 to 1. When T = 0 the curve is located at point P1. When T = 1 the curve is located at point P4. These are the two endpoints.

Although conversion of the theoretical formula to a format which can be used by a microcomputer re-

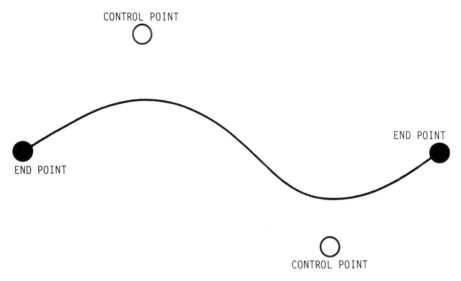

CONTROL POINT

END POINT

END POINT

CONTROL POINT

Fig. 11-1. Control points and endpoints for cubic parametric curves in 2D, also known as free-form curves.

quires an expert understanding of matrix math, the resultant computer algorithm is a standalone curve generator, which can be used without the programmer having to understand the matrices involved. Just as you can drive an automobile without being required to understand the intricate workings of an internal combustion engine, so too can you create free-form curves without the necessity of having a college degree in advanced mathematics.

## 2D FREE-FORM CURVE

Figure 11-3 shows the screen output of the demonstration program in Fig. 11-4. To run this program from the companion diskette, type **LOAD "A-12.BAS",R.**

The formulas which produce the free-form curve are located from line 330 through 450. This free-form curve driver is a subroutine which yields one point on the surface of the curve. By varying the input provided to the curve driver, you can obtain all of the points along the surface of the curve.

Line 260 is a loop which increments the value of T from 0 to 1 in steps of .05. This loop calls the curve driver located at line 350 in order to obtain the SX,SY screen coordinates for each point along the surface of the line. You could reduce the size of the increment from .05 to .01 and thereby increase the smoothness of the free-form curve, but it would take longer to draw

because it would be comprised of more individual points.

To begin to understand how free-form curves work, you might wish to experiment with the location of the control points in this program. By changing the value of X2 and Y2 in line 760 you can see the effect that the first control point has upon the shape of the curve. Line 770 contains the variable values for the second control point. You may wish to try altering these too.

It is interesting to note that you can place both control points above the endpoints and produce a convex curve. If the control points are on opposite sides of the imaginary line between the endpoints, a waveform curve is produced. Moving a control point farther away from an endpoint increases the sharpness of the curve. Moving a control point closer to an endpoint will flatten the free-form curve.

Fig. 11-2. Sub-objects such as aircraft engine cowlings and automobile hoods are best drawn with 3D cubic parametric curves.

114

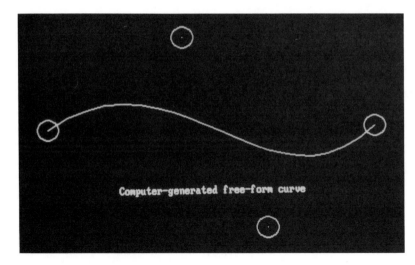

Fig. 11-3. The display image produced by the demonstration program in Fig. 11-4.

Fig. 11-4. Free-form curve.

```
100 'Program A-12.BAS    Free-form curve.
110 'Demonstrates cubic parametric free-form curve
120 '_____
130 '
140   GOTO 540  'configure system
150   GOSUB 730 'assign scalar data
160 '_____
170 '
180 'master routine
190   LOCATE 2,1:PRINT "Free-form curve."
200 'STEP ONE:  establish control points on screen
210   PSET (X1,Y1),C2:CIRCLE (X1,Y1),20,C2:PSET (X2,Y2),C3:CI
RCLE (X2,Y2),20,C3:PSET (X3,Y3),C3:CIRCLE (X3,Y3),20,C3:PSET
 (X4,Y4),C2:CIRCLE (X4,Y4),20,C2
220 '_____
230 '
240 'STEP TWO:  draw free-form curve
250   T=0:T2=T*T:T3=T*T*T:GOSUB 350:PSET (SX,SY),C1  'establi
sh start point
260   FOR T=0 TO 1.01 STEP .05:T2=T*T:T3=T*T*T:GOSUB 350:LINE
-(SX,SY),C1:NEXT T  'must use value slightly greater than 1
to accommodate rounding error in real numbers
270 '_____
280 '
290   SOUND 350,.7
300   GOTO 300
310 '_____
320 '
330 'module:  FREE-FORM curve driver
```

115

```
340 'calculates location of point on cubic parametric curve
350   J1=X1*(-T3+3*T2-3*T+1)    'effect of control point 1
360   J2=X2*(3*T3-6*T2+3*T)     'effect of control point 2
370   J3=X3*(-3*T3+3*T2)         'effect of control point 3
380   J4=X4*T3                   'effect of control point 4
390   SX=J1+J2+J3+J4             'x display coordinate
400   J1=Y1*(-T3+3*T2-3*T+1)    'effect of control point 1
410   J2=Y2*(3*T3-6*T2+3*T)     'effect of control point 2
420   J3=Y3*(-3*T3+3*T2)         'effect of control point 3
430   J4=Y4*T3                   'effect of control point 4
440   SY=J1+J2+J3+J4             'y display coordinate
450   RETURN
460 '_____
470 '
480 'module: return to BASIC interpreter
490   CLS:SCREEN 0,0,0,0:WIDTH 80:COLOR 7,0,0:LOCATE 1,1,1:CL
S:END
500 '_____
510 '
520 'module:   UNIVERSAL
530 'This routine configures the program for the hardware/so
ftware being used.
540   KEY OFF:CLS:ON ERROR GOTO 570  'trap if not Enhanced Di
splay + EGA
550   SCREEN 9,,0,0:COLOR 7,0:PALETTE 1,12:PALETTE 2,9:PALETT
E 3,7:C0=0:C1=1:C2=2:C3=3:LOCATE 1,1:PRINT "ED-EGA 640x350 1
6-color mode"
560   GOTO 670  'jump to screen coordinates set-up
570   RESUME 580
580   ON ERROR GOTO 610 'trap if not Color Display + EGA
590   SCREEN 8,,0,0:COLOR 7,0:PALETTE 1,4:PALETTE 2,9:PALETTE
 3,7:C0=0:C1=1:C2=2:C3=3:LOCATE 1,1:PRINT "CD-EGA 640x200 16
-color mode"
600   GOTO 670  'jump to screen coordinates set-up
610   RESUME 620
620   ON ERROR GOTO 650  'trap if not PCjr
630   CLEAR,,,32768!:SCREEN 6,0,0,0:COLOR 3,0:PALETTE 1,4:PAL
ETTE 2,9:PALETTE 3,7:C0=0:C1=1:C2=2:C3=3:LOCATE 1,1:PRINT "P
Cjr 640x200 4-color mode"
640   GOTO 670  'jump to screen coordinates set-up
650   RESUME 660
660   SCREEN 1,0:COLOR 0,1:C0=0:C1=1:C2=2:C3=3:LOCATE 1,1:PRI
NT "CGA 320x200 4-color mode"
670   ON ERROR GOTO 0  'disable error trapping override
680   WINDOW SCREEN (-399,-299)-(400,300)  'establish device-
independent screen coordinates
690   ON KEY (2) GOSUB 490:KEY (2) ON  'F2 key to exit progra
m
```

```
700   GOTO 150   'return to main program
710 '_____
720 '
730 'module: assign scalar data
740   X1=-300:Y1=20    'start point for curve
750   X4=300:Y4=20     'end point for curve
760   X2=-50:Y2=-160   'first control point for curve
770   X3=100:Y3=220    'second control point for curve
780   RETURN
790 '_____
800 '
810   END 'of program code
```

Although the demonstration program in Fig. 11-4 is fun to tinker with, its usefulness for serious graphics implementations is limited because of its 2D format. Fortunately, there is an easy way to generate free-form curves in 3D on your personal computer.

## 3D FREE-FORM CURVE

The free-form curve subroutine from the previous demonstration program yielded SX,SY display coordinates. But if you consider this output as WORLD COORDINATES and add a standard z-coordinate, you can subject these new WORLD COORDINATES to the standard 3D perspective formulas. You obtain a free-form curve in 3D space, with the curve undulating at a consistent z-coordinate. By varying the R1 (yaw), R2 (roll), and R3 (pitch) angles, you can reposition the free-form curve at any angle and at any location within the 3D axis system. You have, in effect, a cubic parametric curve in 3D, which can be very useful indeed.

The curve by itself, however, is not very helpful for the purposes of 3D modeling. A 3D mesh curve would be more effective. Such a mesh would also provide the opportunity for computer-controlled shading of the curved surface, because the mesh is composed of a series of four-sided polygons.

A simple way to create a 3D free-form mesh is suggested by Fig. 11-5. First, a free-form curve at one end of the mesh is created, and the points along the curve are saved in an array. Second, the same free-form curve is moved to the other end of the mesh by varying the z-coordinate. Again, the points along the curve are saved in an array. Third, the intermediate free-form curves between the two end curves are produced by gradually incrementing the z-coordinate.

Finally, the points which were saved in arrays are connected. The 3D mesh is complete.

For 3D curved surfaces with multiple undulations, the points along the intermediate curves would also be saved in arrays. By connecting the appropriate points, a more detailed 3D mesh can be generated.

Figure 11-6 shows the screen output of the demonstration program in Fig. 11-7. To run this program from the companion diskette, type **LOAD "A-13.BAS",R.**

Note the free-form curve driver subroutine which begins at line 480. This is the same formula used in the previous program, but it has been tightened up to fit on fewer lines. By using the formatting principles discussed in Chapter 3, the code has been made compact and faster-running.

As line 210 indicates, the near edge of the mesh is created at z-coordinate 30. The far edge of the mesh is located at z-coordinate –30, as line 260 shows. The coordinates along the near curve are saved in array B11. The coordinates along the far curve are saved

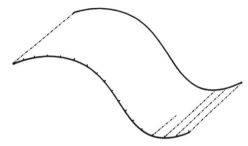

Fig. 11-5. The demonstration program in Fig. 11-7 saves the vertices for the crosshatch lines in a separate array. After the initial parallel free-form curves have been completed, the crosshatch lines are added.

117

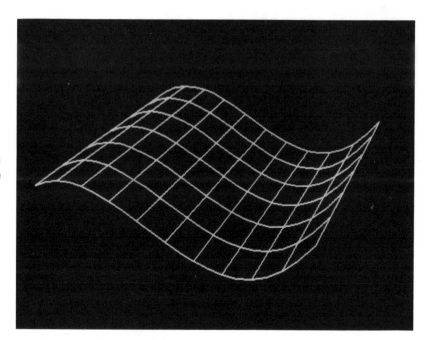

Fig. 11-6. The display image produced by the demonstration program in Fig. 11-7.

Fig. 11-7. Free-form 3D line mesh (cubic parametric curves in 3D).

```
100 'Program A-13.BAS     3D line mesh.
110 'Demonstrates 3D free-form curve mesh.
120 '_____
130 '
140   GOTO 640    'configure system
150   GOSUB 850   'assign variables
160 '_____
170 '
180 'main routine
190   LOCATE 2,1:PRINT "3D free-form mesh"
200 'create near edge curve and save vertices
210   T=0:T2=T*T:T3=T*T*T:GOSUB 500:Z=30:GOSUB 550:PSET (SX,S
Y),C3  'establish start point
220   H=0:FOR T=0 TO 1.01 STEP .05:T2=T*T:T3=T*T*T:GOSUB 500:
Z=30:GOSUB 550:LINE-(SX,SY),C3:B11(H,0)=SX:B11(H,1)=SY:H=H+1
:NEXT T
230 '_____
240 '
250 'create far edge curve and save vertices
260   T=0:T2=T*T:T3=T*T*T:GOSUB 500:Z=-30:GOSUB 550:PSET (SX,
SY),C3  'establish start point
270   H=0:FOR T=0 TO 1.01 STEP .05:T2=T*T:T3=T*T*T:GOSUB 500:
Z=-30:GOSUB 550:LINE-(SX,SY),C3:B12(H,0)=SX:B12(H,1)=SY:H=H+
1:NEXT T
280 '_____
```

```
290 '
300 'draw central curves
310   FOR H=-20 TO 20 STEP 10
320   T=0:T2=T*T:T3=T*T*T:GOSUB 500:Z=H:GOSUB 550:PSET (SX,SY
),C3  'establish start point
330   FOR T=0 TO 1.01 STEP .05:T2=T*T:T3=T*T*T:GOSUB 500:Z=H:
GOSUB 550:LINE-(SX,SY),C3:NEXT T
340   NEXT H
350 '_____
360 '
370 'connect the saved vertices
380   FOR H=0 TO 20 STEP 2
390   SX1=B11(H,0):SY1=B11(H,1):SX2=B12(H,0):SY2=B12(H,1)
400   LINE (SX1,SY1)-(SX2,SY2),C3
410   NEXT H
420 '_____
430 '
440   SOUND 350,.7
450   GOTO 450
460 '_____
470 '
480 'module:   FREE-FORM curve driver
490 'calculates location of point on cubic parametric curve
500   J1=X1*(-T3+3*T2-3*T+1):J2=X2*(3*T3-6*T2+3*T):J3=X3*(-3*
T3+3*T2):J4=X4*T3:X=J1+J2+J3+J4
510   J1=Y1*(-T3+3*T2-3*T+1):J2=Y2*(3*T3-6*T2+3*T):J3=Y3*(-3*
T3+3*T2):J4=Y4*T3:Y=J1+J2+J3+J4:RETURN
520 '_____
530 '
540 'module:   perspective calculations
550   X=(-1)*X:XA=CR1*X-SR1*Z:ZA=SR1*X+CR1*Z:X=CR2*XA+SR2*Y:Y
A=CR2*Y-SR2*XA:Z=CR3*ZA-SR3*YA:Y=SR3*ZA+CR3*YA:X=X+MX:Y=Y+MY
:Z=Z+MZ:SX=D*X/Z:SY=D*Y/Z:RETURN
560 '_____
570 '
580 'module:   return to BASIC interpreter
590   CLS:SCREEN 0,0,0,0:WIDTH 80:COLOR 7,0,0:CLS:LOCATE 1,1,
1:END
600 '_____
610 '
620 'module:   UNIVERSAL
630 'This routine configures the program for the hardware/so
ftware being used.
640   KEY OFF:CLS:ON ERROR GOTO 680  'trap if not Enhanced Di
splay + EGA
650   SCREEN 9,,0,0:COLOR 7,0:PALETTE 1,8:PALETTE 2,1:PALETTE
 3,9:PALETTE 4,11:PALETTE 5,7:PALETTE 6,37:PALETTE 7,7:PALET
TE 8,56:PALETTE 9,34:PALETTE 10,20:PALETTE 11,5:PALETTE 12,4.
```

```
4:PALETTE 13,46:PALETTE 14,55:PALETTE 15,63
660   CO=0:C1=12:C2=9:C3=7:LOCATE 1,1:PRINT "ED-EGA 640x350 1
6-color mode"
670   GOTO 780  'jump to screen coordinates set-up
680   RESUME 690
690   ON ERROR GOTO 720  'trap if not Color Display + EGA
700   SCREEN 8,,0,0:COLOR 7,0:PALETTE 1,0:PALETTE 2,1:PALETTE
 3,9:PALETTE 4,7:PALETTE 8,4:PALETTE 9,2:CO=0:C1=8:C2=9:C3=7
:LOCATE 1,1:PRINT "CD-EGA 640x200 16-color mode"
710   GOTO 780  'jump to screen coordinates set-up
720   RESUME 730
730   ON ERROR GOTO 760  'trap if not PCjr
740   CLEAR,,,32768!:SCREEN 6,0,0,0:COLOR 3,0:PALETTE 1,8:PAL
ETTE 3,7:CO=0:C1=1:C2=2:C3=3:LOCATE 1,1:PRINT "PCjr 640x200
4-color mode"
750   GOTO 780  'jump to screen coordinates set-up
760   RESUME 770
770   SCREEN 1,0:COLOR 0,1:CO=0:C1=1:C2=2:C3=3:LOCATE 1,1:PRI
NT "CGA 320x200 4-color mode"
780   ON ERROR GOTO 0  'disable error trapping override
790   WINDOW SCREEN (-399,-299)-(400,300)
800   ON KEY (2) GOSUB 590:KEY (2) ON  'F2 key to exit progra
m
810   GOTO 150  'return to main program
820 '_____
830 '
840 'module:  assign variables
850   D=1200:R1=5.88319:R2=6.28319:R3=5.79778:MX=0:MY=0:MZ=-1
50  '3D parameter
860   DEFINT H:H=0
870   DIM B11(20,1)  '21 sets sx,sy coordinates near curve
880   DIM B12(20,1)  '21 sets sx,sy coordinates far curve
890   X1=-30:Y1=0:X4=30:Y4=0:X2=-10:Y2=15:X3=10:Y3=-35  'cont
rol points for cubic parametric curve routine
900   X=0:Y=0:Z=0
910   SR1=SIN(R1):CR1=COS(R1):SR2=SIN(R2):CR2=COS(R2):SR3=SIN
(R3):CR3=COS(R3)
920   RETURN
930 '_____
940 '
950   END 'of program code
```

in array B12. These two arrays were dimensioned in lines 870 and 880.

The intermediate free-form curves are drawn by lines 300 through 340. The crosshatching to complete the 3D mesh is performed by the loop at lines 380 through 410.

It is easy to change the shape of this 3D mesh. By altering the values of X2,Y2 and X3,Y3 in line 890 you are moving the control points. All of the free-form curves used in the 3D mesh use the same control points, merely relocated to different z-coordinates, of course. There is no reason preventing you from modifying the program code to use different shaped curves. This has been left as an exercise for you.

In addition, you can easily rotate the 3D mesh by changing the values of R1, R2, and R3 in line 850. You can learn much about curved 3D surfaces by toying with this demonstration program. And you can use the free-form curve driver in any 3D program which requires a curved 3D surface.

After all the mystery and hoopla surrounding free-form curves and 3D curved surfaces, you may be surprised to see how short the demonstration program is. Like all elegant solutions, it is brief and to the point. The lengthiest part of the program is the configuration module which begins at line 620 (and which has nothing whatsoever to do with the generation of cubic parametric curves!).

## SUMMARY

In this chapter you learned how to produce a smooth curve. You discovered how to vary the shape of the curve by manipulating the control points. You learned an easy way to generate free-form curves in 3D. You saw how to construct a 3D mesh from free-form curves.

The next chapter shows you how to map designs onto the surfaces of 3D models. This skill is useful for package design and realistic rendering.

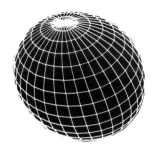

# 12

# *Surface Mapping*

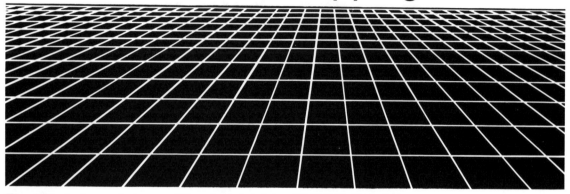

The ability to draw a design on a 3D model is helpful for interactive graphics programs which deal with package design, industrial design, and so forth. Mapping a graphic onto a flat plane located on a 3D model is usually called surface mapping. Plotting a graphic onto a curved surface is often called contour mapping.

In this chapter, you will learn how to map a similar design onto three different models: a cube, a cylinder, and a sphere. The principles introduced in this chapter are refined and enhanced in Chapter 24 when package designs for a film carton and a soft drink container are demonstrated.

## SURFACE MAPPING

You can gain valuable insight into how surface mapping works by considering the cube. If a particular graphic design is to be drawn on one surface of the cube, it is a straightforward task to hold one coordinate constant while the other two coordinates are manipulated to draw the design.

If the surface to be mapped is parallel to the x-axis, for example, the z-coordinate at the surface is held constant while the x-coordinate and the y-coordinate are used to draw the graphics.

## MAPPING THE CUBE

A simple pair of graphics will be mapped onto three different surfaces of the cube, as shown in Fig. 12-1. By stripping open the cube, it is easy to identify the proper coordinates for each graphic. Refer to Fig. 12-2. In addition, it makes it easier to understand how the graphics carry over from one surface to the next. As long as the constant coordinate for each surface is determined, you can identify what the values of the other two coordinates must be in order to draw the graphic.

Figure 12-3 shows the screen output of the demonstration program in Fig. 12-4. To run this program from the demonstration diskette, type **LOAD "A-14.BAS",R.**

If you are using a standard Color/Graphics Adapter, the graphics are displayed as cyan and magenta on a white cube. Otherwise, you will see a blue graphic above a red graphic mapped onto a white cube.

As you can see from lines 220 through 250, this program uses the radial pre-sort method of hidden surface removal. Only the three visible surfaces are drawn, although the database consists of coordinates

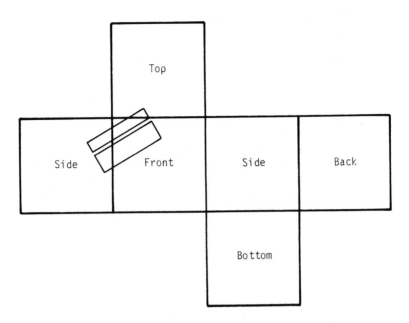

Fig. 12-1. Conceptualization of surface mapping on a 3D cube.

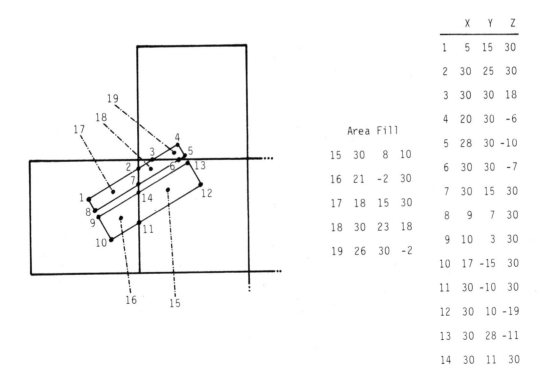

| | X | Y | Z |
|---|---|---|---|
| 1 | 5 | 15 | 30 |
| 2 | 30 | 25 | 30 |
| 3 | 30 | 30 | 18 |
| 4 | 20 | 30 | -6 |
| 5 | 28 | 30 | -10 |
| 6 | 30 | 30 | -7 |
| 7 | 30 | 15 | 30 |
| 8 | 9 | 7 | 30 |
| 9 | 10 | 3 | 30 |
| 10 | 17 | -15 | 30 |
| 11 | 30 | -10 | 30 |
| 12 | 30 | 10 | -19 |
| 13 | 30 | 28 | -11 |
| 14 | 30 | 11 | 30 |

Area Fill

| 15 | 30 | 8 | 10 |
|---|---|---|---|
| 16 | 21 | -2 | 30 |
| 17 | 18 | 15 | 30 |
| 18 | 30 | 23 | 18 |
| 19 | 26 | 30 | -2 |

Fig. 12-2. Surface mapping a 3D cube with axis-dependent coordinates.

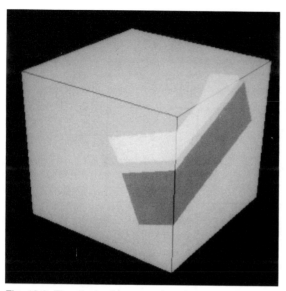

Fig. 12-3. The display image produced by the demonstration program in Fig. 12-4.

Fig. 12-4. Cube: surface mapping.

which describe the entire cube. By using the RESTORE statement in lines 230, 240, and 250, the appropriate coordinates are retrieved from the database.

Lines 280 through 310 merely serve to redraw the outline of the cube in black, making it easier to see where each surface ends.

The top blue graphic is mapped onto the cube by lines 340 through 370. Line 350 maps the design onto surface 3. If you check line 920 in the database, you can see that the z-coordinate is held steady at a value of 30. The x-coordinate and the y-coordinate are used to actually map the design for this surface.

Line 360 maps the design onto surface 4. Again, if you refer to line 930 in the database, you can see that the x-coordinate is held steady while the graphic is created by manipulation of the y-coordinate and the z-coordinate.

Line 370 maps the blue design onto surface 5 by holding the y-coordinate constant.

The red graphic is mapped onto the cube by lines 400 through 420. Although not absolutely necessary,

```
100 'Program A-14.BAS    Surface mapping:   cube.
110 'Demonstrates surface mapping of a 2D design on to a 3D
cube.
120 '_____
130 '
140   GOTO 640    'configure system
150   GOSUB 840   'assign scalar data
160 '_____
170 '
180 'master routine:   draw visible surfaces of cube
190   LOCATE 2,1:PRINT "Map a 2D design onto a 3D cube"
200 '
210 '_____
220 'STEP ONE:   draw visible surfaces of cube
230   RESTORE 890:READ X,Y,Z:GOSUB 550:PSET (SX,SY),C3:FOR T=
1 TO 4 STEP 1:READ X,Y,Z:GOSUB 550:LINE-(SX,SY),C3:NEXT T:RE
AD X,Y,Z:GOSUB 550:PAINT (SX,SY),C3,C3   'surface 3
240   RESTORE 900:READ X,Y,Z:GOSUB 550:PSET (SX,SY),C3:FOR T=
1 TO 4 STEP 1:READ X,Y,Z:GOSUB 550:LINE-(SX,SY),C3:NEXT T:RE
AD X,Y,Z:GOSUB 550:PAINT (SX,SY),C3,C3   'surface 4
250   RESTORE 910:READ X,Y,Z:GOSUB 550:PSET (SX,SY),C3:FOR T=
1 TO 4 STEP 1:READ X,Y,Z:GOSUB 550:LINE-(SX,SY),C3:NEXT T:RE
AD X,Y,Z:GOSUB 550:PAINT (SX,SY),C3,C3   'top surface 5
260 '_____
270 '
```

```
280 'STEP TWO:   add silhouette trim to cube
290   RESTORE 890:READ X,Y,Z:GOSUB 550:PSET (SX,SY),C0:FOR T=
1 TO 4 STEP 1:READ X,Y,Z:GOSUB 550:LINE-(SX,SY),C0:NEXT T   '
surface 3 trim
300   RESTORE 900:READ X,Y,Z:GOSUB 550:PSET (SX,SY),C0:FOR T=
1 TO 4 STEP 1:READ X,Y,Z:GOSUB 550:LINE-(SX,SY),C0:NEXT T   '
surface 4 trim
310   RESTORE 910:READ X,Y,Z:GOSUB 550:PSET (SX,SY),C0:FOR T=
1 TO 4 STEP 1:READ X,Y,Z:GOSUB 550:LINE-(SX,SY),C0:NEXT T   '
top surface 5 trim
320 '_____
330 '
340 'STEP THREE:  map blue graphics on to surfaces of cube
350   RESTORE 920:READ X,Y,Z:GOSUB 550:PSET (SX,SY),C1:FOR T=
1 TO 4 STEP 1:READ X,Y,Z:GOSUB 550:LINE-(SX,SY),C1:NEXT T:RE
AD X,Y,Z:GOSUB 550:PAINT (SX,SY),C1,C1  'blue design on surf
ace 3
360   RESTORE 930:READ X,Y,Z:GOSUB 550:PSET (SX,SY),C1:FOR T=
1 TO 4 STEP 1:READ X,Y,Z:GOSUB 550:LINE-(SX,SY),C1:NEXT T:RE
AD X,Y,Z:GOSUB 550:PAINT (SX,SY),C1,C1  'blue design on surf
ace 4
370   RESTORE 940:READ X,Y,Z:GOSUB 550:PSET (SX,SY),C1:FOR T=
1 TO 4 STEP 1:READ X,Y,Z:GOSUB 550:LINE-(SX,SY),C1:NEXT T:RE
AD X,Y,Z:GOSUB 550:PAINT (SX,SY),C1,C1  'blue design on surf
ace 5
380 '_____
390 '
400 'STEP FOUR:   map red graphics on to surfaces of cube
410   RESTORE 950:READ X,Y,Z:GOSUB 550:PSET (SX,SY),C2:FOR T=
1 TO 4 STEP 1:READ X,Y,Z:GOSUB 550:LINE-(SX,SY),C2:NEXT T:RE
AD X,Y,Z:GOSUB 550:PAINT (SX,SY),C2,C2  'red design on surfa
ce 3
420   RESTORE 960:READ X,Y,Z:GOSUB 550:PSET (SX,SY),C2:FOR T=
1 TO 4 STEP 1:READ X,Y,Z:GOSUB 550:LINE-(SX,SY),C2:NEXT T:RE
AD X,Y,Z:GOSUB 550:PAINT (SX,SY),C2,C2  'red design on surfa
ce 4
430 '_____
440 '
450 'STEP FIVE:   redraw silhouette trim
460   RESTORE 890:READ X,Y,Z:GOSUB 550:PSET (SX,SY),C0:FOR T=
1 TO 4 STEP 1:READ X,Y,Z:GOSUB 550:LINE-(SX,SY),C0:NEXT T   '
surface 3 trim
470   RESTORE 900:READ X,Y,Z:GOSUB 550:PSET (SX,SY),C0:FOR T=
1 TO 4 STEP 1:READ X,Y,Z:GOSUB 550:LINE-(SX,SY),C0:NEXT T   '
surface 4 trim
480   RESTORE 910:READ X,Y,Z:GOSUB 550:PSET (SX,SY),C0:FOR T=
1 TO 4 STEP 1:READ X,Y,Z:GOSUB 550:LINE-(SX,SY),C0:NEXT T   '
top surface 5 trim
```

```
490    SOUND 350,.7
500    GOTO 500
510    END 'of master routine.
520    '_____
530    '
540 'module:    perspective calculations for Cartesian world c
oordinates
550    X=(-1)*X:XA=CR1*X-SR1*Z:ZA=SR1*X+CR1*Z:X=CR2*XA+SR2*Y:Y
A=CR2*Y-SR2*XA:Z=CR3*ZA-SR3*YA:Y=SR3*ZA+CR3*YA:X=X+MX:Y=Y+MY
:Z=Z+MZ:SX=D*X/Z:SY=D*Y/Z:RETURN
560    '_____
570    '
580 'module:    return to BASIC interpreter
590    CLS:WINDOW:SCREEN 0,0,0,0:CLS:WIDTH 80:END
600    '_____
610    '
620 'module:    UNIVERSAL
630 'This routine configures the program for the hardware/so
ftware being used.
640    KEY OFF:CLS:ON ERROR GOTO 670   'trap if not Enhanced Di
splay + EGA
650    SCREEN 9,,0,0:COLOR 7,0:PALETTE 1,9:PALETTE 2,12:PALETT
E 3,7:C0=0:C1=1:C2=2:C3=3:LOCATE 1,1:PRINT "ED-EGA 640x350 1
6-color mode"
660    GOTO 770   'jump to screen coordinates set-up
670    RESUME 680
680    ON ERROR GOTO 710   'trap if not Color Display + EGA
690    SCREEN 8,,0,0:COLOR 7,0:PALETTE 1,9:PALETTE 2,4:PALETTE
 3,7:C0=0:C1=1:C2=2:C3=3:LOCATE 1,1:PRINT "CD-EGA 640x200 16
-color mode"
700    GOTO 770   'jump to screen coordinates set-up
710    RESUME 720
720    ON ERROR GOTO 750   'trap if not PCjr
730    CLEAR,,,32768!:SCREEN 6,0,0,0:COLOR 3,0:PALETTE 1,9:PAL
ETTE 2,4:PALETTE 3,7:C0=0:C1=1:C2=2:C3=3:LOCATE 1,1:PRINT "P
Cjr 640x200 4-color mode"
740    GOTO 770   'jump to screen coordinates set-up
750    RESUME 760
760    SCREEN 1,0:COLOR 0,1:C0=0:C1=1:C2=2:C3=3:LOCATE 1,1:PRI
NT "CGA 320x200 4-color mode"
770    ON ERROR GOTO 0   'disable error trapping override
780    WINDOW SCREEN (-399,-299)-(400,300)
790    ON KEY (2) GOSUB 590:KEY (2) ON   'F2 key to exit progra
m
800    GOTO 150 'return to main program
810    '_____
820    '
830 'module:    assign variables
```

```
840   D=1200:R1=5.68319:R2=6.28319:R3=5.79778:MX=0:MY=0:MZ=-2
50   '3D parameters
850   SR1=SIN(R1):CR1=COS(R1):SR2=SIN(R2):CR2=COS(R2):SR3=SIN
(R3):CR3=COS(R3):RETURN
860 '_____
870 '
880 'module:  database of Cartesian XYZ world coordinates fo
r 3D cube (sorted as bottom surface 0, surface 1, surface 2,
 surface 3, surface 4, top surface 5)
890   DATA   -30,30,30,   30,30,30,   30,-30,30,   -30,-30,30,   -
30,30,30,   0,0,30
900   DATA   30,30,30,   30,30,-30,   30,-30,-30,   30,-30,30,   3
0,30,30,   30,0,0
910   DATA   -30,30,-30,   30,30,-30,   30,30,30,   -30,30,30,   -
30,30,-30,   0,30,0
920   DATA   5,15,30,   9,7,30,   30,15,30,   30,25,30,   5,15,30,
  18,15,30
930   DATA   30,25,30,   30,15,30,   30,30,-7,   30,30,18,   30,25
,30,   30,23,18
940   DATA   30,30,18,   30,30,-7,   28,30,-10,   20,30,-6,   30,3
0,18,   26,30,-2
950   DATA   10,3,30,   17,-15,30,   30,-10,30,   30,11,30,   10,3
,30,   21,-2,30
960   DATA   30,11,30,   30,-10,30,   30,10,-19,   30,28,-11,   30
,11,30,   30,8,10
970 '_____
980 '
990   END 'of program code
```

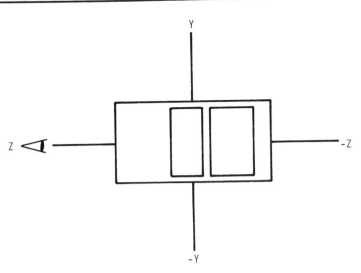

Fig. 12-5. Orientation of the cylinder to be contour-mapped in world coordinate space.

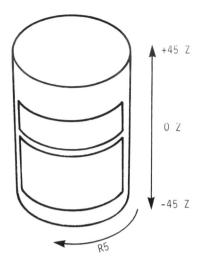

Fig. 12-6. Points on the surface of the 3D cylinder can be located by the z-coordinate and the R5 rotation factor.

the black outline of the cube is redrawn by lines 450 through 480. This re-outlining serves to accent the shape of the graphics which have been mapped onto the cube.

Because the graphics have been linked to the actual surfaces of the model, you can rotate this image by altering the yaw, roll, and pitch values in line 840. Try changing R1 to 4.98319, for example. Then change R3 to 5.49778. Because the radial pre-sort method of hidden surface removal is used, you are limited to rotations which show the three surfaces currently on display. Chapter 25 introduces an algorithm which allows you to rotate a model a full 360 degrees, even when a design has been mapped onto its surface.

## MAPPING THE CYLINDER

The concept for contour mapping is similar to the concept for surface mapping: two coordinates are used to map the design while a third coordinate is held constant. When a cylinder is being mapped, the third coordinate must be held constant at the surface of the curved model.

Figure 12-5 illustrates the orientation of a cylinder within the 3D coordinate space. Obviously, it is easy to obtain the z-coordinates, but how can the x-coordinates and the y-coordinates be obtained from the curved surface of the cylinder?

Figure 12-6 shows the method used to determine WORLD COORDINATES on the surface of the cyl-

inder. The z-coordinate is simply obtained from the z-axis. The y-coordinate and x-coordinate are derived from the angle R5. As you learned in Chapter 10, sine and cosine can be utilized to identify the appropriate WORLD COORDINATES on the surface of the cylinder when angle R5 is known. In essence, R5 and the z-coordinate are the only two tools needed to draw the design.

Figure 12-7 shows the screen output of the demonstration program in Fig. 12-8. To run this program from the companion diskette, type **LOAD "A-15.BAS",R.**

Lines 190 through 240 create a generic cylinder in the same manner as you learned in Chapter 10. The design is mapped onto the cylinder by lines 270 through 340.

When you run the program, it first creates the top end of the cylinder (lines 200 and 210). Then, the visible portion of the bottom end is drawn (lines 220 and 230); and the two lines which connect the ends are drawn (line 240). The cylinder is subjected to white area fill (line 280).

Next, line 290 draws the top line of the lower graphic. Line 300 draws the bottom line of the lower graphic. Both these algorithms operate by incrementing R5 around the cylinder. Then, the two ends of the

Fig. 12-7. The display image produced by the demonstration program in Fig. 12-8.

Fig. 12-8. Cylinder: contour mapping.

```
100 'Program A-15.BAS     Contour mapping: cylinder.
110 'Demonstrates mapping a 2D design onto a 3D cylinder.
120 '_____
130 '
140   GOTO 550  'configure system
150   GOSUB 750 'assign scalar data
160 '_____
170 '
180 'master routine
190 'STEP ONE: prepare line drawing of 3D cylinder
200   X=30:R4=0:R5=0:GOSUB 410:Z=45:GOSUB 460:PSET (SX,SY),C3
:XNT=SX:YNT=SY  'set start point for end of cylinder
210   FOR T=1 TO 72 STEP 1:X=30:R5=R5+.08727:GOSUB 410:Z=45:G
OSUB 460:LINE-(SX,SY),C3:NEXT T  'draw top circumference for
 end of cylinder
220   X=30:R4=0:R5=.17454:GOSUB 410:Z=-45:GOSUB 460:PSET (SX,
SY),C3:XFT=SX:YFT=SY  'set start point for bottom of cylinde
r
230   FOR T=1 TO 32 STEP 1:X=30:R5=R5+.08727:GOSUB 410:Z=-45:
GOSUB 460:LINE-(SX,SY),C3:NEXT T:XFB=SX:YFB=SY  'draw visibl
e portion of circumference of bottom of cylinder
240   LINE (XNT,YNT)-(XFT,YFT),C3:X=0:Z=45:Y=30:GOSUB 460:PSE
T (SX,SY),C3:LINE-(XFB,YFB),C3  'connect top and bottom of c
ylinder
250 '_____
260 '
270 'STEP TWO: apply design to curved surface of 3D cylinder

280   X=0:Z=45:Y=0:GOSUB 460:PAINT (SX,SY),C0,C3:X=30:Y=0:Z=0
:GOSUB 460:PAINT (SX,SY),C3,C3  'paint top of cylinder black
, paint curved surface white
290   X=30:R4=0:R5=.52362:GOSUB 410:Z=0:GOSUB 460:PSET (SX,SY
),C1:XN1=SX:YN1=SY:FOR T=1 TO 24 STEP 1:X=30:R5=R5+.08727:GO
SUB 410:Z=0:GOSUB 460:LINE-(SX,SY),C1:NEXT T:XN2=SX:YN2=SY
300   X=30:R4=0:R5=.52362:GOSUB 410:Z=-40:GOSUB 460:PSET (SX,
SY),C1:XN3=SX:YN3=SY:FOR T=1 TO 24 STEP 1:X=30:R5=R5+.08727:
GOSUB 410:Z=-40:GOSUB 460:LINE-(SX,SY),C1:NEXT T:XN4=SX:YN4=
SY
310   LINE (XN1,YN1)-(XN3,YN3),C1:LINE (XN2,YN2)-(XN4,YN4),C1
:X=30:Z=-20:Y=0:GOSUB 460:PAINT (SX,SY),C1,C1
320   X=30:R4=0:R5=.52362:GOSUB 410:Z=3:GOSUB 460:PSET (SX,SY
),C2:XN1=SX:YN1=SY:FOR T=1 TO 24 STEP 1:X=30:R5=R5+.08727:GO
SUB 410:Z=3:GOSUB 460:LINE-(SX,SY),C2:NEXT T:XN2=SX:YN2=SY
330   X=30:R4=0:R5=.52362:GOSUB 410:Z=20:GOSUB 460:PSET (SX,S
Y),C2:XN3=SX:YN3=SY:FOR T=1 TO 24 STEP 1:X=30:R5=R5+.08727:G
OSUB 410:Z=20:GOSUB 460:LINE-(SX,SY),C2:NEXT T:XN4=SX:YN4=SY
```

```
340   LINE (XN1,YN1)-(XN3,YN3),C2:LINE (XN2,YN2)-(XN4,YN4),C2
:X=30:Z=10:Y=0:GOSUB 460:PAINT (SX,SY),C2,C2
350   BEEP
360   GOTO 360  'clean halt.
370   END 'of master routine.
380 '_____
390 '
400 'module: calculation of 3D world coordinates
410   SR4=SIN(R4):CR4=COS(R4):SR5=SIN(R5):CR5=COS(R5)
420   X1=SR5*X:Y=(-1)*(CR5*X):X=CR4*X1:Z=SR4*X1:RETURN
430 '_____
440 '
450 'module:   perspective calculations for Cartesian world c
oordinates
460   X=(-1)*X:XA=CR1*X-SR1*Z:ZA=SR1*X+CR1*Z:X=CR2*XA+SR2*Y:Y
A=CR2*Y-SR2*XA:Z=CR3*ZA-SR3*YA:Y=SR3*ZA+CR3*YA:X=X+MX:Y=Y+MY
:Z=Z+MZ:SX=D*X/Z:SY=D*Y/Z:RETURN
470 '_____
480 '
490 'module: return to BASIC interpreter
500   CLS:SCREEN 0,0,0,0:WIDTH 80:COLOR 7,0,0:LOCATE 1,1,1:CL
S:END
510 '_____
520 '
530 'module:  UNIVERSAL
540 'This routine configures the program for the hardware/so
ftware being used.
550   KEY OFF:CLS:ON ERROR GOTO 580  'trap if not Enhanced Di
splay + EGA
560   SCREEN 9,,0,0:COLOR 7,0:PALETTE 1,12:PALETTE 2,9:PALETT
E 3,7:C0=0:C1=1:C2=2:C3=3:LOCATE 1,1:PRINT "ED-EGA 640x350 1
6-color mode"
570   GOTO 680  'jump to screen coordinates set-up
580   RESUME 590
590   ON ERROR GOTO 620  'trap if not Color Display + EGA
600   SCREEN 8,,0,0:COLOR 7,0:PALETTE 1,4:PALETTE 2,9:PALETTE
 3,7:C0=0:C1=1:C2=2:C3=3:LOCATE 1,1:PRINT "CD-EGA 640x200 16
-color mode"
610   GOTO 680  'jump to screen coordinates set-up
620   RESUME 630
630   ON ERROR GOTO 660  'trap if not PCjr
640   CLEAR,,,32768!:SCREEN 6,0,0,0:COLOR 3,0:PALETTE 1,4:PAL
ETTE 2,9:PALETTE 3,7:C0=0:C1=1:C2=2:C3=3:LOCATE 1,1:PRINT "P
Cjr 640x200 4-color mode"
650   GOTO 680  'jump to screen coordinates set-up
660   RESUME 670
670   SCREEN 1,0:COLOR 0,1:C0=0:C1=1:C2=2:C3=3:LOCATE 1,1:PRI
NT "CGA 320x200 4-color mode"
```

```
680   ON ERROR GOTO 0  'disable error trapping override
690   WINDOW SCREEN (-399,-299)-(400,300)  'establish device-
independent screen coordinates
700   ON KEY (2) GOSUB 500:KEY (2) ON  'F2 key to exit progra
m
710   GOTO 150  'return to main program
720 '_____
730 '
740 'module: assign scalar data
750   D=1400:R1=5.09448:R2=5.09448:R3=6.28319:MX=0:MY=0:MZ=-3
00    'angular distortion, rotation factors, viewpoint distan.
ce for viewing coordinates
760   X=0:Y=0:Z=0:R4=0:R5=0  'rotation factors for world coor
dinates
770   SR4=SIN(R4):CR4=COS(R4):SR5=SIN(R5):CR5=COS(R5)
780   SR1=SIN(R1):CR1=COS(R1):SR2=SIN(R2):CR2=COS(R2):SR3=SIN
(R3):CR3=COS(R3)
790   RETURN
800 '_____
810 '
820   END 'of program code
```

lower graphic are connected (line 300). The graphic is painted in color C1 by line 310.

The program then constructs the upper graphic. The bottom edge is drawn by line 320; the top edge by line 330. The left and right edge are mapped by line 340, which also invokes the area fill in color C2.

You can change the shape of the mapped graphics quite easily. In line 320, try changing both occurrences of Z to 10 instead of 3. In line 330, change both occurrences of Z to 40. (Hint: you will have to change the value of Z to 15 in line 340 to keep the area fill start point inside the upper graphic.)

The location of the mapped graphics along the length of the cylinder is controlled by the z-coordinate. The location of the mapped graphics around the waist of the cylinder is controlled by the R5 angle. It is left as an exercise for you to experiment with the R5 angle in lines 280 through 340.

## MAPPING THE SPHERE

Mapping a 2D design onto a 3D sphere is the most difficult of the three mapping projects undertaken in this chapter. As Fig. 12-9 shows, the angles of R4 and R5 are used as pointers to draw the graphics on the curved surface of the sphere, much in the same way the polygon belts were drawn in Chapter 10.

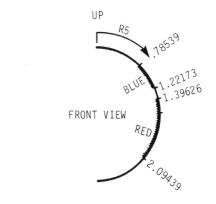

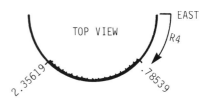

Fig. 12-9. Using the R4 and R5 sine/cosine factors to locate a point on the surface of a 3D sphere.

131

Fig. 12-10. The display image produced by the demonstration program in Fig. 12-11.

Fig. 12-11. Sphere: contour mapping.

```
100 'Program A-16.BAS    Contour mapping:   sphere.
110 'Demonstrates mapping of 2D design on to 3D sphere.
120 '_____
130 '
140   GOTO 660  'configure system
150   GOSUB 860  'assign variables
160 '_____
170 '
180 'master routine
190   LOCATE 2,1:PRINT "Mapping a 2D design on to a 3D sphere
"
200 '_____
210 '
220 'STEP ONE:   draw visible surfaces of sphere
230 'draw longitudinal oval
240   X=30:R5=0:R4=.17453:GOSUB 520:GOSUB 570:PSET (SX,SY),C3

250   FOR T=1 TO 36 STEP 1:X=30:R5=R5+.08727:GOSUB 520:GOSUB
570:LINE-(SX,SY),C3:NEXT T
260   X=30:R5=0:R4=3.14159-.17453:GOSUB 520:GOSUB 570:PSET (S
X,SY),C3
270   FOR T=1 TO 36 STEP 1:X=30:R5=R5+.08727:GOSUB 520:GOSUB
```

```
570:LINE-(SX,SY),C3:NEXT T
280    PAINT (0,0),C3,C3
290    SOUND 350,.7
300 '_____
310 '
320 'STEP TWO:   draw blue graphics on surface of sphere
330    X=30:R5=.78539:R4=.78539:GOSUB 520:GOSUB 570:PSET (SX,S
Y),C2:FOR T=1 TO 5 STEP 1:X=30:R5=R5+.08727:GOSUB 520:GOSUB
570:LINE-(SX,SY),C2:NEXT T
340    X=30:R5=.78539:R4=2.35619:GOSUB 520:GOSUB 570:PSET (SX,
SY),C2:FOR T=1 TO 5 STEP 1:X=30:R5=R5+.08727:GOSUB 520:GOSUB
 570:LINE-(SX,SY),C2:NEXT T
350    X=30:R5=.78539:R4=.78539:GOSUB 520:GOSUB 570:PSET (SX,S
Y),C2:FOR T=1 TO 18 STEP 1:X=30:R4=R4+.08727:GOSUB 520:GOSUB
 570:LINE-(SX,SY),C2:NEXT T
360    X=30:R5=1.22173:R4=.78539:GOSUB 520:GOSUB 570:PSET (SX,
SY),C2:FOR T=1 TO 18 STEP 1:X=30:R4=R4+.08727:GOSUB 520:GOSU
B 570:LINE-(SX,SY),C2:NEXT T
370    X=30:R5=1.00356:R4=1.57079:GOSUB 520:GOSUB 570:PAINT (S
X,SY),C2,C2
380 '_____
390 '
400 'STEP THREE:   draw red graphics on surface of sphere
410    X=30:R5=1.39626:R4=.78539:GOSUB 520:GOSUB 570:PSET (SX,
SY),C1:FOR T=1 TO 8 STEP 1:X=30:R5=R5+.08727:GOSUB 520:GOSUB
 570:LINE-(SX,SY),C1:NEXT T
420    X=30:R5=1.39626:R4=2.35619:GOSUB 520:GOSUB 570:PSET (SX
,SY),C1:FOR T=1 TO 8 STEP 1:X=30:R5=R5+.08727:GOSUB 520:GOSU
B 570:LINE-(SX,SY),C1:NEXT T
430    X=30:R5=1.39626:R4=.78539:GOSUB 520:GOSUB 570:PSET (SX,
SY),C1:FOR T=1 TO 18 STEP 1:X=30:R4=R4+.08727:GOSUB 520:GOSU
B 570:LINE-(SX,SY),C1:NEXT T
440    X=30:R5=2.09439:R4=.78539:GOSUB 520:GOSUB 570:PSET (SX,
SY),C1:FOR T=1 TO 18 STEP 1:X=30:R4=R4+.08727:GOSUB 520:GOSU
B 570:LINE-(SX,SY),C1:NEXT T
450    X=30:R5=1.57079:R4=1.57079:GOSUB 520:GOSUB 570:PAINT (S
X,SY),C1,C1
460    SOUND 350,.7
470    GOTO 470
480    END 'of master routine
490 '_____
500 '
510 'module:   calculation of world coordinates for 3D sphere

520    SR4=SIN(R4):CR4=COS(R4):SR5=SIN(R5):CR5=COS(R5)
530    X1=SR5*X:Y=CR5*X:X=CR4*X1:Z=SR4*X1:RETURN
540 '_____
550 '
```

```
560 'module:   perspective calculations
570   X=(-1)*X:XA=CR1*X-SR1*Z:ZA=SR1*X+CR1*Z:X=CR2*XA+SR2*Y:Y
A=CR2*Y-SR2*XA:Z=CR3*ZA-SR3*YA:Y=SR3*ZA+CR3*YA:X=X+MX:Y=Y+MY
:Z=Z+MZ:SX=D*X/Z:SY=D*Y/Z:RETURN
580 '_____
590 '
600 'module:   clean return to BASIC interpreter
610   CLS:SCREEN 0,0,0,0:WIDTH 80:COLOR 7,0,0:LOCATE 1,1,1:CL
S:END
620 '_____
630 '
640 'module:   UNIVERSAL
650 'This routine configures the program for the hardware/so
ftware being used.
660   KEY OFF:CLS:ON ERROR GOTO 690   'trap if not Enhanced Di
splay + EGA
670   SCREEN 9,,0,0:COLOR 7,0:PALETTE 1,4:PALETTE 2,9:PALETTE
 3,7:C0=0:C1=1:C2=2:C3=3:LOCATE 1,1:PRINT "ED-EGA 640x350 16
-color mode"
680   GOTO 790   'jump to screen coordinates set-up
690   RESUME 700
700   ON ERROR GOTO 730   'trap if not Color Display + EGA
710   SCREEN 8,,0,0:COLOR 7,0:PALETTE 1,4:PALETTE 2,9:PALETTE
 3,7:C0=0:C1=1:C2=2:C3=3:LOCATE 1,1:PRINT "CD-EGA 640x200 16
-color mode"
720   GOTO 790   'jump to screen coordinates set-up
730   RESUME 740
740   ON ERROR GOTO 770   'trap if not PCjr
750   CLEAR,,,32768!:SCREEN 6,0,0,0:COLOR 3,0:PALETTE 1,4:PAL
ETTE 2,9:PALETTE 3,7:C0=0:C1=1:C2=2:C3=3:LOCATE 1,1:PRINT "P
Cjr 640x200 4-color mode"
760   GOTO 790   'jump to screen coordinates set-up
770   RESUME 780
780   SCREEN 1,0:COLOR 0,1:C0=0:C1=1:C2=2:C3=3:LOCATE 1,1:PRI
NT "CGA 320x200 4-color mode"
790   ON ERROR GOTO 0   'disable error trapping override
800   WINDOW SCREEN (-399,-299)-(400,300)
810   ON KEY (2) GOSUB 610:KEY (2) ON   'F2 key to exit progra
m
820   GOTO 150   'return to main program
830 '_____
840 '
850 'assign variables
860   D=1200:R1=0:R2=0:R3=0:MX=0:MY=0:MZ=-150
870   X=0:Y=0:Z=0:C=0:R4=6.28319:R5=6.28319
880   SR4=SIN(R4):CR4=COS(R4):SR5=SIN(R5):CR5=COS(R5)
890   SR1=SIN(R1):CR1=COS(R1):SR2=SIN(R2):CR2=COS(R2):SR3=SIN
(R3):CR3=COS(R3):RETURN
```

```
900 '_____
910 '
920    END 'of program code
```

Figure 12-10 shows the screen output of the demonstration program in Fig. 12-11. To run this program from the companion diskette, type **LOAD "A-16.BAS",R**. The program takes the same graphic design used in the previous two demonstration programs and maps the design onto the sphere.

Lines 240 and 250 draw the right side of the sphere. Lines 260 and 270 draw the left side. The sphere is painted white by line 280.

The upper blue graphic (cyan if you are using a Color/Graphics Adapter) is mapped by lines 320 through 370. The angle R5 is used to bring the coordinate down from the north polar area. Angle R4 is used to sweep the graphic around the sphere parallel to the equator. Unlike the cylinder, there are no straight lines in this graphic design; all lines on the surface of the sphere are curved.

The lower red graphic (magenta on a Color/ Graphics Adapter) is drawn by lines 400 through 450. Note the frequent use of the statement X=30. The internal radius of the sphere is 30 units, just like the internal radius of the cylinder. If you change every occurrence of X in the drawing code, nothing prevents you from modifying this program to create a contour-mapped sphere of, say, radius 45.

If you wish to experiment with this demonstration program, try changing the value of R2 in line 860 to 5.78319. (If the sphere suddenly looks like an oval, your monitor needs adjustment. Try tweaking the V-size control located at the rear of the chassis. If you are using an enhanced color display monitor, adjust V-size 1 if you are in the 640×200 mode; adjust V-size 2 if you are in the 640×350 mode.)

Because the program draws only the silhouette of a sphere, and not the full solid sphere created by the demonstration program in Chapter 10, you might find it interesting to edit line 860 so R3 equals 5.78319.

## SUMMARY

In this chapter you learned how to map simple 2D graphics onto different 3D models. You discovered how to use surface mapping on a cube. You saw how to manipulate R4 and R5 to generate contour mapping on a cylinder and a sphere.

The next chapter provides methods for displaying more than one model and ensuring that distant models cannot be seen through the nearer models.

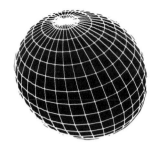

# 13

# *Techniques For Multiple Models*

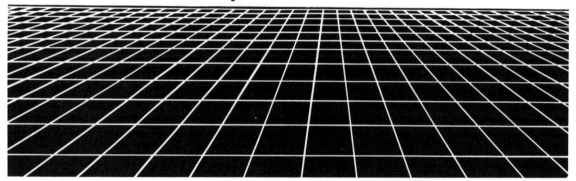

By using the modeling techniques you have learned so far, you can place more than one model in the 3D coordinate system. Provided that you draw the nearer model last, it will conveniently obscure the more distant model(s). However, if you adjust R1 yaw to provide a different point of view, you may find the farther object hiding your view of the nearer object.

There are three primary methods for ensuring the integrity of a multiple-model display. They are the radial presort method, the radial sort method, and the separation plane method.

## SEPARATION PLANE METHOD

The separation plane method adopts the same principle as the plane equation method of hidden surface removal. Refer to Fig. 13-1. By creating (but not displaying) an imaginary plane between the two models, you can use the SP factor generated by the hidden surface routine to alert you which model is nearest the viewpoint. The SP factor tells you which side of the plane is facing you, and because you know which model is on which side of the plane, it then becomes a simple matter to develop an algorithm which draws the farthest model first.

The main advantage enjoyed by the separation plane method is that the environment of the models can be rotated in all three directions: yaw, roll, and pitch. The rotations can be performed individually or simultaneously.

The main disadvantage of the separation plane method is that you must keep track of the inside and outside fascia of the imaginary plane, its relationships to each of the two models, and the relationships of all three objects to you, the viewer.

## RADIAL SORT METHOD

The radial sort method works on the same principle as the cube program in Chapter 8. Because you know in advance the juxtaposition of the two models, you know which will be nearer to the viewpoint for any particular range of yaw angles, for example. This is the method used by the demonstration program in Fig. 13-3. The photograph in Fig. 13-2 shows the screen output of the program. To run this program from the companion diskette, type **LOAD** "A-17 **.BAS**",R.

At start-up, the program draws a pyramid located slightly left and forward of a cube. The pyramid ob-

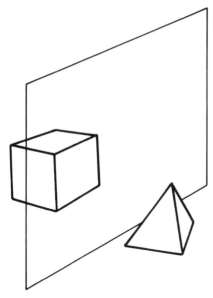

Fig. 13-1. Imposition of an imaginary plane located between two models can be used to determine if one object is positioned in front of (and therefore hides part of) the other object.

trol returns to the main program, line 190 sets the value of L to 1 if the necessary viewing angle has been invoked. If L = 1 the program jumps to line 530 and draws the cube first, otherwise the program simply falls through to line 230 and the pyramid is drawn first. After either model is drawn, an IF. . .THEN statement in line 480 and line 870 determines if the environment has been completed or not.

You may wish to experiment with this demonstration program. Try editing line 1620 by changing R1 to R3, SR1 to SR3, and CR1 to CR3. (Be sure to also change the variable R1 to R3 in lines 190 and 200.) The program will now rotate the entire two-model environment through the pitch plane. As you rotate through the fourth quadrant you will notice that the pyramid seems to disappear. It has been left as an exercise for you to locate and correct this bug, which was created when you switched R1 to R3. (Hint: check the relationship between the L flag and the IF. . . THEN values of R3 during rotation.) If you are puzzled by the occasional failure of the area fill routine in this program, you may wish to review the text which describes the pyramid program in Chapter 9.

scures part of the cube. If you press any key, the global environment will be rotated 10 degrees. As you continuously rotate the environment, you can see that the program always draws the farthest object first. Because the nearer model is always created last, it always obscures part of the more distant model.

By continuing to touch any key, you can eventually rotate the environment through a full 360 degrees, bringing it back to its original position. The double model scenario is drawn correctly by the program through the 360 degree rotation.

The main disadvantage of the radial sort method is that it becomes very complicated if you attempt to rotate more than one axis at the same time. It is not impossible, just difficult. The radial sort method, therefore, is suited very well for architectural models, where the usual rotation is that of yaw.

The pyramid is drawn by lines 230 through 470. The cube is drawn by lines 520 through 860. The techniques used in these sections of code are similar to the methods you have already learned.

Note line 870. If the cube was the first model constructed, the program jumps back to draw the pyramid. The variable L is used as a flag. If L = 1 the cube was drawn first. If L = 0 the pyramid was drawn first. This flag is initially set to value 0 by the keyboard routine in lines 1600 through 1620. When con-

## RADIAL PRESORT METHOD

When two or more different models are being displayed simultaneously in a common 3D environment, the simplest method to ensure proper obscuring is the radial presort method. Because you know the relative juxtaposition of the models, you simply limit the range of views available. In most instances, this means you can shift the viewpoint through a 180 degree sweep

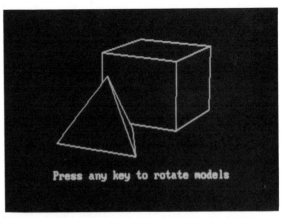

Press any key to rotate models

Fig. 13-2. The display image produced by the demonstration program in Fig. 13-3.

Fig. 13-3. Multiple models.

```
100 'Program A-17.BAS      Cube and pyramid.
110 'Demonstrates hidden surface removal for multiple models
.
120 '_____
130 '
140   GOTO 1010    'configure system
150   GOSUB 1210   'assign variables
160 '_____
170 '
180   LOCATE 2,1:PRINT "Multiple solid models."
190   IF (R1>=0) AND (R1<=1.57079) THEN L=1:GOTO 530
200   IF (R1<=6.28319) AND (R1>=4.71239) THEN L=1:GOTO 530
210 '_____
220 '
230 'module:  calculate/store vertex coordinates for pyramid

240   RESTORE 1400   'beginning of database
250   FOR T=0 TO 3 STEP 1:READ X,Y,Z:GOSUB 920:B1(T,0)=X:B1(T
,1)=Y:B1(T,2)=Z:B2(T,0)=SX:B2(T,1)=SY:NEXT T 'load vertex v
iew coordinates into array B1, load vertex display coordinat
es into array B2
260   FOR T=0 TO 3 STEP 1:READ X,Y,Z:GOSUB 920:B3(T,0)=SX:B3(
T,1)=SY:NEXT T 'load area fill origin display coordinates i
nto array B3
270 '_____
280 '
290 'module:  draw 4 surfaces of pyramid
300 'surface 0 routine
310   X1=B1(0,0):Y1=B1(0,1):Z1=B1(0,2):X2=B1(2,0):Y2=B1(2,1):
Z2=B1(2,2):X3=B1(1,0):Y3=B1(1,1):Z3=B1(1,2):GOSUB 1480:IF SP
>0 THEN 360 'retrieve view coordinates, jump to plane equat
ion routine, test if surface hidden
320   X1=B2(0,0):Y1=B2(0,1):X2=B2(2,0):Y2=B2(2,1):X3=B2(1,0):
Y3=B2(1,1):X4=B3(0,0):Y4=B3(0,1):GOSUB 1520  'assign display
 coordinates and jump to solid surface modeling routine
330 '_____
340 '
350 'surface 1 routine
360   X1=B1(0,0):Y1=B1(0,1):Z1=B1(0,2):X2=B1(1,0):Y2=B1(1,1):
Z2=B1(1,2):X3=B1(3,0):Y3=B1(3,1):Z3=B1(3,2):GOSUB 1480:IF SP
>0 THEN 410
370 X1=B2(0,0):Y1=B2(0,1):X2=B2(1,0):Y2=B2(1,1):X3=B2(3,0):Y
3=B2(3,1):X4=B3(1,0):Y4=B3(1,1):GOSUB 1520
380 '_____
390 '
400 'surface 2 routine
410   X1=B1(1,0):Y1=B1(1,1):Z1=B1(1,2):X2=B1(2,0):Y2=B1(2,1):
```

```
Z2=B1(2,2):X3=B1(3,0):Y3=B1(3,1):Z3=B1(3,2):GOSUB 1480:IF SP
>0 THEN 460
420 X1=B2(1,0):Y1=B2(1,1):X2=B2(2,0):Y2=B2(2,1):X3=B2(3,0):Y
3=B2(3,1):X4=B3(2,0):Y4=B3(2,1):GOSUB 1520
430 '_____
440 '
450 'surface 3 routine
460   X1=B1(2,0):Y1=B1(2,1):Z1=B1(2,2):X2=B1(0,0):Y2=B1(0,1):
Z2=B1(0,2):X3=B1(3,0):Y3=B1(3,1):Z3=B1(3,2):GOSUB 1480:IF SP
>0 THEN 480
470 X1=B2(2,0):Y1=B2(2,1):X2=B2(0,0):Y2=B2(0,1):X3=B2(3,0):Y
3=B2(3,1):X4=B3(3,0):Y4=B3(3,1):GOSUB 1520
480   IF L=0 THEN 530
490   GOSUB 1600
500 '_____
510 '
520 'module:  calculate and store vertex coordinates
530   RESTORE 1320  'beginning of database
540   FOR T=0 TO 7 STEP 1:READ X,Y,Z:GOSUB 920:B1(T,0)=X:B1(T
,1)=Y:B1(T,2)=Z:B2(T,0)=SX:B2(T,1)=SY:NEXT T 'load vertex v
iew coordinates into array B1, load vertex display coordinat
es into array B2
550   FOR T=0 TO 5 STEP 1:READ X,Y,Z:GOSUB 920:B3(T,0)=SX:B3(
T,1)=SY:NEXT T  'load area fill origin display coordinates i
nto array B3
560 '_____
570 '
580 'module:  draw 6 surfaces of cube
590 'surface 0 routine
600   X1=B1(7,0):Y1=B1(7,1):Z1=B1(7,2):X2=B1(0,0):Y2=B1(0,1):
Z2=B1(0,2):X3=B1(3,0):Y3=B1(3,1):Z3=B1(3,2):GOSUB 1480:IF SP
>0 THEN 650  'retrieve view coordinates, jump to plane equat
ion routine, test if surface hidden
610   X1=B2(7,0):Y1=B2(7,1):X2=B2(0,0):Y2=B2(0,1):X3=B2(3,0):
Y3=B2(3,1):X4=B2(6,0):Y4=B2(6,1):X5=B3(0,0):Y5=B3(0,1):GOSUB
 1560  'assign display coordinates and jump to solid surface
 modeling routine
620 '_____
630 '
640 'surface 1 routine
650   X1=B1(6,0):Y1=B1(6,1):Z1=B1(6,2):X2=B1(5,0):Y2=B1(5,1):
Z2=B1(5,2):X3=B1(4,0):Y3=B1(4,1):Z3=B1(4,2):GOSUB 1480:IF SP
>0 THEN 700
660 X1=B2(6,0):Y1=B2(6,1):X2=B2(5,0):Y2=B2(5,1):X3=B2(4,0):Y
3=B2(4,1):X4=B2(7,0):Y4=B2(7,1):X5=B3(1,0):Y5=B3(1,1):GOSUB
1560
670 '_____
680 '
```

```
690 'surface 2 routine
700   X1=B1(3,0):Y1=B1(3,1):Z1=B1(3,2):X2=B1(2,0):Y2=B1(2,1):
Z2=B1(2,2):X3=B1(5,0):Y3=B1(5,1):Z3=B1(5,2):GOSUB 1480:IF SP
>0 THEN 750
710 X1=B2(3,0):Y1=B2(3,1):X2=B2(2,0):Y2=B2(2,1):X3=B2(5,0):Y
3=B2(5,1):X4=B2(6,0):Y4=B2(6,1):X5=B3(2,0):Y5=B3(2,1):GOSUB
1560
720 '_____
730 '
740 'surface 3 routine
750   X1=B1(0,0):Y1=B1(0,1):Z1=B1(0,2):X2=B1(1,0):Y2=B1(1,1):
Z2=B1(1,2):X3=B1(2,0):Y3=B1(2,1):Z3=B1(2,2):GOSUB 1480:IF SP
>0 THEN 800
760 X1=B2(0,0):Y1=B2(0,1):X2=B2(1,0):Y2=B2(1,1):X3=B2(2,0):Y
3=B2(2,1):X4=B2(3,0):Y4=B2(3,1):X5=B3(3,0):Y5=B3(3,1):GOSUB
1560
770 '_____
780 '
790 'surface 4 routine
800   X1=B1(7,0):Y1=B1(7,1):Z1=B1(7,2):X2=B1(4,0):Y2=B1(4,1):
Z2=B1(4,2):X3=B1(1,0):Y3=B1(1,1):Z3=B1(1,2):GOSUB 1480:IF SP
>0 THEN 850
810 X1=B2(7,0):Y1=B2(7,1):X2=B2(4,0):Y2=B2(4,1):X3=B2(1,0):Y
3=B2(1,1):X4=B2(0,0):Y4=B2(0,1):X5=B3(4,0):Y5=B3(4,1):GOSUB
1560
820 '_____
830 '
840 'surface 5 routine
850   X1=B1(1,0):Y1=B1(1,1):Z1=B1(1,2):X2=B1(4,0):Y2=B1(4,1):
Z2=B1(4,2):X3=B1(5,0):Y3=B1(5,1):Z3=B1(5,2):GOSUB 1480:IF SP
>0 THEN 880
860 X1=B2(1,0):Y1=B2(1,1):X2=B2(4,0):Y2=B2(4,1):X3=B2(5,0):Y
3=B2(5,1):X4=B2(2,0):Y4=B2(2,1):X5=B3(5,0):Y5=B3(5,1):GOSUB
1560
870   IF L=1 THEN 220   'if cube drawn first jump back to draw
 pyramid
880   GOSUB 1600
890 '_____
900 '
910 'module:   perspective calculations
920   X=(-1)*X:XA=CR1*X-SR1*Z:ZA=SR1*X+CR1*Z:X=CR2*XA+SR2*Y:Y
A=CR2*Y-SR2*XA:Z=CR3*ZA-SR3*YA:Y=SR3*ZA+CR3*YA:X=X+MX:Y=Y+MY
:Z=Z+MZ:SX=D*X/Z:SY=D*Y/Z:RETURN
930 '_____
940 '
950 'module:   return to BASIC interpreter
960   CLS:WINDOW:SCREEN 0,0,0,0:WIDTH 80:COLOR 7,0,0:CLS:LOCA
TE 1,1,1:END
```

```
970 '_____
980 '
990 'module:  UNIVERSAL
1000 'This routine configures the program for the hardware/s
oftware being used.
1010   KEY OFF:CLS:ON ERROR GOTO 1040   'trap if not Enhanced
Display + EGA
1020   SCREEN 9,,0,0:COLOR 7,0:PALETTE 2,5:PALETTE 3,7:C0=0:C
1=1:C2=2:C3=3:LOCATE 1,1:PRINT "ED-EGA 640x350 16-color mode
"
1030   GOTO 1140   'jump to screen coordinates set-up
1040   RESUME 1050
1050   ON ERROR GOTO 1080   'trap if not Color Display + EGA
1060   SCREEN 8,,0,0:COLOR 7,0:PALETTE 2,5:PALETTE 3,7:C0=0:C
1=1:C2=2:C3=3:LOCATE 1,1:PRINT "CD-EGA 640x200 16-color mode
"
1070   GOTO 1140   'jump to screen coordinates set-up
1080   RESUME 1090
1090   ON ERROR GOTO 1120   'trap if not PCjr
1100   CLEAR,,,32768!:SCREEN 6,0,0,0:COLOR 3,0:C0=0:C1=1:C2=2
:C3=3:LOCATE 1,1:PRINT "PCjr 640x200 4-color mode"
1110   GOTO 1140   'jump to screen coordinates set-up
1120   RESUME 1130
1130   SCREEN 1,0:COLOR 0,1:C0=0:C1=1:C2=2:C3=3:LOCATE 1,1:PR
INT "CGA 320x200 4-color mode"
1140   ON ERROR GOTO 0   'disable error trapping override
1150   WINDOW SCREEN (-399,-299)-(400,300)   'establish device
-independent screen coordinates
1160   ON KEY (2) GOSUB 960:KEY (2) ON   'F2 key to exit progr
am
1170   GOTO 150   'return to main program
1180 '_____
1190 '
1200 'module:   assign variables
1210   D=1200:R1=5.78319:R2=6.28319:R3=5.99778:MX=0:MY=0:MZ=-
500   '3D parameters
1220   DEFINT L:L=0   'control flag for radial sort
1230   DIM B1 (7,2)   '8 sets of XYZ view coordinates
1240   DIM B2 (7,1)   '8 sets of SX,SY display coordinates
1250   DIM B3 (5,1)   '6 sets of SX,SY fill coordinates
1260   XL=.57735:YL=.57735:ZL=.57735   'xyz components of unit
 vector for angle of incidence used in illumination algorith
m
1270   SR1=SIN(R1):CR1=COS(R1):SR2=SIN(R2):CR2=COS(R2):SR3=SI
N(R3):CR3=COS(R3)
1280   RETURN
1290 '_____
1300 '
1310 'module:   database of 8 sets of XYZ world coordinates f
```

or cube vertices
```
1320   DATA  30,-25,-5,  30,30,-5,  -30,30,-5,  -30,-25,-5,
30,30,-65,  -30,30,-65,  -30,-25,-65,  30,-25,-65
1330 '_____
1340 '
1350 'module:  database of 6 sets of XYZ world coordinates f
or area fill origins for 6 surfaces of cube
1360   DATA  0,-25,-35,  0,0,-65,  -30,0,-35,  0,0,-5,  30,0,
-35,  0,30,-35
1370 '_____
1380 '
1390 'module:  4 sets of XYZ world coordinates for pyramid
1400   DATA  -30,-25,55,  30,-25,55,  0,-25,5,  0,25,38
1410 '_____
1420 '
1430 'module:  4 sets of XYZ world coordinates for area fill
 origins for 4 surfaces of pyramid
1440   DATA  0,-25,38,  0,0,47,  6,0,33,  -7,0,33
1450 '_____
1460 '
1470 'module:  plane equation method of hidden surface remov
al
1480   SP1=X1*(Y2*Z3-Y3*Z2):SP1=(-1)*SP1:SP2=X2*(Y3*Z1-Y1*Z3)
:SP3=X3*(Y1*Z2-Y2*Z1):SP=SP1-SP2-SP3:RETURN
1490 '_____
1500 '
1510 'module:  solid surface modeling for 3-sided polygon
1520   LINE (X1,Y1)-(X2,Y2),C2:LINE-(X3,Y3),C2:LINE-(X1,Y1),C
2:PAINT (X4,Y4),C2,C2:LINE (X1,Y1)-(X2,Y2),C3:LINE-(X3,Y3),C
3:LINE-(X1,Y1),C3:PAINT (X4,Y4),C0,C3:RETURN
1530 '_____
1540 '
1550 'module:  solid surface modeling
1560   LINE (X1,Y1)-(X2,Y2),C2:LINE-(X3,Y3),C2:LINE-(X4,Y4),C
2:LINE-(X1,Y1),C2:PAINT (X5,Y5),C2,C2:LINE (X1,Y1)-(X2,Y2),C
3:LINE-(X3,Y3),C3:LINE-(X4,Y4),C3:LINE-(X1,Y1),C3:PAINT (X5,
Y5),C0,C3:RETURN
1570 '_____
1580 '
1590 'module:  keyboard control of rotation
1600   SOUND 350,.7:LOCATE 3,1:PRINT "Press any key to rotate
 models."
1610   K$=INKEY$:IF K$="" THEN 1610
1620   R1=R1-.17453:SR1=SIN(R1):CR1=COS(R1):L=0:CLS:RETURN 18
0
1630 '_____
1640 '
1650   END 'of program code
```

without having to change the order in which the individual models are drawn on the screen. Of course, if you are using an unchanging viewpoint, you are already using the radial presort method by the very fact that you are writing the program to draw certain models before it draws other (nearer) models.

## SUMMARY

In this chapter you learned three methods for coordinating numerous models in a common 3D environment. You saw that the nearest object should be drawn last, in order to ensure that it obscures distant objects.

The next chapter is the beginning of Part Three, which teaches you how to prepare fully-shaded solid models with your personal computer, no matter what type of graphics adapter you are using. You will also learn how to move the light source and have your microcomputer automatically shade the solid model.

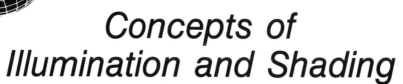

# *14*

# *Concepts of Illumination and Shading*

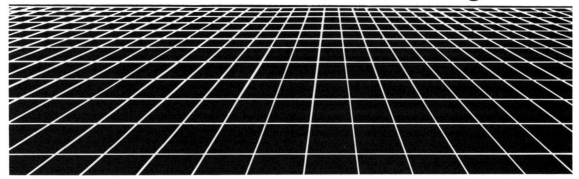

Computer images begin to breathe with a life of their own when rendering techniques are used to add illumination and shading. Professional graphics workstations are noted for the spectacular realism of their displays. Yet, until now, the magnificent potential of personal computers has been overlooked by serious graphics programmers. No matter what type of graphics adapter you are using—EGA, Color/Graphics Adapter, or PCjr video subsystem—you can generate fully-shaded solid models that reflect light just the way real objects do.

## SHADING ALGORITHMS

Two generic algorithms are available for producing realistic shading on solid models. Refer to Fig. 14-1. Polygon mesh models, or models constructed from a series of individual planes, are rendered using the halftone shading technique.

### Halftone Shading

The solid models you learned about in previous chapters were modeled as a group of plane surfaces. Each small polygonal plane on the surface of the model

can be tested in order to determine its relationship to the light source. Each plane can then be shaded (colored) by using a halftoning routine which simply mixes pixels of different colors to produce a particular shade. Halftoning is called bit tiling by IBM and Microsoft. Provided that the individual surfaces are of reasonably small size, the overall shaded model appears very lifelike and realistic. Halftone shading is also called constant shading, flat shading, polygonal shading, and pattern shading.

### Smooth Shading

A more sophisticated technique for shading solid models is that of smooth shading. Refer to Fig. 14-1. Smooth shading is also called variable shading, full shading, ray tracing Gouraud shading, Phong shading, and airbrushing. (Gouraud and Phong were two programmers who developed algorithms to improve the realism of smooth shading on professional graphics workstations.)

In essence, the algorithm is the same as the halftoning technique, except that each individual pixel is tested and colored according to its juxtaposition to the light source. With smooth shading, the gradiation of

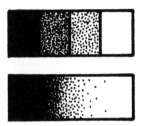

Fig. 14-1. Shading algorithms for personal computers. Top: halftone shading (also called polygonal shading). Bottom: smooth shading.

shades on the model is much more subtle and realistic than the shaded polygons on the surface of a halftone-shaded model, although both techniques can produce pleasing images. Whereas the halftone shading method tests an individual polygon surface, the smooth shading method tests an area the size of an individual pixel.

## ANGLE OF INCIDENCE

The brightness of a surface is regulated by its orientation to the light source. Refer to Fig. 14-2. Specifically, the angle between the rays of light and the surface perpendicular determines how bright the surface will appear to the viewer. This is sometimes called Lambert's Cosine Law, named after a mathematician. A surface perpendicular is a line com-

ing out of the flat surface at a 90 degree angle to the surface. It is sometimes called a surface normal.

A flat surface will appear brightest when the surface perpendicular points directly towards the light source. The greater the angle between the surface perpendicular and the light ray, the dimmer the surface will appear. Refer to Fig. 14-3. The surface will reflect none of the incoming light when the surface is at 90 degrees to the light rays or when the surface is facing away from the light source. In this instance the surface would be illuminated by only ambient light, not by the specific light source under analysis.

## ILLUMINATION AND REFLECTANCE

Different types of illumination produce different effects. These different effects of brightness and color are called reflectance. Refer to Fig. 14-4.

### Diffuse Reflectance

Ambient light is indirect light. The light you see on a heavily overcast or cloudy day is ambient light. The light inside a room with a northern window is

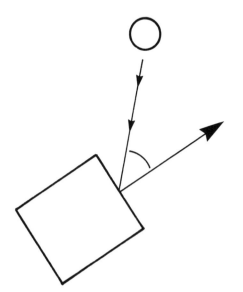

Fig. 14-2. Angle of incidence between surface perpendicular and light source will determine brightness of the surface.

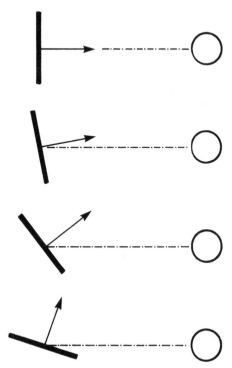

Fig. 14-3. Effect of angle of incidence upon brightness of object. Top: brightest surface. Bottom: dimmest surface.

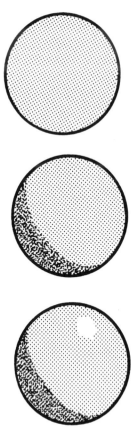

Fig. 14-4. Types of illumination and reflection. Top: 3D sphere exhibiting diffuse reflection from ambient light source. Center: 3D sphere exhibiting ambient reflection from a distributed light source. Bottom: 3D sphere exhibiting ambient reflection and specular reflection (highlight) from a point light source.

usually ambient light (if you haven't turned on any light switches!). In theory, ambient light produces no shadows, as the top sphere in Fig. 14-4 demonstrates. In the real world, however, ambient light is usually stronger from above, so very soft and delicate shadows are often produced. No highlights or bright spots are seen on the model because no strong light sources are present. A solid model being bathed in ambient light is said to be exhibiting diffuse reflectance (or diffuse reflection).

## Ambient Reflectance

Distributed light is a broad source of light which is relatively near the object. A ping pong ball at rest on a table near a northern window is a good example of distributed light. If the ball were illuminated by a fluorescent light tube, it would be lit by distributed light. As the center sphere in Fig. 14-4 shows, distributed light (also called bank light) produces distinct shadows. The light you see on a lightly overcast day or hazy day is distributed light. A solid model being bathed in distributed light is said to be exhibiting ambient reflectance (or ambient reflection).

### Specular Reflectance

A point light source is a single source of light such as a lightbulb, a flashlight, or even the sun. As the bottom sphere in Fig. 14-4 shows, point light produces harsh shadows and a strong highlight. A highlight is called a specular reflection. Whereas diffuse reflectance and ambient reflectance are usually various shades of the color of the object, specular reflections (highlights) are usually the same color as the light source.

### TYPES OF SURFACES

Your perception of the model is influenced by the types of surfaces on the model. Refer to Fig. 14-5. A transparent surface will permit all light rays to penetrate the surface. Glass, plastic film, acrylic, and water are examples of transparent surfaces. A translucent surface will permit only some of the light rays to pass through, reflecting all other rays. Tinted automobile windshields and frosted glass are examples of translucent surfaces. An opaque surface will reflect all the light rays. A brick is an example of an opaque surface.

### What Gives an Object Its Color

It is interesting to note that pure light is white light, composed of all colors. The colors which are absorbed by translucent surfaces and opaque surfaces are lost to the human eye; the colors which are reflected by translucent surfaces and opaque surfaces are the colors which reach the human eye. These reflected colors are the color of the object, so to speak.

### RAY TRACING

Other interesting effects produced by light in the real world can be displayed by your personal computer. The process of calculating these effects is called ray tracing and is most used in generating mirror reflections and shadows.

Mirror reflections follow general laws of geome-

146

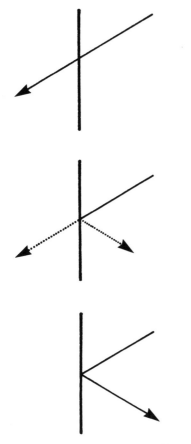

Fig. 14-5. Types of surfaces. Top: transparent. Center: translucent. Bottom: opaque.

try. Refer to Fig. 14-6. If you have developed a program to draw the true model, then it is a straightforward task to generate the mirror reflection, as the demonstration program in Chapter 17 will show.

The location of the mirror image can be extrapolated from geometric intersections and vanishing point construction lines.

Shadows which are cast by solid models can be derived from vanishing point construction lines. Refer to Fig. 14-7. A point light source is considered as a single vanishing point which produces diverging rays of light (shown in Fig. 14-7). A distributed light source will produce parallel rays of light, of course (not shown in Fig. 14-7).

## ILLUMINATION AND
## SHADING FOR PERSONAL COMPUTERS

As described previously, two algorithms are available for shading solid models on your personal computer: halftone shading and smooth shading.

### Smooth Shading on Your Microcomputer

Although you can easily develop program source code to produce smooth shaded models, a hardware limitation holds you back: the number of colors available for a single pixel. In the $640 \times 200$ 16-color mode on the EGA, and in the $640 \times 200$ 4-color mode on the PCjr or Tandy, you can generate two different hues of blue (color 1 and color 9). This means you could have only two different shades of blue on your solid model. Even with four different shades of gray (i.e., black 0, dark gray 8, light gray 7, and white 15), your model would appear very coarse. Clearly, real objects have many more shades than two. Even the $640 \times 350$ 16-color mode of the EGA can only display a total of 12 different blues at one time from the palette of 64 colors, and many of these blues are virtually identical to the human eye.

The IBM Personal System/2 series of microcomputers can produce up to 64 different hues of gray and

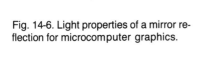

Fig. 14-6. Light properties of a mirror reflection for microcomputer graphics.

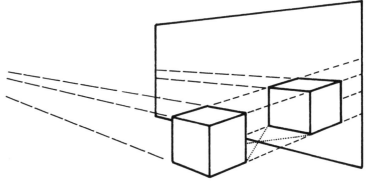

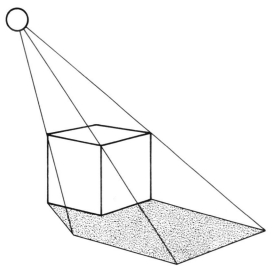

Fig. 14-7. Light properties of a shadow for microcomputer graphics.

up to 256 different colors, depending upon the graphics adapter and display monitor being used. For example, an IBM Personal System/2 Model 50 equipped with the 8514/A Display Adapter and using an IBM 8503 Monochrome Display could easily produce airbrushed, smooth-shaded models using 64 shades of gray. However, a thorough understanding of Assembly Language and hardware architecture would be required, until a version of BASIC which supports these colors becomes available.

On the other hand, the halftone method of producing fully shaded models is supported by a standard Color/Graphics Adapter, by an EGA, and by the PCjr video subsystem.

### Halftone Shading on Your Microcomputer

Halftoning is readily generated by IBM BASICA,

IBM Cartridge BASIC, Compaq BASIC, GW-BASIC, Microsoft BASICA, Microsoft QuickBASIC, and Borland TurboBASIC. Using the halftone method, you can produce up to nine different shades between any two different colors. A standard Color/Graphics Adapter can produce a rendering palette of 17 different shades in the $320 \times 200$ 4-color mode! A PCjr or Tandy can invoke 17 different shades in the $640 \times 200$ 4-color mode! An EGA could produce up to 121 different shades and hues in the $640 \times 350$ mode and the $640 \times 200$ mode (although a palette of 18 shades is used in this book to maintain consistency with the other types of graphics adapters). And by using BASIC's line styling function, you can erase the boundary lines which separate the different shades, thereby producing a smooth, natural effect.

In addition, once you have mastered the techniques of halftone shading, you can modify the formulas to produce airbrush shading if you upgrade your hardware to the IBM Personal System/2 or compatibles. Halftone shading techniques can be used by programmers who prefer BASICA, C, Pascal, or Assembly Language.

### SUMMARY

In this chapter, you learned about two methods for producing fully-shaded solid models on microcomputers: halftone shading and smooth shading. You discovered that the brightness of a surface is determined by the angle of incidence of incoming light rays. You learned about diffuse reflection, ambient reflection, and specular reflection. You read that halftone shading techniques can be implemented on any graphics adapter by using bit tiling and line styling.

The next chapter provides the source code you will need to produce many shades from only a few colors on your personal computer.

# 15

# *Shading Routines for Personal Computers*

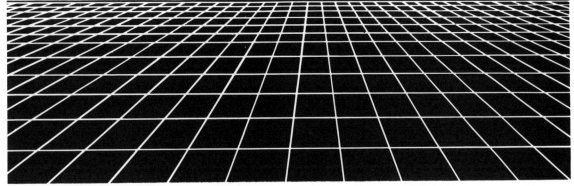

The fundamental technique for producing fully-shaded solid models on microcomputers involves three steps. Refer to Fig. 15-1. First, a polygon mesh model is created from individual plane surfaces. Second, bit tiling is used to create a halftone area fill which paints each surface in an appropriate shade. Third, line styling is used to remove the surface boundary lines.

Although the halftone shading technique is equally effective on different graphics adapters, different hardware architecture makes it necessary to adopt slightly different programming algorithms for the EGA, the Color/Graphics Adapter, and the PCjr video subsystem.

## HALFTONING ON THE EGA

The halftone shading technique is most effective in the two highest screen modes on the EGA: the $640 \times 200$ 16-color mode and the $640 \times 350$ 16-color mode. BASICA supports these modes as SCREEN 8 and SCREEN 9.

Because each pixel on the display screen can be defined as any one of 16 colors, four bits of display memory are required to describe each pixel. In order to improve the screen refresh rate, a series of four bit

planes are used to write graphics data to the display screen. Refer to Fig. 15-2.

Each bit plane can be thought of as a separate screen buffer. Special latching registers in the EGA permit all four bit planes to be decoded simultaneously as the hardware writes the data to the screen. As Fig. 15-2 shows, the four bit planes are sandwiched together, so to speak, and the aggregate total of the four corresponding bits in the bit planes produces the color attribute of the appropriate pixel on the display screen. Each bit can be either 0 or 1. Therefore $2 \times 2 \times 2 \times 2 = 16$ possible colors (i.e., 16 permutations of the four bits).

BASIC's area fill statement can paint in any available solid color. By using bit tiling, the area fill statement can be modified to paint with mixtures of different colors. These mixtures of colors are called halftones. If you are mixing black and white, for example, you might opt to make every even pixel white and every odd pixel black. This bit tiling scheme would result in a gray (called a 50% halftone between black and white). By adding more or fewer pixels of either color, you can create a range of shades between any two colors.

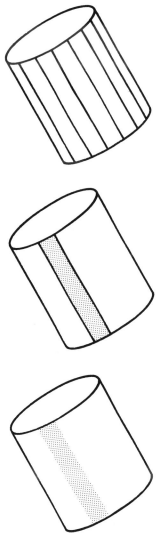

Fig. 15-1. Computer-controlled shading for personal computers. Top: a polygon mesh model is created using the plane equation method of hidden surface removal. Center: halftoning area fill is applied to individual polygons based upon the surface perpendicular method of brightness calculation. Bottom: line dithering is used to remove discontinuities between the shaded polygons.

Figure 15-3 demonstrates how to generate a halftone area fill composed of 50% color 4 and 50% color 5. By stacking the bit planes on top of each other, with bit plane 0 at the bottom and bit plane 4 topmost, the resulting color attribute for each pixel can be decoded by reading the corresponding bits from top to bottom. The rightmost bits, when read from top to bottom,

yield 0101 binary, which is 5 decimal. As Fig. 15-3 demonstrates, these bit codes are translated into hex digits and defined as a string which is used by BASIC's PAINT statement.

## A WORKING PALETTE FOR THE EGA

Because of the different colors available in the $640 \times 350$ and $640 \times 200$ screen modes on the EGA, two different sets of rendering palettes have been developed.

### Halftoning in the EGA 640 × 350 Mode

Although any two colors can be halftoned, a series of dark blues and light blues have been selected from the EGA's palette in order to produce 18 shades for the rendering programs in this book. Refer to Fig. 15-4. Using the PALETTE instruction, the five colors used by the PAINT bit tiling are redefined as follows. Color 1 is defined as hardware color 8 (darkest blue). Color 2 is defined as hardware color 1 (dark blue). Color 3 is defined as hardware color 19 (medium blue). Color 4 is defined as hardware color 11 (light blue). Color 5 is defined as hardware color 7 (light gray or normal white).

As Fig. 15-4 shows, not all of the eight shades possible between any two hues are used. Many halftones appear virtually identical to the human eye because two blues (color 1 and color 2, for example) are relatively near each other in terms of hue content. The matrices used to develop the rendering scheme are illustrated in Fig. 15-5. This is how the pixels will appear on the display screen when the area fill is applied to a polygon.

### Halftoning in the EGA 640 × 200 Mode

Only two different hues of blue are available on the EGA in the $640 \times 200$ 16-color mode. Refer to Fig. 15-6. Color 1 is defined as hardware color 0 (black). Color 2 is defined as hardware color 1 (dark blue). Color 3 is defined as hardware color 9 (light blue). Color 4 is defined as hardware color 7 (light gray or normal white). By invoking bit tiling in the percentages indicated by Fig. 15-6, a pleasing range of shades from near-black to near-white can be generated.

## HALFTONING ON THE COLOR/GRAPHICS ADAPTER AND PCjr

On the PCjr and Tandy, halftone shading is most

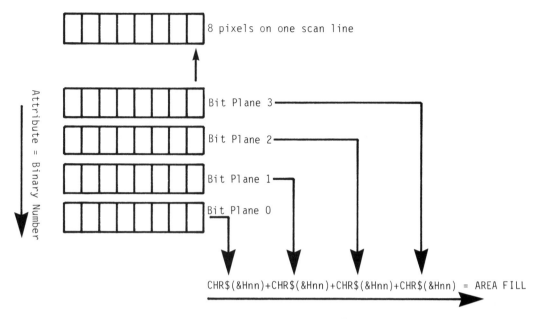

Fig. 15-2. Creating halftone colors using bit plane color mixing with the EGA.

effective on the 640 × 200 screen mode, which is the highest resolution available. On the PCjr, IBM Cartridge BASIC supports this mode as SCREEN 6. On the Tandy, GW-BASIC also supports this mode as SCREEN 6. The Color/Graphics Adapter is limited to the 320x200 mode. All versions of BASIC on all IBM-compatibles support this mode as SCREEN 1.

On the Color/Graphics Adapter, four colors are available in the 320 × 200 mode. On the PCjr and Tandy, four colors are available in the 640 × 200 mode. The halftone rendering palette for both screen modes is shown in Fig. 15-7.

By tiling the pixels between cyan and black and between cyan and white, a full range of 17 shades from black to white can be produced. The third color, magenta, is reserved as an erasing color to remove hid-

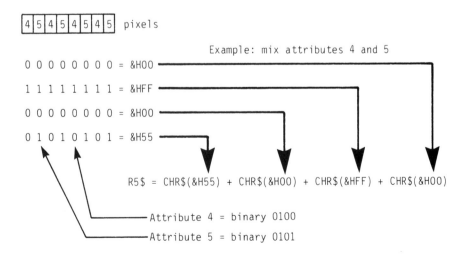

Fig. 15-3. Halftone shade composed of 50% color 4 and 50% color 5.

Blue

| 1 | 12% | 25% | 2 | 12% | 25% | 50% | 75% | 3 | 25% | 50% | 75% | 4 | 12% | 25% | 50% | 75% | 5 |
|---|---|---|---|---|---|---|---|---|---|---|---|---|---|---|---|---|---|
|   | A1 | A2 |   | A5 | A6 | A7 | A8 |   | A10 | A11 | A12 |   | A13 | A14 | A15 | A16 |   |

Fig. 15-4. Halftoning strategy for the EGA.

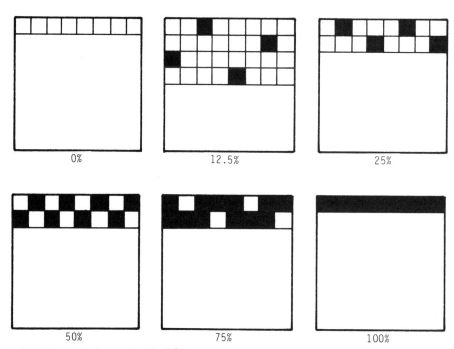

Fig. 15-5. Area fill halftone pixel maps for the EGA.

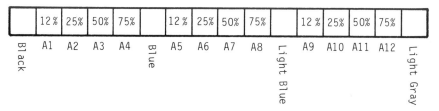

| Black | 12% | 25% | 50% | 75% | Blue | 12% | 25% | 50% | 75% | Light Blue | 12% | 25% | 50% | 75% | Light Gray |
|---|---|---|---|---|---|---|---|---|---|---|---|---|---|---|---|
|   | A1 | A2 | A3 | A4 |   | A5 | A6 | A7 | A8 |   | A9 | A10 | A11 | A12 |   |

PALETTE 1,0:PALETTE 2,1:PALETTE 3,9:PALETTE 4,7

Fig. 15-6. Halftoning strategy for the EGA's 640×200 mode.

|       | 12.5% |     | 37.5% |     | 62.5% |     | 87.5% |       | 12.5% |     | 37.5% |     | 62.5% |     | 87.5% |       |
|-------|-------|-----|-------|-----|-------|-----|-------|-------|-------|-----|-------|-----|-------|-----|-------|-------|
| C0    |       | 25% |       | 50% |       | 75% |       | C1    |       | 25% |       | 50% |       | 75% |       | C3    |
| Black | A1    | A2  | A3    | A4  | A5    | A6  | A7    | Cyan  | A9    | A10 | A12   | A13 | A14   | A15 | A16   | White |

Fig. 15-7. Halftoning strategy for the Color/Graphics Adapter and the PCjr.

152

den surfaces as described in Chapters 6 through 13.

There are no additional bit planes on the Color/Graphics Adapter, PCjr, or Tandy. Only one screen buffer (usually at memory address B80000 hex) is used to hold the bit map for the pixels on the display screen. The bit tiling option in BASIC's PAINT statement is invoked by using a hex digit to describe a four-pixel pattern. By adding a series of hex digit codes, sequential lines of pixels can be tiled in different patterns, as shown in Fig. 15-8. The syntax for this statement is PAINT (x1, y1), halftone-pattern, boundary-color (where halftone-pattern is a two-digit hex number which describes one byte, which is four pixels on the screen).

On the standard Color/Graphics Adapter, a fundamental color palette of black-cyan-magenta-white is available. Solid, fully-shaded models are drawn as cyan objects. On the IBM PCjr and Tandy, the PALETTE instruction can be used to create fully-shaded models in colors other than cyan. Many of the demonstration programs in this book create solid models in shades of gray on the PCjr and Tandy, although you can experiment with blues, greens, and so forth.

## LINE DITHERING

As discussed in Chapter 2, the PAINT instruction in BASIC will apply area fill until a specific boundary line is encountered. The preliminary polygon planes which make up the model to be rendered are drawn as white lines against a black background. If these white lines were left on the model after the halftone shading has been applied, the result would be amateurish. The technique of coloring these lines in a manner which matches the adjacent halftoning pattern is called line dithering. The lines which are to be camouflaged are called discontinuities.

The line styling function available in BASIC provides easy access to the line dithering enhancement. Refer to Fig. 15-9. A four-digit hex code controls the pattern in which a simple line is drawn by BASIC's LINE statement. The syntax follows the form LINE (x1,y1)-(x2,y2),color,,hex-styling-code. The syntax is identical for the EGA, the Color/Graphics Adapter, and the PCjr video subsystem (including Tandy).

By laying down a preparatory line in a desired color before drawing the dithering line, any two colors of pixels can be used in the styled line. Therefore, a

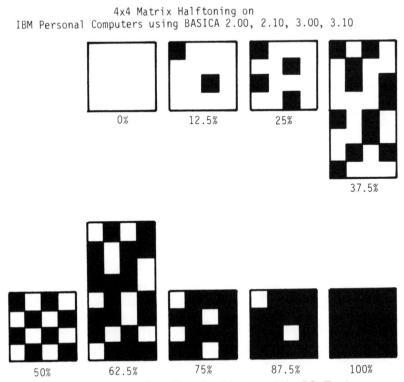

4x4 Matrix Halftoning on
IBM Personal Computers using BASICA 2.00, 2.10, 3.00, 3.10

Fig. 15-8. Area fill halftone pixel map for the Color/Graphics Adapter and the PCjr/Tandy.

pleasing match can be found between any two half-tone shades on the solid model.

As Fig. 15-9 shows, only five sets of hex codes are required. A 25% dither, for example, could be color 2 covered by a 25% dithering line in color 3 or it could be color 3 covered by a 25% dithering line in color 2. The first instance would be 75% between colors 2 and 3; the second instance would be 25% between colors 2 and 3. Both dithering lines were created with the same hex codes, however. The colors of the preparatory line and the styled line determine the final color of the line dithering.

## DEMONSTRATION PROGRAM: HALFTONE SHADING

If you have the companion diskette, you can load the appropriate program which demonstrates the best rendering mode for your particular combination of hardware and software.

To run the program from the companion diskette, type **LOAD** "A-18.BAS",R. If your hardware or software does not support the program, type **LOAD**

```
Line dithering codes for
IBM Personal Computers

LINE (X1,Y1)-(X2,Y2),2,,&Hnnnn

10101010 10101010 = &HAAAA ⎤
01010101 01010101 = &H5555 ⎦ 50%

10010010 01001000 = &H9248 ⎤
01001001 00100100 = &H4924 ⎥ 31.25%
00100100 10010010 = &H2492 ⎦

10001000 10001000 = &H8888 ⎤
00100010 00100010 = &H2222 ⎥ 25%
01000100 01000100 = &H4444 ⎥
00010001 00010001 = &H1111 ⎦

10000100 00100000 = &H8420 ⎤
00000001 00001000 = &H2108 ⎥ 18.75%
10000001 00001000 = &H8108 ⎥
00010000 00100000 = &H1020 ⎦

10000000 10000000 = &H8080 ⎤
00001000 00001000 = &H0808 ⎥ 12.5%
00100000 00100000 = &H2020 ⎥
00000010 00000010 = &H0202 ⎦
```

Fig. 15-9. Line dithering hex codes for the EGA, the Color/Graphics Adapter, and the PCjr/Tandy using the line styling function of BASIC.

"A-19.BAS",R to load and run the next program. Continue with **LOAD** "A-20.BAS",R and **LOAD** "A-21.BAS",R until you determine which program is supported by your particular combination of hardware and software.

If you are typing the program listings from the book, select one listing from the next four program listings, depending upon which graphics adapter, version of BASIC, and display monitor you are using. Refer to Chapters 1, 2, and 5 for more information about the graphics capabilities of different hardware/software configurations.

Figure 15-10 shows the screen output of the demonstration program in Fig. 15-11. This is the master rendering palette for the $640 \times 350$ 16-color mode of the EGA. If you are using IBM BASICA 3.21 or Microsoft QuickBASIC 2.0 or Borland TurboBASIC 1.0, this is the mode in which the demonstration programs will run. You require an enhanced color display in order to generate the $640 \times 350$ 16-color mode with your EGA, of course.

Figure 15-12 shows the screen output of the demonstration program in Fig. 15-13. This is the master rendering palette for the $640 \times 200$ 16-color mode of the EGA. This is the highest resolution mode available from your EGA when you are using a standard color display. If you are using IBM BASICA 3.21 or Microsoft QuickBASIC 2.0 or Borland TurboBASIC 1.0, this is the mode in which the demonstration programs will run.

Figure 15-14 shows the screen output of the demonstration program in Fig. 15-15. This is the master rendering palette for the $320 \times 200$ 4-color mode of the Color/Graphics Adapter. If you are using a Color/Graphics Adapter with any designated version of BASIC and with any display monitor, this is the mode in which the demonstration programs will run. If you are using an EGA with a version of IBM BASICA earlier than 3.21, or with Compaq BASIC, or with GW-BASIC, this is the mode in which the demonstration programs will run.

Figure 15-16 shows the screen output of the demonstration program in Fig. 15-17. This is the master rendering palette for the $640 \times 200$ 4-color mode of the PCjr video subsystem. This mode is identical to the $640 \times 200$ 4-color mode of the Tandy 1000 series of microcomputers. If you are using a PCjr with IBM Cartridge BASIC or a Tandy with GW-BASIC, this is the mode in which the demonstration programs will run.

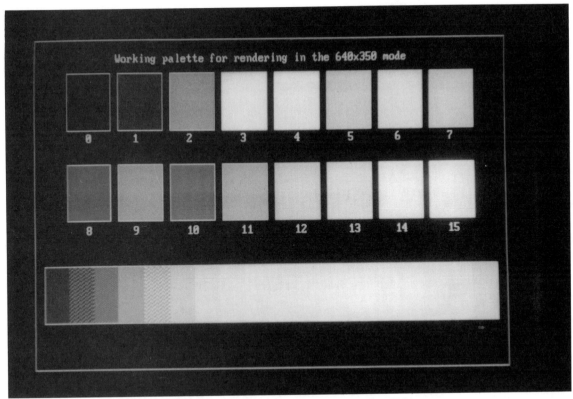

Fig. 15-10. The display image produced by the demonstration program in Fig. 15-11.

Fig. 15-11. Rendering palette for the EGA 640 × 350 mode.

```
100  'Program A-18.BAS    Rendering palette 640x350 mode.
110  'Demonstrates halftoning and dithering techniques.
120  '_____
130  '
140  KEY OFF:CLS:ON ERROR GOTO 870:SCREEN 9,,0,0:COLOR 7,0:C
LS  '640x350 16-color mode.
150  ON ERROR GOTO 0
160  ON KEY (2) GOSUB 630:KEY (2) ON  'enable clean exit.
170  DEFINT T,C
180  PALETTE 1,8:PALETTE 2,1:PALETTE 3,9:PALETTE 4,11:PALETT
E 5,7:PALETTE 6,37:PALETTE 7,7:PALETTE 8,56:PALETTE 9,34:PAL
ETTE 10,20:PALETTE 11,5:PALETTE 12,44:PALETTE 13,46:PALETTE
14,55:PALETTE 15,63
190  GOSUB 670  'assign area fill bit plane hex codes
200  '_____
210  '
220  'module:  create generic screen
230  LINE (0,0)-(639,349),7,B  'outline the entire screen.
```

155

```
240   LOCATE 2,15:PRINT "Working palette for rendering in the
 640x350 mode"
250   X=45:FOR T=1 TO 8 STEP 1:LINE (X,36)-(X+60,96),7,B:X=X+
70:NEXT T
260   LOCATE 8,10:PRINT "0":LOCATE 8,18:PRINT "1":LOCATE 8,27
:PRINT "2":LOCATE 8,36:PRINT "3":LOCATE 8,45:PRINT "4":LOCAT
E 8,54:PRINT "5":LOCATE 8,62:PRINT "6":LOCATE 8,71:PRINT "7"

270   X=45:FOR T=1 TO 8 STEP 1:LINE (X,132)-(X+60,192),7,B:X=
X+70:NEXT T
280   LOCATE 15,10:PRINT "8":LOCATE 15,18:PRINT "9":LOCATE 15
,27:PRINT "10":LOCATE 15,36:PRINT "11":LOCATE 15,45:PRINT "1
2":LOCATE 15,54:PRINT "13":LOCATE 15,62:PRINT "14":LOCATE 15
,71:PRINT "15"
290   X=75:C=0:FOR T=1 TO 8 STEP 1:PAINT (X,40),C,7:X=X+70:C=
C+1:NEXT T
300   X=75:C=8:FOR T=1 TO 8 STEP 1:PAINT (X,140),C,7:X=X+70:C
=C+1:NEXT T
310   X=13:FOR T=1 TO 18 STEP 1:LINE (X,240)-(X+34,300),7,B:X
=X+34:NEXT T
320 '_____
330 '
340 'module:  invoke area fill
350   X=30:PAINT (X,260),1,7:X=X+34:PAINT (X,260),A1$,7:X=X+3
4:PAINT (X,260),A2$,7:X=X+34:PAINT (X,260),2,7
360   X=X+34:PAINT (X,260),A5$,7:X=X+34:PAINT (X,260),A6$,7:X
=X+34:PAINT (X,260),A7$,7:X=X+34:PAINT (X,260),A8$,7:X=X+34:
PAINT (X,260),3,7
370   X=X+34:PAINT (X,260),A10$,7:X=X+34:PAINT (X,260),A11$,7
:X=X+34:PAINT (X,260),A12$,7:X=X+34:PAINT (X,260),4,7
380   X=X+34:PAINT (X,260),A13$,7:X=X+34:PAINT (X,260),A14$,7
:X=X+34:PAINT (X,260),A15$,7:X=X+35:PAINT (X,260),A16$,7:X=X
+34:PAINT (X,260),5,7
390 '_____
400 '
410 'apply dithering
420   X=47:Y1=241:Y2=299:LINE (X,Y1)-(X,Y2),1
430   X=X+34:LINE (X,Y1)-(X,Y2),1:LINE (X,Y1)-(X,Y2),2,,&H888
8
440   X=X+34:LINE (X,Y1)-(X,Y2),2
450   X=X+34:LINE (X,Y1)-(X,Y2),2
460   X=X+34:LINE (X,Y1)-(X,Y2),2:LINE (X,Y1)-(X,Y2),3,,&H888
8
470   X=X+34:LINE (X,Y1)-(X,Y2),2:LINE (X,Y1)-(X,Y2),3,,&HAAA
A
480   X=X+34:LINE (X,Y1)-(X,Y2),3:LINE (X,Y1)-(X,Y2),2,,&HAAA
A
490   X=X+34:LINE (X,Y1)-(X,Y2),3
```

```
500   X=X+34:LINE (X,Y1)-(X,Y2),3
510   X=X+34:LINE (X,Y1)-(X,Y2),3:LINE (X,Y1)-(X,Y2),4,,&HAAA
A
520   X=X+34:LINE (X,Y1)-(X,Y2),4:LINE (X,Y1)-(X,Y2),3,,&HAAA
A
530   X=X+34:LINE (X,Y1)-(X,Y2),4
540   X=X+34:LINE (X,Y1)-(X,Y2),4
550   X=X+34:LINE (X,Y1)-(X,Y2),4:LINE (X,Y1)-(X,Y2),5,,&H888
8
560   X=X+34:LINE (X,Y1)-(X,Y2),4:LINE (X,Y1)-(X,Y2),5,,&HAAA
A
570   X=X+34:LINE (X,Y1)-(X,Y2),5:LINE (X,Y1)-(X,Y2),4,,&HAAA
A
580   BEEP
590   GOTO 590   'clean halt keeps cursor off the screen.
600   '_____
610   '
620   'module:   return to BASIC interpreter
630   CLS:SCREEN 0,0,0,0:WIDTH 80:COLOR 7,0,0:LOCATE 1,1,1:CL
S:END
640   '_____
650   '
660   'module:   area fill bit plane hex codes for 640x350 mode

670   A1$=CHR$(&HDF)+CHR$(&H20)+CHR$(&H0)+CHR$(&H0)+CHR$(&HFD
)+CHR$(&H2)+CHR$(&H0)+CHR$(&H0)+CHR$(&H7F)+CHR$(&H80)+CHR$(&
H0)+CHR$(&H0)+CHR$(&HF7)+CHR$(&H8)+CHR$(&H0)+CHR$(&H0)
680   A2$=CHR$(&HBB)+CHR$(&H44)+CHR$(&H0)+CHR$(&H0)+CHR$(&HEE
)+CHR$(&H11)+CHR$(&H0)+CHR$(&H0)
690   A3$=CHR$(&HAA)+CHR$(&H55)+CHR$(&H0)+CHR$(&H0)+CHR$(&H55
)+CHR$(&HAA)+CHR$(&H0)+CHR$(&H0)
700   A4$=CHR$(&H44)+CHR$(&HBB)+CHR$(&H0)+CHR$(&H0)+CHR$(&H11
)+CHR$(&HEE)+CHR$(&H0)+CHR$(&H0)
710   A5$=CHR$(&H20)+CHR$(&HFF)+CHR$(&H0)+CHR$(&H0)+CHR$(&H2)
+CHR$(&HFF)+CHR$(&H0)+CHR$(&H0)+CHR$(&H80)+CHR$(&HFF)+CHR$(&
H0)+CHR$(&H0)+CHR$(&H8)+CHR$(&HFF)+CHR$(&H0)+CHR$(&H0)
720   A6$=CHR$(&H44)+CHR$(&HFF)+CHR$(&H0)+CHR$(&H0)+CHR$(&H11
)+CHR$(&HFF)+CHR$(&H0)+CHR$(&H0)
730   A7$=CHR$(&H55)+CHR$(&HFF)+CHR$(&H0)+CHR$(&H0)+CHR$(&HAA
)+CHR$(&HFF)+CHR$(&H0)+CHR$(&H0)
740   A8$=CHR$(&HBB)+CHR$(&HFF)+CHR$(&H0)+CHR$(&H0)+CHR$(&HEE
)+CHR$(&HFF)+CHR$(&H0)+CHR$(&H0)
750   A9$=CHR$(&HDF)+CHR$(&HDF)+CHR$(&H20)+CHR$(&H0)+CHR$(&HF
D)+CHR$(&HFD)+CHR$(&H2)+CHR$(&H0)+CHR$(&H7F)+CHR$(&H7F)+CHR$
(&H80)+CHR$(&H0)+CHR$(&HF7)+CHR$(&HF7)+CHR$(&H8)+CHR$(&H0)
760   A10$=CHR$(&HBB)+CHR$(&HBB)+CHR$(&H44)+CHR$(&H0)+CHR$(&H
EE)+CHR$(&HEE)+CHR$(&H11)+CHR$(&H0)
770   A11$=CHR$(&HAA)+CHR$(&HAA)+CHR$(&H55)+CHR$(&H0)+CHR$(&H
```

```
55)+CHR$(&H55)+CHR$(&HAA)+CHR$(&HO)
780   A12$=CHR$(&H44)+CHR$(&H44)+CHR$(&HBB)+CHR$(&HO)+CHR$(&H
11)+CHR$(&H11)+CHR$(&HEE)+CHR$(&HO)
790   A13$=CHR$(&H20)+CHR$(&HO)+CHR$(&HFF)+CHR$(&HO)+CHR$(&H2
)+CHR$(&HO)+CHR$(&HFF)+CHR$(&HO)+CHR$(&H80)+CHR$(&HO)+CHR$(&
HFF)+CHR$(&HO)+CHR$(&H8)+CHR$(&HO)+CHR$(&HFF)+CHR$(&HO)
800   A14$=CHR$(&H44)+CHR$(&HO)+CHR$(&HFF)+CHR$(&HO)+CHR$(&H1
1)+CHR$(&HO)+CHR$(&HFF)+CHR$(&HO)
810   A15$=CHR$(&H55)+CHR$(&HO)+CHR$(&HFF)+CHR$(&HO)+CHR$(&HA
A)+CHR$(&HO)+CHR$(&HFF)+CHR$(&HO)
820   A16$=CHR$(&HBB)+CHR$(&HO)+CHR$(&HFF)+CHR$(&HO)+CHR$(&HE
E)+CHR$(&HO)+CHR$(&HFF)+CHR$(&HO)
830   RETURN
840 '_____
850 '
860 'module:  trap if not EGA and Enhanced Color Display
870   SOUND 350,.7:LOCATE 10,1:PRINT "EGA and Enhanced Displa
y required."
880   LOCATE 12,1:PRINT "Press ESC to return to BASIC..."
890   K$=INKEY$
900   IF K$=CHR$(27) THEN RESUME 920
910   GOTO 890
920   CLS:LOCATE 1,1,1:END
930 '_____
940 '
950   END 'of program code
```

## ANALYSIS OF THE DEMO PROGRAMS

The secret to these four rendering palettes resides in the section of the program listing which defines the area fill hex codes. In Fig. 15-11 these definitions are located at lines 660 through 830. In Fig. 15-13 these definitions are located at lines 640 through 810. In Fig. 15-15 these definitions are located at lines 610 through 760. In Fig. 15-17 these definitions are located at lines 620 through 770. The area fill hex codes are used in a consistent manner for the rendering programs in the book. You can use these four master palette programs to experiment with other codes and colors.

These master palette programs employ an ad hoc approach to line dithering. In later demonstration programs, the dithering matrix shown in Fig. 15-9 will be incorporated into a program algorithm which automatically determines which line styling code is to be used with which halftone shade.

## A SAMPLE APPLICATION

The master rendering palettes produced by the previous four demonstration programs can be readily applied to specific models. In order to fully grasp the full potential of halftone shading, it seems appropriate to explore a fully-shaded solid model by using a manual programming approach.

A frame cube provides a suitable sampler for shading techniques. Using simple fundamental polygons, the complex cube can be created by incremental stages, as Fig. 15-18 shows. Artist's intuition is used to determine the shades to be used for each surface.

Figure 15-19 shows the screen output of the demonstration program in Fig. 15-20. Note that both sets of area fill hex shading codes are incorporated into this program. Lines 1960 through 2130 hold the codes for the EGA. Lines 2160 contain the hex codes for the Color/Graphics Adapter and PCjr video subsystem.

The configuration module located at lines 820 through 1090 determines which hardware and soft-

*(Text continues on page 177)*

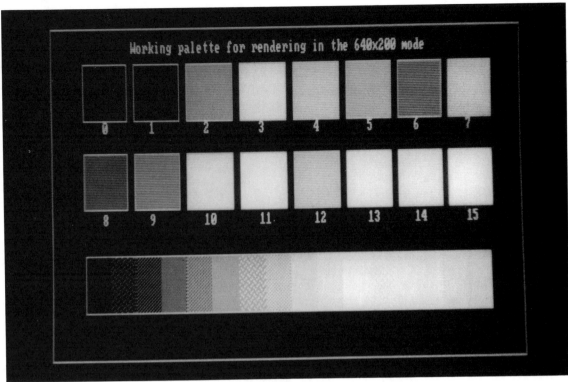

Fig. 15-12. The display image produced by the demonstration program in Fig. 15-13.

Fig. 15-13. Rendering palette for the EGA 640 × 200 mode.

```
100 'Program A-19.BAS      Rendering palette for 640x200 EGA m
ode.
110 'Demonstrates halftoning and dithering techniques.
120 '_____
130 '
140   KEY OFF:CLS:ON ERROR GOTO 850:SCREEN 8,,0,0:COLOR 7,0:C
LS  '640x200 16-color mode.
150   ON ERROR GOTO 0
160   ON KEY (2) GOSUB 610:KEY (2) ON  'enable clean exit.
170   DEFINT T,C
180   PALETTE 1,0:PALETTE 2,1:PALETTE 3,9:PALETTE 4,7:PALETTE
 8,4:PALETTE 9,2
190   GOSUB 650 'assign area fill bit plane hex codes
200 '_____
210 '
220 'module:  create generic screen
230   LINE (0,0)-(639,199),7,B  'outline the entire screen.
```

```
240    LOCATE 2,15:PRINT "Working palette for rendering in the
 640x200 mode"
250    X=45:FOR T=1 TO 8 STEP 1:LINE (X,21)-(X+60,55),7,B:X=X+
70:NEXT T
260    LOCATE 8,10:PRINT "0":LOCATE 8,18:PRINT "1":LOCATE 8,27
:PRINT "2":LOCATE 8,36:PRINT "3":LOCATE 8,45:PRINT "4":LOCAT
E 8,54:PRINT "5":LOCATE 8,62:PRINT "6":LOCATE 8,71:PRINT "7"

270    X=45:FOR T=1 TO 8 STEP 1:LINE (X,75)-(X+60,109),7,B:X=X
+70:NEXT T
280    LOCATE 15,10:PRINT "8":LOCATE 15,18:PRINT "9":LOCATE 15
,27:PRINT "10":LOCATE 15,36:PRINT "11":LOCATE 15,45:PRINT "1
2":LOCATE 15,54:PRINT "13":LOCATE 15,62:PRINT "14":LOCATE 15
,71:PRINT "15"
290    X=75:C=0:FOR T=1 TO 8 STEP 1:PAINT (X,24),C,7:X=X+70:C=
C+1:NEXT T
300    X=75:C=8:FOR T=1 TO 8 STEP 1:PAINT (X,80),C,7:X=X+70:C=
C+1:NEXT T
310    X=47:FOR T=1 TO 16 STEP 1:LINE (X,137)-(X+34,171),7,B:X
=X+34:NEXT T
320 '_____
330 '
340 'module:  invoke area fill
350    X=60:PAINT (X,140),1,7:X=X+34:PAINT (X,140),A1$,7:X=X+3
4:PAINT (X,140),A2$,7:X=X+34:PAINT (X,140),A3$,7:X=X+34:PAIN
T (X,140),A4$,7:X=X+34:PAINT (X,140),2,7
360    X=X+34:PAINT (X,140),A5$,7:X=X+34:PAINT (X,140),A6$,7:X
=X+34:PAINT (X,140),A7$,7:X=X+34:PAINT (X,140),A8$,7:X=X+34:
PAINT (X,140),3,7
370    X=X+34:PAINT (X,140),A9$,7:X=X+34:PAINT (X,140),A10$,7:
X=X+34:PAINT (X,140),A11$,7:X=X+34:PAINT (X,140),A12$,7:X=X+
34:PAINT (X,140),4,7
380 '_____
390 '
400 'apply dithering
410    X=81:Y1=138:Y2=170:LINE (X,Y1)-(X,Y2),1
420    X=X+34:LINE (X,Y1)-(X,Y2),1:LINE (X,Y1)-(X,Y2),2,,&H888
8
430    X=X+34:LINE (X,Y1)-(X,Y2),1:LINE (X,Y1)-(X,Y2),2,,&HAAA
A
440    X=X+34:LINE (X,Y1)-(X,Y2),2:LINE (X,Y1)-(X,Y2),1,,&HAAA
A
450    X=X+34:LINE (X,Y1)-(X,Y2),2
460    X=X+34:LINE (X,Y1)-(X,Y2),2
470    X=X+34:LINE (X,Y1)-(X,Y2),2:LINE (X,Y1)-(X,Y2),3,,&H888
8
480    X=X+34:LINE (X,Y1)-(X,Y2),2:LINE (X,Y1)-(X,Y2),3,,&HAAA
A
```

```
490   X=X+34:LINE (X,Y1)-(X,Y2),3:LINE (X,Y1)-(X,Y2),2,,&HAAA
A
500   X=X+34:LINE (X,Y1)-(X,Y2),3
510   X=X+34:LINE (X,Y1)-(X,Y2),3
520   X=X+34:LINE (X,Y1)-(X,Y2),3:LINE (X,Y1)-(X,Y2),4,,&H888
8
530   X=X+34:LINE (X,Y1)-(X,Y2),3:LINE (X,Y1)-(X,Y2),4,,&HAAA
A
540   X=X+34:LINE (X,Y1)-(X,Y2),4:LINE (X,Y1)-(X,Y2),3,,&HAAA
A
550   X=X+34:LINE (X,Y1)-(X,Y2),4
560   BEEP
570   GOTO 570   'clean halt keeps cursor off the screen.
580   '_____
590   '
600   'module:  return to BASIC interpreter
610   CLS:SCREEN 0,0,0,0:WIDTH 80:CLS:END
620   '_____
630   '
640   'module:  area fill bit plane hex codes for 640x200 mode

650   A1$=CHR$(&HDF)+CHR$(&H20)+CHR$(&H0)+CHR$(&H0)+CHR$(&HFD
)+CHR$(&H2)+CHR$(&H0)+CHR$(&H0)+CHR$(&H7F)+CHR$(&H80)+CHR$(&
H0)+CHR$(&H0)+CHR$(&HF7)+CHR$(&H8)+CHR$(&H0)+CHR$(&H0)
660   A2$=CHR$(&HBB)+CHR$(&H44)+CHR$(&H0)+CHR$(&H0)+CHR$(&HEE
)+CHR$(&H11)+CHR$(&H0)+CHR$(&H0)
670   A3$=CHR$(&HAA)+CHR$(&H55)+CHR$(&H0)+CHR$(&H0)+CHR$(&H55
)+CHR$(&HAA)+CHR$(&H0)+CHR$(&H0)
680   A4$=CHR$(&H44)+CHR$(&HBB)+CHR$(&H0)+CHR$(&H0)+CHR$(&H11
)+CHR$(&HEE)+CHR$(&H0)+CHR$(&H0)
690   A5$=CHR$(&H20)+CHR$(&HFF)+CHR$(&H0)+CHR$(&H0)+CHR$(&H2)
+CHR$(&HFF)+CHR$(&H0)+CHR$(&H0)+CHR$(&H80)+CHR$(&HFF)+CHR$(&
H0)+CHR$(&H0)+CHR$(&H8)+CHR$(&HFF)+CHR$(&H0)+CHR$(&H0)
700   A6$=CHR$(&H44)+CHR$(&HFF)+CHR$(&H0)+CHR$(&H0)+CHR$(&H11
)+CHR$(&HFF)+CHR$(&H0)+CHR$(&H0)
710   A7$=CHR$(&H55)+CHR$(&HFF)+CHR$(&H0)+CHR$(&H0)+CHR$(&HAA
)+CHR$(&HFF)+CHR$(&H0)+CHR$(&H0)
720   A8$=CHR$(&HBB)+CHR$(&HFF)+CHR$(&H0)+CHR$(&H0)+CHR$(&HEE
)+CHR$(&HFF)+CHR$(&H0)+CHR$(&H0)
730   A9$=CHR$(&HDF)+CHR$(&HDF)+CHR$(&H20)+CHR$(&H0)+CHR$(&HF
D)+CHR$(&HFD)+CHR$(&H2)+CHR$(&H0)+CHR$(&H7F)+CHR$(&H7F)+CHR$
(&H80)+CHR$(&H0)+CHR$(&HF7)+CHR$(&HF7)+CHR$(&H8)+CHR$(&H0)
740   A10$=CHR$(&HBB)+CHR$(&HBB)+CHR$(&H44)+CHR$(&H0)+CHR$(&H
EE)+CHR$(&HEE)+CHR$(&H11)+CHR$(&H0)
750   A11$=CHR$(&HAA)+CHR$(&HAA)+CHR$(&H55)+CHR$(&H0)+CHR$(&H
55)+CHR$(&H55)+CHR$(&HAA)+CHR$(&H0)
760   A12$=CHR$(&H44)+CHR$(&H44)+CHR$(&HBB)+CHR$(&H0)+CHR$(&H
11)+CHR$(&H11)+CHR$(&HEE)+CHR$(&H0)
```

```
770    A13$=CHR$(&H20)+CHR$(&HO)+CHR$(&HFF)+CHR$(&HO)+CHR$(&H2
)+CHR$(&HO)+CHR$(&HFF)+CHR$(&HO)+CHR$(&H80)+CHR$(&HO)+CHR$(&
HFF)+CHR$(&HO)+CHR$(&H8)+CHR$(&HO)+CHR$(&HFF)+CHR$(&HO)
780    A14$=CHR$(&H44)+CHR$(&HO)+CHR$(&HFF)+CHR$(&HO)+CHR$(&H1
1)+CHR$(&HO)+CHR$(&HFF)+CHR$(&HO)
790    A15$=CHR$(&H55)+CHR$(&HO)+CHR$(&HFF)+CHR$(&HO)+CHR$(&HA
A)+CHR$(&HO)+CHR$(&HFF)+CHR$(&HO)
800    A16$=CHR$(&HBB)+CHR$(&HO)+CHR$(&HFF)+CHR$(&HO)+CHR$(&HE
E)+CHR$(&HO)+CHR$(&HFF)+CHR$(&HO)
810    RETURN
820    '_____
830    '
840    'module:   trap if not EGA
850    SOUND 350,.7:LOCATE 10,1:PRINT "EGA required."
860    LOCATE 12,1:PRINT "Press ESC to return to BASIC..."
870    K$=INKEY$
880    IF K$=CHR$(27) THEN RESUME 900
890    GOTO 870
900    CLS:LOCATE 1,1,1:END
910    '_____
920    '
930    END 'of program code
```

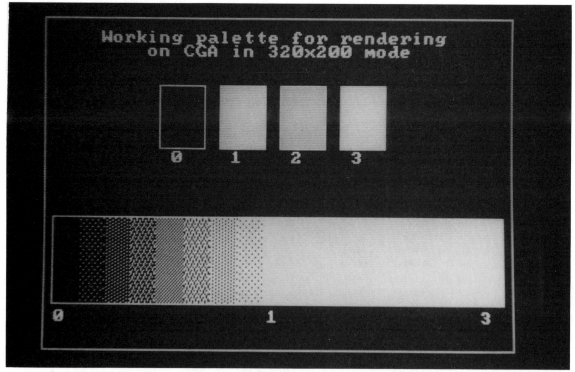

Fig. 15-14. The display image produced by the demonstration program in Fig. 15-15.

Fig. 15-15. Rendering palette for the Color/Graphics Adapter 320 × 200 mode.

```
100 'Program A-20.BAS      Rendering palette for 320x200 CGA m
ode.
110 'Demonstrates halftoning and dithering techniques.
120 '_____
130 '
140   KEY OFF:CLS:SCREEN 1,0:COLOR 0,1   '320x200 4 color mode

150   ON KEY (2) GOSUB 580:KEY (2) ON   'enable clean exit
160   DEFINT T,C
170   WINDOW SCREEN (0,0)-(639,199)
180   GOSUB 620 'assign area fill hex codes
190 '_____
200 '
210 'module:   create generic screen
220   LINE (0,0)-(639,199),3,B  'outline entire screen
230   LOCATE 2,6:PRINT "Working palette for rendering":LOCATE
 3,10:PRINT "on CGA in 320x200 mode"
240   X=13:FOR T=1 TO 17 STEP 1:LINE (X,120)-(X+36,172),3,B:X
=X+36:NEXT T
250   LOCATE 23,2:PRINT "0":LOCATE 23,20:PRINT "1":LOCATE 23,
38:PRINT "3"
260   X=160:FOR T=1 TO 4 STEP 1:LINE (X,40)-(X+60,78),3,B:X=X
+80:NEXT T
270   LOCATE 11,12:PRINT "0":LOCATE 11,17:PRINT "1":LOCATE 11
,22:PRINT "2":LOCATE 11,27:PRINT "3"
280 '_____
290 '
300 'module:   invoke area fill
310   X=170:C=0:FOR T=1 TO 4 STEP 1:PAINT (X,50),C,3:X=X+80:C
=C+1:NEXT T
320   X=24:PAINT (X,130),0,3
330   X=X+36:PAINT (X,130),A2$,3:X=X+36:PAINT (X,130),A3$,3:X
=X+36:PAINT (X,130),A3$,3:X=X+36:PAINT (X,130),A4$,3:X=X+36:
PAINT (X,130),A5$,3:X=X+36:PAINT (X,130),A6$,3:X=X+36:PAINT
(X,130),A7$,3:X=X+36:PAINT (X,130),1,3
340   X=X+36:PAINT (X,130),A9$,3:X=X+36:PAINT (X,130),A10$,3:
X=X+36:PAINT (X,130),A12$,3:X=X+36:PAINT (X,130),A13$,3:X=X+
36:PAINT (X,130),A14$,3:X=X+36:PAINT (X,130),A15$,3:X=X+36:P
AINT (X,130),A16$,3:X=X+36:PAINT (X,130),3,3
350 '_____
360 '
370 'module:   apply dithering
380   X=49:Y1=121:Y2=171:LINE (X,Y1)-(X,Y2),0
390   X=X+36:LINE (X,Y1)-(X,Y2),0:LINE (X,Y1)-(X,Y2),1,,&H842
0
400   X=X+36:LINE (X,Y1)-(X,Y2),0:LINE (X,Y1)-(X,Y2),1,,&HAAA
A
```

```
410  X=X+36:LINE  (X,Y1)-(X,Y2),0:LINE  (X,Y1)-(X,Y2),1,,&H555
5
420  X=X+36:LINE  (X,Y1)-(X,Y2),0:LINE  (X,Y1)-(X,Y2),1,,&H555
5
430  X=X+36:LINE  (X,Y1)-(X,Y2),1:LINE  (X,Y1)-(X,Y2),0,,&H492
4
440  X=X+36:LINE  (X,Y1)-(X,Y2),1:LINE  (X,Y1)-(X,Y2),0,,&H888
8
450  X=X+36:LINE  (X,Y1)-(X,Y2),1
460  X=X+36:LINE  (X,Y1)-(X,Y2),1
470  X=X+36:LINE  (X,Y1)-(X,Y2),1:LINE  (X,Y1)-(X,Y2),3,,&H888
8
480  X=X+36:LINE  (X,Y1)-(X,Y2),1:LINE  (X,Y1)-(X,Y2),3,,&H942
8
490  X=X+36:LINE  (X,Y1)-(X,Y2),1:LINE  (X,Y1)-(X,Y2),3,,&HAAA
A
500  X=X+36:LINE  (X,Y1)-(X,Y2),1:LINE  (X,Y1)-(X,Y2),3,,&HAAA
A
510  X=X+36:LINE  (X,Y1)-(X,Y2),3:LINE  (X,Y1)-(X,Y2),1,,&H555
5
520  X=X+36:LINE  (X,Y1)-(X,Y2),3:LINE  (X,Y1)-(X,Y2),1,,&H111
1
530  BEEP
540  GOTO 540   'clean halt keeps cursor off the screen
550  '_____
560  '
570 'module:   return to BASIC interpreter
580  CLS:SCREEN 0,0,0,0:WIDTH 80:COLOR 7,0,0:LOCATE 1,1,1:CL
S:END
590  '_____
600  '
610 'module:   area fill hex codes for CGA in 320x200 4-color
 mode
620  A1$=CHR$(&H40)+CHR$(&H0)+CHR$(&H4)+CHR$(&H0)
630  A2$=CHR$(&H40)+CHR$(&H4)+CHR$(&H40)+CHR$(&H4)
640  A3$=CHR$(&H44)+CHR$(&H10)+CHR$(&H11)+CHR$(&H1)+CHR$(&H4
4)+CHR$(&H4)+CHR$(&H11)+CHR$(&H40)
650  A4$=CHR$(&H44)+CHR$(&H11)+CHR$(&H44)+CHR$(&H11)
660  A5$=CHR$(&H11)+CHR$(&H45)+CHR$(&H44)+CHR$(&H54)+CHR$(&H
11)+CHR$(&H51)+CHR$(&H44)+CHR$(&H15)
670  A6$=CHR$(&H15)+CHR$(&H51)+CHR$(&H15)+CHR$(&H51)
680  A7$=CHR$(&H15)+CHR$(&H55)+CHR$(&H51)+CHR$(&H55)
690  A9$=CHR$(&HD5)+CHR$(&H55)+CHR$(&H5D)+CHR$(&H55)
700  A10$=CHR$(&HD5)+CHR$(&H5D)+CHR$(&HD5)+CHR$(&H5D)
710  A12$=CHR$(&HDD)+CHR$(&H75)+CHR$(&H77)+CHR$(&H57)+CHR$(&
HDD)+CHR$(&H5D)+CHR$(&H77)+CHR$(&HD5)
720  A13$=CHR$(&HDD)+CHR$(&H77)+CHR$(&HDD)+CHR$(&H77)
730  A14$=CHR$(&H77)+CHR$(&HDF)+CHR$(&HDD)+CHR$(&HFD)+CHR$(&
```

```
     H77)+CHR$(&HF7)+CHR$(&HDD)+CHR$(&H7F)
 740   A15$=CHR$(&H7F)+CHR$(&HF7)+CHR$(&H7F)+CHR$(&HF7)
 750   A16$=CHR$(&H7F)+CHR$(&HFF)+CHR$(&HF7)+CHR$(&HFF)
 760   RETURN
 770 '_____
 780 '
 790   END 'of program code
```

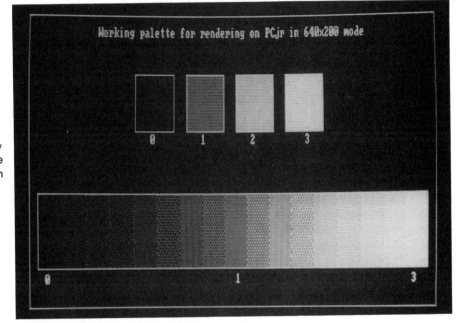

Fig. 15-16. The display image produced by the demonstration program in Fig. 15-17.

Fig. 15-17. Rendering palette for the PCjr and Tandy 640 × 200 mode.

```
100 'Program A-21.BAS      Rendering palette for PCjr 640x200
mode.
110 'Demonstrates halftoning and dithering techniques.
120 '_____
130 '
140   KEY OFF:CLS:ON ERROR GOTO 810:CLEAR,,,32768!:SCREEN 6,0
,0,0:COLOR 3,0   '640x200 4-color mode
150   ON ERROR GOTO 0
160   ON KEY (2) GOSUB 590:KEY (2) ON   'enable clean exit
170   DEFINT T,C
180   PALETTE 0,0:PALETTE 1,8:PALETTE 2,5:PALETTE 3,7
190   GOSUB 630 'assign area fill hex codes
200 '_____
210 '
220 'module:  create generic screen
230   LINE (0,0)-(639,199),3,B 'outline entire screen
```

```
240    LOCATE 2,14:PRINT "Working palette for rendering on PCj
r in 640x200 mode"
250    X=13:FOR T=1 TO 17 STEP 1:LINE (X,120)-(X+36,172),3,B:X
=X+36:NEXT T
260    LOCATE 23,4:PRINT "0":LOCATE 23,41:PRINT "1":LOCATE 23,
76:PRINT "3"
270    X=160:FOR T=1 TO 4 STEP 1:LINE (X,40)-(X+60,78),3,B:X=X
+80:NEXT T
280    LOCATE 11,24:PRINT "0":LOCATE 11,34:PRINT "1":LOCATE 11
,44:PRINT "2":LOCATE 11,55:PRINT "3"
290 '_____
300 '
310 'module:  invoke area fill
320    X=170:C=0:FOR T=1 TO 4 STEP 1:PAINT (X,50),C,3:X=X+80:C
=C+1:NEXT T
330    X=24:PAINT (X,130),0,3
340    X=X+36:PAINT (X,130),A1$,3:X=X+36:PAINT (X,130),A2$,3:X
=X+36:PAINT (X,130),A3$,3:X=X+36:PAINT (X,130),A4$,3:X=X+36:
PAINT (X,130),A5$,3:X=X+36:PAINT (X,130),A6$,3:X=X+36:PAINT
(X,130),A7$,3:X=X+36:PAINT (X,130),1,3
350    X=X+36:PAINT (X,130),A9$,3:X=X+36:PAINT (X,130),A10$,3:
X=X+36:PAINT (X,130),A12$,3:X=X+36:PAINT (X,130),A13$,3:X=X+
36:PAINT (X,130),A14$,3:X=X+36:PAINT (X,130),A15$,3:X=X+36:P
AINT (X,130),A16$,3:X=X+36:PAINT (X,130),3,3
360 '_____
370 '
380 'module:  apply dithering
390    X=49:Y1=121:Y2=171:LINE (X,Y1)-(X,Y2),0
400    X=X+36:LINE (X,Y1)-(X,Y2),0:LINE (X,Y1)-(X,Y2),1,,&H842
0
410    X=X+36:LINE (X,Y1)-(X,Y2),0:LINE (X,Y1)-(X,Y2),1,,&HAAA
A
420    X=X+36:LINE (X,Y1)-(X,Y2),0:LINE (X,Y1)-(X,Y2),1,,&H555
5
430    X=X+36:LINE (X,Y1)-(X,Y2),0:LINE (X,Y1)-(X,Y2),1,,&H555
5
440    X=X+36:LINE (X,Y1)-(X,Y2),1:LINE (X,Y1)-(X,Y2),0,,&H492
4
450    X=X+36:LINE (X,Y1)-(X,Y2),1:LINE (X,Y1)-(X,Y2),0,,&H888
8
460    X=X+36:LINE (X,Y1)-(X,Y2),1
470    X=X+36:LINE (X,Y1)-(X,Y2),1
480    X=X+36:LINE (X,Y1)-(X,Y2),1:LINE (X,Y1)-(X,Y2),3,,&H888
8
490    X=X+36:LINE (X,Y1)-(X,Y2),1:LINE (X,Y1)-(X,Y2),3,,&H942
8
500    X=X+36:LINE (X,Y1)-(X,Y2),1:LINE (X,Y1)-(X,Y2),3,,&HAAA
A
510    X=X+36:LINE (X,Y1)-(X,Y2),1:LINE (X,Y1)-(X,Y2),3,,&HAAA
```

```
A
520   X=X+36:LINE (X,Y1)-(X,Y2),3:LINE (X,Y1)-(X,Y2),1,,&H555
5
530   X=X+36:LINE (X,Y1)-(X,Y2),3:LINE (X,Y1)-(X,Y2),1,,&H111
1
540   BEEP
550   GOTO 550   'clean halt keeps cursor off the screen
560   '_____
570   '
580   'module:  return to BASIC interpreter
590   CLS:SCREEN 0,0,0,0:WIDTH 80:COLOR 7,0,0:LOCATE 1,1,1:CL
S:END
600   '_____
610   '
620   'module:  area fill hex codes for PCjr in 640x200 4-colo
r mode
630   A1$=CHR$(&H40)+CHR$(&H0)+CHR$(&H4)+CHR$(&H0)
640   A2$=CHR$(&H40)+CHR$(&H4)+CHR$(&H40)+CHR$(&H4)
650   A3$=CHR$(&H44)+CHR$(&H10)+CHR$(&H11)+CHR$(&H1)+CHR$(&H4
4)+CHR$(&H4)+CHR$(&H11)+CHR$(&H40)
660   A4$=CHR$(&H44)+CHR$(&H11)+CHR$(&H44)+CHR$(&H11)
670   A5$=CHR$(&H11)+CHR$(&H45)+CHR$(&H44)+CHR$(&H54)+CHR$(&H
11)+CHR$(&H51)+CHR$(&H44)+CHR$(&H15)
680   A6$=CHR$(&H15)+CHR$(&H51)+CHR$(&H15)+CHR$(&H51)
690   A7$=CHR$(&H15)+CHR$(&H55)+CHR$(&H51)+CHR$(&H55)
700   A9$=CHR$(&HD5)+CHR$(&H55)+CHR$(&H5D)+CHR$(&H55)
710   A10$=CHR$(&HD5)+CHR$(&H5D)+CHR$(&HD5)+CHR$(&H5D)
720   A12$=CHR$(&HDD)+CHR$(&H75)+CHR$(&H77)+CHR$(&H57)+CHR$(&
HDD)+CHR$(&H5D)+CHR$(&H77)+CHR$(&HD5)
730   A13$=CHR$(&HDD)+CHR$(&H77)+CHR$(&HDD)+CHR$(&H77)
740   A14$=CHR$(&H77)+CHR$(&HDF)+CHR$(&HDD)+CHR$(&HFD)+CHR$(&
H77)+CHR$(&HF7)+CHR$(&HDD)+CHR$(&H7F)
750   A15$=CHR$(&H7F)+CHR$(&HF7)+CHR$(&H7F)+CHR$(&HF7)
760   A16$=CHR$(&H7F)+CHR$(&HFF)+CHR$(&HF7)+CHR$(&HFF)
770   RETURN
780   '_____
790   '
800   'module:  trap if not PCjr and Cartridge BASIC
810   SOUND 350,.7:LOCATE 10,1:PRINT "PCjr & Cartridge BASIC
required."
820   K$=INKEY$
830   LOCATE 12,1:PRINT "Press ESC to return to BASIC..."
840   IF K$=CHR$(27) THEN RESUME 860
850   GOTO 820
860   CLS:LOCATE 1,1,1:END
870   '_____
880   '
890   END 'of program code
```

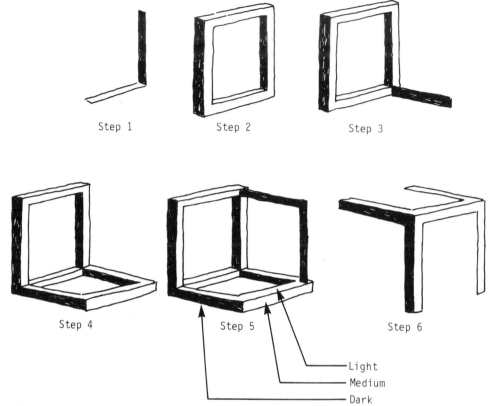

Step 1    Step 2    Step 3

Step 4    Step 5    Step 6

Light
Medium
Dark

Fig. 15-18. Drawing sequence for the fully-shaded frame cube.

Fig. 15-19. The display image produced by the demonstration program in Fig. 15-20.

168

Fig. 15-20. Shaded frame cube.

```
100 'Program A-22.BAS    Frame cube.
110 'Demonstrates intuitive shading of solid models.
120 '_____
130 '
140   GOTO 840  'configure system
150   GOSUB 1130 'assign scalar data
160   ON G GOTO 190, 380, 560  'jump to appropriate master ro
utine
170 '_____
180 '
190 'master routine for EGA and Enhanced Display
200   RESTORE 1190:A$=A3$:C4=1:C5=2:C6=&HAAAA:GOSUB 1360  'su
rface 1
210   RESTORE 1200:A$=A13$:C4=4:C5=5:C6=&H8080:GOSUB 1360   's
urface 2
220   RESTORE 1210:A$=A8$:C4=3:C5=2:C6=&H8888:GOSUB 1480  'su
rface 3
230   RESTORE 1230:A$=A13$:C4=4:C5=5:C6=&H8080:GOSUB 1360   't
op surface 4
240   RESTORE 1240:A$=A3$:C4=1:C5=2:C6=&HAAAA:GOSUB 1360   'su
rface 5
250   RESTORE 1250:A$=A3$:C4=1:C5=2:C6=&HAAAA:GOSUB 1360   'su
rface 6
260   RESTORE 1260:A$=A13$:C4=4:C5=5:C6=&H8080:GOSUB 1650   'l
ower U-shape 7
270   RESTORE 1270:A$=A3$:C4=1:C5=2:C6=&HAAAA:GOSUB 1360   'su
rface 8
280   RESTORE 1280:A$=A8$:C4=3:C5=2:C6=&H8888:GOSUB 1360  'fr
ont surface 9
290   RESTORE 1290:A$=A3$:C4=1:C5=2:C6=&HAAAA:GOSUB 1820  'in
side L-shape 10
300   RESTORE 1300:A$=A13$:C4=4:C5=5:C6=&H8080:GOSUB 1650   't
op U-shape 11
310   RESTORE 1310:A$=A8$:C4=3:C5=2:C6=&H8888:GOSUB 1650  'fr
ont U-shape 12
320   RESTORE 1320:A$=A3$:C4=1:C5=2:C6=&HAAAA:GOSUB 1820  'da
rk L-shape 13
330   BEEP
340   GOTO 340  'clean halt.
350   END 'of master routine.
360 '_____
370 '
380 'master routine for EGA and standard Color Display
390   RESTORE 1190:A$=A3$:C4=1:C5=2:C6=&HAAAA:GOSUB 1360   'su
rface 1
400   RESTORE 1200:A$=A9$:C4=3:C5=4:C6=&H8080:GOSUB 1360   'su
```

```
rface 2
410   RESTORE 1210:A$=A6$:C4=2:C5=3:C6=&H8888:GOSUB 1480     'su
rface 3
420   RESTORE 1230:A$=A9$:C4=3:C5=4:C6=&H8080:GOSUB 1360     'to
p surface 4
430   RESTORE 1240:A$=A3$:C4=1:C5=2:C6=&HAAAA:GOSUB 1360     'su
rface 5
440   RESTORE 1250:A$=A3$:C4=1:C5=2:C6=&HAAAA:GOSUB 1360     'su
rface 6
450   RESTORE 1260:A$=A9$:C4=3:C5=4:C6=&H8080:GOSUB 1650     'lo
wer U-shape 7
460   RESTORE 1270:A$=A3$:C4=1:C5=2:C6=&HAAAA:GOSUB 1360     'su
rface 8
470   RESTORE 1280:A$=A6$:C4=2:C5=3:C6=&H8888:GOSUB 1360     'fr
ont surface 9
480   RESTORE 1290:A$=A3$:C4=1:C5=2:C6=&HAAAA:GOSUB 1820     'in
side L-shape 10
490   RESTORE 1300:A$=A9$:C4=3:C5=4:C6=&H8080:GOSUB 1650     'to
p U-shape 11
500   RESTORE 1310:A$=A6$:C4=2:C5=3:C6=&H8888:GOSUB 1650     'fr
ont U-shape 12
510   RESTORE 1320:A$=A3$:C4=1:C5=2:C6=&HAAAA:GOSUB 1820     'da
rk L-shape 13
520   BEEP
530   GOTO 530   'clean halt.
540 '_____
550 '
560 'master routine for CGA and PCjr
570   RESTORE 1190:A$=A3$:C4=0:C5=1:C6=&H9428:GOSUB 1360     'su
rface 1
580   RESTORE 1200:A$=A13$:C4=1:C5=3:C6=&HAAAA:GOSUB 1360     's
urface 2
590   RESTORE 1210:A$=A7$:C4=1:C5=0:C6=&H8080:GOSUB 1480     'su
rface 3
600   RESTORE 1230:A$=A13$:C4=1:C5=3:C6=&HAAAA:GOSUB 1360     't
op surface 4
610   RESTORE 1240:A$=A3$:C4=0:C5=1:C6=&H9428:GOSUB 1360     'su
rface 5
620   RESTORE 1250:A$=A3$:C4=0:C5=1:C6=&H9428:GOSUB 1360     'su
rface 6
630   RESTORE 1260:A$=A13$:C4=1:C5=3:C6=&HAAAA:GOSUB 1650     'l
ower U-shape 7
640   RESTORE 1270:A$=A3$:C4=0:C5=1:C6=&H9428:GOSUB 1360     'su
rface 8
650   RESTORE 1280:A$=A7$:C4=1:C5=0:C6=&H8080:GOSUB 1360     'fr
ont surface 9
660   RESTORE 1290:A$=A3$:C4=0:C5=1:C6=&H9428:GOSUB 1820     'in
side L-shape 10
```

```
670   RESTORE 1300:A$=A13$:C4=1:C5=3:C6=&HAAAA:GOSUB 1650    't
op U-shape 11
680   RESTORE 1310:A$=A7$:C4=1:C5=0:C6=&H8080:GOSUB 1650    'fr
ont U-shape 12
690   RESTORE 1320:A$=A3$:C4=0:C5=1:C6=&H9428:GOSUB 1820    'da
rk L-shape 13
700   BEEP
710   GOTO 710  'clean halt.
720 '_____
730 '
740 'module:  perspective calculations for Cartesian world c
oordinates
750   X=(-1)*X:XA=CR1*X-SR1*Z:ZA=SR1*X+CR1*Z:X=CR2*XA+SR2*Y:Y
A=CR2*Y-SR2*XA:Z=CR3*ZA-SR3*YA:Y=SR3*ZA+CR3*YA:X=X+MX:Y=Y+MY
:Z=Z+MZ:SX=D*X/Z:SY=D*Y/Z:RETURN
760 '_____
770 '
780 'module: return to BASIC command level
790   CLS:SCREEN 0,0,0,0:WIDTH 80:CLS:END
800 '_____
810 '
820 'module:  UNIVERSAL
830 'This routine configures the program for the hardware/so
ftware being used.
840   KEY OFF:CLS:ON ERROR GOTO 900   'trap if not Enhanced Di
splay + EGA
850   SCREEN 9,,0,0:COLOR 7,0:PALETTE 1,8:PALETTE 2,1:PALETTE
 3,9:PALETTE 4,11:PALETTE 5,7:PALETTE 6,37:PALETTE 7,7:PALET
TE 8,56:PALETTE 9,34:PALETTE 10,20:PALETTE 11,5:PALETTE 12,4
4:PALETTE 13,46:PALETTE 14,55:PALETTE 15,63
860   C0=0:C1=12:C2=9:C3=7:LOCATE 1,1:PRINT "ED-EGA 640x350 1
6-color mode"
870   DEFINT G:G=1  'set flag for ED-EGA mode
880   GOSUB 1970  'assign bit tiling codes for EGA
890   GOTO 1060  'jump to screen coordinates set-up
900   RESUME 910
910   ON ERROR GOTO 960 'trap if not Color Display + EGA
920   SCREEN 8,,0,0:COLOR 7,0:PALETTE 1,0:PALETTE 2,1:PALETTE
 3,9:PALETTE 4,7:PALETTE 8,4:PALETTE 9,2:C0=0:C1=8:C2=9:C3=7
:LOCATE 1,1:PRINT "CD-EGA 640x200 16-color mode"
930   DEFINT G:G=2  'set flag for CD-EGA mode
940   GOSUB 1970  'assign shading codes for EGA
950   GOTO 1060  'jump to screen coordinates set-up
960   RESUME 970
970   ON ERROR GOTO 1020  'trap if not PCjr
980   CLEAR,,,32768!:SCREEN 6,0,0,0:COLOR 3,0:PALETTE 1,8:PAL
ETTE 3,7:C0=0:C1=1:C2=2:C3=3:LOCATE 1,1:PRINT "PCjr 640x200
4-color mode"
```

```
990    DEFINT G:G=3  'set flag for PCjr mode
1000   GOSUB 2170  'assign shading codes for PCjr
1010   GOTO 1060   'jump to screen coordinates set-up
1020   RESUME 1030
1030   SCREEN 1,0:COLOR 0,1:C0=0:C1=1:C2=2:C3=3:LOCATE 1,1:PR
INT "CGA 320x200 4-color mode"
1040   DEFINT G:G=3  'set flag for CGA mode
1050   GOSUB 2170  'assign shading codes for CGA
1060   ON ERROR GOTO 0  'disable error trapping override
1070   WINDOW SCREEN (-399,-299)-(400,300)
1080   ON KEY (2) GOSUB 790:KEY (2) ON  'F2 key to exit progr
am
1090   GOTO 150  'return to main program
1100   '_____
1110   '
1120   'module: assign scalar data
1130   D=1200:R1=.58539:R2=6.28319:R3=5.79778:MX=0:MZ=-220:MY
=0  'angular distortion, rotation factors, viewpoint distan
ce for viewing coordinates
1140   SR1=SIN(R1):CR1=COS(R1):SR2=SIN(R2):CR2=COS(R2):SR3=SI
N(R3):CR3=COS(R3)
1150   RETURN
1160   '_____
1170   '
1180   'module: data base
1190   DATA  25,-25,-30,  25,25,-30,  25,25,-25,  25,-25,-25,
  25,0,-27
1200   DATA  25,-25,-30,  -25,-25,-30,  -25,-25,-25,  25,-25,
-25,  0,-25,-27
1210   DATA  -25,-25,-25,  -25,25,-25,  25,25,-25,  25,-25,-2
5
1220   DATA  -30,-30,-25,  -30,30,-25,  30,30,-25,  30,-30,-2
5,  0,27,-25
1230   DATA  -30,30,-30,  30,30,-30,  30,30,-25,  -30,30,-25,
  0,30,-27
1240   DATA  -30,-30,-30,  -30,30,-30,  -30,30,-25,  -30,-30,
-25,  -30,0,-27
1250   DATA  25,-30,25,  25,-30,-25,  25,-25,-25,  25,-25,25,
  25,-27,0
1260   DATA  30,-25,-25,  30,-25,30,  -30,-25,30,  -30,-25,-2
5,  -25,-25,-25,  -25,-25,25,  25,-25,25,  25,-25,-25,  0,-2
5,27
1270   DATA  -30,-30,-25,  -30,-25,-25,  -30,-25,30,  -30,-30
,30,  -30,-27,0
1280   DATA  -30,-30,30,  -30,-25,30,  30,-25,30,  30,-30,30,
  0,-27,30
```

```
1290   DATA  25,30,-25,   25,30,30,    25,-25,30,   25,-25,25,   2
5,25,25,   25,25,-25,   25,0,27
1300   DATA  30,30,-30,   30,30,30,   -30,30,30,   -30,30,-30,
-25,30,-30,   -25,30,25,   25,30,25,   25,30,-30,   0,30,27
1310   DATA  30,30,30,   30,-30,30,   25,-30,30,   25,25,30,   -2
5,25,30,   -25,-30,30,   -30,-30,30,   -30,30,30,   0,27,30
1320   DATA  -30,30,-30,   -30,30,30,   -30,-30,30,   -30,-30,25
,   -30,25,25,   -30,25,-30,   -30,0,27
1330  '_____
1340  '
1350  'module:  model & render simple polygon
1360   READ X,Y,Z:GOSUB 750:SX1=SX:SY1=SY:READ X,Y,Z:GOSUB 75
0:SX2=SX:SY2=SY:READ X,Y,Z:GOSUB 750:SX3=SX:SY3=SY:READ X,Y,
Z:GOSUB 750:SX4=SX:SY4=SY:READ X,Y,Z:GOSUB 750:SX5=SX:SY5=SY
   'calculate projection coordinates
1370   LINE (SX1,SY1)-(SX2,SY2),C2:LINE-(SX3,SY3),C2:LINE-(SX
4,SY4),C2:LINE-(SX1,SY1),C2:PAINT (SX5,SY5),C2,C2   'key matt
e
1380   LINE (SX1,SY1)-(SX2,SY2),C3:LINE-(SX3,SY3),C3:LINE-(SX
4,SY4),C3:LINE-(SX1,SY1),C3:PAINT (SX5,SY5),C0,C3   'solid mo
del
1390   PAINT (SX5,SY5),A$,C3   'shading
1400   LINE (SX1,SY1)-(SX2,SY2),C4:LINE (SX1,SY1)-(SX2,SY2),C
5,,C6
1410   LINE (SX2,SY2)-(SX3,SY3),C4:LINE (SX2,SY2)-(SX3,SY3),C
5,,C6
1420   LINE (SX3,SY3)-(SX4,SY4),C4:LINE (SX3,SY3)-(SX4,SY4),C
5,,C6
1430   LINE (SX4,SY4)-(SX1,SY1),C4:LINE (SX4,SY4)-(SX1,SY1),C
5,,C6
1440   RETURN
1450  '_____
1460  '
1470  'module:  model & render donut polygon
1480   READ X,Y,Z:GOSUB 750:SX1=SX:SY1=SY:READ X,Y,Z:GOSUB 75
0:SX2=SX:SY2=SY:READ X,Y,Z:GOSUB 750:SX3=SX:SY3=SY:READ X,Y,
Z:GOSUB 750:SX4=SX:SY4=SY
1490   READ X,Y,Z:GOSUB 750:SX5=SX:SY5=SY:READ X,Y,Z:GOSUB 75
0:SX6=SX:SY6=SY:READ X,Y,Z:GOSUB 750:SX7=SX:SY7=SY:READ X,Y,
Z:GOSUB 750:SX8=SX:SY8=SY:READ X,Y,Z:GOSUB 750:SX9=SX:SY9=SY
   'calculate projection coordinates
1500   LINE (SX1,SY1)-(SX2,SY2),C2:LINE-(SX3,SY3),C2:LINE-(SX
4,SY4),C2:LINE-(SX1,SY1),C2:LINE (SX5,SY5)-(SX6,SY6),C2:LINE
-(SX7,SY7),C2:LINE-(SX8,SY8),C2:LINE-(SX5,SY5),C2:PAINT (SX9
,SY9),C2,C2   'key matte
1510   LINE (SX1,SY1)-(SX2,SY2),C3:LINE-(SX3,SY3),C3:LINE-(SX
4,SY4),C3:LINE-(SX1,SY1),C3:LINE (SX5,SY5)-(SX6,SY6),C3:LINE
```

```
-(SX7,SY7),C3:LINE-(SX8,SY8),C3:LINE-(SX5,SY5),C3:PAINT (SX9
,SY9),C0,C3  'solid model
1520   PAINT (SX9,SY9),A$,C3   'shading
1530   LINE (SX1,SY1)-(SX2,SY2),C4:LINE (SX1,SY1)-(SX2,SY2),C
5,,C6
1540   LINE (SX2,SY2)-(SX3,SY3),C4:LINE (SX2,SY2)-(SX3,SY3),C
5,,C6
1550   LINE (SX3,SY3)-(SX4,SY4),C4:LINE (SX3,SY3)-(SX4,SY4),C
5,,C6
1560   LINE (SX4,SY4)-(SX1,SY1),C4:LINE (SX4,SY4)-(SX1,SY1),C
5,,C6
1570   LINE (SX5,SY5)-(SX6,SY6),C4:LINE (SX5,SY5)-(SX6,SY6),C
5,,C6
1580   LINE (SX6,SY6)-(SX7,SY7),C4:LINE (SX6,SY6)-(SX7,SY7),C
5,,C6
1590   LINE (SX7,SY7)-(SX8,SY8),C4:LINE (SX7,SY7)-(SX8,SY8),C
5,,C6
1600   LINE (SX8,SY8)-(SX5,SY5),C4:LINE (SX8,SY8)-(SX5,SY5),C
5,,C6
1610   RETURN
1620 '_____
1630 '
1640 'module:  model & render U-shaped polygon
1650   READ X,Y,Z:GOSUB 750:SX1=SX:SY1=SY:READ X,Y,Z:GOSUB 75
0:SX2=SX:SY2=SY:READ X,Y,Z:GOSUB 750:SX3=SX:SY3=SY:READ X,Y,
Z:GOSUB 750:SX4=SX:SY4=SY
1660   READ X,Y,Z:GOSUB 750:SX5=SX:SY5=SY:READ X,Y,Z:GOSUB 75
0:SX6=SX:SY6=SY:READ X,Y,Z:GOSUB 750:SX7=SX:SY7=SY:READ X,Y,
Z:GOSUB 750:SX8=SX:SY8=SY:READ X,Y,Z:GOSUB 750:SX9=SX:SY9=SY
  'calculate projection coordinates
1670   LINE (SX1,SY1)-(SX2,SY2),C2:LINE-(SX3,SY3),C2:LINE-(SX
4,SY4),C2:LINE-(SX5,SY5),C2:LINE-(SX6,SY6),C2:LINE-(SX7,SY7)
,C2:LINE-(SX8,SY8),C2:LINE-(SX1,SY1),C2:PAINT (SX9,SY9),C2,C
2  'key matte
1680   LINE (SX1,SY1)-(SX2,SY2),C3:LINE-(SX3,SY3),C3:LINE-(SX
4,SY4),C3:LINE-(SX5,SY5),C3:LINE-(SX6,SY6),C3:LINE-(SX7,SY7)
,C3:LINE-(SX8,SY8),C3:LINE-(SX1,SY1),C3:PAINT (SX9,SY9),C0,C
3  'solid model
1690   PAINT (SX9,SY9),A$,C3   'shading
1700   LINE (SX1,SY1)-(SX2,SY2),C4:LINE (SX1,SY1)-(SX2,SY2),C
5,,C6
1710   LINE (SX2,SY2)-(SX3,SY3),C4:LINE (SX2,SY2)-(SX3,SY3),C
5,,C6
1720   LINE (SX3,SY3)-(SX4,SY4),C4:LINE (SX3,SY3)-(SX4,SY4),C
5,,C6
1730   LINE (SX4,SY4)-(SX5,SY5),C4:LINE (SX4,SY4)-(SX5,SY5),C
5,,C6
```

```
1740   LINE (SX5,SY5)-(SX6,SY6),C4:LINE (SX5,SY5)-(SX6,SY6),C
5,,C6
1750   LINE (SX6,SY6)-(SX7,SY7),C4:LINE (SX6,SY6)-(SX7,SY7),C
5,,C6
1760   LINE (SX7,SY7)-(SX8,SY8),C4:LINE (SX7,SY7)-(SX8,SY8),C
5,,C6
1770   LINE (SX8,SY8)-(SX1,SY1),C4:LINE (SX8,SY8)-(SX1,SY1),C
5,,C6
1780   RETURN
1790 '_____
1800 '
1810 'module:   model & render L-shaped polygon
1820   READ X,Y,Z:GOSUB 750:SX1=SX:SY1=SY:READ X,Y,Z:GOSUB 75
0:SX2=SX:SY2=SY:READ X,Y,Z:GOSUB 750:SX3=SX:SY3=SY:READ X,Y,
Z:GOSUB 750:SX4=SX:SY4=SY
1830   READ X,Y,Z:GOSUB 750:SX5=SX:SY5=SY:READ X,Y,Z:GOSUB 75
0:SX6=SX:SY6=SY:READ X,Y,Z:GOSUB 750:SX7=SX:SY7=SY   'calcula
te projection coordinates
1840   LINE (SX1,SY1)-(SX2,SY2),C2:LINE-(SX3,SY3),C2:LINE-(SX
4,SY4),C2:LINE-(SX5,SY5),C2:LINE-(SX6,SY6),C2:LINE-(SX1,SY1)
,C2:PAINT (SX7,SY7),C2,C2  'key matte
1850   LINE (SX1,SY1)-(SX2,SY2),C3:LINE-(SX3,SY3),C3:LINE-(SX
4,SY4),C3:LINE-(SX5,SY5),C3:LINE-(SX6,SY6),C3:LINE-(SX1,SY1)
,C3:PAINT (SX7,SY7),C0,C3  'solid model
1860   PAINT (SX7,SY7),A$,C3  'shading
1870   LINE (SX1,SY1)-(SX2,SY2),C4:LINE (SX1,SY1)-(SX2,SY2),C
5,,C6
1880   LINE (SX2,SY2)-(SX3,SY3),C4:LINE (SX2,SY2)-(SX3,SY3),C
5,,C6
1890   LINE (SX3,SY3)-(SX4,SY4),C4:LINE (SX3,SY3)-(SX4,SY4),C
5,,C6
1900   LINE (SX4,SY4)-(SX5,SY5),C4:LINE (SX4,SY4)-(SX5,SY5),C
5,,C6
1910   LINE (SX5,SY5)-(SX6,SY6),C4:LINE (SX5,SY5)-(SX6,SY6),C
5,,C6
1920   LINE (SX6,SY6)-(SX1,SY1),C4:LINE (SX6,SY6)-(SX1,SY1),C
5,,C6
1930   RETURN
1940 '_____
1950 '
1960 'module:   assign shading codes for EGA
1970   A1$=CHR$(&HDF)+CHR$(&H20)+CHR$(&HO)+CHR$(&HO)+CHR$(&HF
D)+CHR$(&H2)+CHR$(&HO)+CHR$(&HO)+CHR$(&H7F)+CHR$(&H80)+CHR$(
&HO)+CHR$(&HO)+CHR$(&HF7)+CHR$(&H8)+CHR$(&HO)+CHR$(&HO)
1980   A2$=CHR$(&HBB)+CHR$(&H44)+CHR$(&HO)+CHR$(&HO)+CHR$(&HE
E)+CHR$(&H11)+CHR$(&HO)+CHR$(&HO)
```

```
1990   A3$=CHR$(&HAA)+CHR$(&H55)+CHR$(&HO)+CHR$(&HO)+CHR$(&H5
5)+CHR$(&HAA)+CHR$(&HO)+CHR$(&HO)
2000   A4$=CHR$(&H44)+CHR$(&HBB)+CHR$(&HO)+CHR$(&HO)+CHR$(&H1
1)+CHR$(&HEE)+CHR$(&HO)+CHR$(&HO)
2010   A5$=CHR$(&H20)+CHR$(&HFF)+CHR$(&HO)+CHR$(&HO)+CHR$(&H2
)+CHR$(&HFF)+CHR$(&HO)+CHR$(&HO)+CHR$(&H80)+CHR$(&HFF)+CHR$(
&HO)+CHR$(&HO)+CHR$(&H8)+CHR$(&HFF)+CHR$(&HO)+CHR$(&HO)
2020   A6$=CHR$(&H44)+CHR$(&HFF)+CHR$(&HO)+CHR$(&HO)+CHR$(&H1
1)+CHR$(&HFF)+CHR$(&HO)+CHR$(&HO)
2030   A7$=CHR$(&H55)+CHR$(&HFF)+CHR$(&HO)+CHR$(&HO)+CHR$(&HA
A)+CHR$(&HFF)+CHR$(&HO)+CHR$(&HO)
2040   A8$=CHR$(&HBB)+CHR$(&HFF)+CHR$(&HO)+CHR$(&HO)+CHR$(&HE
E)+CHR$(&HFF)+CHR$(&HO)+CHR$(&HO)
2050   A9$=CHR$(&HDF)+CHR$(&HDF)+CHR$(&H20)+CHR$(&HO)+CHR$(&H
FD)+CHR$(&HFD)+CHR$(&H2)+CHR$(&HO)+CHR$(&H7F)+CHR$(&H7F)+CHR
$(&H80)+CHR$(&HO)+CHR$(&HF7)+CHR$(&HF7)+CHR$(&H8)+CHR$(&HO)
2060   A10$=CHR$(&HBB)+CHR$(&HBB)+CHR$(&H44)+CHR$(&HO)+CHR$(&
HEE)+CHR$(&HEE)+CHR$(&H11)+CHR$(&HO)
2070   A11$=CHR$(&HAA)+CHR$(&HAA)+CHR$(&H55)+CHR$(&HO)+CHR$(&
H55)+CHR$(&H55)+CHR$(&HAA)+CHR$(&HO)
2080   A12$=CHR$(&H44)+CHR$(&H44)+CHR$(&HBB)+CHR$(&HO)+CHR$(&
H11)+CHR$(&H11)+CHR$(&HEE)+CHR$(&HO)
2090   A13$=CHR$(&H20)+CHR$(&HO)+CHR$(&HFF)+CHR$(&HO)+CHR$(&H
2)+CHR$(&HO)+CHR$(&HFF)+CHR$(&HO)+CHR$(&H80)+CHR$(&HO)+CHR$(
&HFF)+CHR$(&HO)+CHR$(&H8)+CHR$(&HO)+CHR$(&HFF)+CHR$(&HO)
2100   A14$=CHR$(&H44)+CHR$(&HO)+CHR$(&HFF)+CHR$(&HO)+CHR$(&H
11)+CHR$(&HO)+CHR$(&HFF)+CHR$(&HO)
2110   A15$=CHR$(&H55)+CHR$(&HO)+CHR$(&HFF)+CHR$(&HO)+CHR$(&H
AA)+CHR$(&HO)+CHR$(&HFF)+CHR$(&HO)
2120   A16$=CHR$(&HBB)+CHR$(&HO)+CHR$(&HFF)+CHR$(&HO)+CHR$(&H
EE)+CHR$(&HO)+CHR$(&HFF)+CHR$(&HO)
2130   RETURN
2140 '_____
2150 '
2160 'module:   assign shading codes for CGA and/or PC.jr
2170   A1$=CHR$(&H40)+CHR$(&HO)+CHR$(&H4)+CHR$(&HO)
2180   A2$=CHR$(&H40)+CHR$(&H4)+CHR$(&H40)+CHR$(&H4)
2190   A3$=CHR$(&H44)+CHR$(&H10)+CHR$(&H11)+CHR$(&H1)+CHR$(&H
44)+CHR$(&H4)+CHR$(&H11)+CHR$(&H40)
2200   A4$=CHR$(&H44)+CHR$(&H11)+CHR$(&H44)+CHR$(&H11)
2210   A5$=CHR$(&H11)+CHR$(&H45)+CHR$(&H44)+CHR$(&H54)+CHR$(&
H11)+CHR$(&H51)+CHR$(&H44)+CHR$(&H15)
2220   A6$=CHR$(&H15)+CHR$(&H51)+CHR$(&H15)+CHR$(&H51)
2230   A7$=CHR$(&H15)+CHR$(&H55)+CHR$(&H51)+CHR$(&H55)
2240   A9$=CHR$(&HD5)+CHR$(&H55)+CHR$(&H5D)+CHR$(&H55)
```

176

```
2250    A10$=CHR$(&HD5)+CHR$(&H5D)+CHR$(&HD5)+CHR$(&H5D)
2260    A12$=CHR$(&HDD)+CHR$(&H75)+CHR$(&H77)+CHR$(&H57)+CHR$(
&HDD)+CHR$(&H5D)+CHR$(&H77)+CHR$(&HD5)
2270    A13$=CHR$(&HDD)+CHR$(&H77)+CHR$(&HDD)+CHR$(&H77)
2280    A14$=CHR$(&H77)+CHR$(&HDF)+CHR$(&HDD)+CHR$(&HFD)+CHR$(
&H77)+CHR$(&HF7)+CHR$(&HDD)+CHR$(&H7F)
2290    A15$=CHR$(&H7F)+CHR$(&HF7)+CHR$(&H7F)+CHR$(&HF7)
2300    A16$=CHR$(&H7F)+CHR$(&HFF)+CHR$(&HF7)+CHR$(&HFF)
2310    RETURN
2320    '_____
2330    '
2340    END 'of program code
```

ware is being used. Program control then returns to the appropriate main routine earlier in the program listing. If you are typing in the program, you will be able to run the program on any IBM-compatible microcomputer if you type the entire program listing. Alternatively, you can delete inappropriate sections of code by checking the remarks within the program.

The master routines in the demonstration program follow a uniform format. First, a RESTORE instruction is used to ensure that the correct portion of the database is being addressed. Second, the appropriate halftone shade is assigned to the variable A$. Then, the preparatory color for line dithering is assigned to the variable C4. Next, the overlay color for line dithering is assigned to the variable C5. Finally, the line styling four-digit hex code is assigned to the variable C6. Once all these factors have been defined, the program jumps to a specialized polygon-drawing routine.

Each polygon-drawing routine creates a shaded polygon surface that is outlined with line dithering to make the boundary line undetectable. The subroutine at line 1350 draws a standard four-sided polygon using the variables passed to it by the master routine. The subroutine at line 1470 draws a donut-shaped polygon. (You may find it helpful to refer to Fig. 15-18 for a description of the various shapes required by the drawing code.) The subroutine at line 1640 draws a U-shaped polygon. The subroutine at line 1810 draws an L-shaped polygon.

As you watch this program run, you can see the ordering of the various surfaces. A simple radial presort method has been invoked to ensure that cer-tain surfaces are obscured by other surfaces. By modifying the R1, R2, or R3 variables in line 1130 you can display the frame cube at different yaw, roll, and pitch positions. If you rotate the model past the range permitted in each plane, however, ambiguities will be introduced in the cube by incorrect obscuring.

Note that the upward-facing surfaces of the model have been assigned the brightest shade. The right-facing vertical surfaces are defined as mid-range shades. The left-facing surfaces are the dimmest shades. These attributes were selected by the author, and you can easily change them to suit your own preferences or your own monitor's display characteristics. Simply select the appropriate line of code in the master routine which is being invoked by your particular combination of hardware and software. (Hint: don't forget to change the C4, C5, and C6 line dithering codes too, or else you will be able to see the boundary lines!)

## SUMMARY

In this chapter, you learned how bit tiling and line styling can be implemented on your microcomputer to produce a sophisticated shading palette for 3D modeling and rendering. You saw the graphics effects produced by four demonstration programs. You learned how readily the halftone shading technique can be applied to a specific modeling project.

The next chapter will show you how to instruct your computer to automatically shade the surfaces of the model, depending on the location of the light source.

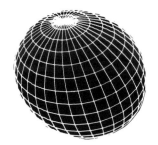

# 16

# Computer-Controlled Shading

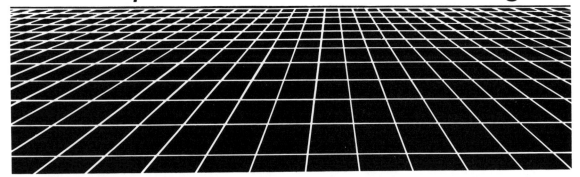

The brightness of a surface is dependent upon the location of the light source. In particular, the angle between the surface perpendicular and the incoming light rays determines the relative brightness or dimness of the surface.

## THE GENERIC ALGORITHM

Three steps are involved in any algorithm for computer-controlled shading of solid models. Refer to Fig. 16-1. First, the surface perpendicular vector for the surface is computed. This vector is also called a surface normal. Second, this vector is converted to a unit vector. A unit vector is a vector whose length equals one unit. Third, the angle between the incoming light unit vector and the surface perpendicular unit vector is determined. This angle is expressed as a decimal value between 0 and 1, where 1 corresponds to maximum brightness and 0 corresponds to minimum brightness.

The amount of light which is reflected from a surface adheres to standard principles of cosine. Refer to Fig. 16-2. Simply stated, vector dot products and vector cross products can be reduced to a simple cosine statement, as the formula in Fig. 16-2 shows. (For

a more detailed discussion of vector mathematics, you may wish to read Appendix B.)

When cosine equals 1, the angle between the surface perpendicular and the light source is nil. In other words, the light source is directly perpendicular to the surface being rendered; the surface is exhibiting maximum brightness. When cosine equals 0, the angle between the surface perpendicular and the light source is 90 degrees. The rays of light are parallel to the surface; the surface is exhibiting minimum brightness. The color of the surface would be determined by ambient light in the environment. When cosine is a negative number, the light source is behind the surface.

## THE SPECIFIC ALGORITHM

As you learned in the previous chapter, a specific rendering palette can be developed for the EGA, the Color/Graphics Adapter, and the PCjr video subsystem. Each shade is described by a hex code assigned to an A$ variable. Figure 16-3 shows how these A$ variables are distributed along the shading arc for a surface. Although Fig. 16-3 refers specifically to the shading routine for the EGA 640 × 350 mode, the other screen modes are similar in concept.

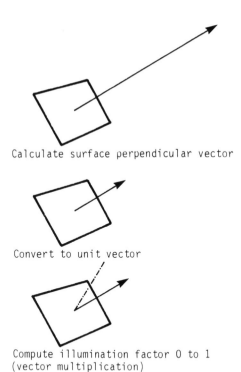

Calculate surface perpendicular vector

Convert to unit vector

Compute illumination factor 0 to 1
(vector multiplication)

Fig. 16-1. Generic algorithm for computer-controlled shading on personal computers.

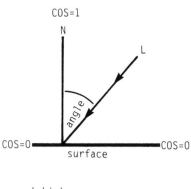

$$|N|\ |L|\ COS\ angle = N\cdot L$$
$$1 \times 1 \times COS\ angle = N\cdot L$$
$$COS\ angle = N\cdot L$$

COS angle = dot product of
vector N and vector L

Fig. 16-2. The intensity of the reflected light depends upon the angle of illumination. When the cosine of the angle is negative, the light source is behind the surface.

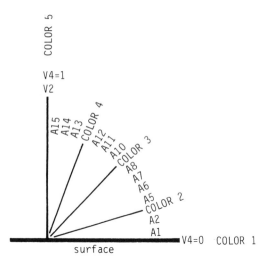

Fig. 16-3. Assignment of halftone codes for computer-controlled shading. V4 is the illumation intensity factor.

Maximum brightness is represented by A15$. Minimum brightness is denoted by A1$. For each shade in the rendering scheme, it is also necessary to define a line dithering algorithm in order to camouflage the boundary lines between different polygon planes on the surface of the model.

### Rendering Matrix for the EGA

The visually appropriate dithering algorithms for the EGA are shown in Fig. 16-4. This dithering matrix will be incorporated into the program listing and the program will automatically select the proper dithering variables for each specific halftone tiling pattern. Note that only four different dithering hex codes are used: 12.5%, 25%, 50%, and 75% (in addition to solid colors, of course). By swapping the color of the preparatory line and the actual dither color the full range of required dithering patterns can be obtained from only four hex codes.

### Rendering Matrix for the CGA and PCjr

Dithering algorithms for the Color/Graphics Adapter and the PCjr video subsystem are shown in Fig. 16-5. Because of the different shading codes used on these adapters, seven different dithering hex codes are used: 12.5%, 25%, 37.5%, 50%, 62.5%, 75%, and 87.5% (in addition to solid colors). Again, by simply swapping line colors the full range of dithering patterns is secured.

179

| | | A$ Tiling Pattern | C4 Preparatory Silhouette | C5 Dither Color | C6 Dither Pattern | |
|---|---|---|---|---|---|---|
| DARK BLUE | Color 1 | | 1 | 1 | &HFFFF | Solid |
| | A1 | A1$ | 1 | 1 | &H0808 | 12.5% |
| | A2 | A2$ | 1 | 2 | &H4444 | 25% |
| MEDIUM BLUE | Color 2 | | 2 | 2 | &HFFFF | Solid |
| | A5 | A5$ | 2 | 3 | &H0808 | 12.5% |
| | A6 | A6$ | 2 | 3 | &H4444 | 25% |
| | A7 | A7$ | 2 | 3 | &HAAAA | 50% |
| | A8 | A8$ | 3 | 2 | &H4444 | 75% |
| LIGHT BLUE | Color 3 | | 3 | 3 | &HFFFF | Solid |
| | A10 | A10$ | 3 | 4 | &H4444 | 25% |
| | A11 | A11$ | 3 | 4 | &HAAAA | 50% |
| | A12 | A12$ | 4 | 3 | &H4444 | 75% |
| LIGHTER BLUE | Color 4 | | 4 | 4 | &HFFFF | Solid |
| | A13 | A13$ | 4 | 5 | &H0808 | 12.5% |
| | A14 | A14$ | 4 | 5 | &H4444 | 25% |
| | A15 | A15$ | 4 | 5 | &HAAAA | 50% |
| | A16 | A16$ | 5 | 4 | &H4444 | 75% |
| WHITE | Color 5 | | 5 | 5 | &HFFFF | Solid |

```
CHR$(&HFF)+CHR$(&H00)+CHR$(&H00)+CHR$(&H00) = color 1
CHR$(&H00)+CHR$(&HFF)+CHR$(&H00)+CHR$(&H00) = color 2
CHR$(&HFF)+CHR$(&HFF)+CHR$(&H00)+CHR$(&H00) = color 3
CHR$(&H00)+CHR$(&H00)+CHR$(&HFF)+CHR$(&H00) = color 4
CHR$(&HFF)+CHR$(&H00)+CHR$(&HFF)+CHR$(&H00) = color 5
```

Fig. 16-4. Shading matrix for the EGA.

| | A$ Tiling Pattern | C4 Preparatory Silhouette | C5 Dither Color | C6 Dither Pattern | |
|---|---|---|---|---|---|
| Color 0 | &H0 | 0 | 0 | &HFFFF | Solid |
| A1 | A1$ | 0 | 1 | &H0808 | 12.5% |
| A2 | A2$ | 0 | 1 | &H4444 | 25% |
| A3 | A3$ | 0 | 1 | &H4924 | 37.5% |
| A4 | A4$ | 0 | 1 | &HAAAA | 50% |
| A5 | A5$ | 1 | 0 | &H4924 | 62.5% |
| A6 | A6$ | 1 | 0 | &H4444 | 75% |
| A7 | A7$ | 1 | 0 | &H0808 | 87.5% |
| Color 1 | &H55 | 1 | 1 | &HFFFF | Solid |
| A9 | A9$ | 1 | 3 | &H0808 | 12.5% |
| A10 | A10$ | 1 | 3 | &H4444 | 25% |
| A12 | A12$ | 1 | 3 | &H4924 | 37.5% |
| A13 | A13$ | 1 | 3 | &HAAAA | 50% |
| A14 | A14$ | 3 | 1 | &H4924 | 62.5% |
| A15 | A15$ | 3 | 1 | &H4444 | 75% |
| A16 | A16$ | 3 | 1 | &H0808 | 87.5% |
| Color 3 | &HFF | 3 | 3 | &HFFFF | Solid |

Fig. 16-5. Shading matrix for the Color/Graphics Adapter.

## Compatibility of Rendering Schemes

Four screen modes are supported by the programs in this book: the EGA 640x350 16-color mode, the EGA 640×200 16-color mode, the Color/Graphics Adapter 320×200 4-color mode, and the PCjr/Tandy 640×200 4-color mode. Although the specific codes used for each mode are different, the generic video which is produced is essentially similar in its visual effect. Refer to Fig. 16-6.

Eighteen shades are available in the 640×350 16-color mode. Sixteen shades are produced in the 640×200 16-color mode. Seventeen shades are available for both the 320×200 4-color mode and the 640×200 4-color mode.

By referring to Fig. 16-6, you can discern that variable A4$ on the PCjr or Color/Graphics Adapter is equal to variable A4$ on the 640×200 EGA mode and A6$ on the 640×350 EGA mode. Accordingly, three sets of shading matrices will be required in any rendering program which is designed to run on all hardware/software configuations.

## COMPUTER-SHADED CUBE

Figure 16-7 shows the screen output produced by the demonstration program in Fig. 16-8. To run this program from the companion diskette, type **LOAD "A-23.BAS",R**. As you watch the program run, you will note a pause of a few seconds before each cube is drawn on the screen. Remember that your computer is precalculating all the various VIEW COORDINATES, DISPLAY COORDINATES, and area fill coordinates before actual drawing begins.

The program generates six different views of a solid 3D cube. Each cube is automatically shaded by the computer according to its position relative to the light source.

The master routine, located at lines 180 through 260, controls the viewing angles for each of the six cubes. To rotate the cube in the upper right corner of the display screen, for example, you need only modify the R1, R2, and R3 variables by changing line 210. (Hint: all the rotation variables were initialized by line 1210.)

The demonstration program constructs the shapes of the cubes by the techniques discussed in the modeling section of the book. You may wish to refer to Fig. 8-7 and Fig. 8-8 in Chapter 8 to review the methodology.

Note line 1250, which identifies the location of the light source, somewhat to the right of your viewing position. If you square each variable in line 1250 and then add them together, you will see they produce a total of one. The location of the light source is defined by a vector composed of three values along the x-axis, y-axis, and z-axis. The unit vector which represents

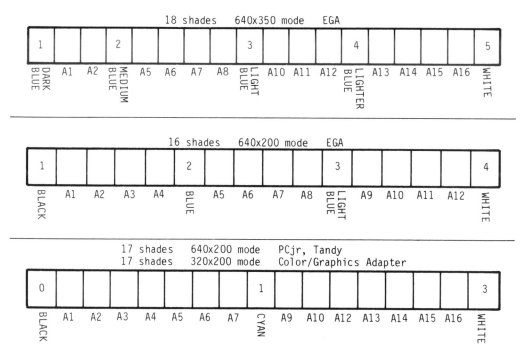

Fig. 16-6. Schematic overview of compatibility issues between different graphics adapters and screen modes for computer-controlled shading.

Fig. 16-7. The display image produced by the demonstration program in Fig. 16-8.

182

Fig. 16-8. Computer-shaded 3D cube.

```
100 'Program A-23.BAS    Six simultaneous views of computer-
shaded cube.
110 'Demonstrates multiple simultaneous viewpoints for same
3D model.
120 '_____
130 '
140   GOTO 840    'configure system
150   GOSUB 1210   'assign variables
160 '_____
170 '
180 'master routine:   simultaneous views of cube
190   R1=4.46141:VIEW (W1,W7)-(W2,W8):GOSUB 2700:GOSUB 300
200   R1=3.76325:R3=6.00009:VIEW (W3,W7)-(W4,W8):GOSUB 2700:G
OSUB 300
210   R1=4.16325:R3=.48319:VIEW (W5,W7)-(W6,W8):GOSUB 2700:GO
SUB 300
220   R1=3.40009:R3=5.89778:VIEW (W1,W9)-(W2,W10):GOSUB 2700:
GOSUB 300
230   R1=3.34159:R3=5.49778:VIEW (W3,W9)-(W4,W10):GOSUB 2700:
GOSUB 300
240   R1=5.29239:R3=5.59778:VIEW (W5,W9)-(W6,W10):GOSUB 2700:
GOSUB 300
250   GOTO 250   'clean halt
260   END 'of main routine
270 '_____
280 '
290 'module:   calculate and store vertex coordinates
300   RESTORE 1310  'beginning of database
310   FOR T=0 TO 7 STEP 1:READ X,Y,Z:GOSUB 750:B1(T,0)=X:B1(T
,1)=Y:B1(T,2)=Z:B2(T,0)=SX:B2(T,1)=SY:NEXT T 'load vertex v
iew coordinates into array B1, load vertex display coordinat
es into array B2
320   FOR T=0 TO 5 STEP 1:READ X,Y,Z:GOSUB 750:B3(T,0)=SX:B3(
T,1)=SY:NEXT T 'load area fill origin display coordinates i
nto array B3
330 '_____
340 '
350 'module:   draw 6 surfaces of cube
360 'surface 0 routine
370   X1=B1(7,0):Y1=B1(7,1):Z1=B1(7,2):X2=B1(0,0):Y2=B1(0,1):
Z2=B1(0,2):X3=B1(3,0):Y3=B1(3,1):Z3=B1(3,2):GOSUB 1390:IF SP
>0 THEN 430 'retrieve view coordinates, jump to plane equat
ion routine, test if surface hidden
380   SX1=B2(7,0):SY1=B2(7,1):SX2=B2(0,0):SY2=B2(0,1):SX3=B2(
3,0):SY3=B2(3,1):SX4=B2(6,0):SY4=B2(6,1):SX5=B3(0,0):SY5=B3(
```

```
0,1):GOSUB 1650    'assign display coordinates and jump to sol
id surface modeling routine
390   GOSUB 1430:PAINT (SX5,SY5),A$,C3:GOSUB 1600   'jump to c
omputer-controlled shading routine, apply halftoning area fi
ll, jump to computer-controlled dithering routine
400 '_____
410 '
420 'surface 1 routine
430   X1=B1(6,0):Y1=B1(6,1):Z1=B1(6,2):X2=B1(5,0):Y2=B1(5,1):
Z2=B1(5,2):X3=B1(4,0):Y3=B1(4,1):Z3=B1(4,2):GOSUB 1390:IF SP
>0 THEN 490
440   SX1=B2(6,0):SY1=B2(6,1):SX2=B2(5,0):SY2=B2(5,1):SX3=B2(
4,0):SY3=B2(4,1):SX4=B2(7,0):SY4=B2(7,1):SX5=B3(1,0):SY5=B3(
1,1):GOSUB 1650
450   GOSUB 1430:PAINT (SX5,SY5),A$,C3:GOSUB 1600
460 '_____
470 '
480 'surface 2 routine
490   X1=B1(3,0):Y1=B1(3,1):Z1=B1(3,2):X2=B1(2,0):Y2=B1(2,1):
Z2=B1(2,2):X3=B1(5,0):Y3=B1(5,1):Z3=B1(5,2):GOSUB 1390:IF SP
>0 THEN 550
500   SX1=B2(3,0):SY1=B2(3,1):SX2=B2(2,0):SY2=B2(2,1):SX3=B2(
5,0):SY3=B2(5,1):SX4=B2(6,0):SY4=B2(6,1):SX5=B3(2,0):SY5=B3(
2,1):GOSUB 1650
510   GOSUB 1430:PAINT (SX5,SY5),A$,C3:GOSUB 1600
520 '_____
530 '
540 'surface 3 routine
550   X1=B1(0,0):Y1=B1(0,1):Z1=B1(0,2):X2=B1(1,0):Y2=B1(1,1):
Z2=B1(1,2):X3=B1(2,0):Y3=B1(2,1):Z3=B1(2,2):GOSUB 1390:IF SP
>0 THEN 610
560   SX1=B2(0,0):SY1=B2(0,1):SX2=B2(1,0):SY2=B2(1,1):SX3=B2(
2,0):SY3=B2(2,1):SX4=B2(3,0):SY4=B2(3,1):SX5=B3(3,0):SY5=B3(
3,1):GOSUB 1650
570   GOSUB 1430:PAINT (SX5,SY5),A$,C3:GOSUB 1600
580 '_____
590 '
600 'surface 4 routine
610   X1=B1(7,0):Y1=B1(7,1):Z1=B1(7,2):X2=B1(4,0):Y2=B1(4,1):
Z2=B1(4,2):X3=B1(1,0):Y3=B1(1,1):Z3=B1(1,2):GOSUB 1390:IF SP
>0 THEN 670
620   SX1=B2(7,0):SY1=B2(7,1):SX2=B2(4,0):SY2=B2(4,1):SX3=B2(
1,0):SY3=B2(1,1):SX4=B2(0,0):SY4=B2(0,1):SX5=B3(4,0):SY5=B3(
4,1):GOSUB 1650
630   GOSUB 1430:PAINT (SX5,SY5),A$,C3:GOSUB 1600
640 '_____
650 '
660 'surface 5 routine
670   X1=B1(1,0):Y1=B1(1,1):Z1=B1(1,2):X2=B1(4,0):Y2=B1(4,1):
```

```
    Z2=B1(4,2):X3=B1(5,0):Y3=B1(5,1):Z3=B1(5,2):GOSUB 1390:IF SP
    >0 THEN 700
680   SX1=B2(1,0):SY1=B2(1,1):SX2=B2(4,0):SY2=B2(4,1):SX3=B2(
    5,0):SY3=B2(5,1):SX4=B2(2,0):SY4=B2(2,1):SX5=B3(5,0):SY5=B3(
    5,1):GOSUB 1650
690   GOSUB 1430:PAINT (SX5,SY5),A$,C3:GOSUB 1600
700   SOUND 550,.7  'model is complete
710   RETURN
720 '_____
730 '
740 'module:   perspective calculations for Cartesian world c
    oordinates
750   X=(-1)*X:XA=CR1*X-SR1*Z:ZA=SR1*X+CR1*Z:X=CR2*XA+SR2*Y:Y
    A=CR2*Y-SR2*XA:Z=CR3*ZA-SR3*YA:Y=SR3*ZA+CR3*YA:X=X+MX:Y=Y+MY
    :Z=Z+MZ:SX=D*X/Z:SY=D*Y/Z:RETURN
760 '_____
770 '
780 'module:   return to BASIC interpreter
790   CLS:WINDOW:SCREEN 0,0,0,0:WIDTH 80:COLOR 7,0,0:CLS:LOCA
    TE 1,1,1:END
800 '_____
810 '
820 'module:   UNIVERSAL
830 'This routine configures the program for the hardware/so
    ftware being used.
840   KEY OFF:CLS:ON ERROR GOTO 920  'trap if not Enhanced Di
    splay + EG
850   SCREEN 9,,0,0:COLOR 7,0:PALETTE 1,8:PALETTE 2,1:PALETTE
     3,9:PALETTE 4,11:PALETTE 5,7:PALETTE 6,37:PALETTE 7,7:PALET
    TE 8,56:PALETTE 9,34:PALETTE 10,20:PALETTE 11,5:PALETTE 12,4
    4:PALETTE 13,46:PALETTE 14,55:PALETTE 15,63
860   C0=0:C1=12:C2=9:C3=7:LOCATE 1,1:PRINT "ED-EGA 640x350 1
    6-color mode"
870   V6=15  'illumination range 0 to 15
880   GOSUB 1690  'assign bit tiling codes for EGA
890   DEFINT G:G=1  'set flag for ED-EGA
900   GOSUB 2740  'set viewports for 640x350 mode
910   GOTO 1140  'jump to screen coordinates set-up
920   RESUME 930
930   ON ERROR GOTO 1000  'trap if not Color Display + EGA
940   SCREEN 8,,0,0:COLOR 7,0:PALETTE 1,0:PALETTE 2,1:PALETTE
     3,9:PALETTE 4,7:PALETTE 8,4:PALETTE 9,2:C0=0:C1=8:C2=9:C3=7
    :LOCATE 1,1:PRINT "CD-EGA 640x200 16-color mode"
950   V6=14  'illumination range 0 to 14
960   GOSUB 1690  'assign shading codes for EGA
970   DEFINT G:G=2  'set flag for CD-EGA
980   GOSUB 2750  'set viewports for 640x200 mode
990   GOTO 1140  'jump to screen coordinates set-up
```

```
1000   RESUME 1010
1010   ON ERROR GOTO 1080  'trap if not PCjr
1020   CLEAR,,,32768!:SCREEN 6,0,0,0:COLOR 3,0:PALETTE 1,8:PA
LETTE 3,7:C0=0:C1=1:C2=2:C3=3:LOCATE 1,1:PRINT "PCjr 640x200
 4-color mode"
1030   V6=14  'illumination range 0 to 14
1040   GOSUB 1890  'assign shading codes for PCjr
1050   DEFINT G:G=3  'set flag for CD-JR
1060   GOSUB 2750  'set viewports for PCjr 640x200 mode
1070   GOTO 1140  'jump to screen coordinates set-up
1080   RESUME 1090
1090   SCREEN 1,0:COLOR 0,1:C0=0:C1=1:C2=2:C3=3:LOCATE 1,1:PR
INT "CGA 320x200 4-color mode"
1100   V6=14  'illumination range 0 to 14
1110   GOSUB 1890  'assign shading codes for CGA
1120   DEFINT G:G=4  'set flag for CD-CGA
1130   GOSUB 2760  'set viewports for CGA 320x200 mode
1140   ON ERROR GOTO 0  'disable error trapping override
1150   WINDOW SCREEN (-399,-299)-(400,300)
1160   ON KEY (2) GOSUB 790:KEY (2) ON  'F2 key to exit progr
am
1170   GOTO 150  'return to main program
1180   '_____
1190   '
1200   'module:  assign variables
1210   D=1200:R1=5.18319:R2=0:R3=5.79778:MX=0:MY=0:MZ=-270  '
3D parameters
1220   DIM B1 (7,2)  '8 sets of XYZ view coordinates
1230   DIM B2 (7,1)  '8 sets of SX,SY display coordinates
1240   DIM B3 (5,1)  '6 sets of SX,SY fill coordinates
1250   XL=.57735:YL=.57735:ZL=.57735  'xyz components of unit
 vector for angle of incidence used in illumination algorith
m
1260   SR1=SIN(R1):CR1=COS(R1):SR2=SIN(R2):CR2=COS(R2):SR3=SI
N(R3):CR3=COS(R3)
1270   RETURN
1280   '_____
1290   '
1300   'module:  8 sets of XYZ world coordinates for vertices
1310   DATA  30,-30,30,  30,30,30,  -30,30,30,  -30,-30,30,
30,30,-30,  -30,30,-30,  -30,-30,-30,  30,-30,-30
1320   '_____
1330   '
1340   'module:  6 sets of XYZ world coordinates for area fill

1350   DATA  0,-30,0,  0,0,-30,  -30,0,0,  0,0,30,  30,0,0,
0,30,0
1360   '_____
1370   '
```

```
1380 'module:   plane equation method of hidden surface remov
al
1390   SP1=X1*(Y2*Z3-Y3*Z2):SP1=(-1)*SP1:SP2=X2*(Y3*Z1-Y1*Z3)
:SP3=X3*(Y1*Z2-Y2*Z1):SP=SP1-SP2-SP3:RETURN
1400 '_____
1410 '
1420 'module:   computer-controlled shading routine
1430   XU=X2-X1:YU=Y2-Y1:ZU=Z2-Z1   'calculate vector from ver
tex 1 to vertex 2
1440   XV=X3-X1:YV=Y3-Y1:ZV=Z3-Z1   'calculate vector from ver
tex 1 to vertex 3
1450   XN=(YU*ZV)-(ZU*YV):YN=(ZU*XV)-(XU*ZV):ZN=(XU*YV)-(YU*X
V)  'calculate surface perpendicular vector
1460   YN=YN*(-1):ZN=ZN*(-1)   'convert vector to cartesian sy
stem
1470 'sub-module:   convert surface perpendicular vector to u
nit vector
1480   V1=(XN*XN)+(YN*YN)+(ZN*ZN):V2=SQR(V1)   'magnitude of s
urface perpendicular vector
1490   V3=1/V2  'ratio of magnitude to unit vector magnitude
1500   XW=V3*XN:YW=V3*YN:ZW=V3*ZN  'XYZ components of surface
 perpendicular unit vector
1510 'sub-module:   calculate illumination factor for surface
 when angle of incidence is 45 degrees elevation and 135 deg
rees yaw
1520   V4=(XW*XL)+(YW*YL)+(ZW*ZL)   'illumination factor 0 to
1
1530   V4=V4*V6:V4=CINT(V4)  'set illumination range
1540   V5=V4+1  'illumination factor from base 1
1550   ON G GOSUB 2070, 2280, 2490, 2490  'jump to device-dep
endent shading routine
1560   RETURN
1570 '_____
1580 '
1590 'module:   computer-controlled dithering routine
1600   LINE (SX1,SY1)-(SX2,SY2),C4:LINE (SX1,SY1)-(SX2,SY2),C
5,,C6:LINE (SX2,SY2)-(SX3,SY3),C4:LINE (SX2,SY2)-(SX3,SY3),C
5,,C6:LINE (SX3,SY3)-(SX4,SY4),C4:LINE (SX3,SY3)-(SX4,SY4),C
5,,C6
1610   LINE (SX4,SY4)-(SX1,SY1),C4:LINE (SX4,SY4)-(SX1,SY1),C
5,,C6:RETURN
1620 '_____
1630 '
1640 'module:   solid surface modeling of 4-sided polygon
1650   LINE (SX1,SY1)-(SX2,SY2),C2:LINE-(SX3,SY3),C2:LINE-(SX
4,SY4),C2:LINE-(SX1,SY1),C2:PAINT (SX5,SY5),C2,C2:LINE (SX1,
SY1)-(SX2,SY2),C3:LINE-(SX3,SY3),C3:LINE-(SX4,SY4),C3:LINE-(
SX1,SY1),C3:PAINT (SX5,SY5),C0,C3:RETURN
1660 '_____
```

```
1670 '
1680 'module:  assign shading codes for EGA
1690    A1$=CHR$(&HDF)+CHR$(&H20)+CHR$(&HO)+CHR$(&HO)+CHR$(&HF
D)+CHR$(&H2)+CHR$(&HO)+CHR$(&HO)+CHR$(&H7F)+CHR$(&H80)+CHR$(
&HO)+CHR$(&HO)+CHR$(&HF7)+CHR$(&H8)+CHR$(&HO)+CHR$(&HO)
1700    A2$=CHR$(&HBB)+CHR$(&H44)+CHR$(&HO)+CHR$(&HO)+CHR$(&HE
E)+CHR$(&H11)+CHR$(&HO)+CHR$(&HO)
1710    A3$=CHR$(&HAA)+CHR$(&H55)+CHR$(&HO)+CHR$(&HO)+CHR$(&H5
5)+CHR$(&HAA)+CHR$(&HO)+CHR$(&HO)
1720    A4$=CHR$(&H44)+CHR$(&HBB)+CHR$(&HO)+CHR$(&HO)+CHR$(&H1
1)+CHR$(&HEE)+CHR$(&HO)+CHR$(&HO)
1730    A5$=CHR$(&H20)+CHR$(&HFF)+CHR$(&HO)+CHR$(&HO)+CHR$(&H2
)+CHR$(&HFF)+CHR$(&HO)+CHR$(&HO)+CHR$(&H80)+CHR$(&HFF)+CHR$(
&HO)+CHR$(&HO)+CHR$(&H8)+CHR$(&HFF)+CHR$(&HO)+CHR$(&HO)
1740    A6$=CHR$(&H44)+CHR$(&HFF)+CHR$(&HO)+CHR$(&HO)+CHR$(&H1
1)+CHR$(&HFF)+CHR$(&HO)+CHR$(&HO)
1750    A7$=CHR$(&H55)+CHR$(&HFF)+CHR$(&HO)+CHR$(&HO)+CHR$(&HA
A)+CHR$(&HFF)+CHR$(&HO)+CHR$(&HO)
1760    A8$=CHR$(&HBB)+CHR$(&HFF)+CHR$(&HO)+CHR$(&HO)+CHR$(&HE
E)+CHR$(&HFF)+CHR$(&HO)+CHR$(&HO)
1770    A9$=CHR$(&HDF)+CHR$(&HDF)+CHR$(&H20)+CHR$(&HO)+CHR$(&H
FD)+CHR$(&HFD)+CHR$(&H2)+CHR$(&HO)+CHR$(&H7F)+CHR$(&H7F)+CHR
$(&H80)+CHR$(&HO)+CHR$(&HF7)+CHR$(&HF7)+CHR$(&H8)+CHR$(&HO)
1780    A10$=CHR$(&HBB)+CHR$(&HBB)+CHR$(&H44)+CHR$(&HO)+CHR$(&
HEE)+CHR$(&HEE)+CHR$(&H11)+CHR$(&HO)
1790    A11$=CHR$(&HAA)+CHR$(&HAA)+CHR$(&H55)+CHR$(&HO)+CHR$(&
H55)+CHR$(&H55)+CHR$(&HAA)+CHR$(&HO)
1800    A12$=CHR$(&H44)+CHR$(&H44)+CHR$(&HBB)+CHR$(&HO)+CHR$(&
H11)+CHR$(&H11)+CHR$(&HEE)+CHR$(&HO)
1810    A13$=CHR$(&H20)+CHR$(&HO)+CHR$(&HFF)+CHR$(&HO)+CHR$(&H
2)+CHR$(&HO)+CHR$(&HFF)+CHR$(&HO)+CHR$(&H80)+CHR$(&HO)+CHR$(
&HFF)+CHR$(&HO)+CHR$(&H8)+CHR$(&HO)+CHR$(&HFF)+CHR$(&HO)
1820    A14$=CHR$(&H44)+CHR$(&HO)+CHR$(&HFF)+CHR$(&HO)+CHR$(&H
11)+CHR$(&HO)+CHR$(&HFF)+CHR$(&HO)
1830    A15$=CHR$(&H55)+CHR$(&HO)+CHR$(&HFF)+CHR$(&HO)+CHR$(&H
AA)+CHR$(&HO)+CHR$(&HFF)+CHR$(&HO)
1840    A16$=CHR$(&HBB)+CHR$(&HO)+CHR$(&HFF)+CHR$(&HO)+CHR$(&H
EE)+CHR$(&HO)+CHR$(&HFF)+CHR$(&HO)
1850    RETURN
1860 '_____
1870 '
1880 'module:  assign shading codes for CGA and/or PC.jr
1890    A1$=CHR$(&H40)+CHR$(&HO)+CHR$(&H4)+CHR$(&HO)
1900    A2$=CHR$(&H40)+CHR$(&H4)+CHR$(&H40)+CHR$(&H4)
1910    A3$=CHR$(&H44)+CHR$(&H10)+CHR$(&H11)+CHR$(&H1)+CHR$(&H
44)+CHR$(&H4)+CHR$(&H11)+CHR$(&H40)
1920    A4$=CHR$(&H44)+CHR$(&H11)+CHR$(&H44)+CHR$(&H11)
1930    A5$=CHR$(&H11)+CHR$(&H45)+CHR$(&H44)+CHR$(&H54)+CHR$(&
H11)+CHR$(&H51)+CHR$(&H44)+CHR$(&H15)
```

188

```
1940    A6$=CHR$(&H15)+CHR$(&H51)+CHR$(&H15)+CHR$(&H51)
1950    A7$=CHR$(&H15)+CHR$(&H55)+CHR$(&H51)+CHR$(&H55)
1960    A9$=CHR$(&HD5)+CHR$(&H55)+CHR$(&H5D)+CHR$(&H55)
1970    A10$=CHR$(&HD5)+CHR$(&H5D)+CHR$(&HD5)+CHR$(&H5D)
1980    A12$=CHR$(&HDD)+CHR$(&H75)+CHR$(&H77)+CHR$(&H57)+CHR$(
&HDD)+CHR$(&H5D)+CHR$(&H77)+CHR$(&HD5)
1990    A13$=CHR$(&HDD)+CHR$(&H77)+CHR$(&HDD)+CHR$(&H77)
2000    A14$=CHR$(&H77)+CHR$(&HDF)+CHR$(&HDD)+CHR$(&HFD)+CHR$(
&H77)+CHR$(&HF7)+CHR$(&HDD)+CHR$(&H7F)
2010    A15$=CHR$(&H7F)+CHR$(&HF7)+CHR$(&H7F)+CHR$(&HF7)
2020    A16$=CHR$(&H7F)+CHR$(&HFF)+CHR$(&HF7)+CHR$(&HFF)
2030    RETURN
2040    '_____
2050    '
2060    'shading routine for ED-EGA 640x350 mode
2070    IF V5<1 THEN GOTO 2090  'if light source is behind sur
face
2080    ON V5 GOTO 2090, 2100, 2110, 2120, 2130, 2140, 2150, 2
160, 2170, 2180, 2190, 2200, 2210, 2220, 2230, 2240
2090    A$=CHR$(&HFF)+CHR$(&HO)+CHR$(&HO)+CHR$(&HO):C4=1:C5=1:
C6=&HFFFF:RETURN
2100    A$=A1$:C4=1:C5=2:C6=&H808:RETURN
2110    A$=A2$:C4=1:C5=2:C6=&H4444:RETURN
2120    A$=CHR$(&HO)+CHR$(&HFF)+CHR$(&HO)+CHR$(&HO):C4=2:C5=2:
C6=&HFFFF:RETURN
2130    A$=A5$:C4=2:C5=3:C6=&H808:RETURN
2140    A$=A6$:C4=2:C5=3:C6=&H4444:RETURN
2150    A$=A7$:C4=2:C5=3:C6=&HAAAA:RETURN
2160    A$=A8$:C4=3:C5=2:C6=&H4444:RETURN
2170    A$=CHR$(&HFF)+CHR$(&HFF)+CHR$(&HO)+CHR$(&HO):C4=3:C5=3
:C6=&HFFFF:RETURN
2180    A$=A10$:C4=3:C5=4:C6=&H4444:RETURN
2190    A$=A11$:C4=3:C5=4:C6=&HAAAA:RETURN
2200    A$=A12$:C4=4:C5=3:C6=&H4444:RETURN
2210    A$=CHR$(&HO)+CHR$(&HO)+CHR$(&HFF)+CHR$(&HO):C4=4:C5=4:
C6=&HFFFF:RETURN
2220    A$=A13$:C4=4:C5=5:C6=&H808:RETURN
2230    A$=A14$:C4=4:C5=5:C6=&H4444:RETURN
2240    A$=A15$:C4=4:C5=5:C6=&HAAAA:RETURN
2250    '_____
2260    '
2270    'shading routine for CD-EGA 640x200 mode
2280    IF V5<1 THEN GOTO 2310  'if light source is behind sur
face
2290    ON V5 GOTO 2310, 2320, 2330, 2340, 2350, 2360, 2370, 2
380, 2390, 2400, 2410, 2420, 2430, 2440, 2450
2300    A$=CHR$(&HFF)+CHR$(&HO)+CHR$(&HO)+CHR$(&HO):C4=1:C5=1:
C6=&HFFFF:RETURN  'solid black is unused
2310    A$=A1$:C4=1:C5=2:C6=&H808:RETURN
```

```
2320    A$=A2$:C4=1:C5=2:C6=&H4444:RETURN
2330    A$=A3$:C4=1:C5=2:C6=&HAAAA:RETURN
2340    A$=A4$:C4=2:C5=1:C6=&H4444:RETURN
2350    A$=CHR$(&HO)+CHR$(&HFF)+CHR$(&HO)+CHR$(&HO):C4=2:C5=2:
C6=&HFFFF:RETURN
2360    A$=A5$:C4=2:C5=3:C6=&H808:RETURN
2370    A$=A6$:C4=2:C5=3:C6=&H4444:RETURN
2380    A$=A7$:C4=2:C5=3:C6=&HAAAA:RETURN
2390    A$=A8$:C4=3:C5=2:C6=&H4444:RETURN
2400    A$=CHR$(&HFF)+CHR$(&HFF)+CHR$(&HO)+CHR$(&HO):C4=3:C5=3
:C6=&HFFFF:RETURN
2410    A$=A9$:C4=3:C5=4:C6=&H8080:RETURN
2420    A$=A10$:C4=3:C5=4:C6=&H4444:RETURN
2430    A$=A11$:C4=3:C5=4:C6=&HAAAA:RETURN
2440    A$=A12$:C4=4:C5=3:C6=&H4444:RETURN
2450    A$=CHR$(&HO)+CHR$(&HO)+CHR$(&HFF)+CHR$(&HO):C4=4:C5=4:
C6=&HFFFF:RETURN
2460 '_____
2470 '
2480 'shading routine for CD-CGA 320x200 mode and CD-JR 640x
200 mode
2490    IF V5<1 THEN GOTO 2520  'if light source is behind sur
face
2500    ON V5 GOTO 2520, 2530, 2540, 2550, 2560, 2570, 2580, 2
590, 2600, 2610, 2620, 2630, 2640, 2650, 2660
2510    A$=CHR$(&HO):C4=0:C5=0:C6=&HFFFF:RETURN   'solid black
-- unused
2520    A$=A1$:C4=0:C5=1:C6=&H2108:RETURN
2530    A$=A2$:C4=0:C5=1:C6=&H4444:RETURN
2540    A$=A4$:C4=0:C5=1:C6=&HAAAA:RETURN
2550    A$=A5$:C4=1:C5=0:C6=&H4924:RETURN
2560    A$=A6$:C4=1:C5=0:C6=&H4444:RETURN
2570    A$=A7$:C4=1:C5=0:C6=&H808:RETURN
2580    A$=CHR$(&H55):C4=1:C5=1:C6=&HFFFF:RETURN
2590    A$=A9$:C4=1:C5=3:C6=&H808:RETURN
2600    A$=A10$:C4=1:C5=3:C6=&H4444:RETURN
2610    A$=A12$:C4=1:C5=3:C6=&H4924:RETURN
2620    A$=A13$:C4=1:C5=3:C6=&HAAAA:RETURN
2630    A$=A14$:C4=3:C5=1:C6=&H4924:RETURN
2640    A$=A15$:C4=3:C5=1:C6=&H4444:RETURN
2650    A$=A16$:C4=3:C5=1:C6=&H808:RETURN
2660    A$=CHR$(&HFF):C4=3:C5=3:C6=&HFFFF:RETURN
2670 '_____
2680 '
2690 'module:  re-assign sine and cosine rotation matrices
2700    SR1=SIN(R1):CR1=COS(R1):SR2=SIN(R2):CR2=COS(R2):SR3=SI
N(R3):CR3=COS(R3):RETURN
2710 '_____
```

```
2720 '
2730 'module:  viewport parameters for 640x350, 640x200, 320
x200
2740    W1=1:W2=319:W3=152:W4=470:W5=320:W6=639:W7=1:W8=174:W9
=175:W10=349:RETURN
2750    W1=1:W2=319:W3=152:W4=470:W5=320:W6=639:W7=1:W8=99:W9=
100:W10=199:RETURN
2760    W1=1:W2=159:W3=76:W4=235:W5=160:W6=319:W7=1:W8=99:W9=1
00:W10=199:RETURN
2770 '_____
2780 '
2790    END 'of program code
```

the relationship of the light source to the 3D coordinate system is essentially the hypotenuse of a 3D triangle. Just as in 2D, where the square of the hypotenuse equals the sum of the squares of the other two sides, in 3D the square of the hypotenuse equals the sum of the squares of the other THREE sides. Appendix B provides details on how to move the light source to other locations. When you move the light source, your computer will shade the models according to the newly-defined source.

The source code which actually decides the dimness or brightness of a particular surface begins at line 1420. This section of code will be used in all demonstration programs in which the computer automatically shades a model.

## ANALYSIS OF THE SHADING ROUTINE

First, the surface perpendicular for the polygon is computed. (Read Appendix B for a full mathematical analysis.)

Line 1430 calculates the vector between the first two corners (vertices) of the surface. Simple subtraction in each of the three axis planes is sufficient to acquire this vector. Line 1440 calculates the vector between the second and third corners of the surface. Finally, line 1450 uses vector math to calculate the raw vector of the surface perpendicular. Simple multiplication by −1 in line 1460 adapts the vector to the +/− layout of the 3D cartesian coordinate system used throughout this book.

Next, the surface perpendicular vector is converted to a unit vector. Remember line 1250, which defined the location of the light source as a unit vector (length one unit). Both vectors must be unit vectors in order for any comparison to be meaningful to the microcomputer.

Line 1480 first calculates the length of the surface perpendicular vector by using the hypotenuse method described earlier in this chapter. Line 1490 calculates the ratio of this length as compared to the length of a unit vector. Line 1500 uses this ratio to modify the three components of the vector.

Next, the brightness of the surface is calculated. Remember, the cosine function describes the value of the angle between the light rays and the surface perpendicular. (Refer to Fig. 16-2 earlier in this chapter.)

Line 1520 calculates this cosine value. If the value falls between 0 and 1 then the light source is having an effect on the surface. If the value is less than 0 then the light source is behind the surface and has no effect on its brightness or dimness.

Line 1530 adjusts this 0-to-1 range to the range of shades present on the software and graphics adapter which you are using. V6 is defined in the configuration module (lines 820 through 1170) to represent the number of shades which will be rendered on your equipment. Because the range was initially defined as starting from 0, line 1540 adjusts the new range to begin at 1 (called base 1 by IBM and Microsoft).

Line 1550 is the pivotal algorithm in the computer-controlled shading routine. Using BASIC's ON ...GOSUB statement, the program is sent to the appropriate shading routine. G has been defined as a flag which identifies the particular hardware/software configuration being used. If you check line 1120 in the configuration module, for example, you will see that G is set equal to 4 for the Color/Graphics Adapter mode. In line 1550 you can see that the 4th GOSUB sends the program to line 2490, which contains the shading routine for the Color/Graphics Adapter. The same concept is used for the two EGA modes and the PCjr/Tandy mode, of course.

The shading routine for the 640×350 16-color mode is located at line 2060. The routine for the 640×200 16-color mode is at line 2270. The shading routine for the 320×200 4-color mode and the 640×200 4-color mode is located at line 2480.

The algorithm used in the 320×200 4-color mode routine at line 2480 is identical in concept to the algorithms used in the other routines. Remember, V5 was defined as the shading range from 1 to 15 for the Color/Graphics Adapter.

Line 2490 checks to see if the light source is behind the surface. If so, it jumps to the dimmest shading line at 2520. Otherwise, line 2500 uses another ON...GOTO instruction to jump to the appropriate hex-defining line, based on the value of V5 (from 1 to 15). The matrix of values in lines 2520 through 2660 corresponds to the conceptual matrix in Fig. 16-5 earlier in this chapter.

When program control returns to the calling routine, the surface is painted with the appropriate A$ area fill bit tiling pattern. (Line 390 is a good example of this.) Then the program jumps to a subroutine at line 1600, which places the preparatory line and the dithering line on all four sides of the polygon, using the C4, C5, and C6 values assigned by the matrix in lines 2520 through 2660.

If you are typing the demonstration programs from the listings in the book, you may wish to use this program to build the other rendering demonstration programs. Many of the modeling and rendering modules are identical. Once you have typed in the various hex codes for halftone shading and line dithering, for example, there is no point typing them in again for another program. Simply use BASIC's MERGE instruction to insert the existing routines into the new program you are working on. When combined with BASIC's renumbering RENUM command, you will often end up with only 20 or so lines of code to type in future programs. If you are using the companion diskette, all the programs are already provided in a ready-to-run format, of course.

For a little experimentation, you can move the location of the light source by changing line 1250 to read as follows: XL = .5477225 : YL = .5477226 : ZL = .6324555. This moves the light source to a position more behind your right shoulder as you look at the models. (Refer to Appendix B for further details.) Note again that the sum of XL*XL + YL*YL + ZL*ZL equals 1. The sum of the squares of the three vectors equals the square of the hypotenuse (i.e., the length of the unit vector).

## COMPUTER-SHADED SPHERE

Figure 16-9 shows the screen output produced by the demonstration program in Fig. 16-10. This is the same polygon mesh sphere which was provided in Chapter 10, except that the computer-controlled shading routines have been appended to the program. To run this program from the companion diskette, type **LOAD "A-24.BAS",R.**

Note the solid surface modeling routine at lines 710 through 830. Line 830 contains the instructions to invoke the halftone shading routines. GOSUB 1550 sends the program to the module which calculates the various vector relationships and illumination levels. Then the polygon is painted by line 830. GOSUB 1720 invokes the generic line dithering routine. These two shading routines are identical to those used in the previous program, which generated a computer-shaded cube instead of a computer-shaded sphere.

Depending upon which graphics adapter and display monitor you are using, you will find it interesting to watch the computer drawing the northern polar region of the sphere. On a Color/Graphics Adapter, some of the small triangles which make up the polar area are simply too tiny to be filled by BASIC's area fill routine. On an EGA these paint failures are fewer in number, because of the finer screen resolution being supported by the EGA. (Hint: you can alleviate these idiosyncracies on your Color/Graphics Adapter by altering the MZ variable in line 1390 to move the sphere closer to your viewpoint, thereby making the polygons larger. BASIC will take care of any parts of the sphere which must be clipped at the edge of the screen. You may wish to adjust the variable MY too, in order to keep the polar region of the sphere near the center of your display screen.) This area fill phenomenon is an excellent example of the limitations imposed by your graphics adapter, display monitor, and version of BASIC.

As the program executes, two alphanumeric readouts in the upper left corner of the screen keep you informed of the surface being rendered and its SP visibility factor. When SP < 0 the polygon surface is visible. If SP > 0 the surface is hidden, of course. During an apparently inactive time near the completion of the program, your computer is actually checking the south polar region for visibility. This area is hidden, of course, so you cannot see any graphics happening on

Fig. 16-9. The display image produced by the demonstration program in Fig. 16-10.

Fig. 16-10. Computer-shaded 3D sphere.

```
100 'Program A-24.BAS    Computer-shaded sphere.
110 'Uses plane equation method of hidden surface removal.
Uses surface perpendicular method of shading.
120 '_____
130 '
140   GOTO 1060    'configure system
150   GOSUB 1390   'assign variables
160 '_____
170 '
180 'main routine:   calculate/store coordinates for belts ar
ound sphere
190 '_____
200 '
210 'step one:   north polar area
220   R5=0:R4=0:X=30:GOSUB 920:GOSUB 970:B11(0,0)=X:B11(0,1)=
Y:B11(0,2)=Z:B21(0,0)=SX:B21(0,1)=SY   'north pole
230   X=30:R5=.17453:R4=0:GOSUB 880
240   SOUND 350,.7:LOCATE 2,1:PRINT "Modeling solid surfaces"
:FOR Q1=0 TO 35 STEP 1:Q2=Q1+1:IF Q2>35 THEN Q2=0
```

```
250   LOCATE 3,1:PRINT Q1"   ":GOSUB 470:NEXT Q1:LOCATE 4,1:PR
INT "                "
260   '_____
270   '
280   'step two:  polygon surfaces along belts on sphere
290   R5=.17453:FOR T2=1 TO 16 STEP 1
300   X=30:R4=0:GOSUB 870:X=30:R5=R5+.17453:R4=0:GOSUB 880
310   SOUND 350,.7:LOCATE 2,1:PRINT "Modeling solid surfaces"
:FOR Q1=0 TO 35 STEP 1:Q2=Q1+1:IF Q2>35 THEN Q2=0   'draw bel
t
320   LOCATE 3,1:PRINT Q1" ":GOSUB 720:NEXT Q1   'draw belt
330   LOCATE 4,1:PRINT "                "
340   NEXT T2
350   '_____
360   '
370   'step three:  south polar area
380   R5=3.14159:R4=0:X=30:GOSUB 920:GOSUB 970:B11(0,0)=X:B11
(0,1)=Y:B11(0,2)=Z:B21(0,0)=SX:B21(0,1)=SY   'south pole
390   X=30:R5=2.96706:R4=0:GOSUB 880
400   SOUND 350,.7:LOCATE 2,1:PRINT "Modeling solid surfaces"
:FOR Q1=0 TO 35 STEP 1:Q2=Q1+1:IF Q2>35 THEN Q2=0
410   LOCATE 3,1:PRINT Q1"   ":GOSUB 580:NEXT Q1:LOCATE 4,1:PR
INT "                "
420   SOUND 550,10:LOCATE 2,1:PRINT "Program completed.      "
:LOCATE 3,1:PRINT "    "
430   GOTO 430
440   '_____
450   '
460   'module:  draw 3-sided polygon for polar areas
470   X1=B12(Q2,0):Y1=B12(Q2,1):Z1=B12(Q2,2)
480   X2=B12(Q1,0):Y2=B12(Q1,1):Z2=B12(Q1,2)
490   X3=B11(0,0):Y3=B11(0,1):Z3=B11(0,2)
500   GOSUB 1510:LOCATE 4,1:PRINT SP:IF SP>0 THEN RETURN
510   SX1=B22(Q2,0):SY1=B22(Q2,1)
520   SX2=B22(Q1,0):SY2=B22(Q1,1)
530   SX3=B21(0,0):SY3=B21(0,1):SX4=SX1:SY4=SY1
540   X4=X1+.5*(X2-X1):Y4=Y1+.5*(Y2-Y1):Z4=Z1+.5*(Z2-Z1):X=X3
+.6*(X4-X3):Y=Y3+.6*(Y4-Y3):Z=Z3+.6*(Z4-Z3)
550   SX5=D*X/Z:SY5=D*Y/Z
560   GOSUB 1770   'jump to solid surface modeling routine
570   GOSUB 1550:PAINT (SX5,SY5),A$,C3:GOSUB 1720:RETURN   'no
rth pole completed
580   X1=B12(Q1,0):Y1=B12(Q1,1):Z1=B12(Q1,2)
590   X2=B12(Q2,0):Y2=B12(Q2,1):Z2=B12(Q2,2)
600   X3=B11(0,0):Y3=B11(0,1):Z3=B11(0,2)
610   GOSUB 1510:LOCATE 4,1:PRINT SP:IF SP>0 THEN RETURN
620   SX1=B22(Q2,0):SY1=B22(Q2,1)
630   SX2=B22(Q1,0):SY2=B22(Q1,1)
```

```
640    SX3=B21(0,0):SY3=B21(0,1):SX4=SX1:SY4=SY1
650    X4=X1+.5*(X2-X1):Y4=Y1+.5*(Y2-Y1):Z4=Z1+.5*(Z2-Z1):X=X3
+.6*(X4-X3):Y=Y3+.6*(Y4-Y3):Z=Z3+.6*(Z4-Z3)
660    SX5=D*X/Z:SY5=D*Y/Z
670    GOSUB 1770
680    GOSUB 1550:PAINT (SX5,SY5),A$,C3:GOSUB 1720:RETURN    'so
uth pole completed
690    '_____
700    '
710    'module:   draw one 4-sided polygon surface on sphere
720    X1=B11(Q1,0):Y1=B11(Q1,1):Z1=B11(Q1,2)
730    X2=B11(Q2,0):Y2=B11(Q2,1):Z2=B11(Q2,2)
740    X3=B12(Q2,0):Y3=B12(Q2,1):Z3=B12(Q2,2)
750    GOSUB 1510:LOCATE 4,1:PRINT SP:IF SP>0 THEN RETURN    'te
st if hidden
760    SX1=B21(Q1,0):SY1=B21(Q1,1)
770    SX2=B21(Q2,0):SY2=B21(Q2,1)
780    SX3=B22(Q2,0):SY3=B22(Q2,1)
790    SX4=B22(Q1,0):SY4=B22(Q1,1)
800    X=X1+.5*(X3-X1):Y=Y1+.5*(Y3-Y1):Z=Z1+.5*(Z3-Z1)   'diago
nal midpoint of polygon's view coordinates
810    SX5=D*X/Z:SY5=D*Y/Z  'area fill coordinates
820    GOSUB 1770  'jump to solid surface modeling routine
830    GOSUB 1550:PAINT (SX5,SY5),A$,C3:GOSUB 1720:RETURN
840    '_____
850    '
860    'module:   calculate/store vertices for sweep 1, sweep 2
870    SOUND 350,.7:LOCATE 2,1:PRINT "Calculating sweep 1
 ":FOR T=0 TO 35 STEP 1:LOCATE 3,1:PRINT T" ":X=30:GOSUB 920
:GOSUB 970:B11(T,0)=X:B11(T,1)=Y:B11(T,2)=Z:B21(T,0)=SX:B21(
T,1)=SY:R4=R4+.17453:NEXT T:RETURN   'sweep 1 coordinates
880    SOUND 350,.7:LOCATE 2,1:PRINT "Calculating sweep 2
 ":FOR T=0 TO 35 STEP 1:LOCATE 3,1:PRINT T" ":X=30:GOSUB 920
:GOSUB 970:B12(T,0)=X:B12(T,1)=Y:B12(T,2)=Z:B22(T,0)=SX:B22(
T,1)=SY:R4=R4+.17453:NEXT T:RETURN   'sweep 2 coordinates
890    '_____
900    '
910    'module:   calculation of world coordinates for 3D sphere

920    SR4=SIN(R4):CR4=COS(R4):SR5=SIN(R5):CR5=COS(R5)
930    X1=SR5*X:Y=CR5*X:X=CR4*X1:Z=SR4*X1:RETURN
940    '_____
950    '
960    'module:   perspective calculations
970    X=(-1)*X:XA=CR1*X-SR1*Z:ZA=SR1*X+CR1*Z:X=CR2*XA+SR2*Y:Y
A=CR2*Y-SR2*XA:Z=CR3*ZA-SR3*YA:Y=SR3*ZA+CR3*YA:X=X+MX:Y=Y+MY
:Z=Z+MZ:SX=D*X/Z:SY=D*Y/Z:RETURN
980    '_____
```

```
990 '
1000 'module:  return to BASIC interpreter
1010  CLS:SCREEN 0,0,0,0:WIDTH 80:COLOR 7,0,0:CLS:LOCATE 1,1
,1:END
1020 '_____
1030 '
1040 'module:  UNIVERSAL
1050 'This routine configures the program for the hardware/s
oftware being used.
1060  KEY OFF:CLS:ON ERROR GOTO 1130  'trap if not Enhanced
Display + EGA
1070  SCREEN 9,,0,0:COLOR 7,0:PALETTE 1,8:PALETTE 2,1:PALETT
E 3,9:PALETTE 4,11:PALETTE 5,7:PALETTE 6,37:PALETTE 7,7:PALE
TTE 8,56:PALETTE 9,34:PALETTE 10,20:PALETTE 11,5:PALETTE 12,
44:PALETTE 13,46:PALETTE 14,55:PALETTE 15,63
1080  C0=0:C1=12:C2=9:C3=7:LOCATE 1,1:PRINT "ED-EGA 640x350
16-color mode"
1090  V6=15  'illumination range 0 to 15
1100  GOSUB 1820  'assign bit tiling codes for EGA
1110  DEFINT G:G=1  'set flag for ED-EGA
1120  GOTO 1320  'jump to screen coordinates set-up
1130  RESUME 1140
1140  ON ERROR GOTO 1200  'trap if not Color Display + EGA
1150  SCREEN 8,,0,0:COLOR 7,0:PALETTE 1,0:PALETTE 2,1:PALETT
E 3,9:PALETTE 4,7:PALETTE 8,4:PALETTE 9,2:C0=0:C1=8:C2=9:C3=
7:LOCATE 1,1:PRINT "CD-EGA 640x200 16-color mode"
1160  V6=14  'illumination range 0 to 14
1170  GOSUB 1820  'assign shading codes for EGA
1180  DEFINT G:G=2  'set flag for CD-EGA
1190  GOTO 1320  'jump to screen coordinates set-up
1200  RESUME 1210
1210  ON ERROR GOTO 1270  'trap if not PCjr
1220  CLEAR,,,32768!:SCREEN 6,0,0,0:COLOR 3,0:PALETTE 1,8:PA
LETTE 3,7:C0=0:C1=1:C2=2:C3=3:LOCATE 1,1:PRINT "PCjr 640x200
 4-color mode"
1230  V6=14  'illumination range 0 to 14
1240  GOSUB 2020  'assign shading codes for PCjr
1250  DEFINT G:G=3  'set flag for CD-JR
1260  GOTO 1320  'jump to screen coordinates set-up
1270  RESUME 1280
1280  SCREEN 1,0:COLOR 0,1:C0=0:C1=1:C2=2:C3=3:LOCATE 1,1:PR
INT "CGA 320x200 4-color mode"
1290  V6=14  'illumination range 0 to 14
1300  GOSUB 2020  'assign shading codes for CGA
1310  DEFINT G:G=4  'set flag for CD-CGA
1320  ON ERROR GOTO 0  'disable error trapping override
1330  WINDOW SCREEN (-399,-299)-(400,300)
```

```
1340   ON KEY (2) GOSUB 1010:KEY (2) ON  'F2 key to exit prog
ram
1350   GOTO 150  'return to main program
1360 '_____
1370 '
1380 'module:   assign variables
1390   D=1200:R1=6.19592:R2=.5235901:R3=5.39778:MX=0:MY=0:MZ=
-150  '3D parameter
1400   DEFINT Q:Q1=0:Q2=0
1410   X=0:Y=0:Z=0:R4=6.28319:R5=6.28319
1420   DIM B11(35,2):DIM B12(35,2)  'two sweeps 36 sets xyz v
iew coords
1430   DIM B21(35,1):DIM B22(35,1)  'two sweeps 36 sets sx,sy
 display coords
1440   XL=.57735:YL=.57735:ZL=.57735  'xyz components of unit
 vector for angle of incidence used in illumination algorith
m
1450   SR1=SIN(R1):CR1=COS(R1):SR2=SIN(R2):CR2=COS(R2):SR3=SI
N(R3):CR3=COS(R3)
1460   SR4=SIN(R4):CR4=COS(R4):SR5=SIN(R5):CR5=COS(R5)
1470   RETURN
1480 '_____
1490 '
1500 'module:   plane equation method of hidden surface remov
al
1510   SP1=X1*(Y2*Z3-Y3*Z2):SP1=(-1)*SP1:SP2=X2*(Y3*Z1-Y1*Z3)
:SP3=X3*(Y1*Z2-Y2*Z1):SP=SP1-SP2-SP3:RETURN
1520 '_____
1530 '
1540 'module:   computer-controlled shading routine
1550   XU=X2-X1:YU=Y2-Y1:ZU=Z2-Z1  'calculate vector from ver
tex 1 to vertex 2
1560   XV=X3-X1:YV=Y3-Y1:ZV=Z3-Z1  'calculate vector from ver
tex 1 to vertex 3
1570   XN=(YU*ZV)-(ZU*YV):YN=(ZU*XV)-(XU*ZV):ZN=(XU*YV)-(YU*X
V)  'calculate surface perpendicular vector
1580   YN=YN*(-1):ZN=ZN*(-1)  'convert vector to cartesian sy
stem
1590 'sub-module:  convert surface perpendicular vector to u
nit vector
1600   V1=(XN*XN)+(YN*YN)+(ZN*ZN):V2=SQR(V1)  'magnitude of s
urface perpendicular vector
1610   V3=1/V2  'ratio of magnitude to unit vector magnitude
1620   XW=V3*XN:YW=V3*YN:ZW=V3*ZN  'XYZ components of surface
 perpendicular unit vector
1630 'sub-module:  calculate illumination factor for surface
 when angle of incidence is 45 degrees elevation and 135 deg
rees yaw
```

```
1640    V4=(XW*XL)+(YW*YL)+(ZW*ZL)   'illumination factor 0 to
1
1650    V4=V4*V6:V4=CINT(V4)   'set illumination range
1660    V5=V4+1  'illumination factor from base 1
1670    ON G GOSUB 2200, 2410, 2620, 2620  'jump to device-dep
endent shading routine
1680    RETURN
1690 '_____
1700 '
1710 'module:   computer-controlled dithering routine
1720    LINE (SX1,SY1)-(SX2,SY2),C4:LINE (SX1,SY1)-(SX2,SY2),C
5,,C6:LINE (SX2,SY2)-(SX3,SY3),C4:LINE (SX2,SY2)-(SX3,SY3),C
5,,C6:LINE (SX3,SY3)-(SX4,SY4),C4:LINE (SX3,SY3)-(SX4,SY4),C
5,,C6
1730    LINE (SX4,SY4)-(SX1,SY1),C4:LINE (SX4,SY4)-(SX1,SY1),C
5,,C6:RETURN
1740 '_____
1750 '
1760 'module:   solid surface modeling of 4-sided polygon
1770    LINE (SX1,SY1)-(SX2,SY2),C2:LINE-(SX3,SY3),C2:LINE-(SX
4,SY4),C2:LINE-(SX1,SY1),C2:PAINT (SX5,SY5),C2,C2
1780    LINE (SX1,SY1)-(SX2,SY2),C3:LINE-(SX3,SY3),C3:LINE-(SX
4,SY4),C3:LINE-(SX1,SY1),C3:PAINT (SX5,SY5),C0,C3:RETURN
1790 '_____
1800 '
1810 'module:   assign shading codes for EGA
1820    A1$=CHR$(&HDF)+CHR$(&H20)+CHR$(&H0)+CHR$(&H0)+CHR$(&HF
D)+CHR$(&H2)+CHR$(&H0)+CHR$(&H0)+CHR$(&H7F)+CHR$(&H80)+CHR$(
&H0)+CHR$(&H0)+CHR$(&HF7)+CHR$(&H8)+CHR$(&H0)+CHR$(&H0)
1830    A2$=CHR$(&HBB)+CHR$(&H44)+CHR$(&H0)+CHR$(&H0)+CHR$(&HE
E)+CHR$(&H11)+CHR$(&H0)+CHR$(&H0)
1840    A3$=CHR$(&HAA)+CHR$(&H55)+CHR$(&H0)+CHR$(&H0)+CHR$(&H5
5)+CHR$(&HAA)+CHR$(&H0)+CHR$(&H0)
1850    A4$=CHR$(&H44)+CHR$(&HBB)+CHR$(&H0)+CHR$(&H0)+CHR$(&H1
1)+CHR$(&HEE)+CHR$(&H0)+CHR$(&H0)
1860    A5$=CHR$(&H20)+CHR$(&HFF)+CHR$(&H0)+CHR$(&H0)+CHR$(&H2
)+CHR$(&HFF)+CHR$(&H0)+CHR$(&H0)+CHR$(&H80)+CHR$(&HFF)+CHR$(
&H0)+CHR$(&H0)+CHR$(&H8)+CHR$(&HFF)+CHR$(&H0)+CHR$(&H0)
1870    A6$=CHR$(&H44)+CHR$(&HFF)+CHR$(&H0)+CHR$(&H0)+CHR$(&H1
1)+CHR$(&HFF)+CHR$(&H0)+CHR$(&H0)
1880    A7$=CHR$(&H55)+CHR$(&HFF)+CHR$(&H0)+CHR$(&H0)+CHR$(&HA
A)+CHR$(&HFF)+CHR$(&H0)+CHR$(&H0)
1890    A8$=CHR$(&HBB)+CHR$(&HFF)+CHR$(&H0)+CHR$(&H0)+CHR$(&HE
E)+CHR$(&HFF)+CHR$(&H0)+CHR$(&H0)
1900    A9$=CHR$(&HDF)+CHR$(&HDF)+CHR$(&H20)+CHR$(&H0)+CHR$(&H
FD)+CHR$(&HFD)+CHR$(&H2)+CHR$(&H0)+CHR$(&H7F)+CHR$(&H7F)+CHR
$(&H80)+CHR$(&H0)+CHR$(&HF7)+CHR$(&HF7)+CHR$(&H8)+CHR$(&H0)
1910    A10$=CHR$(&HBB)+CHR$(&HBB)+CHR$(&H44)+CHR$(&H0)+CHR$(&
```

```basic
     HEE)+CHR$(&HEE)+CHR$(&H11)+CHR$(&HO)
1920    A11$=CHR$(&HAA)+CHR$(&HAA)+CHR$(&H55)+CHR$(&HO)+CHR$(&
H55)+CHR$(&H55)+CHR$(&HAA)+CHR$(&HO)
1930    A12$=CHR$(&H44)+CHR$(&H44)+CHR$(&HBB)+CHR$(&HO)+CHR$(&
H11)+CHR$(&H11)+CHR$(&HEE)+CHR$(&HO)
1940    A13$=CHR$(&H20)+CHR$(&HO)+CHR$(&HFF)+CHR$(&HO)+CHR$(&H
2)+CHR$(&HO)+CHR$(&HFF)+CHR$(&HO)+CHR$(&H80)+CHR$(&HO)+CHR$(
&HFF)+CHR$(&HO)+CHR$(&H8)+CHR$(&HO)+CHR$(&HFF)+CHR$(&HO)
1950    A14$=CHR$(&H44)+CHR$(&HO)+CHR$(&HFF)+CHR$(&HO)+CHR$(&H
11)+CHR$(&HO)+CHR$(&HFF)+CHR$(&HO)
1960    A15$=CHR$(&H55)+CHR$(&HO)+CHR$(&HFF)+CHR$(&HO)+CHR$(&H
AA)+CHR$(&HO)+CHR$(&HFF)+CHR$(&HO)
1970    A16$=CHR$(&HBB)+CHR$(&HO)+CHR$(&HFF)+CHR$(&HO)+CHR$(&H
EE)+CHR$(&HO)+CHR$(&HFF)+CHR$(&HO)
1980    RETURN
1990 '_____
2000 '
2010 'module:   assign shading codes for CGA and/or PCjr
2020    A1$=CHR$(&H40)+CHR$(&HO)+CHR$(&H4)+CHR$(&HO)
2030    A2$=CHR$(&H40)+CHR$(&H4)+CHR$(&H40)+CHR$(&H4)
2040    A3$=CHR$(&H44)+CHR$(&H10)+CHR$(&H11)+CHR$(&H1)+CHR$(&H
44)+CHR$(&H4)+CHR$(&H11)+CHR$(&H40)
2050    A4$=CHR$(&H44)+CHR$(&H11)+CHR$(&H44)+CHR$(&H11)
2060    A5$=CHR$(&H11)+CHR$(&H45)+CHR$(&H44)+CHR$(&H54)+CHR$(&
H11)+CHR$(&H51)+CHR$(&H44)+CHR$(&H15)
2070    A6$=CHR$(&H15)+CHR$(&H51)+CHR$(&H15)+CHR$(&H51)
2080    A7$=CHR$(&H15)+CHR$(&H55)+CHR$(&H51)+CHR$(&H55)
2090    A9$=CHR$(&HD5)+CHR$(&H55)+CHR$(&H5D)+CHR$(&H55)
2100    A10$=CHR$(&HD5)+CHR$(&H5D)+CHR$(&HD5)+CHR$(&H5D)
2110    A12$=CHR$(&HDD)+CHR$(&H75)+CHR$(&H77)+CHR$(&H57)+CHR$(
&HDD)+CHR$(&H5D)+CHR$(&H77)+CHR$(&HD5)
2120    A13$=CHR$(&HDD)+CHR$(&H77)+CHR$(&HDD)+CHR$(&H77)
2130    A14$=CHR$(&H77)+CHR$(&HDF)+CHR$(&HDD)+CHR$(&HFD)+CHR$(
&H77)+CHR$(&HF7)+CHR$(&HDD)+CHR$(&H7F)
2140    A15$=CHR$(&H7F)+CHR$(&HF7)+CHR$(&H7F)+CHR$(&HF7)
2150    A16$=CHR$(&H7F)+CHR$(&HFF)+CHR$(&HF7)+CHR$(&HFF)
2160    RETURN
2170 '_____
2180 '
2190 'shading routine for ED-EGA 640x350 mode
2200    IF V5<1 THEN GOTO 2220  'if light source is behind sur
face
2210    ON V5 GOTO 2220, 2230, 2240, 2250, 2260, 2270, 2280, 2
290, 2300, 2310, 2320, 2330, 2340, 2350, 2360, 2370
2220    A$=CHR$(&HFF)+CHR$(&HO)+CHR$(&HO)+CHR$(&HO):C4=1:C5=1:
C6=&HFFFF:RETURN
2230    A$=A1$:C4=1:C5=2:C6=&H808:RETURN
2240    A$=A2$:C4=1:C5=2:C6=&H4444:RETURN
```

```
2250    A$=CHR$(&HO)+CHR$(&HFF)+CHR$(&HO)+CHR$(&HO):C4=2:C5=2:
C6=&HFFFF:RETURN
2260    A$=A5$:C4=2:C5=3:C6=&H808:RETURN
2270    A$=A6$:C4=2:C5=3:C6=&H4444:RETURN
2280    A$=A7$:C4=2:C5=3:C6=&HAAAA:RETURN
2290    A$=A8$:C4=3:C5=2:C6=&H4444:RETURN
2300    A$=CHR$(&HFF)+CHR$(&HFF)+CHR$(&HO)+CHR$(&HO):C4=3:C5=3
:C6=&HFFFF:RETURN
2310    A$=A10$:C4=3:C5=4:C6=&H4444:RETURN
2320    A$=A11$:C4=3:C5=4:C6=&HAAAA:RETURN
2330    A$=A12$:C4=4:C5=3:C6=&H4444:RETURN
2340    A$=CHR$(&HO)+CHR$(&HO)+CHR$(&HFF)+CHR$(&HO):C4=4:C5=4:
C6=&HFFFF:RETURN
2350    A$=A13$:C4=4:C5=5:C6=&H808:RETURN
2360    A$=A14$:C4=4:C5=5:C6=&H4444:RETURN
2370    A$=A15$:C4=4:C5=5:C6=&HAAAA:RETURN
2380 '_____
2390 '
2400 'shading routine for CD-EGA 640x200 mode
2410    IF V5<1 THEN GOTO 2440  'if light source is behind sur
face
2420    ON V5 GOTO 2440, 2450, 2460, 2470, 2480, 2490, 2500, 2
510, 2520, 2530, 2540, 2550, 2560, 2570, 2580
2430    A$=CHR$(&HFF)+CHR$(&HO)+CHR$(&HO)+CHR$(&HO):C4=1:C5=1:
C6=&HFFFF:RETURN  'solid black is unused
2440    A$=A1$:C4=1:C5=2:C6=&H808:RETURN
2450    A$=A2$:C4=1:C5=2:C6=&H4444:RETURN
2460    A$=A3$:C4=1:C5=2:C6=&HAAAA:RETURN
2470    A$=A4$:C4=2:C5=1:C6=&H4444:RETURN
2480    A$=CHR$(&HO)+CHR$(&HFF)+CHR$(&HO)+CHR$(&HO):C4=2:C5=2:
C6=&HFFFF:RETURN
2490    A$=A5$:C4=2:C5=3:C6=&H808:RETURN
2500    A$=A6$:C4=2:C5=3:C6=&H4444:RETURN
2510    A$=A7$:C4=2:C5=3:C6=&HAAAA:RETURN
2520    A$=A8$:C4=3:C5=2:C6=&H4444:RETURN
2530    A$=CHR$(&HFF)+CHR$(&HFF)+CHR$(&HO)+CHR$(&HO):C4=3:C5=3
:C6=&HFFFF:RETURN
2540    A$=A9$:C4=3:C5=4:C6=&H8080:RETURN
2550    A$=A10$:C4=3:C5=4:C6=&H4444:RETURN
2560    A$=A11$:C4=3:C5=4:C6=&HAAAA:RETURN
2570    A$=A12$:C4=4:C5=3:C6=&H4444:RETURN
2580    A$=CHR$(&HO)+CHR$(&HO)+CHR$(&HFF)+CHR$(&HO):C4=4:C5=4:
C6=&HFFFF:RETURN
2590 '_____
2600 '
2610 'shading routine for CD-CGA 320x200 mode and CD-JR 640x
200 mode
```

```
2620   IF V5<1 THEN GOTO 2650   'if light source is behind sur
face
2630   ON V5 GOTO 2650, 2660, 2670, 2680, 2690, 2700, 2710, 2
720, 2730, 2740, 2750, 2760, 2770, 2780, 2790
2640   A$=CHR$(&H0):C4=0:C5=0:C6=&HFFFF:RETURN   'solid black
-- unused
2650   A$=A1$:C4=0:C5=1:C6=&H2108:RETURN
2660   A$=A2$:C4=0:C5=1:C6=&H4444:RETURN
2670   A$=A4$:C4=0:C5=1:C6=&HAAAA:RETURN
2680   A$=A5$:C4=1:C5=0:C6=&H4924:RETURN
2690   A$=A6$:C4=1:C5=0:C6=&H4444:RETURN
2700   A$=A7$:C4=1:C5=0:C6=&H808:RETURN
2710   A$=CHR$(&H55):C4=1:C5=1:C6=&HFFFF:RETURN
2720   A$=A9$:C4=1:C5=3:C6=&H808:RETURN
2730   A$=A10$:C4=1:C5=3:C6=&H4444:RETURN
2740   A$=A12$:C4=1:C5=3:C6=&H4924:RETURN
2750   A$=A13$:C4=1:C5=3:C6=&HAAAA:RETURN
2760   A$=A14$:C4=3:C5=1:C6=&H4924:RETURN
2770   A$=A15$:C4=3:C5=1:C6=&H4444:RETURN
2780   A$=A16$:C4=3:C5=1:C6=&H808:RETURN
2790   A$=CHR$(&HFF):C4=3:C5=3:C6=&HFFFF:RETURN
2800   '_____
2810   '
2820   END 'of program code
```

the screen. Change the R3 pitch value in line 1390 to tilt the southern pole towards you.

On a standard IBM PC running at 4.77 MHz with an EGA in the 640 × 350 mode, this demonstration program takes 11 minutes 57 seconds to complete the fully-shaded, solid sphere, but the results are well worth the wait. The 3D sphere is the most difficult sub-object which can be shaded, and even a standard Color/Graphics Adapter produces an outstanding display in this instance.

## COMPUTER-SHADED CYLINDER

Figure 16-11 shows the screen output produced by the demonstration program in Fig. 16-12. To run this program from the companion diskette, type **LOAD "A-25.BAS",R**. Although the image produced by this program is just as dramatic as the previous sphere, run-time requires only 73 seconds, the first 28 seconds being used to precalculate all the various coordinates and store them in the appropriate arrays.

Note the loop in lines 370 through 390, which is used to dither the 36 short lines which make up the

circular end of the cylinder. Contrast this with the dithering routine at line 1390, which produces line dithering for a simple four-sided polygon. As you learned in Chapter 10, the curved side of the cylinder is comprised of a series of four-sided, flat polygons.

You may find it illustrative to experiment with different R1, R2, and R3 values in line 1070. A small rotation of the cylinder can produce radical changes in the brightness levels for the various surfaces of the model.

Again, refer to Appendix B if you are interested in changing the location of the light source as defined in line 1120.

## SUMMARY

In this chapter, you learned how to instruct your computer to calculate the brightness or dimness of a surface. You discovered how to add full halftone shading to a cube, sphere, cylinder, and polyhedron middlecrystal. You experimented with model rotations and light source relocation.

The next chapter explores special illumination conditions, such as mirror reflections.

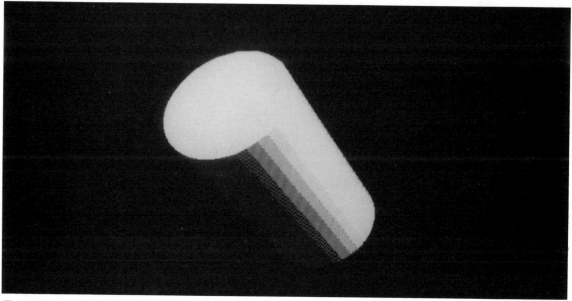

Fig. 16-11. The display image produced by the demonstration program in Fig. 16-12.

Fig. 16-12. Computer-shaded 3D cylinder. For QuickBASIC version, see Appendix C. For TurboBASIC version, see Appendix D.

```
100 'Program A-25.BAS    Computer-shaded cylinder.
110 'Uses plane equation method of hidden surface removal.
Uses surface perpendicular method of shading.
120 '_____
130 '
140   GOTO 740    'configure system
150   GOSUB 1070  'assign variables
160 '_____
170 '
180 'main routine
190   SOUND 350,.7:R5=0:R4=0:FOR T=0 TO 35 STEP 1:LOCATE 2,1:
PRINT "Sweep 1 coordinate"T"   ":X=30:GOSUB 600:Z=Z+60:GOSUB
650:B11(T,0)=X:B11(T,1)=Y:B11(T,2)=Z:B21(T,0)=SX:B21(T,1)=SY
:R5=R5+.17453:NEXT T  'near end of cylinder
200   SOUND 350,.7:R5=0:R4=0:FOR T=0 TO 35 STEP 1:LOCATE 2,1:
PRINT "Sweep 2 coordinate"T"   ":X=30:GOSUB 600:Z=Z-60:GOSUB
650:B12(T,0)=X:B12(T,1)=Y:B12(T,2)=Z:B22(T,0)=SX:B22(T,1)=SY
:R5=R5+.17453:NEXT T  'far end of cylinder
210   SOUND 350,.7:FOR Q1=0 TO 35 STEP 1:Q2=Q1+1:IF Q2>35 THE
N Q2=0
220   LOCATE 2,1:PRINT "Solid surface"Q1"           "
230   GOSUB 450:NEXT Q1
240   SOUND 350,.7:LOCATE 2,1:PRINT "Solid end of cylinder.
    "
```

```
250   X1=B11(0,0):Y1=B11(0,1):Z1=B11(0,2):X2=B11(25,0):Y2=B11
(25,1):Z2=B11(25,2):X3=B11(11,0):Y3=B11(11,1):Z3=B11(11,2)
260   GOSUB 1190:IF SP>0 THEN 400
270   FOR Q1=0 TO 35 STEP 1:Q2=Q1+1:IF Q2>35 THEN Q2=0
280   SX1=B21(Q1,0):SY1=B21(Q1,1):SX2=B21(Q2,0):SY2=B21(Q2,1)

290   LINE (SX1,SY1)-(SX2,SY2),C2:NEXT Q1
300   X=0:Y=0:Z=60:GOSUB 650:PAINT (SX,SY),C2,C2
310   FOR Q1=0 TO 35 STEP 1:Q2=Q1+1:IF Q2>35 THEN Q2=0
320   SX1=B21(Q1,0):SY1=B21(Q1,1):SX2=B21(Q2,0):SY2=B21(Q2,1)

330   LINE (SX1,SY1)-(SX2,SY2),C3:NEXT Q1
340   X=0:Y=0:Z=60:GOSUB 650:PAINT (SX,SY),C0,C3
350   SOUND 350,.7:LOCATE 2,1:PRINT "Shading end of cylinder.
 "
360   X=0:Y=0:Z=60:GOSUB 650:GOSUB 1230:PAINT (SX,SY),A$,C3
'shading of end
370   FOR Q1=0 TO 35 STEP 1:Q2=Q1+1:IF Q2>35 THEN Q2=0
380   SX1=B21(Q1,0):SY1=B21(Q1,1):SX2=B21(Q2,0):SY2=B21(Q2,1)

390   LINE (SX1,SY1)-(SX2,SY2),C4:LINE (SX1,SY1)-(SX2,SY2),C5
,,C6:NEXT Q1 'dithering of end
400   SOUND 650,10:LOCATE 2,1:PRINT "Program completed.
 ":LOCATE 4,1:PRINT "                    "
410   GOTO 410
420 '_____
430 '
440 'module:  draw one 4-sided polygon on surface of cylinde
r
450   X1=B11(Q1,0):Y1=B11(Q1,1):Z1=B11(Q1,2)
460   X2=B11(Q2,0):Y2=B11(Q2,1):Z2=B11(Q2,2)
470   X3=B12(Q2,0):Y3=B12(Q2,1):Z3=B12(Q2,2)
480   GOSUB 1190:LOCATE 4,1:PRINT SP:IF SP>0 THEN RETURN  'te
st if hidden
490   SX1=B21(Q1,0):SY1=B21(Q1,1)
500   SX2=B21(Q2,0):SY2=B21(Q2,1)
510   SX3=B22(Q2,0):SY3=B22(Q2,1)
520   SX4=B22(Q1,0):SY4=B22(Q1,1)
530   X=X1+.5*(X3-X1):Y=Y1+.5*(Y3-Y1):Z=Z1+.5*(Z3-Z1)  'diago
nal midpoint of polygon's view coordinates
540   SX5=D*X/Z:SY5=D*Y/Z 'area fill coordinates
550   GOSUB 1450 'jump to solid surface modeling routine
560   GOSUB 1230:PAINT (SX5,SY5),A$,C3:GOSUB 1400:RETURN
570 '_____
580 '
590 'module:  calculation of world coordinates for 3D cylind
er
600   SR4=SIN(R4):CR4=COS(R4):SR5=SIN(R5):CR5=COS(R5)
```

```
610   X1=SR5*X:Y=CR5*X:X=CR4*X1:Z=SR4*X1:RETURN
620  '_____
630  '
640  'module:   perspective calculations
650   X=(-1)*X:XA=CR1*X-SR1*Z:ZA=SR1*X+CR1*Z:X=CR2*XA+SR2*Y:Y
A=CR2*Y-SR2*XA:Z=CR3*ZA-SR3*YA:Y=SR3*ZA+CR3*YA:X=X+MX:Y=Y+MY
:Z=Z+MZ:SX=D*X/Z:SY=D*Y/Z:RETURN
660  '_____
670  '
680  'module:   return to BASIC interpreter
690   CLS:SCREEN 0,0,0,0:WIDTH 80:COLOR 7,0,0:CLS:LOCATE 1,1,
1:END
700  '_____
710  '
720  'module:   UNIVERSAL
730  'This routine configures the program for the hardware/so
ftware being used.
740   KEY OFF:CLS:ON ERROR GOTO 810   'trap if not Enhanced Di
splay + EGA
750   SCREEN 9,,0,0:COLOR 7,0:PALETTE 1,8:PALETTE 2,1:PALETTE
 3,9:PALETTE 4,11:PALETTE 5,7:PALETTE 6,37:PALETTE 7,7:PALET
TE 8,56:PALETTE 9,34:PALETTE 10,20:PALETTE 11,5:PALETTE 12,4
4:PALETTE 13,46:PALETTE 14,55:PALETTE 15,63
760   C0=0:C1=12:C2=9:C3=7:LOCATE 1,1:PRINT "ED-EGA 640x350 1
6-color mode"
770   V6=15   'illumination range 0 to 15
780   GOSUB 1500   'assign bit tiling codes for EGA
790   DEFINT G:G=1   'set flag for ED-EGA
800   GOTO 1000   'jump to screen coordinates set-up
810   RESUME 820
820   ON ERROR GOTO 880   'trap if not Color Display + EGA
830   SCREEN 8,,0,0:COLOR 7,0:PALETTE 1,0:PALETTE 2,1:PALETTE
 3,9:PALETTE 4,7:PALETTE 8,4:PALETTE 9,2:C0=0:C1=8:C2=9:C3=7
:LOCATE 1,1:PRINT "CD-EGA 640x200 16-color mode"
840   V6=14   'illumination range 0 to 14
850   GOSUB 1500   'assign shading codes for EGA
860   DEFINT G:G=2   'set flag for CD-EGA
870   GOTO 1000   'jump to screen coordinates set-up
880   RESUME 890
890   ON ERROR GOTO 950   'trap if not PCjr
900   CLEAR,,,32768!:SCREEN 6,0,0,0:COLOR 3,0:PALETTE 1,8:PAL
ETTE 3,7:C0=0:C1=1:C2=2:C3=3:LOCATE 1,1:PRINT "PCjr 640x200
4-color mode"
910   V6=14   'illumination range 0 to 14
920   GOSUB 1700   'assign shading codes for PCjr
930   DEFINT G:G=3   'set flag for CD-JR
940   GOTO 1000   'jump to screen coordinates set-up
950   RESUME 960
```

```
960    SCREEN 1,0:COLOR 0,1:C0=0:C1=1:C2=2:C3=3:LOCATE 1,1:PRI
NT "CGA 320x200 4-color mode"
970    V6=14    'illumination range 0 to 14
980    GOSUB 1700  'assign shading codes for CGA
990    DEFINT G:G=4  'set flag for CD-CGA
1000   ON ERROR GOTO 0  'disable error trapping override
1010   WINDOW SCREEN (-399,-299)-(400,300)
1020   ON KEY (2) GOSUB 690:KEY (2) ON  'F2 key to exit progr
am
1030   GOTO 150   'return to main program
1040 '_____
1050 '
1060 'module:   assign variables
1070   D=1200:R1=5.89778:R2=0:R3=.58539:MX=0:MY=0:MZ=-350   '3
D parameter
1080   DEFINT Q:Q1=0:Q2=0
1090   X=0:Y=0:Z=0:R4=6.28319:R5=6.28319
1100   DIM B11(35,2):DIM B12(35,2)   'two sweeps 36 sets xyz v
iew coords
1110   DIM B21(35,1):DIM B22(35,1)   'two sweeps 36 sets sx,sy
 display coords
1120   XL=.57735:YL=.57735:ZL=.57735  'xyz components of unit
 vector for angle of incidence used in illumination algorith
m
1130   SR1=SIN(R1):CR1=COS(R1):SR2=SIN(R2):CR2=COS(R2):SR3=SI
N(R3):CR3=COS(R3)
1140   SR4=SIN(R4):CR4=COS(R4):SR5=SIN(R5):CR5=COS(R5)
1150   RETURN
1160 '_____
1170 '
1180 'module:   plane equation method of hidden surface remov
al
1190   SP1=X1*(Y2*Z3-Y3*Z2):SP1=(-1)*SP1:SP2=X2*(Y3*Z1-Y1*Z3)
:SP3=X3*(Y1*Z2-Y2*Z1):SP=SP1-SP2-SP3:RETURN
1200 '_____
1210 '
1220 'module:   computer-controlled shading routine
1230   XU=X2-X1:YU=Y2-Y1:ZU=Z2-Z1  'calculate vector from ver
tex 1 to vertex 2
1240   XV=X3-X1:YV=Y3-Y1:ZV=Z3-Z1  'calculate vector from ver
tex 1 to vertex 3
1250   XN=(YU*ZV)-(ZU*YV):YN=(ZU*XV)-(XU*ZV):ZN=(XU*YV)-(YU*X
V)  'calculate surface perpendicular vector
1260   YN=YN*(-1):ZN=ZN*(-1)  'convert vector to cartesian sy
stem
1270 'sub-module:   convert surface perpendicular vector to u
nit vector
1280   V1=(XN*XN)+(YN*YN)+(ZN*ZN):V2=SQR(V1)   'magnitude of s
```

urface perpendicular vector
```
1290   V3=1/V2  'ratio of magnitude to unit vector magnitude
1300   XW=V3*XN:YW=V3*YN:ZW=V3*ZN  'XYZ components of surface
  perpendicular unit vector
1310 'sub-module:  calculate illumination factor for surface
  when angle of incidence is 45 degrees elevation and 135 deg
rees yaw
1320   V4=(XW*XL)+(YW*YL)+(ZW*ZL)  'illumination factor 0 to
1
1330   V4=V4*V6:V4=CINT(V4)  'set illumination range
1340   V5=V4+1  'illumination factor from base 1
1350   ON G GOSUB 1880, 2090, 2300, 2300  'jump to device-dep
endent shading routine
1360   RETURN
1370 '_____
1380 '
1390 'module:  computer-controlled dithering routine
1400   LINE (SX1,SY1)-(SX2,SY2),C4:LINE (SX1,SY1)-(SX2,SY2),C
5,,C6:LINE (SX2,SY2)-(SX3,SY3),C4:LINE (SX2,SY2)-(SX3,SY3),C
5,,C6:LINE (SX3,SY3)-(SX4,SY4),C4:LINE (SX3,SY3)-(SX4,SY4),C
5,,C6
1410   LINE (SX4,SY4)-(SX1,SY1),C4:LINE (SX4,SY4)-(SX1,SY1),C
5,,C6:RETURN
1420 '_____
1430 '
1440 'module:  solid surface modeling of 4-sided polygon
1450   LINE (SX1,SY1)-(SX2,SY2),C2:LINE-(SX3,SY3),C2:LINE-(SX
4,SY4),C2:LINE-(SX1,SY1),C2:PAINT (SX5,SY5),C2,C2
1460   LINE (SX1,SY1)-(SX2,SY2),C3:LINE-(SX3,SY3),C3:LINE-(SX
4,SY4),C3:LINE-(SX1,SY1),C3:PAINT (SX5,SY5),C0,C3:RETURN
1470 '_____
1480 '
1490 'module:  assign shading codes for EGA
1500   A1$=CHR$(&HDF)+CHR$(&H20)+CHR$(&H0)+CHR$(&H0)+CHR$(&HF
D)+CHR$(&H2)+CHR$(&H0)+CHR$(&H0)+CHR$(&H7F)+CHR$(&H80)+CHR$(
&H0)+CHR$(&H0)+CHR$(&HF7)+CHR$(&H8)+CHR$(&H0)+CHR$(&H0)
1510   A2$=CHR$(&HBB)+CHR$(&H44)+CHR$(&H0)+CHR$(&H0)+CHR$(&HE
E)+CHR$(&H11)+CHR$(&H0)+CHR$(&H0)
1520   A3$=CHR$(&HAA)+CHR$(&H55)+CHR$(&H0)+CHR$(&H0)+CHR$(&H5
5)+CHR$(&HAA)+CHR$(&H0)+CHR$(&H0)
1530   A4$=CHR$(&H44)+CHR$(&HBB)+CHR$(&H0)+CHR$(&H0)+CHR$(&H1
1)+CHR$(&HEE)+CHR$(&H0)+CHR$(&H0)
1540   A5$=CHR$(&H20)+CHR$(&HFF)+CHR$(&H0)+CHR$(&H0)+CHR$(&H2
)+CHR$(&HFF)+CHR$(&H0)+CHR$(&H0)+CHR$(&H80)+CHR$(&HFF)+CHR$(
&H0)+CHR$(&H0)+CHR$(&H8)+CHR$(&HFF)+CHR$(&H0)+CHR$(&H0)
1550   A6$=CHR$(&H44)+CHR$(&HFF)+CHR$(&H0)+CHR$(&H0)+CHR$(&H1
1)+CHR$(&HFF)+CHR$(&H0)+CHR$(&H0)
```

```
1560    A7$=CHR$(&H55)+CHR$(&HFF)+CHR$(&HO)+CHR$(&HO)+CHR$(&HA
A)+CHR$(&HFF)+CHR$(&HO)+CHR$(&HO)
1570    A8$=CHR$(&HBB)+CHR$(&HFF)+CHR$(&HO)+CHR$(&HO)+CHR$(&HE
E)+CHR$(&HFF)+CHR$(&HO)+CHR$(&HO)
1580    A9$=CHR$(&HDF)+CHR$(&HDF)+CHR$(&H20)+CHR$(&HO)+CHR$(&H
FD)+CHR$(&HFD)+CHR$(&H2)+CHR$(&HO)+CHR$(&H7F)+CHR$(&H7F)+CHR
$(&H80)+CHR$(&HO)+CHR$(&HF7)+CHR$(&HF7)+CHR$(&H8)+CHR$(&HO)
1590    A10$=CHR$(&HBB)+CHR$(&HBB)+CHR$(&H44)+CHR$(&HO)+CHR$(&
HEE)+CHR$(&HEE)+CHR$(&H11)+CHR$(&HO)
1600    A11$=CHR$(&HAA)+CHR$(&HAA)+CHR$(&H55)+CHR$(&HO)+CHR$(&
H55)+CHR$(&H55)+CHR$(&HAA)+CHR$(&HO)
1610    A12$=CHR$(&H44)+CHR$(&H44)+CHR$(&HBB)+CHR$(&HO)+CHR$(&
H11)+CHR$(&H11)+CHR$(&HEE)+CHR$(&HO)
1620    A13$=CHR$(&H20)+CHR$(&HO)+CHR$(&HFF)+CHR$(&HO)+CHR$(&H
2)+CHR$(&HO)+CHR$(&HFF)+CHR$(&HO)+CHR$(&H80)+CHR$(&HO)+CHR$(
&HFF)+CHR$(&HO)+CHR$(&H8)+CHR$(&HO)+CHR$(&HFF)+CHR$(&HO)
1630    A14$=CHR$(&H44)+CHR$(&HO)+CHR$(&HFF)+CHR$(&HO)+CHR$(&H
11)+CHR$(&HO)+CHR$(&HFF)+CHR$(&HO)
1640    A15$=CHR$(&H55)+CHR$(&HO)+CHR$(&HFF)+CHR$(&HO)+CHR$(&H
AA)+CHR$(&HO)+CHR$(&HFF)+CHR$(&HO)
1650    A16$=CHR$(&HBB)+CHR$(&HO)+CHR$(&HFF)+CHR$(&HO)+CHR$(&H
EE)+CHR$(&HO)+CHR$(&HFF)+CHR$(&HO)
1660    RETURN
1670    '_____
1680    '
1690    'module:  assign shading codes for CGA and/or PCjr
1700    A1$=CHR$(&H40)+CHR$(&HO)+CHR$(&H4)+CHR$(&HO)
1710    A2$=CHR$(&H40)+CHR$(&H4)+CHR$(&H40)+CHR$(&H4)
1720    A3$=CHR$(&H44)+CHR$(&H10)+CHR$(&H11)+CHR$(&H1)+CHR$(&H
44)+CHR$(&H4)+CHR$(&H11)+CHR$(&H40)
1730    A4$=CHR$(&H44)+CHR$(&H11)+CHR$(&H44)+CHR$(&H11)
1740    A5$=CHR$(&H11)+CHR$(&H45)+CHR$(&H44)+CHR$(&H54)+CHR$(&
H11)+CHR$(&H51)+CHR$(&H44)+CHR$(&H15)
1750    A6$=CHR$(&H15)+CHR$(&H51)+CHR$(&H15)+CHR$(&H51)
1760    A7$=CHR$(&H15)+CHR$(&H55)+CHR$(&H51)+CHR$(&H55)
1770    A9$=CHR$(&HD5)+CHR$(&H55)+CHR$(&H5D)+CHR$(&H55)
1780    A10$=CHR$(&HD5)+CHR$(&H5D)+CHR$(&HD5)+CHR$(&H5D)
1790    A12$=CHR$(&HDD)+CHR$(&H75)+CHR$(&H77)+CHR$(&H57)+CHR$(
&HDD)+CHR$(&H5D)+CHR$(&H77)+CHR$(&HD5)
1800    A13$=CHR$(&HDD)+CHR$(&H77)+CHR$(&HDD)+CHR$(&H77)
1810    A14$=CHR$(&H77)+CHR$(&HDF)+CHR$(&HDD)+CHR$(&HFD)+CHR$(
&H77)+CHR$(&HF7)+CHR$(&HDD)+CHR$(&H7F)
1820    A15$=CHR$(&H7F)+CHR$(&HF7)+CHR$(&H7F)+CHR$(&HF7)
1830    A16$=CHR$(&H7F)+CHR$(&HFF)+CHR$(&HF7)+CHR$(&HFF)
1840    RETURN
1850    '_____
1860    '
```

```
1870 'shading routine for ED-EGA 640x350 mode
1880    IF V5<1 THEN GOTO 1900  'if light source is behind sur
face
1890    ON V5 GOTO 1900, 1910, 1920, 1930, 1940, 1950, 1960, 1
970, 1980, 1990, 2000, 2010, 2020, 2030, 2040, 2050
1900    A$=CHR$(&HFF)+CHR$(&HO)+CHR$(&HO)+CHR$(&HO):C4=1:C5=1:
C6=&HFFFF:RETURN
1910    A$=A1$:C4=1:C5=2:C6=&H808:RETURN
1920    A$=A2$:C4=1:C5=2:C6=&H4444:RETURN
1930    A$=CHR$(&HO)+CHR$(&HFF)+CHR$(&HO)+CHR$(&HO):C4=2:C5=2:
C6=&HFFFF:RETURN
1940    A$=A5$:C4=2:C5=3:C6=&H808:RETURN
1950    A$=A6$:C4=2:C5=3:C6=&H4444:RETURN
1960    A$=A7$:C4=2:C5=3:C6=&HAAAA:RETURN
1970    A$=A8$:C4=3:C5=2:C6=&H4444:RETURN
1980    A$=CHR$(&HFF)+CHR$(&HFF)+CHR$(&HO)+CHR$(&HO):C4=3:C5=3
:C6=&HFFFF:RETURN
1990    A$=A10$:C4=3:C5=4:C6=&H4444:RETURN
2000    A$=A11$:C4=3:C5=4:C6=&HAAAA:RETURN
2010    A$=A12$:C4=4:C5=3:C6=&H4444:RETURN
2020    A$=CHR$(&HO)+CHR$(&HO)+CHR$(&HFF)+CHR$(&HO):C4=4:C5=4:
C6=&HFFFF:RETURN
2030    A$=A13$:C4=4:C5=5:C6=&H808:RETURN
2040    A$=A14$:C4=4:C5=5:C6=&H4444:RETURN
2050    A$=A15$:C4=4:C5=5:C6=&HAAAA:RETURN
2060 '_____
2070 '
2080 'shading routine for CD-EGA 640x200 mode
2090    IF V5<1 THEN GOTO 2120  'if light source is behind sur
face
2100    ON V5 GOTO 2120, 2130, 2140, 2150, 2160, 2170, 2180, 2
190, 2200, 2210, 2220, 2230, 2240, 2250, 2260
2110    A$=CHR$(&HFF)+CHR$(&HO)+CHR$(&HO)+CHR$(&HO):C4=1:C5=1:
C6=&HFFFF:RETURN   'solid black is unused
2120    A$=A1$:C4=1:C5=2:C6=&H808:RETURN
2130    A$=A2$:C4=1:C5=2:C6=&H4444:RETURN
2140    A$=A3$:C4=1:C5=2:C6=&HAAAA:RETURN
2150    A$=A4$:C4=2:C5=1:C6=&H4444:RETURN
2160    A$=CHR$(&HO)+CHR$(&HFF)+CHR$(&HO)+CHR$(&HO):C4=2:C5=2:
C6=&HFFFF:RETURN
2170    A$=A5$:C4=2:C5=3:C6=&H808:RETURN
2180    A$=A6$:C4=2:C5=3:C6=&H4444:RETURN
2190    A$=A7$:C4=2:C5=3:C6=&HAAAA:RETURN
2200    A$=A8$:C4=3:C5=2:C6=&H4444:RETURN
2210    A$=CHR$(&HFF)+CHR$(&HFF)+CHR$(&HO)+CHR$(&HO):C4=3:C5=3
:C6=&HFFFF:RETURN
2220    A$=A9$:C4=3:C5=4:C6=&H8080:RETURN
2230    A$=A10$:C4=3:C5=4:C6=&H4444:RETURN
```

```
2240    A$=A11$:C4=3:C5=4:C6=&HAAAA:RETURN
2250    A$=A12$:C4=4:C5=3:C6=&H4444:RETURN
2260    A$=CHR$(&HO)+CHR$(&HO)+CHR$(&HFF)+CHR$(&HO):C4=4:C5=4:
C6=&HFFFF:RETURN
2270 '_____
2280 '
2290 'shading routine for CD-CGA 320x200 mode and CD-JR 640x
200 mode
2300    IF V5<1 THEN GOTO 2330    'if light source is behind sur
face
2310    ON V5 GOTO 2330, 2340, 2350, 2360, 2370, 2380, 2390, 2
400, 2410, 2420, 2430, 2440, 2450, 2460, 2470
2320    A$=CHR$(&HO):C4=0:C5=0:C6=&HFFFF:RETURN    'solid black
-- unused
2330    A$=A1$:C4=0:C5=1:C6=&H2108:RETURN
2340    A$=A2$:C4=0:C5=1:C6=&H4444:RETURN
2350    A$=A4$:C4=0:C5=1:C6=&HAAAA:RETURN
2360    A$=A5$:C4=1:C5=0:C6=&H4924:RETURN
2370    A$=A6$:C4=1:C5=0:C6=&H4444:RETURN
2380    A$=A7$:C4=1:C5=0:C6=&H808:RETURN
2390    A$=CHR$(&H55):C4=1:C5=1:C6=&HFFFF:RETURN
2400    A$=A9$:C4=1:C5=3:C6=&H808:RETURN
2410    A$=A10$:C4=1:C5=3:C6=&H4444:RETURN
2420    A$=A12$:C4=1:C5=3:C6=&H4924:RETURN
2430    A$=A13$:C4=1:C5=3:C6=&HAAAA:RETURN
2440    A$=A14$:C4=3:C5=1:C6=&H4924:RETURN
2450    A$=A15$:C4=3:C5=1:C6=&H4444:RETURN
2460    A$=A16$:C4=3:C5=1:C6=&H808:RETURN
2470    A$=CHR$(&HFF):C4=3:C5=3:C6=&HFFFF:RETURN
2480 '_____
2490 '
2500    END 'of program code
```

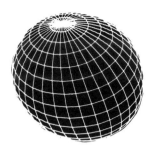

# 17

# *Mirror Reflections and Shadows*

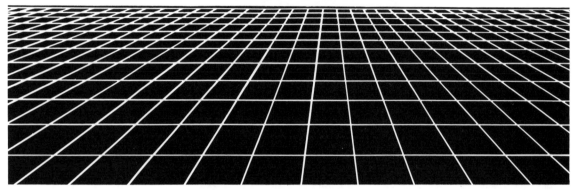

The modeling and rendering routines discussed so far can be easily adapted to generate specialized lighting conditions such as mirror reflections and shadows. Determining the locations of reflections and shadows involves a technique called ray tracing. Simply stated, the lines followed by individual rays of light are traced by geometry to determine their intersections with certain components within the modeling environment.

## MIRROR REFLECTIONS

A cube at rest upon a mirrored platform provides a good example of the geometric principles involved in ray tracing. Refer to Fig. 17-1. The edges of both the true model and its mirror reflection converge on the same vanishing points. This enables an exact replica of the cube to be drawn in the mirror, so to speak. The location of the mirror image is symmetrical to the location of the true model relative to the plane which forms the mirror.

Surface brightness is usually slightly dimmer for the mirror reflection than for the true object. Refer to Fig. 17-2. This is because some light rays are lost as the illumination reflects off the true model and then bounces off the mirror surface before eventually be-

ing captured by your eye. This slight reduction in intensity can be simulated by using an A$ variable one decrement removed from the matrix used in the shading routine. Intensity reduction is heavily influenced by the reflecting qualities of the mirror.

### Geometrical Analysis

The shape and position of a mirror image can be determined by simple geometry. Refer to Fig. 17-3. Simple intersection of diagonal lines can be used to locate the position of the mirror reflection. Visually, the reflection is the same distance from the mirror plane as the true model. For the purposes of this discussion, you can assume that the mirror is at right angles to the true model and the reflected image. (For a detailed discussion of perspective-drawing methods used by graphic artists, engineers, and architects, refer to the author's first book, *High-Speed Animation and Simulation for Microcomputers*, available at your favorite bookstore or direct from TAB BOOKS, Inc.)

### SHADOWS

Shadows can be derived by tracing the rays which originate from a specific light source. Refer to Fig.

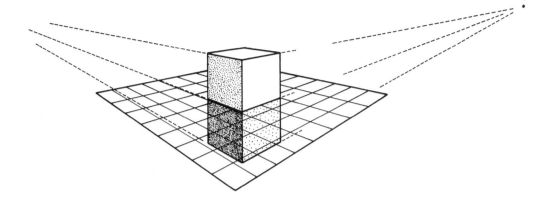

Fig. 17-1. Construction line trace procedure for a cube at rest upon a mirrored surface. Vanishing point symmetry is a universal feature of mirror reflections.

17-4. First, construction lines from a vanishing point are used to locate the position of the ground plane. Next, construction lines from the light source are used to trace the rays of light past the vertices of the model and to their intersection with the ground plane. The area encompassed by these intersections is cloaked in shadow, of course.

Vector mathematics are very useful for developing program algorithms which automatically calculate shadow locations. Refer to Fig. 17-5. Put in its simplest terms, the construction lines which identify the shadow vertices are parts of 3D triangles. If certain angles and/or sides are known, then the remaining angles and sides can be calculated, even in a 3D environment.

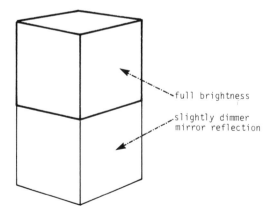

Fig. 17-2. Determination of intuitive light levels exhibited by mirror reflections.

## DEMONSTRATION
## PROGRAM: MIRROR REFLECTION

Figure 17-6 and Fig. 17-7 show the screen output produced by the demonstration program in Fig. 17-8. To run this program from the companion diskette, type **LOAD "A-27.BAS",R.** The program draws a solid cube at rest on a mirrored surface.

Note line 160. Depending upon the value assigned to the G flag by the configuration module (at lines 790 through 1060), program flow is directed to one of three standalone master routines. In order to ensure compatibility with all IBM-compatible hardware/software configurations, this program is really three separate programs in one.

Each master routine builds a solid 3D cube using the radial presort method. The database at lines 1160 through 1270 contains only the coordinates for the visible portions of the cube (and for the visible portions of the mirror image).

As you watch this program running, you will see that the computer first draws the mirror surface. A set of crosshatch lines is etched into the mirror to help keep its surface unambiguous. Next, the true cube is constructed.

The cube is drawn by lines 230 through 250 for the 640 × 350 mode, by lines 410 through 430 for the 640 × 200 mode, and by lines 580 through 600 for the Color/Graphics Adapter and PCjr/Tandy. The A$ halftone shading variable has been assigned intuitively, using artistic judgment. The C4, C5, and C6 linestyling variables have been matched to the A$ variable, of course.

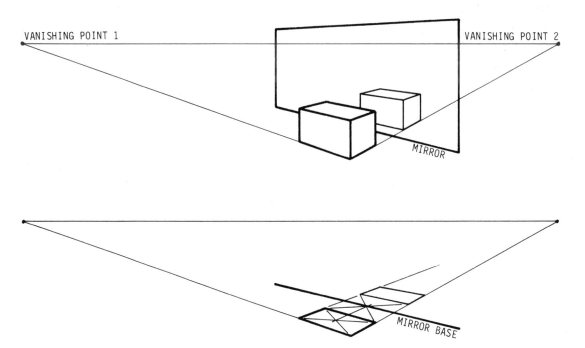

Fig. 17-3. Geometrical proof for positioning of mirror images using vanishing points and the laws of perspective. Top: effect of vanishing points on true image and mirror image. Bottom: using geometry to locate the base position of a mirror image.

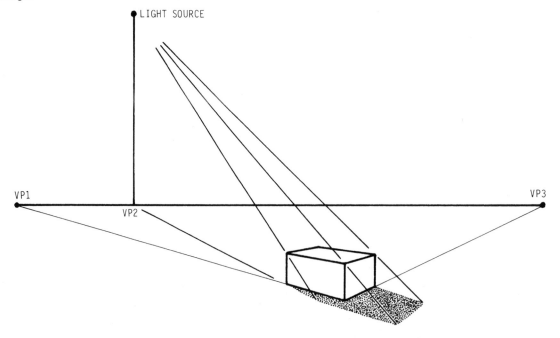

Fig. 17-4. Geometrical proof for positioning of ground shadows.

Colored cubes with shading rotated to various positions.

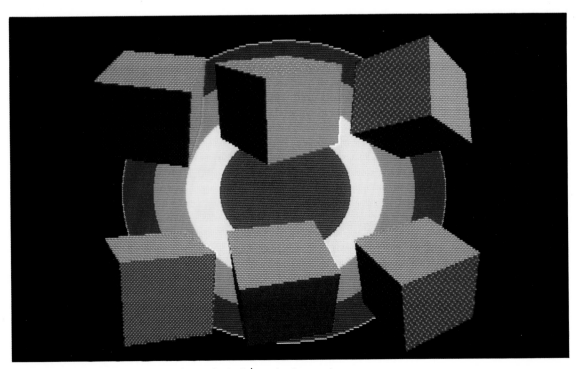

The same colored cubes placed in front of a bulls'-eye background.

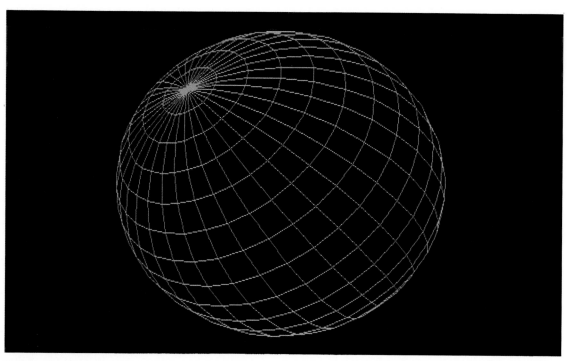

Outline of a globe in space.

The same globe colored and shaded.

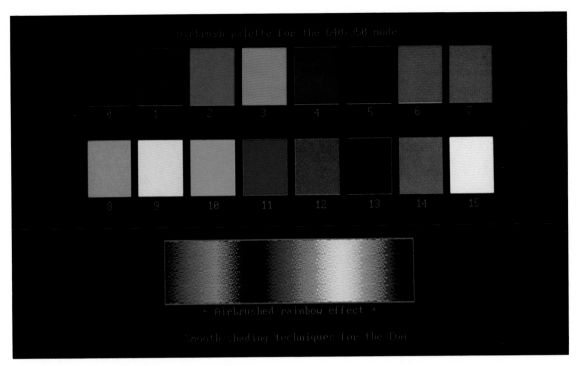

Airbrush palette for the EGA in 640×350 mode.

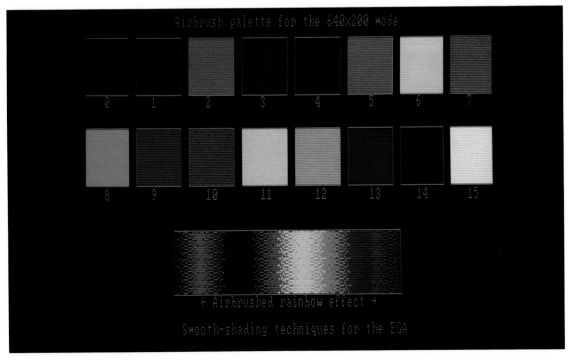

Airbrush palette for the EGA in 640×200 mode.

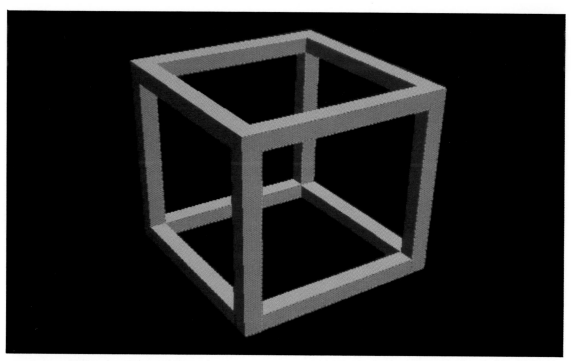

Colored frame cube with shading.

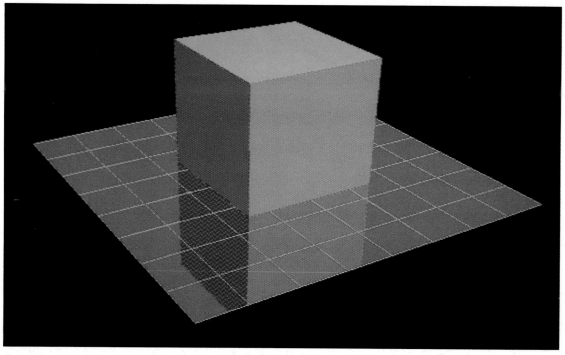

Colored and shaded cube on mirrored grid surface.

Soft drink cans at various rotations.

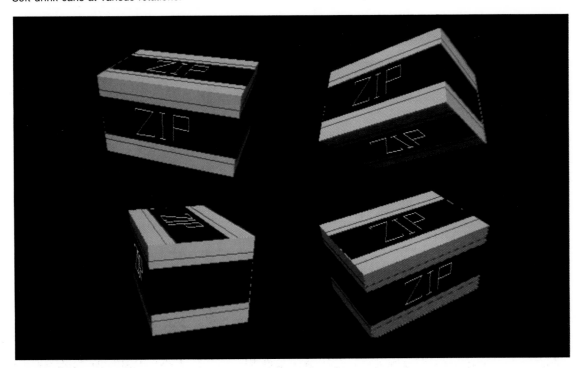

Boxes at various rotations.

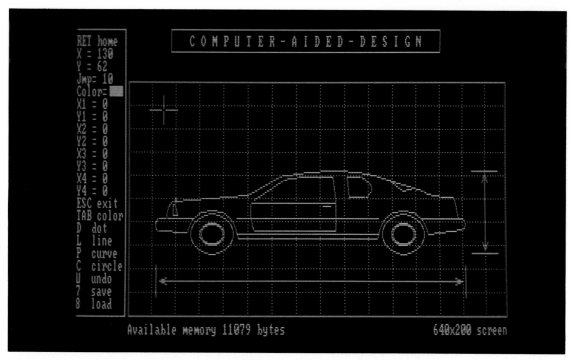

An engineering drawing of a car created with the 2D graphics program listed in Fig. 25-3.

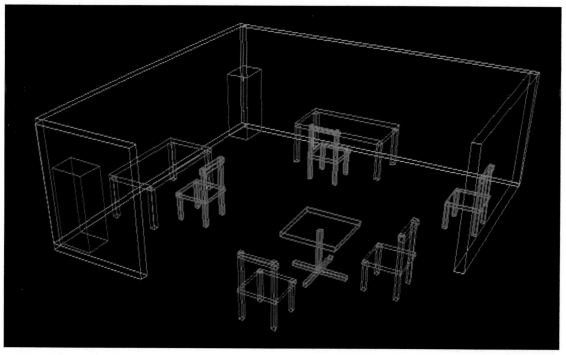

3D interior office design.

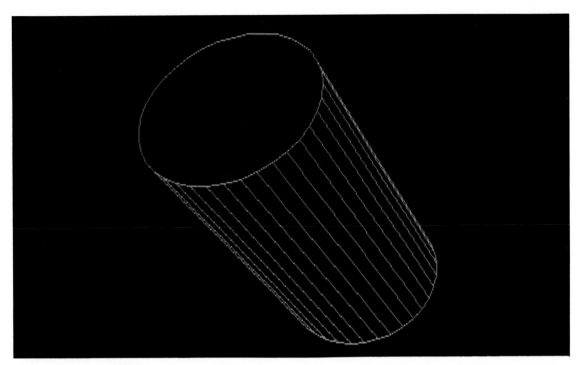

Outline of cylinder in space.

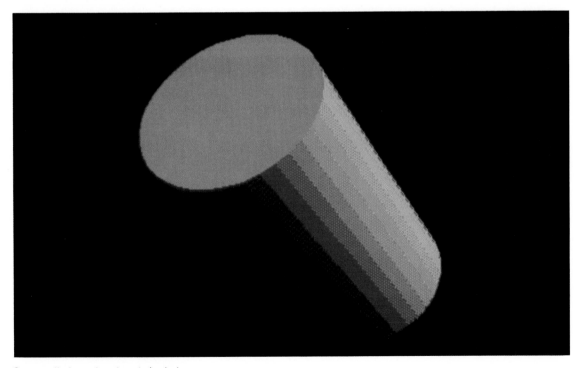

Same cylinder colored and shaded.

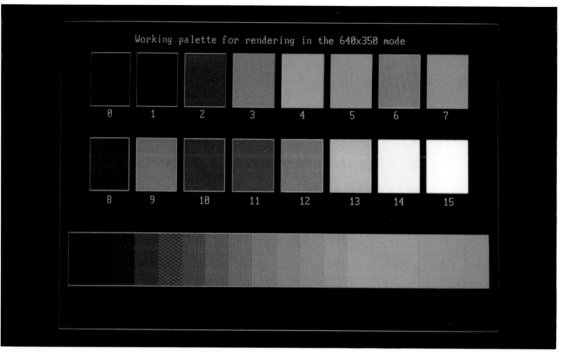

Working palette for the EGA in 640 × 350 mode.

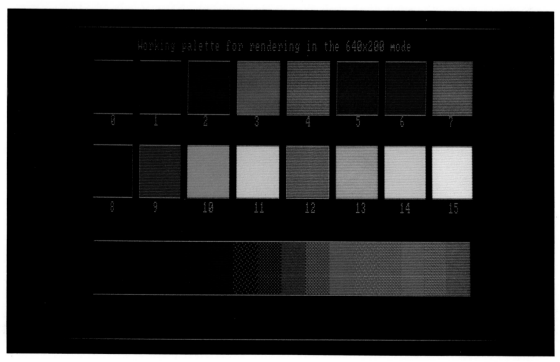

Working palette for the EGA in 640 × 200 mode.

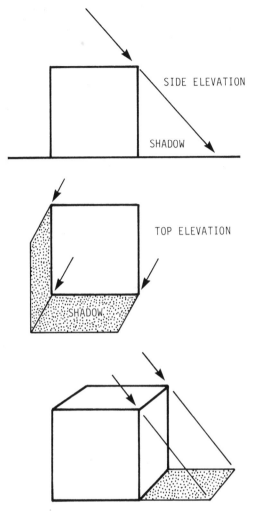

SIDE ELEVATION

SHADOW

TOP ELEVATION

SHADOW

Fig. 17-5. Ground shadow locations can be identified using vectors for 3D models on personal computers.

You may find it interesting to modify the shading on the cube. Refer to Fig. 16-6 in the previous chapter for guidance in selecting alternate shades. Remember to change the dithering variables to match the new A$ code. Refer to Fig. 16-5 in the previous chapter for assistance.

Next, the computer draws the front surface reflection and the side surface reflection. The database contains coordinates which are identical to those used for the true cube, except that the MY height coordinates have been negated (because the mirror surface is at height 0). If a vertex is located at height 30 above the mirror on the true model, then the corresponding vertex on the mirror image is located at height −30 below the mirror. Again, refer to Fig. 17-2.

Note that the mirror reflections fall outside the reflecting surface of the mirror and must be clipped by lines 290, 470, and 640. If you are using a Color/Graphics Adapter, you must be careful if you are experimenting by changing the halftone shades assigned to the reflected surfaces. The PAINT instruction which is used to delete these clipped areas will fail if the screen buffer is already filled with color attributes the same as the color being used for area fill (i.e., black). You can get around this by creating a key matte before you fill in your desired shade, just as the modeling routines do in the demonstration programs throughout this book.

This demonstration program will generate a very lifelike image on an EGA, in both the 640 × 350 16-color mode and the 640 × 200 16-color mode. However, even a standard Color/Graphics Adapter will produce an outstanding display in the 320 × 200 4-color mode. The secret to this program's success is the fact that the mirror image is slightly darker than the true image, and the fact that the mirror image is located symmetrically opposite the true image. The combination of geometric integrity and illumination intensity produces an extremely effective illusion on the 2D display screen.

You may find it interesting to create a mirror reflection of the frame cube produced by the demonstration program in Chapter 15. It is left as an exercise for you to do so. If you are really feeling ambitious, you may wish to take a crack at generating a mirror image of the fully-shaded sphere in Chapter 16. (Hint: the essential code is already in place, all you need do is draw the mirror surface and then modify the MY variable and loop back through the drawing code again! A nitpicky project, yes; an impossible project, no.)

## SUMMARY

In this chapter you learned that geometry can be used to create mirror reflections and shadows on microcomputer displays. You saw how a demonstration program could generate a very realistic mirror image using either an EGA, a Color/Graphics Adapter, or a PCjr video subsystem (Tandy).

The next chapter discusses techniques for producing airbrush displays on your personal computer.

Fig. 17-6. The display image produced by an EGA in the 640 × 350 16-color mode using the demonstration program in Fig. 17-8.

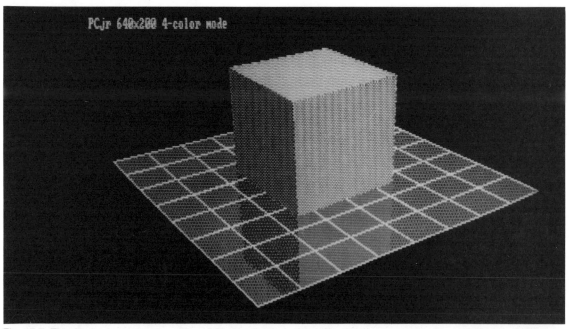

Fig. 17-7. The display image produced by a PCjr or a Tandy in the 640 × 200 4-color mode using the demonstration program in Fig. 17-8.

Fig. 17-8. Cube with mirror reflection.

```
100 'Program A-27.BAS    Cube with mirror reflection.
110 'Demonstrates intuitive shading of solid models.
120 '_____
130 '
140   GOTO 810  'configure system
150   GOSUB 1100 'assign scalar data
160   ON G GOTO 190, 370, 540  'jump to appropriate master ro
utine
170 '_____
180 '
190 'master routine for EGA and Enhanced Display
200   READ X,Y,Z:GOSUB 720:PSET (SX,SY),C3:FOR T=1 TO 4 STEP
1:READ X,Y,Z:GOSUB 720:LINE-(SX,SY),C3:NEXT:READ X,Y,Z:GOSUB
 720:PAINT (SX,SY),A7$,C3  'platform surface
210   FOR T=1 TO 7 STEP 1:READ X,Y,Z:GOSUB 720:PSET (SX,SY),C
3:READ X,Y,Z:GOSUB 720:LINE-(SX,SY),C3:NEXT  'trim on platfo
rm
220   FOR T=1 TO 7 STEP 1:READ X,Y,Z:GOSUB 720:PSET (SX,SY),C
3:READ X,Y,Z:GOSUB 720:LINE-(SX,SY),C3:NEXT  'trim on platfo
rm
230   RESTORE 1190:A$=A15$:C4=5:C5=4:C6=&HAAAA:GOSUB 1310   't
op of cube
240   RESTORE 1200:A$=A10$:C4=3:C5=4:C6=&H8888:GOSUB 1310   'f
ront of cube
250   RESTORE 1210:A$=A6$:C4=2:C5=3:C6=&H8888:GOSUB 1310   'le
ft side of cube
260   RESTORE 1220:A$=A8$:C4=3:C5=2:C6=&H8888:GOSUB 1310   'fr
ont reflection
270   RESTORE 1230:A$=A5$:C4=2:C5=3:C6=&H8080:GOSUB 1310   'si
de reflection
280   READ X,Y,Z:GOSUB 720:PSET (SX,SY),C3:READ X,Y,Z:GOSUB 7
20:LINE-(SX,SY),C3  'redraw near platform boundary
290   READ X,Y,Z:GOSUB 720:PAINT (SX,SY),C0,C3  'delete refle
ction outside bounds of platform
300   FOR T=1 TO 5 STEP 1:READ X,Y,Z:GOSUB 720:PSET (SX,SY),C
3:READ X,Y,Z:GOSUB 720:LINE-(SX,SY),C3:NEXT  'redraw lines o
n platform surface
310   FOR T=1 TO 5 STEP 1:READ X,Y,Z:GOSUB 720:PSET (SX,SY),C
3:READ X,Y,Z:GOSUB 720:LINE-(SX,SY),C3:NEXT  'redraw lines o
n platform surface
320   BEEP
330   GOTO 330  'clean halt.
340   END 'of master routine.
350 '_____
360 '
370 'master routine for EGA and standard Color Display
```

```
380   READ X,Y,Z:GOSUB 720:PSET (SX,SY),C3:FOR T=1 TO 4 STEP
1:READ X,Y,Z:GOSUB 720:LINE-(SX,SY),C3:NEXT:READ X,Y,Z:GOSUB
 720:PAINT (SX,SY),A5$,C3   'platform surface
390   FOR T=1 TO 7 STEP 1:READ X,Y,Z:GOSUB 720:PSET (SX,SY),C
3:READ X,Y,Z:GOSUB 720:LINE-(SX,SY),C3:NEXT   'trim on platfo
rm
400   FOR T=1 TO 7 STEP 1:READ X,Y,Z:GOSUB 720:PSET (SX,SY),C
3:READ X,Y,Z:GOSUB 720:LINE-(SX,SY),C3:NEXT   'trim on platfo
rm
410   RESTORE 1190:A$=A11$:C4=3:C5=4:C6=&HAAAA:GOSUB 1310   't
op of cube
420   RESTORE 1200:A$=A8$:C4=3:C5=2:C6=&H8888:GOSUB 1310   'fr
ont of cube
430   RESTORE 1210:A$=A4$:C4=2:C5=1:C6=&H8888:GOSUB 1310   'le
ft side of cube
440   RESTORE 1220:A$=A6$:C4=2:C5=3:C6=&H8888:GOSUB 1310   'fr
ont reflection
450   RESTORE 1230:A$=A3$:C4=1:C5=2:C6=&HAAAA:GOSUB 1310   'si
de reflection
460   READ X,Y,Z:GOSUB 720:PSET (SX,SY),C3:READ X,Y,Z:GOSUB 7
20:LINE-(SX,SY),C3   'redraw near platform boundary
470   READ X,Y,Z:GOSUB 720:PAINT (SX,SY),C0,C3   'delete refle
ction outside bounds of platform
480   FOR T=1 TO 5 STEP 1:READ X,Y,Z:GOSUB 720:PSET (SX,SY),C
3:READ X,Y,Z:GOSUB 720:LINE-(SX,SY),C3:NEXT   'redraw lines o
n platform surface
490   FOR T=1 TO 5 STEP 1:READ X,Y,Z:GOSUB 720:PSET (SX,SY),C
3:READ X,Y,Z:GOSUB 720:LINE-(SX,SY),C3:NEXT   'redraw lines o
n platform surface
500   BEEP
510   GOTO 510   'clean halt.
520 '_____
530 '
540 'master routine for CGA and PCjr
550   READ X,Y,Z:GOSUB 720:PSET (SX,SY),C3:FOR T=1 TO 4 STEP
1:READ X,Y,Z:GOSUB 720:LINE-(SX,SY),C3:NEXT:READ X,Y,Z:GOSUB
 720:PAINT (SX,SY),A7$,C3   'platform surface
560   FOR T=1 TO 7 STEP 1:READ X,Y,Z:GOSUB 720:PSET (SX,SY),C
3:READ X,Y,Z:GOSUB 720:LINE-(SX,SY),C3:NEXT   'trim on platfo
rm
570   FOR T=1 TO 7 STEP 1:READ X,Y,Z:GOSUB 720:PSET (SX,SY),C
3:READ X,Y,Z:GOSUB 720:LINE-(SX,SY),C3:NEXT   'trim on platfo
rm
580   RESTORE 1190:A$=A13$:C4=1:C5=3:C6=&HAAAA:GOSUB 1310   't
op of cube
590   RESTORE 1200:A$=A10$:C4=1:C5=3:C6=&H8888:GOSUB 1310   'f
ront of cube
600   RESTORE 1210:A$=A6$:C4=1:C5=0:C6=&H8888:GOSUB 1310   'le
ft side of cube
```

```
610   RESTORE 1220:A$=CHR$(&H55):C4=1:C5=1:C6=&HFFFF:GOSUB 13
10   'front reflection
620   RESTORE 1230:A$=A5$:C4=1:C5=0:C6=&H9248:GOSUB 1310   'si
de reflection
630   READ X,Y,Z:GOSUB 720:PSET (SX,SY),C3:READ X,Y,Z:GOSUB 7
20:LINE-(SX,SY),C3   'redraw near platform boundary
640   READ X,Y,Z:GOSUB 720:PAINT (SX,SY),C0,C3   'delete refle
ction outside bounds of platform
650   FOR T=1 TO 5 STEP 1:READ X,Y,Z:GOSUB 720:PSET (SX,SY),C
3:READ X,Y,Z:GOSUB 720:LINE-(SX,SY),C3:NEXT   'redraw lines o
n platform surface
660   FOR T=1 TO 5 STEP 1:READ X,Y,Z:GOSUB 720:PSET (SX,SY),C
3:READ X,Y,Z:GOSUB 720:LINE-(SX,SY),C3:NEXT   'redraw lines o
n platform surface
670   BEEP
680   GOTO 680   'clean halt.
690 '_____
700 '
710 'module:   perspective calculations for Cartesian world c
oordinates
720   X=(-1)*X:XA=CR1*X-SR1*Z:ZA=SR1*X+CR1*Z:X=CR2*XA+SR2*Y:Y
A=CR2*Y-SR2*XA:Z=CR3*ZA-SR3*YA:Y=SR3*ZA+CR3*YA:X=X+MX:Y=Y+MY
:Z=Z+MZ:SX=D*X/Z:SY=D*Y/Z:RETURN
730 '_____
740 '
750 'module: return to BASIC command level
760   CLS:SCREEN 0,0,0,0:WIDTH 80:COLOR 7,0,0:LOCATE 1,1,1:CL
S:END
770 '_____
780 '
790 'module:   UNIVERSAL
800 'This routine configures the program for the hardware/so
ftware being used.
810   KEY OFF:CLS:ON ERROR GOTO 870   'trap if not Enhanced Di
splay + EGA
820   SCREEN 9,,0,0:COLOR 7,0:PALETTE 1,8:PALETTE 2,1:PALETTE
 3,9:PALETTE 4,11:PALETTE 5,7:PALETTE 6,37:PALETTE 7,7:PALET
TE 8,56:PALETTE 9,34:PALETTE 10,20:PALETTE 11,5:PALETTE 12,4
4:PALETTE 13,46:PALETTE 14,55:PALETTE 15,63
830   C0=0:C1=12:C2=9:C3=7:LOCATE 1,1:PRINT "ED-EGA 640x350 1
6-color mode"
840   DEFINT G:G=1   'set flag for ED-EGA mode
850   GOSUB 1430   'assign bit tiling codes for EGA
860   GOTO 1030   'jump to screen coordinates set-up
870   RESUME 880
880   ON ERROR GOTO 930   'trap if not Color Display + EGA
890   SCREEN 8,,0,0:COLOR 7,0:PALETTE 1,0:PALETTE 2,1:PALETTE
 3,9:PALETTE 4,7:PALETTE 8,4:PALETTE 9,2:C0=0:C1=8:C2=9:C3=7
:LOCATE 1,1:PRINT "CD-EGA 640x200 16-color mode"
```

```
900    DEFINT G:G=2  'set flag for CD-EGA mode
910    GOSUB 1430   'assign shading codes for EGA
920    GOTO 1030    'jump to screen coordinates set-up
930    RESUME 940
940    ON ERROR GOTO 990 'trap if not PCjr
950    CLEAR,,,32768!:SCREEN 6,0,0,0:COLOR 3,0:PALETTE 1,8:PAL
ETTE 3,7:C0=0:C1=1:C2=2:C3=3:LOCATE 1,1:PRINT "PCjr 640x200
4-color mode"
960    DEFINT G:G=3  'set flag for PCjr mode
970    GOSUB 1630   'assign shading codes for PCjr
980    GOTO 1030    'jump to screen coordinates set-up
990    RESUME 1000
1000   SCREEN 1,0:COLOR 0,1:C0=0:C1=1:C2=2:C3=3:LOCATE 1,1:PR
INT "CGA 320x200 4-color mode"
1010   DEFINT G:G=3  'set flag for CGA mode
1020   GOSUB 1630   'assign shading codes for CGA
1030   ON ERROR GOTO 0  'disable error trapping override
1040   WINDOW SCREEN (-399,-299)-(400,300)
1050   ON KEY (2) GOSUB 760:KEY (2) ON  'F2 key to exit progr
am
1060   GOTO 150  'return to main program
1070 '_____
1080 '
1090 'module: assign scalar data
1100   D=1200:R1=.58539:R2=6.28319:R3=5.79778:MX=0:MY=0:MZ=-3
54   'angular distortion, rotation factors, viewpoint distan
ce for viewing coordinates
1110   SR1=SIN(R1):CR1=COS(R1):SR2=SIN(R2):CR2=COS(R2):SR3=SI
N(R3):CR3=COS(R3)
1120   RETURN
1130 '_____
1140 '
1150 'module: data base
1160   DATA -80,0,80,  -80,0,-80,  80,0,-80,  80,0,80,  -80,
0,80,  0,0,0
1170   DATA -80,0,-60,  80,0,-60,  -80,0,-40,  80,0,-40,  -8
0,0,-20,  80,0,-20,  -80,0,-0,  80,0,0,  -80,0,20,  80,0,20,
 -80,0,40,  80,0,40,  -80,0,60,  80,0,60
1180   DATA -60,0,80,  -60,0,-80,  -40,0,80,  -40,0,-80,  -2
0,0,80,  -20,0,-80,  0,0,80,  0,0,-80,  20,0,80,  20,0,-80,
 40,0,80,  40,0,-80,  60,0,80,  60,0,-80
1190   DATA -30,60,-30,  30,60,-30,  30,60,30,  -30,60,30,
0,60,0
1200   DATA -30,0,30,  -30,60,30,  30,60,30,  30,0,30,  0,30
,30
1210   DATA -30,0,-30,  -30,60,-30,  -30,60,30,  -30,0,30,
-30,30,0
1220   DATA -30,0,30,  30,0,30,  30,-60,30,  -30,-60,30,  0,
-30,30
```

218

```
1230  DATA  -30,0,30,   -30,-60,30,  -30,-60,-30,   -30,0,-30,
     -30,-30,0
1240  DATA  -80,0,80,  80,0,80
1250  DATA  0,-57,30
1260  DATA  -80,0,-20,  -30,0,-20,  -80,0,0,  -30,0,0,  -80,
  0,20,   -30,0,20,  -80,0,40,  80,0,40,  -80,0,60,  80,0,60
1270  DATA  -60,0,80,  -60,0,-80,  -40,0,80,  -40,0,-80,   -2
  0,0,80,  -20,0,30,  0,0,80,  0,0,30,  20,0,80,  20,0,30
1280  '_____
1290  '
1300  'module:   model & render simple polygon

1310  READ X,Y,Z:GOSUB 720:SX1=SX:SY1=SY:READ X,Y,Z:GOSUB 72
  0:SX2=SX:SY2=SY:READ X,Y,Z:GOSUB 720:SX3=SX:SY3=SY:READ X,Y,
  Z:GOSUB 720:SX4=SX:SY4=SY:READ X,Y,Z:GOSUB 720:SX5=SX:SY5=SY
    'calculate projection coordinates
1320  LINE (SX1,SY1)-(SX2,SY2),C2:LINE-(SX3,SY3),C2:LINE-(SX
  4,SY4),C2:LINE-(SX1,SY1),C2:PAINT (SX5,SY5),C2,C2  'key matt
  e
1330  LINE (SX1,SY1)-(SX2,SY2),C3:LINE-(SX3,SY3),C3:LINE-(SX
  4,SY4),C3:LINE-(SX1,SY1),C3:PAINT (SX5,SY5),C0,C3  'solid mo
  del
1340  PAINT (SX5,SY5),A$,C3  'shading
1350  LINE (SX1,SY1)-(SX2,SY2),C4:LINE (SX1,SY1)-(SX2,SY2),C
  5,,C6
1360  LINE (SX2,SY2)-(SX3,SY3),C4:LINE (SX2,SY2)-(SX3,SY3),C
  5,,C6
1370  LINE (SX3,SY3)-(SX4,SY4),C4:LINE (SX3,SY3)-(SX4,SY4),C
  5,,C6
1380  LINE (SX4,SY4)-(SX1,SY1),C4:LINE (SX4,SY4)-(SX1,SY1),C
  5,,C6
1390  RETURN
1400  '_____
1410  '
1420  'module:   assign shading codes for EGA

1430  A1$=CHR$(&HDF)+CHR$(&H20)+CHR$(&HO)+CHR$(&HO)+CHR$(&HF
  D)+CHR$(&H2)+CHR$(&HO)+CHR$(&HO)+CHR$(&H7F)+CHR$(&H80)+CHR$(
  &HO)+CHR$(&HO)+CHR$(&HF7)+CHR$(&H8)+CHR$(&HO)+CHR$(&HO)
1440  A2$=CHR$(&HBB)+CHR$(&H44)+CHR$(&HO)+CHR$(&HO)+CHR$(&HE
  E)+CHR$(&H11)+CHR$(&HO)+CHR$(&HO)
1450  A3$=CHR$(&HAA)+CHR$(&H55)+CHR$(&HO)+CHR$(&HO)+CHR$(&H5
  5)+CHR$(&HAA)+CHR$(&HO)+CHR$(&HO)
1460  A4$=CHR$(&H44)+CHR$(&HBB)+CHR$(&HO)+CHR$(&HO)+CHR$(&H1
  1)+CHR$(&HEE)+CHR$(&HO)+CHR$(&HO)
1470  A5$=CHR$(&H20)+CHR$(&HFF)+CHR$(&HO)+CHR$(&HO)+CHR$(&H2
  )+CHR$(&HFF)+CHR$(&HO)+CHR$(&HO)+CHR$(&H80)+CHR$(&HFF)+CHR$(
  &HO)+CHR$(&HO)+CHR$(&H8)+CHR$(&HFF)+CHR$(&HO)+CHR$(&HO)
1480  A6$=CHR$(&H44)+CHR$(&HFF)+CHR$(&HO)+CHR$(&HO)+CHR$(&H1
  1)+CHR$(&HFF)+CHR$(&HO)+CHR$(&HO)
```

```
1490   A7$=CHR$(&H55)+CHR$(&HFF)+CHR$(&HO)+CHR$(&HO)+CHR$(&HA
A)+CHR$(&HFF)+CHR$(&HO)+CHR$(&HO)
1500   A8$=CHR$(&HBB)+CHR$(&HFF)+CHR$(&HO)+CHR$(&HO)+CHR$(&HE
E)+CHR$(&HFF)+CHR$(&HO)+CHR$(&HO)
1510   A9$=CHR$(&HDF)+CHR$(&HDF)+CHR$(&H20)+CHR$(&HO)+CHR$(&H
FD)+CHR$(&HFD)+CHR$(&H2)+CHR$(&HO)+CHR$(&H7F)+CHR$(&H7F)+CHR
$(&H80)+CHR$(&HO)+CHR$(&HF7)+CHR$(&HF7)+CHR$(&H8)+CHR$(&HO)
1520   A10$=CHR$(&HBB)+CHR$(&HBB)+CHR$(&H44)+CHR$(&HO)+CHR$(&
HEE)+CHR$(&HEE)+CHR$(&H11)+CHR$(&HO)
1530   A11$=CHR$(&HAA)+CHR$(&HAA)+CHR$(&H55)+CHR$(&HO)+CHR$(&
H55)+CHR$(&H55)+CHR$(&HAA)+CHR$(&HO)
1540   A12$=CHR$(&H44)+CHR$(&H44)+CHR$(&HBB)+CHR$(&HO)+CHR$(&
H11)+CHR$(&H11)+CHR$(&HEE)+CHR$(&HO)
1550   A13$=CHR$(&H20)+CHR$(&HO)+CHR$(&HFF)+CHR$(&HO)+CHR$(&H
2)+CHR$(&HO)+CHR$(&HFF)+CHR$(&HO)+CHR$(&H80)+CHR$(&HO)+CHR$(
&HFF)+CHR$(&HO)+CHR$(&H8)+CHR$(&HO)+CHR$(&HFF)+CHR$(&HO)
1560   A14$=CHR$(&H44)+CHR$(&HO)+CHR$(&HFF)+CHR$(&HO)+CHR$(&H
11)+CHR$(&HO)+CHR$(&HFF)+CHR$(&HO)
1570   A15$=CHR$(&H55)+CHR$(&HO)+CHR$(&HFF)+CHR$(&HO)+CHR$(&H
AA)+CHR$(&HO)+CHR$(&HFF)+CHR$(&HO)
1580   A16$=CHR$(&HBB)+CHR$(&HO)+CHR$(&HFF)+CHR$(&HO)+CHR$(&H
EE)+CHR$(&HO)+CHR$(&HFF)+CHR$(&HO)
1590   RETURN
1600 '_____
1610 '
1620 'module:   assign shading codes for CGA and/or PCjr
1630   A1$=CHR$(&H40)+CHR$(&HO)+CHR$(&H4)+CHR$(&HO)
1640   A2$=CHR$(&H40)+CHR$(&H4)+CHR$(&H40)+CHR$(&H4)
1650   A3$=CHR$(&H44)+CHR$(&H10)+CHR$(&H11)+CHR$(&H1)+CHR$(&H
44)+CHR$(&H4)+CHR$(&H11)+CHR$(&H40)
1660   A4$=CHR$(&H44)+CHR$(&H11)+CHR$(&H44)+CHR$(&H11)
1670   A5$=CHR$(&H11)+CHR$(&H45)+CHR$(&H44)+CHR$(&H54)+CHR$(&
H11)+CHR$(&H51)+CHR$(&H44)+CHR$(&H15)
1680   A6$=CHR$(&H15)+CHR$(&H51)+CHR$(&H15)+CHR$(&H51)
1690   A7$=CHR$(&H15)+CHR$(&H55)+CHR$(&H51)+CHR$(&H55)
1700   A9$=CHR$(&HD5)+CHR$(&H55)+CHR$(&H5D)+CHR$(&H55)
1710   A10$=CHR$(&HD5)+CHR$(&H5D)+CHR$(&HD5)+CHR$(&H5D)
1720   A12$=CHR$(&HDD)+CHR$(&H75)+CHR$(&H77)+CHR$(&H57)+CHR$(
&HDD)+CHR$(&H5D)+CHR$(&H77)+CHR$(&HD5)
1730   A13$=CHR$(&HDD)+CHR$(&H77)+CHR$(&HDD)+CHR$(&H77)
1740   A14$=CHR$(&H77)+CHR$(&HDF)+CHR$(&HDD)+CHR$(&HFD)+CHR$(
&H77)+CHR$(&HF7)+CHR$(&HDD)+CHR$(&H7F)
1750   A15$=CHR$(&H7F)+CHR$(&HF7)+CHR$(&H7F)+CHR$(&HF7)
1760   A16$=CHR$(&H7F)+CHR$(&HFF)+CHR$(&HF7)+CHR$(&HFF)
1770   RETURN
1780 '_____
1790 '
1800   END 'of program code
```

# 18

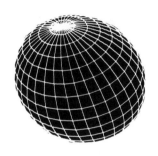

# *Smooth Shading*

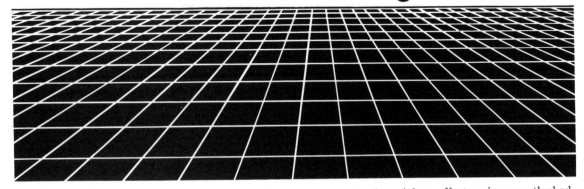

Smooth shading is sometimes called variable shading, airbrushing, or full shading. Simply stated, it involves setting the color attributes for individual pixels. The halftone shading method discussed in previous chapters, on the other hand, sets entire groups of pixels within a polygon surface. (Read Chapter 14 and Chapter 15 for more information about this.)

The highly dramatic images produced by smooth shading are possible, to a limited degree, on off-the-shelf personal computers. Rainbow effects are easily generated, for example. Solid 3D models present problems which are not so easily overcome. (Read Chapter 14 for more on this.) Neither an EGA, nor a Color/Graphics Adapter, nor a PCjr video subsystem offer enough different colors of the same hue to be able to set individual pixels to simulate subtle shading on the model. An individual pixel, after all, is either one color or another color. In the $640 \times 200$ 16-color mode on the EGA, two shades of blue are clearly not enough to render a realistic solid model. (By using the halftone bit tiling method, however, you could produce nine distinct shades between those two hues of blue!)

## RAINBOW GRADIATIONS

Any screen mode which offers 16 colors will sup-

port spectacular rainbow effects using smooth shading. By invoking the line dithering algorithm made possible by BASIC's linestyling function, individual pixels in varying colors can be applied to any portion of the display screen. The syntax for this function is LINE  (x1,y1) - (x2,y2),color,,hex-style-code.  The styling code consists of a four-digit hex number which corresponds to an on-off binary number. For example, &HAAAA translates to 1010 1010 1010 1010 in binary. A pixel is turned on for each 1 in the binary template; no pixel is turned on when a 0 occurs in the binary template. The syntax is consistent across all graphics screen modes.

Figure 18-1 shows the screen output of the demonstration program in Fig. 18-2. To run this program from the companion diskette, type **LOAD** *"A-28.* **BAS***",***R**. The program displays a rainbow-like effect in the $640 \times 350$ 16-color mode on the EGA.

Figure 18-3 shows the screen output of the demonstration program in Fig. 18-4. To run this program from the companion diskette, type **LOAD** *"A-29.* **BAS***",***R**. The program displays a rainbow-like effect in the $320 \times 200$ 16-color mode on the IBM PCjr using Cartridge BASIC and the Tandy using GW-BASIC.

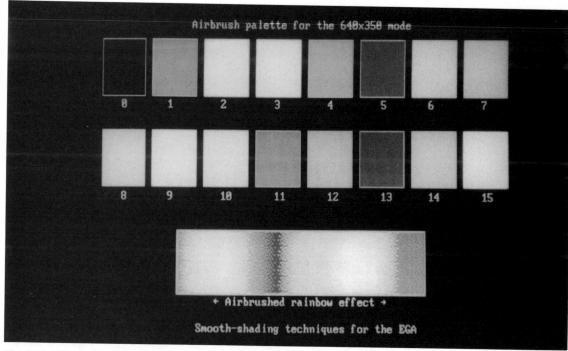

Fig. 18-1. The display image produced by the demonstration program in Fig. 18-2.

Fig. 18-2. Smooth shading in the EGA 640 x 350 16-color mode.

```
100 'Program A-28.BAS    Airbrush palette for 640x350 mode.
110 'Demonstrates dithering techniques.
120 '_____
130 '
140   KEY OFF:CLS:ON ERROR GOTO 940:SCREEN 9,,0,0:COLOR 7,0:C
LS  '640x350 16-color mode.
150   ON ERROR GOTO 0
160   ON KEY (2) GOSUB 900:KEY (2) ON  'enable clean exit.
170   DEFINT C,S,T:SX=0:C4=0:C5=0
180   PALETTE 1,1:PALETTE 2,9:PALETTE 3,11:PALETTE 4,5:PALETT
E 5,4:PALETTE 6,44:PALETTE 7,7:PALETTE 8,46:PALETTE 9,55:PAL
ETTE 10,51:PALETTE 11,34:PALETTE 12,3:PALETTE 13,56:PALETTE
14,7:PALETTE 15,63
190 '_____
200 '
210 'module:  create generic screen
220   LOCATE 25,23:PRINT "Smooth-shading techniques for the E
GA"
230   LOCATE 2,22:PRINT "Airbrush palette for the 640x350 mod
e":LOCATE 23,28:PRINT "Airbrushed rainbow effect"
240   LOCATE 23,26:PRINT CHR$(27):LOCATE 23,54:PRINT CHR$(26)
```

```
250  X=45:FOR T=1 TO 8 STEP 1:LINE (X,36)-(X+60,96),7,B:X=X+
70:NEXT T
260  LOCATE 8,10:PRINT "0":LOCATE 8,18:PRINT "1":LOCATE 8,27
:PRINT "2":LOCATE 8,36:PRINT "3":LOCATE 8,45:PRINT "4":LOCAT
E 8,54:PRINT "5":LOCATE 8,62:PRINT "6":LOCATE 8,71:PRINT "7"
270  X=45:FOR T=1 TO 8 STEP 1:LINE (X,132)-(X+60,192),7,B:X=
X+70:NEXT T
280  LOCATE 15,10:PRINT "8":LOCATE 15,18:PRINT "9":LOCATE 15
,27:PRINT "10":LOCATE 15,36:PRINT "11":LOCATE 15,45:PRINT "1
2":LOCATE 15,54:PRINT "13":LOCATE 15,62:PRINT "14":LOCATE 15
,71:PRINT "15"
290  X=75:C=0:FOR T=1 TO 8 STEP 1:PAINT (X,40),C,7:X=X+70:C=
C+1:NEXT T
300  X=75:C=8:FOR T=1 TO 8 STEP 1:PAINT (X,140),C,7:X=X+70:C
=C+1:NEXT T
310  LINE (150,240)-(482,306),7,B:LINE (149,239)-(483,307),7
,B
320 '_____
330 '
340 'module:   apply airbrush dithering
350  SX=151
360  C4=1:C5=2:GOSUB 500
370  C4=2:C5=3:GOSUB 500
380  C4=3:C5=4:GOSUB 500
390  C4=4:C5=5:GOSUB 500
400  C4=5:C5=6:GOSUB 500
410  C4=6:C5=8:GOSUB 500
420  C4=8:C5=9:GOSUB 500
430  C4=9:C5=10:GOSUB 500
440  C4=10:C5=11:GOSUB 500
450  C4=11:C5=1:GOSUB 500
460  SOUND 350,.7
470  GOTO 470
480 '_____
490 '
500 'module:   airbrush shift from color C4 to color C5
510  LINE (SX,241)-(SX,305),C4
520  LINE (SX,241)-(SX,305),C4
530  SX=SX+1:LINE (SX,241)-(SX,305),C4
540  SX=SX+1:LINE (SX,241)-(SX,305),C4
550  SX=SX+1:LINE (SX,241)-(SX,305),C4:LINE (SX,241)-(SX,305
),C5,,&H80
560  SX=SX+1:LINE (SX,241)-(SX,305),C4:LINE (SX,241)-(SX,305
),C5,,&H800
570  SX=SX+1:LINE (SX,241)-(SX,305),C4:LINE (SX,241)-(SX,305
),C5,,&H808
580  SX=SX+1:LINE (SX,241)-(SX,305),C4:LINE (SX,241)-(SX,305
),C5,,&H8080
```

```
590   SX=SX+1:LINE (SX,241)-(SX,305),C4:LINE (SX,241)-(SX,305
),C5,,&H8420
600   SX=SX+1:LINE (SX,241)-(SX,305),C4:LINE (SX,241)-(SX,305
),C5,,&H2108
610   SX=SX+1:LINE (SX,241)-(SX,305),C4:LINE (SX,241)-(SX,305
),C5,,&H1111
620   SX=SX+1:LINE (SX,241)-(SX,305),C4:LINE (SX,241)-(SX,305
),C5,,&H4444
630   SX=SX+1:LINE (SX,241)-(SX,305),C4:LINE (SX,241)-(SX,305
),C5,,&H9248
640   SX=SX+1:LINE (SX,241)-(SX,305),C4:LINE (SX,241)-(SX,305
),C5,,&H4924
650   SX=SX+1:LINE (SX,241)-(SX,305),C4:LINE (SX,241)-(SX,305
),C5,,&H8A8A
660   SX=SX+1:LINE (SX,241)-(SX,305),C4:LINE (SX,241)-(SX,305
),C5,,&HA8A8
670   SX=SX+1:LINE (SX,241)-(SX,305),C4:LINE (SX,241)-(SX,305
),C5,,&HAAA8
680   SX=SX+1:LINE (SX,241)-(SX,305),C4:LINE (SX,241)-(SX,305
),C5,,&HA8AA
690   SX=SX+1:LINE (SX,241)-(SX,305),C4:LINE (SX,241)-(SX,305
),C5,,&HAAAA
700   SX=SX+1:LINE (SX,241)-(SX,305),C4:LINE (SX,241)-(SX,305
),C5,,&H5555
710   SX=SX+1:LINE (SX,241)-(SX,305),C5:LINE (SX,241)-(SX,305
),C4,,&HAAA8
720   SX=SX+1:LINE (SX,241)-(SX,305),C5:LINE (SX,241)-(SX,305
),C4,,&HA8AA
730   SX=SX+1:LINE (SX,241)-(SX,305),C5:LINE (SX,241)-(SX,305
),C4,,&H8A8A
740   SX=SX+1:LINE (SX,241)-(SX,305),C5:LINE (SX,241)-(SX,305
),C4,,&HA8A8
750   SX=SX+1:LINE (SX,241)-(SX,305),C5:LINE (SX,241)-(SX,305
),C4,,&H9248
760   SX=SX+1:LINE (SX,241)-(SX,305),C5:LINE (SX,241)-(SX,305
),C4,,&H2492
770   SX=SX+1:LINE (SX,241)-(SX,305),C5:LINE (SX,241)-(SX,305
),C4,,&H1111
780   SX=SX+1:LINE (SX,241)-(SX,305),C5:LINE (SX,241)-(SX,305
),C4,,&H4444
790   SX=SX+1:LINE (SX,241)-(SX,305),C5:LINE (SX,241)-(SX,305
),C4,,&H8420
800   SX=SX+1:LINE (SX,241)-(SX,305),C5:LINE (SX,241)-(SX,305
),C4,,&H2108
810   SX=SX+1:LINE (SX,241)-(SX,305),C5:LINE (SX,241)-(SX,305
),C4,,&H808
820   SX=SX+1:LINE (SX,241)-(SX,305),C5:LINE (SX,241)-(SX,305
),C4,,&H8080
```

```
830  SX=SX+1:LINE (SX,241)-(SX,305),C5:LINE (SX,241)-(SX,305
),C4,,&H80
840  SX=SX+1:LINE (SX,241)-(SX,305),C5:LINE (SX,241)-(SX,305
),C4,,&H8000
850  SX=SX+1:LINE (SX,241)-(SX,305),C5
860  RETURN
870  '_____
880  '
890  'module:  return to BASIC interpreter
900  CLS:SCREEN 0,0,0,0:WIDTH 80:COLOR 7,0,0:LOCATE 1,1,1:CL
S:END
910  '_____
920  '
930  'module:  trap if not EGA and Enhanced Color Display
940  SOUND 350,.7:LOCATE 10,1:PRINT "To run this program, yo
u require":LOCATE 11,1:PRINT "an EGA with at least 128Kb,":L
OCATE 12,1:PRINT "an enhanced color display monitor,"
950  LOCATE 13,1:PRINT "and IBM BASICA 3.21 or equivalent,":
LOCATE 14,1:PRINT "or QuickBASIC or TurboBASIC."
960  LOCATE 18,1:PRINT "Press ESC to return to BASIC..."
970  K$=INKEY$
980  IF K$=CHR$(27) THEN RESUME 1000
990  GOTO 970
1000  CLS:LOCATE 1,1,1:END
1010 '_____
1020 '
1030  END 'of program code
```

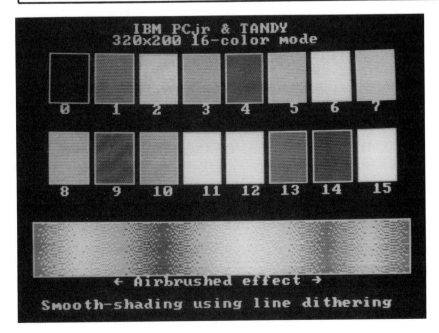

Fig. 18-3. The display image produced by the demonstration program in Fig. 18-4.

Fig. 18-4. Smooth shading in the PCjr/Tandy 320 × 200 16-color mode.

```
100 'Program A-29.BAS    Airbrush palette PCjr or Tandy.
110 'Demonstrates dithering techniques.
120 '_____
130 '
140   KEY OFF:CLS:ON ERROR GOTO 930:CLEAR,,,32768!:SCREEN 5:C
OLOR 7,0:CLS  '320x200 16-color mode.
150   ON ERROR GOTO 0
160   ON KEY (2) GOSUB 890:KEY (2) ON  'enable clean exit.
170   DEFINT C,S,T:SX=0:C4=0:C5=0
180   PALETTE 1,1:PALETTE 2,9:PALETTE 3,5:PALETTE 4,4:PALETTE
 5,12:PALETTE 6,14:PALETTE 7,7:PALETTE 8,10:PALETTE 9,2:PALE
TTE 10,3:PALETTE 11,11:PALETTE 12,13:PALETTE 13,6:PALETTE 14
,8:PALETTE 15,15
190 '_____
200 '
210 'module:  create generic screen
220   LOCATE 25,3:PRINT "Smooth-shading using line dithering"
230   LOCATE 1,12:PRINT "IBM PCjr & TANDY":LOCATE 2,10:PRINT
"320x200 16-color mode":LOCATE 23,12:PRINT "Airbrushed effec
t"
240   LOCATE 23,10:PRINT CHR$(27):LOCATE 23,30:PRINT CHR$(26)

250   X=23:FOR T=1 TO 8 STEP 1:LINE (X,21)-(X+30,55),7,B:X=X+
35:NEXT T
260   LOCATE 8,5:PRINT "0":LOCATE 8,10:PRINT "1":LOCATE 8,14:
PRINT "2":LOCATE 8,19:PRINT "3":LOCATE 8,23:PRINT "4":LOCATE
 8,28:PRINT "5":LOCATE 8,32:PRINT "6":LOCATE 8,36:PRINT "7"
270   X=23:FOR T=1 TO 8 STEP 1:LINE (X,75)-(X+30,110),7,B:X=X
+35:NEXT T
280   LOCATE 15,5:PRINT "8":LOCATE 15,10:PRINT "9":LOCATE 15,
14:PRINT "10":LOCATE 15,19:PRINT "11":LOCATE 15,23:PRINT "12
":LOCATE 15,27:PRINT "13":LOCATE 15,31:PRINT "14":LOCATE 15,
36:PRINT "15"
290   X=38:C=0:FOR T=1 TO 8 STEP 1:PAINT (X,23),C,7:X=X+35:C=
C+1:NEXT T
300   X=38:C=8:FOR T=1 TO 8 STEP 1:PAINT (X,80),C,7:X=X+35:C=
C+1:NEXT T
310   LINE (10,137)-(309,175),7,B
320 '_____
330 '
340 'module:  apply airbrush dithering
350   SX=11
360   C4=1:C5=2:GOSUB 490
370   C4=2:C5=3:GOSUB 490
380   C4=3:C5=4:GOSUB 490
390   C4=4:C5=5:GOSUB 490
```

```
400   C4=5:C5=6:GOSUB 490
410   C4=6:C5=8:GOSUB 490
420   C4=8:C5=9:GOSUB 490
430   C4=9:C5=10:GOSUB 490
440   C4=10:C5=13:GOSUB 490
450   SOUND 350,.7
460   GOTO 460
470   '_____
480   '
490   'module:  airbrush shift from color C4 to color C5
500   LINE (SX,138)-(SX,174),C4
510   LINE (SX,138)-(SX,174),C4
520   SX=SX+1:LINE (SX,138)-(SX,174),C4
530   SX=SX+1:LINE (SX,138)-(SX,174),C4
540   SX=SX+1:LINE (SX,138)-(SX,174),C4:LINE (SX,138)-(SX,174
      ),C5,,&H80
550   SX=SX+1:LINE (SX,138)-(SX,174),C4:LINE (SX,138)-(SX,174
      ),C5,,&H800
560   SX=SX+1:LINE (SX,138)-(SX,174),C4:LINE (SX,138)-(SX,174
      ),C5,,&H808
570   SX=SX+1:LINE (SX,138)-(SX,174),C4:LINE (SX,138)-(SX,174
      ),C5,,&H8080
580   SX=SX+1:LINE (SX,138)-(SX,174),C4:LINE (SX,138)-(SX,174
      ),C5,,&H8420
590   SX=SX+1:LINE (SX,138)-(SX,174),C4:LINE (SX,138)-(SX,174
      ),C5,,&H2108
600   SX=SX+1:LINE (SX,138)-(SX,174),C4:LINE (SX,138)-(SX,174
      ),C5,,&H1111
610   SX=SX+1:LINE (SX,138)-(SX,174),C4:LINE (SX,138)-(SX,174
      ),C5,,&H4444
620   SX=SX+1:LINE (SX,138)-(SX,174),C4:LINE (SX,138)-(SX,174
      ),C5,,&H9248
630   SX=SX+1:LINE (SX,138)-(SX,174),C4:LINE (SX,138)-(SX,174
      ),C5,,&H4924
640   SX=SX+1:LINE (SX,138)-(SX,174),C4:LINE (SX,138)-(SX,174
      ),C5,,&H8A8A
650   SX=SX+1:LINE (SX,138)-(SX,174),C4:LINE (SX,138)-(SX,174
      ),C5,,&HA8A8
660   SX=SX+1:LINE (SX,138)-(SX,174),C4:LINE (SX,138)-(SX,174
      ),C5,,&HAAA8
670   SX=SX+1:LINE (SX,138)-(SX,174),C4:LINE (SX,138)-(SX,174
      ),C5,,&HA8AA
680   SX=SX+1:LINE (SX,138)-(SX,174),C4:LINE (SX,138)-(SX,174
      ),C5,,&HAAAA
690   SX=SX+1:LINE (SX,138)-(SX,174),C4:LINE (SX,138)-(SX,174
      ),C5,,&H5555
700   SX=SX+1:LINE (SX,138)-(SX,174),C5:LINE (SX,138)-(SX,174
      ),C4,,&HAAA8
710   SX=SX+1:LINE (SX,138)-(SX,174),C5:LINE (SX,138)-(SX,174
```

```
),C4,,&HA8AA
 720   SX=SX+1:LINE (SX,138)-(SX,174),C5:LINE (SX,138)-(SX,174
),C4,,&H8A8A
 730   SX=SX+1:LINE (SX,138)-(SX,174),C5:LINE (SX,138)-(SX,174
),C4,,&HA8A8
 740   SX=SX+1:LINE (SX,138)-(SX,174),C5:LINE (SX,138)-(SX,174
),C4,,&H9248
 750   SX=SX+1:LINE (SX,138)-(SX,174),C5:LINE (SX,138)-(SX,174
),C4,,&H2492
 760   SX=SX+1:LINE (SX,138)-(SX,174),C5:LINE (SX,138)-(SX,174
),C4,,&H1111
 770   SX=SX+1:LINE (SX,138)-(SX,174),C5:LINE (SX,138)-(SX,174
),C4,,&H4444
 780   SX=SX+1:LINE (SX,138)-(SX,174),C5:LINE (SX,138)-(SX,174
),C4,,&H8420
 790   SX=SX+1:LINE (SX,138)-(SX,174),C5:LINE (SX,138)-(SX,174
),C4,,&H2108
 800   SX=SX+1:LINE (SX,138)-(SX,174),C5:LINE (SX,138)-(SX,174
),C4,,&H808
 810   SX=SX+1:LINE (SX,138)-(SX,174),C5:LINE (SX,138)-(SX,174
),C4,,&H8080
 820   SX=SX+1:LINE (SX,138)-(SX,174),C5:LINE (SX,138)-(SX,174
),C4,,&H80
 830   SX=SX+1:LINE (SX,138)-(SX,174),C5:LINE (SX,138)-(SX,174
),C4,,&H8000
 840   SX=SX+1:LINE (SX,138)-(SX,174),C5
 850   RETURN
 860   '_____
 870   '
 880   'module:   return to BASIC interpreter
 890   CLS:SCREEN 0,0,0,0:WIDTH 80:CLEAR:COLOR 7,0,0:LOCATE 1,
1,1:CLS:END
 900   '_____
 910   '
 920   'module:   trap if not PCjr or Tandy microcomputer
 930   SOUND 350,.7:LOCATE 10,1:PRINT "To run this program, yo
u require":LOCATE 11,1:PRINT "an IBM PCjr or a Tandy,":LOCAT
E 12,1:PRINT "an RGB color display monitor,"
 940   LOCATE 13,1:PRINT "and IBM Cartridge BASIC,":LOCATE 14,
1:PRINT "or GW BASIC."
 950   LOCATE 18,1:PRINT "Press ESC to return to BASIC..."
 960   K$=INKEY$
 970   IF K$=CHR$(27) THEN RESUME 990
 980   GOTO 960
 990   CLS:LOCATE 1,1,1:END
1000   '_____
1010   '
1020   END 'of program code
```

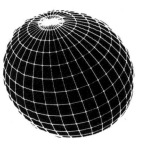

# 19

# *Concepts of High-Speed Animation*

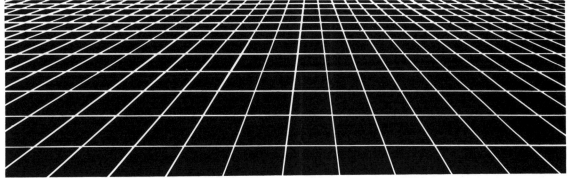

Three distinct methods for producing high-speed animation on microcomputers are available for the programmer who wishes to add movement to 3D models. These methods are: software sprite animation, frame animation, and real-time animation.

## ANIMATION ON PROFESSIONAL WORKSTATIONS

For most purposes, animation on professional graphics workstations means frame animation. Refer to Fig. 19-1. The computer generates a fully-shaded image and stores it in a display buffer (similar to the screen buffer used in your personal computer). Then a sync generator and signal encoder create a video signal which is compatible with television industry standards. Finally, a video controller unit which is capable of starting and stopping a videocassette recorder is used to store the image as a single frame on videotape. This procedure is repeated until enough frames have been created to enable playback of the videotape animation at 30 fps (frames per second). Often, a graphics workstation will be left alone all night to prepare a short segment of videotape, which is ready to

run when the programmer arrives back the next morning.

### Performance Boosters

Unlike the standard IBM PC, XT, AT, PCjr, PS/2, and compatibles, many professional graphics workstations have specialized hardware installed. This dedicated hardware is designed to speed up the modeling, rendering, and animating process. Dedicated line-clipping hardware will clip lines to fit the 2D screen. Dedicated matrix-generating hardware will calculate the rotation, translation, and projection formulas required by 3D models. Special graphics coprocessors (also called DPU drivers) take care of plotting the graphics on the display screen. High-performance workstations which are fully equipped with dedicated hardware can also be used to produce real-time animation sequences (such as flight simulation training modules, for example).

## ANIMATION ON PERSONAL COMPUTERS

No matter what type of graphics adapter you have installed in your personal computer, you can invoke

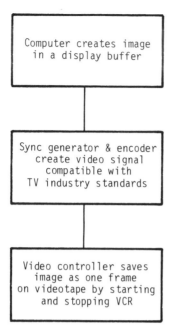

Fig. 19-1. The three steps used to create sequential images on broadcast-quality videotape for frame animation at 30 fps.

three different methods to produce high-speed animation. These methods are: software sprite animation, frame animation, and real-time animation. Each method has its strengths and weaknesses. Each method can be implemented on an EGA, a Color/Graphics Adapter, and a PCjr video subsystem (and Tandy).

## SOFTWARE SPRITE ANIMATION

Software sprite animation is also called graphic array animation, block graphics, and partial-screen animation. Refer to Fig. 19-2. By using BASIC's DIM, PUT, and GET instructions, you can save a rectangular image from the screen buffer and store it in a graphic array inside BASIC's workspace. Animation is created when the graphic array is placed back into the screen buffer (i.e., back onto the display screen).

Software sprite animation is fully supported by all versions of IBM BASIC, IBM Cartridge BASIC, Compaq BASIC, GW-BASIC, Microsoft BASICA, Microsoft QuickBASIC, and Borland TurboBASIC. It is supported by the following screen modes: SCREEN 1, SCREEN 2, SCREEN 4, SCREEN 5, SCREEN 6, SCREEN 7, SCREEN 8, SCREEN 9, SCREEN 11, and SCREEN 12. Graphic arrays are supported by the

standard Color/Graphics Adapter, by the EGA, and by the PCjr video subsystem.

Chapter 20 provides a detailed discussion of software sprite animation, in addition to a demonstration program.

## FRAME ANIMATION

Frame animation is also called full-screen animation and iterative animation. Refer to Fig. 19-3. The microcomputer draws a sequential series of full-screen images, and saves each image in a separate page buffer. When all the pages have been stored, a separate routine in the program merely flips through the pages in the proper sequence, thereby creating animation.

### Frame Animation on the EGA

Frame animation is supported on the EGA by IBM BASICA 3.21, Microsoft QuickBASIC 2.0 and 3.0 (and newer), and by Borland TurboBASIC 1.0 (and newer). Eight graphics pages are available in the SCREEN 7 $320 \times 200$ 16-color mode; four pages are available in the SCREEN 8 $640 \times 200$ 16-color mode; two pages are available in the SCREEN $640 \times 350$ 16-color mode.

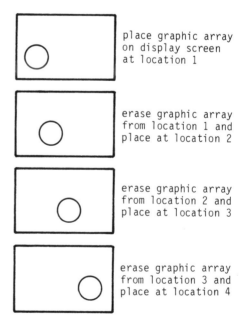

place graphic array on display screen at location 1

erase graphic array from location 1 and place at location 2

erase graphic array from location 2 and place at location 3

erase graphic array from location 3 and place at location 4

Fig. 19-2. The rudimentary mechanics of on-screen graphic array animation.

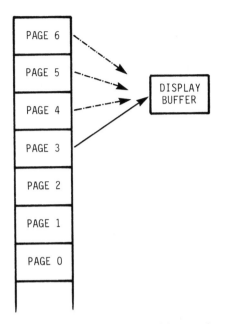

Fig. 19-3. The rudimentary mechanics of frame animation. Fully-formed screen images are saved as separate pages on the EGA or in dynamic RAM on the Color/Graphics Adapter or PCjr. The images are moved onto the display screen in rapid sequence.

## Frame Animation On The PCjr

Frame animation is supported on the IBM PCjr video subsystem by IBM Cartridge BASIC J1.00. Frame animation is supported on Tandy microcomputers by GW-BASIC. On the PCjr, six pages are available in the 320 × 200 4-color mode. On the Tandy, eight pages are available in this screen mode. On the PCjr, three pages are available in the 640 × 200 4-color mode; four pages are available on the Tandy.

## Frame Animation on the Color/Graphics Adapter

Unfortunately, frame animation is not directly supported on the standard Color/Graphics Adapter by any version of BASIC. Because there are only 16384 bytes of display memory on the adapter, there is simply no room for more than one page. A 320 × 200 4-color image (SCREEN 1) requires 16384 bytes, as does a 640 × 200 2-color image (SCREEN 2). There is, however, an innovative way around this limitation.

By using a short assembly language subroutine to create artificial graphics pages in dynamic RAM, high-speed frame animation can be implemented on a Color/Graphics Adapter. As each frame is initially

drawn in the screen buffer at B80000 hex, the assembly language subroutine moves the 16384 bytes of data to a designated area in RAM. After all the frames have been prepared, the assembly language subroutine is used to quickly move the pages back onto the display screen, thereby creating animation. Because the graphics pages in RAM are not damaged during this process, the animation can be cycled over and over again.

Chapter 21 provides a full discussion of frame animation, in addition to a demonstration program for the EGA and PCjr/Tandy, as well as a demonstration program for the Color/Graphics Adapter.

## REAL-TIME ANIMATION

Unlike software sprite animation and frame animation, which draw all the images and save them before beginning the animation sequence, real-time animation draws the images as it animates them.

Real-time animation is also called live animation, ping-pong animation, and dynamic page-flipping animation. A minimum of two separate graphics pages are required. While the computer is drawing an image on one page, the other page is being displayed. When an image is completed, it is displayed on the screen and the computer begins preparing the next image on the other page. The observer never sees the images being drawn, only the completed images. The speed of the animation is limited only by the complexity of the image to be drawn.

### Real-Time Animation on the EGA

Real-time animation is supported on the EGA by IBM BASICA 3.21, by Microsoft QuickBASIC 2.0 and 3.0, and by Borland TurboBASIC 1.0 (and newer). The **SCREEN,,written-to-page,displayed-page** syntax is used to swap the identities of the written-to hidden page and the page being displayed on the monitor. Refer to Fig. 19-4. On the EGA, animation speeds of one frame per second to six seconds per frame per second are normal with interpreted BASIC. Compiled BASIC can produce real-time animation programs running at a respectable 2 fps to 4 fps.

### Real-Time Animation on the PCjr

Real-time animation is supported on the PCjr video subsystem by IBM Cartridge BASIC J1.00. Refer to Fig. 19-4. Real-time animation is supported on the Tandy by GW-BASIC. Again, the SCREEN,,p1,p2

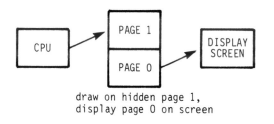

draw on hidden page 1,
display page 0 on screen

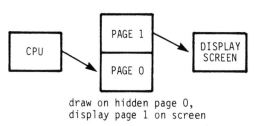

draw on hidden page 0,
display page 1 on screen

Fig. 19-4. The rudimentary mechanics of real-time animation on an EGA, PCjr, or Tandy.

syntax is used to control the mechanics of animation. Real-time animation speeds on the PCjr and Tandy are comparable to speeds which can be achieved on an EGA.

### Real-time Animation On The Color/Graphics Adapter

Unfortunately, real-time animation is not supported on the standard Color/Graphics Adapter. Two limitations come into play here. First, there is simply not enough display memory on the adapter to permit storage of more than one graphics page. Second, there is no version of BASIC which will draw to a hidden page other than the page which is located on the adapter. There is, however, an innovative way to circumvent these difficulties.

By using the POKE instruction, you can physically alter whatever version of BASIC you are using and make it send all graphics output to a memory location of your choosing. Then, by using the assembly language subroutine described earlier in this chapter, you can move the image from the artificial hidden page onto the display screen. Refer to Fig. 19-5. The POKE routines for versions 2.0, 2.1, 3.0, and 3.1 of IBM BASICA are discussed in Chapter 22.

Even Microsoft QuickBASIC can be easily modified to write graphics to an artificial hidden page in dynamic RAM when a standard Color/Graphics Adapter is being used. Flight simulation speeds of 2

frames per second are easily achieved, for example, in BASIC programs compiled by QuickBASIC 2.0. (Editor's note — Compiler modification is outside the scope of this book. You can get further details by writing directly to the author in care of the publisher.)

Chapter 22 provides a full discussion of real-time animation, in addition to a demonstration program for the EGA and PCjr/Tandy, as well as a demonstration program for the Color/Graphics Adapter.

### STRENGTHS AND WEAKNESS

Each method for producing animation has its strengths and weaknesses. By assessing the results you are seeking, you can make a decision regarding the best animation method to use for a particular project.

Frame animation produces the quickest animation. But because all the images have been created in advance, you are limited to those images during the animation sequence. You cannot change horses midstream, so to speak. (For advanced examples of iterative frame animation, refer to the author's first book, *High-Speed Animation and Simulation for Microcomputers,* available at your favorite bookstore or order direct from TAB BOOKS, Inc.)

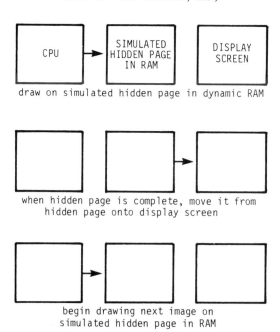

draw on simulated hidden page in dynamic RAM

when hidden page is complete, move it from hidden page onto display screen

begin drawing next image on simulated hidden page in RAM

Fig. 19-5. The rudimentary mechanics of real-time animation on a standard Color/Graphics Adapter.

Software sprite animation (graphic array animation) is not quite as quick as frame animation, but it conserves memory because only selected areas of the screen are being manipulated. Software sprite animation will preserve complicated backgrounds, thereby saving you the time and memory required to redraw the background graphics. Again, however, you are limited to using images which you have presaved in your graphic arrays.

Real-time animation is the most versatile method, but it is also the slowest. Because you are drawing each frame as you animate, you can change the contents of the next frame in the animation sequence. Real-time animation is interactive in the true sense of the definition. By using transparent wire-frame models you can keep drawing time down, animation speeds up, and visual content high.

## SUMMARY

In this chapter you learned about three different ways to generate high-speed animation on your personal computer. You saw that the EGA and the PCjr support all three methods of animation. You saw that the Color/Graphics Adapter requires some innovative programming in order to produce real-time animation and frame animation. Software sprite animation is available on all graphics adapters.

The next chapter explores practical techniques of software sprite animation.

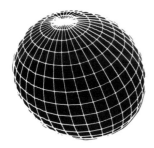

# 20

# *Software Sprite Animation*

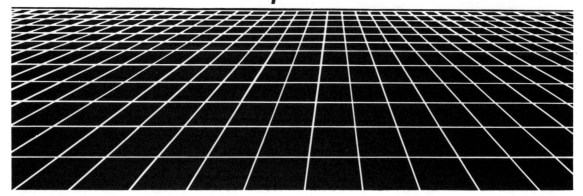

Software sprite animation relies upon graphic arrays to create the illusion of movement. Animation can be created by three mechanisms. First, an unchanging image in a single graphic array can be simply placed at different locations on the display screen to create animation. Second, a changing series of images (each in its own graphic array) can be placed one after the other in the same location on the display screen to create animation. Third, a changing series of images can be placed at different locations on the display screen to create animation.

Some nonIBM, noncompatible brands of personal computers possess built-in graphic array capabilities. In most cases, these hardware routines permitted only very small arrays, which were called software sprites. The term software sprite has become synonymous with the larger images of bona fide graphic arrays. Software-controlled arrays, such as those used in all IBM-compatible microcomputers, are generally much more versatile than hardware-based software sprites.

Animation speeds of one frame per second to a robust six frames per second are achievable if you are using IBM BASICA, IBM Cartridge BASIC, Compaq BASIC, GW-BASIC, or Microsoft BASICA. Even quicker rates are possible with Microsoft QuickBASIC and Borland TurboBASIC.

## GRAPHIC ARRAY MECHANISMS

In order to invoke software sprite animation you must follow three steps. First, use BASIC's DIM statement to dimension the array. This reserves an appropriate amount of memory inside the BASIC workspace. Second, use BASIC's GET instruction to capture the image from the screen buffer and store it in the reserved memory space. Third, use BASIC's PUT statement to place the array back onto the display screen (i.e., back into the screen buffer).

### The GET Statement

The syntax for capturing an image is GET (x1,y1)-(x2,y2),array-name. The coordinates define the upper left corner and lower right corner of an imaginary rectangle which contains the image to be saved in the graphic array. Before you can capture an image, however, you must have previously set aside space to receive the array. The DIM instruction is used to reserve the appropriate amount of space.

## The DIM Statement

The syntax for reserving space in memory to receive the graphic array is DIM array-name(number-of-elements). If you are using the 640 × 200 4-color mode or the 320 × 200 4-color mode, two bits of memory are required to define each pixel. If your graphic array is 51 pixels across by 101 rows down, you would use the following calculations.

**Step One:** Convert the width to bits. 51 pixels × 2 bits-per-pixel equals 102 bits.

**Step Two:** Ensure that the width is expressed in full bytes, because BASIC will not save a portion of a byte in an array. 102 bits divided by 8 equals 12.75 bytes. Add 2 bits to make it an even 13 bytes, which is 104 bits.

**Step Three:** Determine the total number of bits in the graphic array. Width x depth equals size. 104 bits × 101 rows equals 10504 bits.

**Step Four:** Convert this bit quantity to bytes. Remember, there are eight bits in a byte. 10504 divided by 8 equals 1313 bytes.

**Step Five:** BASIC requires an additional four bytes as an information header on the array data. 1313 bytes plus 4 bytes equals 1317 bytes.

**Step Six:** BASIC stores the array in memory as a series of elements. One element is made up of two bytes. Because computer numbering starts at zero, 1317 bytes to you is 1316 bytes to your computer. 1316 bytes divided by 2 bytes-per-element equals 658. The array size needs to be 658 elements.

**Step Seven:** Dimension the array. DIM A1(658). Ensure that A1 has been pre-declared as an integer.

If a graphic array is being created from the 640 × 200 16-color screen or the 320 × 200 16-color screen, the technique is exactly the same as described, except that four bits are required to define each pixel. (It takes four bits to express a number between 0 and 15, which describes all 16 colors, of course.)

## The PUT Statement

The PUT statement retrieves the image from the graphic array and places it back onto the display screen. The syntax for this action is PUT (x1,y1),array-name,action. The coordinates refer to the location where the upper left corner of the array will be placed on the screen. The action argument refers to the logical operator to be used. Refer to Fig. 20-1.

Four logical operators are most often used: they are PSET, OR, AND, and XOR. As Fig. 20-1 shows, PSET will simply overwrite the existing graphics. The image plus the background surrounding it in the rectangular array will be written onto the screen. As Fig. 20-1 shows, the XOR, OR, and AND logical operators will produce a wide range of graphics results, many of them undesirable. Bleed-through and ghosting are typical. However, as Fig. 20-1 also shows, a combination of logical operators can be used to cleanly place an image on the screen in a manner which preserves the silhouette of the image.

## Logical Operators

The four logical operators produce their effects by bit manipulation. Refer to Fig. 20-2. Both the graphic array and the existing background graphics on the screen are simply a series of bits. If the OR logical operator is invoked during a PUT statement, the screen buffer bit will be set to a value of one if either the array or the buffer is a one value, as Fig. 20-2 il-

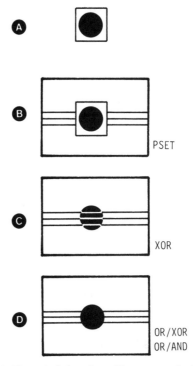

Fig. 20-1. Characteristics of graphic array manipulation. (a) A rectangle containing the image is retrieved from the screen buffer and saved as an array inside BASIC's workspace. (b) The PSET operator will overwrite the entire rectangle over the contents of the screen buffer. (c) The XOR, OR, and AND operators when used individually will result in assorted bleed-throughs. (d) Proper combinations of logical operators can place odd-shaped images onto the screen.

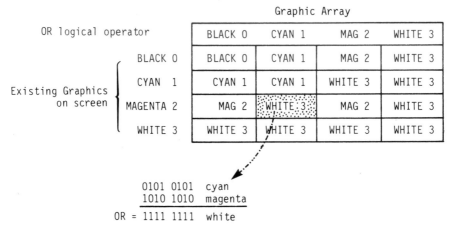

Fig. 20-2. The graphic array operator matrix is derived from the results of bit operation.

lustrates. The other three logical operators adhere to similar concepts of bit analysis, often called boolean logic. (You may wish to refer to Chapter 3 for more information about logical operators.)

### Multiple Operators

By using a preparatory array, you can cleanly place odd-shaped images onto the display screen. The preparatory array is also called a key matte. Refer to Fig. 20-3. If you wish to place a magenta-and-white circle onto the screen, a preparatory array consisting of a white circle on a black background could be used. As the matrix in Fig. 20-3 shows, the OR logical operator would preserve the existing screen background while cleanly placing the white circle onto the screen. Then, the AND operator could be used to place the multicolored circle onto the screen while still preserving the background space. (For a programming demonstration of a multicolored ball bouncing against a multicolored airbrushed background, refer to the author's first book, *High-Speed Animation and Simulation for Microcomputers*, available at your favorite bookstore or direct from TAB BOOKS, Inc.)

### PERFORMANCE BOOSTERS

Both the hardware and the software can dramatically affect the speed of graphic array animation. If the arrays are kept to a shape which is wide horizontally but shallow in terms of depth, speed will be enhanced. BASIC's built-in routine is much more efficient at plotting wide, shallow arrays onto the dis-

play screen. The calculations used to locate the starting point of the next line down are time consuming.

Generally speaking, the smaller the array the quicker the array action will be. If, for example, only one small part of your 3D model is actually moving, then you can substantively improve animation speed by using arrays which only animate that one small component of the overall model.

### HIDDEN PAGE ANIMATION

Hidden page animation can assist in refreshing the background graphics. Each frame in the hidden page animation cycle consists of three components. First, copy the background image from a second hidden page onto the primary hidden page. Second, use PUT to place the graphic array onto the primary hidden page. Third, flip the hidden page up onto the display screen.

If this hidden page method is used, it is not necessary to erase each previous graphic array. Nor is it necessary to keep redrawing complex background graphics. More discussion about hidden pages is undertaken in the next two chapters.

### ON-SCREEN ANIMATION

On-screen animation can be used when the new graphic array will completely cover the old graphic array. This process will only work, however, when simple background graphics are involved.

If the arrays are being placed at different locations on the display screen, on-screen animation can be implemented by using larger-than-necessary borders on

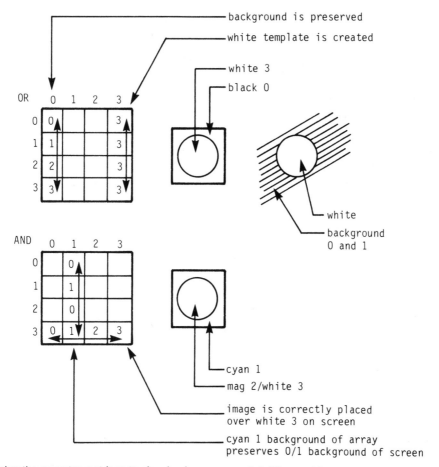

Fig. 20-3. Using the operator matrices to cleanly place a magenta/white graphic over a cyna/black existing screen.

each array. These oversized array backgrounds will cover the previous array image on the screen, even though the location was offset from the current location.

## MEGA ARRAYS

The CAD graphics editor demonstration program in Chapter 25 uses an oversized graphic array to capture almost the entire screen image. The BSAVE instruction is then used to save the data in the array to diskette as an image file.

The maximum size of an array is limited only by the amount of BASIC workspace available. In a typical interpreter environment, this is usually around 50,000 bytes of free memory.

## SOFTWARE SPRITE ANIMATION: DEMONSTRATION

Figure 20-4 shows the screen output of the demonstration program in Fig. 20-6 while the program is creating and saving a series of graphic arrays. Figure 20-5 shows the screen output during the animation cycle. To run this program from the companion diskette, type **LOAD "A-31.BAS",R.** The program produces a solid 3D cube which rotates on the display screen.

Although a fully-shaded, multicolored model can be animated just as easily as a simple black-and-white cube, the emphasis in this demonstration program is on the actual technique of animation. A simple cube is therefore used in this chapter. The same cube is sub-

*(Text continues on page 245)*

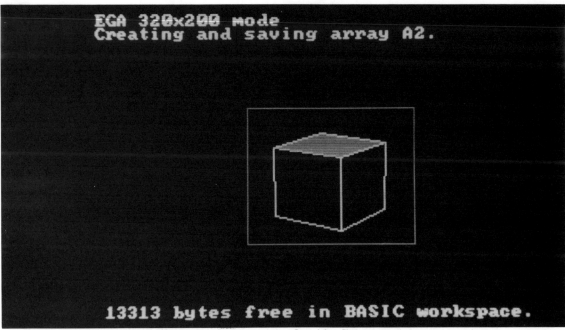

Fig. 20-4. The display image produced by the demonstration program in Fig. 20-6 during saving of the graphic arrays.

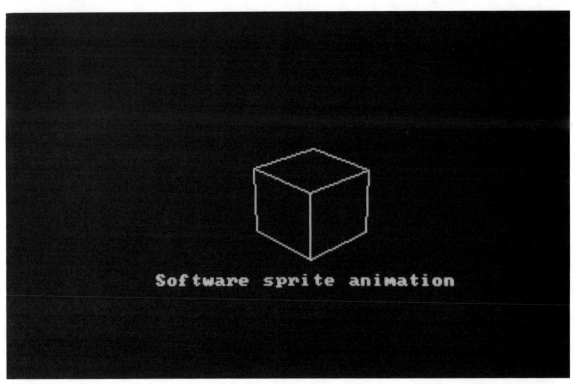

Fig. 20-5. The display image produced by the demonstration program in Fig. 20-6 during the animation sequence.

Fig. 20-6. Software sprite animation of a rotating 3D cube.

```
100  'Program A-31.BAS     Software sprite animation.
110  'Demonstrates on-screen graphic array animation.
120  '_____
130  '
140    GOTO 1530      'configure system
150    GOSUB 1690     'assign variables
160  '_____
170  '
180  'master routine:   save graphic arrays
190    DEFINT A:DIM A1(1149):DIM A2(1149):DIM A3(1149):DIM A4(
1149):DIM A5(1149):DIM A6(1149):DIM A7(1149):DIM A8(1149)
200    DIM A9(1149):DIM A10(1149):DIM A11(1149):DIM A12(1149):
DIM A13(1149):DIM A14(1149):DIM A15(1149):DIM A16(1149)
210    LOCATE 23,1:PRINT FRE(0)"bytes free in BASIC workspace.
"
220    LOCATE 2,1:PRINT "Creating and saving array A1.        "
230    GOSUB 750:WINDOW (0,0)-(319,199):LINE (105,60)-(215,143
),C2,B:GET (106,61)-(214,142),A1:GOSUB 580
240    LOCATE 2,1:PRINT "Creating and saving array A2."
250    GOSUB 750:WINDOW (0,0)-(319,199):GET (106,61)-(214,142)
,A2:GOSUB 580
260    LOCATE 2,1:PRINT "Creating and saving array A3."
270    GOSUB 750:WINDOW (0,0)-(319,199):GET (106,61)-(214,142)
,A3:GOSUB 580
280    LOCATE 2,1:PRINT "Creating and saving array A4."
290    GOSUB 750:WINDOW (0,0)-(319,199):GET (106,61)-(214,142)
,A4:GOSUB 580
300    LOCATE 2,1:PRINT "Creating and saving array A5."
310    GOSUB 750:WINDOW (0,0)-(319,199):GET (106,61)-(214,142)
,A5:GOSUB 580
320    LOCATE 2,1:PRINT "Creating and saving array A6."
330    GOSUB 750:WINDOW (0,0)-(319,199):GET (106,61)-(214,142)
,A6:GOSUB 580
340    LOCATE 2,1:PRINT "Creating and saving array A7."
350    GOSUB 750:WINDOW (0,0)-(319,199):GET (106,61)-(214,142)
,A7:GOSUB 580
360    LOCATE 2,1:PRINT "Creating and saving array A8."
370    GOSUB 750:WINDOW (0,0)-(319,199):GET (106,61)-(214,142)
,A8:GOSUB 580
380    LOCATE 2,1:PRINT "Creating and saving array A9."
390    GOSUB 750:WINDOW (0,0)-(319,199):GET (106,61)-(214,142)
,A9:GOSUB 580
400    LOCATE 2,1:PRINT "Creating and saving array A10."
410    GOSUB 750:WINDOW (0,0)-(319,199):GET (106,61)-(214,142)
,A10:GOSUB 580
420    LOCATE 2,1:PRINT "Creating and saving array A11."
```

```
430    GOSUB 750:WINDOW (0,0)-(319,199):GET (106,61)-(214,142)
,A11:GOSUB 580
440    LOCATE 2,1:PRINT "Creating and saving array A12."
450    GOSUB 750:WINDOW (0,0)-(319,199):GET (106,61)-(214,142)
,A12:GOSUB 580
460    LOCATE 2,1:PRINT "Creating and saving array A13."
470    GOSUB 750:WINDOW (0,0)-(319,199):GET (106,61)-(214,142)
,A13:GOSUB 580
480    LOCATE 2,1:PRINT "Creating and saving array A14."
490    GOSUB 750:WINDOW (0,0)-(319,199):GET (106,61)-(214,142)
,A14:GOSUB 580
500    LOCATE 2,1:PRINT "Creating and saving array A15."
510    GOSUB 750:WINDOW (0,0)-(319,199):GET (106,61)-(214,142)
,A15:GOSUB 580
520    LOCATE 2,1:PRINT "Creating and saving array A16."
530    GOSUB 750:WINDOW (0,0)-(319,199):GET (106,61)-(214,142)
,A16
540    GOTO 620
550    '_____
560    '
570 'module:  refresh rotation factors
580    PAINT (160,100),C0,C2:R1=R1-.01745:SR1=SIN(R1):CR1=COS(
R1):R3=R3-.01745:SR3=SIN(R3):CR3=COS(R3):WINDOW SCREEN (-399
,-299)-(400,300):RETURN
590    '_____
600    '
610 'module:  software sprite animation loop
620    CLS
630    SOUND 450,10:LOCATE 2,1:PRINT "Press <Enter> to begin a
nimation.   "
640    K$=INKEY$:IF K$<>CHR$(13) THEN 640
650    CLS:LOCATE 2,1:PRINT "Software sprite animation of 3D c
ube."
660    PUT (106,61),A2,PSET:PUT (106,61),A3,PSET:PUT (106,61),
A4,PSET:PUT (106,61),A5,PSET:PUT (106,61),A6,PSET:PUT (106,6
1),A7,PSET:PUT (106,61),A8,PSET
670    PUT (106,61),A9,PSET:PUT (106,61),A10,PSET:PUT (106,61)
,A11,PSET:PUT (106,61),A12,PSET:PUT (106,61),A13,PSET:PUT (1
06,61),A14,PSET:PUT (106,61),A15,PSET:PUT (106,61),A16,PSET
680    FOR T=1 TO 400 STEP 1:NEXT
690    PUT (106,61),A15,PSET:PUT (106,61),A14,PSET:PUT (106,61
),A13,PSET:PUT (106,61),A12,PSET:PUT (106,61),A11,PSET:PUT (
106,61),A10,PSET:PUT (106,61),A9,PSET:PUT (106,61),A8,PSET
700    PUT (106,61),A7,PSET:PUT (106,61),A6,PSET:PUT (106,61),
A5,PSET:PUT (106,61),A4,PSET:PUT (106,61),A3,PSET:PUT (106,6
1),A2,PSET:PUT (106,61),A1,PSET
710    FOR T=1 TO 400 STEP 1:NEXT:GOTO 660
720    '_____
```

```
730 '
740 'module:  calculate and store vertex coordinates
750   RESTORE 1790  'beginning of database
760   FOR T=0 TO 7 STEP 1:READ X,Y,Z:GOSUB 1440:B1(T,0)=X:B1(
T,1)=Y:B1(T,2)=Z:B2(T,0)=SX:B2(T,1)=SY:NEXT T  'load vertex
view coordinates into array B1, load vertex display coordina
tes into array B2
770   FOR T=0 TO 5 STEP 1:READ X,Y,Z:GOSUB 1440:B3(T,0)=SX:B3
(T,1)=SY:NEXT T  'load area fill origin display coordinates
into array B3
780 '_____
790 '
800 'main routine:  draw 6 surfaces of cube
810 'surface 0 routine
820   X1=B1(7,0):Y1=B1(7,1):Z1=B1(7,2):X2=B1(0,0):Y2=B1(0,1):
Z2=B1(0,2):X3=B1(3,0):Y3=B1(3,1):Z3=B1(3,2)  'retrieve XYZ v
iewing coordinates for surface 0
830   GOSUB 1870 'jump to plane equation routine
840   IF SP>0 THEN GOTO 920 'if surface hidden jump to next
surface
850   SX=B2(7,0):SY=B2(7,1):PSET (SX,SY),C2:SX=B2(0,0):SY=B2(
0,1):LINE-(SX,SY),C2:SX=B2(3,0):SY=B2(3,1):LINE-(SX,SY),C2:S
X=B2(6,0):SY=B2(6,1):LINE-(SX,SY),C2:SX=B2(7,0):SY=B2(7,1):L
INE-(SX,SY),C2
860   SX=B3(0,0):SY=B3(0,1):PAINT (SX,SY),C2,C2  'key matte f
or surface 0
870   SX=B2(7,0):SY=B2(7,1):PSET (SX,SY),C3:SX=B2(0,0):SY=B2(
0,1):LINE-(SX,SY),C3:SX=B2(3,0):SY=B2(3,1):LINE-(SX,SY),C3:S
X=B2(6,0):SY=B2(6,1):LINE-(SX,SY),C3:SX=B2(7,0):SY=B2(7,1):L
INE-(SX,SY),C3
880   SX=B3(0,0):SY=B3(0,1):PAINT (SX,SY),C0,C3  'solid surfa
ce 0 completed
890 '_____
900 '
910 'surface 1 routine
920   X1=B1(6,0):Y1=B1(6,1):Z1=B1(6,2):X2=B1(5,0):Y2=B1(5,1):
Z2=B1(5,2):X3=B1(4,0):Y3=B1(4,1):Z3=B1(4,2)
930   GOSUB 1870
940   IF SP>0 THEN GOTO 1020
950   SX=B2(6,0):SY=B2(6,1):PSET (SX,SY),C2:SX=B2(5,0):SY=B2(
5,1):LINE-(SX,SY),C2:SX=B2(4,0):SY=B2(4,1):LINE-(SX,SY),C2:S
X=B2(7,0):SY=B2(7,1):LINE-(SX,SY),C2:SX=B2(6,0):SY=B2(6,1):L
INE-(SX,SY),C2
960   SX=B3(1,0):SY=B3(1,1):PAINT (SX,SY),C2,C2
970   SX=B2(6,0):SY=B2(6,1):PSET (SX,SY),C3:SX=B2(5,0):SY=B2(
5,1):LINE-(SX,SY),C3:SX=B2(4,0):SY=B2(4,1):LINE-(SX,SY),C3:S
X=B2(7,0):SY=B2(7,1):LINE-(SX,SY),C3:SX=B2(6,0):SY=B2(6,1):L
INE-(SX,SY),C3
```

```
980   SX=B3(1,0):SY=B3(1,1):PAINT (SX,SY),CO,C3
990 '_____
1000 '
1010 'surface 2 routine
1020   X1=B1(3,0):Y1=B1(3,1):Z1=B1(3,2):X2=B1(2,0):Y2=B1(2,1)
:Z2=B1(2,2):X3=B1(5,0):Y3=B1(5,1):Z3=B1(5,2)
1030   GOSUB 1870
1040   IF SP>0 THEN GOTO 1120
1050   SX=B2(3,0):SY=B2(3,1):PSET (SX,SY),C2:SX=B2(2,0):SY=B2
(2,1):LINE-(SX,SY),C2:SX=B2(5,0):SY=B2(5,1):LINE-(SX,SY),C2:
SX=B2(6,0):SY=B2(6,1):LINE-(SX,SY),C2:SX=B2(3,0):SY=B2(3,1):
LINE-(SX,SY),C2
1060   SX=B3(2,0):SY=B3(2,1):PAINT (SX,SY),C2,C2
1070   SX=B2(3,0):SY=B2(3,1):PSET (SX,SY),C3:SX=B2(2,0):SY=B2
(2,1):LINE-(SX,SY),C3:SX=B2(5,0):SY=B2(5,1):LINE-(SX,SY),C3:
SX=B2(6,0):SY=B2(6,1):LINE-(SX,SY),C3:SX=B2(3,0):SY=B2(3,1):
LINE-(SX,SY),C3
1080   SX=B3(2,0):SY=B3(2,1):PAINT (SX,SY),CO,C3
1090 '_____
1100 '
1110 'surface 3 routine
1120   X1=B1(0,0):Y1=B1(0,1):Z1=B1(0,2):X2=B1(1,0):Y2=B1(1,1)
:Z2=B1(1,2):X3=B1(2,0):Y3=B1(2,1):Z3=B1(2,2)
1130   GOSUB 1870
1140   IF SP>0 THEN GOTO 1220
1150   SX=B2(0,0):SY=B2(0,1):PSET (SX,SY),C2:SX=B2(1,0):SY=B2
(1,1):LINE-(SX,SY),C2:SX=B2(2,0):SY=B2(2,1):LINE-(SX,SY),C2:
SX=B2(3,0):SY=B2(3,1):LINE-(SX,SY),C2:SX=B2(0,0):SY=B2(0,1):
LINE-(SX,SY),C2
1160   SX=B3(3,0):SY=B3(3,1):PAINT (SX,SY),C2,C2
1170   SX=B2(0,0):SY=B2(0,1):PSET (SX,SY),C3:SX=B2(1,0):SY=B2
(1,1):LINE-(SX,SY),C3:SX=B2(2,0):SY=B2(2,1):LINE-(SX,SY),C3:
SX=B2(3,0):SY=B2(3,1):LINE-(SX,SY),C3:SX=B2(0,0):SY=B2(0,1):
LINE-(SX,SY),C3
1180   SX=B3(3,0):SY=B3(3,1):PAINT (SX,SY),CO,C3
1190 '_____
1200 '
1210 'surface 4 routine
1220   X1=B1(7,0):Y1=B1(7,1):Z1=B1(7,2):X2=B1(4,0):Y2=B1(4,1)
:Z2=B1(4,2):X3=B1(1,0):Y3=B1(1,1):Z3=B1(1,2)
1230   GOSUB 1870
1240 IF SP>0 THEN GOTO 1320
1250   SX=B2(7,0):SY=B2(7,1):PSET (SX,SY),C2:SX=B2(4,0):SY=B2
(4,1):LINE-(SX,SY),C2:SX=B2(1,0):SY=B2(1,1):LINE-(SX,SY),C2:
SX=B2(0,0):SY=B2(0,1):LINE-(SX,SY),C2:SX=B2(7,0):SY=B2(7,1):
LINE-(SX,SY),C2
1260   SX=B3(4,0):SY=B3(4,1):PAINT (SX,SY),C2,C2
1270   SX=B2(7,0):SY=B2(7,1):PSET (SX,SY),C3:SX=B2(4,0):SY=B2
```

```
(4,1):LINE-(SX,SY),C3:SX=B2(1,0):SY=B2(1,1):LINE-(SX,SY),C3:
SX=B2(0,0):SY=B2(0,1):LINE-(SX,SY),C3:SX=B2(7,0):SY=B2(7,1):
LINE-(SX,SY),C3
1280   SX=B3(4,0):SY=B3(4,1):PAINT (SX,SY),C0,C3
1290 '_____
1300 '
1310 'surface 5 routine
1320   X1=B1(1,0):Y1=B1(1,1):Z1=B1(1,2):X2=B1(4,0):Y2=B1(4,1)
:Z2=B1(4,2):X3=B1(5,0):Y3=B1(5,1):Z3=B1(5,2)
1330   GOSUB 1870
1340   IF SP>0 THEN GOTO 1400
1350   SX=B2(1,0):SY=B2(1,1):PSET (SX,SY),C2:SX=B2(4,0):SY=B2
(4,1):LINE-(SX,SY),C2:SX=B2(5,0):SY=B2(5,1):LINE-(SX,SY),C2:
SX=B2(2,0):SY=B2(2,1):LINE-(SX,SY),C2:SX=B2(1,0):SY=B2(1,1):
LINE-(SX,SY),C2
1360   SX=B3(5,0):SY=B3(5,1):PAINT (SX,SY),C2,C2
1370   SX=B2(1,0):SY=B2(1,1):PSET (SX,SY),C3:SX=B2(4,0):SY=B2
(4,1):LINE-(SX,SY),C3:SX=B2(5,0):SY=B2(5,1):LINE-(SX,SY),C3:
SX=B2(2,0):SY=B2(2,1):LINE-(SX,SY),C3:SX=B2(1,0):SY=B2(1,1):
LINE-(SX,SY),C3
1380   SX=B3(5,0):SY=B3(5,1):PAINT (SX,SY),C0,C3
1390   SOUND 350,.7
1400   RETURN
1410 '_____
1420 '
1430 'module:   perspective calculations
1440   X=(-1)*X:XA=CR1*X-SR1*Z:ZA=SR1*X+CR1*Z:X=CR2*XA+SR2*Y:
YA=CR2*Y-SR2*XA:Z=CR3*ZA-SR3*YA:Y=SR3*ZA+CR3*YA:X=X+MX:Y=Y+M
Y:Z=Z+MZ:SX=D*X/Z:SY=D*Y/Z:RETURN
1450 '_____
1460 '
1470 'module:   return to BASIC interpreter
1480   CLS:WINDOW:SCREEN 0,0,0,0:WIDTH 80:COLOR 7,0,0:CLS:LOC
ATE 1,1,1:END
1490 '_____
1500 '
1510 'module:   UNIVERSAL
1520 'This routine configures the program for the hardware/s
oftware being used.
1530   KEY OFF:CLS:ON ERROR GOTO 1560 'trap if not EGA
1540   SCREEN 7,,0,0:CLS:SCREEN 1,0:COLOR 0,1:PALETTE 1,1:PAL
ETTE 2,4:PALETTE 3,7:C0=0:C1=1:C2=2:C3=3:LOCATE 1,1:PRINT "E
GA 320x200 mode"
1550   GOTO 1620  'jump to screen coordinates set-up
1560   RESUME 1570
1570   ON ERROR GOTO 1600 'trap if not PCjr
1580   SCREEN 1,0:COLOR 0,1:PALETTE 1,1:PALETTE 2,4:PALETTE 3
,7:C0=0:C1=1:C2=2:C3=3:LOCATE 1,1:PRINT "PCjr 320x200 mode"
```

```
1590   GOTO 1620   'jump to screen coordinates set-up
1600   RESUME 1610
1610   SCREEN 1,0:COLOR 0,1:C0=0:C1=1:C2=2:C3=3:LOCATE 1,1:PR
INT "CGA 320x200 mode"
1620   ON ERROR GOTO 0   'disable error trapping override
1630   WINDOW SCREEN (-399,-299)-(400,300)   'establish device
-independent screen coordinates
1640   ON KEY (2) GOSUB 1480:KEY (2) ON   'F2 key to exit prog
ram
1650   GOTO 150   'return to main program
1660 '_____
1670 '
1680 'module:   assign variables
1690   D=1200:R1=5.68319:R2=6.28319:R3=5.99778:MX=0:MY=0:MZ=-
550   '3D parameters
1700   DIM B1 (7,2)   '8 sets of XYZ view coordinates
1710   DIM B2 (7,1)   '8 sets of SX,SY display coordinates
1720   DIM B3 (5,1)   '6 sets of SX,SY fill coordinates
1730   XL=.57735:YL=.57735:ZL=.57735   'xyz components of unit
 vector for angle of incidence used in illumination algorith
m
1740   SR1=SIN(R1):CR1=COS(R1):SR2=SIN(R2):CR2=COS(R2):SR3=SI
N(R3):CR3=COS(R3)
1750   RETURN
1760 '_____
1770 '
1780 'module:   database of 8 sets of XYZ world coordinates f
or vertices of 3D cube
1790   DATA   30,-30,30,   30,30,30,   -30,30,30,   -30,-30,30,
30,30,-30,   -30,30,-30,   -30,-30,-30,   30,-30,-30
1800 '_____
1810 '
1820 'module:   database of 6 sets of XYZ world coordinates f
or area fill origins for 6 surfaces of 3D cube
1830   DATA   0,-30,0,   0,0,-30,   -30,0,0,   0,0,30,   30,0,0,
0,30,0
1840 '_____
1850 '
1860 'module:   plane equation method of hidden surface remov
al
1870   SP1=X1*(Y2*Z3-Y3*Z2):SP1=(-1)*SP1:SP2=X2*(Y3*Z1-Y1*Z3)
:SP3=X3*(Y1*Z2-Y2*Z1):SP=SP1-SP2-SP3:RETURN
1880 '_____
1890 '
1900   END 'of program code
```

jected in frame animation and real-time animation in later chapters.

Note lines 190 and 200, which allocate space for 16 graphic arrays inside the BASIC workspace. Each array consists of 1149 elements, which is equivalent to 2298 bytes. A total of $2298 \times 16 = 36768$ bytes are required to store all the arrays. An alphanumeric read-out shows you how much free memory is available inside the BASIC workspace on your particular version of BASIC as this program executes.

BASIC is specific in its memory needs. If you change any of the DIM instructions from 1149 to 1148, for example, the program will halt and BASIC will display an error message warning you that not enough space has been set aside to receive the captured image. You can make the DIM values larger, of course, but no purpose would be served other than to waste memory, because no other function can use the memory that has been set aside for a graphic array. (Even though you may have 640K of random access memory, almost all versions of BASIC strictly limit you to a maximum 64K of workspace. When dealing with graphic arrays, memory limitations are important.)

As the program creates and saves each array, an alphanumeric read-out keeps you informed of the count. When all 16 arrays have been saved, the program beeps and waits for you to press <Enter> before beginning the high-speed animation of the rotating cube.

## The Main Routine

The section of code which creates and saves the arrays is located at lines 220 through 540. This routine calls the subroutine at line 580, which updates the sine and cosine rotation matrices. Next, the routine calls the subroutine at line 750, which is the standard code required to produce a transparent wire-frame cube. This algorithm was introduced in Chapter 8.

## The Animating Routine

The loop which actually produces the animation is located at lines 660 through 710. Note that each array is placed on the display screen at the same location: 106,61. It is the different orientation of the cube in each array that creates the illusion of movement. You could, if you wished, increment each x-coordinate by a value of one in order to create a rotating cube which also moves. If you were to employ larger increments, you run the risk of not covering up the previous array, which makes for sloppy animation.

As each cube is originally modeled and saved, note how the program flips back and forth between different WINDOW modes. Line 500 is a good example. The 3D cube must be created in a cartesian coordinate environment, of course. Why, then, does the program flip into a WINDOW (0,0)-(319,199) mode before saving the array?

If you are using IBM BASICA or IBM Cartridge BASIC, you could safely eliminate this $320 \times 200$ WINDOW statement. Here is the reason: IBM BASIC permits you to use either world coordinates or real screen coordinates when dealing with graphic arrays. Both negative coordinates and positive coordinates are legal. GW-BASIC, on the other hand, permits only actual physical screen coordinates: 0,0 to 319,199. The switching back and forth in this demonstration program is needed in order to ensure that the program is fully compatible with all versions of BASIC on all IBM-compatible personal computers.

As you watch the program creating and saving the 16 arrays, you can see that a border is created along the boundary of the array. The array being saved actually fits just inside this border. The border is required only for the PAINT instruction which is used to wipe the previous cube from the work area before the next cube is drawn.

## Screen Ripple

As the animation occurs, you can detect a slight rippling of the images. This is caused when a new array is written over the previous array. The image of the cube in the new array is shifted slightly to the left or to the right of the cube in the previous array. The ripple is caused by the time delay between when BASIC starts writing the array (at the top of the image) and finishes writing (at the bottom of the image). The rippling is less noticeable when QuickBASIC or TurboBASIC is used. Rippling is non-existent if hidden pages are used.

## SUMMARY

In this chapter you learned that four logical operators are used to determine the manner in which a software sprite is placed on the display screen. You discovered how to rotate a solid 3D cube.

The next chapter shows you how to create faster, smoother animation of the same cube by using frame animation.

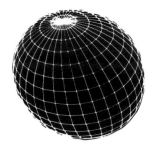

# 21

# Frame Animation

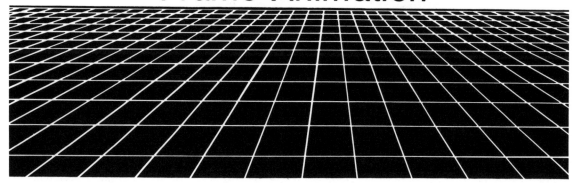

Frame animation is the quickest form of image-oriented animation on personal computers. Complete screens of graphics are saved as pages in memory. Then, an animation routine is used to cycle the pages onto the display screen in rapid sequence, creating the illusion of movement.

Because all the images have been pre-drawn, the computer can focus its attention on animating the images, thereby optimizing the speed of the animation sequence. Using an EGA or a PCjr, you can achieve a maximum rate of nearly 18 fps (frames per second) with IBM BASICA or IBM Cartridge BASIC. Using a standard Color/Graphics Adapter, a maximum speed of roughly 8 fps can be achieved via a short assembly language subroutine.

## FRAME ANIMATION MECHANISMS

Two essential steps are required in frame animation programs. Refer to Fig. 21-1.

First, the computer creates a series of full-screen images and saves each image as a separate graphics page. On the EGA, these pages are stored in the EGA's on-board display memory. With the PCjr and Tandy, these pages are stored in dynamic RAM which

has been reserved for graphics data by the CLEAR,,,n statement. With the Color/Graphics Adapter, these pages are stored in dynamic RAM, away from the memory used by the CGA itself. In fact, there is simply not enough display memory on the CGA to permit storage of more than one page.

Second, an animation routine is used to cycle these pre-saved pages onto the display screen. On the EGA, the PCjr, and the Tandy, a hardware component called the video gate array (VGA) simply points to the beginning of the page to be displayed on the monitor. The SCREEN,,p1,p2 statement adjusts this pointer; no data in memory is moved. On the Color/Graphics Adapter, an assembly language subroutine is used to move the data from each graphics page into the screen buffer at B8000 hex.

### Frame Rates

On the EGA, the PCjr, and the Tandy, the SCREEN,,p1,p2 instruction will flip pages in roughly 1/20th of a second. General overhead reduces that to a realistic achievable run-time rate of 18 fps. (Refer to Chapter 2 for a detailed discussion of the SCREEN statement.)

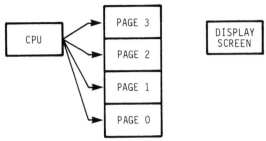

STEP 1: Draw 4 different full-screen images and save as pages in display memory (EGA) or in dynamic RAM (CGA, PCjr, Tandy).

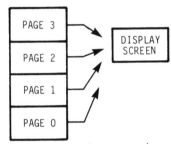

STEP 2: Display the pages on the screen in rapid sequence. On an EGA, PCjr, or Tandy the hardware VGA is pointed to the appropriate memory page, making it the screen buffer. On a Color/Graphics Adapter, the page must be moved into the screen buffer at B80000 hex, but the animation result is the same.

Fig. 21-1. Frame animation principles.

On the Color/Graphics Adapter, the assembly language subroutine moves 16384 bytes of graphics data from the hidden page onto the display screen in approximately 1/11th second. General overhead pulls this down to about 8 fps during run-time.

### Syntax on Professional Workstations

The process of storing a full-screen image as a graphics page is called a frame grab. The process of creating the full-screen image is called frame generation.

## FRAME VOLUME

On the EGA, eight frames (pages) are available in the 320 × 200 16-color mode. Four frames are available in the 640 × 200 16-color mode. Two frames are available in the 640 × 350 16-color mode.

On the PCjr, six frames are available in the 320 × 200 4-color mode. Eight frames are available in this mode on the Tandy. On the PCjr, three frames are available in the 640 × 200 4-color mode. Four frames are available on the Tandy.

On the Color/Graphics Adapter, the number of frames possible is limited by available RAM, because this is where the frames are stored. If your PC carries 640K, you could store more than 30 frames in the 320 × 200 4-color mode, which could be used to produce a relatively lengthy sequence of frame animation. (Refer to Chapter 1 for a memory map.)

## FRAME ANIMATION: DEMONSTRATION

Figure 21-2 shows the screen output produced by the demonstration programs in Fig. 21-3 and Fig. 21-4. The program in Fig. 21-3 is intended for use on an EGA using IBM BASICA 3.21, Microsoft Quick-BASIC 2.0, or Borland TurboBASIC 1.0. The program in Fig. 21-3 will also run on an IBM PCjr or Tandy. The program in Fig. 21-4 is intended for use on a Color/Graphics Adapter using IBM BASICA, Compaq BASIC, GW-BASIC, or Microsoft BASICA.

If you are using the companion diskette, you can run the program for the EGA or PCjr/Tandy by typing **LOAD "A-32.BAS",R**. To run the program for the Color/Graphics Adapter, type **LOAD "A-33.BAS",R**.

The program creates and saves four graphics pages. When all pages have been completed, the program beeps and waits for you to press <Enter> before beginning high-speed animation of the solid 3D cube. This is the same cube which was animated using graphic array animation in the previous chapter. As you can see, however, the animation is much smoother in this program, and there is no screen rippling as was experienced by the graphic array program.

### The EGA/PCjr Program

The program listing for frame animation on the EGA, the PCjr, and the Tandy is shown in Fig. 21-3.

The main routine which coordinates the creation and storage of the four frames is located at lines 180 through 220. Note the use of the PCOPY instruction, which is used to move the completed images into their appropriate pages. All original images are created on page 0 (the displayed page), although there is no technical reason preventing you from modifying this program to draw the images directly onto their proper

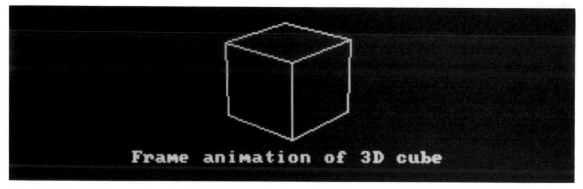

Fig. 21-2. The display image produced by the demonstration programs in Fig. 21-3 and Fig. 21-4.

Fig. 21-3. Frame animation of a rotating 3D cube on an EGA, PCjr, or Tandy.

```
100 'Program A-32.BAS    Frame animation.
110 'Demonstrates frame animation on EGA or PCjr.
120 '_____
130 '
140  GOTO 1140    'configure system
150  GOSUB 1320  'assign variables
160 '_____
170 '
180 'master routine:  create and save frames
190  GOSUB 360:LOCATE 2,1:PRINT "Frame animation of 3D cube.
":PCOPY 0,3
200  CLS:GOSUB 320:LOCATE 2,1:PRINT "Frame animation of 3D c
ube.":GOSUB 360:PCOPY 0,2
210  CLS:GOSUB 320:LOCATE 2,1:PRINT "Frame animation of 3D c
ube.":GOSUB 360:PCOPY 0,1
220  CLS:GOSUB 320:LOCATE 2,1:PRINT "Frame animation of 3D c
ube.":GOSUB 360
230  SOUND 550,5:SOUND 350,5:LOCATE 3,1:PRINT "Press <Enter>
 to begin animation."
240  K$=INKEY$:IF K$<>CHR$(13) THEN 240
250  LOCATE 3,1:PRINT "                                     "
260  SCREEN,,1,1:FOR T=1 TO 100 STEP 1:NEXT T:SCREEN,,2,2:FO
R T=1 TO 100 STEP 1:NEXT T:SCREEN,,3,3
270  FOR T=1 TO 500 STEP 1:NEXT T:SCREEN,,2,2:FOR T=1 TO 100
 STEP 1:NEXT T:SCREEN,,1,1:FOR T=1 TO 100 STEP 1:NEXT T:SCRE
EN,,0,0:FOR T=1 TO 500 STEP 1:NEXT T:GOTO 260
280  END 'of master routine
290 '_____
300 '
310 'module:  refresh rotation factors
320  R1=R1-.04363:SR1=SIN(R1):CR1=COS(R1):R3=R3-.04363:SR3=S
IN(R3):CR3=COS(R3):RETURN
```

```
330 '_____
340 '
350 'module:   calculate and store vertex coordinates
360   RESTORE 1410  'beginning of database
370   FOR T=0 TO 7 STEP 1:READ X,Y,Z:GOSUB 1050:B1(T,0)=X:B1(
T,1)=Y:B1(T,2)=Z:B2(T,0)=SX:B2(T,1)=SY:NEXT T  'load vertex
view coordinates into array B1, load vertex display coordina
tes into array B2
380   FOR T=0 TO 5 STEP 1:READ X,Y,Z:GOSUB 1050:B3(T,0)=SX:B3
(T,1)=SY:NEXT T  'load area fill origin display coordinates
into array B3
390 '_____
400 '
410 'main routine:   draw 6 surfaces of cube
420 'surface 0 routine
430   X1=B1(7,0):Y1=B1(7,1):Z1=B1(7,2):X2=B1(0,0):Y2=B1(0,1):
Z2=B1(0,2):X3=B1(3,0):Y3=B1(3,1):Z3=B1(3,2)  'retrieve XYZ v
iewing coordinates for surface 0
440   GOSUB 1490  'jump to plane equation routine
450   IF SP>0 THEN GOTO 530  'if surface hidden jump to next
surface
460   SX=B2(7,0):SY=B2(7,1):PSET (SX,SY),C2:SX=B2(0,0):SY=B2(
0,1):LINE-(SX,SY),C2:SX=B2(3,0):SY=B2(3,1):LINE-(SX,SY),C2:S
X=B2(6,0):SY=B2(6,1):LINE-(SX,SY),C2:SX=B2(7,0):SY=B2(7,1):L
INE-(SX,SY),C2
470   SX=B3(0,0):SY=B3(0,1):PAINT (SX,SY),C2,C2  'key matte f
or surface 0
480   SX=B2(7,0):SY=B2(7,1):PSET (SX,SY),C3:SX=B2(0,0):SY=B2(
0,1):LINE-(SX,SY),C3:SX=B2(3,0):SY=B2(3,1):LINE-(SX,SY),C3:S
X=B2(6,0):SY=B2(6,1):LINE-(SX,SY),C3:SX=B2(7,0):SY=B2(7,1):L
INE-(SX,SY),C3
490   SX=B3(0,0):SY=B3(0,1):PAINT (SX,SY),C0,C3  'solid surfa
ce 0 completed
500 '_____
510 '
520 'surface 1 routine
530   X1=B1(6,0):Y1=B1(6,1):Z1=B1(6,2):X2=B1(5,0):Y2=B1(5,1):
Z2=B1(5,2):X3=B1(4,0):Y3=B1(4,1):Z3=B1(4,2)
540   GOSUB 1490
550   IF SP>0 THEN GOTO 630
560   SX=B2(6,0):SY=B2(6,1):PSET (SX,SY),C2:SX=B2(5,0):SY=B2(
5,1):LINE-(SX,SY),C2:SX=B2(4,0):SY=B2(4,1):LINE-(SX,SY),C2:S
X=B2(7,0):SY=B2(7,1):LINE-(SX,SY),C2:SX=B2(6,0):SY=B2(6,1):L
INE-(SX,SY),C2
570   SX=B3(1,0):SY=B3(1,1):PAINT (SX,SY),C2,C2
580   SX=B2(6,0):SY=B2(6,1):PSET (SX,SY),C3:SX=B2(5,0):SY=B2(
5,1):LINE-(SX,SY),C3:SX=B2(4,0):SY=B2(4,1):LINE-(SX,SY),C3:S
X=B2(7,0):SY=B2(7,1):LINE-(SX,SY),C3:SX=B2(6,0):SY=B2(6,1):L
```

```
INE-(SX,SY),C3
590   SX=B3(1,0):SY=B3(1,1):PAINT (SX,SY),CO,C3
600  '_____
610  '
620  'surface 2 routine
630   X1=B1(3,0):Y1=B1(3,1):Z1=B1(3,2):X2=B1(2,0):Y2=B1(2,1):
Z2=B1(2,2):X3=B1(5,0):Y3=B1(5,1):Z3=B1(5,2)
640   GOSUB 1490
650   IF SP>0 THEN GOTO 730
660   SX=B2(3,0):SY=B2(3,1):PSET (SX,SY),C2:SX=B2(2,0):SY=B2(
2,1):LINE-(SX,SY),C2:SX=B2(5,0):SY=B2(5,1):LINE-(SX,SY),C2:S
X=B2(6,0):SY=B2(6,1):LINE-(SX,SY),C2:SX=B2(3,0):SY=B2(3,1):L
INE-(SX,SY),C2
670   SX=B3(2,0):SY=B3(2,1):PAINT (SX,SY),C2,C2
680   SX=B2(3,0):SY=B2(3,1):PSET (SX,SY),C3:SX=B2(2,0):SY=B2(
2,1):LINE-(SX,SY),C3:SX=B2(5,0):SY=B2(5,1):LINE-(SX,SY),C3:S
X=B2(6,0):SY=B2(6,1):LINE-(SX,SY),C3:SX=B2(3,0):SY=B2(3,1):L
INE-(SX,SY),C3
690   SX=B3(2,0):SY=B3(2,1):PAINT (SX,SY),CO,C3
700  '_____
710  '
720  'surface 3 routine
730   X1=B1(0,0):Y1=B1(0,1):Z1=B1(0,2):X2=B1(1,0):Y2=B1(1,1):
Z2=B1(1,2):X3=B1(2,0):Y3=B1(2,1):Z3=B1(2,2)
740   GOSUB 1490
750   IF SP>0 THEN GOTO 830
760   SX=B2(0,0):SY=B2(0,1):PSET (SX,SY),C2:SX=B2(1,0):SY=B2(
1,1):LINE-(SX,SY),C2:SX=B2(2,0):SY=B2(2,1):LINE-(SX,SY),C2:S
X=B2(3,0):SY=B2(3,1):LINE-(SX,SY),C2:SX=B2(0,0):SY=B2(0,1):L
INE-(SX,SY),C2
770   SX=B3(3,0):SY=B3(3,1):PAINT (SX,SY),C2,C2
780   SX=B2(0,0):SY=B2(0,1):PSET (SX,SY),C3:SX=B2(1,0):SY=B2(
1,1):LINE-(SX,SY),C3:SX=B2(2,0):SY=B2(2,1):LINE-(SX,SY),C3:S
X=B2(3,0):SY=B2(3,1):LINE-(SX,SY),C3:SX=B2(0,0):SY=B2(0,1):L
INE-(SX,SY),C3
790   SX=B3(3,0):SY=B3(3,1):PAINT (SX,SY),CO,C3
800  '_____
810  '
820  'surface 4 routine
830   X1=B1(7,0):Y1=B1(7,1):Z1=B1(7,2):X2=B1(4,0):Y2=B1(4,1):
Z2=B1(4,2):X3=B1(1,0):Y3=B1(1,1):Z3=B1(1,2)
840   GOSUB 1490
850  IF SP>0 THEN GOTO 930
860   SX=B2(7,0):SY=B2(7,1):PSET (SX,SY),C2:SX=B2(4,0):SY=B2(
4,1):LINE-(SX,SY),C2:SX=B2(1,0):SY=B2(1,1):LINE-(SX,SY),C2:S
X=B2(0,0):SY=B2(0,1):LINE-(SX,SY),C2:SX=B2(7,0):SY=B2(7,1):L
INE-(SX,SY),C2
870   SX=B3(4,0):SY=B3(4,1):PAINT (SX,SY),C2,C2
```

```
880   SX=B2(7,0):SY=B2(7,1):PSET (SX,SY),C3:SX=B2(4,0):SY=B2(
4,1):LINE-(SX,SY),C3:SX=B2(1,0):SY=B2(1,1):LINE-(SX,SY),C3:S
X=B2(0,0):SY=B2(0,1):LINE-(SX,SY),C3:SX=B2(7,0):SY=B2(7,1):L
INE-(SX,SY),C3
890   SX=B3(4,0):SY=B3(4,1):PAINT (SX,SY),C0,C3
900   '_____
910   '
920   'surface 5 routine
930   X1=B1(1,0):Y1=B1(1,1):Z1=B1(1,2):X2=B1(4,0):Y2=B1(4,1):
Z2=B1(4,2):X3=B1(5,0):Y3=B1(5,1):Z3=B1(5,2)
940   GOSUB 1490
950   IF SP>0 THEN GOTO 1010
960   SX=B2(1,0):SY=B2(1,1):PSET (SX,SY),C2:SX=B2(4,0):SY=B2(
4,1):LINE-(SX,SY),C2:SX=B2(5,0):SY=B2(5,1):LINE-(SX,SY),C2:S
X=B2(2,0):SY=B2(2,1):LINE-(SX,SY),C2:SX=B2(1,0):SY=B2(1,1):L
INE-(SX,SY),C2
970   SX=B3(5,0):SY=B3(5,1):PAINT (SX,SY),C2,C2
980   SX=B2(1,0):SY=B2(1,1):PSET (SX,SY),C3:SX=B2(4,0):SY=B2(
4,1):LINE-(SX,SY),C3:SX=B2(5,0):SY=B2(5,1):LINE-(SX,SY),C3:S
X=B2(2,0):SY=B2(2,1):LINE-(SX,SY),C3:SX=B2(1,0):SY=B2(1,1):L
INE-(SX,SY),C3
990   SX=B3(5,0):SY=B3(5,1):PAINT (SX,SY),C0,C3
1000   SOUND 350,.7
1010   RETURN
1020   '_____
1030   '
1040 'module:   perspective calculations
1050   X=(-1)*X:XA=CR1*X-SR1*Z:ZA=SR1*X+CR1*Z:X=CR2*XA+SR2*Y:
YA=CR2*Y-SR2*XA:Z=CR3*ZA-SR3*YA:Y=SR3*ZA+CR3*YA:X=X+MX:Y=Y+M
Y:Z=Z+MZ:SX=D*X/Z:SY=D*Y/Z:RETURN
1060   '_____
1070   '
1080 'module:   return to BASIC interpreter
1090   CLS:WINDOW:SCREEN 0,0,0,0:CLEAR:WIDTH 80:COLOR 7,0,0:C
LS:LOCATE 1,1,1:END
1100   '_____
1110   '
1120 'module:   UNIVERSAL
1130 'This routine configures the program for the hardware/s
oftware being used.
1140   KEY OFF:CLS:ON ERROR GOTO 1170  'trap if not EGA
1150   SCREEN 7,,0,0:COLOR 7,0:PALETTE 1,1:PALETTE 2,4:PALETT
E 3,7:C0=0:C1=1:C2=2:C3=3
1160   GOTO 1250  'jump to screen coordinates set-up
1170   RESUME 1180
1180   ON ERROR GOTO 1210  'trap if not PCjr
1190   CLEAR,,,65536!:SCREEN 1,0:COLOR 0,1:PALETTE 1,1:PALETT
E 2,4:PALETTE 3,7:C0=0:C1=1:C2=2:C3=3
```

```
1200   GOTO 1250   'jump to screen coordinates set-up
1210   RESUME 1220
1220   LOCATE 10,1:PRINT "An EGA or a PCjr is required":LOCAT
E 11,1:PRINT "to run this program.":LOCATE 14,1:PRINT "Press
 <Enter> to return to BASIC."
1230   K$=INKEY$:IF K$<>CHR$(13) THEN 1230
1240   CLS:END
1250   ON ERROR GOTO 0   'disable error trapping override
1260   WINDOW SCREEN (-399,-299)-(400,300)   'establish device
-independent screen coordinates
1270   ON KEY (2) GOSUB 1090:KEY (2) ON   'F2 key to exit prog
ram
1280   GOTO 150   'return to main program
1290 '_____
1300 '
1310 'module:   assign variables
1320   D=1200:R1=5.68319:R2=6.28319:R3=5.99778:MX=0:MY=0:MZ=-
500   '3D parameters
1330   DIM B1 (7,2)   '8 sets of XYZ view coordinates
1340   DIM B2 (7,1)   '8 sets of SX,SY display coordinates
1350   DIM B3 (5,1)   '6 sets of SX,SY fill coordinates
1360   SR1=SIN(R1):CR1=COS(R1):SR2=SIN(R2):CR2=COS(R2):SR3=SI
N(R3):CR3=COS(R3)
1370   RETURN
1380 '_____
1390 '
1400 'module:   database of 8 sets of XYZ world coordinates f
or vertices of 3D cube
1410   DATA   30,-30,30,   30,30,30,   -30,30,30,   -30,-30,30,
30,30,-30,   -30,30,-30,   -30,-30,-30,   30,-30,-30
1420 '_____
1430 '
1440 'module:   database of 6 sets of XYZ world coordinates f
or area fill origins for 6 surfaces of 3D cube
1450   DATA   0,-30,0,   0,0,-30,   -30,0,0,   0,0,30,   30,0,0,
0,30,0
1460 '_____
1470 '
1480 'module:   plane equation method of hidden surface remov
al
1490   SP1=X1*(Y2*Z3-Y3*Z2):SP1=(-1)*SP1:SP2=X2*(Y3*Z1-Y1*Z3)
:SP3=X3*(Y1*Z2-Y2*Z1):SP=SP1-SP2-SP3:RETURN
1500 '_____
1510 '
1520   END 'of program code
```

Fig. 21-4. Frame animation of a rotating 3D cube on a Color/Graphics Adapter.

```
100 'Program A-33.BAS      Frame animation.
110 'Demonstrates frame animation on CGA.
120 '_____
130 '
140    GOTO 1190     'configure system
150    GOSUB 1340    'assign variables
160 '_____
170 '
180 'master routine:  create and save frames
190    GOSUB 410:LOCATE 2,1:PRINT "Frame animation of 3D cube.
    ":DEF SEG=&H2400:POKE &H8,&HB8:POKE &HD,&H34:CALL PCOPY:DEF
SEG   'move to page 3 at 34000 hex
200    CLS:GOSUB 370:LOCATE 2,1:PRINT "Frame animation of 3D c
ube.":GOSUB 410:DEF SEG=&H2400:POKE &HD,&H30:CALL PCOPY:DEF
SEG   'move to page 2 at 30000 hex
210    CLS:GOSUB 370:LOCATE 2,1:PRINT "Frame animation of 3D c
ube.":GOSUB 410:DEF SEG=&H2400:POKE &HD,&H2C:CALL PCOPY:DEF
SEG   'move to page 1 at 2C000 hex
220    CLS:GOSUB 370:LOCATE 2,1:PRINT "Frame animation of 3D c
ube.":GOSUB 410:DEF SEG=&H2400:POKE &HD,&H28:CALL PCOPY:DEF
SEG   'move to page 0 at 28000 hex
230    SOUND 550,5:SOUND 350,5:LOCATE 3,1:PRINT "Press <Enter>
    to begin animation."
240    K$=INKEY$:IF K$<>CHR$(13) THEN 240
250    LOCATE 3,1:PRINT "                                      "
260    CLS:DEF SEG=&H2400:POKE &H8,&H28:POKE &HD,&HB8:CALL PCO
PY:DEF SEG:FOR T=1 TO 100 STEP 1:NEXT T
270    DEF SEG=&H2400:POKE &H8,&H2C:CALL PCOPY:DEF SEG:FOR T=1
    TO 100 STEP 1:NEXT T
280    DEF SEG=&H2400:POKE &H8,&H30:CALL PCOPY:DEF SEG:FOR T=1
    TO 100 STEP 1:NEXT T
290    DEF SEG=&H2400:POKE &H8,&H34:CALL PCOPY:DEF SEG:FOR T=1
    TO 500 STEP 1:NEXT T
300    DEF SEG=&H2400:POKE &H8,&H30:CALL PCOPY:DEF SEG:FOR T=1
    TO 100 STEP 1:NEXT T
310    DEF SEG=&H2400:POKE &H8,&H2C:CALL PCOPY:DEF SEG:FOR T=1
    TO 100 STEP 1:NEXT T
320    DEF SEG=&H2400:POKE &H8,&H28:CALL PCOPY:DEF SEG:FOR T=1
    TO 500 STEP 1:NEXT T:GOTO 270
330    END 'of master routine
340 '_____
350 '
360 'module:  refresh rotation factors
370    R1=R1-.04363:SR1=SIN(R1):CR1=COS(R1):R3=R3-.04363:SR3=S
```

```
IN(R3):CR3=COS(R3):RETURN
380 '_____
390 '
400 'module:  calculate and store vertex coordinates
410   RESTORE 1440  'beginning of database
420   FOR T=0 TO 7 STEP 1:READ X,Y,Z:GOSUB 1100:B1(T,0)=X:B1(
T,1)=Y:B1(T,2)=Z:B2(T,0)=SX:B2(T,1)=SY:NEXT T  'load vertex
view coordinates into array B1, load vertex display coordina
tes into array B2
430   FOR T=0 TO 5 STEP 1:READ X,Y,Z:GOSUB 1100:B3(T,0)=SX:B3
(T,1)=SY:NEXT T  'load area fill origin display coordinates
into array B3
440 '_____
450 '
460 'main routine:  draw 6 surfaces of cube
470 'surface 0 routine
480   X1=B1(7,0):Y1=B1(7,1):Z1=B1(7,2):X2=B1(0,0):Y2=B1(0,1):
Z2=B1(0,2):X3=B1(3,0):Y3=B1(3,1):Z3=B1(3,2)  'retrieve XYZ v
iewing coordinates for surface 0
490   GOSUB 1520  'jump to plane equation routine
500   IF SP>0 THEN GOTO 580  'if surface hidden jump to next
surface
510   SX=B2(7,0):SY=B2(7,1):PSET (SX,SY),C2:SX=B2(0,0):SY=B2(
0,1):LINE-(SX,SY),C2:SX=B2(3,0):SY=B2(3,1):LINE-(SX,SY),C2:S
X=B2(6,0):SY=B2(6,1):LINE-(SX,SY),C2:SX=B2(7,0):SY=B2(7,1):L
INE-(SX,SY),C2
520   SX=B3(0,0):SY=B3(0,1):PAINT (SX,SY),C2,C2  'key matte f
or surface 0
530   SX=B2(7,0):SY=B2(7,1):PSET (SX,SY),C3:SX=B2(0,0):SY=B2(
0,1):LINE-(SX,SY),C3:SX=B2(3,0):SY=B2(3,1):LINE-(SX,SY),C3:S
X=B2(6,0):SY=B2(6,1):LINE-(SX,SY),C3:SX=B2(7,0):SY=B2(7,1):L
INE-(SX,SY),C3
540   SX=B3(0,0):SY=B3(0,1):PAINT (SX,SY),C0,C3  'solid surfa
ce 0 completed
550 '_____
560 '
570 'surface 1 routine
580   X1=B1(6,0):Y1=B1(6,1):Z1=B1(6,2):X2=B1(5,0):Y2=B1(5,1):
Z2=B1(5,2):X3=B1(4,0):Y3=B1(4,1):Z3=B1(4,2)
590   GOSUB 1520
600   IF SP>0 THEN GOTO 680
610   SX=B2(6,0):SY=B2(6,1):PSET (SX,SY),C2:SX=B2(5,0):SY=B2(
5,1):LINE-(SX,SY),C2:SX=B2(4,0):SY=B2(4,1):LINE-(SX,SY),C2:S
X=B2(7,0):SY=B2(7,1):LINE-(SX,SY),C2:SX=B2(6,0):SY=B2(6,1):L
INE-(SX,SY),C2
620   SX=B3(1,0):SY=B3(1,1):PAINT (SX,SY),C2,C2
630   SX=B2(6,0):SY=B2(6,1):PSET (SX,SY),C3:SX=B2(5,0):SY=B2(
5,1):LINE-(SX,SY),C3:SX=B2(4,0):SY=B2(4,1):LINE-(SX,SY),C3:S
```

```
X=B2(7,0):SY=B2(7,1):LINE-(SX,SY),C3:SX=B2(6,0):SY=B2(6,1):L
INE-(SX,SY),C3
640  SX=B3(1,0):SY=B3(1,1):PAINT (SX,SY),C0,C3
650 '_____
660 '
670 'surface 2 routine
680  X1=B1(3,0):Y1=B1(3,1):Z1=B1(3,2):X2=B1(2,0):Y2=B1(2,1):
Z2=B1(2,2):X3=B1(5,0):Y3=B1(5,1):Z3=B1(5,2)
690  GOSUB 1520
700  IF SP>0 THEN GOTO 780
710  SX=B2(3,0):SY=B2(3,1):PSET (SX,SY),C2:SX=B2(2,0):SY=B2(
2,1):LINE-(SX,SY),C2:SX=B2(5,0):SY=B2(5,1):LINE-(SX,SY),C2:S
X=B2(6,0):SY=B2(6,1):LINE-(SX,SY),C2:SX=B2(3,0):SY=B2(3,1):L
INE-(SX,SY),C2
720  SX=B3(2,0):SY=B3(2,1):PAINT (SX,SY),C2,C2
730  SX=B2(3,0):SY=B2(3,1):PSET (SX,SY),C3:SX=B2(2,0):SY=B2(
2,1):LINE-(SX,SY),C3:SX=B2(5,0):SY=B2(5,1):LINE-(SX,SY),C3:S
X=B2(6,0):SY=B2(6,1):LINE-(SX,SY),C3:SX=B2(3,0):SY=B2(3,1):L
INE-(SX,SY),C3
740  SX=B3(2,0):SY=B3(2,1):PAINT (SX,SY),C0,C3
750 '_____
760 '
770 'surface 3 routine
780  X1=B1(0,0):Y1=B1(0,1):Z1=B1(0,2):X2=B1(1,0):Y2=B1(1,1):
Z2=B1(1,2):X3=B1(2,0):Y3=B1(2,1):Z3=B1(2,2)
790  GOSUB 1520
800  IF SP>0 THEN GOTO 880
810  SX=B2(0,0):SY=B2(0,1):PSET (SX,SY),C2:SX=B2(1,0):SY=B2(
1,1):LINE-(SX,SY),C2:SX=B2(2,0):SY=B2(2,1):LINE-(SX,SY),C2:S
X=B2(3,0):SY=B2(3,1):LINE-(SX,SY),C2:SX=B2(0,0):SY=B2(0,1):L
INE-(SX,SY),C2
820  SX=B3(3,0):SY=B3(3,1):PAINT (SX,SY),C2,C2
830  SX=B2(0,0):SY=B2(0,1):PSET (SX,SY),C3:SX=B2(1,0):SY=B2(
1,1):LINE-(SX,SY),C3:SX=B2(2,0):SY=B2(2,1):LINE-(SX,SY),C3:S
X=B2(3,0):SY=B2(3,1):LINE-(SX,SY),C3:SX=B2(0,0):SY=B2(0,1):L
INE-(SX,SY),C3
840  SX=B3(3,0):SY=B3(3,1):PAINT (SX,SY),C0,C3
850 '_____
860 '
870 'surface 4 routine
880  X1=B1(7,0):Y1=B1(7,1):Z1=B1(7,2):X2=B1(4,0):Y2=B1(4,1):
Z2=B1(4,2):X3=B1(1,0):Y3=B1(1,1):Z3=B1(1,2)
890  GOSUB 1520
900 IF SP>0 THEN GOTO 980
910  SX=B2(7,0):SY=B2(7,1):PSET (SX,SY),C2:SX=B2(4,0):SY=B2(
4,1):LINE-(SX,SY),C2:SX=B2(1,0):SY=B2(1,1):LINE-(SX,SY),C2:S
X=B2(0,0):SY=B2(0,1):LINE-(SX,SY),C2:SX=B2(7,0):SY=B2(7,1):L
INE-(SX,SY),C2
```

```
920    SX=B3(4,0):SY=B3(4,1):PAINT (SX,SY),C2,C2
930    SX=B2(7,0):SY=B2(7,1):PSET (SX,SY),C3:SX=B2(4,0):SY=B2(
4,1):LINE-(SX,SY),C3:SX=B2(1,0):SY=B2(1,1):LINE-(SX,SY),C3:S
X=B2(0,0):SY=B2(0,1):LINE-(SX,SY),C3:SX=B2(7,0):SY=B2(7,1):L
INE-(SX,SY),C3
940    SX=B3(4,0):SY=B3(4,1):PAINT (SX,SY),C0,C3
950 '_____
960 '
970 'surface 5 routine
980    X1=B1(1,0):Y1=B1(1,1):Z1=B1(1,2):X2=B1(4,0):Y2=B1(4,1):
Z2=B1(4,2):X3=B1(5,0):Y3=B1(5,1):Z3=B1(5,2)
990    GOSUB 1520
1000    IF SP>0 THEN GOTO 1060
1010    SX=B2(1,0):SY=B2(1,1):PSET (SX,SY),C2:SX=B2(4,0):SY=B2
(4,1):LINE-(SX,SY),C2:SX=B2(5,0):SY=B2(5,1):LINE-(SX,SY),C2:
SX=B2(2,0):SY=B2(2,1):LINE-(SX,SY),C2:SX=B2(1,0):SY=B2(1,1):
LINE-(SX,SY),C2
1020    SX=B3(5,0):SY=B3(5,1):PAINT (SX,SY),C2,C2
1030    SX=B2(1,0):SY=B2(1,1):PSET (SX,SY),C3:SX=B2(4,0):SY=B2
(4,1):LINE-(SX,SY),C3:SX=B2(5,0):SY=B2(5,1):LINE-(SX,SY),C3:
SX=B2(2,0):SY=B2(2,1):LINE-(SX,SY),C3:SX=B2(1,0):SY=B2(1,1):
LINE-(SX,SY),C3
1040    SX=B3(5,0):SY=B3(5,1):PAINT (SX,SY),C0,C3
1050    SOUND 350,.7
1060    RETURN
1070 '_____
1080 '
1090 'module:   perspective calculations
1100    X=(-1)*X:XA=CR1*X-SR1*Z:ZA=SR1*X+CR1*Z:X=CR2*XA+SR2*Y:
YA=CR2*Y-SR2*XA:Z=CR3*ZA-SR3*YA:Y=SR3*ZA+CR3*YA:X=X+MX:Y=Y+M
Y:Z=Z+MZ:SX=D*X/Z:SY=D*Y/Z:RETURN
1110 '_____
1120 '
1130 'module:   return to BASIC interpreter
1140    CLS:WINDOW:SCREEN 0,0,0,0:CLEAR:WIDTH 80:COLOR 7,0,0:C
LS:LOCATE 1,1,1:END
1150 '_____
1160 '
1170 'module:   UNIVERSAL
1180 'This routine configures the program for the hardware/s
oftware being used.
1190    KEY OFF:CLS:ON ERROR GOTO 1240:CLEAR,,,32768!   'trap i
f PCjr
1200    CLS:LOCATE 10,1:PRINT "This program will not run":LOCA
TE 11,1:PRINT "on an IBM PCjr.":LOCATE 12,1:PRINT "An IBM-co
mpatible PC, XT, or AT":LOCATE 13,1:PRINT "with 256Kb is req
uired."
1210    LOCATE 16,1:PRINT "Press <Enter> to return to BASIC."
```

```
1220   K$=INKEY$:IF K$<>CHR$(13) THEN 1220
1230   CLS:SCREEN 0,0,0,0:CLEAR:COLOR 7,0,0:WIDTH 80:LOCATE 1
,1,1:CLS:END
1240   RESUME 1250
1250   SCREEN 1,0:COLOR 0,1:C0=0:C1=1:C2=2:C3=3
1260   ON ERROR GOTO 0   'disable error trapping override
1270   GOSUB 1560  'load PCOPY machine code subroutine
1280   WINDOW SCREEN (-399,-299)-(400,300)   'establish device
-independent screen coordinates
1290   ON KEY (2) GOSUB 1140:KEY (2) ON   'F2 key to exit prog
ram
1300   GOTO 150   'return to main program
1310 '_____
1320 '
1330 'module:   assign variables
1340   D=1200:R1=5.68319:R2=6.28319:R3=5.99778:MX=0:MY=0:MZ=-
500   '3D parameters
1350   DEFINT P:PCOPY=0   'calling protocall for machine code
subroutine
1360   DIM B1 (7,2)   '8 sets of XYZ view coordinates
1370   DIM B2 (7,1)   '8 sets of SX,SY display coordinates
1380   DIM B3 (5,1)   '6 sets of SX,SY fill coordinates
1390   SR1=SIN(R1):CR1=COS(R1):SR2=SIN(R2):CR2=COS(R2):SR3=SI
N(R3):CR3=COS(R3)
1400   RETURN
1410 '_____
1420 '
1430 'module:   database of 8 sets of XYZ world coordinates f
or vertices of 3D cube
1440   DATA   30,-30,30,   30,30,30,   -30,30,30,   -30,-30,30,
30,30,-30,   -30,30,-30,   -30,-30,-30,   30,-30,-30
1450 '_____
1460 '
1470 'module:   database of 6 sets of XYZ world coordinates f
or area fill origins for 6 surfaces of 3D cube
1480   DATA   0,-30,0,   0,0,-30,   -30,0,0,   0,0,30,   30,0,0,
0,30,0
1490 '_____
1500 '
1510 'module:   plane equation method of hidden surface remov
al
1520   SP1=X1*(Y2*Z3-Y3*Z2):SP1=(-1)*SP1:SP2=X2*(Y3*Z1-Y1*Z3)
:SP3=X3*(Y1*Z2-Y2*Z1):SP=SP1-SP2-SP3:RETURN
1530 '_____
1540 '
1550 'subroutine: place PCOPY machine-code subroutine in mem
ory at location &H24000
1560   RESTORE 1600:DEF SEG=&H2400:DEFINT T:FOR T=0 TO 34 STE
```

```
P 1:READ HEX:POKE T,HEX:NEXT:RETURN
1570 '_____
1580 '
1590 'data base: hexadecimal opcodes for machine-code subrou
tine to move 16384 bytes from &H28000 to &HB8000.
1600   DATA  &H51,&H1E,&H06,&H56,&H57,&H9C,&HB9,&H00,&H28,&H8
E,&HD9,&HB9,&H00,&HB8,&H8E,&HC1,&HFC,&HBE,&H00,&H00,&HBF,&H0
0,&H00,&HB9,&H00,&H40,&HF3,&HA4,&H9D,&H5F,&H5E,&H07,&H1F,&H5
9,&HCB
1610 '_____
1620 '
1630   END 'of program code
```

pages. (If you are using QuickBASIC, read Appendix C before you attempt this modification.)

The routine which coordinates the animation is located at lines 260 through 270. Note the use of the FOR T = 1 TO 100 timing loop. This slows down the animation to a speed which is pleasing to the eye. You can experiment with this to produce more pleasing displays on your particular equipment.

The page flip which produces frame animation is implemented by the SCREEN,,p1,p2 instruction. SCREEN,,1,1 makes page 1 the displayed page. SCREEN,,2,2 makes page 2 the displayed page, and so on.

The module at line 310 is used to update the sine and cosine rotation factors as different versions of the cube are being created. You can change the amount of rotation between frames by changing R1 = R1-.04363 to R1 = R1-.08727, for example. The current decrement, .04363 radians, is equal to 2.5 degrees. The cube rotates over an arc of 10 degrees in four frames of animation.

The rest of the program listing is virtually identical to the demonstration program introduced in Chapter 8, which generates a solid 3D cube using the plane equation method of hidden surface removal.

### The Color/Graphics Adapter Program

The program listing for frame animation on the Color/Graphics Adapter is shown in Fig. 21-4.

To understand how this program works, turn your attention to the subroutine at line 1550. This subroutine is called during program start-up.

Line 1560 uses a RESTORE statement to set the database pointer to line 1600. Next, a DEF SEG statement is used to identify a memory location at 24000

hex. Then, a FOR...NEXT loop is used to poke the hex values at line 1600 into memory, starting at 24000 hex. These hex values correspond to the binary machine code values for a short assembly language routine which simply moves 16384 bytes of data from one address to another. Once this assembly language routine has been poked into memory, the environment is ready to produce frame animation.

### The Main Routine

The main routine which creates and saves frame images is located at lines 190 through 220. Line 210 provides a good example of how this process works. The CLS clears the previous image from the display screen. The GOSUB 370 instruction sends the program to the subroutine which decrements the R1 yaw view angle. The GOSUB 410 instruction sends the program to the subroutine which draws the surfaces of the cube using the plane equation method of hidden surface removal.

When control returns to line 210, POKE &HD,&H2C is used to alter the target address used by the assembly language subroutine. If you check line 1600, you will see that the 14th data element is &HB8. This is the target address to which graphics data is moved by the assembly language routine. The source address is the 9th element, &H28. (Line 190 changes this source address to B8 hex, which identifies the B8000 hex address of the screen buffer.)

The command, CALL PCOPY, sends the microprocessor to the assembly language subroutine. Because of the target and source changes made by the POKE instructions, the assembly language moves 16384 bytes of data from B80000 hex to 2C000 hex. As you can see, it is relatively simple to adjust the source and target address. The source address is changed by a POKE &H8 instruction; the target address is changed by a POKE &HD instruction.

### The Animation Routine

The section of code which animates the cube is located at lines 260 through 320. This code essentially does nothing more than adjust the source address before it calls the assembly language subroutine. Page 0 is located at 28000 hex (160K). Page 1 is located at 2C000 hex (176K). Page 2 is located at 30000 hex (192K). Page 3 is located at 34000 hex (208K). Each page is 16K in length. This program will run on any IBM-compatible microcomputer with at least 256K of RAM. Refer to Chapter 1 for a memory map which will help you plan your own frame animation programs with your Color/Graphics Adapter.

If you are using QuickBASIC or TurboBASIC, you should be aware that you might be required to use different memory address for the hidden pages. Both of these compilers use much more memory than does interpreted BASIC. Refer to Chapter 1 for more information on this. Check Appendix C for information about QuickBASIC. Read Appendix D for more information about TurboBASIC.

### ADVANCED MODELING AND RENDERING

As you can see, each frame can consist of extremely detailed images. Computer-shaded models can be rotated smoothly by using the frame animation technique, because animation speed is completely independent of drawing time. Even the computer-shaded 3D sphere in Chapter 10, which takes nearly 12 minutes to generate, could be spun by frame animation at speeds of 8 fps to 18 fps. (For additional demonstration programs using frame animation, refer to the author's first book, *High-Speed Animation and Simulation for Microcomputers,* available at your favorite bookstore or direct from TAB BOOKS, Inc.)

### SUMMARY

In this chapter you learned that two steps are essential to frame animation: creating/saving the frames, and cycling through the presaved pages. You saw that frame animation can be implemented on the EGA, PCjr, and Tandy via the SCREEN,,p1,p2 instruction. You discovered that a short assembly language subroutine can be used to make frame animation possible with a standard Color/Graphics Adapter.

The next chapter introduces the technique of real-time animation, sometimes called ping-pong animation or live animation.

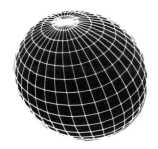

# 22

# *Real-Time Animation*

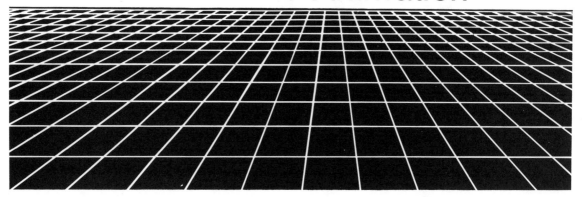

Real-time animation is the most interactive form of animation, but it is also the slowest. The microcomputer is creating the image and animating it simultaneously. With frame animation and graphic array animation, all images have been prepared in advance and the computer can focus all its computational power on merely animating those images, thereby generating quicker animation speeds.

## REAL-TIME ANIMATION MECHANISMS

Real-time animation is also called ping-pong animation, live animation, and dynamic page-flipping animation. While the computer is drawing a new image on a hidden graphics page, the previously-completed image is being displayed. When the new image is completed, it is displayed and the computer begins work on the next image on a hidden page. The actual drawing procedure always occurs on a hidden page. Only completed images are displayed. (Refer to Chapter 19 for a more detailed discussion of the concept of real-time animation.)

The speed of animation is linked to drawing time.

If complex models are being created, the animation rate will be slow. Generally, speeds of one frame per second and slower are typical with interpreted BASIC.

## Real-Time Animation on the EGA and PCjr

The SCREEN,,p1,p2 instruction supports real-time animation on the EGA and on the PCjr (and Tandy). The syntax for this statement is SCREEN,,written-to-page,displayed-page. SCREEN,, 0,1 would draw graphics on hidden page 0 while displaying page 1. SCREEN,,1,0 would flip the pages, now drawing on hidden page 1 and displaying page 0. By continuing this sequence of reciprocal flipping, the real-time animation environment is sustained. (For further discussion of the SCREEN statement in BASIC, consult Chapter 2.)

Because no graphics data is moved by the SCREEN,,p1,p2 instruction, the shift in displayed pages is very quick. The video gate array (VGA) merely alters the starting address pointer for the hardware video display. The flip occurs in approximately 1/20th of a second.

## Real-Time Animation on the Color/Graphics Adapter

The Color/Graphics adapter contains 16384 bytes of display memory: enough for only one graphics page. In order to sustain real-time animation, BASIC must be physically modified to write to a simulated hidden page in dynamic RAM. When the image has been completed, a short assembly language subroutine is used to move the graphics data from the hidden page to the screen buffer (located on the color/graphics adapter).

Because 16384 bytes of graphics data is moved by the assembly language subroutine, the shift of displayed pages is not as quick as the EGA or the PCjr video subsystem. The flip occurs in approximately 1/10th of a second.

## FIVE WAYS TO IMPROVE PERFORMANCE

A number of tactics are available to improve execution times for real-time animation programs. Although real-time animation will never be as quick as frame animation, the need for keyboard interaction often makes real-time animation the preferred choice. With frame animation and graphic array animation, you can only animate images which have been pre-saved. With real-time animation, you are creating the images as you are animating them, so you can use the keyboard to change the shape, location, and identity of the models being animated.

**Method 1:** Keep the image simple. The longer it takes for the computer to create the image, the slower the animation rate. In real-time animation, it is the action which lends credibility to the graphics. Detailing is important, but action is more important. (If you must have detail, use frame animation or graphic array animation instead.)

**Method 2:** If a complex background is required,

create a generic version of the background and store it on a second hidden page. Each frame of the animation sequence would consist of the following algorithm: flip the pages, copy the contents of the background page onto the hidden written-to page, draw the image on the hidden written-to page, flip the completed image up onto the display screen.

**Method 3:** If a 3D model is being merely moved (but not rotated), you can invoke an abbreviated set of perspective formulas. Once you have calculated the sine and cosine rotation results for a model, you can move it to any location with the translation formulas $X = X + MX:Y = Y + MY:Z = Z + MZ$. There is no need to recalculate the rotation formulas SR1, CR1, et al. A model can be moved left, right, up, down, closer, and farther from the viewpoint by just the translation formulas (and the projection formulas, of course). Refer back to Chapter 7 for a detailed discussion of the perspective formulas.

**Method 4:** You can keep animation rates high by using transparent, wire-frame models. Hidden surface routines are time consuming and are best used with frame animation and software sprite animation.

**Method 5:** You can increase animation speed by a factor of 10 or more if you use a compiler such as Microsoft QuickBASIC 2.0 or Borland TurboBASIC 1.0. For example, an air combat simulation written entirely in IBM BASICA 3.21 has been clocked by the author as requiring a full six seconds for each new frame. The same simulator will dash along under QuickBASIC 2.0 at a blazing 2 frames per second: a 12-to-1 improvement in speed!

## DEMONSTRATION OF REAL-TIME ANIMATION

Figure 22-1 shows the screen output of the demonstration programs in Fig. 22-2 and Fig. 22-3.

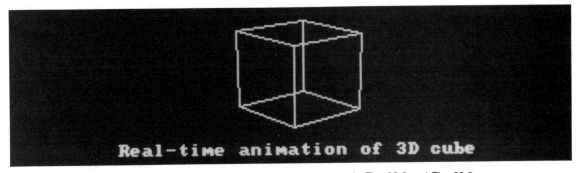

Fig. 22-1. The display image produced by the demonstration programs in Fig. 22-2 and Fig. 22-3.

Fig. 22-2. Real-time animation of a rotating 3D cube on an EGA, PCjr, or Tandy.

```
100 'Program A-34.BAS    Real time animation.
110 'Demonstrates hidden-page animation on EGA or PCjr.
120 '_____
130 '
140   GOTO 410    'configure system
150   GOSUB 590   'assign variables
160 '_____
170 '
180 'master routine:  real time animation
190   LOCATE 2,1:PRINT "Real time animation of 3D cube.":PCOP
Y 0,2
200   SCREEN,,1-P,P  'begin drawing on hidden page
210   RESTORE 680:FOR T=0 TO 7 STEP 1:READ X,Y,Z:GOSUB 320:B2
(T,0)=SX:B2(T,1)=SY:NEXT T
220   SX=B2(7,0):SY=B2(7,1):PSET (SX,SY),C3:SX=B2(0,0):SY=B2(
0,1):LINE-(SX,SY),C3:SX=B2(3,0):SY=B2(3,1):LINE-(SX,SY),C3:S
X=B2(6,0):SY=B2(6,1):LINE-(SX,SY),C3:SX=B2(7,0):SY=B2(7,1):L
INE-(SX,SY),C3
230   SX=B2(6,0):SY=B2(6,1):PSET (SX,SY),C3:SX=B2(5,0):SY=B2(
5,1):LINE-(SX,SY),C3:SX=B2(4,0):SY=B2(4,1):LINE-(SX,SY),C3:S
X=B2(7,0):SY=B2(7,1):LINE-(SX,SY),C3:SX=B2(6,0):SY=B2(6,1):L
INE-(SX,SY),C3
240   SX=B2(3,0):SY=B2(3,1):PSET (SX,SY),C3:SX=B2(2,0):SY=B2(
2,1):LINE-(SX,SY),C3:SX=B2(5,0):SY=B2(5,1):LINE-(SX,SY),C3:S
X=B2(6,0):SY=B2(6,1):LINE-(SX,SY),C3:SX=B2(3,0):SY=B2(3,1):L
INE-(SX,SY),C3
250   SX=B2(0,0):SY=B2(0,1):PSET (SX,SY),C3:SX=B2(1,0):SY=B2(
1,1):LINE-(SX,SY),C3:SX=B2(2,0):SY=B2(2,1):LINE-(SX,SY),C3:S
X=B2(3,0):SY=B2(3,1):LINE-(SX,SY),C3:SX=B2(0,0):SY=B2(0,1):L
INE-(SX,SY),C3
260   SX=B2(7,0):SY=B2(7,1):PSET (SX,SY),C3:SX=B2(4,0):SY=B2(
4,1):LINE-(SX,SY),C3:SX=B2(1,0):SY=B2(1,1):LINE-(SX,SY),C3:S
X=B2(0,0):SY=B2(0,1):LINE-(SX,SY),C3:SX=B2(7,0):SY=B2(7,1):L
INE-(SX,SY),C3
270   SX=B2(1,0):SY=B2(1,1):PSET (SX,SY),C3:SX=B2(4,0):SY=B2(
4,1):LINE-(SX,SY),C3:SX=B2(5,0):SY=B2(5,1):LINE-(SX,SY),C3:S
X=B2(2,0):SY=B2(2,1):LINE-(SX,SY),C3:SX=B2(1,0):SY=B2(1,1):L
INE-(SX,SY),C3
280   R1=R1-.04363:SR1=SIN(R1):CR1=COS(R1):SCREEN,,1-P,P:PCOP
Y 2,1-P:P=1-P:SOUND 350,.7:GOTO 210
290 '_____
300 '
310 'module:  perspective calculations
320   X=(-1)*X:XA=CR1*X-SR1*Z:ZA=SR1*X+CR1*Z:X=CR2*XA+SR2*Y:Y
A=CR2*Y-SR2*XA:Z=CR3*ZA-SR3*YA:Y=SR3*ZA+CR3*YA:X=X+MX:Y=Y+MY
```

```
: Z=Z+MZ:SX=D*X/Z:SY=D*Y/Z:RETURN
330 '_____
340 '
350 'module:   return to BASIC interpreter
360   CLS:WINDOW:SCREEN 0,0,0,0:CLEAR:WIDTH 80:COLOR 7,0,0:CL
S:LOCATE 1,1,1:END
370 '_____
380 '
390 'module:   UNIVERSAL
400 'This routine configures the program for the hardware/so
ftware being used.
410   KEY OFF:CLS:ON ERROR GOTO 440   'trap if not EGA
420   SCREEN 7,,0,0:COLOR 7,0:PALETTE 1,1:PALETTE 2,4:PALETTE
 3,7:C0=0:C1=1:C2=2:C3=3:PCOPY 0,1:PCOPY 0,2
430   GOTO 520   'jump to screen coordinates set-up
440   RESUME 450
450   ON ERROR GOTO 480 'trap if not PCjr
460   CLEAR,,,49152!:SCREEN 1,0:COLOR 0,1:PALETTE 1,1:PALETTE
 2,4:PALETTE 3,7:C0=0:C1=1:C2=2:C3=3:CLS:PCOPY 0,1:PCOPY 0,2

470   GOTO 520   'jump to screen coordinates set-up
480   RESUME 490
490   LOCATE 10,1:PRINT "An EGA or a PCjr is required":LOCATE
 11,1:PRINT "to run this program.":LOCATE 15,1:PRINT "Press
<Enter> to return to BASIC."
500   K$=INKEY$:IF K$<>CHR$(13) THEN 500
510   CLS:SCREEN 0,0,0,0:WIDTH 80:COLOR 7,0,0:LOCATE 1,1,1:CL
S:END
520   ON ERROR GOTO 0   'disable error trapping override
530   WINDOW SCREEN (-399,-299)-(400,300)   'establish device-
independent screen coordinates
540   ON KEY (2) GOSUB 360:KEY (2) ON   'F2 key to exit progra
m
550   GOTO 150   'return to main program
560 '_____
570 '
580 'module:   assign variables
590   D=1200:R1=5.68319:R2=6.28319:R3=5.99778:MX=0:MY=0:MZ=-5
00   '3D parameters
600   DEFINT T   'loop counter
610   DEFINT P:P=0   'page flipping variable
620   DIM B2 (7,1)   '8 sets of SX,SY display coordinates
630   SR1=SIN(R1):CR1=COS(R1):SR2=SIN(R2):CR2=COS(R2):SR3=SIN
(R3):CR3=COS(R3)
640   RETURN
650 '_____
660 '
670 'module:   database of 8 sets of XYZ world coordinates fo
r vertices of 3D cube
```

```
680   DATA  30,-30,30,  30,30,30,  -30,30,30,  -30,-30,30,  3
0,30,-30,  -30,30,-30,  -30,-30,-30,  30,-30,-30
690 '_____
700 '
710   END 'of program code
```

Fig. 22-3. Real-time animation of a rotating 3D cube on a standard Color/Graphics Adapter.

```
100 'Program A-35.BAS    Real time animation.
110 'Demonstrates hidden-page animation on Color/Graphics Ad
apter.
120 '_____
130 '
140   GOTO 370    'configure system
150   GOSUB 600    'assign variables
160 '_____
170 '
180 'master routine:  real time animation
190   CLS:LOCATE 2,1:PRINT "Real time animation of 3D cube":L
OCATE 3,1:PRINT "on Color/Graphics Adapter":DEF SEG=&H2400:P
OKE &H8,&HB8:POKE &HD,&H28:CALL PCOPY   'initialize hidden, w
ritten-to page 1
200   POKE &HD,&H2C:CALL PCOPY:DEF SEG   'initialize page 2
210   RESTORE 690:FOR T=0 TO 7 STEP 1:READ X,Y,Z:GOSUB 320:B2
(T,0)=SX:B2(T,1)=SY:NEXT T
220   SX=B2(7,0):SY=B2(7,1):PSET (SX,SY),C3:SX=B2(0,0):SY=B2(
0,1):LINE-(SX,SY),C3:SX=B2(3,0):SY=B2(3,1):LINE-(SX,SY),C3:S
X=B2(6,0):SY=B2(6,1):LINE-(SX,SY),C3:SX=B2(7,0):SY=B2(7,1):L
INE-(SX,SY),C3
230   SX=B2(6,0):SY=B2(6,1):PSET (SX,SY),C3:SX=B2(5,0):SY=B2(
5,1):LINE-(SX,SY),C3:SX=B2(4,0):SY=B2(4,1):LINE-(SX,SY),C3:S
X=B2(7,0):SY=B2(7,1):LINE-(SX,SY),C3:SX=B2(6,0):SY=B2(6,1):L
INE-(SX,SY),C3
240   SX=B2(3,0):SY=B2(3,1):PSET (SX,SY),C3:SX=B2(2,0):SY=B2(
2,1):LINE-(SX,SY),C3:SX=B2(5,0):SY=B2(5,1):LINE-(SX,SY),C3:S
X=B2(6,0):SY=B2(6,1):LINE-(SX,SY),C3:SX=B2(3,0):SY=B2(3,1):L
INE-(SX,SY),C3
250   SX=B2(0,0):SY=B2(0,1):PSET (SX,SY),C3:SX=B2(1,0):SY=B2(
1,1):LINE-(SX,SY),C3:SX=B2(2,0):SY=B2(2,1):LINE-(SX,SY),C3:S
X=B2(3,0):SY=B2(3,1):LINE-(SX,SY),C3:SX=B2(0,0):SY=B2(0,1):L
INE-(SX,SY),C3
260   SX=B2(7,0):SY=B2(7,1):PSET (SX,SY),C3:SX=B2(4,0):SY=B2(
4,1):LINE-(SX,SY),C3:SX=B2(1,0):SY=B2(1,1):LINE-(SX,SY),C3:S
X=B2(0,0):SY=B2(0,1):LINE-(SX,SY),C3:SX=B2(7,0):SY=B2(7,1):L
INE-(SX,SY),C3
270   SX=B2(1,0):SY=B2(1,1):PSET (SX,SY),C3:SX=B2(4,0):SY=B2(
4,1):LINE-(SX,SY),C3:SX=B2(5,0):SY=B2(5,1):LINE-(SX,SY),C3:S
```

```
X=B2(2,0):SY=B2(2,1):LINE-(SX,SY),C3:SX=B2(1,0):SY=B2(1,1):L
INE-(SX,SY),C3
280   R1=R1-.04363:SR1=SIN(R1):CR1=COS(R1):DEF SEG=&H2400:POK
E &H8,&H28:POKE &HD,&HB8:CALL PCOPY:SOUND 350,.7:POKE &H8,&H
2C:POKE &HD,&H28:CALL PCOPY:DEF SEG:GOTO 210
290 '_____
300 '
310 'module:   perspective calculations
320   X=(-1)*X:XA=CR1*X-SR1*Z:ZA=SR1*X+CR1*Z:X=CR2*XA+SR2*Y:Y
A=CR2*Y-SR2*XA:Z=CR3*ZA-SR3*YA:Y=SR3*ZA+CR3*YA:X=X+MX:Y=Y+MY
:Z=Z+MZ:SX=D*X/Z:SY=D*Y/Z:RETURN
330 '_____
340 '
350 'module:   UNIVERSAL
360 'This routine configures the program for the hardware/so
ftware being used.
370   KEY OFF:CLS:ON ERROR GOTO 420:CLEAR,,,32768!  'trap if
PCjr
380   CLS:LOCATE 10,1:PRINT "This program will not run":LOCAT
E 11,1:PRINT "on an IBM PCjr.":LOCATE 12,1:PRINT "An IBM-com
patible PC, XT, or AT":LOCATE 13,1:PRINT "with 256Kb is requ
ired."
390   LOCATE 16,1:PRINT "Press <Enter> to return to BASIC."
400   K$=INKEY$:IF K$<>CHR$(13) THEN 400
410   CLS:SCREEN 0,0,0,0:CLEAR:COLOR 7,0,0:WIDTH 80:LOCATE 1,
1,1:CLS:END
420   RESUME 430
430   LOCATE 10,1:PRINT "This program requires IBM DOS 2.1":L
OCATE 11,1:PRINT "and IBM BASICA 2.1.":LOCATE 12,1:PRINT "Ot
her versions of DOS and BASICA":LOCATE 13,1:PRINT "will not
support the memory addresses"
440   LOCATE 14,1:PRINT "used in this program."
450   LOCATE 18,1:PRINT "Press <Enter> to continue.":LOCATE 1
9,1:PRINT "Press <ESC> to return to BASIC."
460   K$=INKEY$
470   IF K$=CHR$(13) THEN 500
480   IF K$=CHR$(27) THEN CLS:END
490   GOTO 460
500   SCREEN 1,0:COLOR 0,1:C0=0:C1=1:C2=2:C3=3
510   ON ERROR GOTO 0   'disable error trapping override
520   GOSUB 840   'load PCOPY machine code subroutine
530   GOSUB 790   'start writing graphics to hidden page 1
540   WINDOW SCREEN (-399,-299)-(400,300)   'establish device-
independent screen coordinates
550   ON KEY (2) GOSUB 730:KEY (2) ON   'F2 key to exit progra
m
560   GOTO 150   'return to main program
570 '_____
580 '
```

```
590 'module:   assign variables
600    D=1200:R1=5.68319:R2=6.28319:R3=5.99778:MX=0:MY=0:MZ=-5
00  '3D parameters
610    DEFINT T  'loop counter
620    DEFINT P:PCOPY =0  'calling protocol
630    DIM B2 (7,1)  '8 sets of SX,SY display coordinates
640    SR1=SIN(R1):CR1=COS(R1):SR2=SIN(R2):CR2=COS(R2):SR3=SIN
(R3):CR3=COS(R3)
650    RETURN
660 '_____
670 '
680 'module:   database of 8 sets of XYZ world coordinates fo
r vertices of 3D cube
690    DATA   30,-30,30,   30,30,30,   -30,30,30,   -30,-30,30,   3
0,30,-30,   -30,30,-30,   -30,-30,-30,   30,-30,-30
700 '_____
710 '
720 'subroutine: enhanced exit module to return to BASIC com
mand level
730    CLS:SCREEN 0,0,0,0:WIDTH 80:COLOR 7,0,0:LOCATE 1,1,1
740    DEF SEG=F:POKE &H377D,&HB8:POKE &H37A0,&HB8:POKE &H3890
,&HB8:POKE &H3A6C,&HB8:POKE &H3AE0,&HB8
750    CLS:END
760 '_____
770 '
780 'subroutine: create a hidden written-to graphics page at
 &H28000
790    DEFINT E,F:DEF SEG=0:E=PEEK(&H510)+PEEK(&H511)*256:DEF
SEG=E:F=PEEK(&H702)+PEEK(&H703)*256
800    DEF SEG=F:POKE &H377D,&H28:POKE &H37A0,&H28:POKE &H3890
,&H28:POKE &H3A6C,&H28:POKE &H3AE0,&H28:RETURN
810 '_____
820 '
830 'subroutine: place PCOPY machine-code subroutine in memo
ry at location &H24000
840    RESTORE 880:DEF SEG=&H2400:DEFINT T:FOR T=0 TO 34 STEP
1:READ HEX:POKE T,HEX:NEXT:RETURN
850 '_____
860 '
870 'data base: hexadecimal opcodes for machine-code subrout
ine to move 16384 bytes from &H28000 to &HB8000.
880    DATA   &H51,&H1E,&H06,&H56,&H57,&H9C,&HB9,&H00,&H28,&H8E
,&HD9,&HB9,&H00,&HB8,&H8E,&HC1,&HFC,&HBE,&H00,&H00,&HBF,&H00
,&H00,&HB9,&H00,&H40,&HF3,&HA4,&H9D,&H5F,&H5E,&H07,&H1F,&H59
,&HCB
890 '_____
900 '
910    END 'of program code
```

The programs rotate a 3D, transparent, wire-frame cube using real-time animation. The program in Fig. 22-2 is intended for an EGA or a PCjr (and Tandy). To run this program from the companion diskette, type **LOAD "A-34.BAS",R**. The program in Fig. 22-3 is intended for a color/graphics adapter. To run this program from the companion diskette, type **LOAD "A-35.BAS",R**.

### Analysis of the EGA/PCjr Program

The code section which draws the cube is located at lines 210 through 270. Line 210 restores the database and precalculates all SX,SY DISPLAY COORDINATES, storing them in array B2.

Line 280 is integral to the real-time animation process. First, the R1 yaw angle is decremented. Next, the sine and cosine factors for yaw are refreshed (i.e., SR1 and CR1). Next, a SCREEN instruction is used to flip pages, the computer beeps, and the program is looped back to line 210.

Note the SCREEN,,1-P,P algorithm in line 280. By using a $P = 1 - P$ formula on each pass through the loop, the value of P is swapped between 1 and 0. This saves you the trouble of having to identify page 0 and page 1, keeping the program listing shorter. If P is 1, then $P = 1 - P$ swaps the value to 0, because $1 - 1 = 0$. If P is 0, then $P = 1 - P$ swaps the value to 1, because $1 - 0 = 1$.

The PCOPY instruction in line 280 is used to move a generic background page onto the new hidden page before the computer begins redrawing the cube. It is quicker to copy an existing background page than to reprint the alphanumeric label on each pass through the loop. The generic background page, which is page 2, is initially created by line 190. If you wish, you can add color or additional alphanumerics to this page and they will be displayed during the animation of the cube.

### Analysis of the Color/Graphics Adapter Program

The color/graphics adapter version of the demonstration program uses the same generic principles of real-time animation as the EGA/PCjr version. Only the methods for enabling drawing on a hidden page and moving the graphics from hidden page to display screen are different.

The CGA program uses the same hex codes for the assembly language subroutine as the frame animation program in Chapter 21. Note line 190, for example, which uses POKE &H8 and POKE &HD to alter the source address and target address before calling the PCOPY subroutine to move a page-full of graphics data.

The key line in this program is 280. After refreshing the yaw angles, the program uses a DEF SEG instruction to point to the assembly language subroutine located at 24000 hex in memory. The written-to hidden page at 28000 hex is then moved to the screen buffer at B8000 hex. After issuing a beep, a generic background page located at 2C000 hex to copied onto the hidden written-to page at 28000 hex.

Line 840 loads the assembly language subroutine into memory during program start-up. This is identical to the algorithm used in the previous chapter. However, how is BASICA able to draw graphics on a hidden page in RAM?

### Drawing on a Hidden Page with the CGA

The innovative solution to this programming challenge lies in lines 790 and 800. Line 790 is used to locate BASIC's data area in memory. Line 800 is used to POKE the hex value 28 into five key locations in the BASIC interpreter. This value of &H28 replaces an existing value of &HB8. BASIC no longer sends graphics to the display memory at &HB8000 hex; it now writes graphics to &H28000 hex.

The algorithm in line 800 will work with IBM BASICA 2.10. Because each version of BASICA uses slightly different locations for its data area, you must make the following changes to line 800 if you are using different versions of BASICA on your personal computer.

### BASICA 2.00

```
800 DEF SEG = F: POKE &H36A0,&H28: POKE
&H36C3,&H28: POKE &H378C,&H28: POKE
&H3968,&H28: POKE &H39DC,&H28
```

### BASICA 3.00

```
800 DEF SEG = F: POKE &H39AC,&H28: POKE
&H39CF,&H28: POKE &H3ABF,&H28: POKE
&H3C9B,&H28: POKE &H3D0F,&H28
```

### BASICA 3.10

```
800 DEF SEG = F: POKE &H3B43,&H28: POKE
&H3B66,&H28: POKE &H3C56,&H28: POKE
&H3E32,&H28: POKE &H3EA6,&H28
```

Note also that you must change the five memory addresses in line 740, which switches the &H28 value back to &HB8 when you exit the program. When you are writing your own real-time animation programs, it is important that you do not use the variable F for any other purpose in your program. You require the F value again when you restore BASIC to its native condition when you exit your program.

(For an expanded discussion of real-time animation on the Color/Graphics Adapter, refer to the author's first book, *High-Speed Animation and Simulation for Microcomputers*, available at your favorite bookstore or direct from TAB BOOKS, Inc.)

## SUMMARY

In this chapter, you learned how to generate real-time animation on the EGA, the PCjr, and the color/graphics adapter. You learned five ways to improve animation speed.

The next chapter introduces the first of eight applications programs, which demonstrate the potential uses for modeling, rendering, and animating on your personal computer.

# 23

# Industrial Design and Mechanical Design

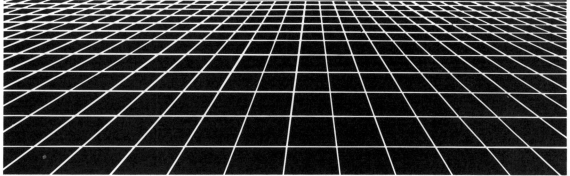

The techniques discussed in previous chapters can be put to work designing assorted industrial parts. In this chapter you will learn how to create a complex part, and you will discover how to generate three different displays of the part: transparent wire-frame model, solid model, and fully-shaded model.

## PREPARATION

The key to serious applications lies in proper preparation. A conceptual understanding of the model to be displayed and manipulated is an integral part of the modeling process. Although some advanced programs provide interactivity at the end-user's level, the demonstration programs in this chapter are interactive at the programmer's level. Changes in size, viewpoint, and shading are easy to achieve, but you must have an understanding of how the program works.

### Preliminary Design

The industrial part to be modeled is shown in Fig. 23-1. It is an angular bracket with a cavity running from one side to the other. Although this particular model is relatively symmetrical, any shape can be modeled and rendered using the principles outlined in this book.

### Vertices

Once the preliminary design has been established, a thumbnail sketch is used in order to identify the vertices which make up the industrial part. Refer to Fig. 23-2. Each vertex can be described by a triplet of x,y,z WORLD COORDINATES. Note that the numbering of the vertices in Fig. 23-2 begins with 0. There are 24 vertices. There are 14 surfaces.

### World Coordinates

Using the 3D axis system, the various elevation views of the model can be positioned against their corresponding x,y, or z axis lines. Refer to Fig. 23-3. The x,y,z WORLD COORDINATES of any particular vertex can then be determined. For this particular model, all the WORLD COORDINATES can be derived from one elevation.

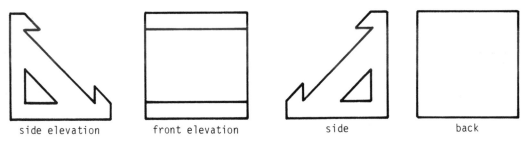

| side elevation | front elevation | side | back |

Fig. 23-1. Elevation views of the industrial part drawn by the demonstration programs.

## Data Tables

The WORLD COORDINATES are first ordered into a table of vertices. The vertices are then ordered into a table of surfaces. The series of vertices which describes a surface is arranged in a counterclockwise order, thereby ensuring the integrity of the plane equation method of hidden surface removal.

After this preliminary preparation has been completed, you can call upon your computer to perform most of the work involved in generating different views of the model. This particular model poses some interesting challenges: the cavity, for example.

## DEMONSTRATION:
## WIRE-FRAME INDUSTRIAL PART

Figure 23-4 shows the screen output of the demonstration program in Fig. 23-5. To run this program from the companion diskette, type **LOAD**

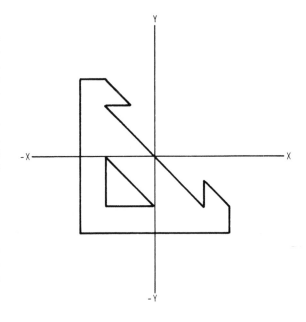

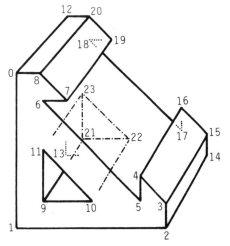

Fig. 23-2. The 24 vertices (corners) used to define the 14 surfaces which make up the industrial part.

| Vertex | X | Y | Z |
|--------|------|------|----|
| 0 | -30 | 30 | 30 |
| 1 | -30 | -30 | 30 |
| 2 | 30 | -30 | 30 |
| 3 | 30 | -10 | 30 |
| 4 | 20 | -10 | 30 |
| 5 | 20 | -20 | 30 |
| 6 | -20 | 20 | 30 |
| 7 | -10 | 20 | 30 |
| 8 | -10 | 30 | 30 |
| 9 | -20 | -20 | 30 |
| 10 | 0 | -20 | 30 |
| 11 | -20 | 0 | 30 |

```
DIM B1(23,2)    '24 sets of x,y,z view coordinates
DIM B2(23,1)    '24 sets of sx,sy display coordinates
DIM B3(13,1)    '14 sets of area fill coordinates
```

Fig. 23-3. Determination of the world coordinates for each vertex of the industrial part.

270

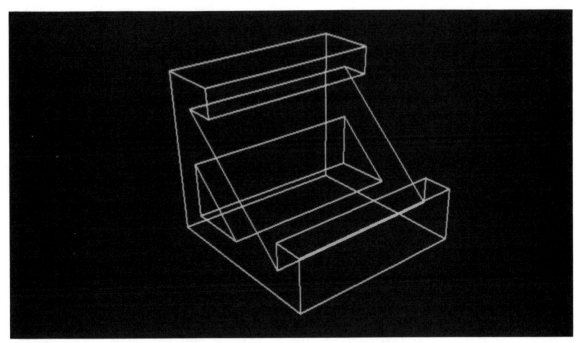

Fig. 23-4. The display image produced by the demonstration program in Fig. 23-5.

Fig. 23-5. Wire-frame industrial part.

```
100 'Program A-36.BAS    Wire frame industrial part.
110 'Demonstrates wire frame model in preparation for full s
hading.
120 '_____
130 '
140   GOTO 1130    'configure system
150   GOSUB 1340    'assign variables
160 '_____
170 '
180 'module:  calculate and store vertex coordinates
190   SOUND 300,.7:LOCATE 2,1:PRINT "Calculating vertex array
"
200   RESTORE 1410:FOR T=0 TO 11 STEP 1:LOCATE 2,25:PRINT T:R
EAD X,Y:Z=30:GOSUB 1040:B2(T,0)=SX:B2(T,1)=SY:NEXT T
210   RESTORE 1410:FOR T=12 TO 23 STEP 1:LOCATE 2,25:PRINT T:
READ X,Y:Z=-30:GOSUB 1040:B2(T,0)=SX:B2(T,1)=SY:NEXT T   'loa
d vertex vertex display coordinates into array B2
220 '_____
230 '
240 'module:  draw 3 inside surfaces of widget
250   LOCATE 2,1:PRINT "Drawing interior surface          "
```

```
260 'surface 0 routine
270   SOUND 300,.7:LOCATE 2,26:PRINT "0    "
280   SX1=B2(11,0):SY1=B2(11,1):SX2=B2(9,0):SY2=B2(9,1):SX3=B
2(21,0):SY3=B2(21,1):SX4=B2(23,0):SY4=B2(23,1):GOSUB 1450   '
assign display coordinates and jump to surface modeling rout
ine
290 '_____
300 '
310 'surface 1 routine
320   SOUND 300,.7:LOCATE 2,26:PRINT "1    "
330   SX1=B2(9,0):SY1=B2(9,1):SX2=B2(10,0):SY2=B2(10,1):SX3=B
2(22,0):SY3=B2(22,1):SX4=B2(21,0):SY4=B2(21,1):GOSUB 1450
340 '_____
350 '
360 'surface 2 routine
370   SOUND 300,.7:LOCATE 2,26:PRINT "2"
380   SX1=B2(23,0):SY1=B2(23,1):SX2=B2(22,0):SY2=B2(22,1):SX3
=B2(10,0):SY3=B2(10,1):SX4=B2(11,0):SY4=B2(11,1):GOSUB 1450
390 '_____
400 '
410 'module:  draw outside surfaces
420   LOCATE 2,1:PRINT "Drawing exterior surface      "
430 'surface 5 routine
440   SOUND 300,.7:LOCATE 2,26:PRINT "5    "
450   SX1=B2(12,0):SY1=B2(12,1):SX2=B2(13,0):SY2=B2(13,1):SX3
=B2(1,0):SY3=B2(1,1):SX4=B2(0,0):SY4=B2(0,1):GOSUB 1450
460 '_____
470 '
480 'surface 6 routine
490   SOUND 300,.7:LOCATE 2,26:PRINT "6    "
500   SX1=B2(2,0):SY1=B2(2,1):SX2=B2(1,0):SY2=B2(1,1):SX3=B2(
13,0):SY3=B2(13,1):SX4=B2(14,0):SY4=B2(14,1):GOSUB 1450
510 '_____
520 '
530 'surface 10 routine
540   SOUND 300,.7:LOCATE 2,26:PRINT "10   "
550   SX1=B2(6,0):SY1=B2(6,1):SX2=B2(5,0):SY2=B2(5,1):SX3=B2(
17,0):SY3=B2(17,1):SX4=B2(18,0):SY4=B2(18,1):GOSUB 1450
560 '_____
570 '
580 'surface 7 routine
590   SOUND 300,.7:LOCATE 2,26:PRINT "7    "
600   SX1=B2(0,0):SY1=B2(0,1):SX2=B2(8,0):SY2=B2(8,1):SX3=B2(
20,0):SY3=B2(20,1):SX4=B2(12,0):SY4=B2(12,1):GOSUB 1450
610 '_____
620 '
630 'surface 8 routine
640   SOUND 300,.7:LOCATE 2,26:PRINT "8    "
```

```
650   SX1=B2(8,0):SY1=B2(8,1):SX2=B2(7,0):SY2=B2(7,1):SX3=B2(
19,0):SY3=B2(19,1):SX4=B2(20,0):SY4=B2(20,1):GOSUB 1450
660   '_____
670   '
680   'surface 9 routine
690   SOUND 300,.7:LOCATE 2,26:PRINT "9    "
700   SX1=B2(7,0):SY1=B2(7,1):SX2=B2(6,0):SY2=B2(6,1):SX3=B2(
18,0):SY3=B2(18,1):SX4=B2(19,0):SY4=B2(19,1):GOSUB 1450
710   '_____
720   '
730   'surface 11 routine
740   SOUND 300,.7:LOCATE 2,26:PRINT "11   "
750   SX1=B2(16,0):SY1=B2(16,1):SX2=B2(17,0):SY2=B2(17,1):SX3
=B2(5,0):SY3=B2(5,1):SX4=B2(4,0):SY4=B2(4,1):GOSUB 1450
760   '_____
770   '
780   'surface 12 routine
790   SOUND 300,.7:LOCATE 2,26:PRINT "12   "
800   SX1=B2(4,0):SY1=B2(4,1):SX2=B2(3,0):SY2=B2(3,1):SX3=B2(
15,0):SY3=B2(15,1):SX4=B2(16,0):SY4=B2(16,1):GOSUB 1450
810   '_____
820   '
830   'surface 13 routine
840   SOUND 300,.7:LOCATE 2,26:PRINT "13   "
850   SX1=B2(3,0):SY1=B2(3,1):SX2=B2(2,0):SY2=B2(2,1):SX3=B2(
14,0):SY3=B2(14,1):SX4=B2(15,0):SY4=B2(15,1):GOSUB 1450
860   '_____
870   '
880   'module:   draw near end and far end of widget
890   SOUND 300,.7:LOCATE 2,1:PRINT "Drawing outside surface
3     "
900   SX1=B2(0,0):SY1=B2(0,1):SX2=B2(1,0):SY2=B2(1,1):SX3=B2(
2,0):SY3=B2(2,1):SX4=B2(3,0):SY4=B2(3,1):SX5=B2(4,0):SY5=B2(
4,1):SX6=B2(5,0):SY6=B2(5,1):SX7=B2(6,0):SY7=B2(6,1):SX8=B2(
7,0):SY8=B2(7,1)
910   SX9=B2(8,0):SY9=B2(8,1):SX10=B2(9,0):SY10=B2(9,1):SX11=
B2(10,0):SY11=B2(10,1):SX12=B2(11,0):SY12=B2(11,1):GOSUB 149
0
920   '_____
930   '
940   SOUND 300,.7:LOCATE 2,25:PRINT "4    "
950   SX1=B2(14,0):SY1=B2(14,1):SX2=B2(13,0):SY2=B2(13,1):SX3
=B2(12,0):SY3=B2(12,1):SX4=B2(20,0):SY4=B2(20,1):SX5=B2(19,0
):SY5=B2(19,1):SX6=B2(18,0):SY6=B2(18,1):SX7=B2(17,0):SY7=B2
(17,1):SX8=B2(16,0):SY8=B2(16,1)
960   SX9=B2(15,0):SY9=B2(15,1):SX10=B2(21,0):SY10=B2(21,1):S
X11=B2(22,0):SY11=B2(22,1):SX12=B2(23,0):SY12=B2(23,1):GOSUB
 1490
```

```
970 '_____
980 '
990   SOUND 550,7:LOCATE 2,1:PRINT "Wire frame model is compl
ete.    "
1000   GOTO 1000
1010 '_____
1020 '
1030 'module:   perspective calculations for Cartesian world
coordinates
1040   X=(-1)*X:XA=CR1*X-SR1*Z:ZA=SR1*X+CR1*Z:X=CR2*XA+SR2*Y:
YA=CR2*Y-SR2*XA:Z=CR3*ZA-SR3*YA:Y=SR3*ZA+CR3*YA:X=X+MX:Y=Y+M
Y:Z=Z+MZ:SX=D*X/Z:SY=D*Y/Z:RETURN
1050 '_____
1060 '
1070 'module:   return to BASIC interpreter
1080   CLS:WINDOW:SCREEN 0,0,0,0:WIDTH 80:COLOR 7,0,0:CLS:LOC
ATE 1,1,1:END
1090 '_____
1100 '
1110 'module:   UNIVERSAL
1120 'This routine configures the program for the hardware/s
oftware being used.
1130   KEY OFF:CLS:ON ERROR GOTO 1170   'trap if not Enhanced
Display + EGA
1140   SCREEN 9,,0,0:COLOR 7,0:PALETTE 1,8:PALETTE 2,1:PALETT
E 3,9:PALETTE 4,11:PALETTE 5,7:PALETTE 6,37:PALETTE 7,7:PALE
TTE 8,56:PALETTE 9,34:PALETTE 10,20:PALETTE 11,5:PALETTE 12,
44:PALETTE 13,46:PALETTE 14,55:PALETTE 15,63
1150   C0=0:C1=12:C2=9:C3=7:LOCATE 1,1:PRINT "ED-EGA 640x350
16-color mode"
1160   GOTO 1270   'jump to screen coordinates set-up
1170   RESUME 1180
1180   ON ERROR GOTO 1210   'trap if not Color Display + EGA
1190   SCREEN 8,,0,0:COLOR 7,0:PALETTE 1,0:PALETTE 2,1:PALETT
E 3,9:PALETTE 4,7:PALETTE 8,4:PALETTE 9,2:C0=0:C1=8:C2=9:C3=
7:LOCATE 1,1:PRINT "CD-EGA 640x200 16-color mode"
1200   GOTO 1270   'jump to screen coordinates set-up
1210   RESUME 1220
1220   ON ERROR GOTO 1250   'trap if not PCjr
1230   CLEAR,,,32768!:SCREEN 6,0,0,0:COLOR 3,0:PALETTE 1,8:C0
=0:C1=1:C2=2:C3=3:LOCATE 1,1:PRINT "PCjr 640x200 4-color mod
e"
1240   GOTO 1270   'jump to screen coordinates set-up
1250   RESUME 1260
1260   SCREEN 1,0:COLOR 0,1:C0=0:C1=1:C2=2:C3=3:LOCATE 1,1:PR
INT "CGA 320x200 4-color mode"
1270   ON ERROR GOTO 0   'disable error trapping override
1280   WINDOW SCREEN (-399,-299)-(400,300)
```

```
1290   ON KEY (2) GOSUB 1080:KEY (2) ON   'F2 key to exit prog
ram
1300   GOTO 150   'return to main program
1310 '_____
1320 '
1330 'module:   assign variables
1340   D=1200:R1=5.39778:R2=0:R3=5.79778:MX=0:MY=0:MZ=-220   '
3D parameters
1350   DIM B2 (23,1)   '24 sets of SX,SY display coordinates
1360   SR1=SIN(R1):CR1=COS(R1):SR2=SIN(R2):CR2=COS(R2):SR3=SI
N(R3):CR3=COS(R3)
1370   RETURN
1380 '_____
1390 '
1400 'module:   12 sets of XY world coordinates for vertices
1410   DATA  -30,30,  -30,-30,  30,-30,  30,-10,  20,-10,  20
,-20,  -20,20,  -10,20,  -10,30,  -20,-20,  0,-20,  -20,0
1420 '_____
1430 '
1440 'module:  wire frame modeling of 4-sided polygon
1450   LINE (SX1,SY1)-(SX2,SY2),C3:LINE-(SX3,SY3),C3:LINE-(SX
4,SY4),C3:LINE-(SX1,SY1),C3:RETURN
1460 '_____
1470 '
1480 'module:  wire frame modeling of 12-sided polygon
1490   LINE (SX1,SY1)-(SX2,SY2),C3:LINE-(SX3,SY3),C3:LINE-(SX
4,SY4),C3:LINE-(SX5,SY5),C3:LINE-(SX6,SY6),C3:LINE-(SX7,SY7)
,C3:LINE-(SX8,SY8),C3:LINE-(SX9,SY9),C3:LINE-(SX1,SY1),C3
1500   LINE (SX10,SY10)-(SX11,SY11),C3:LINE-(SX12,SY12),C3:LI
NE-(SX10,SY10),C3:RETURN
1510 '_____
1520 '
1530   END 'of program code
```

"A-36.BAS,R. The program generates a transparent wire-frame model of the industrial part.

In spite of the numerous vertices to be pre-calculated and the numerous lines to be drawn on the screen, the program completes the model in eight seconds. No hidden surface routines are used. No light sources are analyzed.

The module at lines 180 through 210 calculates all 24 DISPLAY COORDINATES and saves them in array B2. Note the use of Z=30 in line 200. This is the near end of the industrial part. Remember, the z-axis is used to define nearness and farness; the x-axis defines left/right; the y-axis defines up/down. Line 210 uses Z = – 30 to describe the far end of the industrial part. Because the part is generally symmetrical, the x- and y-coordinates are similar for both ends, only the z-coordinates vary.

### The Drawing Code

The module at lines 240 through 380 constructs the three surfaces which make up the interior cavity. Refer to Fig. 23-2 to see how these surfaces are arranged on the model.

The module at lines 410 through 850 draws surfaces 5 through 13, which make up the outside of the model. Then, the module at lines 880 through 960 draws the two ends of the model (surfaces 3 and 4).

275

This program uses an inefficient method to draw the transparent wire-frame model. Many lines are drawn more than once, because a surface approach has been used as opposed to an edge approach. Because one edge can be part of two or more surfaces, a single edge can be (and is) drawn more than once. This redundancy is necessary, however, because the surface concept will be used later to enable the plane equation method of hidden surface removal and the surface perpendicular method of computer-controlled shading.

### Interactive Manipulation

You can easily change the angle of the model by modifying the R1, R2, and R3 variables in line 1340. The location of the model can be varied by manipulating the MX, MY, and MZ variables in line 1340. The angular perspective can be increased or decreased by adjusting D. (Refer to Chapter 7 for a detailed discussion of the perspective formulas and the variables which affect them.)

### The Database

The database is located at line 1410. Because the model is symmetrical (see Fig. 23-3), only the x- and y-coordinates are required in the database. The z-coordinate, which is required to describe the depth of the model, is added by lines 200 and 210 during pre-calculation of the DISPLAY COORDINATES.

### Polygon Modeling

Modeling of standard four-sided polygons is performed by a generic polygon-modeling subroutine located at line 1440. Because each of the two ends of the industrial part is a 12-sided polygon, a specialized polygon-modeling routine at line 1480 is required.

### DEMONSTRATION: SOLID MODEL OF INDUSTRIAL PART

Figure 23-6 shows the screen output of the demonstration program in Fig. 23-7. To run this program from the companion diskette, type **LOAD "A-37.BAS",R**. The program generates a solid model of the industrial part, using the plane equation method of hidden surface removal.

The wisdom in drawing the cavity first now becomes obvious. Technically speaking, the radial pre-sort method of hidden surface removal is also at work in this program. Because any visible surface on the exterior of the model will be closer to the viewpoint

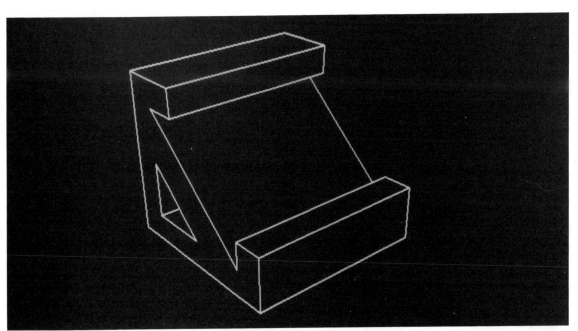

Fig. 23-6. The display image produced by the demonstration program in Fig. 23-7.

Fig. 23-7. Solid industrial part.

```
100 'Program A-37.BAS    Solid model industrial part.
110 'Demonstrates solid model in preparation for full shadin
g.
120 '_____
130 '
140   GOTO 1280    'configure system
150   GOSUB 1490   'assign variables
160 '_____
170 '
180 'module:  calculate and store vertex coordinates
190   SOUND 300,.7:LOCATE 2,1:PRINT "Calculating vertex array
"
200   RESTORE 1580:FOR T=0 TO 11 STEP 1:LOCATE 2,25:PRINT T:R
EAD X,Y:Z=30:GOSUB 1190:B1(T,0)=X:B1(T,1)=Y:B1(T,2)=Z:B2(T,0
)=SX:B2(T,1)=SY:NEXT T
210   RESTORE 1580:FOR T=12 TO 23 STEP 1:LOCATE 2,25:PRINT T:
READ X,Y:Z=-30:GOSUB 1190:B1(T,0)=X:B1(T,1)=Y:B1(T,2)=Z:B2(T
,0)=SX:B2(T,1)=SY:NEXT T  'load vertex view coordinates into
 array B1, load vertex display coordinates into array B2
220   SOUND 300,.7:LOCATE 2,1:PRINT "Calculating fill array
      ":RESTORE 1620:FOR T=0 TO 13 STEP 1:LOCATE 2,23:PRINT T
:READ X,Y,Z:GOSUB 1190:B3(T,0)=SX:B3(T,1)=SY:NEXT T  'load 1
4 area fill origin display coordinates into array B3
230 '_____
240 '
250 'module:  draw 3 inside surfaces of widget
260   LOCATE 2,1:PRINT "Drawing interior surface        "
270 'surface 0 routine
280   SOUND 300,.7:LOCATE 2,26:PRINT "0    "
290   X1=B1(11,0):Y1=B1(11,1):Z1=B1(11,2):X2=B1(9,0):Y2=B1(9,
1):Z2=B1(9,2):X3=B1(21,0):Y3=B1(21,1):Z3=B1(21,2):GOSUB 1660
:IF SP>0 THEN 330  'retrieve view coordinates, jump to plane
 equation routine, test if surface hidden
300   SX1=B2(11,0):SY1=B2(11,1):SX2=B2(9,0):SY2=B2(9,1):SX3=B
2(21,0):SY3=B2(21,1):SX4=B2(23,0):SY4=B2(23,1):SX5=B3(0,0):S
Y5=B3(0,1):GOSUB 1700  'assign display coordinates and jump
to solid surface modeling routine
310 '_____
320 '
330 'surface 1 routine
340   SOUND 300,.7:LOCATE 2,26:PRINT "1    "
350   X1=B1(9,0):Y1=B1(9,1):Z1=B1(9,2):X2=B1(10,0):Y2=B1(10,1
):Z2=B1(10,2):X3=B1(22,0):Y3=B1(22,1):Z3=B1(22,2):GOSUB 1660
:IF SP>0 THEN 390
360   SX1=B2(9,0):SY1=B2(9,1):SX2=B2(10,0):SY2=B2(10,1):SX3=B
```

```
2(22,0):SY3=B2(22,1):SX4=B2(21,0):SY4=B2(21,1):SX5=B3(1,0):S
Y5=B3(1,1):GOSUB 1700
370 '_____
380 '
390 'surface 2 routine
400   SOUND 300,.7:LOCATE 2,26:PRINT "2"
410   X1=B1(23,0):Y1=B1(23,1):Z1=B1(23,2):X2=B1(22,0):Y2=B1(2
2,1):Z2=B1(22,2):X3=B1(10,0):Y3=B1(10,1):Z3=B1(10,2):GOSUB 1
660:IF SP>0 THEN 460
420   SX1=B2(23,0):SY1=B2(23,1):SX2=B2(22,0):SY2=B2(22,1):SX3
=B2(10,0):SY3=B2(10,1):SX4=B2(11,0):SY4=B2(11,1):SX5=B3(2,0)
:SY5=B3(2,1):GOSUB 1700
430 '_____
440 '
450 'module:   draw outside surfaces
460   LOCATE 2,1:PRINT "Drawing exterior surface      "
470 'surface 5 routine
480   SOUND 300,.7:LOCATE 2,26:PRINT "5    "
490   X1=B1(12,0):Y1=B1(12,1):Z1=B1(12,2):X2=B1(13,0):Y2=B1(1
3,1):Z2=B1(13,2):X3=B1(1,0):Y3=B1(1,1):Z3=B1(1,2):GOSUB 1660
:IF SP>0 THEN 540
500   SX1=B2(12,0):SY1=B2(12,1):SX2=B2(13,0):SY2=B2(13,1):SX3
=B2(1,0):SY3=B2(1,1):SX4=B2(0,0):SY4=B2(0,1):SX5=B3(5,0):SY5
=B3(5,1):GOSUB 1700
510 '_____
520 '
530 'surface 6 routine
540   SOUND 300,.7:LOCATE 2,26:PRINT "6    "
550   X1=B1(2,0):Y1=B1(2,1):Z1=B1(2,2):X2=B1(1,0):Y2=B1(1,1):
Z2=B1(1,2):X3=B1(13,0):Y3=B1(13,1):Z3=B1(13,2):GOSUB 1660:IF
 SP>0 THEN 600
560   SX1=B2(2,0):SY1=B2(2,1):SX2=B2(1,0):SY2=B2(1,1):SX3=B2(
13,0):SY3=B2(13,1):SX4=B2(14,0):SY4=B2(14,1):SX5=B3(6,0):SY5
=B3(6,1):GOSUB 1700
570 '_____
580 '
590 'surface 10 routine
600   SOUND 300,.7:LOCATE 2,26:PRINT "10    "
610   X1=B1(6,0):Y1=B1(6,1):Z1=B1(6,2):X2=B1(5,0):Y2=B1(5,1):
Z2=B1(5,2):X3=B1(17,0):Y3=B1(17,1):Z3=B1(17,2):GOSUB 1660:IF
 SP>0 THEN 660
620   SX1=B2(6,0):SY1=B2(6,1):SX2=B2(5,0):SY2=B2(5,1):SX3=B2(
17,0):SY3=B2(17,1):SX4=B2(18,0):SY4=B2(18,1):SX5=B3(10,0):SY
5=B3(10,1):GOSUB 1700
630 '_____
640 '
650 'surface 7 routine
660   SOUND 300,.7:LOCATE 2,26:PRINT "7    "
```

```
670   X1=B1(0,0):Y1=B1(0,1):Z1=B1(0,2):X2=B1(8,0):Y2=B1(8,1):
   Z2=B1(8,2):X3=B1(20,0):Y3=B1(20,1):Z3=B1(20,2):GOSUB 1660:IF
    SP>0 THEN 720
680   SX1=B2(0,0):SY1=B2(0,1):SX2=B2(8,0):SY2=B2(8,1):SX3=B2(
   20,0):SY3=B2(20,1):SX4=B2(12,0):SY4=B2(12,1):SX5=B3(7,0):SY5
   =B3(7,1):GOSUB 1700
690   '_____
700   '
710   'surface 8 routine
720   SOUND 300,.7:LOCATE 2,26:PRINT "8     "
730   X1=B1(8,0):Y1=B1(8,1):Z1=B1(8,2):X2=B1(7,0):Y2=B1(7,1):
   Z2=B1(7,2):X3=B1(19,0):Y3=B1(19,1):Z3=B1(19,2):GOSUB 1660:IF
    SP>0 THEN 780
740   SX1=B2(8,0):SY1=B2(8,1):SX2=B2(7,0):SY2=B2(7,1):SX3=B2(
   19,0):SY3=B2(19,1):SX4=B2(20,0):SY4=B2(20,1):SX5=B3(8,0):SY5
   =B3(8,1):GOSUB 1700
750   '_____
760   '
770   'surface 9 routine
780   SOUND 300,.7:LOCATE 2,26:PRINT "9     "
790   X1=B1(7,0):Y1=B1(7,1):Z1=B1(7,2):X2=B1(6,0):Y2=B1(6,1):
   Z2=B1(6,2):X3=B1(18,0):Y3=B1(18,1):Z3=B1(18,2):GOSUB 1660:IF
    SP>0 THEN 840
800   SX1=B2(7,0):SY1=B2(7,1):SX2=B2(6,0):SY2=B2(6,1):SX3=B2(
   18,0):SY3=B2(18,1):SX4=B2(19,0):SY4=B2(19,1):SX5=B3(9,0):SY5
   =B3(9,1):GOSUB 1700
810   '_____
820   '
830   'surface 11 routine
840   SOUND 300,.7:LOCATE 2,26:PRINT "11    "
850   X1=B1(16,0):Y1=B1(16,1):Z1=B1(16,2):X2=B1(17,0):Y2=B1(1
   7,1):Z2=B1(17,2):X3=B1(5,0):Y3=B1(5,1):Z3=B1(5,2):GOSUB 1660
   :IF SP>0 THEN 900
860   SX1=B2(16,0):SY1=B2(16,1):SX2=B2(17,0):SY2=B2(17,1):SX3
   =B2(5,0):SY3=B2(5,1):SX4=B2(4,0):SY4=B2(4,1):SX5=B3(11,0):SY
   5=B3(11,1):GOSUB 1700
870   '_____
880   '
890   'surface 12 routine
900   SOUND 300,.7:LOCATE 2,26:PRINT "12    "
910   X1=B1(4,0):Y1=B1(4,1):Z1=B1(4,2):X2=B1(3,0):Y2=B1(3,1):
   Z2=B1(3,2):X3=B1(15,0):Y3=B1(15,1):Z3=B1(15,2):GOSUB 1660:IF
    SP>0 THEN 960
920   SX1=B2(4,0):SY1=B2(4,1):SX2=B2(3,0):SY2=B2(3,1):SX3=B2(
   15,0):SY3=B2(15,1):SX4=B2(16,0):SY4=B2(16,1):SX5=B3(12,0):SY
   5=B3(12,1):GOSUB 1700
930   '_____
940   '
```

```
950 'surface 13 routine
960    SOUND 300,.7:LOCATE 2,26:PRINT "13   "
970    X1=B1(3,0):Y1=B1(3,1):Z1=B1(3,2):X2=B1(2,0):Y2=B1(2,1):
Z2=B1(2,2):X3=B1(14,0):Y3=B1(14,1):Z3=B1(14,2):GOSUB 1660:IF
 SP>0 THEN 1020
980    SX1=B2(3,0):SY1=B2(3,1):SX2=B2(2,0):SY2=B2(2,1):SX3=B2(
14,0):SY3=B2(14,1):SX4=B2(15,0):SY4=B2(15,1):SX5=B3(13,0):SY
5=B3(13,1):GOSUB 1700
990 '_____
1000 '
1010 'module:   draw near end and far end of widget
1020    SOUND 300,.7:LOCATE 2,1:PRINT "Drawing outside surface
   3    "
1030    X1=B1(0,0):Y1=B1(0,1):Z1=B1(0,2):X2=B1(1,0):Y2=B1(1,1)
:Z2=B1(1,2):X3=B1(2,0):Y3=B1(2,1):Z3=B1(2,2):GOSUB 1660:IF S
P>0 THEN 1080
1040    SX1=B2(0,0):SY1=B2(0,1):SX2=B2(1,0):SY2=B2(1,1):SX3=B2
(2,0):SY3=B2(2,1):SX4=B2(3,0):SY4=B2(3,1):SX5=B2(4,0):SY5=B2
(4,1):SX6=B2(5,0):SY6=B2(5,1):SX7=B2(6,0):SY7=B2(6,1):SX8=B2
(7,0):SY8=B2(7,1)
1050    SX9=B2(8,0):SY9=B2(8,1):SX10=B2(9,0):SY10=B2(9,1):SX11
=B2(10,0):SY11=B2(10,1):SX12=B2(11,0):SY12=B2(11,1):SX13=B3(
3,0):SY13=B3(3,1):GOSUB 1740
1060 '_____
1070 '
1080    SOUND 300,.7:LOCATE 2,25:PRINT "4    "
1090    X1=B1(14,0):Y1=B1(14,1):Z1=B1(14,2):X2=B1(13,0):Y2=B1(
13,1):Z2=B1(13,2):X3=B1(12,0):Y3=B1(12,1):Z3=B1(12,2):GOSUB
1660:IF SP>0 THEN 1140
1100    SX1=B2(14,0):SY1=B2(14,1):SX2=B2(13,0):SY2=B2(13,1):SX
3=B2(12,0):SY3=B2(12,1):SX4=B2(20,0):SY4=B2(20,1):SX5=B2(19,
0):SY5=B2(19,1):SX6=B2(18,0):SY6=B2(18,1):SX7=B2(17,0):SY7=B
2(17,1):SX8=B2(16,0):SY8=B2(16,1)
1110    SX9=B2(15,0):SY9=B2(15,1):SX10=B2(21,0):SY10=B2(21,1):
SX11=B2(22,0):SY11=B2(22,1):SX12=B2(23,0):SY12=B2(23,1):SX13
=B3(4,0):SY13=B3(4,1):GOSUB 1740
1120 '_____
1130 '
1140    SOUND 550,7:LOCATE 2,1:PRINT "Solid model is complete.
     "
1150    GOTO 1150
1160 '_____
1170 '
1180 'module:   perspective calculations for Cartesian world
coordinates
1190    X=(-1)*X:XA=CR1*X-SR1*Z:ZA=SR1*X+CR1*Z:X=CR2*XA+SR2*Y:
YA=CR2*Y-SR2*XA:Z=CR3*ZA-SR3*YA:Y=SR3*ZA+CR3*YA:X=X+MX:Y=Y+M
Y:Z=Z+MZ:SX=D*X/Z:SY=D*Y/Z:RETURN
```

```
1200 '_____
1210 '
1220 'module:   return to BASIC interpreter
1230  CLS:WINDOW:SCREEN 0,0,0,0:WIDTH 80:COLOR 7,0,0:CLS:LOC
ATE 1,1,1:END
1240 '_____
1250 '
1260 'module:   UNIVERSAL
1270 'This routine configures the program for the hardware/s
oftware being used.
1280  KEY OFF:CLS:ON ERROR GOTO 1320   'trap if not Enhanced
Display + EGA
1290  SCREEN 9,,0,0:COLOR 7,0:PALETTE 1,8:PALETTE 2,1:PALETT
E 3,9:PALETTE 4,11:PALETTE 5,7:PALETTE 6,37:PALETTE 7,7:PALE
TTE 8,56:PALETTE 9,34:PALETTE 10,20:PALETTE 11,5:PALETTE 12,
44:PALETTE 13,46:PALETTE 14,55:PALETTE 15,63
1300  C0=0:C1=12:C2=9:C3=7:LOCATE 1,1:PRINT "ED-EGA 640x350
16-color mode"
1310  GOTO 1420  'jump to screen coordinates set-up
1320  RESUME 1330
1330  ON ERROR GOTO 1360   'trap if not Color Display + EGA
1340  SCREEN 8,,0,0:COLOR 7,0:PALETTE 1,0:PALETTE 2,1:PALETT
E 3,9:PALETTE 4,7:PALETTE 8,4:PALETTE 9,2:C0=0:C1=8:C2=9:C3=
7:LOCATE 1,1:PRINT "CD-EGA 640x200 16-color mode"
1350  GOTO 1420  'jump to screen coordinates set-up
1360  RESUME 1370
1370  ON ERROR GOTO 1400   'trap if not PCjr
1380  CLEAR,,,32768!:SCREEN 6,0,0,0:COLOR 3,0:PALETTE 1,8:C0
=0:C1=1:C2=2:C3=3:LOCATE 1,1:PRINT "PCjr 640x200 4-color mod
e"
1390  GOTO 1420  'jump to screen coordinates set-up
1400  RESUME 1410
1410  SCREEN 1,0:COLOR 0,1:C0=0:C1=1:C2=2:C3=3:LOCATE 1,1:PR
INT "CGA 320x200 4-color mode"
1420  ON ERROR GOTO 0  'disable error trapping override
1430  WINDOW SCREEN (-399,-299)-(400,300)
1440  ON KEY (2) GOSUB 1230:KEY (2) ON   'F2 key to exit prog
ram
1450  GOTO 150  'return to main program
1460 '_____
1470 '
1480 'module:   assign variables
1490  D=1200:R1=5.39778:R2=0:R3=5.79778:MX=0:MY=0:MZ=-220   '
3D parameters
1500  DIM B1 (23,2)   '24 sets of XYZ view coordinates
1510  DIM B2 (23,1)   '24 sets of SX,SY display coordinates
1520  DIM B3 (13,1)   '14 sets of SX,SY fill coordinates
1530  SR1=SIN(R1):CR1=COS(R1):SR2=SIN(R2):CR2=COS(R2):SR3=SI
```

```
N(R3):CR3=COS(R3)
1540   RETURN
1550 '_____
1560 '
1570 'module:   12 sets of XY world coordinates for vertices
1580   DATA  -30,30,  -30,-30,  30,-30,  30,-10,  20,-10,  20
,-20,  -20,20,  -10,20,  -10,30,  -20,-20,  0,-20,  -20,0
1590 '_____
1600 '
1610 'module:   14 sets of XYZ world coordinates for area fil
l
1620   DATA  -20,-10,0,  -10,-20,0,  -10,-10,0,  -10,0,30,  -
10,0,-30,  -30,0,0,  0,-30,0,  -20,30,0,  -10,25,0,  -15,20,
0,  0,0,0,  20,-15,0,  25,-10,0,  30,-20,0
1630 '_____
1640 '
1650 'module:   plane equation method of hidden surface remov
al
1660   SP1=X1*(Y2*Z3-Y3*Z2):SP1=(-1)*SP1:SP2=X2*(Y3*Z1-Y1*Z3)
:SP3=X3*(Y1*Z2-Y2*Z1):SP=SP1-SP2-SP3:RETURN
1670 '_____
1680 '
1690 'module:   solid surface modeling of 4-sided polygon
1700   LINE (SX1,SY1)-(SX2,SY2),C2:LINE-(SX3,SY3),C2:LINE-(SX
4,SY4),C2:LINE-(SX1,SY1),C2:PAINT (SX5,SY5),C2,C2:LINE (SX1,
SY1)-(SX2,SY2),C3:LINE-(SX3,SY3),C3:LINE-(SX4,SY4),C3:LINE-(
SX1,SY1),C3:PAINT (SX5,SY5),C0,C3:RETURN
1710 '_____
1720 '
1730 'module:   solid surface modeling of 12-sided polygon
1740   LINE (SX1,SY1)-(SX2,SY2),C2:LINE-(SX3,SY3),C2:LINE-(SX
4,SY4),C2:LINE-(SX5,SY5),C2:LINE-(SX6,SY6),C2:LINE-(SX7,SY7)
,C2:LINE-(SX8,SY8),C2:LINE-(SX9,SY9),C2:LINE-(SX1,SY1),C2
1750   LINE (SX10,SY10)-(SX11,SY11),C2:LINE-(SX12,SY12),C2:LI
NE-(SX10,SY10),C2:PAINT (SX13,SY13),C2,C2
1760   LINE (SX1,SY1)-(SX2,SY2),C3:LINE-(SX3,SY3),C3:LINE-(SX
4,SY4),C3:LINE-(SX5,SY5),C3:LINE-(SX6,SY6),C3:LINE-(SX7,SY7)
,C3:LINE-(SX8,SY8),C3:LINE-(SX9,SY9),C3:LINE-(SX1,SY1),C3
1770   LINE (SX10,SY10)-(SX11,SY11),C3:LINE-(SX12,SY12),C3:LI
NE-(SX10,SY10),C3:PAINT (SX13,SY13),C0,C3:RETURN
1780 '_____
1790 '
1800   END 'of program code
```

than the interior cavity, these exterior surfaces are drawn after the cavity has been drawn, thereby obscuring the cavity.

## Concave and Convex Polyhedra

Note that the plane equation of hidden surface removal works equally well on the cavity, which is a concave 3D polyhedron (i.e., all its surfaces face inward). Surfaces which face away from you are hidden. Watch as the program draws the cavity to see this happening. Compare this with the creation of the cavity by the previous demonstration program.

The order in which the exterior surfaces are drawn is also important, because the model is a complicated convex 3D polyhedron (i.e., all its surfaces face outward). At some viewing angles, the protrusions at the top and bottom of the model can obscure the opposite protrusion. The nearer protrusion must be drawn last.

### Performance

This program requires 16 seconds to complete the model, as opposed to eight seconds for the previous demonstration program, which generated the same model in a transparent wire-frame format.

### Precalculation of Coordinates

Note the module at lines 180 through 220. In addition to the DISPLAY COORDINATES saved in array B2 by the previous program, this program must also precalculate and save the VIEW COORDINATES in array B1, and the area fill coordinates in array B3. These extra coordinates are required by the hidden surface routine, which performs its hidden/visible analysis on VIEW COORDINATES. The area fill coordinates are required, of course, to support the key matte technique of drawing solid surfaces.

### The Database

In addition to the standard database of vertex coordinates at line 1580, another database at line 1620 is used to define the area fill coordinates. These area fill coordinates could just as easily have been determined by using the geometric algorithm first introduced in the polygon mesh sphere of Chapter 10.

### Solid Surface Modeling

The routines which model a four-sided solid surface and a 12-sided solid surface are located at lines 1690 through 1770. Compare these with their counterparts in the previous demonstration program.

### DEMONSTRATION: COMPUTER-SHADED INDUSTRIAL PART

Figure 23-8 shows the screen output of the demonstration program in Fig. 23-9. To run this program from the companion diskette, type **LOAD**

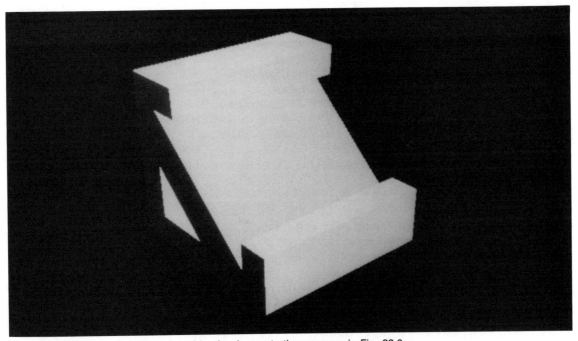

Fig. 23-8. The display image produced by the demonstration program in Fig. 23-9.

Fig. 23-9. Fully-shaded industrial part.

```
100 'Program A-38.BAS    Fully shaded industrial part.
110 'Demonstrates computer-shaded version of wire frame widg
et.
120 '_____
130 '
140   GOTO 1420    'configure system
150   GOSUB 1750    'assign variables
160 '_____
170 '
180 'module:  calculate and store vertex coordinates
190   SOUND 300,.7:LOCATE 2,1:PRINT "Calculating vertex array
"
200   RESTORE 1850:FOR T=0 TO 11 STEP 1:LOCATE 2,25:PRINT T:R
EAD X,Y:Z=30:GOSUB 1330:B1(T,0)=X:B1(T,1)=Y:B1(T,2)=Z:B2(T,0
)=SX:B2(T,1)=SY:NEXT T
210   RESTORE 1850:FOR T=12 TO 23 STEP 1:LOCATE 2,25:PRINT T:
READ X,Y:Z=-30:GOSUB 1330:B1(T,0)=X:B1(T,1)=Y:B1(T,2)=Z:B2(T
,0)=SX:B2(T,1)=SY:NEXT T    'load vertex view coordinates into
 array B1, load vertex display coordinates into array B2
220   SOUND 300,.7:LOCATE 2,1:PRINT "Calculating fill array
      ":RESTORE 1890:FOR T=0 TO 13 STEP 1:LOCATE 2,23:PRINT T
:READ X,Y,Z:GOSUB 1330:B3(T,0)=SX:B3(T,1)=SY:NEXT T    'load 1
4 area fill origin display coordinates into array B3
230 '_____
240 '
250 'module:  draw 3 inside surfaces of widget
260   LOCATE 2,1:PRINT "Drawing interior surface        "
270 'surface 0 routine
280   SOUND 300,.7:LOCATE 2,26:PRINT "0     "
290   X1=B1(11,0):Y1=B1(11,1):Z1=B1(11,2):X2=B1(9,0):Y2=B1(9,
1):Z2=B1(9,2):X3=B1(21,0):Y3=B1(21,1):Z3=B1(21,2):GOSUB 1930
:IF SP>0 THEN 340    'retrieve view coordinates, jump to plane
 equation routine, test if surface hidden
300   SX1=B2(11,0):SY1=B2(11,1):SX2=B2(9,0):SY2=B2(9,1):SX3=B
2(21,0):SY3=B2(21,1):SX4=B2(23,0):SY4=B2(23,1):SX5=B3(0,0):S
Y5=B3(0,1):GOSUB 2260    'assign display coordinates and jump
to solid surface modeling routine
310   GOSUB 1970:PAINT (SX5,SY5),A$,C3:GOSUB 2140    'jump to c
omputer-controlled shading routine, apply halftoning area fi
ll, jump to computer-controlled dithering routine
320 '_____
330 '
340 'surface 1 routine
350   SOUND 300,.7:LOCATE 2,26:PRINT "1     "
360   X1=B1(9,0):Y1=B1(9,1):Z1=B1(9,2):X2=B1(10,0):Y2=B1(10,1
):Z2=B1(10,2):X3=B1(22,0):Y3=B1(22,1):Z3=B1(22,2):GOSUB 1930
```

```
      :IF SP>O THEN 410
370   SX1=B2(9,0):SY1=B2(9,1):SX2=B2(10,0):SY2=B2(10,1):SX3=B
2(22,0):SY3=B2(22,1):SX4=B2(21,0):SY4=B2(21,1):SX5=B3(1,0):S
Y5=B3(1,1):GOSUB 2260
380   GOSUB 1970:PAINT (SX5,SY5),A$,C3:GOSUB 2140
390   '_____
400   '
410   'surface 2 routine
420   SOUND 300,.7:LOCATE 2,26:PRINT "2"
430   X1=B1(23,0):Y1=B1(23,1):Z1=B1(23,2):X2=B1(22,0):Y2=B1(2
2,1):Z2=B1(22,2):X3=B1(10,0):Y3=B1(10,1):Z3=B1(10,2):GOSUB 1
930:IF SP>O THEN 490
440   SX1=B2(23,0):SY1=B2(23,1):SX2=B2(22,0):SY2=B2(22,1):SX3
=B2(10,0):SY3=B2(10,1):SX4=B2(11,0):SY4=B2(11,1):SX5=B3(2,0)
:SY5=B3(2,1):GOSUB 2260
450   GOSUB 1970:PAINT (SX5,SY5),A$,C3:GOSUB 2140
460   '_____
470   '
480   'module:   draw outside surfaces
490   LOCATE 2,1:PRINT "Drawing exterior surface      "
500   'surface 5 routine
510   SOUND 300,.7:LOCATE 2,26:PRINT "5    "
520   X1=B1(12,0):Y1=B1(12,1):Z1=B1(12,2):X2=B1(13,0):Y2=B1(1
3,1):Z2=B1(13,2):X3=B1(1,0):Y3=B1(1,1):Z3=B1(1,2):GOSUB 1930
:IF SP>O THEN 580
530   SX1=B2(12,0):SY1=B2(12,1):SX2=B2(13,0):SY2=B2(13,1):SX3
=B2(1,0):SY3=B2(1,1):SX4=B2(0,0):SY4=B2(0,1):SX5=B3(5,0):SY5
=B3(5,1):GOSUB 2260
540   GOSUB 1970:PAINT (SX5,SY5),A$,C3:GOSUB 2140
550   '_____
560   '
570   'surface 6 routine
580   SOUND 300,.7:LOCATE 2,26:PRINT "6    "
590   X1=B1(2,0):Y1=B1(2,1):Z1=B1(2,2):X2=B1(1,0):Y2=B1(1,1):
Z2=B1(1,2):X3=B1(13,0):Y3=B1(13,1):Z3=B1(13,2):GOSUB 1930:IF
 SP>O THEN 650
600   SX1=B2(2,0):SY1=B2(2,1):SX2=B2(1,0):SY2=B2(1,1):SX3=B2(
13,0):SY3=B2(13,1):SX4=B2(14,0):SY4=B2(14,1):SX5=B3(6,0):SY5
=B3(6,1):GOSUB 2260
610   GOSUB 1970:PAINT (SX5,SY5),A$,C3:GOSUB 2140
620   '_____
630   '
640   'surface 10 routine
650   SOUND 300,.7:LOCATE 2,26:PRINT "10   "
660   X1=B1(6,0):Y1=B1(6,1):Z1=B1(6,2):X2=B1(5,0):Y2=B1(5,1):
Z2=B1(5,2):X3=B1(17,0):Y3=B1(17,1):Z3=B1(17,2):GOSUB 1930:IF
 SP>O THEN 720
670   SX1=B2(6,0):SY1=B2(6,1):SX2=B2(5,0):SY2=B2(5,1):SX3=B2(
```

```
17,0):SY3=B2(17,1):SX4=B2(18,0):SY4=B2(18,1):SX5=B3(10,0):SY
5=B3(10,1):GOSUB 2260
680   GOSUB 1970:PAINT (SX5,SY5),A$,C3:GOSUB 2140
690 '_____
700 '
710 'surface 7 routine
720   SOUND 300,.7:LOCATE 2,26:PRINT "7    "
730   X1=B1(0,0):Y1=B1(0,1):Z1=B1(0,2):X2=B1(8,0):Y2=B1(8,1):
Z2=B1(8,2):X3=B1(20,0):Y3=B1(20,1):Z3=B1(20,2):GOSUB 1930:IF
 SP>0 THEN 790
740   SX1=B2(0,0):SY1=B2(0,1):SX2=B2(8,0):SY2=B2(8,1):SX3=B2(
20,0):SY3=B2(20,1):SX4=B2(12,0):SY4=B2(12,1):SX5=B3(7,0):SY5
=B3(7,1):GOSUB 2260
750   GOSUB 1970:PAINT (SX5,SY5),A$,C3:GOSUB 2140
760 '_____
770 '
780 'surface 8 routine
790   SOUND 300,.7:LOCATE 2,26:PRINT "8    "
800   X1=B1(8,0):Y1=B1(8,1):Z1=B1(8,2):X2=B1(7,0):Y2=B1(7,1):
Z2=B1(7,2):X3=B1(19,0):Y3=B1(19,1):Z3=B1(19,2):GOSUB 1930:IF
 SP>0 THEN 860
810   SX1=B2(8,0):SY1=B2(8,1):SX2=B2(7,0):SY2=B2(7,1):SX3=B2(
19,0):SY3=B2(19,1):SX4=B2(20,0):SY4=B2(20,1):SX5=B3(8,0):SY5
=B3(8,1):GOSUB 2260
820   GOSUB 1970:PAINT (SX5,SY5),A$,C3:GOSUB 2140
830 '_____
840 '
850 'surface 9 routine
860   SOUND 300,.7:LOCATE 2,26:PRINT "9    "
870   X1=B1(7,0):Y1=B1(7,1):Z1=B1(7,2):X2=B1(6,0):Y2=B1(6,1):
Z2=B1(6,2):X3=B1(18,0):Y3=B1(18,1):Z3=B1(18,2):GOSUB 1930:IF
 SP>0 THEN 930
880   SX1=B2(7,0):SY1=B2(7,1):SX2=B2(6,0):SY2=B2(6,1):SX3=B2(
18,0):SY3=B2(18,1):SX4=B2(19,0):SY4=B2(19,1):SX5=B3(9,0):SY5
=B3(9,1):GOSUB 2260
890   GOSUB 1970:PAINT (SX5,SY5),A$,C3:GOSUB 2140
900 '_____
910 '
920 'surface 11 routine
930   SOUND 300,.7:LOCATE 2,26:PRINT "11   "
940   X1=B1(16,0):Y1=B1(16,1):Z1=B1(16,2):X2=B1(17,0):Y2=B1(1
7,1):Z2=B1(17,2):X3=B1(5,0):Y3=B1(5,1):Z3=B1(5,2):GOSUB 1930
:IF SP>0 THEN 1000
950   SX1=B2(16,0):SY1=B2(16,1):SX2=B2(17,0):SY2=B2(17,1):SX3
=B2(5,0):SY3=B2(5,1):SX4=B2(4,0):SY4=B2(4,1):SX5=B3(11,0):SY
5=B3(11,1):GOSUB 2260
960   GOSUB 1970:PAINT (SX5,SY5),A$,C3:GOSUB 2140
970 '_____
```

```
980 '
990 'surface 12 routine
1000    SOUND 300,.7:LOCATE 2,26:PRINT "12   "
1010    X1=B1(4,0):Y1=B1(4,1):Z1=B1(4,2):X2=B1(3,0):Y2=B1(3,1)
:Z2=B1(3,2):X3=B1(15,0):Y3=B1(15,1):Z3=B1(15,2):GOSUB 1930:I
F SP>0 THEN 1070
1020    SX1=B2(4,0):SY1=B2(4,1):SX2=B2(3,0):SY2=B2(3,1):SX3=B2
(15,0):SY3=B2(15,1):SX4=B2(16,0):SY4=B2(16,1):SX5=B3(12,0):S
Y5=B3(12,1):GOSUB 2260
1030    GOSUB 1970:PAINT (SX5,SY5),A$,C3:GOSUB 2140
1040 '_____
1050 '
1060 'surface 13 routine
1070    SOUND 300,.7:LOCATE 2,26:PRINT "13   "
1080    X1=B1(3,0):Y1=B1(3,1):Z1=B1(3,2):X2=B1(2,0):Y2=B1(2,1)
:Z2=B1(2,2):X3=B1(14,0):Y3=B1(14,1):Z3=B1(14,2):GOSUB 1930:I
F SP>0 THEN 1140
1090    SX1=B2(3,0):SY1=B2(3,1):SX2=B2(2,0):SY2=B2(2,1):SX3=B2
(14,0):SY3=B2(14,1):SX4=B2(15,0):SY4=B2(15,1):SX5=B3(13,0):S
Y5=B3(13,1):GOSUB 2260
1100    GOSUB 1970:PAINT (SX5,SY5),A$,C3:GOSUB 2140
1110 '_____
1120 '
1130 'module:   draw near end and far end of widget
1140    SOUND 300,.7:LOCATE 2,1:PRINT "Drawing outside surface
   3    "
1150    X1=B1(0,0):Y1=B1(0,1):Z1=B1(0,2):X2=B1(1,0):Y2=B1(1,1)
:Z2=B1(1,2):X3=B1(2,0):Y3=B1(2,1):Z3=B1(2,2):GOSUB 1930:IF S
P>0 THEN 1210
1160    SX1=B2(0,0):SY1=B2(0,1):SX2=B2(1,0):SY2=B2(1,1):SX3=B2
(2,0):SY3=B2(2,1):SX4=B2(3,0):SY4=B2(3,1):SX5=B2(4,0):SY5=B2
(4,1):SX6=B2(5,0):SY6=B2(5,1):SX7=B2(6,0):SY7=B2(6,1):SX8=B2
(7,0):SY8=B2(7,1)
1170    SX9=B2(8,0):SY9=B2(8,1):SX10=B2(9,0):SY10=B2(9,1):SX11
=B2(10,0):SY11=B2(10,1):SX12=B2(11,0):SY12=B2(11,1):SX13=B3(
3,0):SY13=B3(3,1):GOSUB 2300
1180    GOSUB 1970:PAINT (SX13,SY13),A$,C3:GOSUB 2190
1190 '_____
1200 '
1210    SOUND 300,.7:LOCATE 2,25:PRINT "4    "
1220    X1=B1(14,0):Y1=B1(14,1):Z1=B1(14,2):X2=B1(13,0):Y2=B1(
13,1):Z2=B1(13,2):X3=B1(12,0):Y3=B1(12,1):Z3=B1(12,2):GOSUB
1930:IF SP>0 THEN 1280
1230    SX1=B2(14,0):SY1=B2(14,1):SX2=B2(13,0):SY2=B2(13,1):SX
3=B2(12,0):SY3=B2(12,1):SX4=B2(20,0):SY4=B2(20,1):SX5=B2(19,
0):SY5=B2(19,1):SX6=B2(18,0):SY6=B2(18,1):SX7=B2(17,0):SY7=B
2(17,1):SX8=B2(16,0):SY8=B2(16,1)
1240    SX9=B2(15,0):SY9=B2(15,1):SX10=B2(21,0):SY10=B2(21,1):
```

```
      SX11=B2(22,0):SY11=B2(22,1):SX12=B2(23,0):SY12=B2(23,1):SX13
      =B3(4,0):SY13=B3(4,1):GOSUB 2300
1250    GOSUB 1970:PAINT (SX13,SY13),A$,C3:GOSUB 2190
1260  '_____
1270  '
1280    SOUND 550,7:LOCATE 2,1:PRINT "Fully shaded model is co
mplete. "
1290    GOTO 1290
1300  '_____
1310  '
1320  'module:   perspective calculations for Cartesian world
coordinates
1330    X=(-1)*X:XA=CR1*X-SR1*Z:ZA=SR1*X+CR1*Z:X=CR2*XA+SR2*Y:
YA=CR2*Y-SR2*XA:Z=CR3*ZA-SR3*YA:Y=SR3*ZA+CR3*YA:X=X+MX:Y=Y+M
Y:Z=Z+MZ:SX=D*X/Z:SY=D*Y/Z:RETURN
1340  '_____
1350  '
1360  'module:   return to BASIC interpreter
1370    CLS:WINDOW:SCREEN 0,0,0,0:WIDTH 80:COLOR 7,0,0:CLS:LOC
ATE 1,1,1:END
1380  '_____
1390  '
1400  'module:   UNIVERSAL
1410  'This routine configures the program for the hardware/s
oftware being used.
1420    KEY OFF:CLS:ON ERROR GOTO 1490   'trap if not Enhanced
Display + EGA
1430    SCREEN 9,,0,0:COLOR 7,0:PALETTE 1,8:PALETTE 2,1:PALETT
E 3,9:PALETTE 4,11:PALETTE 5,7:PALETTE 6,37:PALETTE 7,7:PALE
TTE 8,56:PALETTE 9,34:PALETTE 10,20:PALETTE 11,5:PALETTE 12,
44:PALETTE 13,46:PALETTE 14,55:PALETTE 15,63
1440    C0=0:C1=12:C2=9:C3=7:LOCATE 1,1:PRINT "ED-EGA 640x350
16-color mode"
1450    V6=15   'illumination range 0 to 15
1460    GOSUB 2370   'assign bit tiling codes for EGA
1470    DEFINT G:G=1   'set flag for ED-EGA
1480    GOTO 1680   'jump to screen coordinates set-up
1490    RESUME 1500
1500    ON ERROR GOTO 1560   'trap if not Color Display + EGA
1510    SCREEN 8,,0,0:COLOR 7,0:PALETTE 1,0:PALETTE 2,1:PALETT
E 3,9:PALETTE 4,7:PALETTE 8,4:PALETTE 9,2:C0=0:C1=8:C2=9:C3=
7:LOCATE 1,1:PRINT "CD-EGA 640x200 16-color mode"
1520    V6=14   'illumination range 0 to 14
1530    GOSUB 2370   'assign shading codes for EGA
1540    DEFINT G:G=2   'set flag for CD-EGA
1550    GOTO 1680   'jump to screen coordinates set-up
1560    RESUME 1570
1570    ON ERROR GOTO 1630   'trap if not PCjr
```

```
1580    CLEAR,,,32768!:SCREEN 6,0,0,0:COLOR 3,0:PALETTE 1,8:CO
=0:C1=1:C2=2:C3=3:LOCATE 1,1:PRINT "PCjr 640x200 4-color mod
e"
1590    V6=14  'illumination range 0 to 14
1600    GOSUB 2570  'assign shading codes for PCjr
1610    DEFINT G:G=3  'set flag for CD-JR
1620    GOTO 1680  'jump to screen coordinates set-up
1630    RESUME 1640
1640    SCREEN 1,0:COLOR 0,1:C0=0:C1=1:C2=2:C3=3:LOCATE 1,1:PR
INT "CGA 320x200 4-color mode"
1650    V6=14  'illumination range 0 to 14
1660    GOSUB 2570  'assign shading codes for CGA
1670    DEFINT G:G=4  'set flag for CD-CGA
1680    ON ERROR GOTO 0  'disable error trapping override
1690    WINDOW SCREEN (-399,-299)-(400,300)
1700    ON KEY (2) GOSUB 1370:KEY (2) ON  'F2 key to exit prog
ram
1710    GOTO 150  'return to main program
1720    '_____
1730    '
1740    'module:  assign variables
1750    D=1200:R1=5.39778:R2=0:R3=5.79778:MX=0:MY=0:MZ=-220   '
3D parameters
1760    DIM B1 (23,2)  '24 sets of XYZ view coordinates
1770    DIM B2 (23,1)  '24 sets of SX,SY display coordinates
1780    DIM B3 (13,1)  '14 sets of SX,SY fill coordinates
1790    XL=.57735:YL=.57735:ZL=.57735  'xyz components of unit
 vector for angle of incidence used in illumination algorith
m
1800    SR1=SIN(R1):CR1=COS(R1):SR2=SIN(R2):CR2=COS(R2):SR3=SI
N(R3):CR3=COS(R3)
1810    RETURN
1820    '_____
1830    '
1840    'module:  12 sets of XY world coordinates for vertices
1850    DATA  -30,30,  -30,-30,  30,-30,  30,-10,  20,-10,  20
,-20,  -20,20,  -10,20,  -10,30,  -20,-20,  0,-20,  -20,0
1860    '_____
1870    '
1880    'module:  14 sets of XYZ world coordinates for area fil
l
1890    DATA  -20,-10,0,  -10,-20,0,  -10,-10,0,  -10,0,30,  -
10,0,-30,  -30,0,0,  0,-30,0,  -20,30,0,  -10,25,0,  -15,20,
0,  0,0,0,  20,-15,0,  25,-10,0,  30,-20,0
1900    '_____
1910    '
1920    'module:  plane equation method of hidden surface remov
al
```

```
1930   SP1=X1*(Y2*Z3-Y3*Z2):SP1=(-1)*SP1:SP2=X2*(Y3*Z1-Y1*Z3)
:SP3=X3*(Y1*Z2-Y2*Z1):SP=SP1-SP2-SP3:RETURN
1940 '_____
1950 '
1960 'module:   computer-controlled shading routine
1970   XU=X2-X1:YU=Y2-Y1:ZU=Z2-Z1   'calculate vector from ver
tex 1 to vertex 2
1980   XV=X3-X1:YV=Y3-Y1:ZV=Z3-Z1   'calculate vector from ver
tex 1 to vertex 3
1990   XN=(YU*ZV)-(ZU*YV):YN=(ZU*XV)-(XU*ZV):ZN=(XU*YV)-(YU*X
V)   'calculate surface perpendicular vector
2000   YN=YN*(-1):ZN=ZN*(-1)   'convert vector to cartesian sy
stem
2010 'sub-module:   convert surface perpendicular vector to u
nit vector
2020   V1=(XN*XN)+(YN*YN)+(ZN*ZN):V2=SQR(V1)   'magnitude of s
urface perpendicular vector
2030   V3=1/V2 'ratio of magnitude to unit vector magnitude
2040   XW=V3*XN:YW=V3*YN:ZW=V3*ZN   'XYZ components of surface
 perpendicular unit vector
2050 'sub-module:   calculate illumination factor for surface
 when angle of incidence is 45 degrees elevation and 135 deg
rees yaw
2060   V4=(XW*XL)+(YW*YL)+(ZW*ZL)   'illumination factor 0 to
1
2070   V4=V4*V6:V4=CINT(V4)   'set illumination range
2080   V5=V4+1   'illumination factor from base 1
2090   ON G GOSUB 2750, 2960, 3170, 3170   'jump to device-dep
endent shading routine
2100   RETURN
2110 '_____
2120 '
2130 'module:   computer-controlled dithering routine for 4 s
ides
2140   LINE (SX1,SY1)-(SX2,SY2),C4:LINE (SX1,SY1)-(SX2,SY2),C
5,,C6:LINE (SX2,SY2)-(SX3,SY3),C4:LINE (SX2,SY2)-(SX3,SY3),C
5,,C6:LINE (SX3,SY3)-(SX4,SY4),C4:LINE (SX3,SY3)-(SX4,SY4),C
5,,C6
2150   LINE (SX4,SY4)-(SX1,SY1),C4:LINE (SX4,SY4)-(SX1,SY1),C
5,,C6:RETURN
2160 '_____
2170 '
2180 'module:   computer-controlled dithering routine for 12
sides
2190   LINE (SX1,SY1)-(SX2,SY2),C4:LINE (SX1,SY1)-(SX2,SY2),C
5,,C6:LINE (SX2,SY2)-(SX3,SY3),C4:LINE (SX2,SY2)-(SX3,SY3),C
5,,C6:LINE (SX3,SY3)-(SX4,SY4),C4:LINE (SX3,SY3)-(SX4,SY4),C
5,,C6
```

```
2200  LINE (SX4,SY4)-(SX5,SY5),C4:LINE (SX4,SY4)-(SX5,SY5),C
5,,C6:LINE (SX5,SY5)-(SX6,SY6),C4:LINE (SX5,SY5)-(SX6,SY6),C
5,,C6:LINE (SX6,SY6)-(SX7,SY7),C4:LINE (SX6,SY6)-(SX7,SY7),C
5,,C6
2210  LINE (SX7,SY7)-(SX8,SY8),C4:LINE (SX7,SY7)-(SX8,SY8),C
5,,C6:LINE (SX8,SY8)-(SX9,SY9),C4:LINE (SX8,SY8)-(SX9,SY9),C
5,,C6:LINE (SX9,SY9)-(SX1,SY1),C4:LINE (SX9,SY9)-(SX1,SY1),C
5,,C6
2220  LINE (SX10,SY10)-(SX11,SY11),C4:LINE (SX10,SY10)-(SX11
,SY11),C5,,C6:LINE (SX11,SY11)-(SX12,SY12),C4:LINE (SX11,SY1
1)-(SX12,SY12),C5,,C6:LINE (SX12,SY12)-(SX10,SY10),C4:LINE (
SX12,SY12)-(SX10,SY10),C5,,C6:RETURN
2230  '_____
2240  '
2250  'module:  solid surface modeling of 4-sided polygon
2260  LINE (SX1,SY1)-(SX2,SY2),C2:LINE-(SX3,SY3),C2:LINE-(SX
4,SY4),C2:LINE-(SX1,SY1),C2:PAINT (SX5,SY5),C2,C2:LINE (SX1,
SY1)-(SX2,SY2),C3:LINE-(SX3,SY3),C3:LINE-(SX4,SY4),C3:LINE-(
SX1,SY1),C3:PAINT (SX5,SY5),C0,C3:RETURN
2270  '_____
2280  '
2290  'module:  solid surface modeling of 12-sided polygon
2300  LINE (SX1,SY1)-(SX2,SY2),C2:LINE-(SX3,SY3),C2:LINE-(SX
4,SY4),C2:LINE-(SX5,SY5),C2:LINE-(SX6,SY6),C2:LINE-(SX7,SY7)
,C2:LINE-(SX8,SY8),C2:LINE-(SX9,SY9),C2:LINE-(SX1,SY1),C2
2310  LINE (SX10,SY10)-(SX11,SY11),C2:LINE-(SX12,SY12),C2:LI
NE-(SX10,SY10),C2:PAINT (SX13,SY13),C2,C2
2320  LINE (SX1,SY1)-(SX2,SY2),C3:LINE-(SX3,SY3),C3:LINE-(SX
4,SY4),C3:LINE-(SX5,SY5),C3:LINE-(SX6,SY6),C3:LINE-(SX7,SY7)
,C3:LINE-(SX8,SY8),C3:LINE-(SX9,SY9),C3:LINE-(SX1,SY1),C3
2330  LINE (SX10,SY10)-(SX11,SY11),C3:LINE-(SX12,SY12),C3:LI
NE-(SX10,SY10),C3:PAINT (SX13,SY13),C0,C3:RETURN
2340  '_____
2350  '
2360  'module:  assign shading codes for EGA
2370  A1$=CHR$(&HDF)+CHR$(&H20)+CHR$(&HO)+CHR$(&HO)+CHR$(&HF
D)+CHR$(&H2)+CHR$(&HO)+CHR$(&HO)+CHR$(&H7F)+CHR$(&H80)+CHR$(
&HO)+CHR$(&HO)+CHR$(&HF7)+CHR$(&H8)+CHR$(&HO)+CHR$(&HO)
2380  A2$=CHR$(&HBB)+CHR$(&H44)+CHR$(&HO)+CHR$(&HO)+CHR$(&HE
E)+CHR$(&H11)+CHR$(&HO)+CHR$(&HO)
2390  A3$=CHR$(&HAA)+CHR$(&H55)+CHR$(&HO)+CHR$(&HO)+CHR$(&H5
5)+CHR$(&HAA)+CHR$(&HO)+CHR$(&HO)
2400  A4$=CHR$(&H44)+CHR$(&HBB)+CHR$(&HO)+CHR$(&HO)+CHR$(&H1
1)+CHR$(&HEE)+CHR$(&HO)+CHR$(&HO)
2410  A5$=CHR$(&H20)+CHR$(&HFF)+CHR$(&HO)+CHR$(&HO)+CHR$(&H2
)+CHR$(&HFF)+CHR$(&HO)+CHR$(&HO)+CHR$(&H80)+CHR$(&HFF)+CHR$(
&HO)+CHR$(&HO)+CHR$(&H8)+CHR$(&HFF)+CHR$(&HO)+CHR$(&HO)
2420  A6$=CHR$(&H44)+CHR$(&HFF)+CHR$(&HO)+CHR$(&HO)+CHR$(&H1
```

```
               1)+CHR$(&HFF)+CHR$(&HO)+CHR$(&HO)
2430    A7$=CHR$(&H55)+CHR$(&HFF)+CHR$(&HO)+CHR$(&HO)+CHR$(&HA
A)+CHR$(&HFF)+CHR$(&HO)+CHR$(&HO)
2440    A8$=CHR$(&HBB)+CHR$(&HFF)+CHR$(&HO)+CHR$(&HO)+CHR$(&HE
E)+CHR$(&HFF)+CHR$(&HO)+CHR$(&HO)
2450    A9$=CHR$(&HDF)+CHR$(&HDF)+CHR$(&H20)+CHR$(&HO)+CHR$(&H
FD)+CHR$(&HFD)+CHR$(&H2)+CHR$(&HO)+CHR$(&H7F)+CHR$(&H7F)+CHR
$(&H80)+CHR$(&HO)+CHR$(&HF7)+CHR$(&HF7)+CHR$(&H8)+CHR$(&HO)
2460    A10$=CHR$(&HBB)+CHR$(&HBB)+CHR$(&H44)+CHR$(&HO)+CHR$(&
HEE)+CHR$(&HEE)+CHR$(&H11)+CHR$(&HO)
2470    A11$=CHR$(&HAA)+CHR$(&HAA)+CHR$(&H55)+CHR$(&HO)+CHR$(&
H55)+CHR$(&H55)+CHR$(&HAA)+CHR$(&HO)
2480    A12$=CHR$(&H44)+CHR$(&H44)+CHR$(&HBB)+CHR$(&HO)+CHR$(&
H11)+CHR$(&H11)+CHR$(&HEE)+CHR$(&HO)
2490    A13$=CHR$(&H20)+CHR$(&HO)+CHR$(&HFF)+CHR$(&HO)+CHR$(&H
2)+CHR$(&HO)+CHR$(&HFF)+CHR$(&HO)+CHR$(&H80)+CHR$(&HO)+CHR$(
&HFF)+CHR$(&HO)+CHR$(&H8)+CHR$(&HO)+CHR$(&HFF)+CHR$(&HO)
2500    A14$=CHR$(&H44)+CHR$(&HO)+CHR$(&HFF)+CHR$(&HO)+CHR$(&H
11)+CHR$(&HO)+CHR$(&HFF)+CHR$(&HO)
2510    A15$=CHR$(&H55)+CHR$(&HO)+CHR$(&HFF)+CHR$(&HO)+CHR$(&H
AA)+CHR$(&HO)+CHR$(&HFF)+CHR$(&HO)
2520    A16$=CHR$(&HBB)+CHR$(&HO)+CHR$(&HFF)+CHR$(&HO)+CHR$(&H
EE)+CHR$(&HO)+CHR$(&HFF)+CHR$(&HO)
2530    RETURN
2540 '_____
2550 '
2560 'module:   assign shading codes for CGA and/or PCjr
2570    A1$=CHR$(&H40)+CHR$(&HO)+CHR$(&H4)+CHR$(&HO)
2580    A2$=CHR$(&H40)+CHR$(&H4)+CHR$(&H40)+CHR$(&H4)
2590    A3$=CHR$(&H44)+CHR$(&H10)+CHR$(&H11)+CHR$(&H1)+CHR$(&H
44)+CHR$(&H4)+CHR$(&H11)+CHR$(&H40)
2600    A4$=CHR$(&H44)+CHR$(&H11)+CHR$(&H44)+CHR$(&H11)
2610    A5$=CHR$(&H11)+CHR$(&H45)+CHR$(&H44)+CHR$(&H54)+CHR$(&
H11)+CHR$(&H51)+CHR$(&H44)+CHR$(&H15)
2620    A6$=CHR$(&H15)+CHR$(&H51)+CHR$(&H15)+CHR$(&H51)
2630    A7$=CHR$(&H15)+CHR$(&H55)+CHR$(&H51)+CHR$(&H55)
2640    A9$=CHR$(&HD5)+CHR$(&H55)+CHR$(&H5D)+CHR$(&H55)
2650    A10$=CHR$(&HD5)+CHR$(&H5D)+CHR$(&HD5)+CHR$(&H5D)
2660    A12$=CHR$(&HDD)+CHR$(&H75)+CHR$(&H77)+CHR$(&H57)+CHR$(
&HDD)+CHR$(&H5D)+CHR$(&H77)+CHR$(&HD5)
2670    A13$=CHR$(&HDD)+CHR$(&H77)+CHR$(&HDD)+CHR$(&H77)
2680    A14$=CHR$(&H77)+CHR$(&HDF)+CHR$(&HDD)+CHR$(&HFD)+CHR$(
&H77)+CHR$(&HF7)+CHR$(&HDD)+CHR$(&H7F)
2690    A15$=CHR$(&H7F)+CHR$(&HF7)+CHR$(&H7F)+CHR$(&HF7)
2700    A16$=CHR$(&H7F)+CHR$(&HFF)+CHR$(&HF7)+CHR$(&HFF)
2710    RETURN
2720 '_____
2730 '
```

```
2740 'shading routine for ED-EGA 640x350 mode
2750   IF V5<1 THEN GOTO 2770  'if light source is behind sur
face
2760   ON V5 GOTO 2770, 2780, 2790, 2800, 2810, 2820, 2830, 2
840, 2850, 2860, 2870, 2880, 2890, 2900, 2910, 2920
2770   A$=CHR$(&HFF)+CHR$(&HO)+CHR$(&HO)+CHR$(&HO):C4=1:C5=1:
C6=&HFFFF:RETURN
2780   A$=A1$:C4=1:C5=2:C6=&H808:RETURN
2790   A$=A2$:C4=1:C5=2:C6=&H4444:RETURN
2800   A$=CHR$(&HO)+CHR$(&HFF)+CHR$(&HO)+CHR$(&HO):C4=2:C5=2:
C6=&HFFFF:RETURN
2810   A$=A5$:C4=2:C5=3:C6=&H808:RETURN
2820   A$=A6$:C4=2:C5=3:C6=&H4444:RETURN
2830   A$=A7$:C4=2:C5=3:C6=&HAAAA:RETURN
2840   A$=A8$:C4=3:C5=2:C6=&H4444:RETURN
2850   A$=CHR$(&HFF)+CHR$(&HFF)+CHR$(&HO)+CHR$(&HO):C4=3:C5=3
:C6=&HFFFF:RETURN
2860   A$=A10$:C4=3:C5=4:C6=&H4444:RETURN
2870   A$=A11$:C4=3:C5=4:C6=&HAAAA:RETURN
2880   A$=A12$:C4=4:C5=3:C6=&H4444:RETURN
2890   A$=CHR$(&HO)+CHR$(&HO)+CHR$(&HFF)+CHR$(&HO):C4=4:C5=4:
C6=&HFFFF:RETURN
2900   A$=A13$:C4=4:C5=5:C6=&H808:RETURN
2910   A$=A14$:C4=4:C5=5:C6=&H4444:RETURN
2920   A$=A15$:C4=4:C5=5:C6=&HAAAA:RETURN
2930 '_____
2940 '
2950 'shading routine for CD-EGA 640x200 mode
2960   IF V5<1 THEN GOTO 2990  'if light source is behind sur
face
2970   ON V5 GOTO 2990, 3000, 3010, 3020, 3030, 3040, 3050, 3
060, 3070, 3080, 3090, 3100, 3110, 3120, 3130
2980   A$=CHR$(&HFF)+CHR$(&HO)+CHR$(&HO)+CHR$(&HO):C4=1:C5=1:
C6=&HFFFF:RETURN  'solid black is unused
2990   A$=A1$:C4=1:C5=2:C6=&H808:RETURN
3000   A$=A2$:C4=1:C5=2:C6=&H4444:RETURN
3010   A$=A3$:C4=1:C5=2:C6=&HAAAA:RETURN
3020   A$=A4$:C4=2:C5=1:C6=&H4444:RETURN
3030   A$=CHR$(&HO)+CHR$(&HFF)+CHR$(&HO)+CHR$(&HO):C4=2:C5=2:
C6=&HFFFF:RETURN
3040   A$=A5$:C4=2:C5=3:C6=&H808:RETURN
3050   A$=A6$:C4=2:C5=3:C6=&H4444:RETURN
3060   A$=A7$:C4=2:C5=3:C6=&HAAAA:RETURN
3070   A$=A8$:C4=3:C5=2:C6=&H4444:RETURN
3080   A$=CHR$(&HFF)+CHR$(&HFF)+CHR$(&HO)+CHR$(&HO):C4=3:C5=3
:C6=&HFFFF:RETURN
3090   A$=A9$:C4=3:C5=4:C6=&H8080:RETURN
3100   A$=A10$:C4=3:C5=4:C6=&H4444:RETURN
```

```
3110    A$=A11$:C4=3:C5=4:C6=&HAAAA:RETURN
3120    A$=A12$:C4=4:C5=3:C6=&H4444:RETURN
3130    A$=CHR$(&HO)+CHR$(&HO)+CHR$(&HFF)+CHR$(&HO):C4=4:C5=4:
C6=&HFFFF:RETURN
3140    '_____
3150    '
3160    'shading routine for CD-CGA 320x200 mode and CD-JR 640x
200 mode
3170    IF V5<1 THEN GOTO 3200   'if light source is behind sur
face
3180    ON V5 GOTO 3200, 3210, 3220, 3230, 3240, 3250, 3260, 3
270, 3280, 3290, 3300, 3310, 3320, 3330, 3340
3190    A$=CHR$(&HO):C4=0:C5=0:C6=&HFFFF:RETURN    'solid black
-- unused
3200    A$=A1$:C4=0:C5=1:C6=&H2108:RETURN
3210    A$=A2$:C4=0:C5=1:C6=&H4444:RETURN
3220    A$=A4$:C4=0:C5=1:C6=&HAAAA:RETURN
3230    A$=A5$:C4=1:C5=0:C6=&H4924:RETURN
3240    A$=A6$:C4=1:C5=0:C6=&H4444:RETURN
3250    A$=A7$:C4=1:C5=0:C6=&H808:RETURN
3260    A$=CHR$(&H55):C4=1:C5=1:C6=&HFFFF:RETURN
3270    A$=A9$:C4=1:C5=3:C6=&H808:RETURN
3280    A$=A10$:C4=1:C5=3:C6=&H4444:RETURN
3290    A$=A12$:C4=1:C5=3:C6=&H4924:RETURN
3300    A$=A13$:C4=1:C5=3:C6=&HAAAA:RETURN
3310    A$=A14$:C4=3:C5=1:C6=&H4924:RETURN
3320    A$=A15$:C4=3:C5=1:C6=&H4444:RETURN
3330    A$=A16$:C4=3:C5=1:C6=&H808:RETURN
3340    A$=CHR$(&HFF):C4=3:C5=3:C6=&HFFFF:RETURN
3350    '_____
3360    '
3370    END 'of program code
```

**"A-38.BAS",R.** The program generates a fully-shaded model of the industrial part.

The program requires a full 30 seconds to complete the fully-shaded model, as opposed to only 16 seconds for the solid model version, and a mere eight seconds for the wire-frame model version.

This program is similar to the previous demonstration program, except for the addition of the hex shading codes (from lines 2360 through 2710) and the shading routines (from lines 1960 through 2220 and from lines 2740 through 3340). If you are typing in the program listings, you can save yourself some time by simply merging these code fragments from other rendering programs which you have already typed in.

Simply stated, if you are able to create a correct solid model, then it is a simple task to shade the model.

The surfaces which are used to construct the solid model are the same surfaces which are analyzed to determine the shading levels. If you wish to experiment with moving the position of the light source by modifying line 1790, refer to Appendix B. You can experiment with rotations by modifying the R1, R2, and R3 values in line 1750.

## SUMMARY

In this chapter, you learned how to create three different images of an industrial part: a transparent wire-frame model, a solid model, and a fully-shaded model.

The next chapter provides two examples of advanced techniques of package design: a film carton and a soft drink container.

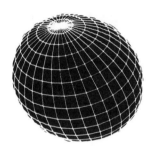

# 24

# *Package Design*

The techniques discussed in previous chapters can be put to work designing assorted packages and containers. In this chapter you will learn how to design a small photographic film carton and a soft drink container. The carton is created using techniques of surface mapping. The drink container employs contour mapping.

### PREPARATION: SOFT DRINK CONTAINER

A preliminary template for a typical cylindrical container is shown in Fig. 24-1. As discussed in Chapter 10, the measurements along the length of the cylinder can be expressed as z-coordinates. Measurements around the curved surface of the cylinder can be expressed as R5 radians. When these R5 units are converted to WORLD COORDINATES, they produce the x-coordinates and y-coordinates needed to complete the x,y,z triplet.

The scale at the top of Fig. 24-1 shows the relationship between angles and radians. The orientation of the model within the 3D axis system is shown in Fig. 24-2. The model is rotated by the projection formulas before being displayed, of course.

By using the template approach, you could map virtually any design onto the surface of a cylinder. This chapter will focus on an imaginary soft drink container.

### DEMONSTRATION: SOFT DRINK CONTAINER

Figure 24-3 shows the screen output of the demonstration program in Fig. 24-4. To run this program from the companion diskette, type **LOAD "A-39.BAS",R**. The program generates six different views of a 3D soft drink container design.

The program uses an algorithm similar to that introduced in Chapter 10, except that a database at lines 1850 through 1950 is employed to store z-coordinates for contour mapping.

#### Drawing the Cylinder

The body of the cylindrical container is produced by lines 280 through 340. Lines 290 and 300 draw the top end. Lines 310 and 320 draw the bottom end. Note how the R5 factor is swept around just far enough to draw only the visible portion of the bottom end of the cylinder. This is a crude, but effective, method for hid-

```
X=30 'radius of cylinder (constant)
R4=0 'leave at 0
R5=.17454 to 2.96718  'sweep around cylinder
GOSUB calculations   'find X,Y world coordinates
Z=45 to -45
GOSUB perspective formulas
```

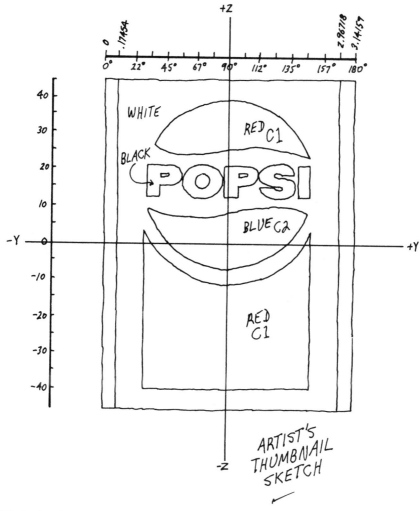

Fig. 24-1. Template for locating the z coordinates and R5 angles for points on the surface of the cylinder.

den surface removal. The cylinder is essentially a transparent wire-frame model which has been painted. It is not polygon mesh, although there is no technical reason preventing you from mapping a fully-shaded, polygon mesh cylinder.

Line 330 connects the two ends of the cylinder by connecting points which were saved while the two ends were being drawn. Line 340 paints the curved

surface white and the end black.

**Drawing the Lower Graphic**

The lower rectangular graphic is drawn by lines 370 through 440. The database is first initialized when the arc at the top of the graphic is constructed. Reading z-coordinate values of the database, line 430 merely

296

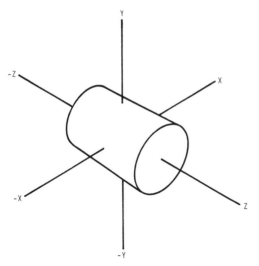

Fig. 24-2. Orientation of the 3D cylindrical container in the axis system.

increments the R5 radian value in order to step around the cylinder. The graphic is painted by line 440.

## Drawing the Circle Graphics

The two half-moon graphics are drawn by lines 470 through 600. Again, a FOR...NEXT loop is used to increment and decrement the R5 factor while the program retrieves z-coordinates from the database. The R5 factor is converted to x-coordinates and y-coordinates by the subroutine at line 1380, of course.

## Drawing the Alphanumerics

The alphabet characters are created by lines 630 through 3120. Although this is time-consuming code from both a programming and a run-time point of view, there is nothing mysterious about it. The algorithm is consistent: select an R5 value, retrieve a z-coordinate value from the database, and use the subroutine at line 1380 to produce the x,y,z WORLD COORDINATES. Once these WORLD COORDINATES are known, the standard perspective formulas can be used to generate the 3D image on the display screen.

The importance of a template becomes obvious as you watch the program drawing the alphanumerics. In order to make the alphabet characters appear smooth, a substantial number of coordinates are required. Simply stated, the more short lines that are used to create the alphanumeric, the more natural the result appears.

Note line 1780, which initializes the variable F.

Fig. 24-3. The display image produced by the demonstration program in Fig. 24-4.

Fig. 24-4. Design for soft drink container.

```
100 'Program A-39.BAS    Soft drink container
110 'Demonstrates package design.
120 '_____
130 '
140   GOTO 1520  'configure system
150   GOSUB 1760 'assign scalar data
160 '_____
170 '
180 'master routine
190   VIEW (W1,W7)-(W2,W8):GOSUB 290
200   VIEW (W3,W7)-(W4,W8):R2=4.89778:GOSUB 1800:GOSUB 290
210   VIEW (W5,W7)-(W6,W8):R2=4.71239:R3=.08539:GOSUB 1800:GO
SUB 290
220   VIEW (W1,W9)-(W2,W10):R2=5.29448:R3=6.08319:GOSUB 1800:
GOSUB 290
230   VIEW (W3,W9)-(W4,W10):R2=4.71239:R3=5.78319:GOSUB 1800:
GOSUB 290
240   VIEW (W5,W9)-(W6,W10):R2=4.41239:R3=6.08319:GOSUB 1800:
GOSUB 290
250   GOTO 250
260 '_____
270 '
280 'STEP ONE: create body of cylinder
290   X=30:R4=0:R5=0:GOSUB 1380:Z=45:GOSUB 1430:PSET (SX,SY),
C3:XNT=SX:YNT=SY  'set start point for end of cylinder
300   FOR T=1 TO 72 STEP 1:X=30:R5=R5+.08727:GOSUB 1380:Z=45:
GOSUB 1430:LINE-(SX,SY),C3:NEXT T  'draw top circumference f
or end of cylinder
310   X=30:R4=0:R5=.17454:GOSUB 1380:Z=-45:GOSUB 1430:PSET (S
X,SY),C3:XFT=SX:YFT=SY  'set start point for bottom of cylin
der
320   FOR T=1 TO 32 STEP 1:X=30:R5=R5+.08727:GOSUB 1380:Z=-45
:GOSUB 1430:LINE-(SX,SY),C3:NEXT T:XFB=SX:YFB=SY  'draw visi
ble portion of circumference of bottom of cylinder
330   LINE (XNT,YNT)-(XFT,YFT),C3:X=0:Z=45:Y=30:GOSUB 1430:PS
ET (SX,SY),C3:LINE-(XFB,YFB),C3  'connect top and bottom of
cylinder
340   X=0:Z=45:Y=0:GOSUB 1430:PAINT (SX,SY),C0,C3:X=30:Y=0:Z=
0:GOSUB 1430:PAINT (SX,SY),C3,C3  'paint top of cylinder bla
ck, paint curved surface white
350 '_____
360 '
370 'STEP TWO: create pedestal graphic on cylinder
380   X=30:R5=2.601631:GOSUB 1380:Z=-40:GOSUB 1430:PSET (SX,S
```

```
Y),C1:X=30:R5=2.601631:GOSUB 1380:Z=2.5:GOSUB 1430:LINE-(SX,
SY),C1
390  X=30:R5=.490874:GOSUB 1380:Z=-40:GOSUB 1430:PSET (SX,SY
),C1:X=30:R5=.490874:GOSUB 1380:Z=2.5:GOSUB 1430:LINE-(SX,SY
),C1
400  X=30:R5=.490874:GOSUB 1380:Z=-40:GOSUB 1430:PSET (SX,SY
),C3
410  FOR R5=.490874 TO 2.601631 STEP .0490873:X=30:GOSUB 138
0:Z=-40:GOSUB 1430:LINE-(SX,SY),C1:NEXT R5
420  RESTORE 1850:R5=.490874:X=30:GOSUB 1380:READ Z:GOSUB 14
30:PSET (SX,SY),C1
430  FOR R5=.490874 TO 2.601631 STEP .0490873:X=30:GOSUB 138
0:READ Z:GOSUB 1430:LINE-(SX,SY),C1:NEXT R5   'arc on pedesta
l graphics
440  X=30:R5=1.570796:GOSUB 1380:Z=-25:GOSUB 1430:PAINT (SX,
SY),C1,C1
450 '_____
460 '
470 'STEP THREE: create upper semi-circle graphic
480  RESTORE 1860:R5=.638136:X=30:GOSUB 1380:READ Z:GOSUB 14
30:PSET (SX,SY),C1
490  FOR R5=.638136 TO 2.552544 STEP .0490873:X=30:GOSUB 138
0:READ Z:GOSUB 1430:LINE-(SX,SY),C1:NEXT R5
500  RESTORE 1870:R5=.638136:X=30:GOSUB 1380:READ Z:GOSUB 14
30:PSET (SX,SY),C1
510  FOR R5=.638136 TO 2.552544 STEP .0490873:X=30:GOSUB 138
0:READ Z:GOSUB 1430:LINE-(SX,SY),C1:NEXT R5
520  X=30:R5=1.570796:GOSUB 1380:Z=32:GOSUB 1430:PAINT (SX,S
Y),C1,C1
530 '_____
540 '
550 'STEP FOUR: create lower semi-circle graphic
560  RESTORE 1880:R5=.638136:X=30:GOSUB 1380:READ Z:GOSUB 14
30:PSET (SX,SY),C2
570  FOR R5=.638136 TO 2.552544 STEP .0490873:X=30:GOSUB 138
0:READ Z:GOSUB 1430:LINE-(SX,SY),C2:NEXT R5
580  RESTORE 1890:R5=.638136:X=30:GOSUB 1380:READ Z:GOSUB 14
30:PSET (SX,SY),C2
590  FOR R5=.638136 TO 2.552544 STEP .0490873:X=30:GOSUB 138
0:READ Z:GOSUB 1430:LINE-(SX,SY),C2:NEXT R5
600  X=30:R5=1.570796:GOSUB 1380:Z=0:GOSUB 1430:PAINT (SX,SY
),C2,C2
610 '_____
620 '
630 'STEP FIVE: create alphanumerics POPSI
640 'draw the first P
650  C=C0  'assign color for alphanumeric drawing code
660  RESTORE 1900:R5=.539961:X=30:GOSUB 1380:READ Z:GOSUB 14
```

```
30:PSET (SX,SY),C
670   X=30:GOSUB 1380:READ Z:GOSUB 1430:LINE-(SX,SY),C
680   F=.0490873:FOR T=1 TO 6 STEP 1:R5=R5+F:X=30:GOSUB 1380:
READ Z:GOSUB 1430:LINE-(SX,SY),C:NEXT T
690   FOR T=1 TO 2 STEP 1:R5=R5+F:X=30:GOSUB 1380:READ Z:GOSU
B 1430:LINE-(SX,SY),C:NEXT T
700   FOR T=1 TO 2 STEP 1:R5=R5+.5*F:X=30:GOSUB 1380:READ Z:G
OSUB 1430:LINE-(SX,SY),C:NEXT T
710   FOR T=1 TO 2 STEP 1:R5=R5-.5*F:X=30:GOSUB 1380:READ Z:G
OSUB 1430:LINE-(SX,SY),C:NEXT T
720   R5=R5-F:X=30:GOSUB 1380:READ Z:GOSUB 1430:LINE-(SX,SY),
C
730   FOR T=1 TO 4 STEP 1:R5=R5-F:X=30:GOSUB 1380:READ Z:GOSU
B 1430:LINE-(SX,SY),C:NEXT T
740   X=30:GOSUB 1380:READ Z:GOSUB 1430:LINE-(SX,SY),C
750   R5=.539961:X=30:GOSUB 1380:READ Z:GOSUB 1430:LINE-(SX,S
Y),C
760   RESTORE 1910:R5=.687223:X=30:GOSUB 1380:READ Z:GOSUB 14
30:PSET (SX,SY),C:X=30:GOSUB 1380:READ Z:GOSUB 1430:LINE-(SX
,SY),C
770   R5=.805398:X=30:GOSUB 1380:READ Z:GOSUB 1430:LINE-(SX,S
Y),C:X=30:GOSUB 1380:READ Z:GOSUB 1430:LINE-(SX,SY),C
780   R5=.687223:X=30:GOSUB 1380:READ Z:GOSUB 1430:LINE-(SX,S
Y),C
790   '————————
800   '
810   'draw the second P
820   RESTORE 1900:R5=1.521709:X=30:GOSUB 1380:READ Z:GOSUB 1
430:PSET (SX,SY),C
830   X=30:GOSUB 1380:READ Z:GOSUB 1430:LINE-(SX,SY),C
840   F=.0490873:FOR T=1 TO 6 STEP 1:R5=R5+F:X=30:GOSUB 1380:
READ Z:GOSUB 1430:LINE-(SX,SY),C:NEXT T
850   FOR T=1 TO 2 STEP 1:R5=R5+F:X=30:GOSUB 1380:READ Z:GOSU
B 1430:LINE-(SX,SY),C:NEXT T
860   FOR T=1 TO 2 STEP 1:R5=R5+.5*F:X=30:GOSUB 1380:READ Z:G
OSUB 1430:LINE-(SX,SY),C:NEXT T
870   FOR T=1 TO 2 STEP 1:R5=R5-.5*F:X=30:GOSUB 1380:READ Z:G
OSUB 1430:LINE-(SX,SY),C:NEXT T
880   R5=R5-F:X=30:GOSUB 1380:READ Z:GOSUB 1430:LINE-(SX,SY),
C
890   FOR T=1 TO 4 STEP 1:R5=R5-F:X=30:GOSUB 1380:READ Z:GOSU
B 1430:LINE-(SX,SY),C:NEXT T
900   X=30:GOSUB 1380:READ Z:GOSUB 1430:LINE-(SX,SY),C
910   R5=1.521709:X=30:GOSUB 1380:READ Z:GOSUB 1430:LINE-(SX,
SY),C
920   RESTORE 1910:R5=1.668971:X=30:GOSUB 1380:READ Z:GOSUB 1
430:PSET (SX,SY),C:X=30:GOSUB 1380:READ Z:GOSUB 1430:LINE-(S
X,SY),C
```

```
930   R5=1.767146:X=30:GOSUB 1380:READ Z:GOSUB 1430:LINE-(SX,
SY),C:X=30:GOSUB 1380:READ Z:GOSUB 1430:LINE-(SX,SY),C
940   R5=1.668971:X=30:GOSUB 1380:READ Z:GOSUB 1430:LINE-(SX,
SY),C
950 '_____
960 '
970 'draw the O
980   RESTORE 1920:R5=.981748:X=30:GOSUB 1380:READ Z:GOSUB 14
30:PSET (SX,SY),C
990   FOR T=1 TO 10 STEP 1:X=30:R5=R5+F:GOSUB 1380:READ Z:GOS
UB 1430:LINE-(SX,SY),C:NEXT T
1000   FOR T=1 TO 2 STEP 1:X=30:R5=R5+.5*F:GOSUB 1380:READ Z:
GOSUB 1430:LINE-(SX,SY),C:NEXT T
1010   FOR T=1 TO 2 STEP 1:X=30:GOSUB 1380:READ Z:GOSUB 1430:
LINE-(SX,SY),C:NEXT T
1020   FOR T=1 TO 2 STEP 1:X=30:R5=R5-.5*F:GOSUB 1380:READ Z:
GOSUB 1430:LINE-(SX,SY),C:NEXT T
1030   FOR T=1 TO 11 STEP 1:X=30:R5=R5-F:GOSUB 1380:READ Z:GO
SUB 1430:LINE-(SX,SY),C:NEXT T
1040   X=30:GOSUB 1380:READ Z:GOSUB 1430:LINE-(SX,SY),C
1050   X=30:R5=.981748:GOSUB 1380:READ Z:GOSUB 1430:LINE-(SX,
SY),C
1060   RESTORE 1930:R5=1.129009:X=30:GOSUB 1380:READ Z:GOSUB
1430:PSET (SX,SY),C
1070   FOR T=1 TO 9 STEP 1:X=30:R5=R5+.5*F:GOSUB 1380:READ Z:
GOSUB 1430:LINE-(SX,SY),C:NEXT T
1080   X=30:GOSUB 1380:READ Z:GOSUB 1430:LINE-(SX,SY),C
1090   FOR T=1 TO 9 STEP 1:X=30:R5=R5-.5*F:GOSUB 1380:READ Z:
GOSUB 1430:LINE-(SX,SY),C:NEXT T
1100 '_____
1110 '
1120 'draw the S
1130   RESTORE 1940:R5=1.963495:X=30:GOSUB 1380:READ Z:GOSUB
1430:PSET (SX,SY),C
1140   FOR T=1 TO 9 STEP 1:X=30:R5=R5+F:GOSUB 1380:READ Z:GOS
UB 1430:LINE-(SX,SY),C:NEXT T
1150   X=30:GOSUB 1380:READ Z:GOSUB 1430:LINE-(SX,SY),C
1160   FOR T=1 TO 6 STEP 1:X=30:R5=R5-F:GOSUB 1380:READ Z:GOS
UB 1430:LINE-(SX,SY),C:NEXT T
1170   FOR T=1 TO 6 STEP 1:X=30:R5=R5+F:GOSUB 1380:READ Z:GOS
UB 1430:LINE-(SX,SY),C:NEXT T
1180   X=30:R5=R5+.5*F:GOSUB 1380:READ Z:GOSUB 1430:LINE-(SX,
SY),C
1190   X=30:R5=R5-.5*F:GOSUB 1380:READ Z:GOSUB 1430:LINE-(SX,
SY),C
1200   FOR T=1 TO 9 STEP 1:X=30:R5=R5-F:GOSUB 1380:READ Z:GOS
UB 1430:LINE-(SX,SY),C:NEXT T
1210   X=30:GOSUB 1380:READ Z:GOSUB 1430:LINE-(SX,SY),C
```

```
1220    FOR T=1 TO 5 STEP 1:X=30:R5=R5+F:GOSUB 1380:READ Z:GOS
UB 1430:LINE-(SX,SY),C:NEXT T
1230    X=30:R5=R5+.5*F:GOSUB 1380:READ Z:GOSUB 1430:LINE-(SX,
SY),C
1240    X=30:R5=R5-.5*F:GOSUB 1380:READ Z:GOSUB 1430:LINE-(SX,
SY),C
1250    FOR T=1 TO 5 STEP 1:X=30:R5=R5-F:GOSUB 1380:READ Z:GOS
UB 1430:LINE-(SX,SY),C:NEXT T
1260    X=30:R5=1.963495:GOSUB 1380:READ Z:GOSUB 1430:LINE-(SX
,SY),C
1270 '_____
1280 '
1290 'draw the I
1300    RESTORE 1950:R5=2.454369:X=30:GOSUB 1380:READ Z:GOSUB
1430:PSET (SX,SY),C:X=30:GOSUB 1380:READ Z:GOSUB 1430:LINE-(
SX,SY),C
1310    R5=2.601631:X=30:GOSUB 1380:READ Z:GOSUB 1430:LINE-(SX
,SY),C:X=30:GOSUB 1380:READ Z:GOSUB 1430:LINE-(SX,SY),C
1320    R5=2.454369:X=30:GOSUB 1380:READ Z:GOSUB 1430:LINE-(SX
,SY),C
1330    BEEP
1340    RETURN
1350 '_____
1360 '
1370 'module: calculation of 3D world coordinates
1380    SR4=SIN(R4):CR4=COS(R4):SR5=SIN(R5):CR5=COS(R5)
1390    X1=SR5*X:Y=(-1)*(CR5*X):X=CR4*X1:Z=SR4*X1:RETURN
1400 '_____
1410 '
1420 'module:   perspective calculations for Cartesian world
coordinates
1430    X=(-1)*X:XA=CR1*X-SR1*Z:ZA=SR1*X+CR1*Z:X=CR2*XA+SR2*Y:
YA=CR2*Y-SR2*XA:Z=CR3*ZA-SR3*YA:Y=SR3*ZA+CR3*YA:X=X+MX:Y=Y+M
Y:Z=Z+MZ:SX=D*X/Z:SY=D*Y/Z:RETURN
1440 '_____
1450 '
1460 'module: return to BASIC interpreter
1470    CLS:SCREEN 0,0,0,0:WIDTH 80:COLOR 7,0,0:LOCATE 1,1,1:C
LS:END
1480 '_____
1490 '
1500 'module:   UNIVERSAL
1510 'This routine configures the program for the hardware/s
oftware being used.
1520    KEY OFF:CLS:ON ERROR GOTO 1560   'trap if not Enhanced
Display + EGA
1530    SCREEN 9,,0,0:COLOR 7,0:PALETTE 1,12:PALETTE 2,9:PALET
TE 3,7:C0=0:C1=1:C2=2:C3=3:LOCATE 1,1:PRINT "ED-EGA 640x350
```

```
16-color mode"
1540    GOSUB 1990  'jump to viewport assignment routine
1550    GOTO 1690  'jump to screen coordinates set-up
1560    RESUME 1570
1570    ON ERROR GOTO 1610  'trap if not Color Display + EGA
1580    SCREEN 8,,0,0:COLOR 7,0:PALETTE 1,4:PALETTE 2,9:PALETT
E 3,7:C0=0:C1=1:C2=2:C3=3:LOCATE 1,1:PRINT "CD-EGA 640x200 1
6-color mode"
1590    GOSUB 2000  'jump to viewport assignment routine
1600    GOTO 1690  'jump to screen coordinates set-up
1610    RESUME 1620
1620    ON ERROR GOTO 1660  'trap if not PCjr
1630    CLEAR,,,32768!:SCREEN 6,0,0,0:COLOR 3,0:PALETTE 1,4:PA
LETTE 2,9:PALETTE 3,7:C0=0:C1=1:C2=2:C3=3:LOCATE 1,1:PRINT "
PCjr 640x200 4-color mode"
1640    GOSUB 2000  'jump to viewport assignment routine
1650    GOTO 1690  'jump to screen coordinates set-up
1660    RESUME 1670
1670    SCREEN 1,0:COLOR 0,1:C0=0:C1=2:C2=1:C3=3:LOCATE 1,1:PR
INT "CGA 320x200 4-color mode"
1680    GOSUB 2010  'jump to viewport assignment routine
1690    ON ERROR GOTO 0  'disable error trapping override
1700    WINDOW SCREEN (-399,-299)-(400,300)  'establish device
-independent screen coordinates
1710    ON KEY (2) GOSUB 1470:KEY (2) ON  'F2 key to exit prog
ram
1720    GOTO 150  'return to main program
1730 '_____
1740 '
1750 'module: assign scalar data
1760    D=1400:R1=5.09448:R2=5.09448:R3=6.28319:MX=0:MY=0:MZ=-
300    'angular distortion, rotation factors, viewpoint dista
nce for viewing coordinates
1770    X=0:Y=0:Z=0:R4=0:R5=0  'rotation factors for world coo
rdinates
1780    F=0  'incremental factor for R5
1790    SR4=SIN(R4):CR4=COS(R4):SR5=SIN(R5):CR5=COS(R5)
1800    SR1=SIN(R1):CR1=COS(R1):SR2=SIN(R2):CR2=COS(R2):SR3=SI
N(R3):CR3=COS(R3)
1810    RETURN
1820 '_____
1830 '
1840 'module:  database of points on surface of cylinder
1850    DATA  2,2,1,-1,-2.5,-3.8,-4.8,-6,-6.7,-7.5,-8,-8.5,-8.
8,-9.2,-10,-10.2,-10.9,-11,-11.2,-11.5,-11.7,-11.9,-12,-12,-
11.9,-11.7,-11.5,-11.2,-11,-10.9,-10.2,-10,-9.2,-8.8,-8.5,-8
,-7.5,-6.7,-6,-4.8,-3.8,-2.5,-1,1,2
1860    DATA  26,26,28,29.2,31,32,33,34,35,35.8,36.5,37,37.2,3
```

303

```
7.5,37.8,38,38.2,38.3,38.5,38.6,38.6,38.6,38.5,38.3,38.2,38,
37.8,37.5,37.2,37,36.5,35.8,35,34,33,32,31,29.2,27.5,25.2,23

1870   DATA   26,26,25.5,25,24.5,24.2,24,23.8,23.7,23.7,23.7,2
3.7,23.7,23.7,23.8,23.9,23.9,24,24.1,24.2,24.5,24.8,25.1,25.
3,25.3,25.5,25.8,26,26,25.8,25.7,25.6,25.5,25.2,25.1,25,24.5
,24.3,23.8,23.7,23
1880   DATA   8.2,7.9,7.5,7.1,7,6.9,6.8,6.7,6.6,6.6,6.6,6.7,6.
7,6.7,6.8,6.9,7,7.1,7.3,7.5,8,8.2,8.6,8.9,9,9.1,9.4,9.6,9.9,
10,10,10,10,9.9,9.8,9.5,9.4,9.1,8.9,8.4,8
1890   DATA   8.2,7,5.5,3.7,2,0,-1,-2,-2.8,-3.8,-4.5,-5.1,-5.7
,-5.9,-6.3,-6.7,-7,-7.2,-7.3,-7.4,-7.5,-7.5,-7.4,-7.3,-7.1,-
7,-6.7,-6.5,-6,-5.5,-4.8,-4,-3.2,-2.5,-1.5,-.5,.5,2.1,3.5,6,
8
1900   DATA   12,21,21,21,21,21,21,21,20.5,20,19,18,17,16,15,1
5,15,15,15,12,12
1910   DATA   18.3,17.5,17.5,18.3,18.3
1920   DATA   18,19,20,20.8,21,21,21,20.8,20.3,20,19,18,17,16,
15,14,13,12.2,12,12,11.8,11.8,12,12.2,12.8,13.2,14,15,16,17
1930   DATA   16.2,17,18,18.5,18.7,18.8,18.7,18,17.5,17,16,15,
14.5,14,14,14,14.4,14.6,15,16.2,
1940   DATA   18,20,20.8,21,21.1,21,20.8,20.5,20,19,18,18,18,1
8,18,18.8,18,17.5,17.4,17.4,17.3,17,16.2,15,14,13,12.1,12,11
.9,11.9,12,12.1,12.5,13.3,14.5,14.5,14.5,14.5,14.5,14,14.5,1
5,15,15.2,15.5,16,16.7,18
1950   DATA   20.8,12,12,20.8,20.8
1960 '_____
1970 '
1980 'module:   viewport parameters for 640x350, 640x200, 320
x200
1990   W1=1:W2=319:W3=152:W4=470:W5=320:W6=639:W7=1:W8=174:W9
=175:W10=349:RETURN
2000   W1=1:W2=319:W3=152:W4=470:W5=320:W6=639:W7=1:W8=99:W9=
100:W10=199:RETURN
2010   W1=1:W2=159:W3=76:W4=235:W5=160:W6=319:W7=1:W8=99:W9=1
00:W10=199:RETURN
2020 '_____
2030 '
2040   END 'of program code
```

This variable is used during the drawing sequence to increment or decrement the R5 factor. Line 680 is a good example of this algorithm. When line 690 is keyed in, only a single keystroke is required to type F, whereas eight keystrokes would have been required to type in the radian value .0490873.

**Disabling the Viewports**

You can modify this program to draw just one large container by making the following revisions.

Change line 190 to read: **GOSUB 290**
Delete lines 200 through 240.

The larger, single container produced by these revisions is better suited to the coarser $320 \times 200$ resolution of the Color/Graphics Adapter.

## PREPARATION: PHOTOGRAPHIC FILM CARTON

The orientation of the film carton design within the 3D axis system is shown in Fig. 24-5. The sides, top, and bottom of the carton all share an identical graphic design. Because of this similarity, a single database can be used to map the graphics onto each of the four surfaces. A separate routine will be developed to convert the standard database to the appropriate x,y,z coordinates for the surface being mapped.

## DEMONSTRATION: FILM CARTON

Figure 24-6 shows the screen output of the demonstration program in Fig. 24-7. To run this program from the companion diskette, type **LOAD "A-40.BAS",R**. The program produces four different views of an imaginary film carton design. Each view is fully-shaded by the computer, depending upon its juxtaposition relative to the light source.

### Drawing the Design

The routine which draws surface number 2 is located at lines 480 through 520. This routine provides a good example of the surface mapping algorithm in action.

Line 490 retrieves the appropriate VIEW COORDINATES from array B1 and jumps to the hidden surface routine at line 1440. If SP is larger than zero the surface is hidden and program control jumps ahead to the next surface routine at line 560. If SP is less than zero then the computer proceeds to draw surface 2, which is one of the sides of the model.

Line 500 retrieves the appropriate DISPLAY COORDINATES from array B2 and the appropriate area fill coordinates from array B3. The program then jumps to the solid surface modeling routine at line 1700.

Line 510 sends the program to the illumination routine at line 1480. After line 580 paints the surface the proper shade of A$, control is passed to the line dithering routine at line 1650.

Line 520 is the key to this program.

### Surface Mapping Routines

Line 520 sends the program to the subroutine at line 2860, which is a specialized surface mapping routine. Note that the variable E is used as a flag to tell the subroutine the orientation of the surface to be mapped.

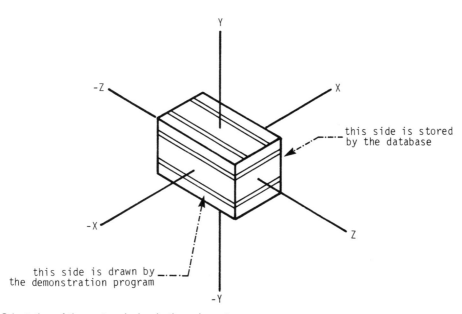

Fig. 24-5. Orientation of the carton design in the axis system.

Fig. 24-6. The display image produced by the demonstration program in Fig. 24-7.

Fig. 24-7. Design for small carton.

```
100 'Program A-40.BAS      Package design.
110 'Demonstrates surface mapping of 3D carton.
120 '_____
130 '
140   GOTO 880    'configure system
150   GOSUB 1250  'assign variables
160 '_____
170 '
180 'master routine:   simultaneous views of carton
190   R1=4.36141:VIEW (W1,W7)-(W2,W8):GOSUB 2750:GOSUB 280
200   R1=4.16325:R3=.58319:VIEW (W5,W7)-(W6,W8):GOSUB 2750:GO
SUB 280
210   R1=3.40009:R3=5.89778:VIEW (W1,W9)-(W2,W10):GOSUB 2750:
GOSUB 280
220   R1=5.29239:R3=5.59778:VIEW (W5,W9)-(W6,W10):GOSUB 2750:
GOSUB 280
230   GOTO 230  'clean halt
240   END 'of main routine
250 '_____
260 '
```

```
270 'module:  calculate and store vertex coordinates
280  RESTORE 1360  'beginning of database
290  FOR T=0 TO 7 STEP 1:READ X,Y,Z:GOSUB 790:B1(T,0)=X:B1(T
,1)=Y:B1(T,2)=Z:B2(T,0)=SX:B2(T,1)=SY:NEXT T  'load vertex v
iew coordinates into array B1, load vertex display coordinat
es into array B2
300  FOR T=0 TO 5 STEP 1:READ X,Y,Z:GOSUB 790:B3(T,0)=SX:B3(
T,1)=SY:NEXT T  'load area fill origin display coordinates i
nto array B3
310 '_____
320 '
330 'module:  draw 6 surfaces of carton
340 'surface 0 routine
350  X1=B1(7,0):Y1=B1(7,1):Z1=B1(7,2):X2=B1(0,0):Y2=B1(0,1):
Z2=B1(0,2):X3=B1(3,0):Y3=B1(3,1):Z3=B1(3,2):GOSUB 1440:IF SP
>0 THEN 420  'retrieve view coordinates, jump to plane equat
ion routine, test if surface hidden
360  SX1=B2(7,0):SY1=B2(7,1):SX2=B2(0,0):SY2=B2(0,1):SX3=B2(
3,0):SY3=B2(3,1):SX4=B2(6,0):SY4=B2(6,1):SX5=B3(0,0):SY5=B3(
0,1):GOSUB 1700  'assign display coordinates and jump to sol
id surface modeling routine
370  GOSUB 1480:PAINT (SX5,SY5),A$,C3:GOSUB 1650  'jump to c
omputer-controlled shading routine, apply halftoning area fi
ll, jump to computer-controlled dithering routine
380  E=1:GOSUB 2860  'jump to generic surface mapping routin
e
390 '_____
400 '
410 'surface 1 routine
420  X1=B1(6,0):Y1=B1(6,1):Z1=B1(6,2):X2=B1(5,0):Y2=B1(5,1):
Z2=B1(5,2):X3=B1(4,0):Y3=B1(4,1):Z3=B1(4,2):GOSUB 1440:IF SP
>0 THEN 490
430  SX1=B2(6,0):SY1=B2(6,1):SX2=B2(5,0):SY2=B2(5,1):SX3=B2(
4,0):SY3=B2(4,1):SX4=B2(7,0):SY4=B2(7,1):SX5=B3(1,0):SY5=B3(
1,1):GOSUB 1700
440  GOSUB 1480:PAINT (SX5,SY5),A$,C3:GOSUB 1650
450  GOSUB 3170  'jump to specialized surface mapping routin
e
460 '_____
470 '
480 'surface 2 routine
490  X1=B1(3,0):Y1=B1(3,1):Z1=B1(3,2):X2=B1(2,0):Y2=B1(2,1):
Z2=B1(2,2):X3=B1(5,0):Y3=B1(5,1):Z3=B1(5,2):GOSUB 1440:IF SP
>0 THEN 560
500  SX1=B2(3,0):SY1=B2(3,1):SX2=B2(2,0):SY2=B2(2,1):SX3=B2(
5,0):SY3=B2(5,1):SX4=B2(6,0):SY4=B2(6,1):SX5=B3(2,0):SY5=B3(
2,1):GOSUB 1700
510  GOSUB 1480:PAINT (SX5,SY5),A$,C3:GOSUB 1650
```

```
520  E=2:GOSUB 2860  'jump to generic surface mapping routin
e
530  '_____
540  '
550  'surface 3 routine
560  X1=B1(0,0):Y1=B1(0,1):Z1=B1(0,2):X2=B1(1,0):Y2=B1(1,1):
Z2=B1(1,2):X3=B1(2,0):Y3=B1(2,1):Z3=B1(2,2):GOSUB 1440:IF SP
>0 THEN 630
570  SX1=B2(0,0):SY1=B2(0,1):SX2=B2(1,0):SY2=B2(1,1):SX3=B2(
2,0):SY3=B2(2,1):SX4=B2(3,0):SY4=B2(3,1):SX5=B3(3,0):SY5=B3(
3,1):GOSUB 1700
580  GOSUB 1480:PAINT (SX5,SY5),A$,C3:GOSUB 1650
590  GOSUB 3230  'jump to specialized surface mapping routin
e
600  '_____
610  '
620  'surface 4 routine
630  X1=B1(7,0):Y1=B1(7,1):Z1=B1(7,2):X2=B1(4,0):Y2=B1(4,1):
Z2=B1(4,2):X3=B1(1,0):Y3=B1(1,1):Z3=B1(1,2):GOSUB 1440:IF SP
>0 THEN 700
640  SX1=B2(7,0):SY1=B2(7,1):SX2=B2(4,0):SY2=B2(4,1):SX3=B2(
1,0):SY3=B2(1,1):SX4=B2(0,0):SY4=B2(0,1):SX5=B3(4,0):SY5=B3(
4,1):GOSUB 1700
650  GOSUB 1480:PAINT (SX5,SY5),A$,C3:GOSUB 1650
660  E=3:GOSUB 2860  'jump to generic surface mapping routin
e
670  '_____
680  '
690  'surface 5 routine
700  X1=B1(1,0):Y1=B1(1,1):Z1=B1(1,2):X2=B1(4,0):Y2=B1(4,1):
Z2=B1(4,2):X3=B1(5,0):Y3=B1(5,1):Z3=B1(5,2):GOSUB 1440:IF SP
>0 THEN 740
710  SX1=B2(1,0):SY1=B2(1,1):SX2=B2(4,0):SY2=B2(4,1):SX3=B2(
5,0):SY3=B2(5,1):SX4=B2(2,0):SY4=B2(2,1):SX5=B3(5,0):SY5=B3(
5,1):GOSUB 1700
720  GOSUB 1480:PAINT (SX5,SY5),A$,C3:GOSUB 1650
730  E=4:GOSUB 2860  'jump to generic surface mapping routin
e
740  SOUND 550,.7  'model is complete
750  RETURN
760  '_____
770  '
780  'module:  perspective calculations for Cartesian world c
oordinates
790  X=(-1)*X:XA=CR1*X-SR1*Z:ZA=SR1*X+CR1*Z:X=CR2*XA+SR2*Y:Y
A=CR2*Y-SR2*XA:Z=CR3*ZA-SR3*YA:Y=SR3*ZA+CR3*YA:X=X+MX:Y=Y+MY
:Z=Z+MZ:SX=D*X/Z:SY=D*Y/Z:RETURN
800  '_____
```

```
810 '
820 'module:   return to BASIC interpreter
830   CLS:WINDOW:SCREEN 0,0,0,0:WIDTH 80:COLOR 7,0,0:CLS:LOCA
TE 1,1,1:END
840 '_____
850 '
860 'module:   UNIVERSAL
870 'This routine configures the program for the hardware/so
ftware being used.
880   KEY OFF:CLS:ON ERROR GOTO 960   'trap if not Enhanced Di
splay + EGA
890   SCREEN 9,,0,0:COLOR 7,0:PALETTE 1,8:PALETTE 2,1:PALETTE
 3,9:PALETTE 4,11:PALETTE 5,7:PALETTE 6,37:PALETTE 7,7:PALET
TE 8,56:PALETTE 9,34:PALETTE 10,20:PALETTE 11,5:PALETTE 12,4
4:PALETTE 13,46:PALETTE 14,55:PALETTE 15,63
900   C0=0:C1=12:C2=9:C3=7:LOCATE 1,1:PRINT "ED-EGA 640x350 1
6-color mode"
910   V6=15   'illumination range 0 to 15
920   GOSUB 1740   'assign bit tiling codes for EGA
930   DEFINT G:G=1   'set flag for ED-EGA
940   GOSUB 2790   'set viewports for 640x350 mode
950   GOTO 1180   'jump to screen coordinates set-up
960   RESUME 970
970   ON ERROR GOTO 1040   'trap if not Color Display + EGA
980   SCREEN 8,,0,0:COLOR 7,0:PALETTE 1,0:PALETTE 2,1:PALETTE
 3,9:PALETTE 4,7:PALETTE 8,4:PALETTE 9,2:C0=0:C1=8:C2=9:C3=7
:LOCATE 1,1:PRINT "CD-EGA 640x200 16-color mode"
990   V6=14   'illumination range 0 to 14
1000   GOSUB 1740   'assign shading codes for EGA
1010   DEFINT G:G=2   'set flag for CD-EGA
1020   GOSUB 2800   'set viewports for 640x200 mode
1030   GOTO 1180   'jump to screen coordinates set-up
1040   RESUME 1050
1050   ON ERROR GOTO 1120   'trap if not PCjr
1060   CLEAR,,,32768!:SCREEN 6,0,0,0:COLOR 3,0:PALETTE 1,8:C0
=0:C1=1:C2=2:C3=3:LOCATE 1,1:PRINT "PCjr 640x200 4-color mod
e"
1070   V6=14   'illumination range 0 to 14
1080   GOSUB 1940   'assign shading codes for PCjr
1090   DEFINT G:G=3   'set flag for CD-JR
1100   GOSUB 2800   'set viewports for PCjr 640x200 mode
1110   GOTO 1180   'jump to screen coordinates set-up
1120   RESUME 1130
1130   SCREEN 1,0:COLOR 0,1:C0=0:C1=1:C2=2:C3=3:LOCATE 1,1:PR
INT "CGA 320x200 4-color mode"
1140   V6=14   'illumination range 0 to 14
1150   GOSUB 1940   'assign shading codes for CGA
1160   DEFINT G:G=4   'set flag for CD-CGA
```

```
1170    GOSUB 2810   'set viewports for CGA 320x200 mode
1180    ON ERROR GOTO 0   'disable error trapping override
1190    WINDOW SCREEN (-399,-299)-(400,300)
1200    ON KEY (2) GOSUB 830:KEY (2) ON   'F2 key to exit progr
am
1210    GOTO 150   'return to main program
1220 '_____
1230 '
1240 'module:   assign variables
1250    D=1200:R1=5.18319:R2=0:R3=5.79778:MX=0:MY=0:MZ=-230   '
3D parameters
1260    DIM B1 (7,2)   '8 sets of XYZ view coordinates
1270    DIM B2 (7,1)   '8 sets of SX,SY display coordinates
1280    DIM B3 (5,1)   '6 sets of SX,SY fill coordinates
1290    XL=0:YL=.4472136:ZL=.8944272   'xyz location of light s
ource
1300    SR1=SIN(R1):CR1=COS(R1):SR2=SIN(R2):CR2=COS(R2):SR3=SI
N(R3):CR3=COS(R3)
1310    DEFINT E:E=0   'flag for surface mapping
1320    RETURN
1330 '_____
1340 '
1350 'module:   8 sets of XYZ world coordinates for vertices
1360    DATA   30,-30,45,   30,30,45,   -30,30,45,   -30,-30,45,
30,30,-45,   -30,30,-45,   -30,-30,-45,   30,-30,-45
1370 '_____
1380 '
1390 'module:   6 sets of XYZ world coordinates for area fill

1400    DATA   0,-30,0,   0,0,-45,   -30,0,0,   0,0,45,   30,0,0,
0,30,0
1410 '_____
1420 '
1430 'module:   plane equation method of hidden surface remov
al
1440    SP1=X1*(Y2*Z3-Y3*Z2):SP1=(-1)*SP1:SP2=X2*(Y3*Z1-Y1*Z3)
:SP3=X3*(Y1*Z2-Y2*Z1):SP=SP1-SP2-SP3:RETURN
1450 '_____
1460 '
1470 'module:   computer-controlled shading routine
1480    XU=X2-X1:YU=Y2-Y1:ZU=Z2-Z1   'calculate vector from ver
tex 1 to vertex 2
1490    XV=X3-X1:YV=Y3-Y1:ZV=Z3-Z1   'calculate vector from ver
tex 1 to vertex 3
1500    XN=(YU*ZV)-(ZU*YV):YN=(ZU*XV)-(XU*ZV):ZN=(XU*YV)-(YU*X
V)   'calculate surface perpendicular vector
1510    YN=YN*(-1):ZN=ZN*(-1)   'convert vector to cartesian sy
stem
```

```
1520 'sub-module:  convert surface perpendicular vector to u
nit vector
1530   V1=(XN*XN)+(YN*YN)+(ZN*ZN):V2=SQR(V1)   'magnitude of s
urface perpendicular vector
1540   V3=1/V2 'ratio of magnitude to unit vector magnitude
1550   XW=V3*XN:YW=V3*YN:ZW=V3*ZN  'XYZ components of surface
 perpendicular unit vector
1560 'sub-module:  calculate illumination factor for surface
 when angle of incidence is 45 degrees elevation and 135 deg
rees yaw
1570   V4=(XW*XL)+(YW*YL)+(ZW*ZL)  'illumination factor 0 to
1
1580   V4=V4*V6:V4=CINT(V4)  'set illumination range
1590   V5=V4+1 'illumination factor from base 1
1600   ON G GOSUB 2120, 2330, 2540, 2540  'jump to device-dep
endent shading routine
1610   RETURN
1620 '_____
1630 '
1640 'module:  computer-controlled dithering routine
1650   LINE (SX1,SY1)-(SX2,SY2),C4:LINE (SX1,SY1)-(SX2,SY2),C
5,,C6:LINE (SX2,SY2)-(SX3,SY3),C4:LINE (SX2,SY2)-(SX3,SY3),C
5,,C6:LINE (SX3,SY3)-(SX4,SY4),C4:LINE (SX3,SY3)-(SX4,SY4),C
5,,C6
1660   LINE (SX4,SY4)-(SX1,SY1),C4:LINE (SX4,SY4)-(SX1,SY1),C
5,,C6:RETURN
1670 '_____
1680 '
1690 'module:  solid surface modeling of 4-sided polygon
1700   LINE (SX1,SY1)-(SX2,SY2),C2:LINE-(SX3,SY3),C2:LINE-(SX
4,SY4),C2:LINE-(SX1,SY1),C2:PAINT (SX5,SY5),C2,C2:LINE (SX1,
SY1)-(SX2,SY2),C3:LINE-(SX3,SY3),C3:LINE-(SX4,SY4),C3:LINE-(
SX1,SY1),C3:PAINT (SX5,SY5),C0,C3:RETURN
1710 '_____
1720 '
1730 'module:  assign shading codes for EGA
1740   A1$=CHR$(&HDF)+CHR$(&H20)+CHR$(&H0)+CHR$(&H0)+CHR$(&HF
D)+CHR$(&H2)+CHR$(&H0)+CHR$(&H0)+CHR$(&H7F)+CHR$(&H80)+CHR$(
&H0)+CHR$(&H0)+CHR$(&HF7)+CHR$(&H8)+CHR$(&H0)+CHR$(&H0)
1750   A2$=CHR$(&HBB)+CHR$(&H44)+CHR$(&H0)+CHR$(&H0)+CHR$(&HE
E)+CHR$(&H11)+CHR$(&H0)+CHR$(&H0)
1760   A3$=CHR$(&HAA)+CHR$(&H55)+CHR$(&H0)+CHR$(&H0)+CHR$(&H5
5)+CHR$(&HAA)+CHR$(&H0)+CHR$(&H0)
1770   A4$=CHR$(&H44)+CHR$(&HBB)+CHR$(&H0)+CHR$(&H0)+CHR$(&H1
1)+CHR$(&HEE)+CHR$(&H0)+CHR$(&H0)
1780   A5$=CHR$(&H20)+CHR$(&HFF)+CHR$(&H0)+CHR$(&H0)+CHR$(&H2
)+CHR$(&HFF)+CHR$(&H0)+CHR$(&H0)+CHR$(&H80)+CHR$(&HFF)+CHR$(
&H0)+CHR$(&H0)+CHR$(&H8)+CHR$(&HFF)+CHR$(&H0)+CHR$(&H0)
```

```
1790    A6$=CHR$(&H44)+CHR$(&HFF)+CHR$(&HO)+CHR$(&HO)+CHR$(&H1
1)+CHR$(&HFF)+CHR$(&HO)+CHR$(&HO)
1800    A7$=CHR$(&H55)+CHR$(&HFF)+CHR$(&HO)+CHR$(&HO)+CHR$(&HA
A)+CHR$(&HFF)+CHR$(&HO)+CHR$(&HO)
1810    A8$=CHR$(&HBB)+CHR$(&HFF)+CHR$(&HO)+CHR$(&HO)+CHR$(&HE
E)+CHR$(&HFF)+CHR$(&HO)+CHR$(&HO)
1820    A9$=CHR$(&HDF)+CHR$(&HDF)+CHR$(&H20)+CHR$(&HO)+CHR$(&H
FD)+CHR$(&HFD)+CHR$(&H2)+CHR$(&HO)+CHR$(&H7F)+CHR$(&H7F)+CHR
$(&H80)+CHR$(&HO)+CHR$(&HF7)+CHR$(&HF7)+CHR$(&H8)+CHR$(&HO)
1830    A10$=CHR$(&HBB)+CHR$(&HBB)+CHR$(&H44)+CHR$(&HO)+CHR$(&
HEE)+CHR$(&HEE)+CHR$(&H11)+CHR$(&HO)
1840    A11$=CHR$(&HAA)+CHR$(&HAA)+CHR$(&H55)+CHR$(&HO)+CHR$(&
H55)+CHR$(&H55)+CHR$(&HAA)+CHR$(&HO)
1850    A12$=CHR$(&H44)+CHR$(&H44)+CHR$(&HBB)+CHR$(&HO)+CHR$(&
H11)+CHR$(&H11)+CHR$(&HEE)+CHR$(&HO)
1860    A13$=CHR$(&H20)+CHR$(&HO)+CHR$(&HFF)+CHR$(&HO)+CHR$(&H
2)+CHR$(&HO)+CHR$(&HFF)+CHR$(&HO)+CHR$(&H80)+CHR$(&HO)+CHR$(
&HFF)+CHR$(&HO)+CHR$(&H8)+CHR$(&HO)+CHR$(&HFF)+CHR$(&HO)
1870    A14$=CHR$(&H44)+CHR$(&HO)+CHR$(&HFF)+CHR$(&HO)+CHR$(&H
11)+CHR$(&HO)+CHR$(&HFF)+CHR$(&HO)
1880    A15$=CHR$(&H55)+CHR$(&HO)+CHR$(&HFF)+CHR$(&HO)+CHR$(&H
AA)+CHR$(&HO)+CHR$(&HFF)+CHR$(&HO)
1890    A16$=CHR$(&HBB)+CHR$(&HO)+CHR$(&HFF)+CHR$(&HO)+CHR$(&H
EE)+CHR$(&HO)+CHR$(&HFF)+CHR$(&HO)
1900    RETURN
1910    '_____
1920    '
1930    'module:   assign shading codes for CGA and/or PCjr
1940    A1$=CHR$(&H40)+CHR$(&HO)+CHR$(&H4)+CHR$(&HO)
1950    A2$=CHR$(&H40)+CHR$(&H4)+CHR$(&H40)+CHR$(&H4)
1960    A3$=CHR$(&H44)+CHR$(&H10)+CHR$(&H11)+CHR$(&H1)+CHR$(&H
44)+CHR$(&H4)+CHR$(&H11)+CHR$(&H40)
1970    A4$=CHR$(&H44)+CHR$(&H11)+CHR$(&H44)+CHR$(&H11)
1980    A5$=CHR$(&H11)+CHR$(&H45)+CHR$(&H44)+CHR$(&H54)+CHR$(&
H11)+CHR$(&H51)+CHR$(&H44)+CHR$(&H15)
1990    A6$=CHR$(&H15)+CHR$(&H51)+CHR$(&H15)+CHR$(&H51)
2000    A7$=CHR$(&H15)+CHR$(&H55)+CHR$(&H51)+CHR$(&H55)
2010    A9$=CHR$(&HD5)+CHR$(&H55)+CHR$(&H5D)+CHR$(&H55)
2020    A10$=CHR$(&HD5)+CHR$(&H5D)+CHR$(&HD5)+CHR$(&H5D)
2030    A12$=CHR$(&HDD)+CHR$(&H75)+CHR$(&H77)+CHR$(&H57)+CHR$(
&HDD)+CHR$(&H5D)+CHR$(&H77)+CHR$(&HD5)
2040    A13$=CHR$(&HDD)+CHR$(&H77)+CHR$(&HDD)+CHR$(&H77)
2050    A14$=CHR$(&H77)+CHR$(&HDF)+CHR$(&HDD)+CHR$(&HFD)+CHR$(
&H77)+CHR$(&HF7)+CHR$(&HDD)+CHR$(&H7F)
2060    A15$=CHR$(&H7F)+CHR$(&HF7)+CHR$(&H7F)+CHR$(&HF7)
2070    A16$=CHR$(&H7F)+CHR$(&HFF)+CHR$(&HF7)+CHR$(&HFF)
2080    RETURN
2090    '_____
```

```
2100 '
2110 'shading routine for ED-EGA 640x350 mode
2120   IF V5<1 THEN GOTO 2140  'if light source is behind sur
face
2130   ON V5 GOTO 2140, 2150, 2160, 2170, 2180, 2190, 2200, 2
210, 2220, 2230, 2240, 2250, 2260, 2270, 2280, 2290
2140   A$=CHR$(&HFF)+CHR$(&HO)+CHR$(&HO)+CHR$(&HO):C4=1:C5=1:
C6=&HFFFF:RETURN
2150   A$=A1$:C4=1:C5=2:C6=&H808:RETURN
2160   A$=A2$:C4=1:C5=2:C6=&H4444:RETURN
2170   A$=CHR$(&HO)+CHR$(&HFF)+CHR$(&HO)+CHR$(&HO):C4=2:C5=2:
C6=&HFFFF:RETURN
2180   A$=A5$:C4=2:C5=3:C6=&H808:RETURN
2190   A$=A6$:C4=2:C5=3:C6=&H4444:RETURN
2200   A$=A7$:C4=2:C5=3:C6=&HAAAA:RETURN
2210   A$=A8$:C4=3:C5=2:C6=&H4444:RETURN
2220   A$=CHR$(&HFF)+CHR$(&HFF)+CHR$(&HO)+CHR$(&HO):C4=3:C5=3
:C6=&HFFFF:RETURN
2230   A$=A10$:C4=3:C5=4:C6=&H4444:RETURN
2240   A$=A11$:C4=3:C5=4:C6=&HAAAA:RETURN
2250   A$=A12$:C4=4:C5=3:C6=&H4444:RETURN
2260   A$=CHR$(&HO)+CHR$(&HO)+CHR$(&HFF)+CHR$(&HO):C4=4:C5=4:
C6=&HFFFF:RETURN
2270   A$=A13$:C4=4:C5=5:C6=&H808:RETURN
2280   A$=A14$:C4=4:C5=5:C6=&H4444:RETURN
2290   A$=A15$:C4=4:C5=5:C6=&HAAAA:RETURN
2300 '_____
2310 '
2320 'shading routine for CD-EGA 640x200 mode
2330   IF V5<1 THEN GOTO 2360  'if light source is behind sur
face
2340   ON V5 GOTO 2360, 2370, 2380, 2390, 2400, 2410, 2420, 2
430, 2440, 2450, 2460, 2470, 2480, 2490, 2500
2350   A$=CHR$(&HFF)+CHR$(&HO)+CHR$(&HO)+CHR$(&HO):C4=1:C5=1:
C6=&HFFFF:RETURN  'solid black is unused
2360   A$=A1$:C4=1:C5=2:C6=&H808:RETURN
2370   A$=A2$:C4=1:C5=2:C6=&H4444:RETURN
2380   A$=A3$:C4=1:C5=2:C6=&HAAAA:RETURN
2390   A$=A4$:C4=2:C5=1:C6=&H4444:RETURN
2400   A$=CHR$(&HO)+CHR$(&HFF)+CHR$(&HO)+CHR$(&HO):C4=2:C5=2:
C6=&HFFFF:RETURN
2410   A$=A5$:C4=2:C5=3:C6=&H808:RETURN
2420   A$=A6$:C4=2:C5=3:C6=&H4444:RETURN
2430   A$=A7$:C4=2:C5=3:C6=&HAAAA:RETURN
2440   A$=A8$:C4=3:C5=2:C6=&H4444:RETURN
2450   A$=CHR$(&HFF)+CHR$(&HFF)+CHR$(&HO)+CHR$(&HO):C4=3:C5=3
:C6=&HFFFF:RETURN
2460   A$=A9$:C4=3:C5=4:C6=&H8080:RETURN
```

```
2470   A$=A10$:C4=3:C5=4:C6=&H4444:RETURN
2480   A$=A11$:C4=3:C5=4:C6=&HAAAA:RETURN
2490   A$=A12$:C4=4:C5=3:C6=&H4444:RETURN
2500   A$=CHR$(&H0)+CHR$(&H0)+CHR$(&HFF)+CHR$(&H0):C4=4:C5=4:
C6=&HFFFF:RETURN
2510 '_____
2520 '
2530 'shading routine for CD-CGA 320x200 mode and CD-JR 640x
200 mode
2540   IF V5<1 THEN GOTO 2570   'if light source is behind sur
face
2550   ON V5 GOTO 2570, 2580, 2590, 2600, 2610, 2620, 2630, 2
640, 2650, 2660, 2670, 2680, 2690, 2700, 2710
2560   A$=CHR$(&H0):C4=0:C5=0:C6=&HFFFF:RETURN   'solid black
-- unused
2570   A$=A1$:C4=0:C5=1:C6=&H2108:RETURN
2580   A$=A2$:C4=0:C5=1:C6=&H4444:RETURN
2590   A$=A4$:C4=0:C5=1:C6=&HAAAA:RETURN
2600   A$=A5$:C4=1:C5=0:C6=&H4924:RETURN
2610   A$=A6$:C4=1:C5=0:C6=&H4444:RETURN
2620   A$=A7$:C4=1:C5=0:C6=&H808:RETURN
2630   A$=CHR$(&H55):C4=1:C5=1:C6=&HFFFF:RETURN
2640   A$=A9$:C4=1:C5=3:C6=&H808:RETURN
2650   A$=A10$:C4=1:C5=3:C6=&H4444:RETURN
2660   A$=A12$:C4=1:C5=3:C6=&H4924:RETURN
2670   A$=A13$:C4=1:C5=3:C6=&HAAAA:RETURN
2680   A$=A14$:C4=3:C5=1:C6=&H4924:RETURN
2690   A$=A15$:C4=3:C5=1:C6=&H4444:RETURN
2700   A$=A16$:C4=3:C5=1:C6=&H808:RETURN
2710   A$=CHR$(&HFF):C4=3:C5=3:C6=&HFFFF:RETURN
2720 '_____
2730 '
2740 'module:   re-assign sine and cosine rotation matrices
2750   SR1=SIN(R1):CR1=COS(R1):SR2=SIN(R2):CR2=COS(R2):SR3=SI
N(R3):CR3=COS(R3):RETURN
2760 '_____
2770 '
2780 'module:    viewport parameters for 640x350, 640x200, 320
x200
2790   W1=1:W2=319:W3=152:W4=470:W5=320:W6=639:W7=1:W8=174:W9
=175:W10=349:RETURN
2800   W1=1:W2=319:W3=152:W4=470:W5=320:W6=639:W7=1:W8=99:W9=
100:W10=199:RETURN
2810   W1=1:W2=159:W3=76:W4=235:W5=160:W6=319:W7=1:W8=99:W9=1
00:W10=199:RETURN
2820 '_____
2830 '
2840 'module:   surface mapping of design onto carton
```

```
2850 'this routine is used to map the same database coordina
tes onto 4 different sides of the carton, by calling a swap
subroutine which swaps the x,y,z coordinates to match the or
ientation of the surface being mapped.
2860   RESTORE 2960:READ Z,Y:X=30:GOSUB 3080:GOSUB 790:PSET (
SX,SY),CO:FOR T=1 TO 4 STEP 1:READ Z,Y:X=30:GOSUB 3080:GOSUB
 790:LINE-(SX,SY),CO:NEXT T:READ Z,Y:X=30:GOSUB 3080:GOSUB 7
90:PAINT (SX,SY),CO,CO  'main graphic on side
2870   RESTORE 2970:FOR T=1 TO 2 STEP 1:READ Z,Y:X=30:GOSUB 3
080:GOSUB 790:PSET (SX,SY),CO:READ Z,Y:X=30:GOSUB 3080:GOSUB
 790:LINE-(SX,SY),CO:NEXT T  'stripes on side
2880   RESTORE 2980:READ Z,Y:X=30:GOSUB 3080:GOSUB 790:PSET (
SX,SY),C3:FOR T=1 TO 5 STEP 1:READ Z,Y:X=30:GOSUB 3080:GOSUB
 790:LINE-(SX,SY),C3:NEXT T  'Z
2890   RESTORE 2990:FOR T=1 TO 3 STEP 1:READ Z,Y:X=30:GOSUB 3
080:GOSUB 790:PSET (SX,SY),C3:READ Z,Y:X=30:GOSUB 3080:GOSUB
 790:LINE-(SX,SY),C3:NEXT T  'I
2900   RESTORE 3000:READ Z,Y:X=30:GOSUB 3080:GOSUB 790:PSET (
SX,SY),C3:FOR T=1 TO 4 STEP 1:READ Z,Y:X=30:GOSUB 3080:GOSUB
 790:LINE-(SX,SY),C3:NEXT T  'P
2910 '_____
2920 '
2930 'module:  database for surface-mapped graphics
2940 'the first two lines in the database contain two-dimens
ional coordinates for the graphics on a side of the carton;
 the next three lines contain two-dimensional coordinates fo
r the alphanumerics on a side of the carton.
2950 'the drawing code calls a swap routine to swap these ge
neric coordinates to match the orientation of the surface be
ing drawn.
2960   DATA  45,-15,  45,15,  -45,15,  -45,-15,  45,-15,  0,0

2970   DATA  45,20,  -45,20,  45,-20,  -45,-20
2980   DATA  20,8,  20,10,  7,10,  20,-10,  7,-10,  7,-8
2990   DATA  3,10,  -1,10,  3,-10,  -1,-10,  1,10,  1,-10
3000   DATA  -6,-10,  -6,10,  -16,10,  -16,0,  -6,0
3010   DATA  30,-15,  30,15,  -30,15,  -30,-15,  30,-15,  0,0

3020   DATA  30,20,  -30,20,  30,-20,  -30,-20
3030   DATA  -30,-15,  -30,15,  30,15,  30,-15,  -30,-15,  0,
0
3040   DATA  -30,20,  30,20,  -30,-20,  30,-20
3050 '_____
3060 '
3070 'module:  swap coordinates for surface mapping
3080   ON E GOTO 3090,3100,3110,3120
3090   X=Y:Y=-30:RETURN  'swap for surface 0 (bottom)
3100   Z=Z*(-1):X=-30:RETURN  'swap for surface 2
```

```
3110    RETURN  'default values for surface 4
3120    X=Y*(-1):Y=30:RETURN   'swap for surface 5
3130 '_____
3140 '
3150 'module:  mapping surface 1 (end)
3160 'this is a specialized routine to draw an end of the ca
rton.
3170    RESTORE 3010:READ X,Y:Z=-45:GOSUB 790:PSET (SX,SY),CO:
FOR T=1 TO 4 STEP 1:READ X,Y:Z=-45:GOSUB 790:LINE-(SX,SY),CO
:NEXT T:READ X,Y:Z=-45:GOSUB 790:PAINT (SX,SY),CO,CO
3180    RESTORE 3020:FOR T=1 TO 2 STEP 1:READ X,Y:Z=-45:GOSUB
790:PSET (SX,SY),CO:READ X,Y:Z=-45:GOSUB 790:LINE-(SX,SY),CO
:NEXT T:RETURN
3190 '_____
3200 '
3210 'module:  mapping surface 3 (end)
3220 'this is a specialized routine to draw an end of the ca
rton.
3230    RESTORE 3030:READ X,Y:Z=45:GOSUB 790:PSET (SX,SY),CO:F
OR T=1 TO 4 STEP 1:READ X,Y:Z=45:GOSUB 790:LINE-(SX,SY),CO:N
EXT T:READ X,Y:Z=45:GOSUB 790:PAINT (SX,SY),CO,CO
3240    RESTORE 3040:FOR T=1 TO 2 STEP 1:READ X,Y:Z=45:GOSUB 7
90:PSET (SX,SY),CO:READ X,Y:Z=45:GOSUB 790:LINE-(SX,SY),CO:N
EXT T:RETURN
3250 '_____
3260 '
3270    END 'of program code
```

Line 2860 retrieves the appropriate design coordinates from the database and then calls the swapping routine at line 3080. Line 3080 uses an ON...GOTO statement to jump to the appropriate swapping algorithm. When $E = 2$ program control jumps to line 3100. Here the z-coordinate is negated, because the database contains coordinates for the graphic design on the opposite side of the carton. X is held steady at $-30$, because the surface being mapped falls in a plane where $X = -30$; only the z- and y-coordinates are permitted to vary while the graphic design is being drawn.

When program control returns to line 2860, the standard perspective formulas at line 790 are called. This process is repeated until all the graphics have been plotted onto the surface.

Because the surface mapping routine is predicated on the visibility of the surface, the hidden surface routine effectively disarms the mapping routine when a surface is round to be hidden. You can, therefore, view the package design from any angle whatsoever and the appropriate graphic designs will be drawn as required. The alphanumerics appear on all four sides. The two ends of the carton contain the stripe graphics, but no alphanumerics. Each end is drawn by a dedicated subroutine, located at lines 3150 and 3210. Only the routine which draws sides is capable of making intelligent decisions concerning surface mapping based upon orientation.

The colors chosen for this demonstration program have been selected for their ability to preserve the illusion of shading. The black and white design graphics look properly illuminated no matter what level of shading has been applied to a surface by the microcomputer. If other colors of graphic design are required, you would have to develop hex shading codes to support those other colors. A 16-color mode, such as that found on the EGA, would be necessary.

## Color/Graphics Adapter

If you are using a Color/Graphics Adapter, the demonstration program will execute in the $320 \times 200$ 4-color mode. You will also notice that a few of the smaller surfaces will suffer from paint failure. As discussed earlier in the book, you can overcome this hardware limitation by making the model larger.

To disable the viewports and instruct your personal computer to generate a single, larger model, make the following changes.

Change line 190 to read: **R1 = 4.36141:GOSUB 280**

Delete lines 200 through 220.

## SUMMARY

In this chapter you learned how to create two package design applications: a cylindrical soft drink container and a rectangular film carton.

The next chapter provides an interactive CAD graphics editor which you can use to create complex designs. It features free-form curves, an undo feature, and the ability to save your drawings to diskette for later editing.

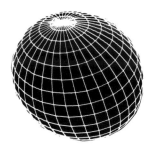

# 25

# *Computer-Aided Design*

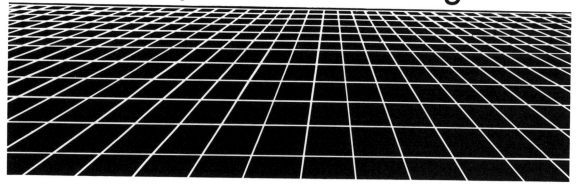

A number of specific keyboard routines and control algorithms are required in order to create a graphics program which is interactive at the end-user level. Mechanisms must be in place which permit the user to control the graphics on the display screen by simple keystrokes. Methods for undoing graphics are also helpful. Routines which enable the image to be saved on diskette and later retrieved are useful.

### DEMONSTRATION: CAD GRAPHICS EDITOR

Figure 25-1 shows the screen output produced by the demonstration program in Fig. 25-3. To run this program from the companion diskette, type **LOAD "A-41.BAS",R**.

The program is a fully-interactive 2D graphics editor. The photograph in Fig. 25-2 illustrates a typical drawing which can be produced in a few minutes using the graphics editor. Programs similar to this prototype are useful for computer-aided-design (CAD), computer-aided-engineering (CAE), and computer-assisted-manufacturing (CAM).

This program runs in the 640 × 200 16-color mode on the EGA, the 640 × 200 4-color mode on the PCjr

and Tandy, and the 640 × 200 2-color mode on the Color/Graphics Adapter.

### PROGRAM START-UP

Line 140 sends program control to the configuration routine at line 770. This is the standard ON ERROR sequence used for all demonstration programs in the book, except that no WINDOW SCREEN statement is used.

When control returns to the main routine, line 150 sends program control to the variable assigning routine at line 900. Line 910 simply initializes all coordinate variables to zero. Line 920 reserves space in memory for a large graphic array (A2) which will be used to save the image created by the user. Line 920 also reserves space for a smaller array (A1) which is the reticle cursor for the editor. Line 930 defines variable U as an integer. This variable is used to locate the graphic array when it is to be written to diskette as an image file.

Line 950 establishes minimum and maximum values for the reticle cursor of the graphics editor. Because the recticle is actually a small graphic array, an

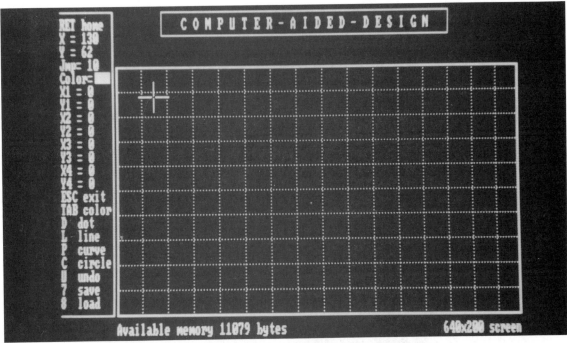

Fig. 25-1. The blank drawing grid produced by the demonstration program in Fig. 25-3.

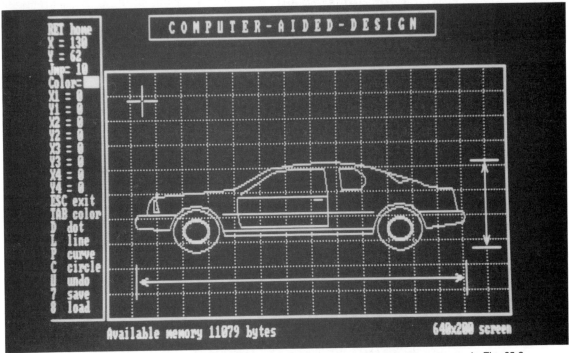

Fig. 25-2. A typical engineering drawing which can be created using the demonstration program in Fig. 25-3.

Fig. 25-3. Full-function 2D graphics editor with lines, free-form curves, circles, undo function, and diskette image files.

```
100 'Program A-41.BAS    Computer-Aided Design
110 'Interactive CAD Editor:  Use keyboard to create technic
al drawings with free-form curves, circles, lines.  Save dra
wings on diskette as binary image files.  Load drawings into
 memory from diskette.
120 '_____
130 '
140   GOTO 770  'configure system
150   GOSUB 900 'assign scalar data
160 '_____
170 '
180 'module:  create crosshair reticle cursor
190   SX=100:SY=100:LINE (SX-20,SY)-(SX-3,SY),C2:LINE (SX+3,S
Y)-(SX+20,SY),C2:LINE (SX,SY-9)-(SX,SY-1),C2:LINE (SX,SY+1)-
(SX,SY+9),C2:GET (SX-20,SY-9)-(SX+20,SY+9),A1  'crosshair re
ticle for 640x200 mode
200   CLS
210 '_____
220 '
230 'module:  create dot mesh
240   LOCATE 25,11:PRINT "Available memory"FRE(0)"bytes":LOCA
TE 25,65:PRINT "640x200 screen"
250   LOCATE 2,22:PRINT "C O M P U T E R - A I D E D - D E S
I G N":LINE (141,4)-(522,18),C3,B
260   FOR SY=37 TO 187 STEP 15:LINE (80,SY)-(623,SY),C3,,&H88
88:NEXT SY:FOR SX=80 TO 623 STEP 34:LINE (SX,37)-(SX,187),C3
,,&HAAAA:NEXT SX
270   LINE (80,37)-(623,187),C1,B
280   SX=110:SY=46:PUT (SX,SY),A1,XOR  'move reticle home
290 '_____
300 '
310 'module:  create menu display
320   LOCATE 3,1:PRINT "X ="CINT(SX+20):LOCATE 4,1:PRINT "Y =
"CINT(SY+16):LOCATE 5,1:PRINT "Jmp="CINT(J)
330   LOCATE 7,1:PRINT "X1 ="CINT(X1):LOCATE 8,1:PRINT "Y1 ="
CINT(Y1):LOCATE 9,1:PRINT "X2 ="CINT(X2):LOCATE 10,1:PRINT "
Y2 ="CINT(Y2)
340   LOCATE 11,1:PRINT "X3 ="CINT(X3):LOCATE 12,1:PRINT "Y3
="CINT(Y3):LOCATE 13,1:PRINT "X4 ="CINT(X4):LOCATE 14,1:PRIN
T "Y4 ="CINT(Y4)
350   LOCATE 2,1:PRINT "RET home":LOCATE 15,1:PRINT "ESC exit
":LOCATE 21,1:PRINT "U  undo":LOCATE 18,1:PRINT "L  line":LO
CATE 19,1:PRINT "P  curve":LOCATE 16,1:PRINT "TAB color":LOC
ATE 6,1:PRINT "Color="
360   LOCATE 20,1:PRINT "C  circle":LOCATE 22,1:PRINT "7  sav
```

```
e":LOCATE 23,1:PRINT "8  load":LOCATE 17,1:PRINT "D  dot"
370  LINE (74,4)-(74,187),C3:LINE (75,4)-(75,187),C3:LINE (0
,187)-(75,187),C3:LINE (0,4)-(74,4),C3
380  GOSUB 1340 'jump to color swatch subroutine
390  SOUND 550,3:SOUND 350,3:SOUND 600,5  'announce ready
400 '_____
410 '
420 'module:  user interface
430  K$=INKEY$:IF K$="" THEN 430
440  IF K$="=" THEN J=J+1:IF J>50 THEN J=50:GOTO 430
450  IF K$="-" THEN J=J-1:IF J<1 THEN J=1:GOTO 430
460  IF K$=CHR$(13) THEN PUT (SX,SY),A1,XOR:SX=110:SY=46:PUT
 (SX,SY),A1,XOR:SOUND 250,.7:GOTO 430
470  IF K$="1" THEN PSET (X1,Y1),CO:SOUND 250,.7:X1=SX+20:Y1
=SY+9:PSET (X1,Y1),C2:GOSUB 1250:GOTO 430
480  IF K$="2" THEN PSET (X2,Y2),CO:SOUND 250,.7:X2=SX+20:Y2
=SY+9:PSET (X2,Y2),C2:GOSUB 1250:GOTO 430
490  IF K$="3" THEN PSET (X3,Y3),CO:SOUND 250,.7:X3=SX+20:Y3
=SY+9:PSET (X3,Y3),C2:GOSUB 1250:GOTO 430
500  IF K$="4" THEN PSET (X4,Y4),CO:SOUND 250,.7:X4=SX+20:Y4
=SY+9:PSET (X4,Y4),C2:GOSUB 1250:GOTO 430
510  IF K$=CHR$(27) THEN SOUND 350,5:GOTO 720
520  IF K$="L" THEN SOUND 250,.7:V1=2:PUT (SX,SY),A1,XOR:LIN
E (X1,Y1)-(X4,Y4),C:PUT (SX,SY),A1,XOR:X1U=X1:Y1U=Y1:X4U=X4:
Y4U=Y4:X1=0:Y1=0:X4=0:Y4=0:GOSUB 1250:GOSUB 1190:GOTO 430
530  IF K$="P" THEN SOUND 250,.7:V1=1:PUT (SX,SY),A1,XOR:GOS
UB 670:SX=SX-20:SY=SY-9:PUT (SX,SY),A1,XOR:PSET (X2,Y2),CO:P
SET (X3,Y3),CO:GOSUB 1250:GOSUB 1190:SOUND 250,.7:GOTO 430
540  IF K$="C" THEN SOUND 250,.7:V1=3:PUT (SX,SY),A1,XOR:R=X
4-X1:CIRCLE (X1,Y1),R,C:PSET (X1,Y1),CO:PUT (SX,SY),A1,XOR:X
1U=X1:Y1U=Y1:X4U=X4:Y4U=Y4:X1=0:Y1=0:X4=0:Y4=0:GOSUB 1250:GO
SUB 1190:GOTO 430
550  IF K$="D" THEN SOUND 250,.7:PUT (SX,SY),A1,XOR:PSET (SX
+20,SY+9),C:PUT (SX,SY),A1,XOR:GOTO 430
560  IF K$=CHR$(9) THEN GOSUB 1300:GOTO 430  'change drawing
 color
570  IF K$="7" THEN SOUND 250,.7:PUT (SX,SY),A1,XOR:GOSUB 14
60:PUT (SX,SY),A1,XOR:SOUND 250,.7:GOTO 430  'save image to
diskette
580  IF K$="8" THEN SOUND 250,.7:PUT (SX,SY),A1,XOR:GOSUB 15
30:PUT (SX,SY),A1,XOR:SOUND 250,.7:GOTO 430  'load image fro
m diskette
590  IF LEN (K$)=2 THEN K$=RIGHT$(K$,1):GOSUB 1030:GOSUB 119
0:GOTO 430
600  IF K$="U" THEN SOUND 250,.7:PUT (SX,SY),A1,XOR:GOSUB 13
80:SOUND 250,.7:GOTO 430
610  GOSUB 1190
620  SOUND 250,.7:GOTO 430
```

```
630 '_____
640 '
650 'module:   FREE-FORM curve driver
660 'calculates location of point on cubic parametric curve
670    T=0:T2=T*T:T3=T*T*T:GOSUB 680:PSET (SX,SY),C:FOR T=0 TO
   1.01 STEP .05:T2=T*T:T3=T*T*T:GOSUB 680:LINE-(SX,SY),C:NEXT
   T:RETURN
680    J1=X1*(-T3+3*T2-3*T+1):J2=X2*(3*T3-6*T2+3*T):J3=X3*(-3*
   T3+3*T2):J4=X4*T3:SX=J1+J2+J3+J4:J1=Y1*(-T3+3*T2-3*T+1):J2=Y
   2*(3*T3-6*T2+3*T):J3=Y3*(-3*T3+3*T2):J4=Y4*T3:SY=J1+J2+J3+J4
   :RETURN
690 '_____
700 '
710 'module: return to BASIC interpreter
720    CLS:SCREEN 0,0,0,0:WIDTH 80:COLOR 7,0,0:LOCATE 1,1,1:CL
S:END
730 '_____
740 '
750 'module:   UNIVERSAL
760 'This routine configures the program for the hardware/so
ftware being used.
770    KEY OFF:CLS:ON ERROR GOTO 800   'trap if not EGA
780    SCREEN 8,,0,0:COLOR 7,0:PALETTE 1,9:PALETTE 2,12:PALETT
E 3,7:C0=0:C1=1:C2=2:C3=3   'EGA 640x200 16-color graphics mo
de
790    GOTO 860   'jump past PCjr and Color/Graphics Adapter tr
aps
800    RESUME 810
810    ON ERROR GOTO 840   'trap if not PCjr
820    CLEAR,,,32768!:SCREEN 6,0,0,0:COLOR 3,0:PALETTE 1,9:PAL
ETTE 2,12:PALETTE 3,7:C0=0:C1=1:C2=2:C3=3   'PCjr 640x200 4-c
olor graphics mode
830    GOTO 860   'jump past Color/Graphics Adapter trap
840    RESUME 850
850    SCREEN 2:C0=0:C1=1:C2=1:C3=1   'Color/Graphics Adapter 6
40x200 2-color graphics mode
860    ON ERROR GOTO 0   'disable error trapping
870    GOTO 150   'return to main program
880 '_____
890 '
900 'module: assign scalar data
910    SX=0:SY=0:X1=0:Y1=0:X2=0:Y2=0:X3=0:Y3=0:X4=0:Y4=0:R=0:T
=0:X1U=0:Y1U=0:X4U=0:Y4U=0:SXU=0:SYU=0
920    DEFINT A:DIM A1(230):DIM A2(20538)   'A1 array for retic
le cursor and A2 array (41076 bytes) for user's graphics
930    DEFINT U:U=0   'used to point to array memory location
940    CF=41   'Y-coordinate for color swatch
950    MINX=62:MINY=29:MAXX=599:MAXY=177   'inhibit cursor rang
e
```

322

```
960    C=C3   'default color
970    J=10   'default jump factor for reticle movement
980    DEFINT V:V=0:V1=1
990    RETURN
1000 '_____
1010 '
1020 'module:   cursor key control
1030   IF K$=CHR$(77) THEN PUT (SX,SY),A1,XOR:SX=SX+J ELSE GO
TO 1060
1040   IF SX>MAXX THEN SX=MAXX:SOUND 250,.7
1050   PUT (SX,SY),A1,XOR:RETURN
1060   IF K$=CHR$(75) THEN PUT (SX,SY),A1,XOR:SX=SX-J ELSE GO
TO 1090
1070   IF SX<MINX THEN SX=MINX:SOUND 250,.7
1080   PUT (SX,SY),A1,XOR:RETURN
1090   IF K$=CHR$(72) THEN PUT (SX,SY),A1,XOR:SY=SY-J ELSE GO
TO 1120
1100   IF SY<MINY THEN SY=MINY:SOUND 250,.7
1110   PUT (SX,SY),A1,XOR:RETURN
1120   IF K$=CHR$(80) THEN PUT (SX,SY),A1,XOR:SY=SY+J ELSE GO
TO 1150
1130   IF SY>MAXY THEN SY=MAXY:SOUND 250,.7
1140   PUT (SX,SY),A1,XOR:RETURN
1150   RETURN
1160 '_____
1170 '
1180 'module:   status display
1190   LOCATE 5,5:PRINT CINT(J)" "
1200   LOCATE 3,4:PRINT CINT(SX+20):LOCATE 4,4:PRINT CINT(SY+
16)
1210   RETURN
1220 '_____
1230 '
1240 'module:   display of control points
1250   LOCATE 7,5:PRINT CINT(X1)" ":LOCATE 8,5:PRINT CINT(Y1)
" ":LOCATE 9,5:PRINT CINT(X2)" ":LOCATE 10,5:PRINT CINT(Y2)"
 ":LOCATE 11,5:PRINT CINT(X3)" ":LOCATE 12,5:PRINT CINT(Y3)"
 ":LOCATE 13,5:PRINT CINT(X4)" ":LOCATE 14,5:PRINT CINT(Y4)"
 "
1260   LINE (74,4)-(74,187),C3:LINE (75,4)-(75,187),C3:RETURN

1270 '_____
1280 '
1290 'module:   default color changer
1300   IF C=C3 THEN SOUND 250,.7:C=C0:GOTO 1340
1310   IF C=C0 THEN SOUND 250,.7:C=C1:GOTO 1340
1320   IF C=C1 THEN SOUND 250,.7:C=C2:GOTO 1340
1330   IF C=C2 THEN SOUND 250,.7:C=C3:GOTO 1340
1340   LINE (50,CF-1)-(70,CF-1),C:LINE (50,CF)-(70,CF),C:LINE
```

```
      (50,CF+1)-(70,CF+1),C:LINE (50,CF+2)-(70,CF+2),C:LINE (50,C
F+3)-(70,CF+3),C:LINE (50,CF+4)-(70,CF+4),C:LINE (50,CF+5)-(
70,CF+5),C:RETURN
1350 '_____
1360 '
1370 'module:  undo last-drawn graphic
1380   ON V1 GOTO 1390,1410,1420
1390   SXU=SX:SYU=SY:T=0:T2=T*T:T3=T*T*T:GOSUB 1400:PSET (SX,
SY),CO:FOR T=0 TO 1.01 STEP .05:T2=T*T:T3=T*T*T:GOSUB 1400:L
INE-(SX,SY),CO:NEXT T:SX=SXU:SY=SYU:PUT (SX,SY),A1,XOR:GOSUB
 1250:GOSUB 1190:RETURN
1400   J1=X1*(-T3+3*T2-3*T+1):J2=X2*(3*T3-6*T2+3*T):J3=X3*(-3
*T3+3*T2):J4=X4*T3:SX=J1+J2+J3+J4:J1=Y1*(-T3+3*T2-3*T+1):J2=
Y2*(3*T3-6*T2+3*T):J3=Y3*(-3*T3+3*T2):J4=Y4*T3:SY=J1+J2+J3+J
4:RETURN
1410   LINE (X1U,Y1U)-(X4U,Y4U),CO:PUT (SX,SY),A1,XOR:GOSUB 1
250:GOSUB 1190:RETURN
1420   R=X4U-X1U:CIRCLE (X1U,Y1U),R,CO:PUT (SX,SY),A1,XOR:GOS
UB 1250:GOSUB 1190:RETURN
1430 '_____
1440 '
1450 'module:  save image to diskette
1460   GET (80,37)-(623,187),A2  'transfer image from screen
buffer into graphic array in BASIC's workspace
1470   U=VARPTR(A2(0))  'identify location of graphic array i
n BASIC's workspace
1480   BSAVE "B:CADIMAGE",U,&HC06C  'save graphic array on di
skette as binary file
1490   RETURN
1500 '_____
1510 '
1520 'module:  load image from diskette
1530   U=VARPTR(A2(0))  'identify location of graphic array A
2 in BASIC's workspace
1540   BLOAD "B:CADIMAGE",U  'transfer binary file from diske
tte to graphic array A2 in BASIC's workspace
1550   PUT (80,37),A2,PSET  'transfer image from graphic arra
y to screen buffer
1560   RETURN
1570 '_____
1580 '
1590   END 'of program code
```

error condition would be generated if the user attempted to run the array off the edge of the screen.

Line 960 establishes the initial drawing color. The user can change this to any one of three other colors while the CAD editor is running. Line 980 sets up the variables V and V1, which are used as flags to control the undo function of the program. Using the undo function, the user can delete the last-drawn graphic and restore the image to its previous condition.

## CREATING THE CAD ENVIRONMENT

The demonstration CAD editor uses a crosshair reticle cursor to indicate the location of graphics about to be created by the user. Line 190 draws the four short lines required to create this crosshair and then stores the image in the graphic array A1. Whenever the cursor is used, A1 will simply be placed on the display screen.

The dot mesh grid which forms the drawing surface is created by line 260, using the linestyling option of the LINE statement. The border around the drawing surface is drawn by line 270. The reticle is established at its starting location by line 280. Note the use of the XOR logical operator with the PUT instruction. If the reticle array is placed at the same location for a second occasion, XOR will cause the pixels to revert back to their original pristine condition. This enables the user to move the reticle about the drawing surface without obliterating any of the drawing or the background graphics.

Lines 240 and 250 place generic housekeeping graphics on the screen.

## THE MENU DISPLAY

Because of the numerous keys used by this program, it is necessary to provide a menu for the user. It is unrealistic to expect the user to memorize a list of keystrokes.

The menu is produced by lines 310 through 380. A series of LOCATE and PRINT statements form the essence of this routine.

Note line 380, which sends program control to a subroutine at 1340. This subroutine draws a small color swatch in the menu, which informs the user about the current drawing color. This subroutine is also called by the program whenever the user wants to change the drawing color.

### Keystroke Analysis

As displayed from top to bottom along the user's menu, keys are used for the following purposes. The RET key, often called the <Enter> key, is used to return the reticle to its home position. The X label is the x-coordinate of the current reticle location on the screen. The Y label is the y-coordinate of the reticle's position. The Jmp label refers to the distance the reticle will skip when it is moved. At start-up, the cursor

will jump 10 pixels every time an arrow key is pressed. This factor is often called snap by packaged CAD systems. The next label is the color swatch, initially set to white during program start-up.

The next eight variables refer to points used by the editor while the user is drawing various lines. X1,Y1 and X4,Y4 are used to hold the endpoints of a straight line or a free-form curve. X2,Y2, and X3,Y3 are used to hold the control points for a free-form curve. X1,Y1 are also used as the center point of a circle; while X4,Y4 hold the radius locator.

The ESC key is used to quit the CAD editor and return to BASIC. TAB is used to rotate through the drawing color options. Simply keep pressing TAB and watch the color swatch change from white to black to blue to red. You can draw in any of the four colors. (A Color/Graphics Adapter can use only black or white.)

Pressing the D key will place a single dot on the screen. Using L will draw a line between the two points contained in the X1,Y1 and X4,Y4 variables. Pressing the P curve will draw a parametric curve, using X1,Y1 and X4,Y4 as the endpoints and X2,Y2/X3,Y3 as the control points. Touching C will produce a circle, using X1,Y1 as the center and using the distance between X1,Y1 and X4,Y4 as the radius.

The U keystroke will delete the last previously-drawn graphic. If a free-form curve was just drawn, for example, it will be deleted by redrawing it in color C0, which is black).

Pressing the 7 key will cause the image on the drawing surface to be saved on diskette as an image file named "CADIMAGE". Touching 8 will cause an image to be retrieved from diskette and placed back onto the display screen. The program in its present form will use drive B to read and write files. You can easily change this to drive A by simply changing B: to A: in lines 1480 and 1540.

When all the alphanumeric labels have been placed on the left side of the display screen, line 370 draws a simple box around the menu. Line 390 produces a short lyrical sound to announce that the interactive CAD editor is ready to be used.

## THE USER INTERFACE MODULE

The user interface routine runs from line 420 through 620. If a key is selected, the routine immediately loops back to line 430 after the instruction is carried out. If no key is pressed, the routine simply loops through 430. If an unrecognized key is pressed, no action occurs and the program falls through to line 620, where a beep advises the user that an inappropriate keystroke was entered. Program control then loops back to line 430.

The user interface routine enables you to draw the following graphics on the display screen.

## Cursor Movement

Press any one of the four cursor arrow keys to move the reticle around the drawing surface. The cursor will not move outside the drawing surface. The x,y location of the cursor is displayed in the menu.

## Adjust Jump

Press the + key to make the jump (snap) factor larger. Press the – key to reduce the jump factor. The new factor is displayed in the menu. The jump factor controls how far the reticle will skip when you press an arrow key.

## Set Control Points

Press the 1 key to set the X1,Y1 coordinates. The coordinates will be displayed in the menu. The current reticle location becomes the X1,Y1 coordinates. Press 2, 3, or 4 to set the other control coordinates as required.

## Change Drawing Color

Press TAB to change the drawing color to black. Press TAB again to change to blue. Press again to switch to red. Press a fourth time to return to white as the drawing color. The color swatch in the menu changes as you scroll through the available colors. (Only black and white are available on a Color/Graphics Adapter.)

## Draw a Dot

Press D to place a dot at the current reticle position. Press U to erase the dot if desired. The dot is drawn in the current drawing color.

## Draw a Line

Use the 1 key to establish the X1,Y1 coordinates. Then use the 4 key to set the X4,Y4 coordinates. Then press L to draw a straight line connecting the coor-dinates. Press U to erase the line if desired. The line is drawn in the current drawing color.

## Draw a Free-Form Curve

Use the 1 key and the 4 key to establish the endpoints. Use the 2 key and the 3 key to establish the control points for the free-form curve. (See Chapter 11 for more information about cubic parametric free-form curves.) Press P to draw the curve in the current drawing color. Press U to delete the curve if desired.

## Draw a Circle

Use the 1 key to establish X1,Y1 as the center of the circle. Move the cursor to a point on the circumference of the circle. Press 4. Press the C key to draw the circle in the current drawing color. Touch U to delete the circle if desired.

## Save Image To Diskette

Press the 7 key to save your drawing as an image file on diskette. Be sure you have a blank diskette in drive B:. The file will be named "CADIMAGE.BAS".

## Retrieve Image From Diskette

Press the 8 key to retrieve your drawing from diskette. You can now perform further graphic editing on the drawing. If you press ESC to quit the program without first using 8 to save the image on diskette, your drawing will be lost when you quit the program.

## HOW THE USER INTERFACE WORKS

The user interface module is located at lines 420 through 620. This module is a closed loop which calls other subroutines in order to execute instructions received from the user via the keyboard.

Line 440 increases the jump factor by one unit if the + key has been pressed. The algorithm checks for the = key only because it is preferable to have the user merely touch = rather than Shift = (which generates the + ASCII code).

Line 450 decreases the jump factor by one unit if the – key has been pressed. Note that both line 440 and line 450 impose a minimum and maximum value. The snap factor will never be less than one nor greater than 50.

Line 460 returns the reticle to the home position at 110,46 if the < Enter > key has been pressed. SX and SY are the coordinates which determine where the reticle graphic array is placed on the screen. SX + 20 and SY + 9 correspond to the center of the reticle crosshairs.

Line 470 plots a point on the screen and sets the value of X1 and Y1 if the 1 key has been pressed. Line 480 does the same for X2,Y2 and the 2 key. Line 490 handles X3,Y3 and the 3 key. Line 500 monitors X4,Y4 and the 4 key.

Line 510 tests if the ESC key has been touched. If so, program control jumps to line 720, which returns the user to the BASIC interpreter in the text mode. No images are saved before quitting the program.

Line 520 draws a straight line between X1,Y1 and X4,Y4. First the V1 undo flag is set. This identifies which graphic is to be drawn if the undo key is later pressed. Next, the XOR operator is used to make the reticle disappear. The line is then drawn and the reticle restored. Then, the coordinates for the undo function are assigned (i.e., X1U etc.). The line endpoints are reset to 0. The program then jumps to a routine at line 1250 which updates the menu display of control points. The routine at line 1190 updates the reticle location display. Then program control returns to the beginning of the keyboard loop at line 430.

Line 530 draws a free-form curve. X1,Y1 and X4,Y4 are the endpoints. X2,Y2 and X3,Y3 are the control points. The curve is actually constructed by a subroutine at line 670. The same general housekeeping details are performed as were undertaken by the line-drawing algorithm in line 520.

Line 540 draws a circle, using X1,Y1 as the center and X4,Y4 as a point on the circumference.

Note that line 520, 530, and 540 each set the V un-do flag to denote which graphic will be undone if the U key is later pressed.

Line 550 places a single dot on the screen if the D key has been pressed.

Line 560 checks for the TAB key. If found, program control jumps to a routine at line 1300, which changes the drawing color defined by the variable C. Note line 1340, which refreshes the color swatch on the menu display whenever the drawing color is altered.

Line 570 calls a routine at line 1460 to save the image to diskette if the 7 key is pressed. Note how the reticle is removed from the screen with the XOR operator before the image is saved. The reticle is

returned when the save is done. Line 1460 in the saving routine captures the entire drawing surface image and places it in a graphic array named A2. Line 1470 identifies the location of this array in memory using the VARPTR (variable-pointer) instruction. Line 1480 uses a BSAVE command to save the graphic array on diskette as "CADIMAGE.BAS". Note that the program uses drive B. You can easily change this to drive A, if you wish.

Line 580 calls a routine at line 1530 which retrieves an image from diskette. Line 1530 uses the VARPTR to find the location of the graphic array inside BASIC's workspace. Line 1540 retrieves the image file "CADIMAGE.BAS" from drive B: and places it into the graphic array. Line 1550 then places the graphic array onto the display screen.

Line 590 tests for the four arrow keys. These are comprised of extended ASCII codes as discussed in Chapter 4. If an extended code is found, program control jumps to a routine at line 1030 which checks to determine which arrow key was pressed. Note how the minimum and maximum values for the location of the reticle are enforced by this routine.

Line 600 controls the undo function. Remember that each routine which draws a graphic sets the V flag. If the undo function at line 1380 is invoked, an ON. . .GOTO statement is used to jump to the appropriate graphic-drawing routine. Undo operates by redrawing in black the most recently-drawn graphic.

### Error Trapping

This prototype is not error-trapped. By using BASIC's ON ERROR GOTO instruction, you can provide a gentle prompt for the user if, for example, no diskette is in drive B: when a save is requested. Simply incorporate the trap into the routines which start at lines 1450 and 1520.

In addition, you may wish to add an alphanumeric display which warns the user to save the image on diskette before quitting the program. The warning should be displayed after the ESC is pressed, but before jumping to the exit module.

### Keyboard Integrity

The user interface routine at lines 420 through 620 is not without fault. While the program is running, try pressing the F2 key and watch what happens. Theoretically, because F2 is not a defined key, nothing should happen. Why does it produce the results it does? It is left as an exercise for you to debug the user interface module. (Hint: check your BASIC manual for the ASCII code for F2 and consider how the program reads the contents of the keyboard buffer on each pass through the INKEY$ loop.)

## SAVING/RETRIEVING IMAGES

The graphic array method for saving and retrieving images has been used in this demonstration program for three reasons.

First, BSAVE and BLOAD will save the entire display screen. This wastes file space on the diskette when only a portion of the screen needs to be saved, as in the demonstration program in this chapter.

Second, because the image is kept inside BASIC's workspace and no specific memory addresses are used (i.e., no hardcoding is used), your program will operate correctly even if future hardware uses a different architecture. BASIC takes care of all memory addresses, including capture and replacement of the image with respect to the screen buffer.

Third, because BSAVE and BLOAD operate differently with an EGA than with a Color/Graphics Adapter, the graphic array approach makes it easier to write a program that will perform correctly on all types of graphics adapters. (Refer to Appendix E for more information about this.)

## 3D ENHANCEMENTS

The CAD graphics editor demonstration program in this chapter can be readily upgraded to produce 3D models. Packaged 3D CAD systems often create the 3D model from a series of layers. For example, you would draw the 2D shape (silhouette) of the model as it exists at a certain altitude. By combining a series of different altitude silhouettes you can create the full 3D model. This technique is called layering or lofting. The current program draws a silhouette at one level of depth only.

By coding your program so it saves these coordinates as they are drawn for different layers, you can then use the standard perspective formulas to generate a true 3D model.

## SUMMARY

In this chapter, you experimented with a user interface which was interactive at the end-user level. You learned how to control graphics on the display screen by accepting keystrokes from the user. You discovered how to save graphic images on diskette.

The next chapter demonstrates an aerospace engineering simulation by animating a vehicle in 3D airspace.

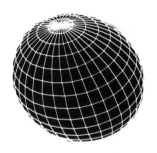

# 26

# Simulation

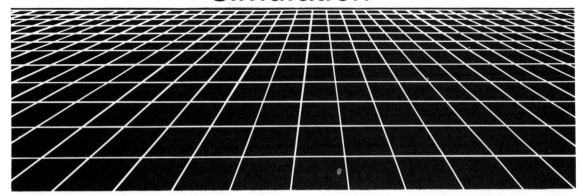

The techniques discussed in previous chapters can be put to work creating simulations of complex real-world events. In this chapter you will learn how to use perspective formulas, dynamic instancing, and real-time animation to simulate an aerospace vehicle in 3D airspace. The vehicle rolls when it changes heading; it pitches up or down when it climbs or dives.

## THE SIMULATION ENVIRONMENT

In order to permit meaningful visual interpretation of the vehicle as it maneuvers through the airspace, the 3D axis system will be incorporated into the visual display. Refer to Fig. 26-1, which shows frame number 12 from the animation sequence. The graphic which portrays the x, y, and z axis lines is called a gnomon by packaged CAD systems.

During the simulation, the gnomon remains in a constant location. The vehicle can be programmed by you to perform all sorts of aerobatic maneuvers. The spatial location of the aerospace vehicle is easily determined because you can always compare it to the 3D axis system. In addition, an alphanumeric readout in the upper left corner of the display screen provides

you with the x,y,z coordinates of the aerospace vehicle.

The vehicle can be programmed to fly outside the area being displayed on the screen. Specialized lineclipping routines for both 2D and 3D modes ensure that no mathematical overload or display error will occur when the vehicle leaves the visible airspace or when it re-enters.

## SIMULATION OUTPUT

During the simulation, the aerospace vehicle enters the 3D airspace from the right edge of the display screen. Refer to Fig. 26-1. As the vehicle nears the x-axis, it begins to roll left and dive. By frame number 24 (see Fig. 26-2), the aerospace vehicle has passed behind the y-axis and is turning back towards you as it continues to lose altitude. The vehicle has completed one full turn around the gnomon by frame 45 (see Fig. 26-3).

A tracer routine provides an exhaust trail which identifies the flight path of the aerospace vehicle. You can readily follow the long-term performance of the simulation, especially once the vehicle begins a second turn around the axis system (see Fig. 26-3).

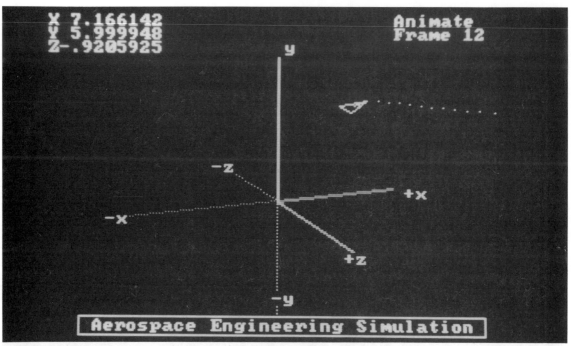

Fig. 26-1. Animation frame 12 from the demonstration program in Fig. 26-4.

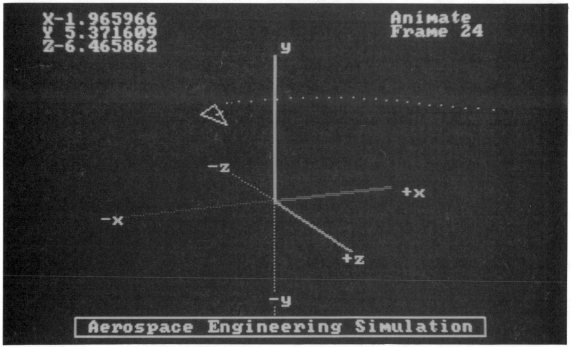

Fig. 26-2. Animation frame 24 from the demonstration program in Fig. 26-4. The aerospace vehicle has begun a roll left and a gentle dive.

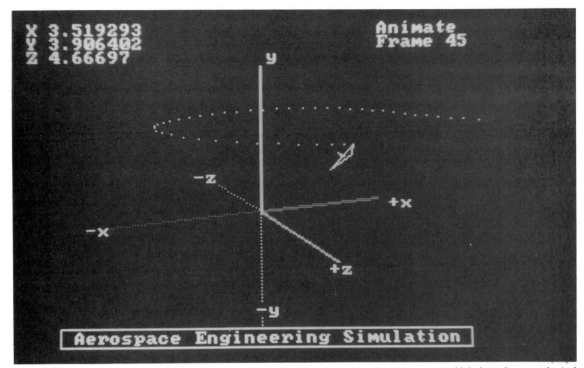

Fig. 26-3. Animation frame 45 from the demonstration program in Fig. 26-4. The aerospace vehicle has circumnavigated the axis system.

## Interactive at the Source Code Level

In its present format, the program follows a pre-defined simulation script. The aerospace vehicle continues to circle and continues to lose altitude until it reaches ground zero, where $Y = 0$. After that point in the simulation, the vehicle merely continues to circle the y-axis at elevation 0. By making a few simple changes to the program listing, however, you can readily instruct the aerospace vehicle to perform different maneuvers.

## Interactive at the End-User Level

Because the program is driven by real-time animation, you can easily modify this simulation to become interactive, thereby permitting you to control the flight path of the aerospace vehicle during the simulation. There will be more discussion about this later in the chapter.

## PROGRAMMING CONCEPTS

The demonstration program in this chapter illustrates a number of important programming concepts. The movement of the aerospace vehicle through 3D airspace is made possible by the technique of dynamic instancing. As you learned in Chapter 6 and Chapter 7, an instance is a single occurrence of a 3D model within a 3D environment.

Each frame of the animation sequence is merely a different instance of the same 3D model in the gnomon airspace. Two factors are at play here: the model (the aerospace vehicle) is rotated and translated according to its current flight attitude, and the model is subjected to ongoing incremental movement (the animated flight). Together, these two factors create an environment of dynamic instancing.

## ANALYSIS OF THE DEMONSTRATION PROGRAM

Figures 26-1, 26-2, and 26-3 show the screen output produced by the demonstration program in Fig. 26-4. The program simulates an aerospace vehicle as it flies through 3D airspace. To run this program from the companion diskette, type **LOAD "A-42.BAS",R.** The program is designed to run on an EGA using IBM BASICA 3.21, a PCjr using IBM Cartridge BASIC, and a Tandy using GW-BASIC.

Fig. 26-4. Aerospace engineering simulation.

```
100 'Program A-42.BAS    Aerospace engineering simulation
110 'Demonstrates flight characteristics of aerospace vehicl
e in 3D airspace.
120 '_____
130 '
140   GOTO 530  'configure system and initialize
150   GOSUB 730  'assign scalar data
160   SCREEN,,1,0  'initialize real-time animation
170 '_____
180 '
190 'create generic background graphics
200   GOSUB 390  'jump to gnomon locating routine
210   GOSUB 880  'jump to draw gnomon routine
220   LOCATE 24,5:PRINT "Aerospace Engineering Simulation"
230   LOCATE 1,30:PRINT "Animate"
240   LOCATE 2,30:PRINT "Frame":LOCATE 3,1:PRINT "Z":LOCATE 1
,1:PRINT "X":LOCATE 2,1:PRINT "Y"
250   LOCATE 14,31:PRINT "+x":LOCATE 16,6:PRINT "-x":LOCATE 3
,20:PRINT "+y":LOCATE 22,20:PRINT "-y":LOCATE 19,26:PRINT "+
z":LOCATE 12,15:PRINT "-z"
260   PCOPY 1,2  'save generic background graphics
270 '_____
280 '
290 'master routine:  animation loop
300   LOCATE 2,35:PRINT T1:LOCATE 3,2:PRINT NZ"       ":LOCATE
1,2:PRINT NX"       ":LOCATE 2,2:PRINT NY"       "
310   G=C3:GOSUB 1590  'set color and jump to vehicle routine

320   IF NZ<0 THEN LINE (S3X,S3Y)-(SOX,SOY),C1:LINE (S3X+1,S3
Y)-(SOX+1,SOY),C1
330   SCREEN,,P,1-P:SOUND 200,.3:PCOPY 2,P:P=1-P:GOTO 300
340   END 'of master routine
350 '_____
360 '
370 'module: 3D axis system
380 'calculates display coordinates for gnomon
390   RESTORE 690:READ X,Y,Z:GOSUB 440:GOSUB 450:SOX=SX:SOY=S
Y:READ X,Y,Z:GOSUB 440:GOSUB 450:S1X=SX:S1Y=SY:READ X,Y,Z:GO
SUB 440:GOSUB 450:S2X=SX:S2Y=SY:READ X,Y,Z:GOSUB 440:GOSUB 4
50:S3X=SX:S3Y=SY:READ X,Y,Z:GOSUB 440:GOSUB 450:S4X=SX:S4Y=S
Y
400   READ X,Y,Z:GOSUB 440:GOSUB 450:S5X=SX:S5Y=SY:READ X,Y,Z
:GOSUB 440:GOSUB 450:S6X=SX:S6Y=SY:RETURN
410 '_____
420 '
430 'module:  generic translation and rotation formulas
```

```
440    X=(-1)*X:X=X-MX:Y=Y+MY:Z=Z+MZ:XA=CR1*X-SR1*Z:ZA=SR1*X+C
R1*Z:Z=CR3*ZA-SR3*Y:YA=SR3*ZA+CR3*Y:X=CR2*XA+SR2*YA:Y=CR2*YA
-SR2*XA:RETURN
450    SX=D*X/Z:SY=D*Y/Z:SX=SX+160:SY=SY+100:RETURN
460    '_____
470    '
480    'module:    provide clean exit with F2 key
490    CLS:SCREEN,,1,0:CLS:SCREEN,,0,0:CLS:SCREEN 0,0,0,0:COLO
R 7,0,0:WIDTH 80:LOCATE 1,1,1:CLS:END
500    '_____
510    '
520    'module:    configure system for EGA or PCjr
530    KEY OFF:CLS:ON ERROR GOTO 560
540    SCREEN 7,,0,0:COLOR 7,0:PALETTE 3,7:C0=0:C1=1:C2=4:C3=3
:C4=2
550    PCOPY 0,1:GOTO 640
560    RESUME 570
570    ON ERROR GOTO 580:CLEAR,,,49152!:SCREEN 1,0:COLOR 0,1:P
ALETTE 1,1:PALETTE 2,4:PALETTE 3,7:C0=0:C1=1:C2=2:C3=3:C4=3:
PCOPY 0,1:GOTO 640
580    RESUME 590
590    SOUND 100,10:LOCATE 10,1:PRINT "This animated program r
equires":LOCATE 11,1:PRINT "an EGA with BASICA 3.2 or":LOCAT
E 12,1:PRINT "a PCjr with Cartridge BASIC."
600    LOCATE 15,1:PRINT "Press <ESC> to return to BASIC."
610    ON ERROR GOTO 0
620    K$=INKEY$:IF K$<>CHR$(27) THEN 620
630    CLS:SOUND 250,.7:END
640    ON ERROR GOTO 0:ON KEY (2) GOSUB 490:KEY (2) ON
650    GOTO 150
660    '_____
670    '
680    'module:    database for gnomon
690    DATA   0,0,0,  10,0,0,  -10,0,0,  0,9,0,  0,-9,0,  0,0,10,  0,
0,-10
700    '_____
710    '
720    'module:    assign variables
730    DEFINT P,T,G,K,I
740    P1=1    'visibility status flag for 3D line clipping
750    T1=1    'frame counter for AI module
760    P=0     'page flipping variable
770    D=270   'angular perspective factor
780    MX=10.4:MY=-7:MZ=-26   'observer's viewpoint
790    R1=.4:R2=0:R3=6.08319   'observer's angle-of-view
800    SR1=SIN(R1):CR1=COS(R1):SR2=SIN(R2):CR2=COS(R2):SR3=SIN
(R3):CR3=COS(R3)
810    N=1    'translation change factor for aerospace vehicle
820    NX=8:NY=6:NZ=10   'starting position of vehicle
```

```
830   R11=0:R21=0:R31=0   'yaw, roll, pitch of vehicle
840   RETURN
850 '_____
860 '
870 'module:  draw gnomon
880   LINE (S1X,S1Y)-(S0X,S0Y),C2:LINE-(S2X,S2Y),C2,,&HAAAA
890   LINE (S1X,S1Y+1)-(S0X,S0Y+1),C2
900   LINE (S5X,S5Y)-(S0X,S0Y),C4:LINE-(S6X,S6Y),C4,,&HAAAA
910   LINE (S5X,S5Y+1)-(S0X,S0Y+1),C4
920   LINE (S3X,S3Y)-(S0X,S0Y),C1:LINE-(S4X,S4Y),C1,,&HAAAA
930   LINE (S3X+1,S3Y)-(S0X+1,S0Y),C1
940   RETURN
950 '_____
960 '
970 'module:  clip 3D view coordinates if behind viewpoint
980 'enter with XA,YA,ZA XB,YB,ZB view coordinates for endpo
ints of line to be clipped in 3D space
990   IF ZA>-1 THEN 1000 ELSE 1010
1000   IF ZB>-1 THEN P1=0:RETURN ELSE SWAP XA,XB:SWAP YA,YB:S
WAP ZA,ZB:GOTO 1030
1010   IF ZB>-1 THEN 1030 ELSE 1020
1020 SXA=D*XA/ZA:SYA=D*YA/ZA:SXB=D*XB/ZB:SYB=D*YB/ZB:RETURN
1030   C=(XA-XB)/(ZA-ZB)*(ZA+1):XC=XA-C:C=(YA-YB)/(ZA-ZB)*(ZA
+1):YC=YA-C:ZC=-1
1040   XB=XC:YB=YC:ZB=ZC:GOTO 990
1050 '_____
1060 '
1070 'module:  clip cartesian display coordinates to fit BAS
IC's standard 320x200 screen
1080   SXA=SXA+160:SYA=SYA+100:SXB=SXB+160:SYB=SYB+100
1090   IF SXA>SXB THEN SWAP SXA,SXB:SWAP SYA,SYB
1100   IF (SXA<0) AND (SXB<0) THEN RETURN
1110   IF (SXA>319) AND (SXB>319) THEN RETURN
1120   IF (SYA<0) AND (SYB<0) THEN RETURN
1130   IF (SYA>199) AND (SYB>199) THEN RETURN
1140   IF SXA<0 THEN 1310
1150   IF SXB>319 THEN 1230
1160   IF SYA>SYB THEN SWAP SYA,SYB:SWAP SXA,SXB
1170   IF SYA<0 THEN 1450
1180   IF SYB>199 THEN 1390
1190   LINE (SXA,SYA)-(SXB,SYB),G:RETURN
1200 '_____
1210 '
1220 'submodule: PUSH LEFT
1230   C=(SYB-SYA)/(SXB-SXA)*(319-SXA)
1240   SXB=319:SYB=SYA+C
1250   IF (SYA<0) AND (SYB<0) THEN RETURN
1260   IF (SYA>199) AND (SYB>199) THEN RETURN
```

```
1270   GOTO 1160
1280 '_____
1290 '
1300 'submodule: PUSH RIGHT
1310   C=(SYB-SYA)/(SXB-SXA)*(SXB)
1320   SXA=0:SYA=SYB-C
1330   IF (SYA<0) AND (SYB<0) THEN RETURN
1340   IF (SYA>199) AND (SYB>199) THEN RETURN
1350   GOTO 1150
1360 '_____
1370 '
1380 'submodule: PUSH UP
1390   C=(SXB-SXA)/(SYB-SYA)*(199-SYA)
1400   SXB=SXA+C:SYB=199
1410   GOTO 1190
1420 '_____
1430 '
1440 'submodule: PUSH DOWN
1450   C=(SXB-SXA)/(SYB-SYA)*(SYB)
1460   SXA=SXB-C:SYA=0
1470   GOTO 1180
1480 '_____
1490 '
1500 'module: aerospace vehicle
1510 'controls position and movement of aerospace vehicle in
  3D airspace
1520 '_____
1530 '
1540 'module:   database for computer-controlled aerospace ve
hicle
1550   DATA  -1,0,1,0,0,-1,1,0,1,0,0,1,0,0,.5,0,.3,1
1560 '_____
1570 '
1580 'submodule:   main routine to calculate view coordinates
  of computer-controlled aerospace vehicle
1590   GOSUB 1760  'jump to instancing direction routine
1600   R21=R21+R2A1:R31=R31+R3A1  'update instancing roll and
  pitch
1610   IF R21>6.28319 THEN R21=R21-6.28319 ELSE IF R21<=0 THE
N R21=R21+6.28319
1620   IF R31>6.28319 THEN R31=R31-6.28319 ELSE IF R31<=0 THE
N R31=R31+6.28319
1630   GOSUB 1830  'jump to instancing yaw change routine
1640   R11=R11+R1A1  'update instancing yaw heading
1650   IF R11>6.28319 THEN R11=R11-6.28319 ELSE IF R11<=0 THE
N R11=R11+6.28319
1660   SR11=SIN(R11):CR11=COS(R11):SR21=SIN(R21):CR21=COS(R21
):SR31=SIN(R31):CR31=COS(R31)
```

```
1670   GOSUB 1910   'jump to instancing translation routine
1680   IF NY<0 THEN NY=0   'prohibit vehicle from penetrating
ground level
1690   GOSUB 2020   'jump to instancing view coordinates locat
ing routine
1700   GOSUB 2300   'jump to instancing --> absolute routine
1710   GOSUB 2200   'jump to drawing routine for vehicle
1720   RETURN   'return to vehicle master routine
1730 '_____
1740 '
1750 'submodule:   artificial intelligence for computer-contr
olled aerospace vehicle
1760   T1=T1+1:IF (T1>5) AND (T1<22) THEN R2A1=-.05 ELSE R2A1
=0
1770   IF (T1>12) AND (T1<20) THEN R3A1=.01 ELSE R3A1=0
1780   RETURN
1790 '_____
1800 '
1810 'submodule: yaw change
1820 'calculates instancing yaw change factor relative to ro
ll heading
1830   IF (R21>=0) AND (R21<=1.57079) THEN R1A1=(R21/.017453)
*.00349:RETURN   'normal roll right
1840   IF (R21<=6.28319) AND (R21>=4.71239) THEN R1A1=((6.283
19-R21)/.017453)*(-.00349):RETURN   'normal roll left
1850   IF (R21>1.57079) AND (R21<=3.14159) THEN R1A1=((3.1415
9-R21)/.017453)*.00349:RETURN   'inverted roll right
1860   IF (R21>3.14159) AND (R21<4.71239) THEN R1A1=((R21-3.1
4159)/.017453)*(-.00349):RETURN   'inverted roll left
1870 '_____
1880 '
1890 'submodule: movement
1900 'calculates instancing translation of vehicle relative
to R11 yaw and R31 pitch
1910   N1=CR31*N   'lateral movement is function of pitch
1920   NY1=(-1)*SR31*N   'link vertical translation to pitch
1930   IF (R31>0!) AND (R31<=1.57079) THEN NY1=CR31*NY1   'air
speed decreases as pitch increases during pitch up mode
1940   IF (R31>1.57079) AND (R31<3.14159) THEN NY1=(-1)*CR31*
NY1   'inverted pitch up mode
1950   NX1=(-1)*SR11*N1:NZ1=CR11*N1   'lateral translation lin
ked to yaw
1960   NX=NX-NX1:NY=NY+NY1:NZ=NZ-NZ1   'update translation fac
tors
1970   RETURN
1980 '_____
1990 '
2000 'submodule: vertex
```

```
2010 'calculates instancing view coordinates of computer-con
trolled aerospace vehicle
2020   RESTORE 1550  'set database pointer
2030   READ X,Y,Z:GOSUB 2140:X1=X:Y1=Y:Z1=Z
2040   READ X,Y,Z:GOSUB 2140:X2=X:Y2=Y:Z2=Z
2050   READ X,Y,Z:GOSUB 2140:X3=X:Y3=Y:Z3=Z
2060   READ X,Y,Z:GOSUB 2140:X4=X:Y4=Y:Z4=Z
2070   READ X,Y,Z:GOSUB 2140:X5=X:Y5=Y:Z5=Z
2080   READ X,Y,Z:GOSUB 2140:X6=X:Y6=Y:Z6=Z
2090   RETURN
2100 '_____
2110 '
2120 'submodule: 3D instancing formulas
2130 'formulas for instancing view coordinates for vehicle u
sing roll + yaw + pitch
2140   X=(-1)*X:XA=CR21*X+SR21*Y:YA=CR21*Y-SR21*X:X=CR11*XA-S
R11*Z:ZA=SR11*XA+CR11*Z:Z=CR31*ZA-SR31*YA:Y=SR31*ZA+CR31*YA:
RETURN
2150 '_____
2160 '
2170 'submodule: 3D drawing
2180 'logic to draw aerospace vehicle
2190 'if P1=0 then line is completely clipped and invisible
2200   XA=X1:YA=Y1:ZA=Z1:XB=X2:YB=Y2:ZB=Z2:P1=1:GOSUB 990:GOS
UB 2410:IF P1=0 THEN 2210 ELSE GOSUB 1080
2210   XA=X2:YA=Y2:ZA=Z2:XB=X3:YB=Y3:ZB=Z3:P1=1:GOSUB 990:IF
P1=0 THEN 2220 ELSE GOSUB 1080
2220   XA=X3:YA=Y3:ZA=Z3:XB=X1:YB=Y1:ZB=Z1:P1=1:GOSUB 990:IF
P1=0 THEN 2230 ELSE GOSUB 1080
2230   XA=X5:YA=Y5:ZA=Z5:XB=X6:YB=Y6:ZB=Z6:P1=1:GOSUB 990:IF
P1=0 THEN 2240 ELSE GOSUB 1080
2240   XA=X6:YA=Y6:ZA=Z6:XB=X4:YB=Y4:ZB=Z4:P1=1:GOSUB 990:IF
P1=0 THEN 2250 ELSE GOSUB 1080
2250   RETURN
2260 '_____
2270 '
2280 'module: instancing change
2290 'converts instancing view coordinates to absolute view
coordinates
2300   X=X1+NX:Y=Y1+NY:Z=Z1+NZ:GOSUB 440:X1=X:Y1=Y:Z1=Z
2310   X=X2+NX:Y=Y2+NY:Z=Z2+NZ:GOSUB 440:X2=X:Y2=Y:Z2=Z
2320   X=X3+NX:Y=Y3+NY:Z=Z3+NZ:GOSUB 440:X3=X:Y3=Y:Z3=Z
2330   X=X4+NX:Y=Y4+NY:Z=Z4+NZ:GOSUB 440:X4=X:Y4=Y:Z4=Z
2340   X=X5+NX:Y=Y5+NY:Z=Z5+NZ:GOSUB 440:X5=X:Y5=Y:Z5=Z
2350   X=X6+NX:Y=Y6+NY:Z=Z6+NZ:GOSUB 440:X6=X:Y6=Y:Z6=Z
2360   RETURN
2370 '_____
2380 '
```

```
2390 'module:  tracer
2400 'traces path of aerospace vehicle through 3D airspace
2410  SXJ=SXA+160:SYJ=SYA+100:PSET (SXJ,SYJ),C3:PCOPY 1-P,2:
RETURN
2420 '_____
2430 '
2440  END 'of program code
```

The program uses three graphics pages. Page 0 and page 1 are flipped between the display page and the hidden written-to page. This is the standard concept of real-time animation introduced in Chapter 22. Page 2 is a generic background page which contains the image of the x,y,z axis system and assorted alphanumeric labels.

Each frame of the animation cycle consists of a number of stages. First, page 0 and page 1 are flipped, using the SCREEN,,P,1-P algorithm discussed in Chapter 22. Second, the background graphics (the gnomon) are copied from hidden page 2 onto the new hidden written-to page. Third, the program calculates the new location of the aerospace vehicle in 3D airspace, submits this data to the perspective formulas, and draws the vehicle in the gnomon environment. Fourth, page 0 and page 1 are again flipped in order to display the new frame. Work then begins on the next frame.

### Program Startup

Line 140 sends the program to a standard configuration module at line 530. The graphics environment is configured for either the EGA or the PCjr/Tandy. This program will not run on a color/graphics adapter in its current form, although you can easily adapt it run on a CGA by incorporating the routines from the real-time animation demonstration program in Chapter 22.

Line 150 sends the program to a routine at line 730 which assigns values to variables. When control returns to the main routine, line 160 establishes page 1 as a hidden written-to page and page 0 as the displayed page. For the next brief while, all graphics will be drawn on a hidden page.

The generic background is created at lines 190 through 260. Line 200 calls the subroutine at line 390, which calculates display coordinates necessary to draw the x,y,z axis system. Line 210 calls the subroutine at line 880 which actually draws the gnomon. Then,

lines 220 through 250 place assorted alphanumeric labels on the axis system image.

Line 260 copies the completed background graphics onto page 2. Whenever a fresh gnomon is needed, page 2 can be copied onto the hidden written-to page. This technique is much quicker than redrawing the axis system from scratch. All general housekeeping functions have now been concluded; the simulation is ready to begin.

### The Animation Loop

The main animation loop is contained in lines 300 through 330. Although this routine is deceptively short, it calls other subroutine which perform functions of considerable complexity.

Line 300 simply displays an alphanumeric readout of the x,y,z position of the aerospace vehicle in 3D airspace. The variable NZ represents the vehicle's north/south position; the variable NX denotes the vehicle's east/west location; the variable NY represents the vehicle's altitude. Refer to Fig. 26-1.

Line 310 sets the drawing color. You can modify the program to draw the aerospace vehicle in some other color by changing the value of G in line 310. C3 is white. The variables C0, C1, and C2 correspond to color attributes defined in the configuration module located at lines 520 through 650.

Line 310 then sends the program to a major subroutine at line 1590. This subroutine controls the movement of the aerospace vehicle. In order to exercise this control, the subroutine at line 1590 calls a number of other subroutines. These control mechanisms will be discussed later.

Line 320 makes it possible for the aerospace vehicle to fly behind the y-axis into the two farthest quadrants of the gnomon. Although the 3D perspective formulas take care of mathematically placing the aerospace vehicle behind the x-axis, so to speak, the y-axis must be redrawn if the vehicle is to appear at a farther distance graphically. If NZ < 0 then the y-axis is redrawn, thereby ensuring that it appears closer to you than the aerospace vehicle because it is drawn after the vehicle is drawn. Parts of the vehicle will be obscured if it is directly behind the y-axis.

Line 330 is the standard algorithm for real-time animation. First, the SCREEN,,P,1-P algorithm is used to flip the displayed page and the hidden written-to page. Then the SOUND statement is used to generate a small beep. Next, the PCOPY instruction copies the generic background graphics from page 2 onto the new hidden written-to page. Then, the value of P is toggled (as described in Chapter 22). Finally, the program is sent looping back to line 300.

## Instancing the Aerospace Vehicle

The placement of one occurrence of the aerospace vehicle in 3D airspace is called instancing. In this case it is dynamic instancing because the vehicle is dynamic: it moves.

Line 310 in the main animation routine calls a major subroutine at line 1590. This subroutine is a substantive program in itself and uses advanced formulas found in many flight simulation programs and air combat programs.

## The Instancing Database

The database for the aerospace vehicle is located at line 1550. The vehicle is drawn as a simple three-sided plane with a stabilizing rudder. Refer to Fig. 26-5. Note the scale of the vehicle. The values in the database range from −1 to +1. The .3 value

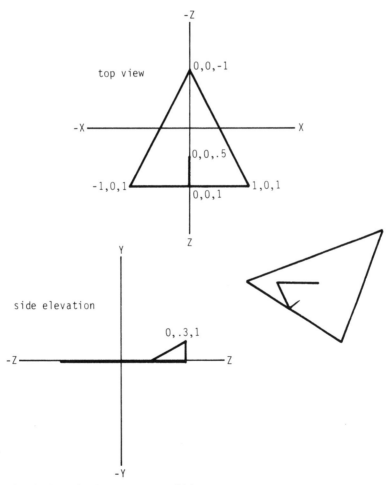

Fig. 26-5. Identifying the database for the aerospace vehicle.

represents the height of the rudder. Refer back to line 690, which contains the database used to draw the axis system. The x-axis, for example, runs from $-10$ to $+10$.

The main routine of the instancing module is located at lines 1580 through 1720. This routine is responsible for calculating the new location (instancing coordinates) of the aerospace vehicle, for translating those new coordinates into VIEW COORDINATES, and DISPLAY COORDINATES. The main routine also ensures that 2D and 3D lines are clipped properly.

## The Artificial Intelligence Routine

Line 1590 calls a subroutine at line 1760. This subroutine is the artificial intelligence for the computer-controlled aerospace vehicle. The term artificial intelligence is used here in its broadest sense, of course.

Note line 1760. The T1 variable is used to count the frames in the animation cycle in order to instruct the aerospace vehicle to begin certain aerobatic maneuvers at certain times during the simulation. R2A1 controls the roll of the vehicle. If $-.05$ is assigned to R2A1, the vehicle rolls (and turns) towards its left. You may wish to experiment with this variable by changing it to $+.05$.

The variable R3A1 in line 1770 controls the climb/dive attitude of the aerospace vehicle. A value of $+.01$ will introduce a shallow dive. You can experiment with this control by changing the value of R3A1 in line 1770 to $+.04$.

The control routine performs operations on only the roll and pitch functions. A separate routine is used later to adjust the vehicle's yaw heading based upon the vehicle's roll attitude. As in the real world, heading is a function of roll and vice versa: the two attitudes are linked.

## Inhibiting the Radian Values

When control returns to the main instancing routine, line 1600 increments the R21 roll factor and the R31 pitch factor.

Lines 1610 through 1620 are used in order to restrict the various radian variables to the range of 0 to 6.28319. Although BASIC can cope with radian values in excess of 6.28319, the aerospace vehicle can perform enough rotations to eventually cause a math overflow in BASIC. Lines 1600, 1610, and 1620 prevent any overflow from happening, thereby ensuring that the aerospace vehicle can fly around this airspace forever, performing any aerobatic maneuver it sees fit, looping back on itself countless times.

If a radian value is less than 0, a value of 6.28319 is added to bump it up into the appropriate range. If a radian value is greater than 6.28319, a value of 6.28319 is subtracted to bump it down into the appropriate range. Remember, there are 6.28319 radians in a full circle.

## Adjusting the Heading

Line 1630 sends the program to a subroutine at line 1830. This subroutine adjusts the yaw heading to match the new roll value introduced by the artificial intelligence routine. The yaw change subroutine can handle full rollovers and upside-down (inverted) flight. If you harbor any ambition of writing your own flight simulation program, this subroutine will be handy. R11 is the yaw (heading) of the aerospace vehicle, expressed in radians. R21 is the roll of the vehicle. R31 is the pitch (climb/dive) attitude.

After the new heading increment has been computed, control returns to the main subroutine at line 1640, which calculates the new R11 yaw heading. Line 1650 inhibits this value to the 0 to 6.28319 range.

## Mathematics

Line 1660 calculates the new sine and cosine values. Line 1670 invokes the instancing translation routine at line 1910. This routine, located at lines 1890 through 1970, calculates the next location of the vehicle in 3D airspace based upon its yaw, roll, and pitch attitudes. Sine and cosine are used to plot its flightpath. Note line 1930, which ensures that airspeed drops as the nose of the vehicle is pointed higher and higher. This subroutine will support a complete pitch up and over of the aircraft to inverted flight.

The subroutine concludes by updating the NX, NY, and NX translation factors for the aerospace vehicle.

## Crash Mode

When control returns to the main subroutine, line 1680 checks the NY altitude of the aerospace vehicle. In its current format, the program merely holds the vehicle steady at ground zero when it crashes, but you can easily cause the program to jump to a crash subroutine if $NY < 0$. It is left as an exercise for you to do so.

## Instancing View Coordinates

Line 1690 sends the program to a subroutine at line 2020, which calculates the location of the aerospace vehicle within the raw 3D airspace. This location is composed of instancing view coordinates (i.e., WORLD COORDINATES). The subroutine in turn calls a set of modified perspective formulas at line 2140. These formulas have been re-ordered to perform roll rotations first, then yaw rotations, then pitch rotations. This re-ordering is necessary to ensure that the aerospace vehicle will move in a fashion consistent with aircraft in the real world. All the instancing view coordinates for the aerospace vehicle are saved as variables X1,Y1,Z1 to X6,Y6,Z6.

## Standard View Coordinates

When control returns to the main subroutine, line 1700 sends the program to a subroutine at line 2300, which converts the instancing view coordinates (i.e., WORLD COORDINATES) into standard VIEW COORDINATES in the axis system. The standard perspective formulas at line 440 are called during this conversion.

## Display Coordinates

Line 1710 sends the program to a subroutine at line 220, which contains the logic to actually draw the aerospace vehicle. For each vertex of the aerospace vehicle, the instancing view coordinates are retrieved, a 3D line-clipping routine at line 990 is called, and the appropriate line is drawn on the display screen.

Note the call to the subroutine at line 1080. This is a windowing routine. The cartesian coordinates produced by the perspective formulas are clipped to fit BASIC's 320 × 200 screen. This windowing routine performs the same function as BASIC's WINDOW SCREEN statement, except that floating point numbers are used, thereby ensuring that no math overflow will occur, no matter where the aerospace vehicle is permitting to fly in the 3D airspace. (For a more detailed discussion of line clipping routines, refer to Appendix B.)

## Tracing the Flight Path

Note line 2200, which is a part of the module which draws the aerospace vehicle on the display screen. The statement GOSUB 2410 sends the program to the tracing module. The first set of DISPLAY COOR-DINATES for the aerospace vehicle is plotted as a simple point on the screen. Then, before any further drawing occurs, the hidden written-to page is copied back onto page 2, the generic background page. This results in a series of single dots on the generic background page. The series forms a graphic history of the flight path of the aerospace vehicle.

When the aerospace vehicle is completed, control returns to line 1720, which in turn returns control to the main animation routine.

## AN OVERVIEW

This program is noteworthy for its demonstration of a complicated simulation environment using the relatively straightforward concept of real-time animation introduced in Chapter 19 and Chapter 22. By using an off-the-shelf personal computer and ordinary BASIC, you can simulate realistic model movement inside 3D space using the same formula concepts used by multimillion dollar mainframe and mini computers. As always, the key lies in the quality of the programming, as opposed to the price tag of the hardware.

## HOW TO MAKE THE PROGRAM FULLY INTERACTIVE

`You can easily modify this program to make it fully interactive at the end-user level. A few IF . . . THEN statements using INKEY$ inserted into the main animation routine will do the trick. You will also be required to disable the artificial intelligence routine, of course.

To give yourself the ability to control the aerospace vehicle's movements from the keyboard, try the following modifications.

Change line 310 to read: **G = C3:GOSUB 1600**

This will cause the program to bypass the artificial intelligence routine. If you run the program without any further changes, the aerospace vehicle will merely fly off into oblivion. It will perform no rolls, climbs, or dives. Its flightpath will be level and straight. Now add the following lines:

```
305   K$ = INKEY$ 'check for any keystrokes
306   IF K$ = "D" THEN R2A1 = .05 'roll right
307   IF K$ = "A" THEN R2A1 = - .05 'roll left
308   IF K$ = "S" THEN R2A1 = 0 'hold roll steady
```

Then, start up the program. If you press D, the aerospace vehicle will begin to roll right. If you touch A, the vehicle will roll left. The craft will continue to roll until you press S to hold it steady in its current attitude. You are now flying the aerospace vehicle through 3D airspace. You control the direction of the aerospace vehicle!

If you wish to incorporate keyboard controls for climbing and diving, add the following lines of code:

**308 IF K\$ = "W" THEN R3A1 = .05 ELSE IF K\$ = "X" THEN R3A1 = – .05 'dive and climb**

**309 IF K\$ = "S" THEN R2A1 = 0:R3A1 = 0 'hold roll and pitch steady**

You now have a complete aircraft control yoke in the A-S-D-W-X key matrix. Using your left hand, press A or D to roll the aerospace vehicle and change direction. Press W or X or cause a nose-up or nose-down attitude. You may wish to change line 1680 to read: **IF NY < – 10 THEN NY = 10.** This will permit you to fly the aerospace vehicle through all quadrants of the gnomon, as opposed to merely above ground zero. (These program revisions have been tested and verified OK on an IBM PC using BASICA 3.21 and on an IBM PCjr using Cartridge BASIC.)

If you are serious about interactive keyboard controls, you should tackle the project in a professional way by putting all the IF . . . THEN keystroke statements in a separate subroutine. Insert a simple GOSUB statement in the main animation routine to jump to the keyboard control subroutine.

## SUMMARY

In this chapter, you learned how to create a very complicated simulation program using the relatively simple concepts of real-time animation. You discovered how easy it is to convert the demonstration program to provide full interactive control.

The next chapter shows you how to create advanced architectural models using static instancing.

# 27

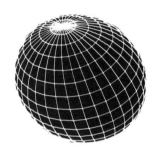

# *Architectural Design*

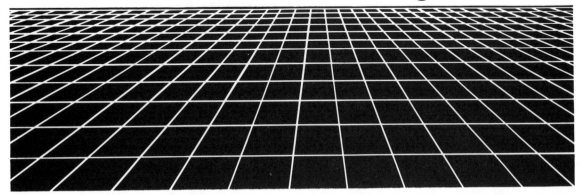

The techniques discussed in previous chapters can be put to work creating realistic architectural designs. In this chapter you will learn how to produce a 3D layout for an interior office design using the advanced programming techniques of instancing and sub-objects.

## PREPARATION

A thorough understanding of two important concepts is necessary before architectural modeling can be undertaken in a serious way. These two concepts are sub-object modeling and static instancing. Both concepts are derived from the fundamental concepts of modeling, rendering, and animation already discussed in the book.

### Sub-Object Modeling

As you discovered in previous sections of the book, simple shapes such as cubes, parallelepipeds, pyramids, spheres, cylinders, and planes can be combined to create more complex objects. These simple shapes are called sub-objects. The industrial part which was generated by the demonstration program in Chapter 23, for example, was constructed from a series of four-sided planes. Even a sub-object like a cylinder can be broken down into more rudimentary sub-objects such as four-sided polygon planes (the curved sides) and 36-sided polygon planes (the ends).

By combining simple parallelepipeds of different sizes, it is a manageable task to prepare a realistic scale drawing of a 3D office interior on your personal computer. A parallelepiped is simply a 3D rectangular object with six surfaces, each of which is a parallelogram. A cube is a parallelepiped. A 3D box of any shape is a parallelepiped.

Six sub-objects can be used to draw a simple office chair, for example. See Fig. 27-1. Even an office courtesy table can be readily generated from simple parallelepipeds. You might wish to think of each occurance of a sub-object in the model as an instancing of the sub-object, although there is a more important use for instancing in architectural modeling.

### Static Instancing

Once a subroutine has been programmed to create the six parallelepipeds which make up a chair, the subroutine can be called to place the chair in a speci-

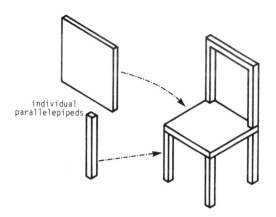

individual
parallelepipeds

Fig. 27-1. Architectural objects can be created by multiple instancing of a parallelepiped.

fied location within the 3D environment. You can then call the subroutine a second time and have it draw the chair in a second location. You now have two instances of the chair. If your subroutine is properly designed, you can call the subroutine a third time and have the chair rotated to face in a new direction. There are now three instances of the chair in your 3D environment.

The ability to use the same routine to produce a variety of instances of the same design is very valuable. You can quickly produce a group of chairs, tables, and filing cabinets to fill an office. Even walls can be rotated and scaled to create the boundaries of the room.

## DEMONSTRATION: ARCHITECTURAL DESIGN

Figure 27-2 shows the screen output of the demonstration program in Fig. 27-3. To run this program from the companion diskette, type **LOAD "A-43.BAS",R**. The program generates a wire-frame representation of a large office filled with numerous chairs, worktables, and filing cabinets.

As you run the program, you will notice that the first components to be drawn are the two far walls of the office. Because the walls have thickness, as well as height and width, they are in fact parallelepipeds.

Next, the program creates two office worktables. For each table, the program first draws four legs, each one a simple parallelepiped. Then the work surfacing is set on top of the legs. The table top is simply a flattened parallelepiped, of course.

Two office filing cabinets are then generated. Each cabinet is simply a tall parallelepiped.

Next, a courtesy table for visitors to the office is drawn. Note how even the crossmembers at the base of the tables can be constructed from two parallelepipeds. Finally, five instances of an office chair are

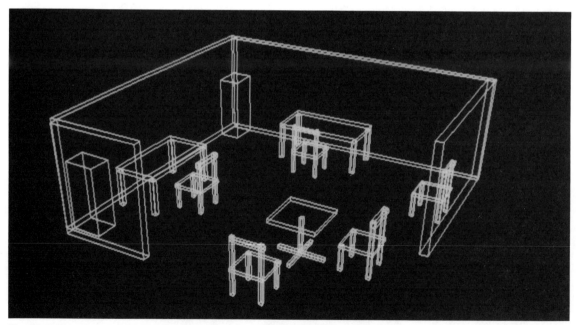

Fig. 27-2. The display image produced by the demonstration program in Fig. 27-3.

344

Fig. 27-3. Interior office design using instancing of sub-objects.

```
100 'Program A-43.BAS     Interior office design.
110 'Demonstrates instancing (rotation and translation) of i
ndependently-constructed subobjects in a 3D environment.
120 '_____
130 '
140   GOTO 650    'configure system
150   GOSUB 850   'assign scalar data
160   LOCATE 2,1:PRINT "INTERIOR OFFICE DESIGN"
170 '_____
180 '
190 'master routine:  define and draw subobjects
200 'draw walls
210   X1=-6:Y1=0:Z1=-6:J=0:D1=20:D2=.5:D3=8:C=C3:GOSUB 1020
'north wall
220   X1=-6:Y1=0:Z1=-6:J=90:D1=20:D2=.5:D3=8:C=C3:GOSUB 1020
 'west wall
230 '_____
240 '
250 'draw work-tables
260   X5=0:Y5=0:Z5=-5:C=C2:J1=0:GOSUB 1320  'table against no
rth wall
270   X5=-5.5:Y5=0:Z5=10:C=C2:J1=270:GOSUB 1320  'table again
st west wall
280 '_____
290 '
300 'draw filing cabinets
310   X1=-6:Y1=0:Z1=-5.5:J=0:D1=1.5:D2=2:D3=5:C=C2:GOSUB 1020

320   X1=-6:Y1=0:Z1=12.3:J=0:D1=2:D2=1.5:D3=5:C=C2:GOSUB 1020

330 '_____
340 '
350 'draw courtesy table
360   X5=6:Y5=0:Z5=8:C=C1:GOSUB 1460
370 '_____
380 '
390 'draw chairs
400   X5=10:Y5=0:Z5=8:J1=270:C=C2:GOSUB 1550
410   X5=11.5:Y5=0:Z5=0:J1=270:C=C1:GOSUB 1550
420   X5=-2:Y5=0:Z5=6.5:J1=270:C=C1:GOSUB 1550
430   X5=2:Y5=0:Z5=-2:J1=0:C=C1:GOSUB 1550
440   X5=6:Y5=0:Z5=13:J1=0:C=C2:GOSUB 1550
450 '_____
460 '
470 'redraw near wall sections
```

```
480    X1=14:Y1=0:Z1=-6:J=90:D1=12:D2=.5:D3=8:C=C3:GOSUB 1020
  'redraw east wall
490    X1=-6:Y1=0:Z1=14:J=0:D1=6:D2=.5:D3=8:C=C3:GOSUB 1020    '
redraw south wall
500    SOUND 250,.7  'done
510    GOTO 510  'clean halt.
520    END 'of master routine.
530    '-----------------------------------------------
540    '
550    'module:   perspective calculations for Cartesian world c
oordinates
560    X=(-1)*X:XA=CR1*X-SR1*Z:ZA=SR1*X+CR1*Z:X=CR2*XA+SR2*Y:Y
A=CR2*Y-SR2*XA:Z=CR3*ZA-SR3*YA:Y=SR3*ZA+CR3*YA:X=X+MX:Y=Y+MY
:Z=Z+MZ:SX=D*X/Z:SY=D*Y/Z:RETURN
570    '_____
580    '
590    'module:   return to BASIC interpreter
600    CLS:WINDOW:SCREEN 0,0,0,0:WIDTH 80:COLOR 7,0,0:CLS:LOCA
TE 1,1,1:END
610    '_____
620    '
630    'module:   UNIVERSAL
640    'This routine configures the program for the hardware/so
ftware being used.
650    KEY OFF:CLS:ON ERROR GOTO 680  'trap if not Enhanced Di
splay + EGA
660    SCREEN 9,,0,0:COLOR 7,0:PALETTE 1,44:PALETTE 2,34:PALET
TE 3,7:C0=0:C1=1:C2=2:C3=3:LOCATE 1,1:PRINT "ED-EGA 640x350
16-color mode"
670    GOTO 780  'jump to screen coordinates set-up
680    RESUME 690
690    ON ERROR GOTO 720  'trap if not Color Display + EGA
700    SCREEN 8,,0,0:COLOR 7,0:PALETTE 1,12:PALETTE 2,2:PALETT
E 3,7:C0=0:C1=1:C2=2:C3=3:LOCATE 1,1:PRINT "CD-EGA 640x200 1
6-color mode"
710    GOTO 780  'jump to screen coordinates set-up
720    RESUME 730
730    ON ERROR GOTO 760  'trap if not PCjr
740    CLEAR,,,32768!:SCREEN 6,0,0,0:COLOR 3,0:PALETTE 1,12:PA
LETTE 2,2:PALETTE 3,7:C0=0:C1=1:C2=2:C3=3:LOCATE 1,1:PRINT "
PCjr 640x200 4-color mode"
750    GOTO 780  'jump to screen coordinates set-up
760    RESUME 770
770    SCREEN 1,0:COLOR 0,1:C0=0:C1=1:C2=2:C3=3:LOCATE 1,1:PRI
NT "CGA 320x200 4-color mode"
780    ON ERROR GOTO 0  'disable error trapping override
790    WINDOW SCREEN (-399,-299)-(400,300)
800    ON KEY (2) GOSUB 600:KEY (2) ON  'F2 key to exit progra
m
```

```
810   GOTO 150   'return to main program
820 '_____
830 '
840 'module:   assign variables
850   D=1200:R1=5.78539:R2=0:R3=5.79778:MX=0:MY=0:MZ=-52   '3D
 parameters
860   DEFINT J:J=0  'instancing rotation factor 0-90-180-270
870   SX=0:SY=0:SX1=0:SY1=0:SX2=0:SY2=0:D1=0:D2=0:D3=0:C=C3:X
1=0:X2=0:X3=0:X4=0:Y1=0:Z1=0:Z2=0:Z3=0:Z4=0   'assorted varia
bles
880   DIM A2(7,1)   '8 sets of sx,sy display coordinates
890   SR1=SIN(R1):CR1=COS(R1):SR2=SIN(R2):CR2=COS(R2):SR3=SIN
(R3):CR3=COS(R3):RETURN
900 '_____
910 '
920 'module:   graphics engine subroutines
930 'called by 3D polygon engine
940   PSET (SX1,SY1),C:RETURN
950   LINE (SX1,SY1)-(SX2,SY2),C:RETURN
960   LINE-(SX2,SY2),C:RETURN
970 '_____
980 '
990 'module:   3D polygon engine subroutine
1000 'this module draws a 3D parallelepiped facing 0, 90, 18
0, or 270 degrees at a position parallel to ground.  Width,
depth, height of parallelepiped are controlled by the callin
g routine.
1010 'this subroutine can be used to build complex 3D subobj
ects from rudimentary components
1020   IF J=0 THEN XF=1:ZF=1
1030   IF J=90 THEN SWAP D1,D2:XF=-1:ZF=1
1040   IF J=180 THEN XF=-1:ZF=-1
1050   IF J=270 THEN SWAP D1,D2:XF=1:ZF=-1
1060   X4=X1:X2=X1+(D1*XF):X3=X2:Z2=Z1:Z4=Z1+(D2*ZF):Z3=Z4
1070   X=X1:Y=Y1:Z=Z1:GOSUB 560:A2(0,0)=SX:A2(0,1)=SY
1080   X=X2:Y=Y1:Z=Z2:GOSUB 560:A2(1,0)=SX:A2(1,1)=SY
1090   X=X3:Y=Y1:Z=Z3:GOSUB 560:A2(2,0)=SX:A2(2,1)=SY
1100   X=X4:Y=Y1:Z=Z4:GOSUB 560:A2(3,0)=SX:A2(3,1)=SY
1110   X=X1:Y=Y1+D3:Z=Z1:GOSUB 560:A2(4,0)=SX:A2(4,1)=SY
1120   X=X2:Y=Y1+D3:Z=Z2:GOSUB 560:A2(5,0)=SX:A2(5,1)=SY
1130   X=X3:Y=Y1+D3:Z=Z3:GOSUB 560:A2(6,0)=SX:A2(6,1)=SY
1140   X=X4:Y=Y1+D3:Z=Z4:GOSUB 560:A2(7,0)=SX:A2(7,1)=SY
1150   SX1=A2(0,0):SY1=A2(0,1):SX2=A2(1,0):SY2=A2(1,1):GOSUB
950
1160   SX2=A2(2,0):SY2=A2(2,1):GOSUB 960
1170   SX2=A2(3,0):SY2=A2(3,1):GOSUB 960
1180   SX2=A2(0,0):SY2=A2(0,1):GOSUB 960
1190   SX2=A2(4,0):SY2=A2(4,1):GOSUB 960
1200   SX2=A2(5,0):SY2=A2(5,1):GOSUB 960
```

```
1210    SX2=A2(6,0):SY2=A2(6,1):GOSUB 960
1220    SX2=A2(7,0):SY2=A2(7,1):GOSUB 960
1230    SX2=A2(4,0):SY2=A2(4,1):GOSUB 960
1240    SX1=A2(7,0):SY1=A2(7,1):SX2=A2(3,0):SY2=A2(3,1):GOSUB
950
1250    SX1=A2(6,0):SY1=A2(6,1):SX2=A2(2,0):SY2=A2(2,1):GOSUB
950
1260    SX1=A2(5,0):SY1=A2(5,1):SX2=A2(1,0):SY2=A2(1,1):GOSUB
950
1270    SOUND 250,.7:RETURN
1280    '--------
1290    '
1300    'module:   subobject instancing of table
1310    'enter with X5,Y5,Z5 location;  C color;  J1 subobject
rotation
1320    IF J1=0 THEN 1340 ELSE IF J1=90 THEN 1360 ELSE IF J1=1
80 THEN 1380 ELSE IF J1=270 THEN 1400
1330    SOUND 100,10:LOCATE 3,1:PRINT "Illegal rotation angle
of subobject":RETURN
1340    D1=.3:D2=.3:D3=2.7:J=0:X1=X5:Y1=Y5:Z1=Z5:GOSUB 1020:X1
=X5+5.7:GOSUB 1020:Z1=Z5+2.7:GOSUB 1020:X1=X5:GOSUB 1020   'l
egs
1350    D1=6:D2=3:D3=.3:J=0:X1=X5:Y1=Y5+2.7:Z1=Z5:GOSUB 1020:R
ETURN   'top
1360    D1=.3:D2=.3:D3=2.7:J=0:X1=X5-.3:Y1=Y5:Z1=Z5:GOSUB 1020
:Z1=Z5+5.7:GOSUB 1020:X1=X5-3:GOSUB 1020:Z1=Z5:GOSUB 1020    '
legs
1370    D1=6:D2=3:D3=.3:J=90:X1=X5:Y1=Y5+2.7:Z1=Z5:GOSUB 1020:
RETURN   'top
1380    D1=.3:D2=.3:D3=2.7:J=0:X1=X5-.3:Y1=Y5:Z1=Z5-.3:GOSUB 1
020:X1=X5-6:GOSUB 1020:Z1=Z5-3:GOSUB 1020:X1=X5-.3:GOSUB 102
0   'legs
1390    D1=6:D2=3:D3=.3:J=180:X1=X5:Y1=Y5+2.7:Z1=Z5:GOSUB 1020
:RETURN   'top
1400    D1=.3:D2=.3:D3=2.7:J=0:X1=X5:Y1=Y5:Z1=Z5-.3:GOSUB 1020
:Z1=Z5-6:GOSUB 1020:X1=X5+2.7:GOSUB 1020:Z1=Z5-.3:GOSUB 1020
   'legs
1410    D1=6:D2=3:D3=.3:J=270:X1=X5:Y1=Y5+2.7:Z1=Z5:GOSUB 1020
:RETURN   'top
1420    '--------
1430    '
1440    'module:   subobject instancing of courtesy table
1450    'enter with X5,Y5,Z5 location;  C color
1460    J=0:D1=3:D2=.2:D3=.2:X1=X5:Y1=Y5:Z1=Z5+1.35:GOSUB 1020
   'brace
1470    J=0:D1=.2:D2=3:D3=.2:X1=X5+1.35:Y1=Y5:Z1=Z5:GOSUB 1020
   'brace
1480    J=0:D1=.2:D2=.2:D3=2.4:X1=X5+1.35:Y1=Y5+.3:Z1=Z5+1.35:
GOSUB 1020   'center post
```

```
1490    J=0:D1=3:D2=3:D3=.3:X1=X5:Y1=Y5+2.7:Z1=Z5:GOSUB 1020
'top
1500    RETURN
1510 '_____
1520 '
1530 'module:   subobject instancing of chair
1540 'enter with X5,Y5,Z5 location;  C color;  J1 subobject
rotation
1550    IF J1=0 THEN 1570 ELSE IF J1=270 THEN 1610
1560    SOUND 100,10:LOCATE 3,1:PRINT "Illegal rotation angle
of subobject":RETURN

1570    D1=.2:D2=.2:D3=1.8:J=0:X1=X5:Y1=Y5:Z1=Z5:GOSUB 1020:X1
=X5+1.7:GOSUB 1020  'front legs
1580    D1=.2:D2=.2:D3=4:J=0:X1=X5:Y1=Y5:Z1=Z5+1.7:GOSUB 1020:
X1=X5+1.7:GOSUB 1020  'back legs
1590    D1=2:D2=2:D3=.2:J=0:X1=X5:Y1=Y5+1.7:Z1=Z5:GOSUB 1020
'seat
1600    D1=2:D2=.2:D3=.2:J=0:X1=X5:Y1=Y5+3.7:Z1=Z5+1.7:GOSUB 1
020:RETURN  'brace
1610    D1=.2:D2=.2:D3=1.8:J=0:X1=X5:Y1=Y5:Z1=Z5:GOSUB 1020:Z1
=Z5+1.7:GOSUB 1020  'front legs
1620    D1=.2:D2=.2:D3=4:J=0:X1=X5+1.7:Y1=Y5:Z1=Z5:GOSUB 1020:
Z1=Z5+1.7:GOSUB 1020  'back legs
1630    D1=2:D2=2:D3=.2:J=0:X1=X5:Y1=Y5+1.7:Z1=Z5:GOSUB 1020
'seat
1640    D1=.3:D2=2:D3=.3:J=0:X1=X5+1.7:Y1=Y5+3.7:Z1=Z5:GOSUB 1
020:RETURN  'brace
1650 '_____
1660 '
1670    END 'of program code
```

created. Each chair is drawn by the same subroutine, only the drawing color, the location, and the rotation of the chairs have been altered for each instance.

After the office furniture has been installed by the program, the two near walls are added. The architectural design is complete.

## INTERACTING WITH THE PROGRAM

You can interact with this program at the source code level. To view the entire office design from a different angle, try changing the value of R1 in line 850 to 4.98539. This affects the yaw rotation of the entire office layout. To alter the pitch angle, try changing the value of R3 in line 850 to 5.39778. This will give you more of a bird's eye view. To gain a flatter viewpoint, try changing R3 in line 850 to 6.08539.

After you are finished experimenting, return to line 850 and restore R1 to 5.78539, R2 to 0, and R3 to 5.79778.

## The Polygon Engine

The most important section of code in this demonstration program is the polygon driver located at lines 990 through 1270. This subroutine draws a simple 3D rectangle (box).

Note lines 1020 through 1050. The subroutine expects to receive certain parameters from the caller. The variable J denotes the direction which the parallelepiped is facing. It can be rotated to either 0 degrees (north), 90 degrees (east), 180 degrees (south), or 270 degrees (west). The D1 variable used by the polygon engine represents the length of the parallelepiped. D2 represents the depth, or thickness. D3 denotes the height. If you check line 210, which calls the polygon engine to draw a wall, you can see that the D1 length of the wall has been set to 20 feet; the D2 thickness of the wall has been set to .5 feet (6 inches); the D3 length of the wall has been set to 8 feet. The C variable in line 210 sets the drawing color to C3, which is white.

Once these parameters have been passed to the polygon engine at lines 990 through 1270, the subroutine swaps various x, y, z coordinate values to ensure that the parallelepiped box is drawn in the correct manner.

Lines 1060 through 1140 calculate the display coordinates for the eight vertices of the box. Note how lines 1110 through 1140 simply add the D3 thickness of the parallelepiped to determine the second four vertices.

Lines 1150 through 1260 simply retrieve these display coordinates and call the appropriate point-setting or line-drawing subroutines at lines 940 through 960 to aid in drawing the box on the display screen.

### Drawing the Walls

As you have seen, line 210 calls the polygon engine to draw the north wall (the far wall on the right side of the screen). The X1, Y1, Z1 variables in line 210 establish the pivotal corner of the box. The J rotation factor simply serves to rotate the parallelepiped around this pivot. Compare line 210 with line 220. Line 220 uses the same pivotal coordinates, but rotates the wall to 90 degrees.

You may wish to experiment with this algorithm by trying a few modifications to the source code. First, try changing the value of Z1 in line 220 to −2. This moves the entire west wall closer to your viewpoint. After watching the program run, try changing the value of J in line 220 to 0. This rotates the west wall so it is parallel to the far north wall. Be sure and restore Z1 to −6 and J to 90 after you are finished tinkering.

### Drawing the Tables

Line 260 in the main routine is responsible for drawing one of the worktables. First, it establishes the location of the pivotal point by defining X5,Y5,Z5. Next, it sets the drawing color to C2 (green on an EGA

or PCjr, magenta on a Color/Graphics Adapter). Finally, it defines the J1 rotation angle to 0 degrees (i.e., north) before calling a sub-object modeling routine at line 1320.

Line 1310 describes the parameters (called arguments by many programmers) which the instancing module expects to receive. As line 1320 illustrates, the routine is currently designed to accept four different rotation angles: 0, 90, 180, and 270 degrees. Based upon the value of J1, the program jumps to the appropriate section of code.

Lines 1340 and 1350 draw the table at rotation angle zero, for example. Each time GOSUB 1020 is used, the subroutine is calling the standard polygon engine to draw a box on the screen. Four boxes are needed to draw the four legs of the table. Line 1350 calls the polygon driver once in order to create the top of the worktable. The height, width, depth, and rotation angle for each polygon is defined by the routine before the polygon engine is called.

You can experiment with this algorithm by modifying line 260. (You can try modifying the table-drawing routine at lines 1300 through 1410, but you run the risk of distorting the fundamental shape of the table.)

Try changing the value of J1 in line 260 to 90. Run the program and observe the results. The table against the north wall has been rotated! You can see how easy it would be to experiment with different furniture arrangements using this demonstration program. Try changing the value of Z5 in line 260 to −14. You have just moved the table into another room on the other side of the north wall!

### Drawing the Filing Cabinets, Courtesy Table, and Chairs

The other pieces of furniture in the office layout are drawn using similar algorithms. The main routine assigns values to expected arguments and then passes these parameters to the appropriate subroutines.

The module at lines 1440 through 1500 draws a courtesy table. Although only one table is drawn in the demonstration program, you can easily add another line to the main routine in order to draw another table at another location in the 3D environment.

The module at lines 1530 through 1640 draws a chair. This module is called five times by the main routine to create the five instances of the office chair in the architectural scene.

## OVERVIEW

You can think of sub-objects as layers of program code. A group of sub-objects (flat planes) can be combined to create a more complex sub-object (a 3D box or parallelepiped). Then, a group of these new sub-objects (parallelepipeds) can be combined to generate an even more complicated sub-object (a chair, for example). Next, a collection of these sub-objects (chairs, tables, filing cabinets) can be ordered together to create a macro sub-object (an entire office). You could, of course, even gather together a group of offices to make up an entire floor.

The important principles to grasp are those of sub-object modeling and static instancing. Using sub-objects, you can draw almost any real-world object. Using instancing, you can place one or more copies of that object at any position in your 3D environment.

You might find it interesting to experiment with this program to create a scale drawing of your office or familyroom. Remember, each x, y, z unit equals one foot in the real world. Make your walls eight feet high.

## SUMMARY

In this chapter, you learned how to use sub-object modeling and static instancing to create complex displays. You discovered how easy it is to experiment with "what-if" options when your personal computer has been programmed to generate architectural designs.

The next chapter discusses some advanced techniques in animation for the EGA.

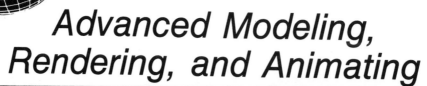

# 28

# Advanced Modeling, Rendering, and Animating

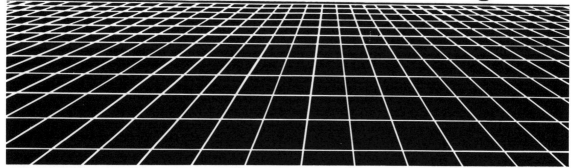

Although the Color/Graphics Adapter and the PCjr video subsystem are somewhat limited in terms of graphics capabilities, the EGA possesses many advanced features. Some of the EGA's capabilities can be put to good use in creating attractive displays, especially animated displays of modeling and rendering programs.

The demonstration program in this chapter is included just for fun. It pushes the EGA to its limits to show you just what the Enhanced Graphics Adapter is capable of in terms of realistic animation of fully-shaded models.

## DEMONSTRATION:
## ADVANCED ANIMATION FOR THE EGA

Figure 28-1 shows the animated screen output produced by the demonstration program in Fig. 28-2. To run this program from the companion diskette, type **LOAD "A-44.BAS",R**. The program individually animates six different cubes, each spinning in a different direction.

As you watch the animated sequence, you can see the brightness of each surface change as the cube rotates its surfaces relative to the light source. Each cube

has been shaded by the computer during preparation of the four graphics pages which make up this program. Because the light source seems to affect each cube during rotation, the sense of realism is almost uncanny. The animation technique used, of course, is frame animation. Check back to Chapters 19 and 22 for more information about animation.

A program like this makes you proud to have an EGA. The animation is effective because enough colors are available with high enough resolution and with enough pages to carry off the illusion of movement and shading. The program runs in the 640 × 200 16-color mode, which offers four pages. (The animation would not be as effective in the 640 × 350 mode, because only two pages are available.) The 320 × 200 4-color mode of the Color/Graphics Adapter can create the shaded cubes, of course, but no extra colors are available to create the bull's eye target, which gives the image its punch. The 640 × 200 4-color mode of the PCjr and Tandy has the resolution, but again only four colors are available.

You can experiment with the position of the light source by modifying the value of XL, YL, and ZL in line 1700. See Appendix B for a more detailed discussion of the geometry involved.

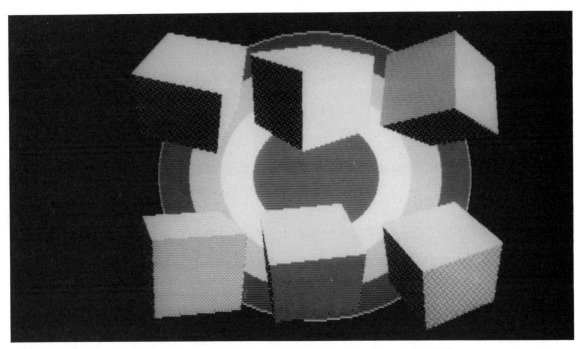

Fig. 28-1. The animated display image produced by the demonstration program in Fig. 28-2.

Fig. 28-2. Advanced animation on the EGA.

```
100 'Program A-44.BAS    Advanced animation for the EGA.
110 'Demonstrates simultaneous multiple rotation of individu
al fully-shaded cubes.  Uses frame animation with 4 graphics
 pages in the 640x200 16-color mode.
120 '_____
130 '
140   GOTO 1560    'configure system
150   GOSUB 1650   'assign variables
160 '_____
170 '
180 'master routine:  create 4 graphics pages, each showing
6 different simultaneous views of a computer-shaded cube
190   GOSUB 2660:R1=4.46141:VIEW (1,1)-(319,99):GOSUB 2520:GO
SUB 570
200   R1=3.76325:R3=6.00009:VIEW (152,1)-(470,99):GOSUB 2520:
GOSUB 570
210   R1=4.16325:R3=.48319:VIEW (320,1)-(639,99):GOSUB 2520:G
OSUB 570
220   R1=3.40009:R3=5.89778:VIEW (1,100)-(319,199):GOSUB 2520
:GOSUB 570
230   R1=3.34159:R3=5.49778:VIEW (152,100)-(470,199):GOSUB 25
20:GOSUB 570
```

```
240   R1=5.29239:R3=5.59778:VIEW (320,100)-(639,199):GOSUB 25
20:GOSUB 570
250   PCOPY 0,3:VIEW:CLS:LOCATE 25,14:PRINT "Simultaneous ANI
MATED views of computer-shaded 3D cube"
260   GOSUB 2660:R1=4.37277:VIEW (1,1)-(319,99):GOSUB 2520:GO
SUB 570
270   R1=3.80689:R3=5.95727:VIEW (152,1)-(470,99):GOSUB 2520:
GOSUB 570
280   R1=4.11962:R3=.43956:VIEW (320,1)-(639,99):GOSUB 2520:G
OSUB 570
290   R1=3.35645:R3=5.89778:VIEW (1,100)-(319,199):GOSUB 2520
:GOSUB 570
300   R1=3.34159:R3=5.54141:VIEW (152,100)-(470,199):GOSUB 25
20:GOSUB 570
310   R1=5.24876:R3=5.55414:VIEW (320,100)-(639,199):GOSUB 25
20:GOSUB 570
320   PCOPY 0,2:VIEW:CLS:LOCATE 25,14:PRINT "Simultaneous ANI
MATED views of computer-shaded 3D cube"
330   GOSUB 2660:R1=4.32914:VIEW (1,1)-(319,99):GOSUB 2520:GO
SUB 570
340   R1=3.85052:R3=5.91364:VIEW (152,1)-(470,99):GOSUB 2520:
GOSUB 570
350   R1=4.07599:R3=.39593:VIEW (320,1)-(639,99):GOSUB 2520:G
OSUB 570
360   R1=3.31282:R3=5.89778:VIEW (1,100)-(319,199):GOSUB 2520
:GOSUB 570
370   R1=3.34158:R3=5.58043:VIEW (152,100)-(470,199):GOSUB 25
20:GOSUB 570
380   R1=5.20513:R3=5.51051:VIEW (320,100)-(639,199):GOSUB 25
20:GOSUB 570
390   PCOPY 0,1:VIEW:CLS:LOCATE 25,14:PRINT "Simultaneous ANI
MATED views of computer-shaded 3D cube"
400   GOSUB 2660:R1=4.28551:VIEW (1,1)-(319,99):GOSUB 2520:GO
SUB 570
410   R1=3.89415:R3=5.87001:VIEW (152,1)-(470,99):GOSUB 2520:
GOSUB 570
420   R1=4.03236:R3=.3523:VIEW (320,1)-(639,99):GOSUB 2520:GO
SUB 570
430   R1=3.26918:R3=5.89778:VIEW (1,100)-(319,199):GOSUB 2520
:GOSUB 570
440   R1=3.34158:R3=5.62406:VIEW (152,100)-(470,199):GOSUB 25
20:GOSUB 570
450   R1=5.1615:R3=5.46688:VIEW (320,100)-(639,199):GOSUB 252
0:GOSUB 570
460   BEEP   'announce ready for animation sequence
470  '_____
480  '
490  'master routine:  animation loop
500   SCREEN,,,3:FOR T=1 TO 1000 STEP 1:NEXT:BEEP
```

```
510  SCREEN,,,3:FOR T=1 TO 600 STEP 1:NEXT:SCREEN,,,2:FOR T=
1 TO 200 STEP 1:NEXT:SCREEN,,,1:FOR T=1 TO 200 STEP 1:NEXT:S
CREEN,,,O:FOR T=1 TO 600 STEP 1:NEXT
520  SCREEN,,,1:FOR T=1 TO 200 STEP 1:NEXT:SCREEN,,,2:FOR T=
1 TO 200 STEP 1:NEXT:GOTO 510
530  GOTO 530
540  '_____
550  '
560  'module:  draw 3D cube using plane equation method of hi
dden surface removal
570  RESTORE 1920  'beginning of database
580  FOR T=0 TO 7 STEP 1:READ X,Y,Z:GOSUB 1480:B1(T,0)=X:B1(
T,1)=Y:B1(T,2)=Z:B2(T,0)=SX:B2(T,1)=SY:NEXT T  'load vertex
view coordinates into array B1, load vertex display coordina
tes into array B2
590  FOR T=0 TO 5 STEP 1:READ X,Y,Z:GOSUB 1480:B3(T,0)=SX:B3
(T,1)=SY:NEXT T  'load area fill origin display coordinates
into array B3
600  '_____
610  '
620  'surface 0 routine
630  X1=B1(7,0):Y1=B1(7,1):Z1=B1(7,2):X2=B1(0,0):Y2=B1(0,1):
Z2=B1(0,2):X3=B1(3,0):Y3=B1(3,1):Z3=B1(3,2)  'retrieve XYZ v
iewing coordinates for surface 0
640  GOSUB 2000  'jump to surface perpendicular routine
650  IF SP>0 THEN GOTO 770
660  SX=B2(7,0):SY=B2(7,1):PSET (SX,SY),C2:SX=B2(0,0):SY=B2(
0,1):LINE-(SX,SY),C2:SX=B2(3,0):SY=B2(3,1):LINE-(SX,SY),C2:S
X=B2(6,0):SY=B2(6,1):LINE-(SX,SY),C2:SX=B2(7,0):SY=B2(7,1):L
INE-(SX,SY),C2
670  SX=B3(0,0):SY=B3(0,1):PAINT (SX,SY),C2,C2  'template fo
r surface 0
680  SX=B2(7,0):SY=B2(7,1):PSET (SX,SY),C3:SX=B2(0,0):SY=B2(
0,1):LINE-(SX,SY),C3:SX=B2(3,0):SY=B2(3,1):LINE-(SX,SY),C3:S
X=B2(6,0):SY=B2(6,1):LINE-(SX,SY),C3:SX=B2(7,0):SY=B2(7,1):L
INE-(SX,SY),C3
690  SX=B3(0,0):SY=B3(0,1):PAINT (SX,SY),0,C3  'surface 0 co
mpleted
700  GOSUB 2040
710  PAINT (SX,SY),A$,C3
720  SX1=B2(7,0):SY1=B2(7,1):SX2=B2(0,0):SY2=B2(0,1):SX3=B2(
3,0):SY3=B2(3,1):SX4=B2(6,0):SY4=B2(6,1)
730  GOSUB 2440
740  '_____
750  '
760  'surface 1 routine
770  X1=B1(6,0):Y1=B1(6,1):Z1=B1(6,2):X2=B1(5,0):Y2=B1(5,1):
Z2=B1(5,2):X3=B1(4,0):Y3=B1(4,1):Z3=B1(4,2)  'retrieve XYZ v
iewing coordinates for surface 1
```

```
780    GOSUB 2000   'jump to surface perpendicular routine
790    IF SP>0 THEN GOTO 910
800    SX=B2(6,0):SY=B2(6,1):PSET (SX,SY),C2:SX=B2(5,0):SY=B2(
5,1):LINE-(SX,SY),C2:SX=B2(4,0):SY=B2(4,1):LINE-(SX,SY),C2:S
X=B2(7,0):SY=B2(7,1):LINE-(SX,SY),C2:SX=B2(6,0):SY=B2(6,1):L
INE-(SX,SY),C2
810    SX=B3(1,0):SY=B3(1,1):PAINT (SX,SY),C2,C2   'template fo
r surface 1
820    SX=B2(6,0):SY=B2(6,1):PSET (SX,SY),C3:SX=B2(5,0):SY=B2(
5,1):LINE-(SX,SY),C3:SX=B2(4,0):SY=B2(4,1):LINE-(SX,SY),C3:S
X=B2(7,0):SY=B2(7,1):LINE-(SX,SY),C3:SX=B2(6,0):SY=B2(6,1):L
INE-(SX,SY),C3
830    SX=B3(1,0):SY=B3(1,1):PAINT (SX,SY),0,C3   'surface 1 co
mpleted
840    GOSUB 2040
850    PAINT (SX,SY),A$,C3
860    SX1=B2(6,0):SY1=B2(6,1):SX2=B2(5,0):SY2=B2(5,1):SX3=B2(
4,0):SY3=B2(4,1):SX4=B2(7,0):SY4=B2(7,1)
870    GOSUB 2440
880  '_____
890  '
900  'surface 2 routine
910    X1=B1(3,0):Y1=B1(3,1):Z1=B1(3,2):X2=B1(2,0):Y2=B1(2,1):
Z2=B1(2,2):X3=B1(5,0):Y3=B1(5,1):Z3=B1(5,2)   'retrieve XYZ v
iewing coordinates for surface 2
920    GOSUB 2000   'jump to surface perpendicular routine
930    IF SP>0 THEN GOTO 1050
940    SX=B2(3,0):SY=B2(3,1):PSET (SX,SY),C2:SX=B2(2,0):SY=B2(
2,1):LINE-(SX,SY),C2:SX=B2(5,0):SY=B2(5,1):LINE-(SX,SY),C2:S
X=B2(6,0):SY=B2(6,1):LINE-(SX,SY),C2:SX=B2(3,0):SY=B2(3,1):L
INE-(SX,SY),C2
950    SX=B3(2,0):SY=B3(2,1):PAINT (SX,SY),C2,C2   'template fo
r surface 2
960    SX=B2(3,0):SY=B2(3,1):PSET (SX,SY),C3:SX=B2(2,0):SY=B2(
2,1):LINE-(SX,SY),C3:SX=B2(5,0):SY=B2(5,1):LINE-(SX,SY),C3:S
X=B2(6,0):SY=B2(6,1):LINE-(SX,SY),C3:SX=B2(3,0):SY=B2(3,1):L
INE-(SX,SY),C3
970    SX=B3(2,0):SY=B3(2,1):PAINT (SX,SY),0,C3   'surface 2 co
mpleted
980    GOSUB 2040
990    PAINT (SX,SY),A$,C3
1000   SX1=B2(3,0):SY1=B2(3,1):SX2=B2(2,0):SY2=B2(2,1):SX3=B2(
5,0):SY3=B2(5,1):SX4=B2(6,0):SY4=B2(6,1)
1010   GOSUB 2440
1020 '_____
1030 '
1040 'surface 3 routine
1050   X1=B1(0,0):Y1=B1(0,1):Z1=B1(0,2):X2=B1(1,0):Y2=B1(1,1)
```

356

```
:Z2=B1(1,2):X3=B1(2,0):Y3=B1(2,1):Z3=B1(2,2)   'retrieve XYZ
viewing coordinates for surface 3
1060   GOSUB 2000  'jump to surface perpendicular routine
1070   IF SP>0 THEN GOTO 1190
1080   SX=B2(0,0):SY=B2(0,1):PSET (SX,SY),C2:SX=B2(1,0):SY=B2
(1,1):LINE-(SX,SY),C2:SX=B2(2,0):SY=B2(2,1):LINE-(SX,SY),C2:
SX=B2(3,0):SY=B2(3,1):LINE-(SX,SY),C2:SX=B2(0,0):SY=B2(0,1):
LINE-(SX,SY),C2
1090   SX=B3(3,0):SY=B3(3,1):PAINT (SX,SY),C2,C2  'template f
or surface 3
1100   SX=B2(0,0):SY=B2(0,1):PSET (SX,SY),C3:SX=B2(1,0):SY=B2
(1,1):LINE-(SX,SY),C3:SX=B2(2,0):SY=B2(2,1):LINE-(SX,SY),C3:
SX=B2(3,0):SY=B2(3,1):LINE-(SX,SY),C3:SX=B2(0,0):SY=B2(0,1):
LINE-(SX,SY),C3
1110   SX=B3(3,0):SY=B3(3,1):PAINT (SX,SY),0,C3  'surface 3 c
ompleted
1120   GOSUB 2040
1130   PAINT (SX,SY),A$,C3
1140   SX1=B2(0,0):SY1=B2(0,1):SX2=B2(1,0):SY2=B2(1,1):SX3=B2
(2,0):SY3=B2(2,1):SX4=B2(3,0):SY4=B2(3,1)
1150   GOSUB 2440
1160 '_____
1170 '
1180 'surface 4 routine
1190   X1=B1(7,0):Y1=B1(7,1):Z1=B1(7,2):X2=B1(4,0):Y2=B1(4,1)
:Z2=B1(4,2):X3=B1(1,0):Y3=B1(1,1):Z3=B1(1,2)   'retrieve XYZ
viewing coordinates for surface 4
1200   GOSUB 2000  'jump to surface perpendicular routine
1210 IF SP>0 THEN GOTO 1330
1220   SX=B2(7,0):SY=B2(7,1):PSET (SX,SY),C2:SX=B2(4,0):SY=B2
(4,1):LINE-(SX,SY),C2:SX=B2(1,0):SY=B2(1,1):LINE-(SX,SY),C2:
SX=B2(0,0):SY=B2(0,1):LINE-(SX,SY),C2:SX=B2(7,0):SY=B2(7,1):
LINE-(SX,SY),C2
1230   SX=B3(4,0):SY=B3(4,1):PAINT (SX,SY),C2,C2  'template f
or surface 4
1240   SX=B2(7,0):SY=B2(7,1):PSET (SX,SY),C3:SX=B2(4,0):SY=B2
(4,1):LINE-(SX,SY),C3:SX=B2(1,0):SY=B2(1,1):LINE-(SX,SY),C3:
SX=B2(0,0):SY=B2(0,1):LINE-(SX,SY),C3:SX=B2(7,0):SY=B2(7,1):
LINE-(SX,SY),C3
1250   SX=B3(4,0):SY=B3(4,1):PAINT (SX,SY),0,C3  'surface 4 c
ompleted
1260   GOSUB 2040
1270   PAINT (SX,SY),A$,C3
1280   SX1=B2(7,0):SY1=B2(7,1):SX2=B2(4,0):SY2=B2(4,1):SX3=B2
(1,0):SY3=B2(1,1):SX4=B2(0,0):SY4=B2(0,1)
1290   GOSUB 2440
1300 '_____
1310 '
```

```
1320 'surface 5 routine
1330   X1=B1(1,0):Y1=B1(1,1):Z1=B1(1,2):X2=B1(4,0):Y2=B1(4,1)
:Z2=B1(4,2):X3=B1(5,0):Y3=B1(5,1):Z3=B1(5,2)   'retrieve XYZ
viewing coordinates for surface 5
1340   GOSUB 2000  'jump to surface perpendicular routine
1350   IF SP>0 THEN GOTO 1440
1360   SX=B2(1,0):SY=B2(1,1):PSET (SX,SY),C2:SX=B2(4,0):SY=B2
(4,1):LINE-(SX,SY),C2:SX=B2(5,0):SY=B2(5,1):LINE-(SX,SY),C2:
SX=B2(2,0):SY=B2(2,1):LINE-(SX,SY),C2:SX=B2(1,0):SY=B2(1,1):
LINE-(SX,SY),C2
1370   SX=B3(5,0):SY=B3(5,1):PAINT (SX,SY),C2,C2  'template f
or surface 5
1380   SX=B2(1,0):SY=B2(1,1):PSET (SX,SY),C3:SX=B2(4,0):SY=B2
(4,1):LINE-(SX,SY),C3:SX=B2(5,0):SY=B2(5,1):LINE-(SX,SY),C3:
SX=B2(2,0):SY=B2(2,1):LINE-(SX,SY),C3:SX=B2(1,0):SY=B2(1,1):
LINE-(SX,SY),C3
1390   SX=B3(5,0):SY=B3(5,1):PAINT (SX,SY),0,C3  'surface 5 c
ompleted
1400   GOSUB 2040
1410   PAINT (SX,SY),A$,C3
1420 SX1=B2(1,0):SY1=B2(1,1):SX2=B2(4,0):SY2=B2(4,1):SX3=B2(
5,0):SY3=B2(5,1):SX4=B2(2,0):SY4=B2(2,1)
1430   GOSUB 2440
1440   BEEP:RETURN
1450 '--------------------------------------------------
1460 '
1470 'module:   perspective calculations for Cartesian world
coordinates
1480   X=(-1)*X:XA=CR1*X-SR1*Z:ZA=SR1*X+CR1*Z:X=CR2*XA+SR2*Y:
YA=CR2*Y-SR2*XA:Z=CR3*ZA-SR3*YA:Y=SR3*ZA+CR3*YA:X=X+MX:Y=Y+M
Y:Z=Z+MZ:SX=D*X/Z:SY=D*Y/Z:RETURN
1490 '_____
1500 '
1510 'module:   return to BASIC command level
1520   CLS:SCREEN 0,0,0,0:WIDTH 80:COLOR 7,0:LOCATE 1,1,1:CLS
:END
1530 '_____
1540 '
1550 'module:   configure system for 640x200 mode
1560   KEY OFF:CLS:ON ERROR GOTO 2560:SCREEN 8,,0,0:COLOR 7,0
:PALETTE 1,0:PALETTE 2,1:PALETTE 3,9:PALETTE 4,7:PALETTE 8,4
:PALETTE 9,2:PALETTE 10,4:PALETTE 11,12:PALETTE 12,14:PALETT
E 13,8
1570   ON ERROR GOTO 0:WINDOW SCREEN (-399,-299)-(400,300)   '
establish device-independent normalized coordinates
1580   ON KEY (2) GOSUB 1520:KEY (2) ON   'F2 toggle to exit p
rogram
1590   DEFINT T  'loop counter
```

```
1600    LOCATE 25,14:PRINT "Simultaneous ANIMATED views of com
puter-shaded 3D cube"
1610    GOTO 150
1620    '_____
1630    '
1640    'module:  assign scalar data
1650    G=0:D=1200:R1=5.68319:R2=6.28319:R3=5.79778:MX=0:MY=0:
MZ=-270  '3D parameters
1660    DIM B1 (7,2)  '8 sets of XYZ view coordinates
1670    DIM B2 (7,1)  '8 sets of SX,SY display coordinates
1680    DIM B3 (5,1)  '6 sets of SX,SY fill coordinates
1690    C1=8:C2=9:C3=7  'color attributes for drawing code
1700    XL=.57735:YL=.57735:ZL=.57735  'xyz components of unit
 vector for angle of incidence used in illumination algorith
m
1710    SR1=SIN(R1):CR1=COS(R1):SR2=SIN(R2):CR2=COS(R2):SR3=SI
N(R3):CR3=COS(R3)
1720    A1$=CHR$(&HDF)+CHR$(&H20)+CHR$(&HO)+CHR$(&HO)+CHR$(&HF
D)+CHR$(&H2)+CHR$(&HO)+CHR$(&HO)+CHR$(&H7F)+CHR$(&H80)+CHR$(
&HO)+CHR$(&HO)+CHR$(&HF7)+CHR$(&H8)+CHR$(&HO)+CHR$(&HO)
1730    A2$=CHR$(&HBB)+CHR$(&H44)+CHR$(&HO)+CHR$(&HO)+CHR$(&HE
E)+CHR$(&H11)+CHR$(&HO)+CHR$(&HO)
1740    A3$=CHR$(&HAA)+CHR$(&H55)+CHR$(&HO)+CHR$(&HO)+CHR$(&H5
5)+CHR$(&HAA)+CHR$(&HO)+CHR$(&HO)
1750    A4$=CHR$(&H44)+CHR$(&HBB)+CHR$(&HO)+CHR$(&HO)+CHR$(&H1
1)+CHR$(&HEE)+CHR$(&HO)+CHR$(&HO)
1760    A5$=CHR$(&H20)+CHR$(&HFF)+CHR$(&HO)+CHR$(&HO)+CHR$(&H2
)+CHR$(&HFF)+CHR$(&HO)+CHR$(&HO)+CHR$(&H80)+CHR$(&HFF)+CHR$(
&HO)+CHR$(&HO)+CHR$(&H8)+CHR$(&HFF)+CHR$(&HO)+CHR$(&HO)
1770    A6$=CHR$(&H44)+CHR$(&HFF)+CHR$(&HO)+CHR$(&HO)+CHR$(&H1
1)+CHR$(&HFF)+CHR$(&HO)+CHR$(&HO)
1780    A7$=CHR$(&H55)+CHR$(&HFF)+CHR$(&HO)+CHR$(&HO)+CHR$(&HA
A)+CHR$(&HFF)+CHR$(&HO)+CHR$(&HO)
1790    A8$=CHR$(&HBB)+CHR$(&HFF)+CHR$(&HO)+CHR$(&HO)+CHR$(&HE
E)+CHR$(&HFF)+CHR$(&HO)+CHR$(&HO)
1800    A9$=CHR$(&HDF)+CHR$(&HDF)+CHR$(&H20)+CHR$(&HO)+CHR$(&H
FD)+CHR$(&HFD)+CHR$(&H2)+CHR$(&HO)+CHR$(&H7F)+CHR$(&H7F)+CHR
$(&H80)+CHR$(&HO)+CHR$(&HF7)+CHR$(&HF7)+CHR$(&H8)+CHR$(&HO)
1810    A10$=CHR$(&HBB)+CHR$(&HBB)+CHR$(&H44)+CHR$(&HO)+CHR$(&
HEE)+CHR$(&HEE)+CHR$(&H11)+CHR$(&HO)
1820    A11$=CHR$(&HAA)+CHR$(&HAA)+CHR$(&H55)+CHR$(&HO)+CHR$(&
H55)+CHR$(&H55)+CHR$(&HAA)+CHR$(&HO)
1830    A12$=CHR$(&H44)+CHR$(&H44)+CHR$(&HBB)+CHR$(&HO)+CHR$(&
H11)+CHR$(&H11)+CHR$(&HEE)+CHR$(&HO)
1840    A13$=CHR$(&H20)+CHR$(&HO)+CHR$(&HFF)+CHR$(&HO)+CHR$(&H
2)+CHR$(&HO)+CHR$(&HFF)+CHR$(&HO)+CHR$(&H80)+CHR$(&HO)+CHR$(
&HFF)+CHR$(&HO)+CHR$(&H8)+CHR$(&HO)+CHR$(&HFF)+CHR$(&HO)
1850    A14$=CHR$(&H44)+CHR$(&HO)+CHR$(&HFF)+CHR$(&HO)+CHR$(&H
```

```
 11)+CHR$(&HO)+CHR$(&HFF)+CHR$(&HO)
 1860   A15$=CHR$(&H55)+CHR$(&HO)+CHR$(&HFF)+CHR$(&HO)+CHR$(&H
 AA)+CHR$(&HO)+CHR$(&HFF)+CHR$(&HO)
 1870   A16$=CHR$(&HBB)+CHR$(&HO)+CHR$(&HFF)+CHR$(&HO)+CHR$(&H
 EE)+CHR$(&HO)+CHR$(&HFF)+CHR$(&HO)
 1880   RETURN
 1890 '_____
 1900 '
 1910 'module:   database of 8 sets of XYZ world coordinates f
 or vertices of 3D cube
 1920   DATA   30,-30,30,   30,30,30,   -30,30,30,   -30,-30,30,
 30,30,-30,   -30,30,-30,   -30,-30,-30,   30,-30,-30
 1930 '_____
 1940 '
 1950 'module:   database of 6 sets of XYZ world coordinates f
 or area fill origins for 6 surfaces of 3D cube
 1960   DATA   0,-30,0,   0,0,-30,   -30,0,0,   0,0,30,   30,0,0,
 0,30,0
 1970 '_____
 1980 '
 1990 'module:   plane equation method of hidden surface remov
 al
 2000   SP1=X1*(Y2*Z3-Y3*Z2):SP1=(-1)*SP1:SP2=X2*(Y3*Z1-Y1*Z3)
 :SP3=X3*(Y1*Z2-Y2*Z1):SP=SP1-SP2-SP3:RETURN
 2010 '_____
 2020 '
 2030 'module:   illumination algorithm
 2040   XU=X2-X1:YU=Y2-Y1:ZU=Z2-Z1   'calculate vector from ver
 tex 1 to vertex 2
 2050   XV=X3-X1:YV=Y3-Y1:ZV=Z3-Z1   'calculate vector from ver
 tex 1 to vertex 3
 2060   XN=(YU*ZV)-(ZU*YV):YN=(ZU*XV)-(XU*ZV):ZN=(XU*YV)-(YU*X
 V)   'calculate surface perpendicular vector
 2070   YN=YN*(-1):ZN=ZN*(-1)   'convert vector to cartesian sy
 stem
 2080 '_____
 2090 '
 2100 'sub-module:   convert surface perpendicular vector to u
 nit vector
 2110   V1=(XN*XN)+(YN*YN)+(ZN*ZN):V2=SQR(V1)   'magnitude of s
 urface perpendicular vector
 2120   V3=1/V2   'ratio of magnitude to unit vector magnitude
 2130   XW=V3*XN:YW=V3*YN:ZW=V3*ZN   'XYZ components of surface
  perpendicular unit vector
 2140 '_____
 2150 '
 2160 'sub-module:   calculate illumination factor for surface
  when angle of incidence is 45 degrees elevation and 135 deg
 rees yaw
```

```
2170    V4=(XW*XL)+(YW*YL)+(ZW*ZL)   'illumination factor 0 to
1
2180    V4=V4*14:V4=CINT(V4)   'illumination factor 0 to 14
2190    V5=V4+1  'illumination factor range 1 to 15
2200  '_____
2210  '
2220  'sub-module:   assign halftone codes for area fill and d
ithering
2230    IF V5<1 THEN GOTO 2260  'if light source is behind sur
face
2240    ON V5 GOTO 2260, 2270, 2280, 2290, 2300, 2310, 2320, 2
330, 2340, 2350, 2360, 2370, 2380, 2390, 2400
2250    A$=CHR$(&HFF)+CHR$(&H0)+CHR$(&H0)+CHR$(&H0):C4=1:C5=1:
C6=&HFFFF:RETURN  'solid black is unused
2260    A$=A1$:C4=1:C5=2:C6=&H808:RETURN
2270    A$=A2$:C4=1:C5=2:C6=&H4444:RETURN
2280    A$=A3$:C4=1:C5=2:C6=&HAAAA:RETURN
2290    A$=A4$:C4=2:C5=1:C6=&H4444:RETURN
2300    A$=CHR$(&H0)+CHR$(&HFF)+CHR$(&H0)+CHR$(&H0):C4=2:C5=2:
C6=&HFFFF:RETURN
2310    A$=A5$:C4=2:C5=3:C6=&H808:RETURN
2320    A$=A6$:C4=2:C5=3:C6=&H4444:RETURN
2330    A$=A7$:C4=2:C5=3:C6=&HAAAA:RETURN
2340    A$=A8$:C4=3:C5=2:C6=&H4444:RETURN
2350    A$=CHR$(&HFF)+CHR$(&HFF)+CHR$(&H0)+CHR$(&H0):C4=3:C5=3
:C6=&HFFFF:RETURN
2360    A$=A9$:C4=3:C5=4:C6=&H8080:RETURN
2370    A$=A10$:C4=3:C5=4:C6=&H4444:RETURN
2380    A$=A11$:C4=3:C5=4:C6=&HAAAA:RETURN
2390    A$=A12$:C4=4:C5=3:C6=&H4444:RETURN
2400    A$=CHR$(&H0)+CHR$(&H0)+CHR$(&HFF)+CHR$(&H0):C4=4:C5=4:
C6=&HFFFF:RETURN
2410  '_____
2420  '
2430  'module:   dithering
2440    LINE (SX1,SY1)-(SX2,SY2),C4:LINE (SX1,SY1)-(SX2,SY2),C
5,,C6
2450    LINE (SX2,SY2)-(SX3,SY3),C4:LINE (SX2,SY2)-(SX3,SY3),C
5,,C6
2460    LINE (SX3,SY3)-(SX4,SY4),C4:LINE (SX3,SY3)-(SX4,SY4),C
5,,C6
2470    LINE (SX4,SY4)-(SX1,SY1),C4:LINE (SX4,SY4)-(SX1,SY1),C
5,,C6
2480    RETURN
2490  '_____
2500  '
2510  'module:   re-assign sine and cosine values
2520    SR1=SIN(R1):CR1=COS(R1):SR2=SIN(R2):CR2=COS(R2):SR3=SI
N(R3):CR3=COS(R3):RETURN
```

```
2530 '_____
2540 '
2550 'module:   trap program execution if Color/Graphics Adap
ter or PCjr or pre-3.21 version of BASICA.
2560   CLS:SOUND 100,18
2570   LOCATE 5,1:PRINT "This advanced animation program":LOC
ATE 6,1:PRINT "requires the following software/hardware:"
2580   LOCATE 8,1:PRINT "1.  An IBM-compatible EGA with 256K
graphics RAM,":LOCATE 9,1:PRINT "2.   IBM BASICA 3.21 or high
er":LOCATE 10,1:PRINT "     (or a compiler which supports EGA
 functions,"
2590   LOCATE 11,1:PRINT "     such as QuickBASIC or TurboBASI
C)":LOCATE 12,1:PRINT "3.  a standard color display (SCD) or
 an":LOCATE 13,1:PRINT "enhanced color display (ECD)."
2600   LOCATE 18,1:PRINT "Press ESC to return to BASIC..."
2610   K$=INKEY$:IF K$<>CHR$(27) THEN 2610
2620   CLS:END
2630 '_____
2640 '
2650 'module:   background graphics
2660   CIRCLE (0,0),250,10:PAINT (0,0),10,10:CIRCLE (0,0),200
,11:PAINT (0,0),11,11:CIRCLE (0,0),150,12:PAINT (0,0),12,12:
CIRCLE (0,0),100,13:PAINT (0,0),13,13
2670   CIRCLE (0,0),250,4
2680   RETURN
2690 '_____
2700 '
2710   END 'of program code
```

# A

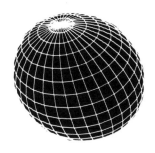

# *Dictionary of Variables*

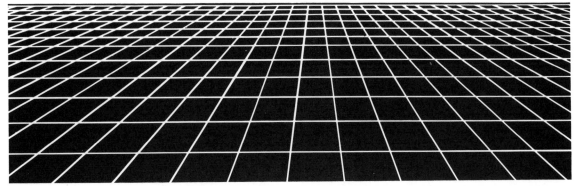

BASIC interpreters such as IBM BASICA, Microsoft BASICA, COMPAQ BASIC, and GW-BASIC are useful for graphics programming because of the immediate feedback they provide during program development. However, the manner in which the BASIC interpreter handles program variables can produce both benefits and hazards for your graphics programs.

A global variable is one which can be used by all portions of the program, including subroutines and assembly language CALLs. The main part of your program can manipulate and change the value of a variable, and a subroutine can also manipulate and change the value of that same variable. Nearly all BASIC interpreters use global variables. Although this environment makes data manipulation very easy during program development, it also means that you can quickly run out of names for your variables!

The dictionary of variables in this appendix serves to organize the variable labels which were used throughout the book. During development of the demonstration programs, I took care to maintain compatibility of variable names from program to program. This means that if you wished to add full shading capabilities to the interactive CAD program (in the Applica-

tions section of the book), you would not be faced with a large number of variables with redundant names. In addition, during your study of the program listings throughout the book, you may find it easier to follow the flow of logic by referring to the dictionary of variables.

If you are using QuickBASIC or TurboBASIC, you have the option of using either global variables or local variables. A local variable can only be used in specified sections of your program. You can, for example, define a particular variable as local to a particular subroutine. Although the subroutine can manipulate and change the variable, the changes do not affect the rest of the program. The main program or other subroutines can even use a local variable with the same name and there will be no conflict.

Note: Most variables are floating point numbers accurate to six digits. These numbers are sometimes called single-precision numbers in your BASIC manual. Where noted in this dictionary, some variables are specifically declared as either integers or strings. The following syntax is used in the dictionary: W1,W2 . . . W10 is intended to mean W1,W2,W3,W4, W5,W6,W7,W8,W9,W10.

A1, A2 . . . — graphic arrays (integer)

A$ — generic hex shading pattern (string)

A1$, A2$ . . . — specific hex shading patterns (string)

B1, B2 . . . — scalar arrays for 3D vertices

CR1,CR2,CR3,CR4,CR5 — cosine rotation factors

C,C0,C1,C2,C3 — color for drawing instructions (C2 is often used as universal key matte color, C3 is often used as universal solid surface silhouette color)

C4 — sets color for preparatory line used in line dithering routine

C5 — sets background color for line dithering

C6 — hex value used during line dithering

CF — y-coordinate location of color swatch in interactive CAD program (hardware-dependent)

C — length of logical right-angle triangle used in line clipping routine in dynamic instancing program. (Note: G is used as color variable in this case)

D — angular perspective factor

D1,D2,D3 — width, depth, height of instancing subobject in static instancing program

E — used to invoke hidden graphics page on the Color/Graphics Adapter (integer)

E — used to identify surface orientation in package design

F — used to invoke hidden graphics page on the Color/Graphics Adapter (integer)

G — hardware flag used to identify EGA or Color/Graphics Adapter or PCjr in universal configuration module (integer)

H — counter used during 3D free-form curves (integer)

J — movement factor for crosshair cursor in interactive CAD program

J,J1 — rotation angle for instancing of subobjects

J1,J2,J3,J4 — effects of control points on free-form curves

K$ — keyboard input (string)

L — surface counter, radial sort hidden surface removal (integer)

MX,MY,MZ — 3D translation factors for viewpoint

MINX,MINY,MAXX,MAXY — used to define minimum and maximum legal screen coordinates in interactive CAD program

NX,NY,NZ — translation factors in dynamic instancing programs

N1 — lateral movement factor in dynamic instancing programs

NY1 — vertical movement factor in dynamic instancing of subobjects

P — offset indicator for assembly language subroutine

used in Color/Graphics Adapter real-time animation; page indicator used on EGA and PCjr for real-time animation and frame animation (integer)

Q1 — loop counter for solid surface creation: sphere and cylinder

Q2 — used to identify scalar array of vertices during loop creation of solid surfaces on sphere, cylinder

R1,R2,R3,R4,R5 — yaw, roll, pitch factors in radians

R11,R21,R31 — yaw, roll, pitch of subobject in dynamic instancing program

R1A1,R2A1,R3A1 — change in yaw, roll, pitch used in dynamic instancing program

SP — visibility factor used in hidden surface routine (if SP > 0 then surface is hidden)

SX,SY — screen display coordinates

SX1,SY1 . . . SX5,SY5 — screen display coordinates used during solid surface modeling and computer-controlled shading

SR1,SR2,SR3,SR4,SR5 — sine rotation factors

S0X,S0Y . . . S6X,S6Y — gnomon display coordinates in engineering simulation program

SXJ,SYJ — tracer display coordinates in dynamic instancing program

SXU,SYU — temporary storage of cursor location in interactive CAD program

SXA,SYA,SXB,SYB — endpoints of line to be clipped in 3D space and in 2D space

T — generic loop counter

T1 — frame counter for real-time animation

T2,T3 — interim values used in free-form curve routine

U — used to locate a RAM address in interactive CAD program

V1,V2 — used to calculate magnitude of surface perpendicular vector used in hidden surface routine

V1 — graphics function flag used in interactive CAD program

V3 — ratio of surface perpendicular magnitude to unit vector magnitude

V4 — illumination factor, expressed as 0 to 1 range (i.e., from option base 0)

V5 — illumination factor, expressed as 1 to V6 range where V6 = 14 or 15 depending upon hardware

V6 — hardware-dependent illumination range factor

X,Y,Z — world coordinates in database

XA,YA,ZA — interim variables in 3D formulas

X1,X2 . . . Y1,Y2 . . . Z1,Z2 . . . — coordinates for hidden surface routine, solid surface modeling, computer-controlled shading

XL,YL,ZL — components of unit vector used to

describe location of light source in computer-controlled shading

XF,YF — direction factors for subobject in static instancing routine

XU,YU,ZU — vector from vertex 1 to 2 in hidden surface routine

XV,YV,ZV — vector from vertex 1 to 3 in hidden surface routine

XN,YN,ZN — surface perpendicular vector used in hidden surface routine

XW,YW,ZW — world coordinates of surface perpendicular vector used in hidden surface routine

X1,Y1 . . . X4,Y4 — endpoints and control points for graphics functions in interactive CAD program

X1U,Y1U,X4U,Y4U — used to store endpoints for undo function of interactive CAD program

W1,W2 . . . W10 — viewport parameters for $640 \times 350$ mode, $640 \times 200$ mode, $320 \times 200$ mode

# B

## Mathematics for Computer Graphics

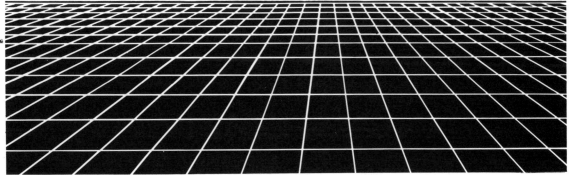

If you understand math, you understand computer graphics, it's as simple as that.

A variety of different mathematical disciplines are used in the generation of modeling, rendering, and animation displays on microcomputers. These include geometry, trigonometry, cubic parametrics, vector dot products, vector cross products, matrix multiplication, and others.

Although no single appendix can ever replace a good mathematics text, an overview of important formulas and concepts is presented here for your quick reference.

### MOVING THE LIGHT SOURCE

You can move the location of the light source for any of the computer-controlled shading programs in this book. Refer to Fig. B-1. Because the vector which describes the incoming light is a unit vector (where vector length = one unit), a simple formula can be used to derive the x,y,z components of the vector.

In any two-dimensional, right-angle triangle, the square of the hypotenuse is equal to the sum of the squares of the other two sides. The same concept ap-

plies to the x,y,z descriptors of a vector in 3D space. Simply stated, the sum of the squares of the x,y,z components equals the square of the hypotenuse, where the hypotenuse is the length of the vector. Because the length of the vector is one unit, one squared equals one. Therefore, the sum of the squares of the x,y,z descriptors equals one.

To move the light source to a position of 45 degrees inclination (up) located directly behind the viewpoint (due south), you can see from Fig. B-1 that XL would equal 0, the z-displacement would be .5, and the y-displacement would be .5. Because $XL^2 + YL^2 + ZL^2 = 1$, you know that $0 + YL^2 + ZL^2 = 1$. The square root of .5 is .7071068. Therefore, you would define XL as 0, YL as .7071068, and ZL as .7071068 in your program.

To move the light source to a position behind your right shoulder at east-south-east and approximately 30 degrees inclination (up), you can see from Fig. B-1 that each component of the vector would be equal. In otherwords, 3.333 + 3.333 + 3.333 = 1. Because the square root of 3.333 is .5773503, you would define XL,YL,ZL as each being .5773503 in your program.

You can experiment with different light source lo-

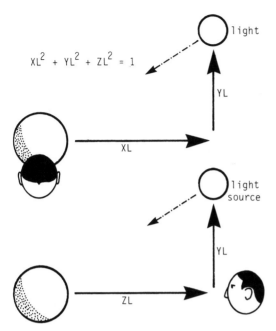

$$XL^2 + YL^2 + ZL^2 = 1$$

XL

YL

light

YL

light source

ZL

Fig. B-1. Displacements which describe the location of the light source for 3D rendering programs.

cations by using the following variable assignments in the computer-controlled shading programs in this book.

Directly behind you at due south at 45 degrees inclination:

**XL = 0:YL = .7071068:ZL = .7071068**

To your right at due east at 45 degrees inclination:

**XL = .7071068:YL = .7071068:ZL = 0**

To your left at due west at 45 degrees inclination:

**XL = .7071068:YL = .7071068:ZL = 0**

Directly in front of you at due north at 45 degrees inclination:

**XL = 0:YL = .7071068:ZL = − .7071068**

Behind your right shoulder at East-south-east (from heading 135) at 45 degrees inclination:

**XL = .5773503:YL = .5773503:ZL = .5773503**

Behind your right shoulder at East-south-east (from heading 135) at 30 degrees inclination:

**XL = .5477225:YL = .5477226:ZL = .6324555**

Behind your left shoulder at West-south-west (from heading 225) at 45 degrees inclination:

**XL = − .5773503:YL = .5773503:ZL = .5773503**

Behind your left shoulder at West-south-west (from heading 225) at 30 degrees inclination:

**XL = − .5477225:YL = .5477226:ZL = .6324555**

## PRINCIPLES OF TRIGONOMETRY

Trigonometry formulas are concerned with the relationships between an angle and the sides of a right-angle triangle. The fundamental concepts are shown in Fig. B-2.

The sine of angle R is equal to the result of the length of the opposite side B divided by the length of the hypotenuse A. The cosine of angle R is equal to the result of the length of the adjacent side C divided by the length of the hypotenuse A.

If you know the size of the angle and the length of one side, you can quickly calculate the length of the other two sides. If you know the length of two or three sides, you can quickly calculate the sine and cosine values. Sine and cosine are the fundamental functions used in the 3D perspective formulas in order to rotate the model through different angles in each axis, thereby creating VIEW COORDINATES.

The relationship of the lengths of the three sides in a right-angle triangle is also useful for some

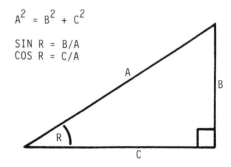

$$A^2 = B^2 + C^2$$

$$SIN\ R = B/A$$
$$COS\ R = C/A$$

A

B

R

C

Fig. B-2. Principles of trigonometry.

programming applications. The square of hypotenuse A equals the sum of the squares of the other two sides.

## PRINCIPLES OF GEOMETRY

Geometry formulas are concerned with common ratios between the sides of different right-angle triangles which share a common oblique angle. The fundamental concepts are shown in Fig. B-3.

Simply stated, the ratio of any two sides in one triangle is equal to the ratio of the corresponding two sides in the other triangle. These ratios are the fundamental building blocks for 2D and 3D line-clipping routines described later in this appendix. Geometric ratios are also used in the projection formulas used to place the 3D VIEW COORDINATES onto the 2D display screen. See Chapter 7 for a geometric proof of the projection formulas $SX = D*X/Z$ and $SY = D*Y/Z$.

## RADIAN MEASUREMENTS

When dealing with circles and angles, computers do not usually use degrees for making their calculations. Degrees in a circle are not based upon any scientific or geometric logic. The choice of 360 degrees to represent a full sweep around a circle is an arbitrary one; there is no reason preventing the adoption of 345 degrees to describe a circle, for example.

Radians, on the other hand, are based upon geometric principles. Refer to Fig. B-4. A unit circle has a radius of one unit. As you probably remember from high school math, the circumference of a circle can be found by the formula CIRCUMFERENCE = $2(\pi)$RADIUS, where $\pi$ equals approximately 3.14159. As Fig. B-4 shows, because the radius is one unit, the circumference can be described as 6.28319 radians. In other words, the arc produced by any angle can be expressed as radians.

## WINDOWING FORMULAS

The WINDOW and WINDOW SCREEN state-

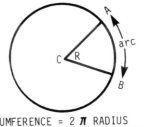

CIRCUMFERENCE = 2 $\pi$ RADIUS
CIRCUMFERENCE = (2)(3.14159)(1)
CIRCUMFERENCE = 6.28319 radians

Fig. B-4. A unit circle provides the proof theorem for radian measurements.

ments in BASIC can be used to map positive and negative world coordinates onto the display screen. Refer to Fig. B-5. Although this ability seems almost like magic to many computer-users, the mathematics involved are relatively straightforward.

If you prefer to perform these calculations yourself, or if you are using a programming language which does not support a graphical windowing function (such as C, Pascal, or Assembly Language), you can use the windowing utility shown in Fig. B-6. The routine accepts SX,SY display coordinates in the range of (-399,-299)-(400,300) and maps them onto the 640×200 display screen.

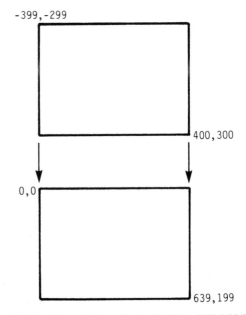

Fig. B-5. Mapping world coordinates (-399,-299)-(400,300) to the 640×200 screen.

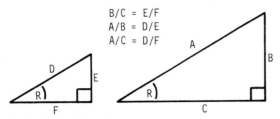

$B/C = E/F$
$A/B = D/E$
$A/C = D/F$

Fig. B-3. Principles of geometry.

Fig. B-6. Windowing utility for use with BASIC. The algorithm is compatible with C, Pascal, Assembly Language.

```
5000 'subroutine:  WINDOW_SCREEN
5010 'Places world coordinates on the physical 640x200 scree
n.  Simulates a WINDOW SCREEN (-399,-299)-(400,300) instruct
ion in BASIC.
5020 'Enter with SX,SY world coordinates.  X must be within
range -399 to +400.  Y must be within range -299 to +300.
5030 'Exit with SX,SY coordinates which fit 640x200 screen.
5040 '_____
5050 '
5060   SX=SX+399:SY=SY+299  'convert low end to 0,0
5070   RX=639/799  'calculate ratio to convert X high end to
639
5080   RY=199/599  'calculate ratio to convert Y high end to
199
5090   SX=SX*RX  'calculate physical display coordinate for
X
5100   SY=SY*RY  'calculate physical display coordinate for
Y
5110   RETURN
```

The algorithm follows three steps. First, simple addition is used to translate the low limits of the world coordinates so they match the low limits of the physical screen. Second, the ratio of world coordinates gross size to physical screen coordinates gross size is calculated. Third, the world coordinates to be mapped are multiplied by this ratio to yield the proper x,y coordinates for the physical screen.

### Translate to Low End Range

Line 5060 adds 399 to SX in order to shift the low end of the world coordinates x-range (–399) over to the low end of the screen coordinates x-range (0). Then, 299 is added to the SY coordinate to shift the low end of the world coordinates y-range (–299) over to the low end of the screen coordinates y-range (0). The world coordinates now fall in an effective range of (0,0)-(799,599). The problem now becomes that of converting (0,0)-(799,599) to (0,0)-(639,199).

### Determine the Conversion Ratio

Line 5070 divides the x-length of the physical screen by the x-length of the world coordinates range to determine an x-conversion ratio RX. Line 5080 divides the y-length of the physical screen by the y-length of the world coordinates range to determine a y-conversion ratio RY.

### Calculate the Screen Coordinates

Line 5090 multiplies the SX world coordinate by the x-conversion ratio RX to generate the correct SX physical screen coordinate. Line 5100 multiplies the SY world coordinate by the y-conversion ratio RY to generate the correct SY physical screen coordinate.

### Mapping to the 320 × 200 Mode

You can easily modify this algorithm to map world coordinates to the 320 × 200 display screen. Simply change the constant 639 in line 5070 to 319. You can also easily change the range of legal world coordinates by modifying the constants in line 5060 and by changing the divisors in lines 5070 and 5080.

### VIEWPORT FORMULAS

The VIEW statement in BASIC can be used to map graphics onto a small portion of the display screen. Refer to Fig. B-7. The effect is similar to creating a small display screen inside the larger whole display screen. Again, the math involved is relatively straightforward.

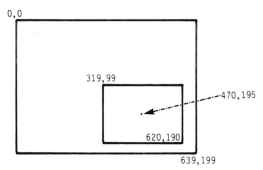

0,0

319,99

470,195

620,190

639,199

Fig. B-7. Mapping a viewport at (319,99)-(620,190).

Many programming languages do not directly support a VIEW function. You can do the math calculations yourself by using the viewport utility in Fig. B-8.

In its current format, the utility accepts SX,SY coordinates for the 640×200 screen and maps them into a viewport located in the lower right quadrant at (319,199)-(620,190). In other words, the entire screen is condensed to fit into the lower right hand corner.

### Viewport Mapping Algorithm

The algorithm follows three steps. First, addition is used to translate the 0,0 low end of the physical screen coordinates to the low end coordinates of the viewport (in this case 319,99). Second, the ratios of the x-length and y-length of the full screen and the

viewport or calculate. Third, the ratios are used to multiply the SX,SY screen coordinates to produce the SX,SY viewport coordinates.

### Translate to Low End Range

Line 5060 adds 319 to the SX physical screen coordinate and adds 99 to the SY physical screen coordinate. This moves the low end of the (0,0)-(639,199) range to (319,99), which is the low end of the viewport range (319,199)-(620,190).

### Determine the Conversion Ratio

Line 5070 divides the gross x-length of the viewport by the gross x-length of the physical screen in order to generate an x-conversion ratio RX. Line 5080 divides the gross y-length of the viewport by the gross y-length of the physical screen in order to generate a y-conversion ratio RY.

### Calculate the Screen Coordinates

Line 5090 multiplies the SX input coordinate by the x-conversion ratio RX to generate the proper coordinate within the logical viewport. Line 5100 multiplies the SY input coordinate by the y-conversion ratio RY to produce the proper coordinate with the viewport.

Fig. B-8. Viewport utility for use with BASIC. The algorithm is compatible with C, Pascal, Assembly Language.

```
5000 'subroutine:  VIEWPORT
5010 'Places a viewport anywhere on the 640x200 screen.
5020 'Enter with SX,SY coordinates within range 0,0 to 639,1
99.
5030 'Exit with SX,SY coordinates mapped to a viewport locat
ed within the rectangle bounded by (319,99)-(620,140).
5040 '_____
5050 '
5060   SX=SX+319:SY=SY+99
5070   RX=301/639  'X conversion ratio is length of viewport
divided by length of physical screen
5080   RY=91/199   'Y conversion ratio is height of viewport
divided by height of physical screen
5090   SX=SX*RX    'calculate SX within viewport
5100   SY=SY*RY    'calculate SY within viewport
5110   RETURN
```

## Mapping Other Viewports

You can easily modify the utility to map to different viewports. The value of 301 in line 5070 is found by subtracting 319 from 620. The value of 41 in line 5080 is derived by subtracting 99 from 190. The comments in the source code are self-explanatory.

## HIDDEN SURFACE REMOVAL

The hidden surface routines in this book use the standard equation for a plane to test for visibility. Refer to Fig. B-9. Because the viewpoint for 3D computer graphics is always located at 0,0,0, the location of this viewpoint relative to the orientation of the surface of a plane can be used to determine if the plane is visible or hidden.

Matrix math is used to calculate the A,B,C,D constants for the plane equation. Refer to Fig. B-10. The x,y,z coordinates used to compute the A,B,C,D constants must be plotted in a counterclockwise location around the perimeter of the plane (when the plane is imagined to be part of a convex polyhedron such as a cube, for example).

Then, if the equation produces zero when a set of X,Y,Z coordinates are used, the point defined by those coordinates resides on the surface of the plane. If the equation produces a result greater than zero, the point is on the inside of a convex polyhedron. (The surface is hidden.) If the result is less than zero, the point is on the outside surface of a convex polyhedron. (The surface is visible.)

## VECTOR MULTIPLICATION

Vector multiplication is used in this book for calculating the brightness level of a surface. Two forms

```
AX+BY+CZ+D=0
```

```
EQUATION FOR A PLANE
where X,Y,Z is a point
on the surface of the plane.

A,B,C,D are constants derived
from 3 points on the plane.

If AX+BY+CZ+D > 0 then X,Y,Z is
on inside surface of convex polyhedron.

If AX+BY+CZ+D < 0 then X,Y,Z is
on outside surface of convex polyhedron
```

Fig. B-9. Generic equation for a plane, where x,y,z is the viewpoint.

```
A = Y1(Z2-Z3)+Y2(Z3-Z1)+Y3(Z1-Z2)

B = Z1(X2-X2)+Z2(X3-X1)+Z3(X1-X2)

C = X1(Y2-Y3)+X2(Y3-Y1)+X3(Y1-Y2)

D = -X1(Y2Z3-Y3Z2)-X2(Y3Z1-Y1Z3)-X3(Y1Z2-Y2Z1)
```

Fig. B-10. Constants derived from three non-collinear points on the surface of a plane.

of vector multiplication are invoked: vector dot products and vector cross-products.

## Vector Dot Products

By definition, $|N|\ |L|\ \text{COS(angle)} = N \cdot L$, where $N \cdot L$ is algebraic notation for the dot product of vectors N and L. The length of vector N is expressed as $|N|$. The length of vector L is expressed as $|L|$.

If vector U equals (a,b,c) and if vector V equals (d,e,f), then the dot product $U \cdot V = (a,b,c)\ (d,e,f) = (ad + be + cf) = $ a numerical value (i.e., not a vector).

If the vectors are unit vectors, then the length of each vector is one unit. Therefore, $1*1*\text{COS(angle)} = N \cdot L$.

This, of course, reduces to $\text{COS(angle)} = N \cdot L$. In otherwords, the cosine of the angle between the two vectors N and L is equal to the dot product of the vectors N and L.

Vector dot products are used in this book to invoke computer-controlled shading of solid models. The dot product of two vectors (XW,YW,ZW) (XL,YL,ZL) can be expressed in algebraic notation as (XW*XL)+(YW*YL)+(ZW*ZL), where XW,YW,ZW is a surface perpendicular vector and ZL,YL,ZL represents a vector of the incoming light rays. Refer to Chapter 16 for an explanation of the shading algorithm.

## Vector Cross-Products

By definition, the cross-product of two vectors produces a vector which is perpendicular to the plane of the two vectors. Refer to Fig. B-11.

If vector U equals (a,b,c) and if vector V equals (d,e,f), then the cross-product $U*V = (a,b,c)*(d,e,f) = $ (bf-ce, cd-af, ae-bd) = a vector (i.e., not a numerical value).

In 3D space, vector U can be described as (x2 − x1, y2 − y1, z2 − z1). The computer code is written as XU = X2-X1:YU = Y2-Y1:ZU = Z2-Z1. Vector V can be

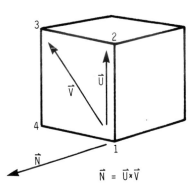

Fig. B-11. The cross-product of two vectors produces a vector which is perpendicular to the plane holding the two vectors.

described by (x3 – x1, y3 – y1, z3 – z1). The computer code is written as $XV = X3-X1:YV = Y3-Y1:ZV = Z3-Z1$.

The surface perpendicular can be calculated thus: vector N equals the cross-product of vector U and vector V.

$N = U * V$, where vector U and vector V are written in the computer code previously described. The surface perpendicular can be described, therefore, in computer code as:

$XN = (YU*ZV) - (ZU*YV):YN = (ZU*XV) - (XU*ZV):ZN = (XU*YV) - (YU*XV)$

### Scalar Multiplication of Vectors

Multiplying a vector by a positive scalar will change the length of the vector, but will not affect its direction.

If vector U equals (a,b), then multiplication of vector U by T will yield $T*(a,b)$, which is the same as $(T*a, T*b)$.

### COMPUTER-CONTROLLED SHADING

A surface normal is a vector which is perpendicular to the surface of a plane. Refer to Fig. B-11.

Provided that the points on perimeter of a plane have been described in a counterclockwise order as viewed from the outside of the polyhedron, then the cross-product of two vectors on the surface of the plane will produce a vector which is an outside perpendicular to the surface of the plane. (If the points are clockwise, the result will be an perpendicular which points to the inside of the model containing the plane.)

The computer-controlled shading routines in this

book operate by comparing the angle between the surface perpendicular of the plane and the angle of incidence of incoming light. The comparison is made by converting the vectors to unit vectors.

### 3D ROTATION FORMULAS

The rotation of a point in 3D space is best implemented via matrix multiplication. As you discovered throughout the book, the three rotations of yaw, roll, and pitch are controlled by a separate set of formulas.

### Yaw: Rotation Around the Y Axis

$$(X,Y,Z,1) \begin{bmatrix} COS & SIN & 0 & 0 \\ -SIN & COS & 0 & 0 \\ 0 & 0 & 1 & 0 \\ 0 & 0 & 0 & 1 \end{bmatrix}$$

The resulting computer code is $XA = CR1*X - SR1*Z:ZA = SR1*X + CR1*Z$, where SR1 refers to the sine of the yaw viewing angle R1 and CR1 refers to the cosine of the yaw viewing angle R1.

### Roll: Rotation Around the Z Axis

$$(X,Y,Z,1) \begin{bmatrix} COS & 0 & -SIN & 0 \\ 0 & 1 & 0 & 0 \\ SIN & 0 & COS & 0 \\ 0 & 0 & 0 & 1 \end{bmatrix}$$

The resulting computer code is $X = CR2*XA + SR2*Y:YA = CR2*Y - SR2*XA$.

### Pitch: Rotation Around the X Axis

$$(X,Y,Z,1) \begin{bmatrix} 1 & 0 & 0 & 0 \\ 0 & COS & SIN & 0 \\ 0 & -SIN & COS & 0 \\ 0 & 0 & 0 & 1 \end{bmatrix}$$

The resulting computer code is $Z = CR3*ZA - SR3*YA:Y = SR3*ZA + CR3*YA$

After the point has been rotated through the yaw, roll, and pitch planes, simple addition and subtraction along the x,y,z axes will translate the rotated model to an appropriate location.

## Mirror Reflections

The demonstration program in Chapter 17 used geometric principles and artistic intuition to locate the mirror reflection. Matrix math can be used to create a formula which automatically generates a mirror image. For example, a reflection through the x,y plane can be expressed thus:

$$(X,Y,Z,1) \begin{bmatrix} 1 & 0 & 0 & 0 \\ 0 & 1 & 0 & 0 \\ 0 & 0 & -1 & 0 \\ 0 & 0 & 0 & 1 \end{bmatrix}$$

which can be expressed algebraically as $(X,Y,(-1*Z),1)$

## CUBIC PARAMETRIC CURVES

During the generation of computer graphics, matrix math finds its most useful implementation in the generation of free-form curves. Figure B-12 illustrates the matrix components of cubic parametric curves. In order to implement this logic on a microcomputer, the matrix multiplication must be expressed in standard algebraic notation, as shown in Fig. B-13.

Converting the algebraic notation to syntax which can be understood by the computer yields the loop shown in Fig. B-14. In its current format, the formula will generate the x-coordinate for a single point on the free-form curve. The y-coordinate can be derived by swapping Y for X in the formula.

```
Cubic Parametric Curve

four control points: P1, P2, P3, P4
```

$$C(T) = \begin{bmatrix} T^3 T^2 T^1 \end{bmatrix} B \begin{bmatrix} P1 \\ P2 \\ P3 \\ P4 \end{bmatrix}$$

```
where B =
```

$$\begin{bmatrix} -1 & 3 & -3 & 1 \\ 3 & -6 & 3 & 0 \\ -3 & 3 & 0 & 0 \\ 1 & 0 & 0 & 0 \end{bmatrix}$$

```
When T=0 the curve is on point P1.

When T=1 the curve is on point P4.
```

Fig. B-12. Matrix components of free-form curves.

$$X(T) = (-T^3+3T^2-3T+1)P1^X + \\ (3T^3-6T^2+3T)P2^X + \\ (-3T^3+3T^2)P3^X+T^3P4^X$$

```
where P1^X = x-coordinate for X1
where P2^X = x-coordinate for X2
where P3^X = x-coordinate for X3
where P4^X = x-coordinate for X4
```

Fig. B-13. Algebraic notation for the x-coordinate of points located along the surface of a free-form curve (cubic parametric).

## 3D LINE-CLIPPING

If you are using the 3D perspective formulas in this book to create models or environments which could stretch behind the viewpoint, you should use a 3D line-clipping routine. If the computer is permitted to attempt to display lines or points behind the viewpoint, those graphics will be displayed upside down and backwards.

The 3D line-clipping utility in Fig. B-15 will clip all lines which contain z-coordinates which fall behind the viewpoint (which is located at the origin of the axis system, where $Z=0$, of course.) Imagine it like this: if you are looking at a scene through a window where your nose is right up against the glass, the 3D line-clipping utility in Fig. B-15 will clip lines so that none penetrate the window, so to speak.

The utility operates in 3D VIEW COORDINATE space. The resulting clipped line will not penetrate past $Z=0$ in 3D space. (To keep the math running fast by preventing excessively large X-VIEW COORDINATES, the parameter is set to $-1$ in this utility.) The resulting projection DISPLAY COORDINATES produced by the projection formulas may have to be further clipped to fit the 2D display screen. Refer to the demonstration program in Chapter 26 to see this algorithm in action.

The algorithm uses geometry to compare the ratios of the sides of triangles in different axial planes.

```
FOR T=0 TO 1 STEP .025:

SX = ((-1)*(T*T*T)+3*(T*T)-3*T+1)*X1
    +(3*(T*T*T)-(6*T*T)+(3*T))*X2
    +((-1)*(T*T*T)+(3*T*T))*X3
    +(T*T*T)*X4
```

Fig. B-14. Computer-ready notation for SX display coordinates on the surface of a free-form curve (cubic parametric).

Fig. B-15. 3D line-clipping utility for interpreted or compiled BASIC.

```
5000 'subroutine: CLIP3D
5010 'Enter with XA,YA,ZA and XB,YB,ZB rotated view coordina
tes for endpoints of line to be clipped in 3D space.
5020 'Exit with SXA,SYA and SXB,SYB display coordinates of l
ine.  This resulting line requires further 2D clipping to fi
t display screen.
5030 '_____
5040 '
5050   IF ZA>-1 THEN 5060 ELSE 5070
5060   IF ZB>-1 THEN P1=0:RETURN ELSE SWAP XA,XB:SWAP YA,YB:S
WAP ZA,ZB:GOTO 5090
5070   IF ZB>-1 THEN 5090 ELSE 5080
5080   SXA=D*XA/ZA:SYA=D*YA/ZA:SXB=D*XB/ZB:SYB=D*YB/ZB:RETURN

5090   C=(XA-XB)/(ZA-ZB)*(ZA+1):XC=XA-C:C=(YA-YB)/(ZA-ZB)*(ZA
+1):YC=YA-C:ZC=-1
5100   XB=XC:YB=YC:ZB=ZC:GOTO 5050
```

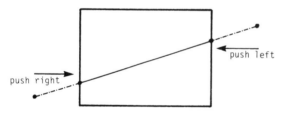

Fig. B-16. Principles of 2D line-clipping.

## 2D LINE-CLIPPING

Lines whose endpoints are located outside the display screen limits must be clipped. Refer to Fig. B-16. A point located to the right of the display screen must be pushed left, so to speak. Simple geometry is used to compare the ratios of right-angled triangles in order to accomplish this pushing operation.

Although BASIC automatically clips lines which

Fig. B-17. 2D line-clipping utility for interpreted or compiled BASIC.

```
5000 'subroutine: CLIP2D
5010 'Clips lines to fit BASIC's standard 320x200 screen.
5020 'Enter with SXA,SYA and SXB,SYB as endpoints of line to
 be clipped.  These initial coordinates can be negative or p
ositive values.
5030 'NOTE:  Instruction 5170 of this subroutine draws the l
ine on the screen.  You can change the color of the line as
required, or use a variable (which can be controlled from ou
tside this subroutine).
5040 '_____
5050 '
5060   SXA=SXA+160:SYA=SYA+100:SXB=SXB+160:SYB=SYB+100
5070   IF SXA>SXB THEN SWAP SXA,SXB:SWAP SYA,SYB
```

```
5080   IF (SXA<0) AND (SXB<0) THEN RETURN
5090   IF (SXA>319) AND (SXB>319) THEN RETURN
5100   IF (SYA<0) AND (SYB<0) THEN RETURN
5110   IF (SYA>199) AND (SYB>199) THEN RETURN
5120   IF SXA<0 THEN 5290
5130   IF SXB>319 THEN 5210
5140   IF SYA>SYB THEN SWAP SYA,SYB:SWAP SXA,SXB
5150   IF SYA<0 THEN 5430
5160   IF SYB>199 THEN 5370
5170   LINE (SXA,SYA)-(SXB,SYB),1:RETURN
5180   '_____
5190   '
5200   'submodule: PUSH LEFT
5210   C=(SYB-SYA)/(SXB-SXA)*(319-SXA)
5220   SXB=319:SYB=SYA+C
5230   IF (SYA<0) AND (SYB<0) THEN RETURN
5240   IF (SYA>199) AND (SYB>199) THEN RETURN
5250   GOTO 5140
5260   '_____
5270   '
5280   'submodule: PUSH RIGHT
5290   C=(SYB-SYA)/(SXB-SXA)*(SXB)
5300   SXA=0:SYA=SYB-C
5310   IF (SYA<0) AND (SYB<0) THEN RETURN
5320   IF (SYA>199) AND (SYB>199) THEN RETURN
5330   GOTO 5130
5340   '_____
5350   '
5360   'submodule: PUSH UP
5370   C=(SXB-SXA)/(SYB-SYA)*(199-SYA)
5380   SXB=SXA+C:SYB=199
5390   GOTO 5170
5400   '_____
5410   '
5420   'submodule: PUSH DOWN
5430   C=(SXB-SXA)/(SYB-SYA)*(SYB)
5440   SXA=SXB-C:SYA=0
5450   GOTO 5160
```

fall outside the physical boundaries of the display screen, it will produce a math overflow condition if the coordinates to be clipped are smaller than −32768 or larger than +32767. The 2D line-clipping utility in Fig. B-17 overcomes this problem by using floating point numbers.

CLIP2D will clip lines to fit the 320×200 display screen. If you use C, Pascal, or Assembly Language, you will find this utility to be very handy. The code

at lines 5060 through 5170 continues to call the submodules to push the endpoints left, right, up, and down until the line has been successfully clipped. Line 5170 plots the graphic on the display screen.

To see this section of code in action, refer to the aerospace vehicle simulation in Chapter 26, which employs it to ensure that the aircraft is properly drawn no matter how close to the viewpoint it is (i.e., no matter how large the vehicle appears).

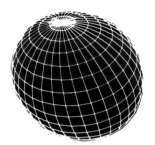

# C

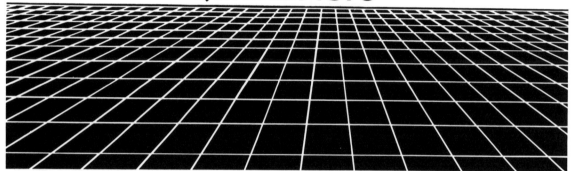

# *QuickBASIC*

By making three simple changes, you can run the programs in this book with QuickBASIC version 2.0 or newer. Refer to Fig. C-1.

Graphics programs compiled with QuickBASIC can execute three times to ten times faster than under the IBM BASICA interpreter. Because of Microsoft's commitment to maintaining compatibility with BASICA, the advanced modeling and rendering programs in this book can be easily run under the QuickBASIC interactive compiler.

## THE QUICKBASIC ENVIRONMENT

Under normal conditions QuickBASIC generates compiled machine code from your source code and it places the executable machine code into RAM memory. A complex graphics program of 200 lines typically requires fewer than 15 seconds to compile. A 400-line program will compile in 40 seconds. The compiled program can then be run from within the QuickBASIC programming environment. Simply touch Ctrl R to run. When the program is finished, control returns to the QuickBASIC editor.

Because the QuickBASIC editor requires approximately 200K of memory (the QB.EXE file is 186256 bytes on diskette), only very short and simple programs can be compiled into memory and run on a 256K microcomputer. A system with 384K to 640K is required in order to work with programs of reasonable size, because both your source code and the compiled machine code must exist in RAM simultaneously. The demonstration program in this appendix was converted, compiled, and run on an IBM PC with 640K (although the program will run in less than 384K).

The QuickBASIC compiler can compile various sorts of executable machine code directly to diskette, but a discussion of compilation options is beyond the scope of this book. Refer to your QuickBASIC user's manual for further details.

## HOW TO CONVERT
## BASICA PROGRAMS TO QUICKBASIC

**Step 1.** If you are typing in the program from the listing in this book, start with Step 2. If you have the companion diskette, skip Step 2 and go directly to Step 3.

**Step 2.** Load DOS. Then insert your Quick-BASIC master diskette in drive A. From the DOS prompt, load the QuickBASIC editor with the key-

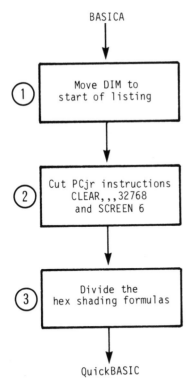

BASICA

① Move DIM to
start of listing

② Cut PCjr instructions
CLEAR,,,32768
and SCREEN 6

③ Divide the
hex shading formulas

QuickBASIC

Fig. C-1. A schematic representation of the three simple steps to adapt the demonstration programs for use with QuickBASIC.

board command **A:QB /V/D/S**. Using the QuickBASIC editor, type in the program listing exactly as printed in the book. Skip Step 3 and Step 4 and go instead directly to Step 5.

**Step 3.** If you have the companion diskette, use BASICA (which you will find on your DOS diskette) to load the program which you wish to convert. Then save the program on a separate diskette using ASCII format. For example, if you were working on program A-25.BAS (the computer-shaded cylinder), you would save the program to diskette with the keyboard command **SAVE "A-25.BAS",A**. QuickBASIC can only read diskette files which are in ASCII format; it cannot understand the tokenized format which BASIC normally uses to write files to diskette. Tokenized format is merely a form of abbreviated symbols which BASIC uses in order to save diskette space.

**Step 4.** Exit BASICA and return to DOS. Insert your QuickBASIC master diskette in drive A. From the DOS prompt, load the QuickBASIC editor with the keyboard command **A:QB /V/D/S**.

**Step 5.** For safety's sake, save the program under a new name before continuing.

**Step 6.** If any DIM instructions are present in the source code, move them to the beginning of the program. DIM is used to size scalar arrays in the 3D modeling programs and the 3D rendering programs. DIM is also used to size graphic arrays in the software sprite animation programs. QuickBASIC considers the DIM instruction to be a nonexecutable statement. The arrays defined by DIM are dimensioned during compilation, but the DIM instruction is not executed by the microprocessor during run-time.

**Step 7.** If any GET and PUT instructions are present in the source code, be certain that they use actual screen coordinates. Under QuickBASIC, world coordinates which have been established by a WINDOW SCREEN instruction are not legal as arguments to GET and PUT. The BASICA interpreter allows both actual screen coordinates and world coordinates. GW-BASIC permits only actual screen coordinates. The programs in this book employ coordinates which match the actual screen coordinates in order to maintain software compatibility, so if you are adapting a program from this book you do not have to worry about the GET and PUT instructions.

**Step 8.** Delete any lines of source code which refer to the PCjr or TANDY, such as CLEAR,,,32768 and SCREEN 6. The QuickBASIC editor does not support any of the PCjr modes (which are also found in GW-BASIC on the TANDY). Because most of the programs in the book contain code which ensures compatibility with the PCjr, you will be required to remove these lines from the compatibility module named UNIVERSAL before QuickBASIC will compile the program.

**Step 9.** If any complex string definitions are present in the source code (such as the computer-controlled shading formulas), you may encounter an error message from QuickBASIC which says "Statement Too Complex". Simply break up the string definition into two shorter definitions, then define the original string as being composed of the two shortened strings. Refer to the demonstration program in this appendix to see how easily this is done.

**Step 10.** Save the modified source code on diskette.

**Step 11.** Use the F5 key to compile the program into memory. The /V/D/S options which you used to start up QuickBASIC will ensure that the resultant machine code is optimized for speed and error trapping.

(Tip: You can make the programs run even faster by removing the ON KEY and KEY ON instructions from the source code. This allows you to reconfigure the compile dialog box of QuickBASIC to eliminate checking between statements.)

**Step 12.** Touch Ctrl-R to run the compiled program.

### QUICKBASIC COMPATIBILITY WITH BASICA:

If you are modifying the programs in this book for your own purposes, or if you are writing your own original modeling and rendering programs, you may find the following comments helpful.

Remember that an INKEY$ instruction in a compiled program can actually read the Ctrl Break key combination just like any other keystrokes if the /D option is not used during compilation. Always use the /D option until you are certain that your program is completely bug-free.

BLOAD and BSAVE will function correctly if they are used to identify address locations within the display memory segments (such as B8000 hex, A0000 hex, and so forth). If you use areas in dynamic RAM, however, you may run into trouble by inadvertently writing over important areas of run-time memory. QuickBASIC does not organize the microcomputer's RAM in the same manner as BASICA does. Refer to Chapter 1 or refer to your QuickBASIC user's manual for a map of run-time memory conditions. (If you are using an EGA with QuickBASIC, refer to Appendix E for guidance on using BSAVE.)

QuickBASIC does not support the following instructions within a program: LOAD, MERGE, LIST, LLIST, NEW, SAVE.

QuickBASIC supports the SCREEN 1 and SCREEN 2 graphics modes on the Color/Graphics Adapter.

QuickBASIC supports the SCREEN 7, SCREEN 8, SCREEN 9, and SCREEN 10 graphics modes on the EGA (Enhanced Graphics Adapter).

QuickBASIC 2.0 and 2.1 permit only one page in the SCREEN 0 text mode. QuickBASIC version 3.0 and newer permit multiple pages in the SCREEN 0 text mode.

QuickBASIC does not support SCREEN 3, SCREEN 4, SCREEN 5, or SCREEN 6 as used on the IBM PCjr. If you wish to compile BASIC source code for the PCjr, you should use the IBM BASIC Compiler version 2.0 or newer. Because of its size, the QuickBASIC editor cannot even be loaded into a standard 128K PCjr, although standalone executable programs created by QuickBASIC will run on a PCjr if they use either the SCREEN 1 or SCREEN 2 graphics modes.

QuickBASIC does not support SCREEN 3, SCREEN 4, SCREEN 5, or SCREEN 6 as used on TANDY microcomputers with GW-BASIC. For all practical purposes, you are limited to SCREEN 0, SCREEN 1, and SCREEN 2 on a TANDY when using the QuickBASIC editor.

Some EGAs will not write graphics to a hidden page when using some versions of QuickBASIC. Under these conditions real-time animation requires special coding, although the programming techniques of frame animation and software sprite animation will work as discussed in Part Four of this book.

### ANALYSIS OF THE DEMONSTRATION PROGRAM:

The demonstration program in Fig. C-2 is the

Fig. C-2. QuickBASIC version of the computer-shaded cylinder from Chapter 16.

```
100 'Program C-05.BAS     QuickBASIC fully-shaded cylinder.
110 'Demonstrates the compatibility of QuickBASIC 2.0 with I
BM BASICA for modeling and rendering.
111 'DIM instructions are moved to start of program.   See li
nes 145 and 146.
112 'All PCjr code has been deleted from the set-up module.
    QuickBASIC does not support PCjr modes.   See line 890.
113 'Because some hex shading formulas for the EGA are too c
omplex for QuickBASIC, the formulas have been built from two
    smaller sections.   See lines 1500, 1540, 1580, 1620.
```

```
114 'On an IBM PC, the program takes 29 seconds to compile.
115 'Program execution takes 34 seconds, compared to 73 seco
nds if BASICA is used.
120 '_____
130 '
140   GOTO 740   'configure system
145   DIM B11(35,2):DIM B12(35,2)   'this code moved to here f
rom line 1100
146   DIM B21(35,1):DIM B22(35,1)   'this code moved to here f
rom line 1110
150   GOSUB 1070   'assign variables
160 '_____
170 '
180 'main routine
190   SOUND 350,.7:R5=0:R4=0:FOR T=0 TO 35 STEP 1:LOCATE 2,1:
PRINT "Sweep 1 coordinate"T"  ":X=30:GOSUB 600:Z=Z+60:GOSUB
650:B11(T,0)=X:B11(T,1)=Y:B11(T,2)=Z:B21(T,0)=SX:B21(T,1)=SY
:R5=R5+.17453:NEXT T   'near end of cylinder
200   SOUND 350,.7:R5=0:R4=0:FOR T=0 TO 35 STEP 1:LOCATE 2,1:
PRINT "Sweep 2 coordinate"T"  ":X=30:GOSUB 600:Z=Z-60:GOSUB
650:B12(T,0)=X:B12(T,1)=Y:B12(T,2)=Z:B22(T,0)=SX:B22(T,1)=SY
:R5=R5+.17453:NEXT T   'far end of cylinder
210   SOUND 350,.7:FOR Q1=0 TO 35 STEP 1:Q2=Q1+1:IF Q2>35 THE
N Q2=0
220   LOCATE 2,1:PRINT "Solid surface"Q1"          "
230   GOSUB 450:NEXT Q1
240   SOUND 350,.7:LOCATE 2,1:PRINT "Solid end of cylinder.
    "
250   X1=B11(0,0):Y1=B11(0,1):Z1=B11(0,2):X2=B11(25,0):Y2=B11
(25,1):Z2=B11(25,2):X3=B11(11,0):Y3=B11(11,1):Z3=B11(11,2)
260   GOSUB 1190:IF SP>0 THEN 400
270   FOR Q1=0 TO 35 STEP 1:Q2=Q1+1:IF Q2>35 THEN Q2=0
280   SX1=B21(Q1,0):SY1=B21(Q1,1):SX2=B21(Q2,0):SY2=B21(Q2,1)
290   LINE (SX1,SY1)-(SX2,SY2),C2:NEXT Q1
300   X=0:Y=0:Z=60:GOSUB 650:PAINT (SX,SY),C2,C2
310   FOR Q1=0 TO 35 STEP 1:Q2=Q1+1:IF Q2>35 THEN Q2=0
320   SX1=B21(Q1,0):SY1=B21(Q1,1):SX2=B21(Q2,0):SY2=B21(Q2,1)

330   LINE (SX1,SY1)-(SX2,SY2),C3:NEXT Q1
340   X=0:Y=0:Z=60:GOSUB 650:PAINT (SX,SY),C0,C3
350   SOUND 350,.7:LOCATE 2,1:PRINT "Shading end of cylinder.
    "
360   X=0:Y=0:Z=60:GOSUB 650:GOSUB 1230:PAINT (SX,SY),A$,C3
'shading of end
370   FOR Q1=0 TO 35 STEP 1:Q2=Q1+1:IF Q2>35 THEN Q2=0
380   SX1=B21(Q1,0):SY1=B21(Q1,1):SX2=B21(Q2,0):SY2=B21(Q2,1)

390   LINE (SX1,SY1)-(SX2,SY2),C4:LINE (SX1,SY1)-(SX2,SY2),C5
```

```
,,C6:NEXT Q1    'dithering of end
400    SOUND 650,10:LOCATE 2,1:PRINT "Program completed.
  ":LOCATE 4,1:PRINT "                          "
410    GOTO 410
420 '_____
430 '
440 'module:    draw one 4-sided polygon on surface of cylinde
r
450    X1=B11(Q1,0):Y1=B11(Q1,1):Z1=B11(Q1,2)
460    X2=B11(Q2,0):Y2=B11(Q2,1):Z2=B11(Q2,2)
470    X3=B12(Q2,0):Y3=B12(Q2,1):Z3=B12(Q2,2)
480    GOSUB 1190:LOCATE 4,1:PRINT SP:IF SP>0 THEN RETURN
490    SX1=B21(Q1,0):SY1=B21(Q1,1)
500    SX2=B21(Q2,0):SY2=B21(Q2,1)
510    SX3=B22(Q2,0):SY3=B22(Q2,1)
520    SX4=B22(Q1,0):SY4=B22(Q1,1)
530    X=X1+.5*(X3-X1):Y=Y1+.5*(Y3-Y1):Z=Z1+.5*(Z3-Z1)
540    SX5=D*X/Z:SY5=D*Y/Z
550    GOSUB 1450
560    GOSUB 1230:PAINT (SX5,SY5),A$,C3:GOSUB 1400:RETURN
570 '_____
580 '
590 'module:    calculation of world coordinates for 3D cylind
er
600    SR4=SIN(R4):CR4=COS(R4):SR5=SIN(R5):CR5=COS(R5)
610    X1=SR5*X:Y=CR5*X:X=CR4*X1:Z=SR4*X1:RETURN
620 '_____
630 '
640 'module:    perspective calculations
650    X=(-1)*X:XA=CR1*X-SR1*Z:ZA=SR1*X+CR1*Z:X=CR2*XA+SR2*Y:Y
A=CR2*Y-SR2*XA:Z=CR3*ZA-SR3*YA:Y=SR3*ZA+CR3*YA:X=X+MX:Y=Y+MY
:Z=Z+MZ:SX=D*X/Z:SY=D*Y/Z:RETURN
660 '_____
670 '
680 'module:    return to QuickBASIC editor
690    CLS:SCREEN 0,0,0,0:WIDTH 80:COLOR 7,0,0:CLS:LOCATE 1,1,
1:END
700 '_____
710 '
720 'module:    UNIVERSAL
730 'This routine configures the program for the hardware/so
ftware being used on a PC, XT, or AT.
740    KEY OFF:CLS:ON ERROR GOTO 810    'trap if not Enhanced Di
splay + EGA
750    SCREEN 9,,0,0:COLOR 7,0:PALETTE 1,8:PALETTE 2,1:PALETTE
 3,9:PALETTE 4,11:PALETTE 5,7:PALETTE 6,37:PALETTE 7,7:PALET
TE 8,56:PALETTE 9,34:PALETTE 10,20:PALETTE 11,5:PALETTE 12,4
4:PALETTE 13,46:PALETTE 14,55:PALETTE 15,63
```

```
760    C0=0:C1=12:C2=9:C3=7:LOCATE 1,1:PRINT "ED-EGA 640x350 1
6-color mode"
770    V6=15
780    GOSUB 1500
790    DEFINT G:G=1
800    GOTO 1000
810    RESUME 820
820    ON ERROR GOTO 880   'trap if not Color Display + EGA
830    SCREEN 8,,0,0:COLOR 7,0:PALETTE 1,0:PALETTE 2,1:PALETTE
 3,9:PALETTE 4,7:PALETTE 8,4:PALETTE 9,2:C0=0:C1=8:C2=9:C3=7
:LOCATE 1,1:PRINT "CD-EGA 640x200 16-color mode"
840    V6=14
850    GOSUB 1500
860    DEFINT G:G=2
870    GOTO 1000
880    RESUME 960
890 '*** NOTE:   The PCjr set-up code has been deleted, becau
se QuickBASIC does not support screen modes 3,4,5,6.   PCjr w
ill run in CGA mode.
960    SCREEN 1,0:COLOR 0,1:C0=0:C1=1:C2=2:C3=3:LOCATE 1,1:PRI
NT "CGA 320x200 4-color mode"
970    V6=14
980    GOSUB 1700
990    DEFINT G:G=4
1000   ON ERROR GOTO 0
1010   WINDOW SCREEN (-399,-299)-(400,300)
1020   ON KEY (2) GOSUB 690:KEY (2) ON
1030   GOTO 150
1040 '_____
1050 '
1060 'module:   assign variables
1070   D=1200:R1=5.89778:R2=0:R3=.58539:MX=0:MY=0:MZ=-350
1080   DEFINT Q:Q1=0:Q2=0
1090   X=0:Y=0:Z=0:R4=6.28319:R5=6.28319
1120   XL=.57735:YL=.57735:ZL=.57735
1130   SR1=SIN(R1):CR1=COS(R1):SR2=SIN(R2):CR2=COS(R2):SR3=SI
N(R3):CR3=COS(R3)
1140   SR4=SIN(R4):CR4=COS(R4):SR5=SIN(R5):CR5=COS(R5)
1150   RETURN
1160 '_____
1170 '
1180 'module:   plane equation method of hidden surface remov
al
1190   SP1=X1*(Y2*Z3-Y3*Z2):SP1=(-1)*SP1:SP2=X2*(Y3*Z1-Y1*Z3)
:SP3=X3*(Y1*Z2-Y2*Z1):SP=SP1-SP2-SP3:RETURN
1200 '_____
1210 '
1220 'module:   computer-controlled shading routine
```

```
1230   XU=X2-X1:YU=Y2-Y1:ZU=Z2-Z1
1240   XV=X3-X1:YV=Y3-Y1:ZV=Z3-Z1
1250   XN=(YU*ZV)-(ZU*YV):YN=(ZU*XV)-(XU*ZV):ZN=(XU*YV)-(YU*X
V)
1260   YN=YN*(-1):ZN=ZN*(-1)
1270 'sub-module:   convert surface perpendicular vector to u
nit vector
1280   V1=(XN*XN)+(YN*YN)+(ZN*ZN):V2=SQR(V1)
1290   V3=1/V2
1300   XW=V3*XN:YW=V3*YN:ZW=V3*ZN
1310 'sub-module:   calculate illumination factor for surface
 when angle of incidence is 45 degrees elevation and 135 deg
rees yaw
1320   V4=(XW*XL)+(YW*YL)+(ZW*ZL)
1330   V4=V4*V6:V4=CINT(V4)
1340   V5=V4+1
1350   ON G GOSUB 1880, 2090, 2300, 2300  'jump to device-dep
endent shading routine
1360   RETURN
1370 '_____
1380 '
1390 'module:   computer-controlled dithering routine
1400   LINE (SX1,SY1)-(SX2,SY2),C4:LINE (SX1,SY1)-(SX2,SY2),C
5,,C6:LINE (SX2,SY2)-(SX3,SY3),C4:LINE (SX2,SY2)-(SX3,SY3),C
5,,C6:LINE (SX3,SY3)-(SX4,SY4),C4:LINE (SX3,SY3)-(SX4,SY4),C
5,,C6
1410   LINE (SX4,SY4)-(SX1,SY1),C4:LINE (SX4,SY4)-(SX1,SY1),C
5,,C6:RETURN
1420 '_____
1430 '
1440 'module:   solid surface modeling of 4-sided polygon
1450   LINE (SX1,SY1)-(SX2,SY2),C2:LINE-(SX3,SY3),C2:LINE-(SX
4,SY4),C2:LINE-(SX1,SY1),C2:PAINT (SX5,SY5),C2,C2
1460   LINE (SX1,SY1)-(SX2,SY2),C3:LINE-(SX3,SY3),C3:LINE-(SX
4,SY4),C3:LINE-(SX1,SY1),C3:PAINT (SX5,SY5),C0,C3:RETURN
1470 '_____
1480 '
1490 'module:   assign shading codes for EGA
1500   A1A$=CHR$(&HDF)+CHR$(&H20)+CHR$(&H0)+CHR$(&H0)+CHR$(&H
FD)+CHR$(&H2):A1$=A1A$+CHR$(&H0)+CHR$(&H0)+CHR$(&H7F)+CHR$(&
H80)+CHR$(&H0)+CHR$(&H0)+CHR$(&HF7)+CHR$(&H8)+CHR$(&H0)+CHR$
(&H0)
1510   A2$=CHR$(&HBB)+CHR$(&H44)+CHR$(&H0)+CHR$(&H0)+CHR$(&HE
E)+CHR$(&H11)+CHR$(&H0)+CHR$(&H0)
1520   A3$=CHR$(&HAA)+CHR$(&H55)+CHR$(&H0)+CHR$(&H0)+CHR$(&H5
5)+CHR$(&HAA)+CHR$(&H0)+CHR$(&H0)
1530   A4$=CHR$(&H44)+CHR$(&HBB)+CHR$(&H0)+CHR$(&H0)+CHR$(&H1
1)+CHR$(&HEE)+CHR$(&H0)+CHR$(&H0)
```

```
1540    A5A$=CHR$(&H20)+CHR$(&HFF)+CHR$(&HO)+CHR$(&HO)+CHR$(&H
2)+CHR$(&HFF):A5$=A5A$+CHR$(&HO)+CHR$(&HO)+CHR$(&H80)+CHR$(&
HFF)+CHR$(&HO)+CHR$(&HO)+CHR$(&H8)+CHR$(&HFF)+CHR$(&HO)+CHR$
(&HO)
1550    A6$=CHR$(&H44)+CHR$(&HFF)+CHR$(&HO)+CHR$(&HO)+CHR$(&H1
1)+CHR$(&HFF)+CHR$(&HO)+CHR$(&HO)
1560    A7$=CHR$(&H55)+CHR$(&HFF)+CHR$(&HO)+CHR$(&HO)+CHR$(&HA
A)+CHR$(&HFF)+CHR$(&HO)+CHR$(&HO)
1570    A8$=CHR$(&HBB)+CHR$(&HFF)+CHR$(&HO)+CHR$(&HO)+CHR$(&HE
E)+CHR$(&HFF)+CHR$(&HO)+CHR$(&HO)
1580    A9A$=CHR$(&HDF)+CHR$(&HDF)+CHR$(&H20)+CHR$(&HO)+CHR$(&
HFD)+CHR$(&HFD):A9$=A9A$+CHR$(&H2)+CHR$(&HO)+CHR$(&H7F)+CHR$
(&H7F)+CHR$(&H80)+CHR$(&HO)+CHR$(&HF7)+CHR$(&HF7)+CHR$(&H8)+
CHR$(&HO)
1590    A10$=CHR$(&HBB)+CHR$(&HBB)+CHR$(&H44)+CHR$(&HO)+CHR$(&
HEE)+CHR$(&HEE)+CHR$(&H11)+CHR$(&HO)
1600    A11$=CHR$(&HAA)+CHR$(&HAA)+CHR$(&H55)+CHR$(&HO)+CHR$(&
H55)+CHR$(&H55)+CHR$(&HAA)+CHR$(&HO)
1610    A12$=CHR$(&H44)+CHR$(&H44)+CHR$(&HBB)+CHR$(&HO)+CHR$(&
H11)+CHR$(&H11)+CHR$(&HEE)+CHR$(&HO)
1620    A13A$=CHR$(&H20)+CHR$(&HO)+CHR$(&HFF)+CHR$(&HO)+CHR$(&
H2)+CHR$(&HO):A13$=A13A$+CHR$(&HFF)+CHR$(&HO)+CHR$(&H80)+CHR
$(&HO)+CHR$(&HFF)+CHR$(&HO)+CHR$(&H8)+CHR$(&HO)+CHR$(&HFF)+C
HR$(&HO)
1630    A14$=CHR$(&H44)+CHR$(&HO)+CHR$(&HFF)+CHR$(&HO)+CHR$(&H
11)+CHR$(&HO)+CHR$(&HFF)+CHR$(&HO)
1640    A15$=CHR$(&H55)+CHR$(&HO)+CHR$(&HFF)+CHR$(&HO)+CHR$(&H
AA)+CHR$(&HO)+CHR$(&HFF)+CHR$(&HO)
1650    A16$=CHR$(&HBB)+CHR$(&HO)+CHR$(&HFF)+CHR$(&HO)+CHR$(&H
EE)+CHR$(&HO)+CHR$(&HFF)+CHR$(&HO)
1660    RETURN
1670    '_____
1680    '
1690    'module:  assign shading codes for CGA and/or PC.jr
1700    A1$=CHR$(&H40)+CHR$(&HO)+CHR$(&H4)+CHR$(&HO)
1710    A2$=CHR$(&H40)+CHR$(&H4)+CHR$(&H40)+CHR$(&H4)
1720    A3$=CHR$(&H44)+CHR$(&H10)+CHR$(&H11)+CHR$(&H1)+CHR$(&H
44)+CHR$(&H4)+CHR$(&H11)+CHR$(&H40)
1730    A4$=CHR$(&H44)+CHR$(&H11)+CHR$(&H44)+CHR$(&H11)
1740    A5$=CHR$(&H11)+CHR$(&H45)+CHR$(&H44)+CHR$(&H54)+CHR$(&
H11)+CHR$(&H51)+CHR$(&H44)+CHR$(&H15)
1750    A6$=CHR$(&H15)+CHR$(&H51)+CHR$(&H51)+CHR$(&H55)
1760    A7$=CHR$(&H15)+CHR$(&H55)+CHR$(&H51)+CHR$(&H55)
1770    A9$=CHR$(&HD5)+CHR$(&H55)+CHR$(&H5D)+CHR$(&H55)
1780    A10$=CHR$(&HD5)+CHR$(&H5D)+CHR$(&HD5)+CHR$(&H5D)
1790    A12$=CHR$(&HDD)+CHR$(&H75)+CHR$(&H77)+CHR$(&H57)+CHR$(
&HDD)+CHR$(&H5D)+CHR$(&H77)+CHR$(&HD5)
1800    A13$=CHR$(&HDD)+CHR$(&H77)+CHR$(&HDD)+CHR$(&H77)
```

```
1810    A14$=CHR$(&H77)+CHR$(&HDF)+CHR$(&HDD)+CHR$(&HFD)+CHR$(
&H77)+CHR$(&HF7)+CHR$(&HDD)+CHR$(&H7F)
1820    A15$=CHR$(&H7F)+CHR$(&HF7)+CHR$(&H7F)+CHR$(&HF7)
1830    A16$=CHR$(&H7F)+CHR$(&HFF)+CHR$(&HF7)+CHR$(&HFF)
1840    RETURN
1850  '_____
1860  '
1870  'shading routine for ED-EGA 640x350 mode
1880    IF V5<1 THEN GOTO 1900  'if light source is behind sur
face
1890    ON V5 GOTO 1900, 1910, 1920, 1930, 1940, 1950, 1960, 1
970, 1980, 1990, 2000, 2010, 2020, 2030, 2040, 2050
1900    A$=CHR$(&HFF)+CHR$(&HO)+CHR$(&HO)+CHR$(&HO):C4=1:C5=1:
C6=&HFFFF:RETURN
1910    A$=A1$:C4=1:C5=2:C6=&H808:RETURN
1920    A$=A2$:C4=1:C5=2:C6=&H4444:RETURN
1930    A$=CHR$(&HO)+CHR$(&HFF)+CHR$(&HO)+CHR$(&HO):C4=2:C5=2:
C6=&HFFFF:RETURN
1940    A$=A5$:C4=2:C5=3:C6=&H808:RETURN
1950    A$=A6$:C4=2:C5=3:C6=&H4444:RETURN
1960    A$=A7$:C4=2:C5=3:C6=&HAAAA:RETURN
1970    A$=A8$:C4=3:C5=2:C6=&H4444:RETURN
1980    A$=CHR$(&HFF)+CHR$(&HFF)+CHR$(&HO)+CHR$(&HO):C4=3:C5=3
:C6=&HFFFF:RETURN
1990    A$=A10$:C4=3:C5=4:C6=&H4444:RETURN
2000    A$=A11$:C4=3:C5=4:C6=&HAAAA:RETURN
2010    A$=A12$:C4=4:C5=3:C6=&H4444:RETURN
2020    A$=CHR$(&HO)+CHR$(&HO)+CHR$(&HFF)+CHR$(&HO):C4=4:C5=4:
C6=&HFFFF:RETURN
2030    A$=A13$:C4=4:C5=5:C6=&H808:RETURN
2040    A$=A14$:C4=4:C5=5:C6=&H4444:RETURN
2050    A$=A15$:C4=4:C5=5:C6=&HAAAA:RETURN
2060  '_____
2070  '
2080  'shading routine for CD-EGA 640x200 mode
2090    IF V5<1 THEN GOTO 2120  'if light source is behind sur
face
2100    ON V5 GOTO 2120, 2130, 2140, 2150, 2160, 2170, 2180, 2
190, 2200, 2210, 2220, 2230, 2240, 2250, 2260
2110    A$=CHR$(&HFF)+CHR$(&HO)+CHR$(&HO)+CHR$(&HO):C4=1:C5=1:
C6=&HFFFF:RETURN  'solid black is unused
2120    A$=A1$:C4=1:C5=2:C6=&H808:RETURN
2130    A$=A2$:C4=1:C5=2:C6=&H4444:RETURN
2140    A$=A3$:C4=1:C5=2:C6=&HAAAA:RETURN
2150    A$=A4$:C4=2:C5=1:C6=&H4444:RETURN
2160    A$=CHR$(&HO)+CHR$(&HFF)+CHR$(&HO)+CHR$(&HO):C4=2:C5=2:
C6=&HFFFF:RETURN
2170    A$=A5$:C4=2:C5=3:C6=&H808:RETURN
```

```
2180    A$=A6$:C4=2:C5=3:C6=&H4444:RETURN
2190    A$=A7$:C4=2:C5=3:C6=&HAAAA:RETURN
2200    A$=A8$:C4=3:C5=2:C6=&H4444:RETURN
2210    A$=CHR$(&HFF)+CHR$(&HFF)+CHR$(&HO)+CHR$(&HO):C4=3:C5=3
:C6=&HFFFF:RETURN
2220    A$=A9$:C4=3:C5=4:C6=&H8080:RETURN
2230    A$=A10$:C4=3:C5=4:C6=&H4444:RETURN
2240    A$=A11$:C4=3:C5=4:C6=&HAAAA:RETURN
2250    A$=A12$:C4=4:C5=3:C6=&H4444:RETURN
2260    A$=CHR$(&HO)+CHR$(&HO)+CHR$(&HFF)+CHR$(&HO):C4=4:C5=4:
C6=&HFFFF:RETURN
2270    '_____
2280    '
2290    'shading routine for CD-CGA 320x200 mode and CD-JR 640x
200 mode
2300    IF V5<1 THEN GOTO 2330   'if light source is behind sur
face
2310    ON V5 GOTO 2330, 2340, 2350, 2360, 2370, 2380, 2390, 2
400, 2410, 2420, 2430, 2440, 2450, 2460, 2470
2320    A$=CHR$(&HO):C4=0:C5=0:C6=&HFFFF:RETURN    'solid black
-- unused
2330    A$=A1$:C4=0:C5=1:C6=&H2108:RETURN
2340    A$=A2$:C4=0:C5=1:C6=&H4444:RETURN
2350    A$=A4$:C4=0:C5=1:C6=&HAAAA:RETURN
2360    A$=A5$:C4=1:C5=0:C6=&H4924:RETURN
2370    A$=A6$:C4=1:C5=0:C6=&H4444:RETURN
2380    A$=A7$:C4=1:C5=0:C6=&H808:RETURN
2390    A$=CHR$(&H55):C4=1:C5=1:C6=&HFFFF:RETURN
2400    A$=A9$:C4=1:C5=3:C6=&H808:RETURN
2410    A$=A10$:C4=1:C5=3:C6=&H4444:RETURN
2420    A$=A12$:C4=1:C5=3:C6=&H4924:RETURN
2430    A$=A13$:C4=1:C5=3:C6=&HAAAA:RETURN
2440    A$=A14$:C4=3:C5=1:C6=&H4924:RETURN
2450    A$=A15$:C4=3:C5=1:C6=&H4444:RETURN
2460    A$=A16$:C4=3:C5=1:C6=&H808:RETURN
2470    A$=CHR$(&HFF):C4=3:C5=3:C6=&HFFFF:RETURN
2480    '_____
2490    '
2500    END 'of program code
```

QuickBASIC version of the fully-shaded cylinder discussed in Chapter 16.

The source code takes only 29 seconds to compile when the compilation options are set to /V/D/S. It is interesting to note that BASICA will draw the cylinder in 73 seconds on an IBM PC. QuickBASIC will run the same program in less than 34 seconds . . . more than twice as fast!

Note that lines 145 and 146 contain the DIM instructions which were originally located in lines 1100 and 1110. When using QuickBASIC, these DIM instructions must be physically located in the program listing before the arrays which they define.

Lines 890 to 950 have been deleted from the source code. This section of code was originally used to configure the program to run on an IBM PCjr or a TANDY. QuickBASIC does not support the CLEAR,,,n instruction or the SCREEN 6 instruction which is used for the PCjr and TANDY code.

Note the minor changes in lines 1500, 1540, 1580, and 1620. Although the hex formulas for computer-controlled shading are identical to the original versions, the formulas have been broken up into two shorter pieces. QuickBASIC will generate a "Statement Too Complex" error message if the formulas are left in their original format.

When the original version of this program runs under BASICA, the first executable instruction at line 140 is GOTO 740. This sends the processor to the configuration module. After the program has configured itself to match the hardware and software environment in which it is running, the instruction in line 1030 sends the processor back to line 150. This means that in the QuickBASIC version of the program, lines 145 and 146 are never encountered during run-time. Although this situation would be fatal to BASICA, it causes no adverse effect on QuickBASIC because the DIM instructions were executed during compilation of the program; they are not executed during run-time with QuickBASIC. To ensure that the program in Fig. D-1 will run under BASICA, simply change line 1030 to state GOTO 145.

Simply stated, to adapt the programs in this book (or on the companion diskette) to run on QuickBASIC version 2.0 or newer, you must make three changes:

1. Move the DIM instructions to the beginning of the program.

2. Delete any code which refers to the PCjr screen modes.

3. Break up the longest hex shading formulas into two shorter formulas.

# D

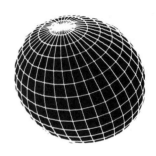

# *TurboBASIC*

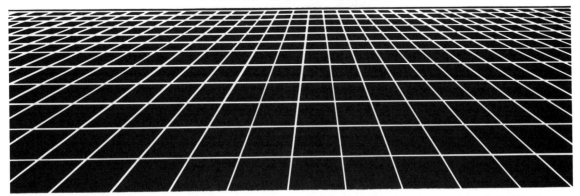

By making three simple changes, you can run the programs in this book with TurboBASIC version 1.0 or newer.

Graphics programs compiled with TurboBASIC can execute three times to ten times faster than under the IBM BASICA interpreter. Because of Borland's commitment to maintaining compatibility with BASICA, the advanced modeling and rendering programs in this book can be easily run under the TurboBASIC interactive compiler.

## THE TurboBASIC ENVIRONMENT

Under normal conditions TurboBASIC generates compiled machine code from your source code and it places the executable machine code into RAM memory. A complex graphics program of 200 lines typically requires fewer than 12 seconds to compile. A 400-line program will compile in 32 seconds. The compiled program can then be run from within the TurboBASIC programming environment. Simply use the cursor arrow key to choose Run from the options bar and press <Enter> to run. When the program is fin-

ished, control returns to the TurboBASIC editor.

Because the TurboBASIC editor and compiler require approximately 220K of memory (the TB.EXE file is 204312 bytes on diskette), a system with 384K to 640K is required in order to work with programs of reasonable size, because both your source code and the compiled machine code must exist in RAM simultaneously. The demonstration program in this appendix was converted, compiled, and run on an IBM PC with 640K (although the program will run in less than 384K).

The TurboBASIC compiler can compile .EXE files (executable machine code) directly to diskette. Refer to your TurboBASIC user's manual for further details on how to use the Options menu.

Because TurboBASIC supports integers, long integers, single-precision, and double-precision numbers, you have much more control over the mathematical component of your graphics programs. By bumping the numbers up into the appropriate range, you can use TurboBASIC's long integer format to increase the performance of the perspective formulas used in this book.

## HOW TO CONVERT BASICA
## PROGRAMS TO TurboBASIC

**Step 1.** If you are typing in the program from the listing in this book, start with Step 2. If you have the companion diskette, skip Step 2 and go directly to Step 3.

**Step 2.** Load DOS. Then insert your Turbo-BASIC master diskette in drive A. From the DOS prompt, load TurboBASIC with the keyboard command **A:TB**. Activate the editor by using the cursor arrow key to select Edit from the options bar and press <Enter>. Using the TurboBASIC editor, type in the program listing exactly as printed in the book. Skip Step 3 and Step 4 and go instead directly to Step 5.

**Step 3.** If you have the companion diskette, use BASICA (which you will find on your DOS diskette) to load the program which you wish to convert. Then save the program on a separate diskette using ASCII format. For example, if you were working on program A-25.BAS (the computer-shaded cylinder), you would save the program to diskette with the keyboard command **SAVE "A-25.BAS",A**. TurboBASIC can only read diskette files which are in ASCII format; it cannot understand the tokenized format which BASIC normally uses to write files to diskette. Tokenized format is merely a form of abbreviated symbols which BASIC uses in order to save diskette space.

**Step 4.** Exit BASICA and return to DOS. Insert your TurboBASIC master diskette in drive A. From the DOS prompt, load TurboBASIC with the keyboard command **A:TB**.

**Step 5.** For safety's sake, save the program under a new name before continuing. Use the cursor arrow key to select File from the options bar and press <Enter>. Type in a new name when TurboBASIC asks you to. Then, select Edit from the options bar and press <Enter> to activate the TurboBASIC editor.

**Step 6.** If any DIM instructions are present in the source code, move them to the beginning of the program. DIM is used to size scalar arrays in the 3D modeling programs and the 3D rendering programs. DIM is also used to size graphic arrays in the software sprite animation programs. TurboBASIC considers the DIM instruction to be a nonexecutable statement. The arrays defined by DIM are dimensioned during compilation, but the DIM instruction is not executed by the microprocessor during run-time.

**Step 7.** If any GET and PUT instructions are

present in the source code, be certain that they use actual screen coordinates. Under TurboBASIC, world coordinates which have been established by a WINDOW SCREEN instruction are not legal as arguments to GET and PUT. The BASICA interpreter allows both actual screen coordinates and world coordinates. GW-BASIC permits only actual screen coordinates. The programs in this book employ coordinates which match the actual screen coordinates in order to maintain software compatibility, so if you are adapting a program from this book you do not have to worry about the GET and PUT instructions.

**Step 8.** Delete any lines of source code which refer to the PCjr or TANDY, such as CLEAR,,,32768 and SCREEN 6. TurboBASIC does not support any of the PCjr modes (which are also found in GW-BASIC on the TANDY). Because most of the programs in the book contain code which ensures compatibility with the PCjr, you will be required to remove these lines from the compatibility module named UNIVERSAL before TurboBASIC will compile the program.

**Step 9.** If any complex string definitions are present in the source code (such as the computer-controlled shading formulas), you may encounter an error message from TurboBASIC which says "401 Expression Too Complex" or "402 Statement Too Complex". Simply break up the string definition into two shorter definitions, then define the original string as being composed of the two shortened strings. Refer to the demonstration program in this appendix to see how easily this is done.

**Step 10.** Save the modified source code on diskette. Use the short-cut key, F2, if you wish.

**Step 11.** Use the cursor arrow key to select the Options menu from the option bar and press <Enter>. Scroll down to the Keyboard break toggle and press <Enter>. Use the cursor arrow key to select Compile and touch <Enter> to compile the program into memory. The Keyboard break option will ensure that you can use Ctrl-Break to exit any program that hangs.

**Step 12.** Use the cursor arrow key to select Run from the option bar and press <Enter> to run the compiled program.

## TurboBASIC COMPATIBILITY WITH BASICA:

If you are modifying the programs in this book for your own purposes, or if you are writing your own original modeling and rendering programs, you may find the following comments helpful.

BLOAD and BSAVE will function correctly if they are used to identify address locations within the display memory segments (such as B8000 hex, A0000 hex, and so forth). If you use areas in dynamic RAM, however, you may run into trouble by inadvertently writing over important areas of run-time memory. TurboBASIC does not organize the microcomputer's RAM in the same manner as BASICA does. Refer to your TurboBASIC user's manual for a map of run-time memory conditions. (If you are using an EGA with TurboBASIC, read Appendix E for guidelines on saving images to diskette with BSAVE.)

TurboBASIC does not support the following instructions: AUTO, LOAD, DELETE, EDIT, MERGE, LIST, NEW, SAVE, RENUM, CONT. Many of these statements are useful only in the context of interpreted BASIC.

TurboBASIC supports the SCREEN 1 and SCREEN 2 graphics modes on the Color/Graphics Adapter.

TurboBASIC supports the SCREEN 7, SCREEN 8, SCREEN 9, and SCREEN 10 graphics modes on the EGA (Enhanced Graphics Adapter).

TurboBASIC supports the SCREEN 11 and SCREEN 12 graphics modes on the IBM Personal System/2 series of microcomputers.

TurboBASIC does not support SCREEN 3, SCREEN 4, SCREEN 5, or SCREEN 6 as used on the IBM PCjr. If you wish to compile BASIC source code for the PCjr, you should use the IBM BASIC Compiler version 1.0 or newer. Because of its size, Turbo-BASIC editor cannot even be loaded into a standard 128K PCjr, although standalone executable programs created by TurboBASIC will run on a PCjr if they use either the SCREEN 1 or SCREEN 2 graphics modes.

TurboBASIC does not support SCREEN 3, SCREEN 4, SCREEN 5, or SCREEN 6 as used on TANDY microcomputers with GW-BASIC. For all practical purposes, you are limited to SCREEN 0, SCREEN 1, and SCREEN 2 on a TANDY when using the TurboBASIC editor.

There is no PCOPY instruction in TurboBASIC 1.0. For frame animation (as demonstrated in Chapter 21), you should draw the graphics directly onto the appropriate page by using the SCREEN,,p1,p2 algorithm. For real-time animation (as demonstrated in Chapter 22), you should use the CLS instruction to clear the new hidden written-to page before you begin drawing the next frame in the animation sequence.

Some EGAs will not write graphics to a hidden page when using some versions of TurboBASIC. Under these conditions animation requires special coding, although the programming technique of software sprite animation will work as described in Part Four of this book.

TurboBASIC supports the 8087 and 80287 math coprocessors. If you have a coprocessor, set the appropriate toggle switch in the Options menu to activate TurboBASIC's coprocessor support. Programs can run 10 to 100 times faster.

Because TurboBASIC's default mode is double-precision math, some of the alphanumeric displays used in the demonstration programs in this book will appear much longer than with BASICA. In the computer-shaded cylinder, for example, a single alphanumeric is left on the screen because not enough blanks were written over the last number displayed. This is a minor problem which you can easily correct, of course.

### ANALYSIS OF THE DEMONSTRATION PROGRAM:

The demonstration program in Fig. E-1 is the TurboBASIC version of the fully-shaded cylinder discussed in Chapter 16.

The source code takes only 22 seconds to compile. It is interesting to note that BASICA will draw the cylinder in 73 seconds on an IBM PC. Turbo-BASIC will run the same program in 45 seconds (when no math coprocessor is present) . . . nearly twice as fast!

Note that lines 145 and 146 contain the DIM instructions which were originally located in lines 1100 and 1110. When using TurboBASIC, these DIM instructions must be physically located in the program listing before the arrays which they define.

Lines 890 to 950 have been deleted from the source code. This section of code was originally used to configure the program to run on an IBM PCjr or a TANDY. TurboBASIC does not support the CLEAR,,,n instruction or the SCREEN 6 instruction which is used for the PCjr and TANDY code.

Note the minor changes in lines 1500, 1540, 1580, and 1620. Although the hex formulas for computer-controlled shading are identical to the original versions, the formulas have been broken up into two shorter pieces. TurboBASIC will generate a "402 Statement Too Complex" error message if the formulas are left in their original format.

Fig. D-1. TurboBASIC version of the computer-shaded cylinder from Chapter 16.

```
100 'Program C-06.BAS     TurboBASIC fully-shaded cylinder.
110 'Demonstrates the compatibility of TurboBASIC 1.0 with I
BM BASICA for modeling and rendering.
111 'DIM instructions are moved to start of program.  See li
nes 145 and 146.
112 'All PCjr code has been deleted from the set-up module.
 TurboBASIC does not support PCjr modes.  See line 890.
113 'Because some hex shading formulas for the EGA are too c
omplex for TurboBASIC, the formulas have been built from two
 smaller sections.  See lines 1500, 1540, 1580, 1620.
114 'On an IBM PC, the program takes 22 seconds to compile.
115 'Program execution takes 45 seconds, compared to 82 seco
nds if BASICA is used.
120 '_____
130 '
140  GOTO 740    'configure system
145  DIM B11(35,2):DIM B12(35,2)  'this code moved to here f
rom line 1100
146  DIM B21(35,1):DIM B22(35,1)  'this code moved to here f
rom line 1110
150  GOSUB 1070   'assign variables
160 '_____
170 '
180 'main routine
190  SOUND 350,.7:R5=0:R4=0:FOR T=0 TO 35 STEP 1:LOCATE 2,1:
PRINT "Sweep 1 coordinate"T"   ":X=30:GOSUB 600:Z=Z+60:GOSUB
650:B11(T,0)=X:B11(T,1)=Y:B11(T,2)=Z:B21(T,0)=SX:B21(T,1)=SY
:R5=R5+.17453:NEXT T  'near end of cylinder
200  SOUND 350,.7:R5=0:R4=0:FOR T=0 TO 35 STEP 1:LOCATE 2,1:
PRINT "Sweep 2 coordinate"T"   ":X=30:GOSUB 600:Z=Z-60:GOSUB
650:B12(T,0)=X:B12(T,1)=Y:B12(T,2)=Z:B22(T,0)=SX:B22(T,1)=SY
:R5=R5+.17453:NEXT T   'far end of cylinder
210  SOUND 350,.7:FOR Q1=0 TO 35 STEP 1:Q2=Q1+1:IF Q2>35 THE
N Q2=0
220  LOCATE 2,1:PRINT "Solid surface"Q1"          "
230  GOSUB 450:NEXT Q1
240  SOUND 350,.7:LOCATE 2,1:PRINT "Solid end of cylinder.
   "
250  X1=B11(0,0):Y1=B11(0,1):Z1=B11(0,2):X2=B11(25,0):Y2=B11
(25,1):Z2=B11(25,2):X3=B11(11,0):Y3=B11(11,1):Z3=B11(11,2)
260  GOSUB 1190:IF SP>0 THEN 400
270  FOR Q1=0 TO 35 STEP 1:Q2=Q1+1:IF Q2>35 THEN Q2=0
280  SX1=B21(Q1,0):SY1=B21(Q1,1):SX2=B21(Q2,0):SY2=B21(Q2,1)

290  LINE (SX1,SY1)-(SX2,SY2),C2:NEXT Q1
300  X=0:Y=0:Z=60:GOSUB 650:PAINT (SX,SY),C2,C2
```

```
310   FOR Q1=0 TO 35 STEP 1:Q2=Q1+1:IF Q2>35 THEN Q2=0
320   SX1=B21(Q1,0):SY1=B21(Q1,1):SX2=B21(Q2,0):SY2=B21(Q2,1)
330   LINE (SX1,SY1)-(SX2,SY2),C3:NEXT Q1
340   X=0:Y=0:Z=60:GOSUB 650:PAINT (SX,SY),C0,C3
350   SOUND 350,.7:LOCATE 2,1:PRINT "Shading end of cylinder.
   "
360   X=0:Y=0:Z=60:GOSUB 650:GOSUB 1230:PAINT (SX,SY),A$,C3
'shading of end
370   FOR Q1=0 TO 35 STEP 1:Q2=Q1+1:IF Q2>35 THEN Q2=0
380   SX1=B21(Q1,0):SY1=B21(Q1,1):SX2=B21(Q2,0):SY2=B21(Q2,1)

390   LINE (SX1,SY1)-(SX2,SY2),C4:LINE (SX1,SY1)-(SX2,SY2),C5
,,C6:NEXT Q1   'dithering of end
400   SOUND 650,10:LOCATE 2,1:PRINT "Program completed.
   ":LOCATE 4,1:PRINT "                     "
410   GOTO 410
420   '_____
430   '
440   'module:   draw one 4-sided polygon on surface of cylinde
r
450   X1=B11(Q1,0):Y1=B11(Q1,1):Z1=B11(Q1,2)
460   X2=B11(Q2,0):Y2=B11(Q2,1):Z2=B11(Q2,2)
470   X3=B12(Q2,0):Y3=B12(Q2,1):Z3=B12(Q2,2)
480   GOSUB 1190:LOCATE 4,1:PRINT SP:IF SP>0 THEN RETURN
490   SX1=B21(Q1,0):SY1=B21(Q1,1)
500   SX2=B21(Q2,0):SY2=B21(Q2,1)
510   SX3=B22(Q2,0):SY3=B22(Q2,1)
520   SX4=B22(Q1,0):SY4=B22(Q1,1)
530   X=X1+.5*(X3-X1):Y=Y1+.5*(Y3-Y1):Z=Z1+.5*(Z3-Z1)
540   SX5=D*X/Z:SY5=D*Y/Z
550   GOSUB 1450
560   GOSUB 1230:PAINT (SX5,SY5),A$,C3:GOSUB 1400:RETURN
570   '_____
580   '
590   'module:   calculation of world coordinates for 3D cylind
er
600   SR4=SIN(R4):CR4=COS(R4):SR5=SIN(R5):CR5=COS(R5)
610   X1=SR5*X:Y=CR5*X:X=CR4*X1:Z=SR4*X1:RETURN
620   '_____
630   '
640   'module:   perspective calculations
650   X=(-1)*X:XA=CR1*X-SR1*Z:ZA=SR1*X+CR1*Z:X=CR2*XA+SR2*Y:Y
A=CR2*Y-SR2*XA:Z=CR3*ZA-SR3*YA:Y=SR3*ZA+CR3*YA:X=X+MX:Y=Y+MY
:Z=Z+MZ:SX=D*X/Z:SY=D*Y/Z:RETURN
660   '_____
670   '
680   'module:   return to TurboBASIC editor
690   CLS:SCREEN 0,0,0,0:WIDTH 80:COLOR 7,0,0:CLS:LOCATE 1,1,
```

```
  1:END
700 '_____
710 '
720 'module:   UNIVERSAL
730 'This routine configures the program for the hardware/so
ftware being used on a PC, XT, or AT.
740   KEY OFF:CLS:ON ERROR GOTO 810  'trap if not Enhanced Di
splay + EGA
750   SCREEN 9,,0,0:COLOR 7,0:PALETTE 1,8:PALETTE 2,1:PALETTE
 3,9:PALETTE 4,11:PALETTE 5,7:PALETTE 6,37:PALETTE 7,7:PALET
TE 8,56:PALETTE 9,34:PALETTE 10,20:PALETTE 11,5:PALETTE 12,4
4:PALETTE 13,46:PALETTE 14,55:PALETTE 15,63
760   CO=0:C1=12:C2=9:C3=7:LOCATE 1,1:PRINT "ED-EGA 640x350 1
6-color mode"
770   V6=15
780   GOSUB 1500
790   DEFINT G:G=1
800   GOTO 1000
810   RESUME 820
820   ON ERROR GOTO 880  'trap if not Color Display + EGA
830   SCREEN 8,,0,0:COLOR 7,0:PALETTE 1,0:PALETTE 2,1:PALETTE
 3,9:PALETTE 4,7:PALETTE 8,4:PALETTE 9,2:CO=0:C1=8:C2=9:C3=7
:LOCATE 1,1:PRINT "CD-EGA 640x200 16-color mode"
840   V6=14
850   GOSUB 1500
860   DEFINT G:G=2
870   GOTO 1000
880   RESUME 960
890 '*** NOTE:   The PCjr set-up code has been deleted, becau
se TurboBASIC does not support screen modes 3,4,5,6.   PCjr w
ill run in CGA mode.
960   SCREEN 1,0:COLOR 0,1:CO=0:C1=1:C2=2:C3=3:LOCATE 1,1:PRI
NT "CGA 320x200 4-color mode"
970   V6=14
980   GOSUB 1700
990   DEFINT G:G=4
1000   ON ERROR GOTO 0
1010   WINDOW SCREEN (-399,-299)-(400,300)
1020   ON KEY (2) GOSUB 690:KEY (2) ON
1030   GOTO 150
1040 '_____
1050 '
1060 'module:   assign variables
1070   D=1200:R1=5.89778:R2=0:R3=.58539:MX=0:MY=0:MZ=-350
1080   DEFINT Q:Q1=0:Q2=0
1090   X=0:Y=0:Z=0:R4=6.28319:R5=6.28319
1120   XL=.57735:YL=.57735:ZL=.57735
1130   SR1=SIN(R1):CR1=COS(R1):SR2=SIN(R2):CR2=COS(R2):SR3=SI
N(R3):CR3=COS(R3)
```

```
1140   SR4=SIN(R4):CR4=COS(R4):SR5=SIN(R5):CR5=COS(R5)
1150   RETURN
1160 '_____
1170 '
1180 'module:   plane equation method of hidden surface remov
al
1190   SP1=X1*(Y2*Z3-Y3*Z2):SP1=(-1)*SP1:SP2=X2*(Y3*Z1-Y1*Z3)
:SP3=X3*(Y1*Z2-Y2*Z1):SP=SP1-SP2-SP3:RETURN
1200 '_____
1210 '
1220 'module:   computer-controlled shading routine
1230   XU=X2-X1:YU=Y2-Y1:ZU=Z2-Z1
1240   XV=X3-X1:YV=Y3-Y1:ZV=Z3-Z1
1250   XN=(YU*ZV)-(ZU*YV):YN=(ZU*XV)-(XU*ZV):ZN=(XU*YV)-(YU*X
V)
1260   YN=YN*(-1):ZN=ZN*(-1)
1270 'sub-module:   convert surface perpendicular vector to u
nit vector
1280   V1=(XN*XN)+(YN*YN)+(ZN*ZN):V2=SQR(V1)
1290   V3=1/V2
1300   XW=V3*XN:YW=V3*YN:ZW=V3*ZN
1310 'sub-module:   calculate illumination factor for surface
 when angle of incidence is 45 degrees elevation and 135 deg
rees yaw
1320   V4=(XW*XL)+(YW*YL)+(ZW*ZL)
1330   V4=V4*V6:V4=CINT(V4)
1340   V5=V4+1
1350   ON G GOSUB 1880, 2090, 2300, 2300   'jump to device-dep
endent shading routine
1360   RETURN
1370 '_____
1380 '
1390 'module:   computer-controlled dithering routine
1400   LINE (SX1,SY1)-(SX2,SY2),C4:LINE (SX1,SY1)-(SX2,SY2),C
5,,C6:LINE (SX2,SY2)-(SX3,SY3),C4:LINE (SX2,SY2)-(SX3,SY3),C
5,,C6:LINE (SX3,SY3)-(SX4,SY4),C4:LINE (SX3,SY3)-(SX4,SY4),C
5,,C6
1410   LINE (SX4,SY4)-(SX1,SY1),C4:LINE (SX4,SY4)-(SX1,SY1),C
5,,C6:RETURN
1420 '_____
1430 '
1440 'module:   solid surface modeling of 4-sided polygon
1450   LINE (SX1,SY1)-(SX2,SY2),C2:LINE-(SX3,SY3),C2:LINE-(SX
4,SY4),C2:LINE-(SX1,SY1),C2:PAINT (SX5,SY5),C2,C2
1460   LINE (SX1,SY1)-(SX2,SY2),C3:LINE-(SX3,SY3),C3:LINE-(SX
4,SY4),C3:LINE-(SX1,SY1),C3:PAINT (SX5,SY5),C0,C3:RETURN
1470 '_____
1480 '
1490 'module:   assign shading codes for EGA
```

```
1500   A1A$=CHR$(&HDF)+CHR$(&H20)+CHR$(&HO)+CHR$(&HO)+CHR$(&H
FD)+CHR$(&H2):A1$=A1A$+CHR$(&HO)+CHR$(&HO)+CHR$(&H7F)+CHR$(&
H80)+CHR$(&HO)+CHR$(&HO)+CHR$(&HF7)+CHR$(&H8)+CHR$(&HO)+CHR$
(&HO)
1510   A2$=CHR$(&HBB)+CHR$(&H44)+CHR$(&HO)+CHR$(&HO)+CHR$(&HE
E)+CHR$(&H11)+CHR$(&HO)+CHR$(&HO)
1520   A3$=CHR$(&HAA)+CHR$(&H55)+CHR$(&HO)+CHR$(&HO)+CHR$(&H5
5)+CHR$(&HAA)+CHR$(&HO)+CHR$(&HO)
1530   A4$=CHR$(&H44)+CHR$(&HBB)+CHR$(&HO)+CHR$(&HO)+CHR$(&H1
1)+CHR$(&HEE)+CHR$(&HO)+CHR$(&HO)
1540   A5A$=CHR$(&H20)+CHR$(&HFF)+CHR$(&HO)+CHR$(&HO)+CHR$(&H
2)+CHR$(&HFF):A5$=A5A$+CHR$(&HO)+CHR$(&HO)+CHR$(&H80)+CHR$(&
HFF)+CHR$(&HO)+CHR$(&HO)+CHR$(&H8)+CHR$(&HFF)+CHR$(&HO)+CHR$
(&HO)
1550   A6$=CHR$(&H44)+CHR$(&HFF)+CHR$(&HO)+CHR$(&HO)+CHR$(&H1
1)+CHR$(&HFF)+CHR$(&HO)+CHR$(&HO)
1560   A7$=CHR$(&H55)+CHR$(&HFF)+CHR$(&HO)+CHR$(&HO)+CHR$(&HA
A)+CHR$(&HFF)+CHR$(&HO)+CHR$(&HO)
1570   A8$=CHR$(&HBB)+CHR$(&HFF)+CHR$(&HO)+CHR$(&HO)+CHR$(&HE
E)+CHR$(&HFF)+CHR$(&HO)+CHR$(&HO)
1580   A9A$=CHR$(&HDF)+CHR$(&HDF)+CHR$(&H20)+CHR$(&HO)+CHR$(&
HFD)+CHR$(&HFD):A9$=A9A$+CHR$(&H2)+CHR$(&HO)+CHR$(&H7F)+CHR$
(&H7F)+CHR$(&H80)+CHR$(&HO)+CHR$(&HF7)+CHR$(&HF7)+CHR$(&H8)+
CHR$(&HO)
1590   A10$=CHR$(&HBB)+CHR$(&HBB)+CHR$(&H44)+CHR$(&HO)+CHR$(&
HEE)+CHR$(&HEE)+CHR$(&H11)+CHR$(&HO)
1600   A11$=CHR$(&HAA)+CHR$(&HAA)+CHR$(&H55)+CHR$(&HO)+CHR$(&
H55)+CHR$(&H55)+CHR$(&HAA)+CHR$(&HO)
1610   A12$=CHR$(&H44)+CHR$(&H44)+CHR$(&HBB)+CHR$(&HO)+CHR$(&
H11)+CHR$(&H11)+CHR$(&HEE)+CHR$(&HO)
1620   A13A$=CHR$(&H20)+CHR$(&HO)+CHR$(&HFF)+CHR$(&HO)+CHR$(&
H2)+CHR$(&HO):A13$=A13A$+CHR$(&HFF)+CHR$(&HO)+CHR$(&H80)+CHR
$(&HO)+CHR$(&HFF)+CHR$(&HO)+CHR$(&H8)+CHR$(&HO)+CHR$(&HFF)+C
HR$(&HO)
1630   A14$=CHR$(&H44)+CHR$(&HO)+CHR$(&HFF)+CHR$(&HO)+CHR$(&H
11)+CHR$(&HO)+CHR$(&HFF)+CHR$(&HO)
1640   A15$=CHR$(&H55)+CHR$(&HO)+CHR$(&HFF)+CHR$(&HO)+CHR$(&H
AA)+CHR$(&HO)+CHR$(&HFF)+CHR$(&HO)
1650   A16$=CHR$(&HBB)+CHR$(&HO)+CHR$(&HFF)+CHR$(&HO)+CHR$(&H
EE)+CHR$(&HO)+CHR$(&HFF)+CHR$(&HO)
1660   RETURN
1670 '_____
1680 '
1690 'module:   assign shading codes for CGA and/or PCjr
1700   A1$=CHR$(&H40)+CHR$(&HO)+CHR$(&H4)+CHR$(&HO)
1710   A2$=CHR$(&H40)+CHR$(&H4)+CHR$(&H40)+CHR$(&H4)
1720   A3$=CHR$(&H44)+CHR$(&H10)+CHR$(&H11)+CHR$(&H1)+CHR$(&H
44)+CHR$(&H4)+CHR$(&H11)+CHR$(&H40)
1730   A4$=CHR$(&H44)+CHR$(&H11)+CHR$(&H44)+CHR$(&H11)
```

```
1740    A5$=CHR$(&H11)+CHR$(&H45)+CHR$(&H44)+CHR$(&H54)+CHR$(&
H11)+CHR$(&H51)+CHR$(&H44)+CHR$(&H15)
1750    A6$=CHR$(&H15)+CHR$(&H51)+CHR$(&H15)+CHR$(&H51)
1760    A7$=CHR$(&H15)+CHR$(&H55)+CHR$(&H51)+CHR$(&H55)
1770    A9$=CHR$(&HD5)+CHR$(&H55)+CHR$(&H5D)+CHR$(&H55)
1780    A10$=CHR$(&HD5)+CHR$(&H5D)+CHR$(&HD5)+CHR$(&H5D)
1790    A12$=CHR$(&HDD)+CHR$(&H75)+CHR$(&H77)+CHR$(&H57)+CHR$(
&HDD)+CHR$(&H5D)+CHR$(&H77)+CHR$(&HD5)
1800    A13$=CHR$(&HDD)+CHR$(&H77)+CHR$(&HDD)+CHR$(&H77)
1810    A14$=CHR$(&H77)+CHR$(&HDF)+CHR$(&HDD)+CHR$(&HFD)+CHR$(
&H77)+CHR$(&HF7)+CHR$(&HDD)+CHR$(&H7F)
1820    A15$=CHR$(&H7F)+CHR$(&HF7)+CHR$(&H7F)+CHR$(&HF7)
1830    A16$=CHR$(&H7F)+CHR$(&HFF)+CHR$(&HF7)+CHR$(&HFF)
1840    RETURN
1850 '_____
1860 '
1870 'shading routine for ED-EGA 640x350 mode
1880    IF V5<1 THEN GOTO 1900    'if light source is behind sur
face
1890    ON V5 GOTO 1900, 1910, 1920, 1930, 1940, 1950, 1960, 1
970, 1980, 1990, 2000, 2010, 2020, 2030, 2040, 2050
1900    A$=CHR$(&HFF)+CHR$(&H0)+CHR$(&H0)+CHR$(&H0):C4=1:C5=1:
C6=&HFFFF:RETURN
1910    A$=A1$:C4=1:C5=2:C6=&H808:RETURN
1920    A$=A2$:C4=1:C5=2:C6=&H4444:RETURN
1930    A$=CHR$(&H0)+CHR$(&HFF)+CHR$(&H0)+CHR$(&H0):C4=2:C5=2:
C6=&HFFFF:RETURN
1940    A$=A5$:C4=2:C5=3:C6=&H808:RETURN
1950    A$=A6$:C4=2:C5=3:C6=&H4444:RETURN
1960    A$=A7$:C4=2:C5=3:C6=&HAAAA:RETURN
1970    A$=A8$:C4=3:C5=2:C6=&H4444:RETURN
1980    A$=CHR$(&HFF)+CHR$(&HFF)+CHR$(&H0)+CHR$(&H0):C4=3:C5=3
:C6=&HFFFF:RETURN
1990    A$=A10$:C4=3:C5=4:C6=&H4444:RETURN
2000    A$=A11$:C4=3:C5=4:C6=&HAAAA:RETURN
2010    A$=A12$:C4=4:C5=3:C6=&H4444:RETURN
2020    A$=CHR$(&H0)+CHR$(&H0)+CHR$(&HFF)+CHR$(&H0):C4=4:C5=4:
C6=&HFFFF:RETURN
2030    A$=A13$:C4=4:C5=5:C6=&H808:RETURN
2040    A$=A14$:C4=4:C5=5:C6=&H4444:RETURN
2050    A$=A15$:C4=4:C5=5:C6=&HAAAA:RETURN
2060 '_____
2070 '
2080 'shading routine for CD-EGA 640x200 mode
2090    IF V5<1 THEN GOTO 2120    'if light source is behind sur
face
2100    ON V5 GOTO 2120, 2130, 2140, 2150, 2160, 2170, 2180, 2
190, 2200, 2210, 2220, 2230, 2240, 2250, 2260
2110    A$=CHR$(&HFF)+CHR$(&H0)+CHR$(&H0)+CHR$(&H0):C4=1:C5=1:
```

```
        C6=&HFFFF:RETURN   'solid black is unused
 2120   A$=A1$:C4=1:C5=2:C6=&H808:RETURN
 2130   A$=A2$:C4=1:C5=2:C6=&H4444:RETURN
 2140   A$=A3$:C4=1:C5=2:C6=&HAAAA:RETURN
 2150   A$=A4$:C4=2:C5=1:C6=&H4444:RETURN
 2160   A$=CHR$(&HO)+CHR$(&HFF)+CHR$(&HO)+CHR$(&HO):C4=2:C5=2:
        C6=&HFFFF:RETURN
 2170   A$=A5$:C4=2:C5=3:C6=&H808:RETURN
 2180   A$=A6$:C4=2:C5=3:C6=&H4444:RETURN
 2190   A$=A7$:C4=2:C5=3:C6=&HAAAA:RETURN
 2200   A$=A8$:C4=3:C5=2:C6=&H4444:RETURN
 2210   A$=CHR$(&HFF)+CHR$(&HFF)+CHR$(&HO)+CHR$(&HO):C4=3:C5=3
        :C6=&HFFFF:RETURN
 2220   A$=A9$:C4=3:C5=4:C6=&H8080:RETURN
 2230   A$=A10$:C4=3:C5=4:C6=&H4444:RETURN
 2240   A$=A11$:C4=3:C5=4:C6=&HAAAA:RETURN
 2250   A$=A12$:C4=4:C5=3:C6=&H4444:RETURN
 2260   A$=CHR$(&HO)+CHR$(&HO)+CHR$(&HFF)+CHR$(&HO):C4=4:C5=4:
        C6=&HFFFF:RETURN
 2270 '_____
 2280 '
 2290 'shading routine for CD-CGA 320x200 mode and CD-JR 640x
      200 mode
 2300   IF V5<1 THEN GOTO 2330   'if light source is behind sur
      face
 2310   ON V5 GOTO 2330, 2340, 2350, 2360, 2370, 2380, 2390, 2
      400, 2410, 2420, 2430, 2440, 2450, 2460, 2470
 2320   A$=CHR$(&HO):C4=0:C5=0:C6=&HFFFF:RETURN   'solid black
      -- unused
 2330   A$=A1$:C4=0:C5=1:C6=&H2108:RETURN
 2340   A$=A2$:C4=0:C5=1:C6=&H4444:RETURN
 2350   A$=A4$:C4=0:C5=1:C6=&HAAAA:RETURN
 2360   A$=A5$:C4=1:C5=0:C6=&H4924:RETURN
 2370   A$=A6$:C4=1:C5=0:C6=&H4444:RETURN
 2380   A$=A7$:C4=1:C5=0:C6=&H808:RETURN
 2390   A$=CHR$(&H55):C4=1:C5=1:C6=&HFFFF:RETURN
 2400   A$=A9$:C4=1:C5=3:C6=&H808:RETURN
 2410   A$=A10$:C4=1:C5=3:C6=&H4444:RETURN
 2420   A$=A12$:C4=1:C5=3:C6=&H4924:RETURN
 2430   A$=A13$:C4=1:C5=3:C6=&HAAAA:RETURN
 2440   A$=A14$:C4=3:C5=1:C6=&H4924:RETURN
 2450   A$=A15$:C4=3:C5=1:C6=&H4444:RETURN
 2460   A$=A16$:C4=3:C5=1:C6=&H808:RETURN
 2470   A$=CHR$(&HFF):C4=3:C5=3:C6=&HFFFF:RETURN
 2480 '_____
 2490 '
 2500   END 'of program code
```

When the original version of this program runs under BASICA, the first executable instruction at line 140 is GOTO 740. This sends the processor to the configuration module. After the program has configured itself to match the hardware and software environment in which it is running, the instruction in line 1030 sends the processor back to line 150. This means that in the TurboBASIC version of the program, lines 145 and 146 are never encountered during run-time. Although this situation would be fatal to BASICA, it causes no adverse effect on TurboBASIC because the DIM instructions were executed during compilation of the program; they are not executed during run-time with TurboBASIC. To ensure that the program in Fig. E-1 will run under BASICA, simply change line 1030 to state GOTO 145.

Simply stated, to adapt the programs in this book (or on the companion diskette) to run on TurboBASIC version 1.0 or newer, you must make three changes:

1. Move the DIM instructions to the beginning of the program.
2. Delete any code which refers to the PCjr screen modes.
3. Break up the longest hex shading formulas into two shorter formulas.

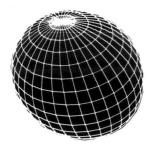

# E

# Quadram's EGA Boards

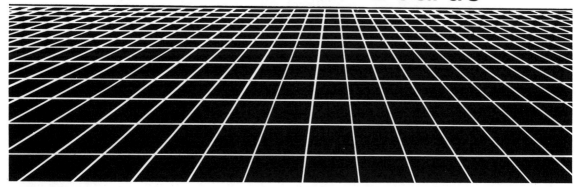

The demonstration programs throughout this book were developed on an IBM PC equipped with a QuadEGA + Enhanced Graphics Adapter manufactured by Quadram Corporation.

The QuadEGA + board is typical of many IBM workalike EGAs. It offers near-100% compatibility with IBM's product, yet the QuadEGA + is significantly less expensive and more versatile than the IBM EGA. Quadram's Model QC8601 is a compact, half-length board which requires minimal space inside the computer (see Fig. F-1). It is designed for easy owner-installation and comes with a comprehensive user's manual.

The QuadEGA + carries 256K of display memory. This means that you can choose any palette of 16 colors from a total of 64 available colors in the 640 × 350 mode. IBM's EGA comes with only 64K on-board memory, which can produce only four colors in the 640 × 350 mode. IBM offers a memory expansion kit for the EGA at extra cost.

For the purposes of graphics generation, the QuadEGA + will drive either an enhanced color display monitor or a standard RGB color display moni-

tor. Like the IBM EGA, it will not drive a composite monitor or color television.

The QuadEGA + board will generate a 640 × 350 16-color mode (SCREEN 9), a 640 × 200 16-color mode (SCREEN 8), and a 320 × 200 16-color mode (SCREEN 7). In addition, the QuadEGA + will produce the standard Color/Graphics Adapter modes of 320 × 200 4-color (SCREEN 1) and 640 × 200 2-color (SCREEN 2). The EGA graphics modes are accessible by any version of BASIC which supports the EGA, including IBM BASICA version 3.21 (and newer), QuickBASIC versions 2.0 and 3.0 (and newer), and TurboBASIC version 1.0 (and newer). Like the IBM EGA, the QuadEGA + will also generate a SCREEN 10 mode, which is not used in this book, however.

### MEMORY MAPPING THE QUADEGA +

The display memory on an EGA is organized into bit planes in order to maintain high-speed creation of graphics in spite of the massive amount of data which must be written for each screen mode. Simply stated, special registers inside the EGA's 82C431 Graphics Controller microchip are able to write bytes of data

Fig. E-1. The QuadEGA+ enhanced graphics adapter, manufactured by Quadram Corporation of Norcross, Georgia, USA. The board will generate 640×350 16-color graphics, 640×200 16-color graphics, and 320×200 16-color graphics when used with IBM BASICA 3.21, QuickBASIC 2.0/3.0 and newer, TurboBASIC 1.0 and newer. The standard Color/Graphics Adapter modes of 320×200 4-color and 640×200 2-color are also available on the QuadEGA+.

to all four bit planes simultaneously. Each bit plane contains a vital portion of the binary value which controls each pixel on the screen. The EGA's 82C434 CRT Controller microchip reads the corresponding bit in all four bit planes simultaneously, adds up the values of the bits, and uses the result to determine which color the pixel should be. The hex shading formulas used throughout this book take advantage of the additive nature of the EGA's bit plane hardware. (See Chapter 15.) Although assembly language programming of graphics on an EGA is a complicated undertaking, EGA-compatible languages like BASICA 3.21 (and newer), QuickBASIC 2.0/3.0 (and newer), and Turbo-BASIC 1.0 (and newer) have taken all the drudgery out of programming the EGA.

On the QuadEGA+, four graphics pages are available in the 640×200 16-color mode. Refer to Fig. F-2. The 256K display memory is divided into four 64K segments. Bit plane 0 of pages one through four is located in the first 64K segment. Bit plane 1 of each page is stored in the next 64K, and so on.

Page 0, bit plane 0, is located at memory address A0000 hex. Page 1 starts at A4000 hex. Page 2 begins at A8000 hex. Page 3 starts at AC000 hex. Each page in the 640×200 16-color mode requires 64000 bytes of display memory. Each bit plane requires 16000 bytes.

It is interesting to note that you cannot directly address any of the higher 64K segments. The computer literally tricks itself into believing that all four bit planes for page 0 are located at memory address A0000 hex. The latching registers of the EGA's 82C431 Graphics Controller must be manipulated in order to write data to bit planes 1, 2, and 3 of page 0. The higher bit planes are actually stored at memory addresses B0000 hex and so forth, but the hardware engineers want you to send graphics data via the EGA's latching registers.

Two separate graphics pages are available in the 640×350 16-color mode. Refer to Fig. F-3. Each page requires a full 112000 bytes of display memory. Each bit plane uses 28000 bytes of memory. Page 0, bit plane 0, occupies memory space from A0000 hex to A6D60 hex. Page 1, bit plane 0, uses memory space

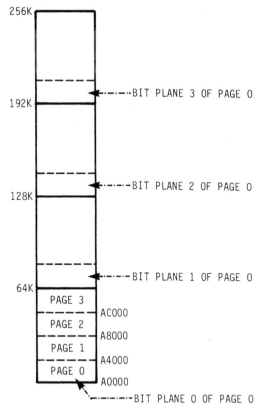

Fig. E-2. Memory allocation when the QuadEGA+ enhanced graphics adapter is in the 640×200 16-color mode. Four pages are available for frame animation or hidden-page drawing.

A8000 hex to AED60 hex. The portion of display memory between the end of page 0 and the beginning of page 1 is unused.

When the QuadEGA+ is emulating a Color/Graphics Adapter, display memory is located at the standard B8000 hex address. You can BLOAD, BSAVE, POKE, and PEEK to this address just as if it were a genuine Color/Graphics Adapter.

## HIGH-SPEED AREA FILL

The ability of any EGA to write simultaneous bytes has some definite advantages in high-speed area fill applications: BASIC's PAINT instruction, for example. The EGA writes area fill data on a double-word basis. During a PAINT operation, four full bytes of area fill are written at one time. In spite of the increased number of bytes which must be written in the 640×200 16-color mode, an EGA will fill an area with

color nearly three times quicker than a standard Color/Graphics Adapter can fill areas on the 320×200 4-color screen! Accordingly, the demonstration programs in this book which generate fully-shaded models will execute faster with an EGA than with a CGA, especially in the 640×200 16-color mode.

## SAVING EGA IMAGES ON DISKETTE

Neither a genuine IBM EGA nor a QuadEGA+ can use a simple BSAVE instruction to save a 640×350 screen image to diskette. One of the reasons for this situation is the single-segment limitation of the BSAVE instruction. No more than 65535 bytes can be saved with a single BSAVE command, but the 640×350 screen takes up a whopping 112000 bytes! Another, more important reason is the fact that all four bit planes occupy the same logical address in memory. Used by itself, a BSAVE instruction would merely read the first bit plane at &HA0000. (If you attempt

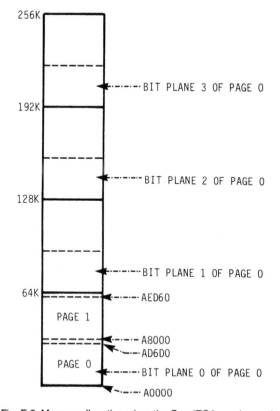

Fig. E-3. Memory allocation when the QuadEGA+ enhanced graphics adapter is in the 640×350 16-color mode. Two pages are available.

a simple BSAVE instruction, the image eventually returned by a subsequent BLOAD statement will be monochrome: white and black only.)

There are two ways to circumvent this limitation if you want to save images to diskette from any of the EGA modes.

### Saving Images to Diskette with GET/PUT

As the CAD program in Chapter 25 demonstrates, graphic arrays can be used to precisely identify a portion of the screen buffer which you wish to save. First, a DIM instruction is used to reserve memory inside BASIC's workspace to receive the image data. Second, GET is used to take a graphic array from the screen buffer and save it inside the array defined by the DIM instruction. Third, BSAVE is used to write the contents of the array to diskette. The procedure is simply reversed to retrieve an image from diskette. This technique will work in any graphics mode on any EGA or Color/Graphics Adapter. Because data is never written to dynamic RAM (it is only written to array space inside BASIC's workspace) you need not worry about memory incompatibilities with future versions of DOS or future hardware architecture.

### Saving Images to Diskette with BSAVE/BLOAD/OUT

IBM issued a caveat in the IBM BASICA 3.21 manual, stating that BSAVE cannot be used to save a $640 \times 350$ screen image. With all due respect to IBM, the BSAVE and BLOAD instructions can do the job, notwithstanding some fancy footwork, however. If the EGA's latching registers are manipulated so that the BSAVE and BLOAD instructions can be used to move graphics data to and from individual bit planes, then it is possible to save diskette image files of the $640 \times 350$ 16-color mode, the $640 \times 200$ 16-color mode, and the $320 \times 200$ 16-color mode. BASIC's OUT statement will modify the EGA's latching registers.

The following code will save the $640 \times 350$ 16-color screen image to diskette, provided that your program is already in the SCREEN 9 mode.

```
660  DEF SEG = &HA000 'set up segment
670  OUT &H3CE,4:OUT &H3CF,0:BSAVE "IMAGE0.
     BAS",0,28000 'bsave bit plane 0
680  OUT &H3CE,4:OUT &H3CF,1:BSAVE "IMAGE1.
     BAS",0,28000 'bsave bit plane 1
690  OUT &H3CE,4:OUT &H3CF,2:BSAVE "IMAGE2.
     BAS",0,28000 'bsave bit plane 2
700  OUT &H3CE,4:OUT &H3CF,3:BSAVE "IMAGE3.
     BAS",0,28000 'bsave bit plane 3
710  OUT &H3CE,4:OUT &H3CF,0:DEF SEG 'restore
EGA registers
```

Note that the preceding routine will create four image files on your diskette, one for each bit plane. Each image file will be approximately 28000 bytes in length; all four image files will occupy over 112000 bytes on diskette. (Considering the large amount of diskette space required, you may wish to use the graphic array method instead of the BSAVE/BLOAD/OUT method when the image being saved does not fill the entire screen.)

The following code segment will retrieve the image files from diskette and return the graphic image to the $640 \times 350$ 16-color screen. It is assumed that your program is already in the SCREEN 9 mode.

```
820  DEF SEG = &HA000 'set up segment
830  OUT &H3C4,2:OUT &H3C5,1:BLOAD "IMAGE0.
     BAS",0 'bload bit plane 0
840  OUT &H3C4,2:OUT &H3C5,2:BLOAD "IMAGE1.
     BAS",0 'bload bit plane 1
850  OUT &H3C4,2:OUT &H3C5,4:BLOAD "IMAGE2.
     BAS",0 'bload bit plane 2
860  OUT &H3C4,2:OUT &H3C5,8:BLOAD "IMAGE3.
     BAS",0 'bload bit plane 3
870  OUT &H3C4,2:OUT &H3C5,&HF:DEF SEG 're-
store EGA registers
```

The preceding code fragments have been tested and verified on an IBM PC equipped with an IBM Enhanced Color Display and a Quadram QuadEGA + enhanced graphics adapter, using IBM BASICA 3.21.

# Index